Data Envelopment Analysis (DEA) Methods for Maximizing Efficiency

Adeyemi Abel Ajibesin
American University of Nigeria, Nigeria

Narasimha Rao Vajjhala
University of New York Tirana, Albania

A volume in the Advances in Business Information
Systems and Analytics (ABISA) Book Series

Published in the United States of America by
IGI Global
Business Science Reference (an imprint of IGI Global)
701 E. Chocolate Avenue
Hershey PA, USA 17033
Tel: 717-533-8845
Fax: 717-533-8661
E-mail: cust@igi-global.com
Web site: http://www.igi-global.com

Library of Congress Cataloging-in-Publication Data
CIP Data in progress

Title: Data Envelopment Analysis (DEA) Methods for Maximizing Efficiency
ISBN: 9798369302552

This book is published in the IGI Global book series Advances in Business Information Systems and Analytics (ABISA) (ISSN: 2327-3275; eISSN: 2327-3283)

British Cataloguing in Publication Data
A Cataloguing in Publication record for this book is available from the British Library.

For electronic access to this publication, please contact: eresources@igi-global.com.

Advances in Business Information Systems and Analytics (ABISA) Book Series

Madjid Tavana
La Salle University, USA

ISSN:2327-3275
EISSN:2327-3283

MISSION

The successful development and management of information systems and business analytics is crucial to the success of an organization. New technological developments and methods for data analysis have allowed organizations to not only improve their processes and allow for greater productivity, but have also provided businesses with a venue through which to cut costs, plan for the future, and maintain competitive advantage in the information age.

The **Advances in Business Information Systems and Analytics (ABISA) Book Series** aims to present diverse and timely research in the development, deployment, and management of business information systems and business analytics for continued organizational development and improved business value.

COVERAGE

- Data Governance
- Legal information systems
- Business Decision Making
- Strategic Information Systems
- Big Data
- Forecasting
- Business models
- Decision Support Systems
- Business Process Management
- Data Management

IGI Global is currently accepting manuscripts for publication within this series. To submit a proposal for a volume in this series, please contact our Acquisition Editors at Acquisitions@igi-global.com or visit: http://www.igi-global.com/publish/.

Titles in this Series

For a list of additional titles in this series, please visit: www.igi-global.com/book-series

701 East Chocolate Avenue, Hershey, PA 17033, USA
Tel: 717-533-8845 x100 • Fax: 717-533-8661
E-Mail: cust@igi-global.com • www.igi-global.com

Editorial Advisory Board

Table of Contents

Detailed Table of Contents

Chapter 1

Effects of Public Capital Investments on the Productivity of the United States, 1992-2022 1
Brian Sloboda, University of Maryland, Global Campus, USA
Yaya Sissoko, Indiana University of Pennsylvania, USA

This chapter examines the productivity of the public sectors throughout the United States from 1992 through 2022. Because there is heterogeneity across states regarding public services provided, this could impact its productivity and efficiency. The services provided by the public sector have come under increased scrutiny with the ongoing reform process in recent years. In the public sector, unlike the private sector, and the information and incentives provided by these markets, performance information, particularly comparative performance measures, have been used to gauge the productivity of the public service sector. This chapter examines the productivity of the public sector across states using the standard date envelopment analysis (DEA) and efficiency measures given by the Malmquist productivity index. Then, the DEA analysis was followed by panel regression analysis.

Chapter 2

Data Envelopment Analysis Advantages and Problems Demonstrated in a University Comparison Study 18
Kenneth David Strang, W3 Research, USA

This chapter explains the variations of DEA with visual examples and test data in a way that can be understood by business practitioners, students, and stakeholders who are not mathematicians. DEA input and output-focused approaches are discussed along with constant returns to scale, variable returns to scale, and increasing and decreasing returns to scale. Radial movements and slack estimates are explained to achieve the efficient frontier. A small example dataset is used, and a larger real-world secondary higher education dataset is processed from the U.S. Department of Education. DEA is compared with nonparametric statistics. This chapter also exposes the problems of using DEA and how to use methods and data triangulation to check reliability and validity. The most surprising finding was that the research questions could not be answered, and independent data revealed some paradoxically contrasting results for some of the sample data cases. The chapter will interest managers, decision-makers in any industry, students, government regulators, and researchers.

Karim Iddouch, Ibn Zohr University, Morocco

Khalid El Badraoui, Ibn Zohr University, Morocco & Mohammed VI Polytechnic University,
Morocco

Jamal Ouenniche, The University of Edinburgh, UK & Mohammed VI Polytechnic
University, Morocco

This chapter surveys the literature on the productivity profiles of Islamic Banks (IBs), with a specific
emphasis on Malmquist Productivity Indices (MPIs) estimated using Data Envelopment Analysis (DEA)
methodologies. It examines 68 publications from 2006 to 2022, offering a comprehensive categorization
of the literature based on four key aspects: (1) the type of DEA analysis, (2) productivity measurement
methodologies, (3) variables for DEA model specification and corresponding evaluation approaches,
and (4) the drivers of productivity along with their theoretical foundations. This paper also provides
a critical analysis of the existing literature, identifying gaps, inconsistencies, and potential sources of
discrepancies in the findings, thereby paving the way for future research to address these limitations.

Leonardo H. Talero-Sarmiento, Universidad Autónoma de Bucaramanga, Colombia

Laura Yeraldin Escobar Rodriguez, Universidad Autónoma de Bucaramanga, Colombia

This study advances healthcare process optimization, focusing on surgery roadmaps in the healthcare
system, a scenario exemplifying optimization challenges due to limited information. This chapter
emphasizes enhancing efficiency and resource utilization by employing lean manufacturing, operational
research, simulation, data envelopment analysis, and non-dominance analysis. This study discovers
32 correlated patient pathways, showing shared activities and simultaneous multi-route impact from
optimization strategies. Instead of merely analyzing pathway performance, the study applies data
envelopment analysis to various investment scenarios, providing insights for healthcare decision-makers
on improving patient care quality and efficiency. The juxtaposition of data envelopment analysis with
a non-dominance algorithm in this mixed-method approach offers a robust framework for addressing
healthcare operational challenges, particularly under information scarcity, and promotes continuous
process improvement.

Edlira Martiri, University of Tirana, Albania

This chapter offers a comprehensive examination of contemporary practices in synthetic data generation.
Its primary objective is to analyze and synthesize the methodologies, techniques, applications, and
challenges associated with synthetic data across diverse scientific disciplines. The motivation behind the
use of synthetic data stems from data privacy concerns, limitations in data availability, and the necessity
for diverse, representative datasets. This chapter delves into various synthetic data generation methods,
such as statistical modeling, generative adversarial networks (GANs), simulation-based techniques,

and data envelopment analysis (DEA). It also scrutinizes the evaluation metrics for assessing synthetic data quality and privacy preservation. The chapter highlights applications in healthcare, finance, social sciences, and computer vision, and discusses emerging trends, including deep learning integration and domain adaptation. Researchers, practitioners, and policymakers will gain valuable insights into the state-of-the-art in synthetic data generation.

Chapter 6

Muhammed Abiodun Adebimpe, American University of Nigeria, Nigeria
Adeyemi Abel Ajibesin, American University of Nigeria, Nigeria
Franklin Tchakounté, University of Ngaoundere, Cameroon

The growth of wireless technology due to global population growth and urbanization has increased internet usage, intensifying network energy demands. Researchers and professionals prioritize energy efficiency to cut costs and reduce emissions, with a focus on wireless networks. This chapter explores energy efficiency's importance, particularly in ad hoc wireless and sensor networks. This study seeks to maintain energy efficiency while maximizing resources like node numbers, using computational methods and data envelopment analysis (DEA) with multicast incremental power (MIP) and coded packet algorithms as DEA inputs. An output-oriented DEA approach enhances network performance by increasing output while maintaining input resources. This research contributes significantly to understanding energy efficiency in wireless networks, providing valuable insights for network administrators and decision-makers, particularly in ad hoc wireless networks.

Chapter 7

Rajasekhara Mouly Potluri, Kazakh British Technical University, Kazakhstan
Narasimha Rao Vajjhala, University of New York Tirana, Albania

In the modern era, disruptive technologies, ranging from artificial intelligence to big data analytics and virtual reality to drone technology, have profoundly impacted India's lifestyles and employment dynamics. This chapter deeply explores these innovations' history, meaning, theory, and significance, focusing mainly on their transformative influence on the Indian industries, health, transport, and energy sectors. Beyond just an exploration, this study employs DEA for efficiency benchmarking, offering a structured assessment of how well these sectors have harnessed the potential of disruptive technologies. The analysis underscores the diverse issues, challenges, and opportunities arising from integrating these technologies and the subsequent shifts in employer-employee relationships and challenges posed to governance. Furthermore, the chapter elaborates on the real-world implementations of these technologies and their broader ramifications, including cost reductions, sustainability, and socially responsible practices in the concerned sectors.

Chapter 8

Uetutiza C. C. Kuzatjike, Namibia University of Science and Technology, Namibia
K. S. Sastry Musti, Namibia University of Science and Technology, Namibia

Microgrid configurations provide a reliable and sustainable energy supply to off-grid settlements. Various energy sources, including renewable and non-renewables, are currently used to power the microgrids. Scheduling these energy resources and managing the microgrids can be challenging due to various constraints. Data envelopment analysis (DEA) is one of the well-known solution methodologies that can be effectively used for energy management studies. This chapter applies a multi-objective DEA to the energy management of a typical rural, remote micro-grid supplied by a solar plant and diesel generator sets. The methodology utilizes the DEA algorithm to identify microgrid optimal configurations by considering technical, environmental, and economic factors. The Tsumkwe rural region of Namibia is considered for studying the DEA application and analysis. The study evaluated the energy system's performance under varying efficiencies, fuel consumptions, and generator capacities.

This chapter investigates data envelopment analysis (DEA) in the context of supply chain management. DEA, a non-parametric method for assessing productive efficiency with many inputs and outputs, has considerably impacted research and practical implementation. It enables performance analysis across organizations with complicated input-output interactions. DEA provides user-friendly and customizable criterion weighting, simplifies analysis by eliminating the need for production function calculation, and delivers comprehensive efficiency measurements. This chapter examines existing research on the use of DEA in supply chains to assess present practices, recent breakthroughs, and techniques critically. This chapter addresses the central research question, "What are the latest advancements and methodologies in applying DEA to the supply chain?" The findings of this study add to the understanding of current practices at the confluence of DEA and supply chain management, which is critical in today's complex corporate context.

Renewable energy systems have gained significant attention in recent years due to their potential to mitigate climate change and reduce reliance on fossil fuels. However, ensuring the efficient utilization of resources and optimizing the performance of these systems remain critical challenges. This chapter focuses on applying data envelopment analysis (DEA) as a valuable tool for assessing and optimizing the efficiency of renewable energy systems in various scientific, information technology, and engineering contexts. The chapter overviews DEA principles, methodologies, and models and explores its specific application in renewable energy systems. The integration of DEA with other analytical tools, such as life cycle assessment (LCA) and optimization techniques, is also examined. The chapter highlights data availability and quality challenges and identifies future research directions in DEA for renewable energy systems.

Chapter 11

This chapter explores the applications, contributions, limitations, and challenges of data envelopment analysis (DEA) in healthcare management. DEA, a non-parametric method used for evaluating the efficiency of decision-making units, has found extensive applications in healthcare sectors such as hospital management, nursing, and outpatient services. The review consolidates findings from a broad range of studies, highlighting DEA's significant contributions to efficiency measurement, benchmarking, resource allocation and optimization, and performance evaluation. However, despite DEA's robust applications, the chapter also identifies several limitations and challenges, including the selection of inputs and outputs, sensitivity to outliers, inability to handle statistical noise, lack of inherent uncertainty measures, homogeneity assumption, and the static nature of traditional DEA models. These challenges underscore the need for further research and methodological advancements in applying DEA in healthcare management.

The digital divide in Africa, particularly Nigeria, has raised concerns about the efficiency of internet service providers (ISPs) in providing quality services to their subscribers. This research focuses on evaluating the efficiencies of the major ISPs in Nigeria, including MTN, Glo, Airtel, and 9mobile, using data envelopment analysis (DEA). The study examines vital efficiency metrics such as internet speed, cost of data, years of existence, and subscriber base over five years from 2015 to 2019. The results reveal varying levels of efficiency among ISPs, with MTN consistently ranking as the most efficient. These findings have implications for improving the quality of internet services and promoting healthy competition within the Nigerian telecommunications industry. The study also highlights the importance of considering multiple parameters in assessing ISP efficiency, shedding light on areas for future research and regulatory interventions by the Nigeria Communications Commission.

Chapter 13

The chapter aims to analyze and compare the cost and profit efficiency of public sector banks (PSBs) in India after the post-banking sector reforms of 1991. The data was gathered and analyzed from 1995 to 2017, i.e., from the post-liberalization period until the significant State Bank of India merger in 2017. Average profit efficiency (PE) and cost efficiency (CE) scores were analyzed year-wise for each PSB in India. The distribution and median of efficiency scores in two sub-periods were also assessed using non-parametric Friedman's two-way ANOVA and Wilcoxon signed-rank test. The results revealed profit inefficiencies among PSBs in the selected period. Over the whole period, PE is less than the CE scores. The findings also revealed wide variations across public sector banks from 1995 to 2017. Moreover, the

PE of PSBs has declined since the banking sector reform in 1991 in India.

Chapter 14

Trilochan Jena, Birla Global University, India
Pradipta Kumar Sanyal, Birla Global University, India
- Sreekumar, Rourkela Institute of Management Studies, India

In today's changing business environment characterized by complexity and volatility, the Indian banking sector is witnessing tough competition from national and multinational players. In this study, the authors studied the Indian bank mergers between 2006 and 2018 to measure the impact of mergers and acquisitions (M&A) on efficiency in financial performance. A sample of four Indian banks—State Bank of India, Bank of Baroda, HDFC Bank, and Kotak Mahindra Bank—was selected based on market capitalization. This chapter evaluated five years of pre- and post-merger financial efficiency to measure the impact of M&A on efficiency in financial performance. The authors considered seven critical variables impacting the performance of Indian banks for the study. The non-parametric technique data envelopment analysis (DEA) is used for efficiency measurement over the period. The study shows that mergers and acquisitions positively impact the enhancement of financial efficiency.

Foreword

It is with great pleasure that I introduce the forthcoming publication, *Data Envelopment Analysis (DEA) Methods for Maximizing Efficiency*, edited by Adeyemi Abel Ajibesin and Narasimha Rao Vajjhala. This comprehensive volume, compiled by esteemed experts in the field, promises to be an invaluable resource for scholars, researchers, consultants, and decision-makers interested in efficiency analysis and performance measurement. The editors, Narasimha Rao Vajjhala and Adeyemi Abel Ajibesin, bring a wealth of experience and expertise to this project. Dr. Vajjhala, an Associate Professor at the Faculty of Engineering and Architecture at the University of New York Tirana, Albania, has over 20 years of experience teaching and consulting in technology firms across Europe and Africa. His role as the Editor-in-Chief of the International Journal of Risk and Contingency Management underscores his commitment to advancing knowledge in the field. Dr. Ajibesin's contributions as an editor and author enhance the depth and breadth of this compilation, bringing together a diverse range of perspectives and insights.

The book begins with a strong foundation in the basics of DEA, exploring various models and methodologies. It progresses seamlessly from fundamental concepts to advanced techniques, showcasing practical applications through real-world examples and case studies. The editors have succeeded in creating a resource that is both accessible to a broad audience and informative for experts in the field. The chapters cover a wide range of topics, including applications of DEA in diverse industries such as healthcare, finance, supply chain management, environmental management, education management, and public sector management. Furthermore, chapters in this book explore future developments and emerging trends in DEA research, ensuring that readers stay abreast of the latest advancements.

One notable strength of this book is its attention to addressing real-world challenges. Chapters like "Efficiency Analysis of a Surgery Roadmap Based on Lean Manufacturing Techniques, Simulation, and Data Envelopment Analysis" and "Data Envelopment Analysis in Healthcare Management: Overview of the Latest Trends" provide practical insights that resonate with current issues in healthcare optimization. The diverse perspectives offered in chapters like "Synthetic Data Generation: Methods, Applications, and Multidisciplinary Use Cases" demonstrate the interdisciplinary nature of DEA and its relevance across various scientific disciplines.

As you delve into the chapters of this book, you will find a rich tapestry of knowledge, insights, and methodologies that contribute to the advancement of efficiency analysis. Whether you are a student, researcher, consultant, decision-maker, or simply someone with a general interest in data analysis and performance measurement, *Data Envelopment Analysis (DEA) Methods for Maximizing Efficiency* is sure to be a valuable addition to your library. I commend the editors and authors for their dedication to producing a work that not only reflects the current state of the field but also sets the stage for future advancements. I am confident that this book will be a cornerstone in the literature on DEA, inspiring further research and application in the quest for maximizing efficiency across diverse domains.

Best wishes for an enlightening and informative reading experience.

Ali Emrouznejad
Centre for Business Analytics in Practice, Surrey Business School, Guildford, UK

Ali Emrouznejad *is a Professor and Chair in Business Analytics at Surrey Business School, UK. He also serves as the director of the Centre for Business Analytics in Practice, leading research efforts in various fields, including performance measurement and management, efficiency and productivity analysis, as well as AI and big data. Ali Emrouznejad has been acknowledged as one of the top 2% most influential scientists globally by Stanford University. With an h-index of over 60, he has been listed among the 'World Top 100 Business & Management/Business Administration Scientists 2024.' Prof. Emrouznejad serves as the editor or associate editor in numerous reputable journals. He has authored or co-authored over 250 articles and published over 10 books.*

Preface

INTRODUCTION

As the editors of *Data Envelopment Analysis (DEA) Methods for Maximizing Efficiency*, we are thrilled to present a comprehensive and timely resource for researchers, practitioners, and students in science and engineering. This book fills a significant gap in the literature by addressing the application of DEA, a critical and evolving tool in measuring and enhancing technical efficiency, particularly in scientific and engineering contexts. Since its inception by Michael Farrell in 1957, DEA has primarily been applied in economic and management fields. However, its potential in science and engineering has remained largely untapped. This gap can be attributed to both a need for more relevant data in these fields and a limited understanding of how DEA can be effectively applied to assess and improve decision-making processes. Recognizing this, our book embarks on an interdisciplinary journey, showcasing how DEA can be a vital instrument for performance measurement and improvement in various technical domains. It delves into the practicalities and complexities of applying DEA in scientific and engineering disciplines, which involve highly technical processes and decision-making units (DMUs). A total of 31 authors from 12 countries contributed a total of 14 chapters. A total of 19 chapters were submitted, and following a double-blind peer-review process, the editors rejected five chapters.

CHAPTER OVERVIEW

In Chapter 1, "Effects of Public Capital Investments on Productivity of the United States, 1992-2022," Brian Sloboda and Yaya Sissoko provide an in-depth analysis of public sector productivity in the United States from 1992 to 2022, a period characterized by significant heterogeneity across states in terms of public services delivery. This diversity has implications for both productivity and efficiency within the public sector. The chapter addresses the increasing scrutiny of public services amidst ongoing reform processes. Unlike the private sector, where market forces primarily inform performance, the public sector relies on comparative performance measures to assess productivity. This study investigates the productivity of the public sector across various states using standard Data Envelopment Analysis (DEA) and the Malmquist Productivity Index (MPI) for efficiency measurement. The DEA analysis is complemented by panel regression analysis to provide a more comprehensive understanding of public sector productivity, considering the unique challenges and dynamics of public service delivery in different states. This approach offers valuable insights into the performance of the public sector, highlighting areas for improvement and reform in the context of an evolving administrative landscape.

In Chapter 2, "Data Envelopment Analysis Advantages and Problems Demonstrated in a University Comparison Study," Kenneth David Strang explores the multifaceted aspects of DEA, presented in a manner accessible to a diverse audience, including business professionals, students, and various stakeholders. This chapter intricately explores DEA's input and output-oriented approaches, encompassing a spectrum of returns to scale – constant, variable, and those exhibiting increasing or decreasing trends. Crucial concepts such as radial movements and slack estimates are elucidated, paving the way to achieving an efficient frontier. Central to the discussion is the application of DEA through two distinctive datasets: a concise, illustrative example and a more extensive, real-world dataset derived from secondary higher education statistics provided by the U.S. Department of Education. This exploration offers a comparative perspective between DEA and nonparametric statistical methods. Furthermore, this chapter addresses the inherent challenges associated with utilizing DEA, highlighting the importance of employing methods and data triangulation to assure the reliability and validity of findings. One of the most striking revelations of this study is the inability to conclusively answer the research questions posed, underscored by independent data, which paradoxically presented contrasting results for some instances within the sample data. This chapter promises to be of significant interest to a wide array of individuals, including managers, decision-makers across various industries, students, government regulators, and researchers, providing them with valuable insights into the application and nuances of DEA.

In Chapter 3, "Productivity Profiles of Islamic Banks using Data Envelopment Analysis-Based Malmquist Productivity Indices (MPIs): Survey, Classification, and Critical Analysis," Karim Iddouch, Khalid El Badraoui, and Jamal Ouenniche present an in-depth systematic literature review focusing on the productivity of Islamic Banks (IBs). The study, which scrutinizes 68 publications from 2006 to 2022, emphasizes explicitly using Malmquist Productivity Indices (MPIs) estimated through DEA methodologies. The authors have meticulously categorized the existing literature into four distinct areas: the types of DEA analysis employed, the methods used for measuring productivity, the variables involved in DEA model specification, their evaluation approaches, and the underlying drivers and theoretical frameworks of productivity. Additionally, the chapter critically examines the literature to unearth gaps, inconsistencies, and potential sources of discrepancies, thereby shedding light on areas that future research might explore further to enhance our understanding of productivity in Islamic Banks.

In Chapter 4, "Efficiency Analysis of a Surgery Roadmap Based on Lean Manufacturing Techniques, Simulation, and Data Envelopment Analysis (DEA)," Leonardo H. Talero-Sarmiento and Laura Yeraldin Escobar Rodriguez focus on optimizing healthcare processes, particularly in the context of surgery roadmaps within healthcare systems. The study addresses the challenges of optimization in scenarios characterized by limited information. This chapter explores various methodologies, including lean manufacturing, operational research, simulation, DEA, and non-dominance analysis, to enhance efficiency and resource utilization in healthcare. The study identifies 32 interrelated patient pathways, revealing the shared activities and the extensive impact of optimization strategies across multiple routes. Unlike conventional analysis of pathway performance, this study utilizes DEA across various investment scenarios, offering vital insights for healthcare decision-makers on enhancing patient care quality and efficiency. The novel approach of combining DEA with a non-dominance algorithm provides a comprehensive and robust framework. This mixed-method approach is particularly effective in tackling operational challenges in healthcare, especially in situations of limited information, and underscores the importance of continuous process improvement.

In Chapter 5, "Synthetic Data Generation: Methods, Applications, and Multidisciplinary Use Cases," Edlira Martiri provides an in-depth examination of the current state of synthetic data generation, encompassing its methodologies, applications, and challenges across various scientific fields. This chapter addresses the growing need for synthetic data, driven by concerns over data privacy, limited availability of real datasets, and the requirement for diverse, representative data. The chapter explores a range of methods for generating synthetic data, including statistical modeling, generative adversarial networks (GANs), simulation-based approaches, and DEA. This chapter also discusses the importance of evaluating synthetic data in terms of quality and privacy preservation. Key applications in sectors such as healthcare, finance, social sciences, and computer vision are highlighted, along with emerging trends like the integration of deep learning and domain adaptation. The chapter is a valuable resource for researchers, practitioners, and policymakers, offering insights into the advanced practices of synthetic data generation.

In Chapter 6, "Data Envelopment Analysis-Based Approach for Maximizing Energy Efficiency in Ad Hoc Networks," Muhammed Abiodun Adebimpe, Adeyemi Abel Ajibesin, and Franklin Tchakounté explore the escalating energy demands of wireless networks driven by global population growth and urbanization, which have led to increased internet usage. The chapter underscores the growing importance of energy efficiency, especially in wireless networks, in response to rising costs and the need to reduce emissions. It focuses mainly on ad hoc wireless and sensor networks. The study employs computational methods and data envelopment analysis (DEA), incorporating Multicast Incremental Power (MIP) and Coded Packet algorithms as inputs to DEA to optimize energy efficiency while maximizing network resources such as node numbers. An output-oriented DEA approach is highlighted, aiming to enhance network performance by increasing output while conserving input resources. This research provides significant insights into the energy efficiency of wireless networks, offering practical guidance for network administrators and decision-makers, with a particular emphasis on ad hoc wireless networks.

In Chapter 7, "Efficiency Benchmarking Through Data Envelopment Analysis: Evaluating Disruptive Technologies in India's Key Sectors," Rajasekhara Mouly Potluri and Narasimha Rao Vajjhala provide an in-depth analysis of how disruptive technologies, including artificial intelligence, big data analytics, virtual reality, and drone technology, are reshaping lifestyles and employment dynamics in India. This chapter explores these innovations' history, meaning, theory, and significance, explicitly focusing on their transformative impact on critical sectors such as industry, healthcare, transportation, and energy in India. Employing DEA for efficiency benchmarking, the study systematically evaluates the extent to which these sectors have effectively leveraged disruptive technologies. The analysis highlights the various challenges, opportunities, changes in employer-employee relationships, and governance issues that have emerged from integrating these technologies. Additionally, the chapter examines the real-world applications of these innovations, emphasizing their implications for cost reduction, sustainability, and socially responsible practices in the respective sectors.

In Chapter 8, "Data Envelopment Analysis for Improving the Microgrid Operations," Uetutiza C.C. Kuzatjike and K.S. Sastry Musti explore the application of multi-objective DEA in managing and optimizing energy resources in microgrids, with a particular focus on off-grid settlements. Microgrids, which can be powered by a mix of renewable and non-renewable energy sources, offer a sustainable and reliable energy supply but pose significant scheduling and management challenges due to various constraints. The chapter demonstrates how DEA, a well-known solution methodology, can be effectively used in energy management studies. Specifically, it applies a multi-objective DEA to a rural, remote microgrid in the Tsumkwe region of Namibia, which solar plants and diesel generators supply. This approach utilizes the DEA algorithm to identify the optimal configuration of the microgrid by considering technical, environmental, and economic factors. The study assesses the energy system's performance under different conditions, including varying efficiencies, fuel consumptions, and generator capacities, providing valuable insights into optimizing energy management in remote microgrids.

In Chapter 9, "Advancing Supply Chain Efficiency and Sustainability: A Comprehensive Review of Data Envelopment Analysis (DEA) Applications," Natasha Cecilia Edeh provides an insightful examination of DEA within the realm of supply chain management. DEA, known for its non-parametric approach in evaluating productive efficiency involving multiple inputs and outputs, has significantly influenced both academic research and practical applications. The method is particularly adept at analyzing performance in organizations where complex input-output relationships are prevalent. One of DEA's key advantages is its user-friendliness and the flexibility it offers in criterion weighting, which simplifies the analysis by obviating the need for calculating production functions and provides comprehensive efficiency assessments. The chapter critically reviews existing research on DEA's application in supply chains, aiming to identify current practices, recent innovations, and methodologies. The central research question addressed is, "What are the latest advancements and methodologies in applying DEA to the supply chain?" This study contributes to a deeper understanding of the intersection of DEA and supply chain management, an area of great significance in the intricate landscape of modern business.

In Chapter 10, "Efficiency Assessment and Optimization in Renewable Energy Systems Using Data Envelopment Analysis," Tarun Kumar Vashishth, Vikas Sharma, Kewal Krishan Sharma, Bhupendra Kumar, Rajneesh Panwar, and Sachin Chaudhary explore the burgeoning field of renewable energy systems, spotlighting their role in combating climate change and reducing dependence on fossil fuels. A key focus is the utilization of DEA, a potent tool for evaluating and enhancing the efficiency of these systems within scientific, information technology, and engineering frameworks. The chapter provides a comprehensive overview of DEA, covering its fundamental principles, methodologies, and models, and specifically discusses its application in the context of renewable energy systems. It also examines how DEA can be integrated with other analytical tools, such as life cycle assessment (LCA) and optimization techniques, to further refine the efficiency assessment of renewable energy sources. Additionally, the chapter addresses challenges related to data availability and quality and outlines potential avenues for future research in applying DEA to renewable energy systems. This exploration is essential for advancing the efficient and effective use of renewable energy in an era increasingly focused on sustainable practices.

In Chapter 11, "Data Envelopment Analysis in Healthcare Management: Overview of the Latest Trends," Narasimha Rao Vajjhala and Philip Eappen provide an insightful exploration of DEA within the context of healthcare management. DEA, recognized for its non-parametric approach in assessing the efficiency of decision-making units, is widely applied in various healthcare sectors, including hospital management, nursing, and outpatient services. The chapter synthesizes findings from numerous studies, emphasizing DEA's crucial role in efficiency measurement, benchmarking, resource allocation, optimization, and performance evaluation in healthcare. Despite its extensive use, the chapter also sheds light on several limitations and challenges associated with DEA. These include issues related to the selection of inputs and outputs, sensitivity to outliers, an inability to deal with statistical noise, the absence of measures for inherent uncertainty, assumptions of homogeneity, and the static nature of traditional DEA models. These identified challenges highlight the necessity for ongoing research and methodological improvements in applying DEA to healthcare management, aiming to enhance its effectiveness and reliability in this critical sector.

In Chapter 12, "Exploring Productivity by Evaluating ISP Efficiency in Nigeria's Telecommunications Sector," Yakub Akinmoyede, Adeyemi Abel Ajibesin, Senthil Kumar Thangavel, and Ridwan Salahudeen address the digital divide in Africa, specifically focusing on the efficiency of Internet Service Providers

(ISPs) in Nigeria. The research evaluates the performance of major Nigerian ISPs - MTN, Glo, Airtel, and 9mobile - using Data Envelopment Analysis (DEA). The study investigates key efficiency metrics, including internet speed, cost of data, years of operation, and subscriber base, over five years from 2015 to 2019. The findings indicate diverse efficiency levels among the ISPs, with MTN emerging as the most consistently efficient provider. These results significantly enhance internet service quality and foster competitive practices in Nigeria's telecommunications sector. The study underscores the importance of considering a range of factors in evaluating ISP efficiency, providing insights for future research, and guiding potential regulatory actions by the Nigeria Communications Commission. This analysis is crucial for understanding and addressing the challenges of the digital divide in Nigeria and potentially other parts of Africa.

In Chapter 13, "Comparison of Cost and Profit Efficiencies of Indian Public Sector Banks in the Post-Reform Period," Vipul Gupta presents a comprehensive analysis of the cost and profit efficiency of Public Sector Banks (PSBs) in India in the aftermath of the banking sector reforms introduced in 1991. The study covers a period from 1995 to 2017, which includes the post-liberalization era and extends up to the significant merger of the State Bank of India in 2017. It entails a year-wise examination of average profit efficiency (PE) and cost efficiency (CE) scores for each PSB in India. Additionally, the distribution and median of these efficiency scores across two sub-periods were evaluated using non-parametric methods, specifically Friedman's two-way ANOVA and the Wilcoxon signed-rank test. The findings highlight a trend of profit inefficiencies among PSBs during the selected period, with PE scores generally being lower than CE scores. The study also reveals considerable variations in efficiency among different Public Sector Banks throughout the 1995-2017 timeframe. Notably, there has been a decline in the PE of PSBs since the onset of banking sector reforms in 1991, offering critical insights into the impacts of these reforms on the operational efficiencies of India's PSBs.

In the book's final chapter, "Impact of Mergers and Acquisitions on the Shareholders Wealth of Indian Banks: A Data Envelopment Analysis Approach," Trilochan Jena, Pradipta Kumar Sanyal, and Sree Kumar present a study on the impact of mergers and acquisitions (M&A) on financial performance efficiency in the Indian banking sector, a domain marked by intense competition and dynamic changes. This study analyzes four major Indian banks —State Bank of India, Bank of Baroda, HDFC Bank, and Kotak Mahindra Bank—selected based on their market capitalization and focuses on the period between 2006 and 2018. It evaluates the financial efficiency of these banks over five years, both before and after the mergers, to assess the effects of M&A. The authors incorporate seven critical variables that influence the performance of these banks. Using the non-parametric method of Data Envelopment Analysis (DEA) for efficiency measurement, the study concludes that mergers and acquisitions positively impact banks' financial efficiency, highlighting the strategic value of M&A in enhancing performance in the competitive Indian banking landscape.

This book is the product of contributions from leading experts in the field. It is designed to be a valuable resource for those new to DEA as well as for seasoned practitioners and researchers seeking to deepen their understanding and application of this methodology in science and engineering contexts. We hope that this book will inspire new research directions, foster the development of innovative applications of DEA, and contribute to the broader discourse on efficiency and productivity in the scientific and engineering communities.

Adeyemi Abel Ajibesin
American University of Nigeria, Nigeria

Preface

Narasimha Rao Vajjhala
University of New York Tirana, Albania

Acknowledgment

Assoc. Prof. Adeyemi Abel Ajibesin

To my beloved wife, Mrs. Olajimoke Olufemi Ajibesin, and my cherished children, Wisdom and Eunice Ajibesin, your unwavering support is my greatest treasure. Thank you for being my constant inspiration and the heartbeat of our family.

Assoc. Prof. Narasimha Rao Vajjhala

I want to thank my family members, particularly my mother, Mrs. Rajeswari Vajjhala, for her blessings and for instilling in me the virtues of perseverance and commitment.

We extend our heartfelt gratitude to Professor Ali Emrouznejad, esteemed Chair in Business Analytics at Surrey Business School, UK, for his invaluable contribution in writing the foreword of this book. His expertise and insightful perspectives have greatly enriched the content, offering readers a profound understanding of the subject matter.

Chapter 1
Effects of Public Capital Investments on the Productivity of the United States, 1992–2022

Brian Sloboda
ⓘ https://orcid.org/0000-0003-0007-1725
University of Maryland, Global Campus, USA

Yaya Sissoko
Indiana University of Pennsylvania, USA

ABSTRACT

This chapter examines the productivity of the public sectors throughout the United States from 1992 through 2022. Because there is heterogeneity across states regarding public services provided, this could impact its productivity and efficiency. The services provided by the public sector have come under increased scrutiny with the ongoing reform process in recent years. In the public sector, unlike the private sector, and the information and incentives provided by these markets, performance information, particularly comparative performance measures, have been used to gauge the productivity of the public service sector. This chapter examines the productivity of the public sector across states using the standard date envelopment analysis (DEA) and efficiency measures given by the Malmquist productivity index. Then, the DEA analysis was followed by panel regression analysis.

INTRODUCTION

What are the empirical effects of public capital on private output or productivity? Policymakers in the United States is greatly interested in measuring productivity in the public sector across states, as many states are confronted with budget deficits. Consequently, policymakers want to know if the state governments are using their limited resources efficiently and cost-effectively to the taxpayers. In general, there

DOI: 10.4018/979-8-3693-0255-2.ch001

have been opposite positions on the subject: those who believe that government investments in general are not efficient, and those who believe that they are efficient which contributes positively to economic growth. While strong arguments exist on both sides of the issue, the empirical results have been mixed. This chapter analyzed the efficiency of the public sector involving all fifty states throughout the United States, focusing on productivity, i.e., technical efficiency. Technical efficiency is commonly defined as the production of maximum output with the most efficient usage of inputs and is frequently used as a necessary condition for measuring efficiency. More specifically, this chapter examined the current state of efficiency of the public sector in the United States in terms of resource use and its impact on the economy, as measured by public capital from 1992 through 2022.

The first contribution of this chapter is the annual expenditure data from the National Association of Budget Officers (NASBO) to measure public capital, not the Census of Government by the Bureau of the Census. Prior studies would often use the Census of Government as a measure of inputs (different expenditure programs) and/or output (aggregate expenditure) to measure the impact of the public sector on economic growth or productivity. More importantly, the data from NASBO differs from the Census of Government as the NASBO provides more granular data for expenditures by each state. In contrast, the Census of Government provides their data at an aggregated level. The second contribution of this chapter is another approach to measuring the effects of public capital and labor on total factor productivity (TFP) using the Malmquist productivity index. The primary problem in measuring public capital is that measures of public capital do not exist. To derive measures of public capital, prior researchers would determine the value of the public capital stock by adding gross investment flows and subtracting the depreciation of public capital stock based on the life spans for each of the public capital estimated. The latter approach is called the perpetual inventory method (PIM).[1]

This chapter is divided into four sections: the first section provides a literature of review highlighting the hypotheses presented over the years; the second section provides a discussion of the data and the methodology; the third section summarizes the empirical results; and the final section concludes the chapter.

MAIN FOCUS OF THE CHAPTER

Issues, Controversies, Problems

The assessment of the relationship between public investment and economic growth has existed for quite some time in the economics and public administration literature, not just for the United States, but other countries and regions. However, the degree to which these public investments are impacted based on empirical results on economic growth evidence has been mixed. Some empirical results supported the position that public investments in infrastructure, e.g., roads, bridges, highways, and services, contribute to economic growth. In contrast, some empirical results support the notion that public investments do not impact economic growth. Empirically, the approach used to assess the effects of public capital on productivity via a production function approach was used extensively following the seminal work of Aschauer (1989).

The seminal work by Aschauer (1989) reinforced the acknowledgment of the positive relationship between increased public spending, especially non-defense spending, and economic growth. Aschauer's work is vital because it attributes the problem of declining productivity to the declining government spending on infrastructure. He concluded that a one percent increase in public capital would increase productivity by 0.39 in the United States. He concluded that a one percent increase in public capital was highly productive in the United States. Given the latter conclusion, it promulgated additional studies about the effects of public capital on productivity. Munnell (1990) also reached conclusions like Aschauer, although her estimates of the relative effects of public investments were smaller than those of Aschauer. The main criticism of the empirical results by Munnell (1990) and Aschauer (1989) is that they used the aggregate data at the national level, ignoring trends in the time series. More importantly, subsequent empirical work showed that the estimate of the output elasticity of public capital differs across studies (ranging from -0.11 to 0.73), which spurs the validity of the production function approach and data used in these studies.

Since the advent of Aschauer (1989), future researchers have also used enhanced empirical estimation techniques to examine the effects of public capital on productivity. The subsequent empirical work removed the trends, considered any missing explanatory variables, such as oil price shocks, and estimated an elasticity close to zero. In addition, future empirical work used other state-level data sources to assess the role of public capital and economic growth. Some of these empirical models are simple extensions of the neoclassical growth model of Solow (1957). To examine the role of public capital and productivity more closely, researchers used different data sets to investigate the linkages between the role of public capital and the macroeconomy. Many authors have made use of state-level data using various approaches to look at the importance of infrastructure to productivity ((Sloboda and Yao, (2008) used state-level data to assess spillover effects; and costs of production in manufacturing sectors used on the state level as espoused by Holtz-Eakin & Schwartz, 1995). Specifically, using the production function approach is not the problem but the econometric problems that often arise reverse causation, and non-stationarity of time series data (spurious correlation). Some research has revealed nonlinearity between the role of public capital and economic growth on the state level.

Using panel data, Murova and Khan (2017) used a stochastic frontier analysis (SFA) to estimate the efficiency of public investments and their impact on economic growth in the United States from 1992 to 2012. Their empirical results showed a highly significant and positive relationship between gross state product (GSP) and expenditures on education, transportation, health, welfare, and public safety (police and fire), but negative but significant relationships between output and employment in health care and public safety. They examined the efficiency of government expenditures in five service sectors: education, transportation, health, welfare, and public safety (police and fire), using data from the Bureau of Economic Analysis and government expenditures from the Bureau of the Census. They used GSP as the dependent variable and government expenditure on the five service sectors as the independent (input) variables. They found that the public sector's technical efficiency (TE) was high. The average TE score across all years and all states was 0.878, which suggested that the public sector operated at a relatively high efficiency level.

Aschauer (2000) provided one such explanation that the benefits of public capital rise at a diminishing rate, but the costs of providing public capital (e.g., through distorting taxation) rise at a constant rate. Garcia-Milà et al. (1996) estimated the Cobb-Douglas production function with three types of public capital as inputs via a panel regression for 48 contiguous US states from 1970 to 1983. After controlling for fixed effects, they found that highways and water/sewers contributed 0.127 percent and 0.064 percent for the United States using a production function. In comparison, other capital spending contributed –0.071 percent to the economic growth. The empirical results from the literature focused on the United States. What does the empirical evidence say from international studies? Santiago et al. (2020) analyzed the relationship between public capital stock, private capital stock, and economic growth for a group of thirty Latin American and Caribbean countries from 1970 to 2014 via a panel vector autoregression methodology, panel dynamic ordinary least squares, and panel fully modified ordinary least squares estimators. Their results showed that public and private capital positively affect the countries' long-term economic growth. On the other hand, their estimates showed that the public capital seemed to crowd private capital in the short run, possibly explaining the adverse effect of public capital stock on growth. Despite these findings, governments throughout Latin America and the Caribbean should continue to support public and private investment projects because both types of capital affect long-term economic growth positively.

Straub, Vellutini, and Warlters (2008) used the growth accounting model and cross-country regressions and determined an insignificant relationship between infrastructure, productivity, and growth in East Asia. Boopen (2006) used a dynamic panel model and found that transport capital contributed significantly to the economic growth of Sub-Saharan African countries. Canning and Pedroni (2004) investigated the long-run effects of telephones, electricity generation, and paved roads on per capita income in a panel of countries from 1950 to 1992. Their results determined that infrastructure did induce long-run growth effects with a variation across countries used in their study. Ho and Iyke (2020) applied the autoregressive distributed lag (ARDL) testing procedure to investigate Ghana's economic growth determinants and how government expenditure only influences short-term economic growth. Similarly, Diyoke et al. (2017) investigated the impact of government spending on economic growth in Sub-Saharan African countries (SSA) from 1980 to 2015. They applied static panel regressions and Arellano and Bond GMM estimators. Their findings revealed that government spending has a significant positive impact on SSA's economic growth. Campo and Mendoza (2018) studied the impact of public spending on regional GDP in 24 Colombian areas. Their findings revealed that public spending significantly and positively affects GDP.

The earlier literature, e.g., Ashauer (1989), Munnell (1990), Garcia-Mila & McGuire (1992), public investment has a higher return to private-sector economic performance than private capital investment. Their findings imply that augmenting public infrastructure investment could enhance U.S. productivity. However, on the other hand, some studies have shown no clear consensus on the degree of impact of public investments on total factor productivity. Despite these differences in the literature, there seems to be a general agreement that public investments contribute to economic growth and productivity (Kalyvitis & Vella, 2011; Lithgart and Suarez, 2011; Warner, 2014).

METHODOLOGY AND DATA SOURCES

Dataset and Statistical Sources

The input data has been collected and tabulated by the United States Department of Commerce Census Bureau to study the long-term productivity trends of the public sector in the United States. To illustrate the cross-section efficiency models, we focused on 1992 through 2022, while productivity trends corresponding to the Malmquist index are calculated using panel data from 1992 through 2022. The dataset consists of one output (public capital for each state) and three inputs (total labor, full-time equivalent (FTE), and payroll). Public capital is measured by the National Association of State Budget Officers (NASBO). The NASBO does not collect data for the District of Columbia (DC), so DC was omitted

Table 1. Summary of the variables in this analysis

Variable	Shorthand	Data Source
Public Capital	out_pubcap	National Association of State Budget Officers (NASBO)
Fulltime Equivalent	in_FTE	Employment and Payroll Survey, Census Bureau
Payroll	in_Payroll	Employment and Payroll Survey, Census Bureau
Total Labor	in_Total	Employment and Payroll Survey, Census Bureau

from the analysis. Using the fiscal data from NASBO enables us to improve the data measures of public capital and distinguish the contributions of public capital to productivity. Compared with accounting data based on capital stock and depreciation schedules, these fiscal data have certain advantages, particularly reliability, because they represent actual spending by the state governments. Also, these data are a more objective measure, which avoids the controversy of estimating public capital by state (Munnell, 1990). The public capital is deflated using the price index from the Bureau of Economic Analysis (BEA) for private fixed investment in structures because a public spending deflator is currently unavailable.[2]

For the inputs on labor, a common variable used in public sector productivity studies is obtained from the Census Bureau's Employment and Payroll Survey. The Bureau of the Census conducts a Census of Governments of all state and local government organization units every five years, for years ending in 2 and 7, coinciding with the Economic Census, as required by law. Because of the infrequency of the Census of Governments, we used the Employment and Payroll Survey to provide the annual data. In this analysis, we used full-time equivalent (FTE) for labor and a measure of payroll for all workers, including part-time. In productivity studies, it is best to use the number of hours of full-time labor. However, the Census Bureau does not collect such data, so we used the payroll data over the FTE of workers by the state government. Table 1 summarizes the variables used in this chapter.

Methodology of Malmquist Productivity Index

The data structure underlying the Malmquist Productivity Index or data envelopment analysis in general measures the productive and economic performance of a set of $j = 1, 2, \ldots, n$ observed DMUs, e.g., firms, activities, countries, individuals, etc. These observations transform a vector of $i = 1, 2, \ldots, m$ positive inputs $x \in R_{++}^m$ into a vector of $i = 1, 2, \ldots, s$ positive outputs $x \in R_{++}^s$ using the technology represented by the following constant returns to scale production possibility set:

Pcrs = $\{(x, y) \mid x \geq X\lambda, y \leq \lambda, \lambda > 0\}$, where X = $(x)_j \in R^{s \times n}$, Y = $(y)_j \in R^{m \times n}$ and $\lambda = (\lambda_1, \ldots, \lambda_n)^T >$ is a semipositive vector.

Charnes, Cooper, and Rhodes (1978) introduced an innovative linear programming approach to comparing decision-making unit (DMUs) efficiencies based on observed values of the DMUs' inputs and outputs in each time period. Their method imputes the weights for the inputs and outputs and is then used to produce a ratio of weighted outputs to weighted inputs, a measure of efficiency.

Using the data matrix inputs and outputs from the DMUs, we can estimate the input-oriented efficiency of each observation by solving n times the following linear programming problem under the assumption of constant returns to scale (CRS):

$$\min_{\theta,\lambda} \theta s.t. - y_i + Y\lambda \geq 0 \tag{1}$$

$$\theta xi - x\lambda \geq 0$$

where y is the column vector of outputs, x is the column vector of inputs, X is the input matrix, Y is the output matrix. θ represents the measure of the efficiency of the ratio between the weighted average of the outputs (y) produced and the weighted average of the inputs (x) used.

The linear programming model in equation (1) can be easily modified to include variables returns to scale (VRS) by adding the convexity constraint that ensures that an inefficient firm is only benchmarked against firms of similar size. The modified linear programming becomes:

$$\min_{\theta,\lambda} \theta s.t. - y_i + Y\lambda \geq 0 \tag{2}$$

$$\theta xi - x\lambda \geq 03$$

$$n1'» = 1$$

$$\lambda \geq 0$$

Malmquist Productivity Index measures productivity changes along with time variations and can be decomposed into changes in efficiency and technology with a DEA-like nonparametric approach. Productivity decomposition into technical change and efficiency catch-up necessitates using a contemporaneous version of the data and the time variants of technology in the study period. The MPI can be expressed in terms of distance function (E) as Equation (3) and Equation (4) using the observations at time t and t+1 as shown below:

$$MPI_I^t = \frac{E_I^t\left(x^{t+1}y^{t+1}\right)}{E_I^t\left(x^t y^t\right)} \tag{3}$$

$$MPI_I^{t+1} = \frac{E_I^{t+1}\left(x^{t+1}y^{t+1}\right)}{E_I^{t+1}\left(x^t y^t\right)} \tag{4}$$

where I denotes the orientation of the Malmquist Productivity Index (MPI), e.g., increasing returns to scale, constant returns to scale, variable returns to scale etc. The geometric mean of two MPI in Equation (3) and Equation (4) then becomes:

$$MPI_I^G = \left(MPI_I^t * MPI_I^{t+1}\right)^{1/2} = \left[\left(\frac{E_I^t\left(x^{t+1}y^{t+1}\right)}{E_I^t\left(x^t y^t\right)} * \frac{E_I^{t+1}\left(x^{t+1}y^{t+1}\right)}{E_I^{t+1}\left(x^t y^t\right)}\right)\right]^{1/2} \tag{5}$$

Equation (6) shows the input oriented geometric mean of MPI as denoted by G decomposed into the input oriented technical change (TECH) and input oriented efficiency change(EFF).

$$MPI_I^G = EFF_I * TECH_I^G = \frac{E_I^t\left(x^{t+1}y^{t+1}\right)}{E_I^t\left(x^t y^t\right)} * \left[\left(\frac{E_I^t\left(x^t y^t\right)}{E_I^{t+1}\left(x^t y^t\right)} * \frac{E_I^t\left(x^{t+1}y^{t+1}\right)}{E_I^{t+1}\left(x^{t+1}y^{t+1}\right)}\right)\right]^{1/2} \tag{6}$$

The Malmquist Productivity Index (MPI) as represented by Equation (5) and Equation (6) can be defined via DEA like distance functions. Put in another way, the components of Malmquist Productivity Index (MPI) are derived from the estimation of distance functions based on some frontier technology as shown by (Fare, Grosskopf, Norris, and Zhang, 1994)

After we can apply the CRS and VRS DEA frontiers to Equation (6) to estimate the distance functions, the measure of technical efficiency can be disaggregated into scale efficiency and pure technical efficiency. The scale efficiency be given in Equation (7)

$$SCALE = \left[\left(\frac{E_{vrs}^{t+1}(x^{t+1}y^{t+1} / E_{crs}^{t+1}\left(x^{t+1}y^{t+1}\right)}{E_{vrs}^{t+1}\left(x^t y^t\right) / E_{crs}^{t+1}\left(x^t y^t\right)} * \frac{E_{vrs}^t(x^{t+1}y^{t+1} / E_{crs}^t\left(x^{t+1}y^{t+1}\right)}{E_{vrs}^t\left(x^t y^t\right) / E_{crs}^t\left(x^t y^t\right)}\right)\right]^{1/2} \tag{7}$$

Finally, Equation (8), pure technical efficiency can be given as

$$PURE = \frac{E_{vrs}^{t+1}\left(x^{t+1}y^{t+1}\right)}{E_{crs}^t\left(x^t y^t\right)} \tag{8}$$

To calculate the Malmquist productivity index, the following linear programming problems need to be solved and these linear programming problems are represented as distance functions:

$$\left(d_0^t\left(x_t, y_t\right)\right)^{-1} = \max_{\theta,\lambda} \theta \, s.t. -\theta y_i + Y\lambda \geq 0 - x_{i,t} + X_t\lambda \geq 0, \lambda \geq 0 \tag{9}$$

$$\left(d_0^t\left(x_{t+1}, y_{t+1}\right)\right)^{-1} = \max_{\theta,\lambda} \theta \, s.t. -\theta y_i + Y_{t+1}\lambda \geq 0 - x_{i,t+1} + X_{t+1}\lambda \geq 0, \lambda \geq 0 \tag{1}$$

$$\left(d_0^t\left(x_{t+1},y_{t+1}\right)\right)^{-1} = \max_{\theta,\lambda} \theta s.t. -\theta y_i + Y_{t+1}\lambda \geq 0 - x_{i,t+1} + X_t\lambda \geq 0, \lambda \geq 0 \tag{11}$$

$$\left(d_0^{t+1}\left(x_t,y_t\right)\right)^{-1} = \max_{\theta,\lambda} \theta s.t. -\theta y_i + Y_{t+1}\lambda \geq 0 - x_{i,t+1} + X_t\lambda \geq 0, \lambda \geq 0 \tag{12}$$

The Method using the Parametric Approach

After the estimation of the results from the Malmquist productivity index, a regression analysis is used to test for the significance of the factor inputs and TFP in assessing the variation of the productivity level across US states. Each of the variables apart from the TFP are expressed in growth rates and recall that the estimates of the TFP from the Malmquist productivity index are merely the differences between pair-wise years and treated as a rate of change. A general Cobb-Douglas was estimated using a panel regression of the form:

$$\log\left(y_{i,t}\right) = \beta_0 + \beta_L \log\left(L_{i,t}\right) + \beta_K \log\left(K_{i,t}\right) + \mu_{i,t}, i = 1,\ldots N, t = 1,\ldots T \tag{13}$$

which I denotes the cross-section dimension of the fifty states in the United States, and t denotes the time series dimension where T= 31 (1992-2022). For a given state of i at time t, y_{it} is the measure of total factor productivity, L_{it} is the measure labor input of payroll for the number of full-time employees (FTE), and K_{it} is the measure of public capital. Finally, $\mu i_{,t}$ is the error term of this panel regression. However, TFP from the Malmquist productivity index are merely the differences between pair-wise years and treated as a rate of change, the measures of Li_t and Ki_t would also be expressed as rate of change. The revised specification of Equation (13) would be:

$$\Delta\log\left(y_{i,t}\right) = \beta_0 + \beta_L\Delta\log\left(L_{i,t}\right) + \beta_K\Delta\log\left(K_{i,t}\right) + \mu_{i,t}, i = 1,\ldots N, t = 1,\ldots T \tag{14}$$

EMPIRICAL RESULTS

Descriptive Statistics

From table 2, we can see that California and Texas has the largest number of full-time and part-time state employees (in_total) and (in_FTE) while the states of Vermont and Wyoming have the least number of state employees. As for the payroll (in_Payroll), California, New York, and Texas have the largest payrolls of state employees while South Dakota and Wyoming have the smallest payroll for its state employees. Finally, for the public capital (out_pubcap), California and New York have largest amount while Texas came in a distant third while the state of South Dakota had the lowest estimates and North Dakota and New Hampshire had close estimates to South Dakota.

Table 2. Descriptive statistics (means) for variables across states (in millions), 1992-2022

DMU	in_total	in_FTE	in_Payroll	out_pubcap
ALABAMA	3,255,803	2,704,720	9,865,848,260	1,357,434,487
ALASKA	861,899	759,681	3,574,502,110	600,723,874
ARIZONA	2,608,604	2,101,078	8,006,653,185	1,655,359,109
ARKANSAS	2,042,175	1,761,850	6,031,665,455	1,005,004,942
CALIFORNIA	14,741,472	12,028,026	66,803,374,024	11,717,243,684
COLORADO	2,869,692	2,236,909	10,161,170,173	1,282,281,608
CONNECTICUT	2,300,488	1,903,525	9,519,082,446	1,550,617,453
DELAWARE	917,851	767,697	2,985,632,950	472,036,276
FLORIDA	6,493,898	5,618,827	20,014,339,272	4,302,134,339
GEORGIA	4,626,077	3,801,645	13,253,700,100	2,265,088,154
HAWAII	2,152,520	1,731,969	6,559,005,537	707,786,474
IDAHO	903,079	711,677	2,681,325,843	359,373,957
ILLINOIS	4,920,146	4,059,700	17,602,979,068	3,211,302,521
INDIANA	3,513,394	2,749,030	9,791,077,869	1,496,694,673
IOWA	2,055,121	1,610,073	7,179,916,494	1,005,182,917
KANSAS	1,825,105	1,477,406	5,490,607,281	793,240,166
KENTUCKY	2,905,678	2,440,119	8,606,002,458	1,396,983,092
LOUISIANA	3,158,769	2,682,903	9,286,927,988	1,503,656,806
MAINE	822,935	654,044	2,376,530,197	434,183,993
MARYLAND	3,004,978	2,738,698	11,542,266,282	1,897,804,432
MASSACHUSETTS	3,539,390	2,916,104	13,757,185,261	2,574,146,264
MICHIGAN	5,574,236	4,374,766	19,649,938,245	2,804,974,903
MINNESOTA	2,925,969	2,390,384	10,964,323,476	1,717,564,777
MISSISSIPPI	1,930,495	1,691,241	5,465,268,093	917,859,319
MISSOURI	3,219,470	2,687,094	8,444,396,934	1,287,970,228
MONTANA	797,901	613,250	2,165,896,625	286,260,880
NEBRASKA	1,176,225	993,367	3,330,975,547	549,070,054
NEVADA	972,259	800,755	3,390,738,149	488,020,430
NEW HAMPSHIRE	761,715	575,792	2,238,811,117	284,968,797
NEW JERSEY	4,875,029	4,299,993	21,607,431,357	2,869,596,282
NEW MEXICO	1,702,765	1,420,740	5,049,263,632	784,570,982
NEW YORK	8,667,459	7,783,446	37,974,277,714	7,205,145,942
NORTH CAROLINA	4,941,738	4,202,350	15,944,474,904	2,357,806,805
NORTH DAKOTA	722,084	542,485	1,953,247,301	270,754,599
OHIO	5,593,283	4,266,474	17,302,716,818	3,372,817,023
OKLAHOMA	2,574,095	2,082,461	6,854,990,623	1,092,830,199
OREGON	2,387,179	1,905,368	8,260,027,419	1,504,775,787
PENNSYLVANNIA	5,901,666	4,835,725	20,704,865,557	3,563,633,184

continued on following page

Table 2. Continued

DMU	in_total	in_FTE	in_Payroll	out_pubcap
RHODE ISLAND	754,377	607,199	2,802,524,201	462,153,854
SOUTH CAROLINA	2,859,494	2,451,695	8,160,283,845	1,150,938,696
SOUTH DAKOTA	551,766	429,353	1,475,127,207	234,152,531
TENNESSEE	3,000,121	2,514,264	8,610,025,278	1,623,181,298
TEXAS	10,296,518	8,902,053	35,180,821,944	4,730,361,799
UTAH	2,047,412	1,612,338	6,306,263,963	677,935,087
VERMONT	491,730	426,572	1,785,682,964	297,550,577
VIRGINIA	4,778,400	3,777,851	14,830,358,041	2,166,447,144
WASHINGTON	4,588,792	3,618,517	15,926,849,822	2,009,671,482
WEST VIRGINIA	1,372,854	1,150,315	3,730,555,223	942,494,369
WISCONSIN	2,956,033	2,147,636	9,121,783,750	2,045,810,626
WYOMING	454,844	380,872	1,346,746,802	301,721,476

Results from the Data Envelopment Analysis (DEA) and the Malmquist Productivity Index (MPI)

We estimated the single period or Farrell's measure – efficiency change and technical change – for the fifty states from 1992-2022. These results are summarized in table 3 as averages for fifty states for each year.[4]

Table 3. Average annual changes of single period efficiency scores--Farrell's measure

Year	Efficiency Score	Year	Efficiency Score	Year	Efficiency Score
1992	0.644	2007	0.713	2022	0.703
1993	0.749	2008	0.721		
1994	0.712	2009	0.720		
1995	0.749	2010	0.725		
1996	0.799	2011	0.720		
1997	0.380	2012	0.712		
1998	0.769	2013	0.697		
1999	0.762	2014	0.738		
2000	0.748	2015	0.795		
2001	0.772	2016	0.707		
2002	0.685	2017	0.811		
2003	0.676	2018	0.796		
2004	0.684	2019	0.787		
2005	0.674	2020	0.671		
2006	0.668	2021	0.712		

Notes: 1. The estimates were prepared using the Data Envelopment Analysis Online Software. https://deaos.com/login.aspx?ReturnUrl=%2f.
2. The estimates used variables returns to scale (VRS).

Table 4. Average annual changes of the Malmquist productivity index, 1992-2022

Period	Efficiency Change (EC)	Pure Efficiency Change (PEC)	Scale Efficiency Change (SEC)	Technical Change (TC)	Malmquist Productivity Index (MPI)
1992-1993	0.982	1.079	0.938	1.050	1.033
1993-1994	0.996	0.955	1.044	1.067	1.063
1994-1995	1.064	1.056	1.008	0.973	1.034
1995-1996	1.096	1.079	1.006	0.923	1.006
1996-1997	0.242	0.467	0.553	6.058	1.490
1997-1998	0.240	0.463	0.547	5.998	1.475
1998-1999	0.956	0.993	0.966	1.049	1.004
1999-2000	0.942	0.988	0.943	1.081	1.017
2000-2001	1.063	1.037	1.026	0.950	1.009
2001-2002	0.898	0.887	1.032	1.204	1.080
2002-2003	0.946	0.986	0.960	1.082	1.023
2003-2004	1.015	1.015	1.002	1.041	1.057
2004-2005	0.950	0.996	0.963	1.141	1.083
2005-2006	0.981	0.996	0.990	1.080	1.059
2006-2007	1.131	1.090	1.043	0.922	1.043
2007-2008	1.041	1.019	1.023	0.983	1.024
2008-2009	0.970	0.998	0.975	1.078	1.045
2009-2010	1.055	1.015	1.041	0.995	1.049
2010-2011	1.005	0.997	1.011	1.021	1.026
2011-2012	0.982	0.999	0.984	1.005	0.986
2012-2013	0.903	0.971	0.937	1.133	1.023
2013-2014	1.203	1.075	1.124	0.849	1.022
2014-2015	1.083	1.084	1.002	0.957	1.036
2015-2016	0.959	1.016	0.945	1.045	1.002
2016-2017	1.029	1.009	1.020	0.978	1.006
2017-2018	0.978	0.980	0.998	1.032	1.009
2018-2019	1.000	0.991	1.009	1.024	1.025
2019-2020	0.747	0.844	0.892	1.433	1.068
2020-2021	1.141	1.073	1.065	1.009	1.146
2021-2022	0.976	0.986	0.986	1.094	1.064
Average	0.952	0.971	0.967	1.375	1.067

Note: The estimates were prepared using the Data Envelopment Analysis Online Software.
https://deaos.com/login.aspx?ReturnUrl=%2f.

We estimated these measures using the variable returns to scale (VRS) because not all states are endogenous and the VRS would estimate the measures of a state that are like them. The constant returns to scale (CRS) would not do the latter.[5] Because each year is less than unity, none of these years exhibit total efficiency. The lowest year reported was 1997 with an efficiency score of 0.380 while highest year was in 2017 with an efficiency score of 0.811. Given the state-by-state measures of each year, Wyoming, Florida, and Wyoming was efficient in most years. Other states such as Tennessee, and New York. West Virginia started off with inefficient scores but over time achieved efficiency from West Virginia were inefficient and gradually achieved efficiency in 2002 and maintained this status until 2020 then their estimates declined by a large amount. For some states such as Iowa, Alabama, and Georgia maintained a consistent pattern in its technical inefficiency scores from 1992 to 2022. The average TE score across all years and all states was which suggested that the public sector operates at a moderate level of efficiency of 0.7160.

Results From the Malmquist Productivity Index (MPI)

We estimated the MPI and its two components – efficiency change and technical change – for the US states for each pair of years from 1992-2022. In addition, to the efficiency and technical change, pure efficiency change, and the scale efficiency change are also estimated. Most states experienced progress in productivity during the period. The averages for each of the measures were estimated for the period 1992-2022. During 1992-2022, the annual productivity growth of the US states was 6.7 percent which indicates modest progress. The overall technical improvement rate increased by 37.5 percent and thus contributed to the growth of the TFP of the US states during this period. The annual TFP change showed a rising trend during most of the period. Overall, the US states were shown to have positive technical change, indicating that there is innovation occurring across the states. On the other hand, the average annual EC rate from 1992-2022 declined modestly by 4.8 percent indicating that the technical efficiency of the US states was declining. Instead of improvements in efficiency like we expected, there was a decline. More specifically, a positive efficiency measure would be evidence of catching up (to the best practices frontier), but the estimates do not reveal a catching up.

By breaking down the EC into the PEC and SEC, we see that these measures contributed to the decline of the overall EC in the US states as revealed by the 2.9 percent (PEC) and the 3.2 percent (SEC). Despite these declines in the EC, the TC provided the greatest contribution to the overall improvement in the TFP for the US states.

The Regression Analysis as Follow-up from the Nonparametric Estimation

Table 4 showed that technological change drives its TFP growth while efficiency showed a decline. Each state showed an improvement in their technology that is reflected as an improvement in their productivity change over time despite a decline in performance in terms of their efficiency change. Then, a regression analysis based on Equation (14) was used to test for the significance of the factor inputs and the TFP to determine growth. Table 5 summarizes the results from the pooled regression, panel regression, and generalized method of moments (GMM).

The regression results show that public capital stock or capital accumulation growth is directly linked to state economic growth. A pooled regression and panel regression showed a positive contribution of public capital to productivity. GMM also showed a high contribution to productivity across states given the instruments of lfte and ltotal which are the logarithmic transformation of in_fte and in_total, respectively. The latter would be like the conclusions by Ashauer (1989, 1990), Munnell (1990), Sloboda et al (2008) and others.

Table 5. Results from the panel regression analysis

	Pooled Regression		Panel Regression		Generalized Method of Moments (GMM)	
	Coefficient	Standard Error	Coefficient	Standard Error	Coefficient	Standard Error
Constant	-0.00023	0.003266	1.974	0.430341	-0.00035	0.001239
D(L(Pay)	-0.73728*	0.022352	-0.6643*	0.137596	-1.13193*	0.167193
D(L(Cap)	0.702568*	0.021349	0.471*	0.102297	1.070293*	0.167409

Note: * denotes statistical significance at .05. For GMM, the instruments used include the constant, lfte and ltotal. For GMM, the weighting matrix estimation used HAC (Newey West).

For the labor variables, each regression showed a negative contribution of state employees to the productivity across states. The latter could be consistent with the literature that effects of labor could have a negative effect on productivity (Warner, et al, 2021). They found higher contributions from labor in states with a higher concentration of unionization, but lower labor contributions in states with a conservative legislature and more penetration of state legislatures with corporate special interests.

CONCLUSION AND FUTURE RESEARCH DIRECTIONS

The states experienced high economic growth in recent decades via the Malmquist productivity index, and this remarkable growth has been attributed to technical change, not efficiency. Efficiency measures the improvements in resources. The state governments do not appear to use its resources well to enable productivity growth. From the empirical analysis, technological change is the main driver of growth for all the states but does not emerge as the driving force for growth across states. However, the efficiency measure does not contribute to productivity. That is, there are factors that are reasons why the efficiency measure is not contributing to productivity. The results also require a careful interpretation of the empirical results because the empirical evidence shows that productivity and public capital or state expenditures by each state are procyclical. That is, the regression results would not imply a causality from productivity growth to productivity growth in the long run. From this analysis, the evidence for labor to promote productivity does not appear promising.

A contribution of this chapter is another approach to measuring the effects of public capital and labor on total factor productivity (TFP) using the Malmquist productivity index. Prior empirical studies used the standard neoclassical production function to assess the impacts of public capital on productivity. Another contribution of this chapter is the use of the fiscal data from National Association of State Budget Officers (NASBO) enabled us to improve the data measures of public capital and distinguish the contributions of public capital on productivity across states. Earlier productivity studies emphasized the use of perpetual inventory method (PIM) to estimate public capital since the data availability for public capital is scant.

Though the literature on the effects of public capital on productivity has been largely dormant in recent years, there are still potential avenues for future research. Future research should focus on convergence because convergence by countries even by states, or regions that are poorer, e.g., per capita income, grows faster than countries (states, region) that are richer. In regional economics, the latter is known as the β convergence and the reasons for convergence include capital accumulation to steady state; labor migration; technology transfer; and other factors. Baumol (1986, 1994) posited conditional convergence. That is, how can nations join the "club"? There are several ways for the latter to occur: openness to trade, financial markets, educational attainment of the population. That is, convergence among U.S. states: "reversal of fortune" of the South because of the differences in economic development across states. The purpose of the convergence analysis would allow using the data mining technics to reduce heterogeneity across states by clustering on the dynamics of the states. More important, the latter analysis would increase the accuracy of the productivity estimates and determine leaders and catcher-ups clubs based on productivity across the states.

ACKNOWLEDGMENT

This research received no specific grant from any funding agency in the public, commercial, or not-for-profit sectors. We like to thank the participants, especially Allison Shwachman Kaminaga from the 2022 Pennsylvania Economics Association (PEA) Meeting for her comments and feedback.

REFERENCES

Arrow, K. J., Chenery, H. B., Minhas, B. S., & Solow, R. M. (1961). Capital labor substitution and economic efficiency. *The Review of Economics and Statistics*, *18*(4), 225–250. doi:10.2307/1927286

Aschauer, D. A. (1989). Is public expenditure productive? *Journal of Monetary Economics*, *23*(2), 177–200. doi:10.1016/0304-3932(89)90047-0

Aschauer, D. A. (2000). Public capital and economic growth: Issues of quantity, finance, and efficiency. *Economic Development and Cultural Change*, *48*(2), 391–406. doi:10.1086/452464

Baumol, W. J. (1986). Productivity growth, convergence, and welfare: What the long run data show. *The American Economic Review*, 1072–1085.

Baumol, W.J. (1994). Multivariate growth patterns: contagion and common forces as possible sources of convergence. *Convergence of productivity*, 62-85.

Boopen, S. (2006). Transport infrastructure and economic growth: Evidence from Africa using dynamic panel estimates. *The Empirical Economics Letters*, *5*(1), 37–52.

Campo, J., & Mendoza, H. (2018). Public expenditure and economic growth: A regional analysis for Colombia, 1984-2012. *Lecturas de Economía*, *88*, 77–108.

Canning, D., & Pedroni, P. (2004). *The Effect of Infrastructure on Long-Run Economic Growth* (Department of Economics Working Papers 2004-04). Department of Economics, Williams College. Available at: https://web.williams.edu/Economics/wp/pedroniinfrastructure.pdf

Charnes, A., Cooper, W. W., & Rhodes, E. (1978). Measuring the efficiency of decision making units. *European Journal of Operational Research*, *2*(6), 429–444. doi:10.1016/0377-2217(78)90138-8

Diyoke, K., Yusuf, A., & Demirbas, E. (2017). Government expenditure and economic growth in lower middle income countries in Sub-Saharan Africa: An empirical investigation. *Asian Journal of Economics. Business and Accounting, 5*(4), 1–11.

Fare, R., Grosskopf, S., Norris, M., & Zhang, Z. (1994). Productivity growth, technical progress, and efficiency change in industrialized countries. *The American Economic Review*, 66–83.

Farrell, M. J. (1957). The measurement of productive efficiency. *Journal of the Royal Statistical Society. Series A (General), 120*(3), 253–281. doi:10.2307/2343100

Garcia-Milà, T., McGuire, T. J., & Porter, R. H. (1996). The effect of public capital in state-level production functions reconsidered. *The Review of Economics and Statistics, 78*(1), 177–180. doi:10.2307/2109857

Ho, S. Y., & Iyke, B. N. (2020). The determinants of economic growth in Ghana: New empirical evidence. *Global Business Review, 21*(3), 626–644. doi:10.1177/0972150918779282

Holtz-Eakin, D., & Schwartz, A. E. (1995). Spatial productivity spillovers from public infrastructure: Evidence from state highways. *International Tax and Public Finance, 12*(4), 459–468.

Kalyvitis, S., & Vella, E. (2011). Public capital maintenance, decentralization, and US productivity growth. *Public Finance Review, 39*(6), 784–809. doi:10.1177/1091142111422439

Lithgart, J. E., & Suarez, R. M. (2011). The productivity of public capital: a meta-analysis. In W. Jonkhoff & W. Manshanden (Eds.), *Infrastructure Productivity Evaluation* (pp. 5–32). Springer.

Munnell, A. H. (1990). Why has productivity growth declined? Productivity and public investment. *New England Economic Review*, 3–22.

Munnell, A. H., & Cook, L. M. (1990). How does public infrastructure affect regional economic performance? *New England Economic Review*, 11–33.

Murova, O., & Khan, A. (2017). Public investments, productivity and economic growth: A cross-state study of selected public expenditures in the United States. *International Journal of Productivity and Performance Management, 66*(2), 251–265. doi:10.1108/IJPPM-12-2015-0190

Santiago, R., Koengkan, M., Fuinhas, J. A., & Marques, A. C. (2020). The relationship between public capital stock, private capital stock and economic growth in the Latin American and Caribbean countries. *International Review of Economics, 67*(3), 293–317. doi:10.100712232-019-00340-x

Sloboda, B. W., & Yao, V. W. (2008). Interstate spillovers of private capital and public spending. *The Annals of Regional Science, 42*(4), 505–518. doi:10.100700168-007-0181-z

Solow, R. M. (1957). Technical change and the aggregate production function. *The Review of Economics and Statistics, 39*(3), 312–320. doi:10.2307/1926047

Straub, S., Vellutini, C., & Warlters, M. (2008). *Infrastructure and Economic Growth in East Asia* (Policy Research Working Paper 4589). World Bank.

Sturm, J. E., & De Haan, J. (1995). Is public expenditure really productive?: New evidence for the USA and The Netherlands. *Economic Modelling, 12*(1), 60–72. doi:10.1016/0264-9993(94)P4156-A

Warner, A. M. (2014). *Public investment as an engine of growth.* Working Paper No. WP/14/148, International Monetary Fund. doi:10.1093/cjres/rsaa040

Warner, M. E., & Xu, Y. (2021). Productivity divergence: State policy, corporate capture and labour power in the USA. *Cambridge Journal of Regions, Economy and Society, 14*(1), 51–68. doi:10.1093/cjres/rsaa040

ADDITIONAL READING

Caves, D. W., Christensen, L. R., & Diewert, W. E. (1982). The economic theory of index Numbers and the measurement of input, output, and productivity. *Econometrica, 50*(6), 1393–1414. doi:10.2307/1913388

Coelli, T. J., Rao, D. S. P., O'Donnell, C. J., & Battese, G. E. (1995). *An introduction to efficiency and productivity analysis.* Springer Science & Business Media.

Fare, R., Grifell-Tatje, E., Grosskopf, S., & Lovell, C. A. K. (1997). Biased technical change and the Malmquist productivity index. *The Scandinavian Journal of Economics, 99*(1), 119–127. doi:10.1111/1467-9442.00051

Fare, R., Grosskopf, S., Lindgren, B., & Roos, P. (1992). Productivity changes in Swedish Pharmacies 1980-89: A nonparametric Malmquist Approach. *Journal of Productivity Analysis, 3*(3), 85–101.

Grifell-Tatje, E., & Lovell, C. A. K. (1999). A generalized Malmquist productivity index. *Top (Madrid), 7*(1), 81–101. doi:10.1007/BF02564713

Pastor, J. T., & Lovell, C. A. K. (2005). A global Malmquist productivity index. *Economics Letters, 88*(2), 266–271. doi:10.1016/j.econlet.2005.02.013

Ray, S. C., & Desli, E. (1997). Productivity growth, technical progress, and efficiency change in industrialized countries. *The American Economic Review, 87*(5), 1033–1039.

Shestalova, V. (2003). Sequential Malmquist indices of productivity growth: An application to OECD industrial activities. *Journal of Productivity Analysis, 19*(2/3), 211–226. doi:10.1023/A:1022857501478

KEY TERMS AND DEFINITIONS

Allocatively Efficient: A firm makes an efficient allocation in terms of choosing optimal input and output combinations given its resources.

Constant Returns to Scale: If a firm increases its inputs by x% results in x% increase in outputs.

Convexity: For each pair of points, every point on the line segment that joins them is covered by the set.

Distance Function: The maximal radial contraction (equivalently, the minimal radial expansion) of an input vector consistent with the technological feasibility of producing a given output vector.

Economically Efficient: A firm that is both technically and allocatively efficient in its use of resources.

Public Capital: Tangible capital stock owned by the public sector excluding military structures and equipment.

Transformation: The resources of a firms, activities, countries, individuals to be transformed from inputs into outputs.

Variable Returns to Scale: It helps to estimate efficiencies whether an increase or decrease in input or outputs does not result in a proportional change in the outputs or inputs respectively. While working in a problem, it can use constant returns to scale, increasing returns to scale, and decreasing returns to scale.

ENDNOTES

[1] For a good background on the perpetual inventory method (PIM), the reader should consult Sturm and DeHaan(1995).

[2] BEA currently does not have an index to deflate the public data because of the lack of public capital data to develop such an index.

[3] Charnes, Cooper, and Rhodes (1978) initially developed Farrell's (1957) idea to propose data envelopment analysis (DEA), which was called the CCR model. It is a linear programming technique that assesses decision-making units' technical efficiency (TE) measures (DMUs). This approach uses multiple inputs to produce outputs under the assumption of constant returns to scale (CRS).

[4] The averages are reported in this table. Farrell's measures are reported for each state, available from the authors, and not reported here for brevity.

Chapter 2
Data Envelopment Analysis Advantages and Problems Demonstrated in a University Comparison Study

Kenneth David Strang
https://orcid.org/0000-0002-4333-4399
W3 Research, USA

ABSTRACT

This chapter explains the variations of DEA with visual examples and test data in a way that can be understood by business practitioners, students, and stakeholders who are not mathematicians. DEA input and output-focused approaches are discussed along with constant returns to scale, variable returns to scale, and increasing and decreasing returns to scale. Radial movements and slack estimates are explained to achieve the efficient frontier. A small example dataset is used, and a larger real-world secondary higher education dataset is processed from the U.S. Department of Education. DEA is compared with nonparametric statistics. This chapter also exposes the problems of using DEA and how to use methods and data triangulation to check reliability and validity. The most surprising finding was that the research questions could not be answered, and independent data revealed some paradoxically contrasting results for some of the sample data cases. The chapter will interest managers, decision-makers in any industry, students, government regulators, and researchers.

INTRODUCTION

Everyone must make decisions, and there are numerous techniques to assist when the scenario is complicated. However, one of the biggest challenges for decision-makers is when the data is complex and when you need to know more than which is the best alternative. Only a few techniques are available to rank alternatives and identify improvements across numerous variables and cases. Most techniques allow only a few data types, they accept a limited number of independent or dependent variables, and

DOI: 10.4018/979-8-3693-0255-2.ch002

the routines will either identify something good or bad, rank the metrics, or predict the best value when a model has been developed - but rarely can one decision-making technique perform all these tasks.

Let's consider an example of a complex problem. How would a large multinational corporation leader decide which divisions or locations to terminate (or create) given the high volume of measurement data available? Furthermore, how could that same leader identify what needed to be improved in the lower-performing divisions so that perhaps no one needed to be hired or terminated? Likewise, given the high volume of marketing and benchmarking information available, how do students know which universities are the best choice? Alternatively, how do regulators determine which institutions under their supervision can be deemed safe for the public, or in contrast, which companies need to be improved and how? These are complicated managerial research questions requiring more than statistical correlation or predictive regression to solve!

That is the purpose of this chapter: to illustrate how a complex managerial decision-making approach can be applied to a complex situation. Additionally, the objective is to illustrate the advantages and disadvantages of applying a single best-in-class technique to solve a managerial problem. This chapter will review the literature to identify several critical factors relevant to managerial decision-making technique selection and implementation. The literature review will explain how several relevant techniques function and provide applied examples cited from the literature. The remainder of the chapter will apply the methodology in a study of universities, following the general approach conducted by a U.S.-based higher education association while using secondary data collected by the U.S. Department of Education. The results will be explained, and the implications will be provided to the stakeholders.

Specifically, the chapter aims to explain the data envelopment analysis (DEA) technique, the underlying theories, the advantages, and the disadvantages in a factual higher education comparative university study. There are several variations of how to design and apply DEA. These variations are discussed, and advice is provided about which design to choose based on the managerial research question and the available data types. There are three managerial research questions (RQ) driving this study. The first RQ is how the universities in the sample compare using benchmarks developed by the U.S. Department of Education (e.g., tuition, tenured faculty, etc.). The second RQ is how the lower-performing universities could improve their resource utilization or production compared to the best-in-class institutions within their peer group. A third RQ is also addressed regarding research quality: What are the statistical problems of using the DEA technique, which can be proven through detailed observations of the sample study, and how can the limitations be overcome in future studies? However, one of the challenges with DEA is that it is difficult to explain and understand for managers or nonmathematicians. In this chapter, the author explains the basics of DEA with examples in spreadsheet graphs to give the reader a theoretical understanding. Additionally, the author provides applied examples of DEA, with the estimates interpreted along with implications generalized to stakeholders.

In terms of generalizing the results of this study, the techniques and implications are transferable to any industry and managerial problem with a similar context of decision variables. The primary stakeholders are managerial decision-makers in any industry, within and beyond higher education. Decision-makers in this context include leaders, managers, administrators, government regulators, and policymakers. Secondary stakeholders interested in this chapter include consumers such as students or customers of services, where decisions need to be made when a high volume of complex numeric benchmarking or metrics are available for comparison. Thus, this chapter will benefit anyone needing to make a complex decision when the factors - the metrics - are readily available but in high volume and difficult to distinguish between. This chapter would also benefit researchers, scholars, and students concentrating in operations research or management science. Finally, this chapter will be of extreme value to management science consulting organizations and professionals because the techniques described herein are useful for helping organizations benchmark their efficiency against comparable peers or competitors and identify opportunities for productivity improvement.

BACKGROUND LITERATURE REVIEW

Data-driven decision-making can be achieved using three basic types of data - qualitative, quantitative, and or mixed combinations - each of which can be analyzed with appropriate techniques. Qualitative data includes images, open-ended questions, text, and non-numeric types. Qualitative data sounds numeric, but for certain research designs and techniques, numeric refers to strictly continuous or interval types (such as currency, ratios, and temperatures). A new form of mixed data has been identified in the last decade - big data, which customarily describes highly dispersed data characterized by a large volume, high arrival velocity, diverse variety, integrity, and value - to decision-makers. This is described in the literature as the five V's of big data – volume, velocity, veracity, value, and variety (Seiford & Zhu, 2002; Strang, 2019). It may also be noted that data can be transformed from one type to another, such as converting nominal labels into a meaningful interval scale to accommodate statistical techniques. Machine learning and artificial intelligence programs convert image and voice data into structured binary or hexadecimal tags to uniquely summarize patterns in the data stream, thereby accommodating nonparametric analysis. An example application of that would be facial recognition algorithms.

Techniques for analyzing qualitative and mixed data have been called interpretative or constructive approaches, including thematic analysis, critical analysis, comparative case studies, etc. Machine learning (ML) and software programming have been used to analyze mixed big data and all data types. ML applications often include statistical routines for evaluating predictive models developed using conditional processing and artificial intelligence concepts. In the positivist paradigm, parametric and nonparametric statistical approaches are customarily applied to numeric data types, and these include numerous techniques from description to correlation, as well as advanced mean-variance, regression, and time series analysis - to mention a few. A family of operations research techniques, including linear programming and statistical techniques, exist conceptually as positivist or interpretive approaches that may be applied to numeric data (or transformed data types). This last group is where DEA fits in, as an operations research technique in the management science field to assist decision-makers when analyzing complex numeric data. However, there are numerous decision-making techniques, which are briefly reviewed next.

Overall Landscape of Decision-Making Techniques Leading to DEA

Not surprisingly, decision-making techniques date back to the early management science literature. According to Rosacker and Olson (2008), the earlier decision-making approaches were based on qualitative data to evaluate tacit or intangible requirements using visual and persuasive techniques such as 'acts of faith' and 'instinct.' Qualitative decision-making techniques emerged using attribute models such as 'sacred cow' (suggestions by high-ranking executives), operating necessity (crisis), competitive necessity (industry pressures), product line expansion (market modernization), and benefit comparisons such as the 'Q-Sort' of perceived staff priorities (Meredith & Mantel, 2006).

Some decision-making approaches include embedded research methods such as expert team brainstorming (instead of a single person) to select the best alternative and the nominal group or Delphi consensus techniques (Strang, 2012). Numerous multi-criteria decision-making techniques and models emerged in the financial and economics literature, which embedded financial ratios like payback period, average or internal rate of return, discounted cash flow, or a profitability index (Meredith & Mantel, 2006). Advanced techniques from the financial field included Monte Carlo simulation, portfolio model selection, scenario development, and sensitivity analysis (Strang, 2012).

Numerous other weighting models emerged, all following the principles of transforming the original numeric factors into more representative indexes. An interesting decision-making technique called the analytical hierarchy process was developed by Saaty (1994), which allowed complex qualitative factors to be transformed into numeric indexes for ranking using pairwise comparisons and normalization factoring. Statistical principles are often embedded into techniques when quantitative data are being used. One of the weaknesses of the parametric statistical techniques is the requirement for the sample data to approximate a specific distribution, and many procedures have several additional assumptions. Even the nonparametric statistical techniques have limitations, such as the number of variables and lack of precision in the resulting estimate(s). A general weakness of all statistical techniques is that they commonly answer one ranking or prediction RQ through a hypothesis but are usually unable to identify improvements in the independent factors or dependent variables.

Overview of DEA

DEA is derived from vector math and distance analysis techniques based on calculus and trigonometry principles. Similar techniques are Euclidean Distance, correspondence analysis, and radial analysis. When algebra formulas and computer programming were added to these routines, nonlinear and linear programming (LP) approaches began to surface (Strang, 2012). In parallel, some statistical techniques and distance analysis procedures were extended and combined with programming, which many researchers would claim was the emergence of machine learning and artificial intelligence. Although ML is powerful and could help solve complex managerial problems, this is beyond the scope of the chapter and the RQs. DEA emerged to go beyond statistical and distance techniques to calculate multiple input and output variable improvements in supply chain production and transportation problems.

DEA is conceptually implemented as a multidimensional graph, where the various axes provide space for plotting the existing data. Then, the most theoretically efficient frontier line is created using the underlying linear programming calculations to solve multiple objective functions to maximize or minimize the resulting lambda technical efficiency weights. A maximization goal is used when the manager focuses on outputs by adjusting inputs. A minimization goal is applied when the focus is on adjusting the output to accommodate the inputs better. There are various combinations of the maximize versus minimize goals in DEA, known as the multi-stage approach, where the efficient frontier is approached to examine cost efficiency and optimize either inputs or outputs. The inputs and outputs are the production variables, determined or calculated by managers, and the decision variables are the lambda technical efficiency weights estimated to achieve the most efficient frontier (the best-sloping line on the conceptual graph). Functionally, DEA is commonly used to adjust inputs to maximize the output-to-input ratio, known as a maximization objective function in linear programming. The term constant returns to scale is often applied, meaning that a linear frontier is a straight line rather than a curved one. Variable returns to sale mean that the efficient frontier line can be sloped. In more detail, the variable returns scale can be increasing returns to scale (sloping up) or decreasing returns to scale (sloping down).

One of the key limitations of the various multicriteria, distance-based, and LP techniques is that they are deterministic, assuming all variables are known and produce a single best solution, or at best, a ranking of solutions. Some of the techniques have been modified to overcome those limitations. Still, for theoretical purposes, it wasn't until DEA, computer programming, and spreadsheet models began to be used that managers could add more input and output numeric variables along with production constraints to make complex decisions. This is where DEA becomes an advantage over similar tools when there are many numeric input and output variables, each in different base units, along with production or consumption constraints. DEA matured as a better-controlled decision-making approach than spreadsheet models and linear programming (although the latter is used within DEA). On the other hand, as noted earlier, DEA can be difficult for managers and decision-makers to understand. Consequently, if the decision-maker understands the DEA, it will be easier to apply a DEA technique to solve a complicated decision-making problem, or worse, the DEA application could be incorrectly designed, resulting in a fatally flawed solution for a business—technical examples of how DEA functions will be shown and discussed later in the 'Methodology' section.

Brief Review of a Few Interesting DEA Industry Applications

In reviewing the literature, it seems clear the original idea for DEA could be attributed to Farrell (1957), who applied it to analyze agriculture, that, is, farm production efficiency across 48 states in the U.S. Additionally, there were two other sources in the early literature contributing to the development of DEA. Fi, first Debreu (1951) developed the coefficient of resource utilization based on vector set arithmetic instead of calculus or linear equations. In parallel, Koopmans (1951) had been working on a similar technique using calculus and the graphing approach, but his unique contribution was introduced to the objective function subject to constraints. This basic model of the objective function subject to constraints has driven much of today's linear and nonlinear programming in management science. The DEA technique was further perfected as an operations research technique in management science by Charles Cooper and Rhodes (1979). They introduced the terminality decision-making units (DMUs) to represent the lambda technical efficient weights needed for each case or firm in the data under analysis. Interestingly, they developed DEA and applied it to assess (compare) the health systems across 35 countries in the African continent.

Since those earlier papers advanced the development of DEA, many researchers have applied DEA across other industries and added enhancements to the technique. A Google Scholar search returned over 1 million papers where DEA was mentioned. This chapter will briefly mention a few novel implementations of DEA implementations. Authors in early literature have categorized DEA as a nonlinear nonparametric technique. However, since linear programming is used, where balancing algebra equations are commonly used to solve for the optimal variable solutions, one could say DEA has a linear design, although calculus concepts are applied to estimate radial distances. The basic idea of simultaneous algebraic equations and linear programming is that the values of the decision variables will be proportional to the inputs and outputs. The end goal of DEA is, as mentioned above, to estimate efficiency scores, or weights, called lambdas, referring to adjustments needed for each variable under consideration to bring it closer, either up (in maximization) or down (in minimization), towards the best possible solution, the efficient frontier. A secondary goal or result of DEA is to rank the input cases or firms in terms of their overall efficiency (considering all inputs and outputs), which is a comparative research approach. Therefore, DEA is an operations research technique to compare the production efficiency of cases in management science, which would be conceptually similar to ANOVA (parametric) or Kruskall Wallis (nonparametric) techniques in the statistical field of practice. ANOVA is used much more than DEA.

In these early implementations of DEA cited above, much of the work was done through hand calculations and computer programming. Today, software, or even spreadsheets, is used to implement DEA. DEA has often been applied to analyze supply chain, logistics, and transportation production efficiency. One of the more interesting applications of DEA was by Paradi, Vela, and Zhu (2010), where they applied DEA to benchmark (compare) the e-commerce efficiency across two large banks in Canada. It was interesting because they added cultural indexes to capture the effectiveness of corporate strategies in dealing with multinational customers.

Another group of interesting models was developed along with supporting studies by Seiford and Zhu (2002). They produced DEA models using CRS, VRS, and RTS designs while adding variations for structure in the constraints, isolating the undesirable inputs and the efficiency adjustment weights. A useful concept they mentioned was the idea of bootstrapping to increase the size of the data sample, which would theoretically allow small samples to be processed using parametric statistical techniques if additional estimates were needed, including predictive model development of selected factors (inputs) regressed on dependent variables (outputs). This idea is useful because decision managers would identify high-performing efficient divisions or cases and then take a subset of the variables to identify predictive patterns in production. In that situation, a researcher would likely select several relevant inputs with widely varying values and perhaps one or two of the most critical outputs of the greatest strategic value to the manager. This way, multiple regression or multivariate regression (using generalized linear models) could be applied to develop a predictive model to aid strategic production planning.

Certainly, one of the more creative applications of DEA was by Liang, Cook, and Zhu (2008), where they demonstrated various DEA models to measure the efficiency of leader and follower peer decision-making units. They provided a comprehensive literature review on DEA (useful for other researchers). They developed a two-stage DEA process, showing various approaches to decompose the linear programming equations and test the efficiency scores. Another interesting practice they shared was using two large global data sets and a randomly generated data set to prove the model behaved reliably across complex data. This would certainly interest decision-makers in large multinationals where the number of variables and cases available is approaching the big data threshold. They also noted how the DEA Malmquist technique was ideal for time series input data, how that changed the basic and two-stage DEA models, and how to structure the data for correct analysis.

The author is familiar with two other recent studies of DEA. A DEA model was developed by Strang (2019) using a spreadsheet to assist regulatory policy decision-making in the U.S. government to monitor and help local electricity generation plants. His study aimed to apply DEA on data from a clean energy renewable hydroelectricity plant located in a natural park preserve (in New York). The clean energy plant study was interesting because it was among the first to apply DEA in the environmental conservation/ climate protection research category. Additionally, the study used two novel features, the first being a minimization goal and the second being a beta distribution as input. Another valuable feature was that the researcher developed and implemented the entire DEA model in a Microsoft Excel spreadsheet. In the study, the DEA's objective function was to make the minimum changes to the proposed policy rates for hydroelectricity generation subject to the known capabilities and risks calculated from a beta distribution. The DEA decision variables were the proposed changes to the policy rates for each month.

The simplex linear programming technique was used to implement DEA in a spreadsheet. Screenshots were included to illustrate how a manager or likely their information technology department could set up the DEA model in the spreadsheet software.

Finally, an interesting book reviewed most DEA techniques, with examples, and illustrated how to use DEA with R and other programming languages. Lotfi, Ebrahimnejad, Vaez-Ghasemi, and Moghaddas (2020) reviewed the DEA literature and discussed the concepts of deterministic and fuzzy analysis, where solutions could be more precise due to the complexity of the context. They combined the concept of DEA with fuzzy decision-making frameworks to solve optimization problems with the R programming language. They provided several examples of each DEA approach using datasets available in the public domain. This way, research students or management science practitioners could learn DEA and R.

METHODOLOGY

Scientific research begins with a research question and the explicit or implied unit of analysis, which identifies variables of interest and the data type. This chapter focuses on analyzing quantitative data from several universities to answer the managerial decision-maker question (MQ): How do the universities in the sample compare in performance based on industry-accepted benchmarking variables, and how could the lower performers improve their efficiency? The unit of analysis here is university efficiency according to several *a priori* variables to be measured. The variables are quantitative except for the university entity and its location. This is a comparative type of design, comparing quantitative data types - the performance variables of several universities. If we only wanted to contrast the means of student-teacher ratios, or some other metric, between the universities, then this would be a simple group comparison. For straight-forward group comparisons, the T-Test (if only two universities), ANOVA, or MANOVA techniques could be applied (more than two universities), or possibly CANOVA if an independent factor were numeric and known to vary in *a priori* studies as a component of another factor. We will apply the ANOVA technique in the case study to illustrate how this works.

On the other hand, ANOVA and its alternatives cannot solve the second part of the question, which is to identify how lower-performing universities could improve. This latter task requires an operations research technique within the linear programming category, such as DEA. As a general guideline, the researcher in this chapter applied the eight guidelines that Strang (2023) elaborated for reporting on quantitative scientific and scholarly studies. These are the guidelines:

- Formulate research questions in estimation terms, mentioning the anticipated effect size if possible but not testing hypotheses of no difference.
- Effect sizes should relate to the research questions, such as a measure of goodness of fit if a predictive regression model is being developed.
- Describe sample size, procedures, and data analysis techniques.
- In the results section, calculate point estimates and control intervals (CIs) in the relevant publication style; an APA example citing a fictitious mean is $M=9.5$, 95% CI [9.1, 9.7].
- Create figures to illustrate results where practical, including CIs, using error bars to depict 95% CIs.

- In the results, explain effect size estimates and how they were calculated because, for example, unlike r^2, Cohen's *d* has alternative denominators, plus state precision of CIs to answer research questions.
- In the discussion, consider theoretical and practical implications, express findings in ways they may be cited in future meta-analysis studies, and recommend how the study could be extended or replicated.
- Transparently describe the research to establish integrity, preferably including or making available the raw data to other researchers. [Adapted from Strang (2023)].

The above research guidelines are aligned with the scientific method post-positivistic ideology described by Strang (2023), which he explained is deductive theory-driven, fact-seeking data collection, and quantitative estimate testing. The ideology applied in this study was pragmatic, which Strang defined as a philosophy on a continuum between the extreme positions of positivist (deductive theory-driven, fact-oriented) and interpretative (inductive qualitative, meaning-focused (Strang, 2023). Strang further asserted that pragmatic researchers often use theories to guide the analysis rather than apply a single, generally accepted formal method; they may validate or refine theories after gathering mixed (quantitative and qualitative) data types and then using pluralistic combinations of techniques. Thus, when applying pragmatic ideology, it is acceptable to collect mixed data types (qualitative and or quantitative) and to apply combinations of techniques, including parametric or nonparametric statistics or general analytical procedures. Nevertheless, most of the guidelines cannot be applied to DEA, such as the statistical estimates, because DEA is not based on any underlying statistical distribution or inferential concepts. The first and last two guidelines are certainly applicable for this study or any study where DEA is applied.

Sample Data and Protocol

The sample was drawn from secondary data already collected and verified by the U.S. Department of Education (USDE, 2023). The source was selected because the University of Delaware had published an earlier study. DEA was applied to compare many higher education institutions using the same or similar metrics such as those identified by the University of Delaware (2023). The full data study contained approximately 1,000 performance benchmarks of 6543 private and public universities - the sample frame - collected by the U.S. Department of Education across all States, last updated on April 23, 2023 (USDE, 2023). The author recommends that other researchers utilize this USDE (2023) dataset. The data contains institution-level (university, college) data files for 1996-97 through 2020-21 containing aggregate data for each university or college. The level of analysis is at the college site, so there are multiple records for many of the larger universities since each campus site submits its responses individually. The dataset had almost a thousand fields, capturing information on university campus characteristics, enrollment numbers, student aid amounts, costs, and important student outcomes. A small subsample of four universities was taken from the sample frame to facilitate the discussion of DEA in this chapter. This was done to limit the high volume of results that would need to be discussed, given that the main objective of this chapter was to address the DEA technique rather than examine university metrics. Additionally, only a few of the most important fields were analyzed.

The sampling technique was purposive and then random. The purpose was to select an equal balance of similarly sized public and private universities from different states. First, the filter was set to include only medium-sized universities. Medium-sized institutions were chosen because the author felt smaller or larger universities may yield unusual metrics due to their uniqueness, as middle-tier universities would more likely be identical in productivity and quality. Then, a random private and a random public university were selected from each state (resulting in 104 total records). Although several universities had multiple campuses, only one was selected, exactly as it was provided to USDE (2023). This meant that only one specific site was selected for any university in the subsample, whether a main campus or a secondary site, and that site was considered a medium-sized institution.

The subsample was further reduced to 26 by eliminating records with unavailable metrics of interest (that is, data not provided on purpose by the institution). Next, two private and two public universities were randomly selected in different states to create the subsample of two private universities (one in Pennsylvania, one in Connecticut) and two public universities (one in New Jersey and one in California). The four universities were given generic abbreviations in the dataset, starting with 'Uni', to preserve the confidentiality of the institutions (given the good and bad results identified) and allow the reader to understand the interpretation of the DEA estimates and diagrams. Notwithstanding the need for confidentiality, a scholar must also balance the scientific requirement of revealing the exact evidence to other researchers. Therefore, the references were accurate, without concealing the sources, to make the evidence clear and truthful to other researchers and the global scientific community.

DEA Application Procedures

DEA can be applied for point-in-time and time series data. This chapter is restricted to point-in-time data (as described in the sampling protocol above). DEA can focus on optimizing the solution for inputs (the most common approach), outputs, or for costs (often by adding price data to calculate the extended costs). As explained earlier, DEA is a mathematical linear programming tool to develop ratios between the output and input variables, and then determine which adjustments or weights need to be applied to the variables to bring each case close to the conceptual efficient frontier line. A simple way to think of this is that when the focus is on inputs, these become the denominator in the formula, so the goal is usually to maximize outputs while minimizing inputs. Usually a best case (or multiple cases) is (are) selected within the data, called peer reference groups, to represent the efficient frontier. Alternatively, some DEA algorithms develop a hypothetical efficient frontier.

When focusing on the outputs, the goal is often to vary inputs while holding outputs constant, in order to bring a. This raises another aspect of DEA, which is the focus on linear constant proportions known as constant returns to scale (CRS), as compared to variable returns to scale (VRS), where the latter may be increasing returns to scale (IRS) or decreasing returns to scale (RTS). As the literature review describes, the CRS is the simplest DEA implementation where the so-called efficiency frontier is a straight line. We will look at a simple example below to explain the DEA procedures to a non-mathematician, such as a managerial decision-maker. A variation of an R routine is utilized to apply the DEA. For statistical and mathematical completeness, the following very basic linear programming equation 1 is provided, which can be implemented in the DEA routine for one of the variables (it would be repeated for each of the variables, using either a maximum or minimum objective goal:

Objective function: $0 \leq \Lambda \leq 1$ (1)

Subject to: $\frac{U}{D} \leq 1$

Table 1. Example inputs-focused DEA data inputs, outputs, costs

Company Cases	Input Workers (X)	Output Units (Y)	Labor Cost (Z)	Output / Input Ratio (W)	Unit Sell Price (P)	Revenue (R)	Net Profit (N)
Company A	15	200	600	13.333	10	2000	1400
Company B	5	80	200	16.000	10	800	600
Company C	10	150	400	15.000	10	1500	1100
Formulas:			$40 / worker	Y / X		Y * P	R-Z or Y*P-Z

$$y \leqq 1$$

Where λ is the optimized adjustment weight for one variable on one dimension or plane, x and y are two deterministic constraints (often there are many more).

The example produced by the author is a subset of the textile production industry, where a small group of workers at three different companies are compared using DEA. The number of inputs is 1, which is how many employees are clocked in for the production run in the group for each company site. The number of outputs is how many finished dresses each group produced per company. The author also added the known direct costs associated with the total units produced per group per company. Additionally, the author revealed the price each unit was being sold for as a distribution company in the upstream supply chain, where the goods would then be sold at another marked-up price at the retail point (we can ignore the retail price for this example). For simplicity, we will also assume a constant return to scale (CRS) and apply the multistage DEA. According to Paradi, Vela, and Zhu (2010), the multistage DEA is considered the most robust and accurate of all DEA variations because it encompasses both minimization and maximization objectives, one feeding into the other since a straight linear slope can be approximated for the efficient frontier.

Table 1 shows the example data across each of the three companies (which are the cases). The input workers (X) for company A are 15, and they produced 200 dresses (output units) in the sample production cycle. The company pays each worker $40. Therefore, the direct labor cost for all the units was $600. Since the selling price to the distributor was $10 per unit, the revenue for company A was $10 * 2000 = $2,000. Thus, the net profit was revenue minus costs, or $2,000 - $600 = $1,400 for company A. The formulas are listed at the bottom of the table (a slash means to divide, and the asterisk means to multiply). A key estimate was added to Table 1 (it was a result, but there was no room in Table 2 to add that metric). The key estimate was the output-to-input ratio (W). This illustrates the nature of DEA, which focuses on inputs in the denominator, and outputs become measured relative to each group.

When the DEA was applied to the above data, using the CRS and multistage options, the estimates are calculated as summarized in Table 2. This DEA result table shows that company B is the most efficient of the sample, with a technical efficiency of 1. Next is Company C, followed by Company A. The technical efficiency scores are ratios known as the Lambda. The highest performing group - B here - becomes the peer group used to benchmark the remaining cases in the sample. The efficiency ratio (TE in Table 2) is based on the output-to-input ratio (W) described above and listed in Table 1. The technical efficiency score is calculated by locating the highest output: input ratio (W) and using their Lambda as the basis or peer group to evaluate the remaining cases. For example, company A has a W of 13.3, calculated as

Table 2. Example inputs-focused DEA estimates to explain methodology

Company/Group	Technical Efficiency Ratio (TE Lambda)	Lambda Weight	X Adjustment (Xa)	New Xx	New Output / Input Ratio Efficient Frontier (Ww)
Company A	0.833	2.5	-2.5	12.5	16.00
Company B	1.000	1	0	5	16.00
Company C	0.938	1.875	-0.625	9.375	16.00
Formulas:	W/Max(W peer)	Xx/Xx peer	W-Max(W)*X	X+Xa	

200 / 15. The technical efficiency of 0.833 for company A was calculated as 13.333 / 16. Other equations were used to calculate the Lambda weight and radial X adjustment (Xa), listed in Table 2. For the example, the Xa if -2.5 for company A was calculated as the Lambda weight of 0.833 - the highest (peer) of 1 multiplied by the input X, or: (0.833 - 1) * 15 = -2.5 (note there are more decimals of precision in the software and dataset so a simple calculator may produce a different number). The new adjusted input Xx is calculated as 15 - 2.5 = 12.5 (again, beware of higher decimal precision in DEA). The Lamdha weight is calculated as the newly adjusted input Xx divided by the highest peer input (never adjusted), or 12.5 / 5 = 2.5 (again, beware of higher precision in DEA software). The new output: input ratio (Ww) in Table 2 is the efficient frontier. Ww creates a straight line since we use the DEA CRS option.

A visual explanation will also help explain how DEA works. Figure 1 is a graphical representation illustrating the data from Tables 1 and 2. The Y scale on the left represents the output: input ratio (W), while the Y scale on the right corresponds to the number of output units produced, all cast across the three companies on the X axis shown on the bottom. In Figure 1, the red line at the top, with triangles at the points, represents the efficient frontier across the three companies set at 16. The blue line with circles on the points represents the input (workers) data, while the yellow line with squares on the points presents the output units produced. Looking at the first company A values in Figure 1 (and cross-referencing to Tables 1 and 2), we can observe that the approximate distance between the blue circle (at 12.5 on the left Y axis) and the red triangle (at 16 on the left Y axis) is 2.5 units, which is the adjustment needed in company A's production team to achieve the most efficient frontier.

Likewise, the remaining company C has an adjustment of 1.875 required to decrease inputs from 10 to 9.375 to achieve optimal resource utilization levels, at least according to the calculated DEA frontier. Note that the DEA calculated the most optimal frontier based on selecting the highest performing case in the data, the company, referred to as the peer group. This illustrates one limitation of DEA: it can establish the most efficient frontier based only on inputs and outputs. Therefore, the theoretical most efficient frontier may never be known to managers. Nevertheless, the DEA technique appears capable of identifying the most efficient frontier as the peer comparison group and then ranking the remaining cases in terms of their relative production efficiency based on the data inputs and outputs. The benefit of DEA in doing this is the ability to analyze numerous input and output variables in vastly different base units.

This DEA procedure was applied to the full sample dataset from the USDE (2023) and the subsample. The DEA software was rerun with CRS and VRS, as well as multi-stage versus single-stage variations. This DEA application was input-focused, so only the inputs were examined by the linear programming equations in the software to determine if they needed adjustments. The DEA could also be implemented with an output focus (not included in this example). Again, in this example, only the most informative

Figure 1. Chart of DEA example to explain methodology

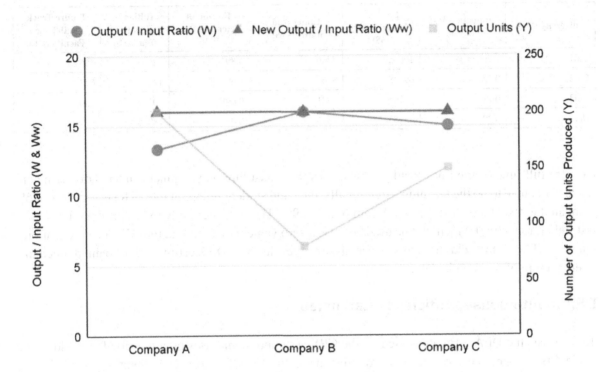

results were selected and discussed to explain the methodology to readers non technically without confusing business managers using the Newtonian formula convention style.

RESULTS AND DISCUSSION

Sample Descriptive Data

First, the sample's descriptive statistics are summarized to follow common practice. As explained earlier, all four universities were classified by USED (2023) as medium-sized. The average size of the sampled university campuses was 7865 students. Table 3 lists the data captured in the subsample (N=4) for processing in DEA. The output fields for DEA are GR and S$. The inputs to DEA are S#, RR, T$, and FT. This makes sense for the decision maker in the case study because graduation rates and student mean salaries are expected outcomes, benchmarks of the program after the students have graduated. In contrast to the decision-making model, the remaining fields would be controlled by management and serve as input to the conceptual process of providing students with accredited degrees. Here, the outputs comprised the number of students, how many stayed after the first semester, the tuition fees, and how many faculty were available to teach. The fields in Table 3 are abbreviated to facilitate discussion.

A quick observation of Table 3 reveals the descriptive statistics. We may observe that the graduation rate (GR) of Uni4 is significantly lower than all others (ranging from 71% to 90%). Additionally, Uni4

Table 3. Descriptive fields from university subsample data (n=4)

University (Uni)	Graduation Rate (GR)	Student Median Salary (S$)	Undergrad Students (S#)	Freshman Retention Rate (RR)	Tuition + Fees Per Year (T$)	Tenure Track Full-Time Faculty (FT)
Uni1	0.90	100559	5446	0.89	32698	566
Uni2	0.72	69748	8066	0.69	12807	673
Uni3	0.71	63365	8321	0.69	10751	250
Uni4	0.29	48155	7086	0.06	18325	0

has zero full-time tenure track faculty. This means they must hire only adjuncts under short-term contracts per course to do the teaching. Additionally, the Uni4 student retention rate (RR) is very low at 6% compared to the others, which ranged from 69% to 89%. These are certainly red flags about Uni4. The last field for faculty (FT) will not be used because a zero value will confound the DEA linear equations, but we will keep this field in mind as we analyze the results. The DEA estimates will paint a much different picture of the sample data.

DEA Input-Focused Efficiency Estimates

Table 4 lists the DEA estimates based on the CRS assumption and uses only the first four fields from Table 4 (since Uni4 does not employ any full-time tenure-track faculty). The abbreviations in Table 4 follow the convention explained in the methodology section. The new variable names refer to the graduation rate (GR), student tuition fees (S$), and first-year freshman retention rate (RR). The term 'radial adjustment' is based on the calculus and graphing principles of the distance between two points. Still, in DEA models, a radial movement is usually a downward change in the X or Y axis towards a more optimal state value point (assuming a maximization objective function goal) towards the efficient frontier. In a similar convention, the term 'slack' represents an upward or positive adjustment in the X or Y access toward a more optimal data value point in the graph toward the conceptual efficient frontier line.

Table 4 lists only relevant DEA estimates, such as the slack and radial adjustments and the calculated new values. For example, the column 'slack S$' is listed in Table 4 because DEA identified a nonzero value needed for at least one of the cases for the variable student tuition fees (S$). Still, there were no radial adjustments for S$, so that component was not included in Table 4 (it would have been a redundant column of zeros). The DEA estimates in Table 4 clearly show that Uni2 (86.9%) and Uni3 (84.8%) are less efficient than the other peers. Uni1 and Uni4 rank as 100% efficient (at least based on the input and DEA), so these two groups are positioned as the peer groups for the adjacent cases (to use when benchmarking Uni2 and Uni3). The Lambda weights for the output: input ratios adjust the inputs and outputs. The cells of interest in Table 4 are highlighted with background shading and italics.

First, it can be observed in Table 4 that Uni2 should attempt to help students get placements with higher salaries after graduation, by the average amount of $88,275. This is what the slack S$ refers to. Similarly, Uni3 should help its students increase starting salaries by $87,475. The two radial adjustment columns in Table 4 refer to downward or point movements on the conceptual DEA graph (assuming a maximization objective function goal, or the opposite if a minimization linear programming function is being implemented for the particular variable), as contrasted with the slack (upward) adjustments

Table 4. Key inputs-focused DEA estimates from university subsample data (n=4)

	Technical Efficiency (TE)	Cost Efficiency (CE)	GR Lambda Weight (Wgr)	S$ Lambda Weight (Ws$)	Slack S$	New S$	Radial adjustment S#	New S#	Radial adj, RR	New RR
Uni1	1	1	1	1	0	$100,559	0	5446	0	0.89
Uni2	0.869	0.54	0.497	0.64	18527	$88,275	-1060	7006	-0.091	0.599
Uni3	0.848	0.516	0.517	0.622	24110	$87,475	-1268	7053	-0.105	0.585
Uni4	1	0.368	1	1	0	$48,155	0	7086	0	0.06
Note: Numbers rounded to tenths decimal precision (beware of different precision if using calculators)										

calculated in the DEA (upward, again assuming a maximization goal or the opposite - downwards for a minimization linear programming goal). According to the DEA results in Table 4, Uni2 should decrease enrolled students by 1060, and likewise, Uni3 ought to decrease their student population by 1268. Paradoxically, the DEA proposed that these two universities decrease their graduation rates by 9.1% (Uni2) and 15% (Uni3), respectively.

As can be seen by these results, the DEA needs to make more sense to a university decision-maker who is focused on accommodating the key higher education stakeholders, the students, the accreditation associations, and the college campus community. The DEA estimates in Table 4 would serve only to make the mathematical model balance to achieve an efficient frontier. Thus, the biggest limitation of DEA is that it may need to be revised for the key stakeholder perspective, only for decision-makers. This means the DEA technique may show only part of the truth regarding comparative productivity metrics. The DEA model is only as effective as selecting input and output variables.

DEA Output-Focused Efficiency Coefficients

Given the surprising and overall uninformative estimates provided by the DEA input-focused analysis in Table 4, another DEA model was developed; this time, it was output-focused, but all the same variables were carried forward. Table 5 summarizes the key estimates from the DEA output-focused implementation using a CRS approach and a cost analysis.

Most DEA output-focused estimates shown in Table 5 were identical to the input-focused coefficients explained in Table 4. The TE rates were the same, and both Uni2 and Uni3 were identified as inefficient, requiring adjustments to their critical variables, using Uni1 and Uni4 as their nearest peer group in the data, respectively. However, there were two key differences since the DEA routine underlying the model explained in Table 5 used the output-focused variables as an objective function goal in the linear programming. Table 5 adjusted the two variable student salaries after graduation (S$) with radial movements and slack. In Table 5, another difference was that the graduation rate (GR) variable was given positive radial movement adjustments. This GR variable adjustment contrasts with the DEA input-focused analysis from Table 4 in that those earlier coefficients were negative adjustments, and the previous variable selected was the first-year freshman retention rate (RR), as contrasted with this new output-focused DEA model in Table 5.

In Table 5, the revised adjustment for student starting salary (S$) requires a slack of $21330 and a radial movement of $10,554 towards the new salary of $101,632 (rounded). Uni3 had a similar adjustment

Table 5. Key output-focused DEA estimates from university subsample data (n=4)

Case	Technical Efficiency (TE)	Cost Efficiency (CE)	GR Lambda Weight (Wgr)	S$ Lambda Weight (Ws$)	Slack S$	Radial adj. S$	New S$	Radial adj, GR	New GR
Uni1	1	1	1	1	0	0	100,559.00	0	0.9
Uni2	0.869	0.54	0.572	0.737	21330	10,554.12	101,632.31	0.109	0.829
Uni3	0.848	0.516	0.734	0.61	28445	11,392.53	103,202.64	0.128	0.838
Uni4	1	0.368	1		0	48,155.00	96,310.00	0	0.29
Note: Numbers rounded to tenths decimal precision (beware of different precision if using calculators)									

for S$, with a slack of $28445 and a positive radial movement of $11,392, resulting in a proposed new student starting salary of $103,203 (rounded). The graduation rates were adjusted for Uni2 (by +0.109) and Uni3 (by +0.128), thus raising their recommended graduation rates to 83% and 84%, respectively. As with the previous DEA input-focused analysis from Table 4, the DEA output-focused coefficients in Table 5 seemed to overlook the obvious low-performing Uni4, allowing Uni4 to serve as the peer group to Uni3 to define the efficient frontier.

Again, there is a decision-maker caveat here in that the DEA linear programming routines do not always make logical business choices. Instead, it is a mathematical choice based on linear programming loops. In linear programming, what occurs is that the entire set of possible values for a variable of interest is tested (that is subject to the constraints), one by one, and when a solution is found, the looping is ended since an optimal solution has been identified. Therefore, a weakness in linear programming is that it will only stop when the first optimal solution is found if the program has additional artificial intelligence logic.

Triangulation of Method and Data

Although this step was not specifically annotated in the methodology section, one of the most important requirements for generating high-quality scholarly scientific outcomes is to ensure the reliability and validity of the data as well as selected methods (the statistical or DEA techniques). Since this was a small subsample, taken by resampling the larger secondary data from USDE (2023), it would make sense to apply a different category of analysis procedure and to collect additional facts (data) to corroborate the results. In this chapter, given the ideology and methods identified earlier, performing a complementary nonparametric or parametric statistical technique makes sense, and collecting additional data points makes sense.

The additional statistical technique, being that this was a small sample of N=4, with no reliable statistical distribution to rely on, a nonparametric technique would be best. The most appropriate nonparametric group comparison technique is the Kruskal Wallis (KW) program so that it will be run. Additionally, a limited scholarly literature search will be done in an attempt to validate the ranking of the universities in the subsample to determine from sources outside of USDE (2023) what inputs or outputs may have been published - this could include a search of generic media and generic databases as long as the sources are independent of the university in question (in other words, the web sites of the universities would not be selected as independent sources of data to triangulate earlier findings). The KW routine is

Table 6. Kruskal-Wallis nonparametric test of university subsample data (n=4)

Case / Variable Ranks	GR	S$	S#	RR	T$	FT
Uni1	4	4	1	3	4	3
Uni2	3	3	3	2	2	4
Uni3	2	2	4	2	1	2
Uni4	1	1	2	1	3	1
Results	M=2.5, H=3, DF=3, P=.392	M=2.5, H=3, DF=3, P=.392	M=2.5, H=3, DF=3, P=.392	M=2.7, H=3, DF=3, P=.44	M=2.5, H=3, DF=3, P=.392	M=2.5, H=3, DF=3, P=.392
Hypothesis	Rejected	Rejected	Rejected	Rejected	Rejected	Rejected

a x lower in rank as compared to the others, and the median of the rank numbers (which would not be useful in a small sample). As mentioned in the methodology section, the confidence level was 95%, so the P value must be less than or equal to .05 to accept the hypothesis that the tested variable has at least some significantly higher or lower values.

Table 6 summarizes the critical coefficients, results, and hypothesis test interpretations from the KW tests of all the variables. The values shown in the columns are the ranks of the medians (not the medians or raw data values). At the bottom, the results row summarized the statistical coefficient reliability estimates, including the average rank, DF, H, and P value. If the P value is $\leq$.05, the variable cannot be considered a significant factor; the values between the cases or universities being compared are not significantly different. Here, the desired hypothesis is a p $\leq$.05 for all the variables, indicating they are significantly different. Then, we would look for the largest ranked value in the column to identify which university had the highest or best efficiency score.

The results from the KW nonparametric analysis listed in Table 6 are not favorable to a decision maker. All variables failed the hypothesis test of being significantly different, better, or worse than the others. Even for Uni4, with zero tenure track full-time faculty, there was not a statistically significant result (KW: average ranks=2.5, H=3, DF=3, p=.392). Although this was disappointing, we have one avenue for collecting additional data from different sources to triangulate the earlier DEA results when small sample sizes are used. To accomplish the triangulation of data sources, the generic literature was researched using the legal entity name of each university. Reliable government sources (e.g., USDE and federal government sources) or well-known independent review associations such as the Better Business Bureau (BBB) were used. Additionally, the well-established newspapers, such as the New York Times and

The results of the data source triangulation were surprising and significantly different from some of the DEA estimates. Uni1 could be informally considered one of the best-performing universities from a student standpoint since it had the highest graduation and retention rates and starting salaries. However, the tuition was over twice as high as the other three universities. This is a strong argument for managerial decision-making; the university graduates 90% of students (compared to 72% for Uni2, 71% for Uni3, and 29% for Uni4). Uni1 assures students they will start at a salary of approximately $100,000 after graduation, compared to around $70,000 for Uni2, $63,000 for Uni3, and $48,000 for Uni4. Uni1 has the smallest student population but is like the other universities. The more surprising finding in the data was that Uni4 had an almost unbelievably low rate of 6% for first-year student retention (RR) but the second highest tuition of $18,325 (next to Uni1 tuition of $32,698). Paradoxically, Uni4 had zero tenure track full-time faculty.

During the data triangulation, it became clear that Uni1 had positive student reviews in the literature, but there was a negative case in the public records. Uni1 recently settled a litigation with the U.S. Department of Justice (USDOJ, 2020, July 31). In that case, Dr. Yujie Ding, formerly a professor at and since terminated by the university, was convicted of wire fraud due to setting up a fake business and winning several small business grants. Ding was sentenced to a year and a day in prison for his role in the fraud; He was also ordered to pay a fine of $3,000 and restitution of $72,000, while his wife, Yuliya Zotova, was sentenced to 3 months in prison, given a fine and restitution to pay. Uni1 was fined $200,000 for failing to manage and prevent Ding's illegal activities at the university. There was also a blind student who complained that Uni1 failed to accommodate her disabilities, including not providing course materials in braille (Wolman, 2020, January 25) - but that case was not finalized at the time of writing. From a managerial decision-making perspective, the additional data did not necessarily overrule or change the earlier interpretation that Uni1 seems to be the highest-performing university and likely the best choice for a student.

Some independent data were found for Uni2, but it was not linked to the decision-making variables (e.g., not linked to student graduation rate, retention rate, tuition, faculty load, etc.). The one piece of data was in the court records (Justia, 2022), which involved a group of athletes in the basketball team who were self-declared as being in the LBTQ category, suing their coach and Uni2 for mistreatment during field practices and games. Given that the independent reviews of the university in BBB and other sources were positive, there seems to be no reason to question that Uni2 tended to be ranked as second best along with Uni3 when looking at Table 3 (descriptive statistics) and Table 6 (KW rank tests). This means Uni2 seemed equivalent to Uni3 on most efficiency scores, although Uni1 still ranked at the top. Uni3 had very little negative information and a lot of positive data found in the independent sources. There is little to be said of it except that, as with many universities, they could anticipate some activity from students in the 'Black Matters' category, which has seen many litigation cases citing discrimination as the cause. Ironically, Uni3 students seem to be promoting freedom-of-speech because their students criticized their Chancellor, in writing, for charging too high a security fee at a recent public event (Van-Voorhis, 2018, March 2).

The independent data collected to triangulate Uni4 was very negative, so much so that when considering the full-time faculty of zero, the 6% student retention rate, and the 29% graduation rate, any reasonable decision-maker would likely discredit the earlier DEA results that indicated no efficiency problems. For example, the first place searched was the BBB (2023), which contained 38 complaints in the last three years, 13 complaints in the last 12 months, an overall rating of 1.3 out of 5, and many negative responses by Uni4's customers. A search of government sites returned several federal cases by students and government departments, decided against Uni4. For example, Green (2022, April 8) summarized several lawsuits against Uni4. The first was by a former student, Carroll, who entered the business doctoral program at Uni4 with a 4.0 GPA from her master's degree. She was told it would take 18 months to complete it. Still, the university delayed her on purpose, extending the duration by an additional three years, costing "tens of thousands of dollars in unexpected tuition costs later" (Green, 2022, April 8). The case stated, "The school overcharged students by over $28.5 million" (Green, 2022, April 8). Another student, Fair, earned a Doctor of Business Administration from Uni4 but ended up owing $89,000 in loans that covered what became a four-and-a-half-year endeavor when she was originally told: "she could complete her degree in two and a half years and that with a military discount and a scholarship, she would pay a little more than $26,200" (Green, 2022, April 8).

The literature corresponding to Uni4 continued. In another independent court document, students Wright, Callahan, Harrison, Holubz, and Gardiner sued Uni4 and its parent company (Classaction, 2016). The students claimed they and thousands of similarly situated doctoral students were harmed by Uni4's false representations and omissions and by a dissertation process intended to ensure that it would be difficult, if not impossible, for students to complete. Another student - Thornhill - sued Uni4 for similar causes (Casetext, 2017). Schecter (2016) reported Thornhill, a former Uni4 student, was "a veteran, a single mother, and a schoolteacher in California with a sympathetic story of how [Uni4] stole six years of her life and left her in debt" and that Uni4 used "false advertising." Another student, Aaron Bleess, filed a similar lawsuit against Uni4 (Torres, 2017), claiming damages due to the university's false promises of finishing the doctorate in a shorter time and at a stated projected cost. Additional litigation cases against Uni4 were found (see Justia, 2011). It seems the triangulation casts a lot of unreliability and doubt on the DEA results for Uni4.

Going back to the RQs described in the introduction. Unfortunately, this chapter cannot positively answer those since the findings were unreliable from the DEA as well as from the non-parametric statistical tests. The DEA and independent triangulated data raise many questions above and beyond this chapter, which are out of scope. Still, there are valid issues for other researchers to explore, particularly for those in higher education and justice disciplines. This data triangulation analysis shows that decision-makers and managers must be careful of using only a handful of data points to make significant choices or decisions. The study also proves that small samples with only a few data points can also lead to fatally flawed results even when nonparametric statistical techniques are applied. Data triangulation through different independent sources and methods with alternative compatible techniques must be done, especially with small samples. Data triangulation is a recommended best practice even when the sample size is large.

CONCLUSION

This chapter was not a run-of-the-mill positive demonstration of DEA, one that would join millions of *a priori* literature claiming the technique was valuable and possibly including illustrations or sample data. But no, this chapter did something very different. This chapter explained DEA and how the model works, not only scientifically but in a way understandable by a businessperson, a leader, or a decision-maker. This chapter further demonstrated a simplistic example of DEA, using both the input and output-focused approaches, with and without cost data applied within the model. Text and graphic charts explained how DEA's minimization and maximization linear programming equations conceptually work to achieve productivity estimates towards a theoretical best-case efficient frontier. The data was provided, which another researcher would immediately use, either by typing the values from Table 1 into one's DEA software, likewise with Table 3, or by referencing the secondary sample data from the USDE (2023).

This chapter went much further. Comparative nonparametric statistical techniques were used to illustrate the triangulation of the method, using an alternative compatible technique to ensure the results from DEA made sense to achieve external validity and reliability. The chapter further demonstrated how to triangulate the data from the DEA by researching independent sources to corroborate or refute the DEA findings. It was this last section where the most surprising results emerged. For example, one of the cases scored high in the DEA results but low in the nonparametric tests, and numerous litigations against the entity was in the literature. DEA was found to require additional thinking when designing studies, which should include triangulation of method and data to achieve reliability and validity.

In conclusion, although the original managerial RQs could not be affirmatively answered due to the unreliability of the DEA estimates, and due to the unreliability of the nonparametric statistical results, given the triangulated data and method results, there were other usable outcomes to report. Most importantly, the data triangulation analysis demonstrated that decision-makers and managers must be careful of using only a handful of data points in DEA (or any technique) to make significant choices or decisions. Data triangulation through different independent sources and methods with alternative compatible techniques must be done when small samples are used. It should also be noted that this chapter did not prove that DEA was a good or bad technique, only that stakeholders need to be aware of how it works, and especially to be wary of using small samples with only a few decision-making variables. The same could be said of the nonparametric statistical techniques applied in the current study. Furthermore, collecting qualitative data from government and reputable media sources, as was done in the current study for triangulation, cannot be assumed to be reliable as the primary single technique to answer important managerial RQs. What is being recommended here is to use more than one technique, with as many relevant variables as practical, collected from more than one data source, to answer important managerial decision-making questions.

One important limitation associated with this chapter is that only a few techniques were discussed (and illustrated) and limited literature was provided to describe the entire background of each technique. Certainly, this chapter does not cover all the possible topics and foundations which would assist the reader and stakeholders. To do so would require a book rather than a chapter, where the latter has defined space limitations. To that end, the entire book, particularly the other chapters, will assist in filling those gaps not covered in the current chapter, by covering more background of DEA, the alternatives to DEA, and variations for how DEA can and should be applied. Another important point, in keeping with research best-practices, is that the results were reported honestly even though the RQ and implied hypotheses were not answered or supported. It may be tempting for researchers to discard the data and collect new data and possibly a larger sample. This would be permissible, but it would be a different study. It is not ethically acceptable for a researcher to go back and alter the data after the results provided undesirable results. Another interesting future study would be to further investigate the interesting findings from the triangulated qualitative data (collected from government and reputable media sources). There may be a potential hypothesis that the quality of higher education institutions could be measured by certain key factors, such as their use of full-time employees, student complaints to reputable outlets including the courts, along with graduation rates at different points during the degree process. Other researchers are encouraged to explore that alternative as well, using new techniques and larger data samples from the same or additional populations.

REFERENCES

BBB. (2023). *Customer Reviews and Business Profile for Walden University*. Arlington, VA: Better Business Bureau (BBB). https://www.bbb.org/us/mn/minneapolis/profile/college-and-un iversity/walden-university-llc-0704-5722

Casetext. (2017). *Latonya Thornhill v. Walden University and Laureate Education.* Ohio District Court. https://casetext.com/case/thornhill-v-walden-univ-llc-1

Charnes, A., Cooper, W. W., & Rhodes, E. (1978). Measuring the Efficiency of Decision Making Units. *European Journal of Operational Research, 2*(1), 429–444. doi:10.1016/0377-2217(78)90138-8

ClassAction. (2016). *Jennifer Wright, Kelli Callahan, Janet Harrison, Pete Holubz, and Kelly Gardiner (class action) v. Walden University and Laureate Education,* 1-145. District Court of Minnesota. https://www.classaction.org/news/walden-university-laureate-education-inc-hit-with

Debreu, G. (1951). The Coefficient of Resource Utilization. *Econometrica, 19*(3), 273–292. doi:10.2307/1906814

Farrell, M. J. (1957). The measurement of productive efficiency. *Journal of the Royal Statistical Society. Series A (General), 120*(3), 253–281. doi:10.2307/2343100

Green, E. L. (2022, April 8). Lawsuit Charges For-Profit University Preyed on Black and Female Students. *NY Times.* https://www.nytimes.com/2022/04/08/us/politics/walden-university-lawsuit.html

Justia. (2011). *Yolanda Rene Travis, Leah Zitter, and Abbie Goldbas v. Walden University and Laureate Education.* https://cases.justia.com/federal/district-courts/maryland/mddce/1:2015cv00235/304055/304033/304050.pdf?ts=1446286879

Justia. (2022), *Kevin Morris et al., VS Rutgers-Newark University, et al.* [Court Case]. New Jersey Superior Court, Appellate Division. https://law.justia.com/cases/new-jersey/appellate-division-published/2022/a-0582-21.html

Koopmans, T. C. (1951). An Analysis of Production as an Efficient Combination of Activities. In T. C. Koopmans (Ed.), *Activity Analysis of Production and Allocation.* NY: Cowles Commission for Research in Economics. https://www.scirp.org/%28S%28351jmbntvnsjt1aadkposzje%29%29/reference/referencespapers.aspx?referenceid=3107432

Liang, L., Cook, W. D., & Zhu, J. (2008). DEA models for two-stage processes: Game approach and efficiency decomposition. *Naval Research Logistics, 55*(7), 643–653. doi:10.1002/nav.20308

Lotfi, F. H., Ebrahimnejad, A., Vaez-Ghasemi, M., & Moghaddas, Z. (2020). *Data Envelopment Analysis with R Ebook.* Springer. doi:10.1007/978-3-030-24277-0

Paradi, J. C., Vela, S. A., & Zhu, H. (2010). A new DEA model was applied to a merged bank to adjust for cultural differences. *Journal of Productivity Analysis, 33*(2), 109–123. doi:10.100711123-009-0158-2

Schecter, A. R. (2016). *For-Profit Walden U., Once Tied to Bill Clinton, Put Under Review.* NBC News https://www.nbcnews.com/news/us-news/student-sues-walden-university-i-wasted-six-years-my-life-n690706

Seiford, L. M., & Zhu, J. (2002). Modeling Undesirable Factors in Efficiency Evaluation. *European Journal of Operational Research, 142*(1), 16–20. doi:10.1016/S0377-2217(01)00293-4

Strang, K. D. (2012). Applied financial non-linear programming models for decision making. *International Journal of Applied Decision Sciences, 5*(4), 370–395. doi:10.1504/IJADS.2012.050023

Strang, K. D. (2019). Novel hydroelectricity data envelopment analysis model. *International Journal of Energy Technology and Policy, 15*(4), 436–456. doi:10.1504/IJETP.2019.102661

University of Delaware. (2023). *The Cost Study: The National Study of Instructional Costs and Productivity.* Institutional Research and Effectiveness, Higher Education Consortia at the University of Delaware. https://ire.udel.edu/cost/reports/cost-study-reports/

USDE. (2023). *College Scorecard* [national data as of April 25, 2023]. U.S. Department of Education (USDE), https://collegescorecard.ed.gov/compare/?toggle%3Dinstitutions%26s%3D125231%26s%3D213543%26s%3D186399%26s%3D445188

USDOJ. (2020, July 31). *Lehigh University Agrees to Pay $200,000 Settlement to Resolve False Claims Act Allegations Arising from Convicted Professor's Grant Fraud* [Court Case]. U.S. Department of Justice, Attorney General's Office (USDOJ). https://www.justice.gov/usao-edpa/pr/lehigh-university-agrees-pay-200000-settlement-resolve-false-claims-act-allegations

Van-Voorhis, P. (2018, March 2). UC Merced charges College Republicans $17,000 for Ben Shapiro event. *Washington Examiner.* https://www.washingtonexaminer.com/uc-merced-charges-college-republicans-17-000-for-ben-shapiro-event

Wolman, J. (2020, January 25). Class action lawsuit against Lehigh University, BASD asks for $54 million in damages. *The Brown and White.* https://thebrownandwhite.com/2020/01/25/breaking-class-action-lawsuit-against-lehigh-university-basd-asks-for-54-million-in-damages/

ADDITIONAL READING

Abramo, G., Cicero, T., & D'Angelo, C. A. (2011). A field-standardized application of DEA to national-scale research assessment of universities. *Journal of Informetrics, 5*(4), 618–628. doi:10.1016/j.joi.2011.06.001

Do, Q. H., & Chen, J. F. (2014). A hybrid fuzzy AHP-DEA approach for assessing university performance. *WSEAS Transactions on Business and Economics, 11*(1), 386-397.

Noh, Y. (2011). Evaluation of the resource utilization efficiency of university libraries using DEA techniques and a proposal of alternative evaluation variables. *Library Hi Tech, 29*(4), 697–724. doi:10.1108/07378831111189787

Rostamzadeh, R., Akbarian, O., Banaitis, A., & Soltani, Z. (2021). Application of DEA in benchmarking: A systematic literature review from 2003–2020. *Technological and Economic Development of Economy, 27*(1), 175–222. doi:10.3846/tede.2021.13406

Tomkins, C., & Green, R. (1988). An experiment in the use of data envelopment analysis for evaluating the efficiency of UK university departments of accounting. *Financial Accountability & Management*, *4*(2), 147–164. doi:10.1111/j.1468-0408.1988.tb00066.x

KEY TERMS AND DEFINITIONS

Benchmarking: The process of comparing one's business processes and performance metrics to industry bests or best practices from other companies. In the context of higher education, this involves comparing universities on various performance indicators.

Data Envelopment Analysis (DEA): A nonparametric method in operations research and economics for the estimation of production frontiers. It is used to empirically measure productive efficiency of decision-making units (or DMUs).

Decision-Making Units (DMUs): In DEA, these are the entities being evaluated, often characterized by their inputs and outputs. In the context of higher education, universities or colleges can be considered DMUs.

Efficient Frontier: In DEA, this is a set of decision-making units that are deemed most efficient, serving as a benchmark against which the efficiency of other units is measured.

Higher Education Effectiveness: A measure of how well higher education institutions achieve their intended outcomes, such as producing graduates, conducting research, and providing community services.

Linear Programming: A method to achieve the best outcome in a mathematical model whose requirements are represented by linear relationships. It's a key component of DEA when determining the efficient frontier.

Nonparametric Statistics: Statistical methods not based on parameterized families of probability distributions. They are used to analyze data that doesn't fit well with standard parametric models.

Radial Movements: In the context of DEA, these refer to movements along a ray from the origin to a point of observed production, used to measure efficiency improvements.

Returns To Scale: An economic concept that describes how the output of a production process changes as the scale of production is increased. In DEA, it refers to how changes in inputs affect outputs in decision-making units.

Triangulation of Data: The use of multiple data sources in an investigation to produce understanding. In DEA studies, it refers to using different datasets to validate or cross-check findings.

Triangulation of Method: The use of more than one research method to study a phenomenon. In the context of DEA, it refers to using various methods like statistical analysis to complement the findings from DEA.

Chapter 3
Productivity Profiles of Islamic Banks Using Data Envelopment Analysis–Based Malmquist Productivity Indices (MPIs):
Survey, Classification, and Critical Analysis

Karim Iddouch
https://orcid.org/0000-0003-3197-7693
Ibn Zohr University, Morocco

Khalid El Badraoui
Ibn Zohr University, Morocco & Mohammed VI Polytechnic University, Morocco

Jamal Ouenniche
The University of Edinburgh, UK & Mohammed VI Polytechnic University, Morocco

ABSTRACT

This chapter surveys the literature on the productivity profiles of Islamic Banks (IBs), with a specific emphasis on Malmquist Productivity Indices (MPIs) estimated using Data Envelopment Analysis (DEA) methodologies. It examines 68 publications from 2006 to 2022, offering a comprehensive categorization of the literature based on four key aspects: (1) the type of DEA analysis, (2) productivity measurement methodologies, (3) variables for DEA model specification and corresponding evaluation approaches, and (4) the drivers of productivity along with their theoretical foundations. This paper also provides a critical analysis of the existing literature, identifying gaps, inconsistencies, and potential sources of discrepancies in the findings, thereby paving the way for future research to address these limitations.

DOI: 10.4018/979-8-3693-0255-2.ch003

1. INTRODUCTION

Banking systems are critical drivers of economic growth and financial stability in countries (Jokipii & Monnin, 2013; Athari et al., 2023). In recent decades, the global banking industry has witnessed significant transformations due to the rise of Islamic Banks (IBs) (Alam, 2013; Imam and Kpodar, 2016). Empirical studies by Hasan and Dridi (2010) and Farooq and Zaheer (2015), along with the 2010 International Monetary Fund (IMF) survey, have demonstrated that IBs were more resilient than Conventional Banks (CBs) during the Global Financial Crisis (GFC) of 2007-2008. This resilience is attributed to their higher intermediation ratio, better asset quality, and stronger capitalization compared to CBs (Beck et al., 2013). Furthermore, the General Council for Islamic Banks and Financial Institutions (CIBAFI) reported in 2022 that Islamic assets under management experienced a growth of 13.7% in 2020 during the COVID-19 pandemic, and over the last decade, the sector expanded by 300%, with assets under management nearly reaching $200 billion. These facts and the empirical evidence of IBs' resilience have generated considerable interest from various stakeholders, such as policymakers, regulators, investors, and academics, in examining the productivity of IBs.

The motivation for studying the productivity of IBs arises from both general arguments common to the entire banking industry and arguments specific to Islamic banking. General arguments include the insights productivity studies can offer to managers and regulators regarding changes in efficiency over time (Alhassan and Biekpe, 2015; Nartey et al., 2019), the informative decompositions of productivity change for stakeholders (Khoveyni and Eslami, 2014), the expectation that increased productivity leads to better bank performance, competitive prices, improved quality of services, and better resource allocation, and the impact of recent changes in the financial services industry and technological advancements on banks' productivity (Berger and Mester, 2003). Emrouznejad and Yang (2018) further revealed an exponential increase in the number of publications on productivity studies over the past four decades. On the other hand, the Islamic banking-specific arguments are primarily concerned with the differences between the business models of IBs and CBs due to Sharia constraints, which can affect their cost, profit, risk, and productivity profiles (Beck et al., 2013; Bitar et al., 2020). Two key distinctive features of IBs' business models are finance for the real economy and risk-sharing between capital-providers and capital-users. IBs' modes of financing, such as Murabaha (sales contract / cost plus financing contract), Ijarah (leasing contract), and Istisnā (manufacturing contract), are more connected to the real economy, as all transactions and financial instruments must be real asset-linked. According to Sharia principles, IBs are prohibited from engaging in leveraged (and speculative) transactions with weak or no links to real economic activities. Moreover, IBs do not invest in toxic assets and mortgage-backed securities, which were the primary causes of the GFC of 2007-2008 (Chapra, 2008, 2011). As to the risk-sharing aspect, some Islamic banking contracts, such as Musharakah (partnerships) and Muḍārabah (Trustee finance), are based on risk-sharing between fund-providers and fund-users, in contrast to the conventional banking system where depositors transfer the risk to the bank, which guarantees a pre-specified rate of return for their investments.

The literature on the productivity of IBs has increased and diversified in aims over the past two decades. While several studies have investigated the productivity of IBs compared to CBs (Omar et al., 2006; Johnes et al., 2014; Isik et al., 2016; Abdul-Wahab and Haron, 2017; Alexakis et al., 2019; Alsharif et al., 2019; Saleh et al., 2020; Kamarudin et al., 2022), others have focused on comparing the productivity of different groups of IBs, such as foreign-owned vs. domestically-owned IBs (e.g., Sufian, 2007; Sufian, 2010; Hadad et al., 2011; Azad et al., 2017; Kamarudin et al., 2017; Basri et al., 2018), full-fledged IBs vs. Islamic windows (e.g., Sufian, 2009a; Khan and Shah, 2015; Salami and Adeyemi, 2015; Alendejani and Asutay, 2017), old vs. new IBs (e.g., Alsharif et al., 2019), and large vs. small IBs (e.g., Alsharif et al., 2019). Moreover, some studies have investigated the impact of specific events on the productivity of IBs, such as the GFC of 2007-2008 (e.g., Bahrini, 2015; Ganouati and Essid, 2017; Kamarudin et al., 2022) and the Basel III accord (e.g., Alsharif et al., 2019). One of the aims of our survey is to summarize, discuss, and critically analyse the findings of the literature we cover.

Previous surveys on bank productivity have mainly focused on the conventional banking sector (Colwell and Davis, 1992; Sharma et al., 2013; Bhatia et al., 2018), except for Rusydiana et al. (2019), which concentrated on studies within the Islamic economics and finance sectors. However, literature surveys specifically addressing the productivity of IBs remain scarce, and our survey aims to fill this gap.

Our survey covers 68 documents published over 17 years classifies the literature on Islamic banking productivity using MPIs estimated with a DEA methodology according to various criteria, providing a detailed analysis of the findings and a critical examination of both methodological and empirical aspects of the papers surveyed. Specifically, our classification criteria fall under the following categories: (1) type of DEA analysis and underlying research problems or questions; (2) productivity measurement methodologies; (3) evaluation approaches and categories of variables for model specification; and (4) drivers of productivity. Additionally, we provide the theoretical justifications for empirical results and a critical analysis of the literature, identifying gaps, inconsistencies, and potential sources of discrepancies in the findings.

The remainder of this paper is organized as follows. Section 2 summarizes the design decisions of our survey. Section 3 surveys the literature on the productivity profiles of IBs and offers several classifications. Section 4 presents a critical analysis of the literature, including methodological shortcomings, inconsistencies, and research gaps. Finally, Section 5 concludes the paper.

2. SELECTION PROCESS OF THE RELEVANT LITERATURE ON THE PRODUCTIVITY OF ISLAMIC BANKS

We present a comprehensive survey that aims to classify, summarize, and critique the existing literature on IBs' productivity, as measured by MPI estimated with DEA models. We employ a two-step process of bibliographic search, including a search in various electronic databases such as Scopus, ResearchGate, SSRN, and Google Scholar, to identify relevant papers for the survey. We employed a list of keywords to ensure the inclusion of all relevant documents in our review. These keywords encompass "Malmquist," "DEA," "Malmquist Productivity Index", "MPI", "Total Factor Productivity Change", "TFP," "Productivity", "Islamic banks", and "Shariah bank".

Initially, we conducted a search on the Scopus database using the aforementioned keywords, which generated 25 documents. Of these, 21 were deemed relevant for the survey. To supplement our sample, we performed another search using the same keywords on the Web of Science (WoS) database, which returned 17 documents. However, these were duplicate records already found in the Scopus list, and thus were excluded. In the second stage of our selection process, we searched Google Scholar, ResearchGate, and SSRN, which yielded an additional 50 relevant documents on productivity. Upon screening these documents based on the survey's objective, we identified 46 articles and 1 book chapter that met our selection criteria.

Figure 1. Distribution of DEA-based MPI studies on Islamic banking

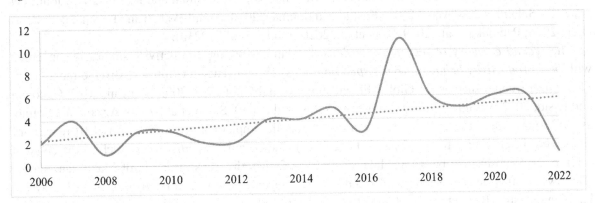

Our final sample for the survey comprises 68 references (66 articles and 2 book chapters) published over a span of 17 years (from January 2006 to January 2022). We initiated the paper retrieval process on October 31st, 2021, and updated it until February 6th, 2022. Figure 1 depicts the distribution of DEA-based MPI papers in Islamic banking in the final sample, indicating that publications implementing DEA-based MPIs in Islamic banking tend to follow a cyclical pattern, exhibiting an increasing trend over time.

3. LITERATURE SURVEY ON THE PRODUCTIVITY OF ISLAMIC BANKS

Our survey of the academic literature on the productivity of IBs using DEA-based MPIs is organised around a classification of papers into two meaningful categories depending on the type of DEA analysis performed, namely, single stage analysis and two-stage analysis.

3.1 Single Stage Analyses of Islamic Banks' Productivity

3.1.1 Research Problem and Related Research Questions

In productivity studies, a typical single stage analysis is concerned with assessing the productivity profiles of a given set of entities (e.g., IBs), commonly referred to as decision marking units (DMUs), over a specific period of time. Alongside this *research problem*, one is often interested in addressing a number of related *research questions*. In Islamic banking productivity studies using DEA-based MPIs, only 2 papers (Al-Muharrami, 2007; Karanlioglu and Musajeva, 2017) out of 68 explicitly stated research questions; however, we made an effort to identify the implicit research questions addressed in the remaining 66 studies and classified them into the following four main categories:

The *first category of research questions* is concerned with *how the productivity of Islamic banks behaves over the period of analysis*. This line of inquiry can be divided into two main categories: non-persistent changes over time (e.g., Sufian, 2007; Hadi and Saad, 2010; Arjomandi et al., 2012; Othman et al., 2013; Ada and Dalkilic, 2014; Abbas et al., 2015; Isik et al., 2016; Yildirim, 2017; Aisyah and Hosen, 2018; Alsharif et al., 2019; Chowdhury and Haron, 2021; Kamarudin et al., 2022), and persistent changes in productivity, characterised by *upward or downward trends over time* (e.g., Hassan, 2006;

Al-Muharrami, 2007; Johnes et al., 2009; Abu-Alkheil et al., 2012; Ismail and Rahim, 2013; Johnes et al., 2014; Salami and Adeyemi, 2015; Rashid and Rehman, 2016; Abdul-Wahab and Haron, 2017; Basri et al., 2018; Pambuko et al., 2019; Rani et al., 2020; Jubilee et al., 2021a).

The *second category of research questions* in Islamic banking productivity studies is concerned with *how productivity behaves around specific events*. These events encompass a diverse range, from *global occurrences* such as the Global Financial Crisis (GFC) of 2007-2009 (Bahrini, 2015; Ganouati and Essid, 2017; Wahid and Harun, 2019; Alexakis et al., 2019; Saleh et al., 2020; Azzam and Rettab, 2020; Kamarudin et al., 2022) to *regional events* like the implementation of the Basel III regulatory framework in GCC countries (Alsharif et al., 2019), and *country-specific events* such as the entry of foreign De Novo Islamic banks in Malaysia (Sufian, 2010), the transformation of Malaysian Islamic windows into full-fledged Islamic banks (Salami and Adeyemi, 2015), the liberalization of the Malaysian banking industry (Basri et al., 2018), and the spin-off of Indonesian Islamic banks into social funds like Zakat, Infaq, Sadaqah, and financial funds (Pambuko et al., 2019). Several key inferences can be made from these event studies. *First*, the productivity of IBs is sensitive to various events, demonstrating that their performance is closely intertwined with global, regional, and country-specific developments. This highlights the importance of considering the broader context when analyzing the productivity of IBs. *Second*, the examination of productivity behavior around specific events can offer valuable insights into the resilience and adaptability of IBs in response to changing economic and regulatory environments. This can help identify the strengths and weaknesses of the Islamic banking industry and inform strategic decision-making. *Third*, the diversity of events considered in these studies underlines the complex interplay between the Islamic banking industry and its surrounding context.

The *third category of research questions* is concerned with *whether there are significant differences in productivity between different groups of banks or different categories of bank features*. This generic research question has been addressed for *specific groups of banks*, namely, (1) *type of the bank;* i.e., Islamic vs. Conventional (e.g., Omar et al., 2006; Johnes et al., 2009; Johnes et al., 2014; Abbas et al., 2015; Abdul-Wahab and Haron, 2017; Alsharif et al., 2019; Saleh et al., 2020; Kamarudin et al., 2022); and (2) *type of operating structure of the bank*; i.e., full-fledged IBs vs. Islamic windows (e.g., Sufian, 2009a; Siddique and Rahim, 2013; Alandejani, 2014; Alendejani and Asutay, 2017), and *specific categories of bank features*, namely, (1) *ownership type of the bank*; i.e., domestic vs. foreign (e.g., Sufian, 2007; Sufian and Haron, 2008; Abdul-Wahab and Haron, 2017; Kamarudin et al., 2017; Basri et al., 2018), (2) *size of the bank*; i.e., small vs. large (Alsharif et al., 2019), (3) *age of the bank*; i.e., old vs. new banks (Alsharif et al., 2019), (4) *listing status*; i.e., listed vs. unlisted banks (Hadad et al., 2011), and (5) the *geographic location or countries these banks operate in.*

These geographic locations can be divided into three main categories: (a) the first category consists of *single country focused studies* – see Figure 2 – and covers *Indonesian banks* (e.g., Omar et al., 2006; Afiatun and Wiryono, 2010; Rani et al., 2017; Firmansyah, 2018; Usman et al., 2019; Otaviya and Rani, 2020; Octrina and Mariam, 2021), *Malaysian banks* (e.g., Sufian, 2007; Sufian and Haron, 2008; Hadi and Saad, 2010; Othman et al., 2013; Salami and Adeyemi, 2015; Basri et al., 2018; Wahid and Harun, 2019), *Pakistani banks* (e.g., Siddique and Rahim, 2013; Abbas et al., 2015; Rashid and Rehman, 2016), *Qatari banks* (Abdul-Wahab and Haron, 2017), *Yemeni banks* (Bushara et al., 2018), *Bengali banks* (Abduh et al., 2013; Ara, 2016; Jahan, 2019), *Turkish banks* (Alpay and Hassan, 2007; Boyacioglu et al., 2014), *Iranian banks* (Arjomandi et al., 2012), *Jordanian banks* (Isik et al., 2016), and *Sudanese banks* (Onour and Abdalla, 2011); (b) the second category consists of *multi-country focused studies* and covers countries; Indonesia, Malaysia and Pakistan (Rodoni et al., 2017), 10 countries, namely,

Figure 2. Distribution of single country-focused studies in Islamic banking literature on productivity

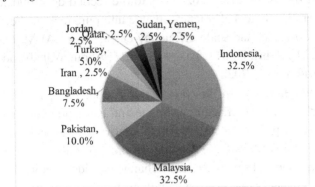

Qatar, Saudi Arabia, Kuwait, Bahrain, U.A.E, Malaysia, Turkey, Azerbaijan, UK, Bosnia – Herzegovina (Abu-Alkheil et al., 2012); Malaysia and Turkey (Ada and Dalkilic, 2014; Yildirim, 2015); 13 countries (Ganouati and Essid, 2017); 21 countries (Hassan, 2006); Brunei, Indonesia, and Malaysia (Kamarudin et al., 2017); Malaysia, Indonesia, Brunei and Singapore (Kamarudin et al., 2022); Iran, Saudi Arabia, Malaysia, United Arab Emirates, Qatar, Kuwait, Bahrain, Indonesia, Turkey, and Bangladesh (Nugrohowati et al., 2020); Indonesia, Malaysia and Brunei Darussalam (Rani et al., 2020); Indonesia, Malaysia, and Pakistan (Rodoni et al., 2017); 15 countries, namely, Malaysia, Bangladesh, Indonesia, Pakistan, Iran, UAE, Qatar, Kuwait, Bahrain, Saudi Arabia, Yemen, Egypt, Sudan, Jordan, and Turkey (Romdhane and Alhakimi, 2018); Indonesia, Malaysia, Brunei Darussalam and Thailand (Rusydiana and Assalafiyah, 2021); and Qatar, Indonesia, Saudi Arabia, Malaysia, UAE and Turkey (Yildirim, 2017), (c) the third category consists of *region focused studies* and covers regions such as *Gulf Cooperation Council (GCC)* (e.g., Al-Muharrami, 2007; Johnes et al., 2009; Johnes et al., 2014; Alandejani, 2014; Alendejani and Asutay, 2017; Alsharif et al., 2019; Alexakis et al., 2019; Saleh et al., 2020), *MENA region* (Bahrini, 2015), *Southeast Asia (SEA)* (e.g., Chowdhury and Haron, 2021; Jubilee et al., 2021b); and (d) the fourth and final category focused on *multiple regions* such as *Middle East, Southeast Asia, and South Asia* (Jubilee et al., 2021a), and *Middle east and Southeast Asia* (Yaumidin, 2007). We can draw the following inferences from this third research question. *First*, there are significant differences in productivity between different groups of banks and various categories of bank features, suggesting that factors such as bank type, operating structure, ownership, size, age, and listing status can significantly impact productivity in the Islamic banking sector. *Second*, the variation in productivity across different countries and regions highlights the importance of considering the local context and regulatory environment when evaluating the performance of IBs. This suggests that strategies and best practices may not be universally applicable, and banks may need to tailor their approaches to the specific circumstances of their operating environment.

Finally, the *fourth category of research questions* is concerned with the *identification of the sources of productivity change of IBs (i.e., overall technical efficiency change and/or technological change; pure technical efficiency change, scale efficiency change, and/or technological change)?* Answers to this research question have been addressed through two types of decomposition of productivity change. The first decomposition considers two components; namely, overall technical efficiency change – also referred to as "catching-up" effect, and technological change – also referred to as "frontier shift" effect (e.g., Al-Muharrami, 2007; Johnes et al., 2009; Onour and Abdalla, 2011; Hadad et al., 2011; Johnes et al., 2014; Azad et al., 2017; Saleh et al., 2020). As to the second decomposition, it refines the first one by breaking down overall technical efficiency change into pure technical efficiency change, which reflects management performance, and scale efficiency change (e.g., Al-Muharrami, 2007; Johnes et al., 2009; Johnes et al., 2014;; Bahrini, 2015; Isik et al., 2016; Abdul-Wahab and Haron, 2017; Alsharif et al., 2019; 2021; Kamarudin et al., 2022).

Several insights can be derived from this research question. *First*, IBs' productivity change can be attributed to both overall technical efficiency change and technological change. This suggests that improvements in management performance, as well as innovations in technology and processes, can significantly impact productivity. *Second*, the decomposition of overall technical efficiency change into pure technical efficiency change and scale efficiency change provides a more nuanced understanding of the sources of productivity change. This allows stakeholders to better identify areas where improvements can be made to enhance productivity. *Finally*, the variety of studies employing different decomposition methods highlights the need for a consistent and comprehensive approach to understanding the sources of productivity change in IBs. This will enable more accurate comparisons between studies and facilitate the development of targeted strategies for improvement.

Also, papers on DEA-based MPIs concerned with the productivity of IBs can be classified into two groups. The first group focuses exclusively on the *productivity profiles of banks* (e.g., Al-Muharrami, 2007; Sufian, 2010; Abbas et al., 2015; Rani et al., 2017; Romdhane and Alhakimi, 2018; Alsharif et al., 2019; Salleh and Rani, 2020; Kamarudin et al., 2022). The second group considers *both efficiency and productivity profiles of banks* (e.g., Omar et al., 2006; Sufian, 2007; Johnes et al., 2009; Abu-Alkheil et al., 2012; Johnes et al., 2014; Salami and Adeyemi, 2015; Abdul-Wahab and Haron, 2017; Nugrohowati et al., 2020; Sapanji et al., 2021). Furthermore, while most studies have compared the efficiency and/or productivity profiles of *IBs and CBs* (e.g., Alpay and Hassan, 2007; Johnes et al., 2009; Hadad et al., 2011; Othman et al., 2013; Abbas et al., 2015; Isik et al., 2016; Abdul-Wahab and Haron, 2017; Alexakis et al., 2019; Wahid and Harun, 2019; Salleh and Rani, 2020; Jubilee et al., 2021b), other studies have focused *solely on IBs* (e.g., Sufian and Haron, 2008; Sufian, 2009a; Onour and Abdalla, 2011; Siddique and Rahim, 2013; Bahrini, 2015; Ganouati and Essid, 2017; Kamarudin et al., 2017; Basri et al., 2018; Usman et al., 2019; Nugrohowati et al., 2020; Chowdhury and Haron, 2021). We can draw the following inferences from this classification: (1) the variety of studies concerned with the productivity and efficiency profiles indicates the significance of understanding the performance of both IBs and CBs. The comparison helps identify the strengths and weaknesses of each banking model and contributes to the development of strategies to enhance their performance; in addition, such comparison provides information that can help inform stakeholders, including policymakers, regulators, and bank managers, on areas where improvements can be made to enhance the overall performance of the financial sector; (2) the exclusive focus on IBs in some studies highlights the growing interest in understanding the unique characteristics of this banking sector; and (3) the dual focus on efficiency and productivity profiles underscores the importance of considering both aspects when assessing the performance of banks.

3.1.2 Productivity Estimation Models in Islamic Banking

Our survey of the academic literature on the productivity profiles of IBs revealed that productivity is generally measured by the *Malmquist Productivity Index (MPI)1*, which could be estimated using a variety of methodologies including DEA models and SFA models. In the Islamic banking literature, studies such as Omar et al., 2006; Sufian, 2009a; Johnes et al., 2009; Afiatun and Wiryono, Onour and

Abdalla, 2011; Arjomandi et al., 2012; Abduh et al., 2013; Ismail and Rahim, 2013; Alandejani, 2014; Ada and Dalkilic, 2014; Johnes et al., 2014; Bahrini, 2015; Salami and Adeyemi, 2015; Ara, 2016; Isik et al., 2016; Azad et al., 2017; Alsharif et al., 2019; Saleh et al., 2020; Chowdhury and Haron, 2021; and Kamarudin et al., 2022, have focused on estimating MPIs using DEA models. These studies have made significant contributions to understanding productivity in the Islamic banking sector. By employing DEA-based MPI estimation, researchers can investigate productivity changes, efficiency improvements, and technological advancements of IBs over time. This analysis is essential for identifying factors that influence the performance of IBs and can provide valuable insights for stakeholders to determine areas where improvements can be made, ultimately enhancing the overall performance of the financial sector.

In the academic literature on the productivity profiles of IBs, the *Adjacent MPI* is the prevailing methodology employed by researchers for estimating productivity (e.g., Hassan, 2006; Omar et al., 2006; Sufian, 2007). The *Global MPI* methodology has been just used once (Azad et al., 2017). Most MPI scores in the Islamic banking productivity literature using DEA-based MPIs were estimated by solving radial models under *CRS regime*, i.e., CCR models (e.g., Al-Muharrami, 2007; Johnes et al., 2009; Onour and Abdalla, 2011), or under *VRS regime*, i.e., BCC models (e.g., Siddique and Rahim, 2013; Yildirim, 2015). Some studies used *both CRS and VRS regimes*, i.e., CCR and BCC models respectively (e.g., Omar et al., 2006; Sufian and Haron, 2008; Johnes et al., 2009), while others employed the *Semi-Oriented Radial Measure* (SORM) (Hadad et al., 2011). One notable exception is Saleh et al. (2020), who used a *non-radial model*, namely, the weighted directional distance model, to estimate the MPI scores. To the best of our knowledge, no study in the Islamic banking productivity literature amongst the ones surveyed has ever utilized the popular non-radial models, such as Slack-Based Measure (SBM) models.

The MPI indices mentioned above can be used within input-oriented analyses, output-oriented analyses, or both. In *input-oriented analyses*, the focus is on minimizing the use of inputs while maintaining the same level of outputs. Conversely, *output-oriented analyses* aim to maximize the outputs while maintaining the same level of inputs. In the Islamic banking productivity literature, MPIs are mostly computed under an output orientation (e.g., Omar et al., 2006; Sufian, 2007; Sufian and Haron, 2008; Sufian, 2009a; Johnes et al., 2009; Abdul-Wahab and Haron, 2017; Azad et al., 2017; Aisyah and Hosen, 2018; Wahid and Harun, 2019; Nugrohowati et al., 2020; Chowdhury and Haron, 2021; Kamarudin et al., 2022), followed by an input orientation (e.g., Al-Muharrami, 2007; Onour and Abdalla, 2011; Ismail and Rahim, 2013; Othman et al., 2013; Yildirim, 2015; Isik et al., 2016), or under both input and output orientations (e.g., Karanlioglu and Musajeva, 2017; Yildirim, 2017; Sapanji et al., 2021). One notable exception is Saleh et al. (2020), who performed the analysis under a non-oriented setup. In sum, various DEA-based MPIs are widely used in the literature to analyze the productivity of Islamic banks. The choice of input-oriented or output-oriented analyses depends on the research focus and the specific goals of the analysis. The use of radial models to estimate MPIs prevails in the literature. The use of non-radial models however remains scarce in the Islamic banking productivity literature (Saleh et al., 2020).

When examining the productivity of IBs, researchers often use MPIs to identify the potential sources of productivity change. Empirical studies in this field can be classified into two categories based on the decomposition of the productivity index. The first category decomposes *MPIs as the product of technical efficiency change and technological change* (e.g., Johnes et al., 2009; Saleh et al., 2020; Azad et al., 2017). This decomposition enables researchers to study how changes in efficiency within the banks and changes in technology or best practices over time impact productivity. The second category further breaks down technical efficiency into pure technical efficiency and scale efficiency, resulting in the decomposition of *MPIs as the product of pure technical efficiency change, scale efficiency change, and technological change* (e.g., Omar et al., 2006; Sufian, 2009; Salami and Adeyemi, 2015; Kamarudin et al., 2017; Alexakis et al., 2019; Firmansyah, 2018; Alsharif et al., 2019; Nugrohowati et al., 2020; Chowdhury and Haron, 2021; Kamarudin et al., 2022). This approach allows for a more detailed analysis of the sources of productivity change. However, Hadad et al. (2011) took a unique approach by incorporating Risk Management (RM) into the two categories of decompositions. They proposed two variations: (1) MPI is computed as the product of RM technical efficiency change and frontier shift due to RM efficiency change; and (2) MPI is calculated as the product of RM effect on technical change and frontier shift due to RM effect. This approach highlights the importance of risk management in the productivity analysis of Islamic banks.

Finally, to compare the productivity scores of banks amongst different *groups of banks* (i.e., IBs vs CBs; domestic vs foreign banks; full-fledged IBs vs Islamic windows) or *categories of features* (i.e., small vs. large banks), several *parametric and non-parametric statistical tests* were performed. To be more specific, the parametric tests used are *ANOVA* (Sufian, 2007; Sufian, 2009; Alpay and Hassan, 2007) and *t-test* (Sufian, 2007; Sufian, 2009; Johnes et al., 2009; Sufian, 2010; Afiatun and Wiryono, 2010; Johnes et al., 2014; Abbas et al., 2015; Kamarudin et al., 2017; Alsharif et al., 2019; Jubilee et al., 2021a; Jubilee et al., 2021b; Kamarudin et al., 2022), whereas the non-parametric tests used are *Kolmogorov-Smirnov test* (Sufian, 2007; Sufian, 2009; Sufian, 2010; Johnes et al., 2014; Abbas et al., 2015; Kamarudin et al., 2017; Alsharif et al., 2019), *Mann-Whitney test* (Sufian, 2007; Sufian, 2009; Johnes et al., 2009; Sufian, 2010; Johnes et al., 2014; Abbas et al., 2015; Kamarudin et al., 2017; Alsharif et al., 2019; Pambuko et al., 2019; Saleh et al., 2020; Jubilee et al., 2021a; Jubilee et al., 2021b; Kamarudin et al., 2022), and *Kruskall-Wallis test* (Sufian, 2007; Sufian, 2009; Johnes et al., 2009; Ganouati and Essid, 2017; Jubilee et al., 2021a; Jubilee et al., 2021b; Kamarudin et al., 2022). Finally, Sufian (2010) tested the impact of the entry of foreign De Novo IBs on the productivity of the existing banks in Malaysia using both parametric and non-parametric statistical tests, namely, *t-test, Kolmogorov-Smirnov test*, and *Mann-Whitney test*.

3.1.3 Evaluation Approaches and Variables Used for the Specification of DEA Models and Their Classifications

The choice of the variables for the specification of DEA models used for estimating MPIs are shaped by the choice of the conceptual model of the bank, also referred to as the bank behaviour model or evaluation approach. There are six main conceptual models in banking; namely, the *intermediation approach* or IA for short, the *production approach* or PA short for, the *asset approach* or AA short for, the *profit-oriented approach* or POA short for, the *user-cost approach* or UCA short for, and the *value-added approach* or VAA short for. However, in the literature on Islamic banking productivity, only three evaluation approaches were used, namely, the IA, which is by far the most used one (e.g., Omar et al., 2006; Sufian, 2007; Johnes et al., 2009; Johnes et al., 2014; Azad et al., 2017; Alexakis et al., 2019; Jubilee et al., 2021b; Kamarudin et al., 2022), followed by the PA (e.g., Isik et al., 2016; Azad et al., 2017; Romdhane and Alhakimi, 2018) and the POA (Azad et al., 2017; Karanlioglu and Musajeva, 2017), which are the least used ones, see Figure 4. These findings are in congruence with the findings of the literature survey by Sharma et al. (2013) on the conventional banking sector. Similarly, the results by Bhatia et al. (2018) also suggest that IA is the dominant approach, followed by PA. Note that 11 research papers out of 68 were not explicit about the evaluation approach being used for the specification of inputs and outputs.

For a complete summary of the evaluation approaches, typical inputs and outputs used under each bank behaviour model, and pros and cons of each approach, we refer the reader to Iddouch et al. (2023).

In this paper, we classify the inputs and outputs used in the Islamic banking literature on productivity using DEA-based MPIs into several categories based on the following criteria: *accounting variables (those reported in the IBs' financial statements)* vs. *extra-accounting variables*, *absolute variables* vs. *composite/relative variables*, *balance sheet items* vs. *income statement items*, and *cost-based variables* vs. *return-based variables* – see Figure 5 and Table 1 for a detailed description of inputs and outputs used in the literature on Islamic banking productivity.

Table 2 in the appendix classifies the input-and-output vectors using two levels of classifications along with their frequency and frequency percentage distribution according to each evaluation approach. Note that this table considers all productivity studies (57 papers) where authors explicitly specify the evaluation approach being used. As to the IA, total deposits, personnel expenses, and physical capital are the most frequently used inputs, whereas total loans, investments, and other earning assets are the most predominant outputs. These choices made by authors are consistent with the rationale of the IA which considers banks as financial intermediaries who collect funds to provide financial services and expand assets. On the topic of the PA, authors have shown consistency in their specification process of inputs and outputs with the conceptual model, which views banks as production units who transform inputs into outputs or produce deposit accounts and loan services. Along the same vein, consistency in choices of inputs and outputs being made were also shown in studies using the POA, which is obviously in agreement with the rationale of the approach viewing banking institutions as revenue generating units which aim at maximising profit and thus capture the final monetary effect of the financial intermediation function.

3.1.4 Findings of Single Stage Analyses and Their Classifications

The single-stage DEA analysis has been used to estimate MPI scores using various criteria in the banking industry. The empirical findings have produced mixed patterns that are categorized into three main panels based on different criteria; (1) *Panel A* classifies the results of bank type criterion into three main points. Firstly, Islamic Banks (IBs) are more productive than Conventional Banks (CBs). Secondly, IBs are less productive than CBs. Finally, there is no significant difference in productivity between IBs and CBs; (2) *Panel B* classifies the results of the ownership type criterion into three main outcomes. Firstly, foreign IBs are more productive than domestic IBs. Secondly, foreign IBs are less productive than domestic IBs. Finally, there is no significant difference in productivity between foreign and domestic IBs; and (3) *Panel C* classifies the findings on the operating structure type criterion into two main outcomes. Firstly, Islamic windows are more productive than full-fledged IBs. Secondly, Islamic windows are less productive than full-fledged IBs. The reasons behind these conflicting results are discussed in Subsection 6.7. Table 1 provides a comprehensive synopsis of the mixed empirical results of each panel along with specifics of each study.

Some other empirical results have been reached based on different criteria. Ganouati and Essid (2017) found no significant difference between changes in MPI components of IBs under both IA and PA. Similarly, Isik et al. (2016) reached the same conclusion but with a focus on both IBs and CBs. However, Azad et al. (2017) provided evidence that there are significant differences in MPI components of bank type (Islamic vs. Conventional) and ownership type (foreign vs. domestic IBs) under IA, PA, and POA. Usman et al. (2019) found that social funds of IBs are more productive than financial funds of IBs. Pambuko et al. (2019) found that the spin-off decision has no significant impact on social funds' productivity in IBs. Azzam and Rettab (2020) and Saleh et al. (2020) found that the productivity of IBs is less affected by the GFC than CBs' productivity. Bahrini (2015), Ganouati and Essid (2017), Wahid and Harun (2019) and Alexakis et al. (2019) found that the GFC of 2007-2008 has a negative effect on the productivity of IBs. Alsharif et al. (2019) found that the productivity of IBs is adversely more affected by the Basel III accord introduction than the productivity of CBs. Alsharif et al. (2019) found that the productivity of old IBs (respectively, CBs) is negatively and significantly more impacted by the introduction of Basel III than the productivity of new IBs (respectively, CBs). Finally, Alsharif et al. (2019) found that the productivity of big IBs (respectively, CBs) is negatively and significantly more affected by the Basel III requirements than the productivity of small IBs (respectively, CBs).

3.2 Two-Stage Analyses of Productivity of Islamic Banks

In productivity studies, a two-stage analysis is concerned with identifying the drivers of productivity; to be more specific, in the first stage productivity indexes are computed – typically using a specific MPI methodology, then in the second stage these productivity indexes are regressed on a potential set of drivers to identify the effective ones. It is worth noting that DEA-based MPI single stage analysis studies are the most dominant studies, followed by two-stage analysis studies by a lower proportion (9 papers out of 68 in our sample), see Figure 3. Alongside the above-mentioned *research problem*, studies performing a two-stage DEA analysis on IBs' productivity have addressed the following *research question – what are the drivers of productivity of IBs?* – to determine what are the drivers of productivity, be they bank-specific or country-specific (Sufian and Haron, 2008; Othman et al., 2013; Bahrini, 2015; Azad et al., 2017; Rani et al., 2017; Kamarudin et al., 2017; Otaviya and Rani, 2020; Jubilee et al., 2021b; Kamarudin et al., 2022).

To address this research question on the drivers of productivity, several regression frameworks can be used and the ones that have been identified in DEA-based MPI studies on Islamic banking are *Ordinary Least Squares (OLS) panel regression (*Kamarudin et al., 2017; Rani et al., 2017; Otaviya and Rani, 2020), *Generalised Method of Moments (GMM) panel regression* (Jubilee et al., 2021b), *bootstrapped fixed effects panel regression* (Bahrini, 2015*), fixed effects Generalised Least Squares (GLS) panel regression* (Sufian and Haron, 2008), *both fixed and random effects GLS panel regressions* (Kamarudin et al., 2022), *double bootstrap truncated panel regression* (Azad et al., 2017), and *Tobit panel regression* (Othman et al., 2013). In addition, the drivers of productivity used in the Islamic banking literature can

Figure 3. Distribution of DEA-based MPI studies in Islamic banking by type of DEA analysis

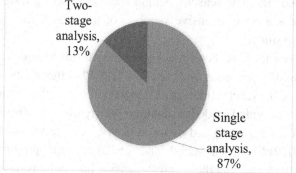

Figure 4. Distribution of evaluation approaches used in Islamic banking productivity literature

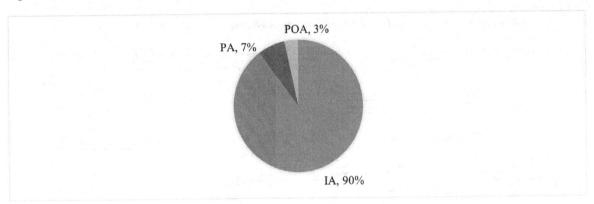

be divided into two broad categories – *internal environment-related variables* and *external environment-related variables*. On one hand, internal environment-related variables (i.e., bank-specific factors) are those controlled by the managers of the bank and reflect their various internal policies and decisions. On the other hand, external environment-related variables (i.e., country-specific factors) are not under the control of the bank management being factors reflecting the country's economic and legal environment. In this section, we shall provide a classification of the drivers of productivity used in the DEA-based MPI literature on Islamic banking into meaningful categories along with the percentage of studies that used each variable (see Table 3 in the appendix). The internal environment-related variables are further sub-divided into several sub-categories; namely, (1) *bank risk variables* which represent the risks banks are exposed to such as credit risk, insolvency risk; (2) *bank profitability measures* which capture the overall performance of the bank using ratios such as ROA, ROE; (3) *bank liquidity variables* which reflect the ability of the bank to meet its financial obligations as they fall due; (4) *bank cost efficiency variables* which capture the ability of the bank to manage its expenses; e.g., operating costs; (5) *bank business model variables* reflect the extent to which banks are able to diversity their activities among traditional and non-traditional banking operations; (6) *bank governance variables* which capture ownership type of the bank (e.g. domestic vs. foreign); and (7) *bank intrinsic variables* capture those characteristics that are inherent to the bank such as bank size, bank type (Islamic vs. conventional), and market power. On the other hand, external environment-related variables are further sub-divided into (1) *macroeconomic variables* which capture trends in the economy, (2) *country governance variables* which consist of six major dimensions provided by the World Bank; i.e., government effectiveness, rule of law, regulatory quality, political stability and absence of violence, voice and accountability, and control of corruption, and (3) *globalisation variables* which consist of six-dimensional globalisation indicators created by Dreher (2006), namely trade globalisation, financial globalisation, interpersonal globalisation, informational globalisation, cultural globalisation and political globalisation. Furthermore, the reader is referred to Figure 6 for the distribution of the main drivers of productivity. Hereafter, we shall summarise some of the main findings by subcategory of drivers and shall provide supporting theories to explain the relationship between these drivers and IBs' productivity.

Figure 5. General framework of the variables (inputs, outputs, links, carry-overs) in the Islamic banking MPI literature
Notes: (*) variables that have not been used in the Islamic banking productivity literature on DEA

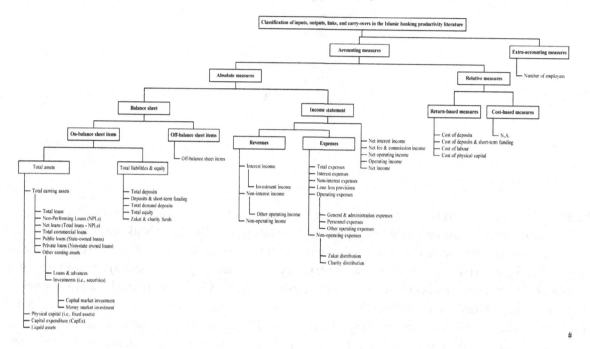

Figure 6. Distribution of the drivers of productivity in Islamic banking MPI literature. For the sake of clarity, only the drivers of productivity used at least two times (14 out of 54 drivers)

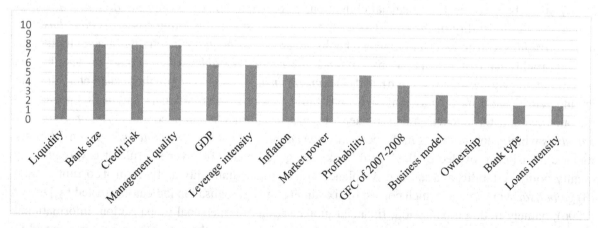

3.2.1 Impact of Bank Internal Environment Variables on Islamic Banks' Productivity

Bank risk variables. Two types of risk have been considered as drivers of productivity in the Islamic banking literature: *credit (or default) risk* and *solvency risk*. The research on the association between credit risk and productivity profiles of Islamic banks (IBs) has produced mixed conclusions.

- *Credit Risk*: Studies have employed various proxies for credit risk, such as loan loss provisions (LLPs) expressed as a percentage of total assets, the ratio of LLPs to gross loans, and non-performing loans (NPLs) to gross loans. Some findings suggest that IBs' productivity is negatively affected by default risk (Azad et al., 2017; Kamarudin et al., 2017), while others indicate a positive effect (Kamarudin et al., 2022). This counter-intuitive result could be explained by the *skimping hypothesis* (Berger and DeYoung, 1997), which suggests that banks might reduce short-term operating costs at the expense of long-term loan performance issues. However, some studies using alternative proxies have found no significant effect of credit risk on IBs' productivity (Sufian and Haron, 2008; Bahrini, 2015; Rani et al., 2017; Kamarudin et al., 2017; Otaviya and Rani, 2020; Jubilee et al., 2021b).

- *Solvency Risk*: Empirical research has also explored the IBs' productivity profiles from an insolvency standpoint. Researchers have measured insolvency risk using proxies such as leverage intensity (the ratio of total shareholders' equity to total assets) and capital adequacy ratio (the sum of Tier 1 capital and Tier 2 capital divided by risk-weighted assets). Some studies have found a significant negative relationship between IBs' leverage intensity and their productivity (Sufian and Haron, 2008; Bahrini, 2015; Kamarudin et al., 2017), while others documented a positive and significant coefficient (Azad et al., 2017; Jubilee et al., 2021b; Kamarudin et al., 2022). The positive correlation supports the *underinvestment problem theory* (Myers, 1977), which posits that highly indebted firms tend to forego productivity-enhancing investment opportunities due to financial creditors capturing a significant portion of the project cash flows. In contrast, the negative correlation aligns with the *free cash-flow theory* (Jensen, 1986) suggesting that debt could deter managers from spending excess cash flows on unproductive investments in firms with abundant cash flows. Finally, Rani et al. (2017) found no significant impact of capital adequacy ratio on IBs' productivity when using it as a proxy for solvency risk.

Bank profitability variables. Two measures of profitability have been identified in the Islamic banking productivity literature: *return on assets (ROA)* and *return on equity (ROE)*. ROA is measured by the ratio of net income to total assets, while ROE is measured by the ratio of net income to total shareholders' equity. The relationship between IBs' profitability and MPI scores has yielded mixed results.

- Some studies, such as Sufian and Haron (2008), Bahrini (2015), and Azad et al. (2017), have found a significant positive association between Islamic bank profitability and MPI scores. According to Sufian and Haron (2008), this positive relationship indicates that clients prefer highly profitable banks over less profitable ones, enabling banks to capture a larger market share of deposits and attract more credit-worthy borrowers. In turn, such a favorable banking environment encourages banks to be more productive from an intermediation perspective. Conversely, other empirical studies, like Rani et al. (2017) and Otaviya and Rani (2020), suggest that there is no significant relationship between the profitability of IBs and their productivity profiles.

Bank liquidity variables. Bank liquidity refers to a bank's ability to meet its short-term obligations and is generally measured by the level of cash and other liquid assets it has readily available. Studies on Islamic bank productivity using two-stage analysis have employed various proxies for liquidity, including the *ratio of total loans to total deposits, cash-to-assets ratio, ratio of net loans to total loans*, and the *ratio of total loans to total assets*. The use of these different liquidity proxies as potential drivers of Islamic banks' (IBs) productivity has led to mixed findings.

- Some empirical studies, such as Bahrini (2015), Azad et al. (2017), and Kamarudin et al. (2022), suggest that less liquid IBs tend to exhibit higher MPI scores. These results imply that IBs improve their productivity by generating more loans from existing deposits. However, this productivity enhancement may come at the cost of increased liquidity risk, as fewer liquid assets would be available for the bank to meet its obligations when they fall due for payment. On the other hand, findings from Bahrini (2015) and Jubilee et al. (2021b) reveal a significant positive impact of IBs' liquidity on their productivity, suggesting that highly liquid IBs tend to be more productive. Other studies, such as Kamarudin et al. (2017), Rani et al. (2017), and Otaviya and Rani (2020), have found an insignificant nexus between liquidity and productivity of IBs in various contexts under investigation.

Bank cost efficiency variables. The bank cost efficiency ratio, calculated as *non-interest expenses to total assets*, is widely employed to approximate management quality, capturing the bank managers' ability to control overhead expenses. Research on the relationship between management quality and IBs productivity has yielded mixed results.

- Empirical studies by Sufian and Haron (2008) and Bahrini (2015) found that an increase in overhead expenses (including personnel expenses, general and administrative expenses, and other operating expenses) leads to a significant improvement in IBs' productivity. This is consistent with the views of Berger (1995) and Sathye (2001), who suggest that banks with qualified managerial staff are expected to enjoy high levels of efficiency, despite the higher remuneration packages. This is particularly true for IBs, which require qualified managers and Shariah advisors to develop a full range of financial instruments to compete with CBs. A significant positive effect of managerial behaviour on IBs' productivity profiles can be attributed to the *expense-preference theory*, developed by Williamson (1963) and modified by Rees (1974). This theory posits that, under certain circumstances, managers may recruit more staff, spend more on office furniture and equipment, and allocate more resources to other perquisites, leading to increased productivity as new opportunities arise. Contrastingly, Azad et al. (2017) and Kamarudin et al. (2022) found evidence supporting a negative association between management quality and IBs' productivity change, suggesting that overstaffing and poor management may weaken IBs' productivity. Meanwhile, Rani et al. (2017), Kamarudin et al. (2017), Otaviya and Rani (2020), and Jubilee et al. (2021b) reported no significant link between management quality and IBs' productivity across various geographical locations.

Bank business model variables. The bank's business model is based on revenue generation through interest-based (or traditional banking) activities, which involve accepting deposits and offering loans, and non-interest-based operations (or non-traditional banking) activities, which generate fees. In the literature on Islamic bank productivity, the ratio of non-interest income to total assets is used as a proxy for *non-traditional banking activities*, while the ratio of total loans to total bank assets is employed as a proxy for *traditional banking activities*. Findings are mixed in studies examining the impact of IB business models on MPI profiles.

- Bahrini (2015) found that traditional banking activities have a significant positive effect on the productivity profiles of IBs. Similarly, Othman et al. (2013) discovered that IBs with high loans-to-assets ratios experience substantial increases in their productivity, along with improvements in overall technical efficiency changes and technological change. These findings suggest that specialized IBs, focusing more on Islamic modes of financing, are more productive than diversified ones. This is consistent with the *strategic-focus hypothesis* (Berger et al., 2000), which argues that more diversified firms are likely to incur additional costs in monitoring a broad range of business branches. Conversely, Azad et al. (2017) reported that IBs diversifying their portfolio of activities toward non-traditional transactions achieve high levels of productivity growth. This finding aligns with the *conglomeration hypothesis* (Berger, 2016), which posits that firms owning and operating a broad range of businesses can exploit shared resources at multiple points in the value chain, enabling them to realize revenue and profit scope economies and thereby operate close to best practice frontiers. Lastly, studies by Sufian and Haron (2008), Rani et al. (2017), and Otaviya and Rani (2020) found no statistically significant link between IBs' business models and their productivity.

Bank governance variables. Studies investigating the relationship between *bank ownership* and IBs' productivity have generally reached the conclusion that foreign-owned IBs are more productive than domestically-owned ones (Azad et al., 2017; Kamarudin et al., 2017). This finding aligns with the works of Isik and Hassan (2003) and Sufian and Kamarudin (2014). The higher productivity of foreign-owned banks compared to domestically-owned ones is consistent with the *limited global advantage hypothesis*, which posits that foreign-owned banking institutions in a host nation benefit from competitive advantages, available labour, and the use of advanced technology (Berger et al., 2000). These advantages provide foreign-owned banks with a favourable context in which to enhance their productivity more easily. Another explanation for the higher productivity of foreign-owned banks is that multinational firms (of which foreign firms are a subset) are, on average, more productive than purely domestic firms. This observation leads to the idea that there may be knowledge spillovers from more productive foreign firms to less productive domestic firms in the host country (Griffith et al., 2004). Such spillovers can result from foreign firms introducing new technologies, best practices, and management techniques to the host country, thereby indirectly improving the productivity of domestic firms through imitation, learning, and competition.

Bank intrinsic variables. Bank intrinsic variables reflect inherent attributes of IBs. In the literature on Islamic banking, three main intrinsic variables were identified as drivers of productivity: bank size, *bank market power, bank type*, and *Zakat*.

- *Bank size*: The majority of studies examining the association between bank size (proxied by the natural logarithm of total assets of the bank) and IBs productivity found a positive and significant correlation (Sufian and Haron, 2008; Othman et al., 2013; Kamarudin et al., 2017; Azad et al., 2017; Rani et al., 2017; Kamarudin et al., 2022), which is consistent with Llorens et al. (2020). This suggests that larger IBs tend to be more productive than medium- and smaller-sized IBs. However, Bahrini (2015) and Jubilee et al. (2021b) found no significant link between bank size and productivity of IBs in various contexts investigated in their respective studies.

- *Bank market power*: Studies examining the association between bank market power and the productivity profiles of IBs generally found a statistically significant negative influence (Sufian and Haron, 2008; Azad et al., 2017; Kamarudin et al., 2017; Kamarudin et al., 2022), which is in congruence with Sufian and Noor (2009). This suggests that more productive IBs are associated with a lower market share, thus diminishing the market leadership argument. However, Jubilee et al. (2021b) found that market power has a significant positive impact on the productivity profiles of IBs, which is in line with the structure-conduct-performance (SCP) framework. It suggests that banks with significant market power are likely to raise the cost of services such as loans and advances as well as non-conventional activities, while simultaneously lowering interest rates on customer deposits.

- *Bank type*: The relationship between bank type and productivity profiles of IBs establishes a common positive conclusion. Specifically, Othman et al. (2013) and Azad et al. (2017) found that bank type is statistically significant in determining the total factor productivity change scores of IBs.

- *Zakat*: The effect of the payment of Zakat by Malaysian IBs on productivity was found to be not statistically significant by Sufian and Haron (2008).

3.2.2 Impact of Bank External Environment Variables on Islamic Banks' Productivity

Bank macroeconomic variables. GDP is widely used as an economic growth indicator, representing a country's progress within a specific time frame. Three GDP measures analysed for their impact on IBs' productivity are: (1) *real GDP*, (2) *real GDP growth*, and (3) *GDP per capita*.

- For the first measure, real GDP, studies have reported mixed findings concerning its relationship with IBs' productivity. Azad et al. (2017), Otaviya and Rani (2020), and Kamarudin et al. (2022) found a significant positive impact of real GDP on IBs' productivity, which aligns with research from other regions (e.g., Jalilian et al., 2007). This positive impact can be attributed to favourable economic conditions that increase the supply and demand for loans and deposits, encouraging firms to seek more capital for growth (Kosmidou, 2008). In the case of IBs, high economic growth drives them to offer more financing and enhance their asset quality. However, Kamarudin et al. (2017) and Jubilee et al. (2021b) observed a significant negative impact of economic growth on IBs' productivity, while Bahrini (2015) found no significant relationship between real GDP and IBs' productivity.

- Regarding the second measure, real GDP growth, Azad et al. (2017) discovered that future GDP estimates and business expansion opportunities significantly and positively influence bank productivity, consistent with the findings of Arazmuradov et al. (2014) and Leimbach et al. (2017).

- For the third measure, GDP per capita, Othman et al. (2013) found no impact on IBs' productivity, which contradicts previous research findings (e.g., Sissoko et al., 2018; Ozbugday et al., 2019).

- Research on the relationship between inflation and IBs' productivity levels has produced varying results. Azad et al. (2017) and Kamarudin et al. (2022) demonstrated that inflation has a significant negative effect on IBs' productivity, corroborating the common findings of Bulman and Simon (2003). Conversely, Jubilee et al. (2021b) identified a significant positive effect of the consumer price index on IBs' productivity. Perry (1992) empirically established that inflation's impact on bank performance depends on whether it is anticipated or unanticipated. Anticipated inflation allows banks to adjust interest rates accordingly, resulting in a faster revenue increase compared to costs, positively impacting bank performance. However, unanticipated inflation may cause banks to adjust interest rates slowly, negatively affecting interest margins due to increased costs. Kamarudin et al. (2017) and Otaviya and Rani (2020) suggested that the relationship between inflation and bank productivity is not significant, although it is negative.

The relationship between the *Global Financial Crisis of 2007-2009 (GFC)* and IBs' productivity has produced mixed findings. On one hand, studies by Kamarudin et al. (2017), Jubilee et al. (2021b), and Kamarudin et al. (2022) incorporated the GFC as a dummy variable and demonstrated a statistically significant positive impact on IBs' productivity levels. This aligns with other research highlighting the performance of IBs during the 2007-2009 economic turmoil (Bourkhis and Nabi, 2013; Mobarek and Kalonov, 2014). Mollah et al. (2016) argued that the governance structure of IBs played a crucial role in their financial success during the GFC. On the other hand, Bahrini (2015) found that the GFC had a significant negative influence on IBs' productivity, suggesting that higher levels of financial crisis were associated with lower bank productivity.

Other factors, such as unemployment rate, exports, banking sector development, financial market development, reference interest rate, and currency exchange rate, have also been examined in relation to bank productivity. Othman et al. (2013) found a statistically significant relationship between the *unemployment rate* and bank productivity. However, they discovered that the level of exports had no impact on bank productivity. Bahrini (2015) studied *banking sector development*, measured by the ratio of credits to the private sector divided by GDP, and found no significant effect on IBs' productivity levels. Bahrini (2015) also found that a *developed financial market*, as indicated by the stock market capitalization to GDP ratio, had a significant positive relationship with bank productivity. Otaviya and Rani (2020) investigated the impact of *reference interest rates* and *currency exchange rates* on the productivity of IBs. They found a statistically significant impact of reference interest rates on IBs' productivity, while currency exchange rates showed no effect on productivity levels.

Country governance variables have been incorporated by Kamarudin et al. (2022) to assess their impact on the productivity profiles of IBs. Their findings show that all indicators, including political stability and absence of violence, government effectiveness, regulatory quality, rule of law, and control of corruption, have a statistically significant negative impact on IBs' productivity levels, except for voice and accountability. This latter indicator is positively and significantly correlated with the productivity profiles of IBs, aligning with findings by Kamarudin et al. (2016) and Chortareas et al. (2012).

The positive impact of voice and accountability on productivity suggests that increased voice and accountability lead to higher productivity levels. This may be attributed to the active role of citizens and state institutions in promoting democracy and reducing poverty, which can improve banks' performance.

Conversely, the negative effects of the remaining indicators can be explained as follows:

- *Political stability and absence of violence*: A stable political environment and freedom from violence and terrorism may contribute to lower productivity levels in IBs, possibly because an overly stable environment could hinder growth.
- *Government effectiveness*: Higher credibility and quality of government policies that benefit the public could lead to lower productivity levels for IBs.
- *Regulatory quality*: A negative relationship with productivity suggests that higher-quality regulation may result in lower productivity levels.
- *Rule of law*: A negative association indicates that higher-quality rule of law may contribute to lower bank productivity levels. The *theory of judicial behavior* posits that quality rule of law can drive economic efficiency (Sherwood et al., 1994).

• *Control of corruption:* A negative relationship suggests that greater control of corruption reduces banks' productivity levels. The *theory of supervision* argues that a robust supervisory agency that directly disciplines and monitors banks can improve the banking industry's efficiency by reducing corruption in bank lending (Beck et al., 2006).

Globalization variables have been examined by Jubilee et al. (2021b) to determine their impact on the productivity of Islamic banks (IBs). They used the six-dimensional globalization indicators created by Dreher (2006), which include Trade Globalization, Financial Globalization, Interpersonal Globalization, Informational Globalization, Cultural Globalization, and Political Globalization. These six dimensions can be divided into de facto and de jure globalization, with de facto globalization measuring real international flows and activities, while de jure globalization measures policies and requirements that, in theory, facilitate and promote flows and activities. *Cultural globalization, informational globalization,* and *political globalization* were found to have a negative but statistically insignificant correlation with IBs' productivity. Conversely, *financial globalization, interpersonal globalization,* and *trade globalization* were observed to have a positive but statistically insignificant impact on the productivity profiles of IBs. It has often been the case in international trade, as demonstrated by various research studies (Choudhri and Hakura, 2000), that increased international trade with industrial nations boosts productivity growth in developing nations through research and development (R&D) spillovers.

4. CRITICAL ANALYSIS OF DEA-BASED MPI STUDIES ON ISLAMIC BANKING PRODUCTIVITY

This section presents a critical examination of several aspects of the surveyed literature on Islamic banking productivity using DEA-based MPIs. These critical aspects are divided into three sections: (1) critical analysis of methodological and empirical aspects of the surveyed literature and identification of research gaps, (2) critical analysis of inconsistencies in the productivity literature (including methodological inconsistencies), and (3) critical analysis of mixed findings identified in both single stage and two-stage analyses as well as their justifications.

4.1 Critical Analysis of the Methodological and Empirical Choices

There are four methodological issues worth addressing. The *first one* arises from the fact that all previous cross-country DEA-based MPI studies on Islamic banking have focused on either estimating MPI scores of IBs (using single stage DEA analysis) or determining the drivers of productivity of IBs (using two-stage DEA analysis), and thus have failed to account for the possibility of technological differences across countries or differences in the operating (economic & banking) environments, which may bias the findings and provide under- or over-estimated productivity measures for IBs as a result of the heterogeneity of such environments. The *second methodological issue* is concerned with MPIs' various methodologies for estimating them. These methodologies can be broadly categorised into five significant contributions, namely, *Adjacent MPI* by Fare et al. (1992), *Sequential MPI* by Shestalova (2003), *Global MPI* by Pastor and Lovell (2005), *Common Weight Global MPI* by Kao (2010), and *Biennial MPI* by Pastor et al. (2011). Almost all DEA-based MPI research on Islamic banking computed MPI scores using an Adjacent MPI approach, followed by sparing usage of the Global MPI methodology. The productivity results obtained with the Adjacent MPI approach may be questionable since such index is not immune to the infeasibility of the DEA models used for estimating the index. In addition, this index is not circular. Therefore, one should use the Global MPI index instead as it overcomes these issues by design. Note however that as pointed out by Bjurek (1996), who proposed the Hicks–Moorsteen productivity index, and empirically investigated by Kerstens and de Woestyne (2014) who compared these indices, the Hicks–Moorsteen productivity index is by design superior to the above mentioned MPIs in that it overcomes their weaknesses including the returns-to-scale issue. Therefore, future research should use the Hicks–Moorsteen productivity index instead of MPIs in the estimation of productivity. The *third methodological issue* is the absence of popular non-radial models, namely SBM models, to compute MPIs and therefore, so far MPI scores of IBs and related conclusions have overlooked slacks which might result in overestimated MPI scores. Finally, the *fourth methodological issue* is that all DEA-based MPI studies on Islamic banking have estimated MPIs using black-box models, namely, CCR and BCC. To overcome this issue, one could use an open-box model to estimate MPIs.

On the other hand, there are also empirical issues. The *first one* is that research investigating the drivers of IBs' productivity are relatively scarce, with most of these studies focusing on Southeast Asian nations, namely, Malaysia and Indonesia. As a result, further empirical research is required to identify the most appropriate drivers for specific countries or regions that a variety of stakeholders could act upon. The *second empirical issue* lies in the fact that all previous studies on IB productivity, with a focus on identifying the drivers of productivity, were mainly concerned with the drivers of the overall productivity score and therefore failed to identify the drivers of their components (i.e., technology change, efficiency change) which would be highly insightful for practitioners as well as policy makers.

Finally, the *third empirical issue* has to do with incorporating risk factors in the estimation of MPI scores. In fact, most previous research ignores factors of risk in designing MPIs for IBs. However, the literature on CBs addressed this issue – see for example Khanal & Bhatta (2017).

Overall, the above-mentioned issues demonstrate the need for further research in the area of productivity analysis in Islamic banking. Addressing these issues can improve the accuracy and reliability of the findings. Such research can benefit various stakeholders, including policymakers, regulators, and investors, by providing them with a better understanding of the performance of IBs and informing their decision-making processes.

4.2 Inconsistencies in Islamic Banking Productivity Literature Using DEA-Based MPIs

We have identified several inconsistencies of different categories while surveying DEA-based MPI studies on Islamic banking productivity. First, it is well established in DEA applications in the banking area that bank behaviour models – also known as evaluation approaches, should be explicitly mentioned as they help researchers provide justified choices of inputs and outputs for the specification of DEA models. However, several studies on Islamic banking productivity (17%) did not explicitly state what type of evaluation approach they used for the selection of inputs and outputs. *Second*, few studies failed to report the details on the proxies they used for the input and output variables to specify the DEA models, which makes their studies non-reproduceable, on one hand, and comparisons across papers infeasible, on the other hand. Third, in Islamic banking productivity, some studies compared different groups of banks using only the mean values of the groups as opposed to performing formal statistical tests whether parametric or non-parametric. Fourth, few studies concerned with identifying the drivers of productivity have chosen factors (e.g., inflation) that are known to have a bidirectional relationship with productivity, but opted for a regression framework that doesn't account for such bidirectional relationship resulting in an endogeneity issue. Finally, from an empirical analysis perspective, several studies failed to engage with the literature, provide an explanation for inconsistent findings, or back up their findings with the relevant theories.

4.3 Critical Analysis of the Mixed Findings Identified in Both Single Stage Analysis and Two-Stage Analysis and their Justifications

In this section, we look into the mixed findings in the Islamic banking productivity literature using DEA-based MPIs. Such mixed findings can be divided into two primary categories: (1) *conflicting productivity findings* of single stage analyses and (2) *conflicting effects of drivers of productivity* in two-stage analyses. These conflicting findings are summarised in Table 1 in the appendix, which is organised into panels each concerned with a different criterion (i.e., type of bank: Islamic vs. Conventional; type of ownership: foreign vs. domestic IBs; and type of modus operandi: full-fledged IBs vs. Islamic windows).

The conclusions of panel A concerning the *bank type* criterion are threefold: (1) IBs are more productive than CBs, (2) IBs are less productive than CBs, and (3) there is no significant difference between IB and CB productivity. We found that the panel B regarding the *ownership type* criterion yield opposing results and are threefold: (1) foreign IBs are more productive than domestic IBs, (2) foreign IBs are less productive than domestic IBs, and (3) there is no significant difference between the productivity of foreign and domestic IBs. Panel C's results regarding the *modus operandi type* criterion yield conflicting conclusions: (1) Islamic windows are more productive than full-fledged IBs, and (2) Islamic windows are less productive than full-fledged IBs. These findings and their sources of differences revealed that these inconsistencies in findings may be attributed to differences in sample composition, period of analysis, sources of data or databases, inconsistencies in the reporting of data providers, evaluation approaches and selection of variables for the specification of DEA models in the estimation of an MPI, type of MPI, type of orientation(s), and types of DEA models used for estimating the productivity profiles of banks. In addition to the above-mentioned sources of mixed findings across all criteria, other sources specific to the bank type include (1) differences in Sharia-compliant product implementations across various jurisdictions (e.g., Beck et al., 2013; Asmild et al., 2019); (2) differences in business models of IBs and CBs (e.g., Beck et al., 2013); (3) differences in risk profiles as IBs are exposed to a set of specific types of risks other than the common ones to both types of banks (e.g., Sharia non-compliance risk, displaced commercial risk; Oz et al. 2016); (4) the governance structure of IBs differs significantly from that of CBs due to the existence of Shariah supervisory boards (e.g., Mollah et al., 2017); (6) differences in maturity of the sector in that the Islamic banking industry is a relatively young industry (Johnes et al., 2018) as compared to the conventional banking industry, which dates back to about two hundred years.

Moreover, the following additional factors are likely to drive these mixed findings: (1) differences in *regulatory and supervisory frameworks* across countries and regions may influence the productivity of IBs. For instance, stricter regulations may lead to higher compliance costs for banks, potentially affecting their productivity. However, in some cases, strict regulations may prompt banks to become more efficient and productive to maintain profitability; (2) *market competition* could influence the productivity of IBs differently. In highly competitive markets, banks may be pressured to improve their efficiency and productivity to maintain market share and profitability. On the other hand, in less competitive markets, banks may not face the same level of pressure to optimize their operations; (3) *financial innovation and technological advancements* may affect the productivity of IBs differently. Banks that invest in and adopt new technologies and offer innovative products may experience productivity gains, while those that are slow to adapt may lag behind; and (4) *size and scale of banks' operations* may also contribute to the mixed results in productivity. Larger banks may benefit from economies of scale, leading to higher productivity, while smaller banks may struggle to achieve the same level of efficiency.

On the other hand, the *conflicting effects of drivers of productivity* (i.e., *statistically significant positive relationship, statistically significant negative relationship, or no statistically significant relationship*) could be due to the use of different proxies for the same driver, the variables used for the specification of the DEA model for its estimation, the regression framework used as well as differences in sample composition and period of analysis. In cross-country analyses, however mixed findings could result from differences in the banking and economic environments, which could be more or less favourable than others.

5. CONCLUDING REMARKS AND FUTURE RESEARCH DIRECTIONS

In this review paper, we classified the 68 papers on Islamic banking productivity using DEA-based MPIs, published between 2006 and 2022, into several meaningful categories and provided a critical analysis of papers within each category and across categories to help new researchers avoid some methodological or empirical shortcomings while crafting their papers. Some of the identified shortcomings themselves represent future research avenues for someone concerned with addressing them.

By covering a variety of the most important aspects of the productivity literature on Islamic banking utilising DEA-based MPIs, we provided a painting of the landscape of research in this field. Regarding the future research agenda, as mentioned above, addressing each of the shortcomings identified in our critical analysis is in itself future research; however, some are more pressing than others. For example, purging IBs' productivity scores from the effect of their operating environments is a priority for banking productivity to be comparable across types of banks and countries. Estimating productivity using MPIs with desirable properties and using open box DEA models to estimate MPIs to provide more realistic productivity profiles are other priorities.

REFERENCES

Abbas, M., Hammad, R. S., Elshahat, M. F., & Azid, T. (2015). Efficiency, productivity and Islamic banks: An application of DEA and Malmquist index. *Humanomics, 31*(1), 118–131. doi:10.1108/H-03-2013-0022

Abduh, M., Hasan, S. M., & Pananjung, A. G. (2013). Efficiency and Performance of Islamic Banks in Bangladesh. *Journal of Islamic Banking and Finance, 30*(2), 94–106.

Abdul-Wahab, A.-H., & Haron, R. (2017). Efficiency of Qatari banking industry: An empirical investigation. *International Journal of Bank Marketing. Unit, 07*, 1–5.

Abu-Alkheil, A. M., Burghof, H. P., & Khan, W. A. (2012). Comparison of efficiency and productivity changes of Islamic and conventional banks: Evidence from Europe and Muslim-Majority countries? *Journal of Applied Business Research, 28*(6), 1385–1412. doi:10.19030/jabr.v28i6.7351

Ada, A. A., & Dalkılıç, N. (2014). Efficiency Analysis in Islamic Banks: A Study for Malaysia and Turkey. *BDDK Bankacılık ve Finansal Piyasalar, 8*(1), 9–33.

Afiatun, P., & Wiryono, S. (2010). Efficiency and Productivity of Indonesian Islamic Banking. *Journal of Technology Management, 9*(3), 264–278.

Aisyah, S., & Hosen, M. N. (2018). Total Factor Productivity and Efficiency Analysis on Islamic Banks in Indonesia. *Jurnal Keuangan Dan Perbankan, 22*(1), 137–147. doi:10.26905/jkdp.v22i1.1333

Ajija, S. R., Yasin, M. Z., & Albra, R. (2017). Indonesian Banking Efficiency: Transmission to the Financial Stability Confronting ASEAN Economic Community. *Jurnal Ekonomi Pembangunan, 18*(2), 183. doi:10.23917/jep.v18i2.5095

Al-Muharrami, S. (2007). The causes of productivity change in GCC banking industry. *International Journal of Productivity and Performance Management, 56*(8), 731–743. doi:10.1108/17410400710833029

Alam, N. (2013). Impact of banking regulation on risk and efficiency in Islamic banking. *Journal of Financial Reporting and Accounting, 11*(1), 29–50. doi:10.1108/JFRA-03-2013-0010

Alandejani, M. (2014). *Efficiency, Survival, and Non-Performing Loans in Islamic and Conventional Banking in the GCC. Durham Theses.* Durham University.

Alendejani, M., & Asutay, M. (2017). Determining the Efficiency of Islamic and Conventional Commercial Banks in the GCC. In *Islamic Finance* (Vol. 3, pp. 11–50). Performance and Efficiency. doi:10.2307/j.ctt1df4hbd.4

Alexakis, C., Izzeldin, M., Johnes, J., & Pappas, V. (2019). Performance and Productivity in Islamic and Conventional Banks: Evidence from the Global Financial Crisis. *Economic Modelling, 79*, 1–14. Advance online publication. doi:10.1016/j.econmod.2018.09.030

Alhassan, A. L., & Biekpe, N. (2015). Explaining Bank Productivity in Ghana. *MDE. Managerial and Decision Economics, 37*(8), 563–573. doi:10.1002/mde.2748

Alpay, S., & Hassan, M. K. (2007). A Comparative Efficiency Analysis of Interest Free Financial Institutions and Conventional Banks: A Case Study on Turkey. *Working Paper, 0714*, 1–18.

Alsharif, M., Md Nassir, A., Kamarudin, F., & Zariyawati, M. A. (2019). The productivity of GCC Islamic and conventional banks after Basel III announcement. *Journal of Islamic Accounting and Business Research, 10*(5), 770–792. doi:10.1108/JIABR-04-2017-0050

Ara, S. (2016). Comparison between conventional banking and islamic banking in terms of x-efficiency using data envelopment analysis and malmquist productivity index analysis. *Proceedings of the 14th International Conference of DEA.*

Arazmuradov, A., Martini, G., & Scotti, D. (2014). Determinants of total factor productivity in former Soviet Union economies: A stochastic frontier approach. *Economic Systems, 38*(1), 115–135. doi:10.1016/j.ecosys.2013.07.007

Arjomandi, A., Harvie, C., & Valadkhani, A. (2012). An empirical analysis of Iran's banking performance. *Studies in Economics and Finance, 29*(4), 287–300. doi:10.1108/10867371211266928

Athari, S. A., Irani, F., & Hadood, A. A. (2023). Country risk factors and banking sector stability: Do countries' income and risk-level matter? Evidence from global study. *Heliyon, 10*(9), e20398. doi:10.1016/j.heliyon.2023.e20398 PMID:37780769

Azad, M. A. K., Munisamy, S., Masum, A. K. M., Saona, P., & Wanke, P. (2017). Bank efficiency in Malaysia: A use of Malmquist meta-frontier analysis. *Eurasian Business Review, 7*(2), 287–311. doi:10.100740821-016-0054-4

Azzam, A., & Rettab, B. (2020). Comparative TFP Growth Between GCC Conventional and Islamic Banks Before and After the 2008 Financial Crisis. *The Singapore Economic Review*. Advance online publication. doi:10.1142/S0217590820420047

Bahrini, R. (2015). Productivity of MENA Islamic banks: A bootstrapped Malmquist index approach. *International Journal of Islamic and Middle Eastern Finance and Management, 8*(4), 508–528. doi:10.1108/IMEFM-11-2014-0114

Basri, M. F., Muhamat, A. A., & Jaafar, M. N. (2018). The efficiency of Islamic banks in Malaysia: Based on DEA and Malmquist productivity index. *Journal of Emerging Economies and Islamic Research, 6*(3), 15. doi:10.24191/jeeir.v6i3.8784

Beck, T., Demirgüç-Kunt, A., & Levine, R. (2006). Bank supervision and corruption in lending. *Journal of Monetary Economics, 53*(8), 2131–2163. doi:10.1016/j.jmoneco.2005.10.014

Beck, T., Demirgüç-Kunt, A., & Merrouche, O. (2013). Islamic vs. conventional banking: Business model, efficiency and stability. *Journal of Banking & Finance, 37*(2), 433–447. doi:10.1016/j.jbankfin.2012.09.016

Berger, A. N., Cummins, J. D. D., Weiss, M. A., & Zi, H. (2000). Conglomeration Versus Strategic Focus: Evidence from the Insurance Industry. SSRN *Electronic Journal*. doi:10.2139/ssrn.174810

Berger, A. N., & DeYoung, R. (1997). Problem loans and cost efficiency in commercial banks. *Journal of Banking & Finance, 21*(6), 849–870. doi:10.1016/S0378-4266(97)00003-4

Berger, A. N., DeYoung, R., Genay, H., & Udell, G. F. (2000). Globalization of Financial Institutions: Evidence from Cross-Border Banking Performance. *Brookings-Wharton Papers on Financial Service, 3*(1), 23–120. doi:10.1353/pfs.2000.0001

Berger, A. N., & Mester, L. J. (2003). Explaining the dramatic changes in performance of US banks: Technological change, deregulation, and dynamic changes in competition. *Journal of Financial Intermediation, 12*(1), 57–95. doi:10.1016/S1042-9573(02)00006-2

Bhatia, V., Basu, S., Mitra, S. K., & Dash, P. (2018). *A review of bank efficiency and productivity.* OPSEARCH., doi:10.100712597-018-0332-2

Bitar, M., Naceur, S. B., Ayadi, R., & Walker, T. (2020). Basel Compliance and Financial Stability: Evidence from Islamic Banks. *Journal of Financial Services Research, 60*(1), 81–134. doi:10.100710693-020-00337-6

Bjurek, H. (1996). The Malmquist Total Factor Productivity Index. *The Scandinavian Journal of Economics, 98*(2), 303–313. doi:10.2307/3440861

Bourkhis, K., & Nabi, M. S. (2013). Islamic and Conventional Banks' Soundness during the 2007-2008 Financial Crisis. *Review of Financial Economics, 22*(2), 68–77. doi:10.1016/j.rfe.2013.01.001

Boyacioglu, M. A., & Şahin, İ. E. (2014). A Comparison of the Financial Efficiencies of Commercial Banks and Participation Banks: The Case of Turkey. *11th International Academic Conference*, Reykjavik, 7–26.

Bushara, M. O., Aziz, Y. A., & Hussain, A. I. (2018). The sources of productivity change in Yemen Islamic banks: An application of Malmquist productivity index. *International Journal of Financial Management and Economics, 1*(1), 39–45. doi:10.33545/26179210.2018.v1.i1a.8

Chapra, M. U. (2011). The Global Financial Crisis: Can Islamic Finance Help? *Islamic Economics and Finance*, 135–142. doi:10.1057/9780230361133_5

Chapra, U. M., (2008). The Global Financial Crisis - Economic Challenges and Prospects for Islamic Finance. *ICR Journal, 1*(2).

Chortareas, G. E., Girardone, C., & Ventouri, A. (2012). Bank supervision, regulation, and efficiency: Evidence from the European Union. *Journal of Financial Stability, 8*(4), 292–302. doi:10.1016/j.jfs.2011.12.001

Choudhri, E. U., & Hakura, D. S. (2000). International Trade and Productivity Growth: Exploring the Sectoral Effects for Developing Countries. *IMF Staff Papers, 47*(1), 1–2. doi:10.2307/3867624

Chowdhury, M. A. M., & Haron, R. (2021). The efficiency of Islamic Banks in the Southeast Asia (SEA) Region. *Future Business Journal, 7*(16), 1–16. doi:10.118643093-021-00062-z

Dreher, A. (2006). Does globalization affect growth? Evidence from a new index of globalization. *Applied Economics, 38*(10), 1091–1110. doi:10.1080/00036840500392078

Emrouznejad, A., & Yang, G. L. (2018). A Survey And Analysis Of The First 40 Years Of Scholarly Literature In DEA: 1978-2016. *Socio-Economic Planning Sciences, 61*(1), 4–8. doi:10.1016/j.seps.2017.01.008

Fare, R., Grosskopf, S., Lindgren, B., & Roos, P. (1992). Productivity Changes in Swedish Pharmacies 1980-1989: A Non-Parametric Malmquist Approach. *Journal of Productivity Analysis, 3*, 85–101. doi:10.1007/BF00158770

Faruk, U., Disman, D., & Nugraha, N. (2017). Efficiency and Productivity Growth Analysis of the Islamic Banking in Indonesia: Data Envelopment Analysis and Malmquist Productivity Index Approach. *1st International Conference on Islamic Economics, Business, and Philanthropy*, 213–218. 10.5220/0007079502130218

Firmansyah, I. (2018). Measuring of Islamic Banking Productivity in Indonesia Using Malmquist Index. *International Conference on Life, Innovation, Change, and Knowledge, 203*, 251–254. 10.2991/iclick-18.2019.51

Ganouati, J., & Essid, H. (2017). The sources of productivity change and efficiency in Islamic banking: Application of Malmquist productivity index. *The Central European Review of Economics and Management, 1*(4), 35–67. doi:10.29015/cerem.555

Griffith, R., Redding, S. J., & Van Reenen, J. M. (2000). Mapping the two Faces of R&D: Productivity Growth in a Panel of OECD Industries. *SSRN*, *86*(4), 442–448. doi:10.2139srn.229400

Gygli, S., Haelg, F., Potrafke, N., & Sturm, J.-E. (2019). The KOF Globalisation Index – revisited. *The Review of International Organizations*, *14*(3), 543–574. Advance online publication. doi:10.100711558-019-09344-2

Hadad, M. D., Hall, M. J. B., Kenjegaliev, K. A., Santoso, W., & Simper, R. (2011). Productivity changes and risk management in Indonesian banking: A Malmquist analysis. *Applied Financial Economics*, *21*(12), 847–861. doi:10.1080/09603107.2010.537636

Hadi, F. S. A., & Saad, N. M. (2010). An analysis on the efficiency of the Malaysian Islamic banking industry: Domestic vs. foreign. *Review of Islamic Economics*, *14*(1), 27–47.

Hassan, M. K. (2006). The X-Efficiency in Islamic Banks. *Islamic Economic Studies*, *13*(2), 49–78.

Iddouch, K., El Badraoui, K., & Ouenniche, J. (2023). Landscape of research on the efficiency profiles of Islamic banks using DEA: Survey, classification and critical analysis of the literature. *International Journal of Business*, *28*(3), 1–46. Advance online publication. doi:10.55802/IJB.028(3).004

Imam, P., & Kpodar, K. (2016). Islamic banking: Good for growth? *Economic Modelling*, *59*, 387–401. doi:10.1016/j.econmod.2016.08.004

Isik, I., Kulali, I., & Agcayazi-Yilmaz, B. (2016). Total Factor Productivity Change in the Middle East Banking: The Case of Jordanian Banks at the Turn of the Millennium. *International Journal of Research in Business and Social Science, 5*(3), 1–29. doi:10.20525/ijrbs.v5i3.296

Ismail, F., & Rahim, R. A. (2013). Productivity of Islamic and Conventional Banks of Malaysia: An Empirical Analysis. *The IUP Journal of Telecommunications*, *12*(3), 7–20.

Jahan, N. (2019). Productivity Analysis of Commercial Banks of Bangladesh: A Malmquist Productivity Index Approach. *International Journal of Economics and Financial Issues*, *9*(1), 108–115.

Jalilian, H., Kirkpatrick, C., & Parker, D. (2007). The Impact of Regulation on Economic Growth in Developing Countries: A Cross-Country Analysis. *World Development*, *35*(1), 87–103. doi:10.1016/j.worlddev.2006.09.005

Jensen, M. C. (1986). Agency Cost of Free Cash Flow, Corporate Finance, and Takeovers. *SSRN*, *76*(2), 323–329. doi:10.2139srn.99580

Johnes, J., Izzeldin, M., & Pappas, V. (2009). *The efficiency of Islamic and conventional banks in the Gulf Cooperation Council (GCC) countries: An analysis using financial ratios and data envelopment analysis*. Working Paper.

Johnes, J., Izzeldin, M., & Pappas, V. (2014). Efficiency in Islamic and Conventional Banks: Evidence from the Gulf Cooperation Council Countries. SSRN *Electronic Journal*, 1–36. doi:10.2139/ssrn.2411974

Jokipii, T., & Monnin, P. (2013). The impact of banking sector stability on the real economy. *Journal of International Money and Finance*, *32*, 1–16. doi:10.1016/j.jimonfin.2012.02.008

Jubilee, R. V. W., Kamarudin, F., Latiff, A. R. A., Hussain, H. I., & Tan, K. M. (2021a). Do Islamic versus conventional banks progress or regress in productivity level? *Future Business Journal, 7*(1), 22. Advance online publication. doi:10.118643093-021-00065-w

Jubilee, R. V. W., Razman, A., & Latiff, A. (2021b). (in press). Does globalisation have an impact on dual banking system productivity in selected Southeast Asian banking industry? *Asia-Pacific Journal of Business Administration.* Advance online publication. doi:10.1108/APJBA-09-2020-0343

Kamarudin, F., Hue, C. Z., Sufian, F., & Mohamad Anwar, N. A. (2017). Does productivity of Islamic banks endure progress or regress? Empirical evidence using data envelopment analysis-based Malmquist Productivity Index. *Humanomics, 33*(1), 84–118. doi:10.1108/H-08-2016-0059

Kamarudin, F., Mohamad Anwar, N. A., Md. Nassir, A., Sufian, F., Tan, K. M., & Iqbal Hussain, H. (2022). Does country governance and bank productivity Nexus matters? *Journal of Islamic Marketing, 13*(2), 329–380. doi:10.1108/JIMA-05-2019-0109

Kamarudin, F., Sufian, F., & Nassir, A. M. (2016). Global financial crisis, ownership and bank profit efficiency in the Bangladesh's state owned and private commercial banks. *Contaduría y Administración, 61*(4), 705–745. doi:10.1016/j.cya.2016.07.006

Kao, C. (2010). Malmquist productivity index based on common-weights DEA: The case of Taiwan forests after reorganization. *Omega, 38*(6), 484–491. doi:10.1016/j.omega.2009.12.005

Karanlioglu, G., & Musajeva, S. (2017). *Comparison of Efficiency and Productivity between Islamic Banks in the GCC region A quantitative study using DEA and Malmquist index.* Academic Press.

Kerstens, K., & de Woestyn, I. V. (2014). Comparing Malmquist and Hicks–Moorsteen productivity indices: Exploring the impact of unbalanced vs. balanced panel data. *European Journal of Operational Research, 233*(4), 749–758. doi:10.1016/j.ejor.2013.09.009

Khan, M. I., & Shah, I. A. (2015). Cost Efficiency and Total Factor Productivity of Islamic and Conventional Banks in Pakistan. *Research Journal of Finance and Accounting, 6*(5), 135–146.

Khanal, S., & Bhatta, B. P. (2017). Evaluating Efficiency of Personnel in Nepalese Commercial Banks. *International Advances in Economic Research, 23*(4), 379–394. doi:10.100711294-017-9654-8

Khoveyni, M., & Eslami, R. (2022). Merging two-stage series network structures: A DEA-based approach Merging two-stage series network structures: A DEA-based approach. *OR-Spektrum, 44*(1), 273–302. doi:10.100700291-021-00653-w

Kosmidou, K. (2008). The determinants of banks' profits in Greece during the period of EU financial integration. *Managerial Finance, 34*(3), 146–159. doi:10.1108/03074350810848036

Leimbach, M., Kriegler, E., Roming, N., & Schwanitz, J. (2017). Future growth patterns of world regions – A GDP scenario approach. *Global Environmental Change, 42*, 215–225. doi:10.1016/j.gloenvcha.2015.02.005

Llorens, V., Martín-Oliver, A., & Salas-Fumas, V. (2020). Productivity, competition and bank restructuring process. *SERIEs, 11*(3), 313–340. doi:10.100713209-020-00214-4

Mobarek, A., & Kalonov, A. (2014). Comparative performance analysis between conventional and Islamic banks: Empirical evidence from OIC countries. *Applied Economics*, *46*(3), 253–270. doi:10.1080/00036846.2013.839863

Mollah, S., Hassan, M. K., Al Farooque, O., & Mobarek, A. (2016). The governance, risk-taking, and performance of Islamic banks. *Journal of Financial Services Research*, *51*(2), 195–219. doi:10.1007/10693-016-0245-2

Myers, S. C. (1977). Determinants of corporate borrowing. *Journal of Financial Economics*, *5*(2), 147–175. doi:10.1016/0304-405X(77)90015-0

Nartey, A. B., Osei, K. A., & Sarpong-Kumankoma, E. (2019). Bank productivity in Africa. *International Journal of Productivity and Performance Management*, *69*(9), 1973–1997. doi:10.1108/IJPPM-09-2018-0328

Nugrohowati, R. N. I., Fakhrunnas, F., & Haron, R. (2020). Examining Technological and Productivity Change in the Islamic Banking Industry. *Pertanika Journal of Social Science & Humanities*, *28*(4), 3355–3374. doi:10.47836/pjssh.28.4.47

Octrina, F., & Mariam, A. G. S. (2021). Productivity of Islamic Banking in Indonesia. *Jurnal Perspektif Pembiayaan Dan Pembangunan Daerah*, *9*(1), 19–28. doi:10.22437/ppd.v9i1.11041

Omar, M. A., Abd. Majid, M. S., & Rulindo, R. (2006). Efficiency and Productivity Performance of the National Private Banks in Indonesia. *Gadjah Mada International Journal of Business*, *9*(1), 1. doi:10.22146/gamaijb.5603

Onour, I. A., & Abdalla, A. M. A. (2011). Efficiency of Islamic Banks in Sudan: A non-parametric Approach. *Journal of Islamic Economics. Banking and Finance*, *7*(4), 79–92.

Otaviya, S. A., & Rani, L. N. (2020). Productivity and its Determinants in Islamic Banks: Evidence from Indonesia. *Journal of Islamic Monetary Economics and Finance*, *6*(1), 189–212. doi:10.21098/jimf.v6i1.1146

Othman, A., Kari, F., & Hamdan, R. (2013). A Comparative Analysis of the Co-operative, Islamic and Conventional Banks in Malaysia. *American Journal of Economics*, *3*(5C), 184–190. doi:10.5923/c.economics.201301.31

Ozbugday, F. C., Tirgil, A., & Kose, E. G. (2019). Efficiency changes in long-term care in OECD countries: A non-parametric Malmquist Index approach. *Socio-Economic Planning Sciences*, *100733*. Advance online publication. doi:10.1016/j.seps.2019.100733

Pambuko, Z. B., Usman, N., & Andriyani, L. (2019). Spin-off and Social Funds' Productivity of Islamic Banking Industry in Indonesia. *1st International Conference on Progressive Civil Society (IConProCS 2019)*, *317*, 7–10. 10.2991/iconprocs-19.2019.2

Pastor, J. T., Asmild, M., & Lovell, C. K. (2011). The biennial Malmquist productivity change index. *Socio-Economic Planning Sciences*, *45*(1), 10–15. doi:10.1016/j.seps.2010.09.001

Pastor, J. T., & Lovell, C. K. (2005). A global Malmquist productivity index. *Economics Letters*, *88*(2), 266–271. doi:10.1016/j.econlet.2005.02.013

Perry, P. (1992). Do banks gain or lose from inflation. *Journal of Retail Banking, 14*(2), 25–30.

Rani, L. N., Sukmaningrum, P. S., & Salleh, M. C. M. (2020). A Comparative Analysis of the Productivity of Islamic Banking in Indonesia, Malaysia and Brunei Darussalam during the period 2012-2017. *International Journal of Innovation, Creativity and Change, 11*(11), 470–491.

Rani, L. N., Widiastuti, T., & Rusydiana, A. S. (2017). Comparative Analysis of Islamic Bank's Productivity and Conventional Bank's in Indonesia Period 2008-2016. *1st International Conference on Islamic Economics, Business, and Philanthropy (ICIEBP 2017)*, 118–123. 10.5220/0007077901180123

Rashid, A., & Rehman, U. Z. (2016). Measurement and decomposition of productivity change in banking: Islamic and conventional banks in Pakistan. *Journal of Islamic Business and Management, 6*(2), 55–75.

Rees, R. (1974). A reconsideration of the expense preference theory of the firm. *Econometrica, 41*, 295–307.

Rodoni, A., Salim, M. A., Amalia, E., & Rakhmadi, R. S. (2017). Comparing Efficiency and Productivity in Islamic Banking: Case Study Indonesia, Malaysia and Pakistan. *Al-Iqtishad: Journal of Islamic Economics, 9*(2), 227–242. doi:10.15408/aiq.v9i2.5153

Romdhane, M., & Alhakimi, S. S. (2018). Productivity and technical efficiency in Islamic banks: Cross-country analysis. *Asian Journal of Economic Modelling, 6*(1), 1–7. doi:10.18488/journal.8.2018.61.1.7

Rusydiana, A. S., & Assalafiyah, A. (2021). Advancement and Setback in Islamic Banking Productivity in Asean: Do Technological Changes Matter? *Journal of Islamic Monetary Economics and Finance, 7*(3), 583–604. doi:10.21098/jimf.v7i3.1322

Salami, O. L., & Adeyemi, A. A. (2015). Malaysian Islamic banks' efficiency: An intra-bank comparative analysis of Islamic windows and full-fledged subsidiaries. *International Journal of Business and Society, 16*(1), 19–38. doi:10.33736/ijbs.551.2015

Saleh, A. S., Moradi-Motlagh, A., & Zeitun, R. (2020). What are the drivers of inefficiency in the Gulf Cooperation Council banking industry? A comparison between conventional and Islamic banks. *Pacific Basin Finance Journal, 60*, 101266. https://doi.org/ doi:10.1016/j.pacfin.2020.101266

Salleh, M. C. M., & Rani, L. N. (2020). Productivity Comparation of Islamic and Conventional Banks in Indonesia. *Al-Uqud: Journal of Islamic Economics, 4*(28), 69–82. doi:10.26740/al-uqud.v4n1.p69-82

Sapanji, R. A. E. V. T., Athoillah, A., Solehudin, E., & Mohamad, S. (2021). Analysis of the Technical Efficiency, Malmquist Productivity Index, and Tobit Regression of the eleven Islamic Commercial Banks in Indonesia between 2010 and 2019. *Turkish Journal of Computer and Mathematics Education, 12*(8), 505–522.

Sharma, A. K., & Barua, M. K. (2013). Efficiency and productivity of banking sector. *Qualitative Research in Financial Markets, 5*(2), 195–224. doi:10.1108/QRFM-10-2011-0025

Sherwood, R. M., Shepherd, G., & De Souza, C. M. (1994). Judicial systems and economic performance. *The Quarterly Review of Economics and Finance, 34*, 101–116. doi:10.1016/1062-9769(94)90038-8

Shestalova, V. (2003). Sequential Malmquist indices of productivity growth: An application to OECD industrial activities. *Journal of Productivity Analysis*, *19*(2-3), 211–226. doi:10.1023/A:1022857501478

Siddique, M. A., & Rahim, M. (2013). Efficiency analysis of full-fledged Islamic banks and standalone Islamic branches of conventional banks in Pakistan: A comparative study for the period of 2007-2012. *Journal of Islamic Business and Management*, *3*(2), 129–149. doi:10.12816/0005000

Sissoko, Y., Sloboda Brian, W., & Kone, S. (2018). Is it Factor Accumulation or Total Factor Productivity Explaining the Economic Growth in ECOWAS? An Empirical Assessment. *African Journal of Economic Review*, *5*(2), 30–45.

Sufian, F. (2007). Malmquist indices of productivity change in Malaysian Islamic banking industry: Foreign versus domestic banks. *Journal of Economic Cooperation*, *28*(1), 115–150.

Sufian, F. (2009a). Sources of TFP growth in the Malaysian Islamic banking sector. *Service Industries Journal*, *29*(9), 1273–1291. doi:10.1080/02642060801911128

Sufian, F. (2009b). Total factor productivity change of the Malaysian Islamic banking sector: An empirical study. *Journal of Islamic Economics. Banking and Finance*, *5*(1), 73–88.

Sufian, F. (2010). Productivity, technology and efficiency of De Novo Islamic banks: Empirical evidence from Malaysia. *Journal of Financial Services Marketing*, *15*(July), 241–258. doi:10.1057/fsm.2010.20

Sufian, F., & Haron, R. (2008). The sources and determinants of productivity growth in the Malaysian Islamic banking sector: A nonstochastic frontier approach. *International Journal of Accounting and Finance*, *1*(2), 193–215. doi:10.1504/IJAF.2008.020303

Usman, N., Andriyani, L., & Pambuko, Z. B. (2019). Productivity of Islamic banks in Indonesia: Social funds versus financial funds. *Journal of Asian Finance. Economics and Business*, *6*(3), 115–122. doi:10.13106/jafeb.2019.vol6.no3.115

Wahid, M. A., & Harun, M. S. (2019). Productivity of Islamic and Conventional Banks in Malaysia –During the Pre and Post Global Financial Crisis. *The Journal of Muamalat and Islamic Finance Research*, *16*(2), 86–95. doi:10.33102/jmifr.v16i2.225

Williamson, O. (1963). Managerial discretion and business behavior. *The American Economic Review*, *53*, 1032–1057.

Yaumidin, U. K. (2007). Efficiency in Islamic Banking: A Non-Parametric Approach. *Buletin Ekonomi Moneter Dan Perbankan*, *9*(4), 23–54. doi:10.21098/bemp.v9i4.213

Yildirim, I. (2015). Financial efficiency analysis in Islamic banks: Turkey and Malaysia models. *Pressacademia*, *2*(3), 289–289. doi:10.17261/Pressacademia.2015312956

Yıldırım, İ. (2017). Financial Efficiency Analysis of Islamic Banks in the Qismut Countries. *Journal of Islamic Economics and Finance*, *3*(2), 187–216.

ADDITIONAL READING

Granadillo, E. D. L. H., Gomez, J. M., & Herrera, T. J. F. (2019). Methodology with multivariate calculation to define and evaluate financial productivity profiles of the chemical sector in Colombia. *International Journal of Productivity and Quality Management*, 27(2), 144–160. doi:10.1504/IJPQM.2019.100141

Iddouch, K., El Badraoui, K., & Ouenniche, J. (2023). Landscape of Research on the Efficiency Profiles of Islamic Banks using DEA: Survey, Classification and Critical Analysis of the Literature. *International Journal of Business*, 28(3).

Rahimpour, K., Shirouyehzad, H., Asadpour, M., & Karbasian, M. (2020). A PCA-DEA method for organizational performance evaluation based on intellectual capital and employee loyalty: A case study. *Journal of Modelling in Management*, 15(4), 1479–1513. doi:10.1108/JM2-03-2019-0060

Rusydiana, A. S., & As-Salafiyah, A. (2021). DEA Window Analysis of Indonesian Islamic Bank Efficiency. *Journal of Islamic Monetary Economics and Finance*, 7(4), 733–758. doi:10.21098/jimf.v7i4.1410

Shahzad, A., Mahmood, T., & Shahzad, M. (2021). A Comparative Study of Banking Sectors of Pakistan and India: An Application of Data Envelopment Analysis. *Lahore Journal of Business*, 9(2).

KEY TERMS AND DEFINITIONS

Banking Efficiency: A measure of how effectively a bank uses its resources to generate income and provide services. In the context of Islamic Banks, it often involves assessing how well these institutions balance profit-making with adherence to Islamic financial principles.

Data Envelopment Analysis (DEA): A nonparametric method in operations research used for efficiency measurement. It evaluates the performance of decision-making units (such as banks) by comparing their input and output data.

Evaluation Approaches: The methods and criteria used to assess and interpret the results obtained from DEA and other productivity measurement methodologies in the context of Islamic Banks.

Islamic Banks (IBs): Financial institutions that operate in accordance with the principles of Islamic law (Sharia). This includes the prohibition of interest (riba) and the assurance that investments adhere to Islamic ethical standards.

Literature Survey: A comprehensive review of scholarly articles, books, and other academic publications. In this context, it refers to the systematic examination of literature concerning the productivity of Islamic Banks.

Malmquist Productivity Indices (MPIs): A method for calculating productivity change over time, often used in conjunction with DEA. It measures the shift in the production frontier and the change in relative efficiency of decision-making units.

Productivity: In the context of banks, productivity refers to the efficiency and effectiveness with which they convert inputs (like capital, labor) into outputs (like loans, financial services).

Productivity Measurement Methodologies: The various approaches and techniques used to evaluate and quantify productivity. In the context of DEA, this refers to the specific methods applied to measure the productivity of Islamic Banks.

Theoretical Foundations: The underlying theories and principles that support the methodologies and analyses used in a study. In the context of this chapter, it refers to the economic and financial theories underpinning the assessment of banking productivity.

Variables For DEA Model Specification: The specific input and output variables chosen to define the DEA model in a study. These variables are critical in accurately measuring the efficiency and productivity of the decision-making units under consideration.

ENDNOTES

[1]   Two exceptions use the Hicks–Moorsteen TFP index proposed by Bjurek (1996) instead of the Malmquist index, namely, Arjomandi et al. (2012) and Rashid & Rehman (2016).

APPENDIX

Table 1. Synopsis of the mixed empirical findings of single stage analysis on productivity in Islamic banking literature

Author(s)	Type of MPI, Orientation(s), DEA model(s), and type of RTS regime(s)	Type(s) of MPI decompositions	Type of MPI change	Evaluation approach	Variables for the specification of DEA Models		Country or region of analysis	Sample size	Period of analysis
					Inputs	Outputs			
Panel A: Key empirical findings based on bank type (Islamic vs. Conventional)									
(1) IBs are more productive than CBs									
Johnes et al. (2009)	**Adjacent MPI-OO** estimated by solving CCR models	MPI is the product of OTE Change and Technical Change	Progress in productivity is mainly due to technological change	IA	Deposits & short-term funding Physical capital Equity General & administration expenses	Total loans Other earning assets	GCC countries	19 IBs & 50 CBs	2004-2007
Ismail & Rahim (2013)	**Adjacent MPI-IO** under CRS & VRS regimes	(1) MPI as the product of OTE Change and Technical Change. (2) MPI as the product of PTE Change, SE Change and Technical Change	Progress in Technological change is the main source of productivity	IA	Deposits & short-term funding Personnel expenses Physical capital Cost of deposits Cost of labour Cost of physical capital	Total loans Other earning assets Off-balance sheet items	Malaysia	8 IBs & 9 CBs	2006-2009
Johnes et al. (2014)	**Adjacent MPI-OO** under both CRS & VRS regimes	MPI as the product of OTE Change and Technical Change.	Source of productivity decline is mainly due to OTE change	IA	Deposits & short-term funding Physical capital Equity General & administration expenses	Total loans Other earning assets	GCC countries	19 IBs & 50 CBs	2004-2007
Boyacioglu et al. (2014)			Progress of productivity is due to both OTE change and technological change	IA	Total deposits Personnel expenses Interest expenses	Loans & advances Interest income Net fee & commission income	Turkey	4 IBs & 16 CBs	2011-2013
Khan & Shah (2015)			OTE change is mainly the source of productivity growth	IA	Total deposits Physical capital Number of employees	Total loans Investments Other operating income	Pakistan	5 IBs, 5 CBs & 5 IWs	2007-2011
Ara (2016)	**Adjacent MPI-OO** under both CRS & VRS regimes	(1) MPI as the product of OTE Change and Technical Change. (2) MPI as the product of PTE Change, SE Change and Technical Change	Source of productivity progress is mainly attributed to OTE change and its components (PTE and SE change)	Not specified	Interest expenses Non-interest expenses	Interest income Non-interest income	Bangladesh	7 IBs & 23 CBs	2009-2012

Author(s)	Type of MPI, Orientation(s), DEA model(s), and type of RTS regime(s)	Type(s) of MPI decompositions	Type of MPI change	Evaluation approach	Variables for the specification of DEA Models		Country or region of analysis	Sample size	Period of analysis
					Inputs	Outputs			
Azad et al. (2017)	**Global / meta-frontier MPI-OO** (Pastor and Lovell, 2005) estimated by solving radial models under CRS regime	MPI as the product of OTE Change and Technical Change	Progress in OTE change and Technological change are both considered sources of productivity progress	IA	Total deposits Personnel expenses Physical capital	Total loans	Malaysia	16 IBs & 27 CBs	2009-2013
				PA	Personnel expenses Physical capital Interest expenses	Total loans Total deposits			
				POA	Interest expenses Non-interest expenses Personnel expenses	Interest income Net income			
Wahid & Harun (2019)	**Adjacent MPI-OO under VRS regime**	(1) MPI as the product of OTE Change and Technical Change. (2) MPI as the product of PTE Change, SE Change and Technical Change	The decline in productivity is mainly attributed to SE change (i.e., banks operate at a wrong optimal scale of operations)	IA	Total deposits Personnel expenses Physical capital	Total loans Investments Non-interest income	Malaysia	17 IBs & 21 CBs	2004-2013
Azzam & Rettab (2020)			Productivity growth/ progress is driven by both OTE change and technological change	IA	Total deposits Personnel expenses Physical capital Cost of deposits Cost of labour Cost of physical capital	Get the main article ???!!	GCC countries	10 IBs & 45 CBs	1998-2012
Jubilee et al. (2021a)	**Adjacent MPI-OO** (Fare et al., 1992) estimated by solving radial models	(1) MPI as the product of OTE Change and Technical Change. (2) MPI as the product of PTE Change, SE Change and Technical Change	Progress in productivity is due to OTE change	IA	Deposits & short-term funding Personnel expenses Physical capital	Net loans Investments	Middle East, Southeast Asia, and South Asia	66 IBs & 319 CBs	2008-2017
Jubilee et al. (2021b)			The increase in productivity is mainly assigned to technological change	IA	Deposits & short-term funding Personnel expenses Physical capital	Total loans Investments	Brunei, Indonesia, Malaysia, and Singapore	23 IBs & 132 CBs	2008-2017
Kamarudin et al. (2022)	**Adjacent MPI-OO** (Fare et al., 1992) estimated by solving radial models under VRS and CRS regimes	(1) MPI as the product of OTE Change and Technical Change. (2) MPI as the product of PTE Change, SE Change and Technical Change	The progress in productivity is attributed to OTE change, specifically to its component PTE change	IA	Total deposits Personnel expenses Total assets	Total loans Investments	Southeast Asian countries (Malaysia, Indonesia, Brunei and Singapore)	30 IBs & 137 CBs	2006-2016

Author(s)	Type of MPI, Orientation(s), DEA model(s), and type of RTS regime(s)	Type(s) of MPI decompositions	Type of MPI change	Evaluation approach	Variables for the specification of DEA Models		Country or region of analysis	Sample size	Period of analysis
					Inputs	Outputs			
(2) IBs are less productive than CBs									
Abu-Alkheil et al. (2012)	**Adjacent MPI-OO** under CRS & VRS regimes	(1) MPI as the product of OTE Change and Technical Change. (2) MPI as the product of PTE Change, SE Change and Technical Change	Source of the increasing productivity is due to OTE change	IA	Deposits & short-term funding Personnel expenses Total expenses	Total loans Total income	Qatar, Saudi Arabia, Kuwait, Bahrain, U.A.E, Malaysia, Turkey, Azerbaijan, UK, and Bosnia – Herzegovina	23 IBs & 12 CBs	2005-2008
Rashid & Rehman (2016)			The decline in productivity is attributed to OTE, particularity to SE change	IA	Personnel expenses Physical capital Total deposits	Total demand deposits Public sector organisations loans Private loans	Pakistan	4 IBs & 20 CBs	2007-2013
Isik et al. (2016)	**Adjacent MPI-IO** under VRS regime	(1) MPI as the product of OTE Change and Technical Change. (2) MPI as the product of PTE Change, SE Change and Technical Change	Source of productivity growth is mainly due to technological change	IA	Total deposits Personnel expenses Physical capital	Total loans Investments	Jordan	2 IBs & 16 CBs	1996-2001
				PA	Personnel expenses Physical capital	Total loans Total deposits Investments			
Jahan (2019)	**Adjacent MPI-OO** estimated by solving CCR-OO model	(1) MPI as the product of OTE Change and Technical Change. (2) MPI as the product of PTE Change, SE Change and Technical Change	Progress in productivity is mainly due to OTE change	IA	Interest expenses Non-interest expenses	Interest income Non-interest income	Bangladesh	6 IBs & 23 CBs	2011-2015
Alsharif et al. (2019)	**Adjacent MPI-OO** (Fare et al., 1992) estimated by solving radial models	(1) MPI as the product of OTE Change and Technical Change. (2) MPI as the product of PTE Change, SE Change and Technical Change	Source of regress in productivity is mainly due to technological change	IA	Deposits & short-term funding Personnel expenses Physical capital	Total loans Other earning assets	GCC region	28 IBs & 45 CBs	2005-2015

Author(s)	Type of MPI, Orientation(s), DEA model(s), and type of RTS regime(s)	Type(s) of MPI decompositions	Type of MPI change	Evaluation approach	Variables for the specification of DEA Models		Country or region of analysis	Sample size	Period of analysis
					Inputs	Outputs			
Salleh & Rani (2020)			Source of productivity growth is mainly due to technological change	IA	Total deposits Personnel expenses Physical capital	Total loans Investments Total operating income	Indonesia	7 IBs & 7 CBs	2011-2018
(3) There is no significant difference in productivity between IBs and CBs									
Alpay & Hassan (2007)			Source of productivity decline is majorly attributed to technological change	Not specified	Total deposits Personnel expenses Physical capital	Total loans	Turkey	4 IBs & 49 CBs	1990-2000
Afiatun and Wiryono (2010)	**Adjacent MPI-OO** under both CRS & VRS regimes	(1) MPI as the product of OTE Change and Technical Change. (2) MPI as the product of PTE Change, SE Change and Technical Change	The overall decline of productivity is mostly due to technological change	IA	Total deposits Total expenses	Total loans Other earning assets	Indonesia	3 IBs & 10 CBs	2004-2009
Othman et al. (2013)	**Adjacent MPI-IO** under CRS & VRS regimes	(1) MPI as the product of OTE Change and Technical Change. (2) MPI as the product of PTE Change, SE Change and Technical Change	Source of productivity progress is mainly assigned to technological change	IA	Personnel expenses Total assets	Total loans	Malaysia	5 IBs & 9 CBs	2006-2010
Abbas et al. (2015)	**Adjacent MPI-OO** estimated by solving radial models (i.e., CCR-OO and BCC-OO)	(1) MPI as the product of OTE Change and Technical Change. (2) MPI as the product of PTE Change, SE Change and Technical Change	Technological change index is a major source of productivity growth	IA	Total deposits Personnel expenses Physical capital Equity	Loans & advances Investments Other operating income Interest income	Pakistan	8 IBs & 12 CBs	2005-2009
Ajija et al. (2017)			Source of productivity growth is mainly due to technological change	Not specified	Physical capital Equity	Total loans Net income	Indonesia	9 IBs & 9 CBs	2011-2014
Rani et al. (2017)			Productivity decline is attributed to both OTE change and technological change	IA	Total deposits Personnel expenses Physical capital	Total loans Investments Net operating income	Indonesia	5 IBs & 5 CBs	2008-2016
Panel B: Key empirical findings based on ownership type (foreign vs. domestic IBs)									
(1) Foreign IBs are more productive than domestic IBs									

Author(s)	Type of MPI, Orientation(s), DEA model(s), and type of RTS regime(s)	Type(s) of MPI decompositions	Type of MPI change	Evaluation approach	Variables for the specification of DEA Models		Country or region of analysis	Sample size	Period of analysis
					Inputs	Outputs			
Sufian (2010)	**Adjacent MPI-OO** (Fare et al., 1992) estimated by solving radial models	(1) MPI as the product of OTE Change and Technical Change. (2) MPI as the product of PTE Change, SE Change and Technical Change	Productivity progress is attributed to increase in technological change rather than OTE change	IA	Total deposits Personnel expenses	Total loans Investments	Malaysia	11 domestic IBs & 7 foreign IBs banks	2001-2008
Azad et al. (2017)	**Global / meta-frontier MPI-OO** (Pastor and Lovell, 2005) estimated by solving radial models under CRS regime	MPI as the product of OTE Change and Technical Change	Progress in OTE change and Technological change are both considered sources of productivity progress	IA	Total deposits Personnel expenses Physical capital	Total loans	Malaysia	10 domestic IBs & 6 foreign IBs	2009-2013
				PA	Personnel expenses Physical capital Interest expenses	Total loans Total deposits			
				POA	Interest expenses Non-interest expenses Personnel expenses	Interest income Net income			
(2) Foreign IBs are less productive than domestic IBs									
Sufian (2007)	**Adjacent MPI-OO** under both CRS & VRS regimes	(1) MPI as the product of OTE Change and Technical Change. (2) MPI as the product of PTE Change, SE Change and Technical Change	The progress in productivity is mainly attributable to technological change rather OTE change (PTE change)	IA	Total deposits Personnel expenses Physical capital	Total loans Total income	Malaysia	11 domestic IBs & 4 foreign IBs	2001-2004
Sufian and Haron (2008)	**Adjacent MPI-OO** (Fare et al., 1992) estimated by solving radial models under VRS and CRS regimes	(1) MPI as the product of OTE Change and Technical Change. (2) MPI as the product of PTE Change, SE Change and Technical Change	Source of productivity growth is attributed to an increase in OTE change rather than to technological change	IA	Total deposits Personnel expenses	Total loans Investments	Malaysia	11 domestic IBs & 4 foreign IBs	2001-2005
Sufian (2009b)	**Adjacent MPI-OO** under CRS & VRS regimes	(1) MPI as the product of OTE Change and Technical Change. (2) MPI as the product of PTE Change, SE Change and Technical Change	Technological change is the reason behind the slight downward in productivity	IA	Total deposits Personnel expenses	Total loans Investments	Malaysia	11 domestic IBs & 4 foreign IBs	2001-2005

Author(s)	Type of MPI, Orientation(s), DEA model(s), and type of RTS regime(s)	Type(s) of MPI decompositions	Type of MPI change	Evaluation approach	Variables for the specification of DEA Models		Country or region of analysis	Sample size	Period of analysis
					Inputs	Outputs			
Hadi & Saad (2010)	**Adjacent MPI-OO** under CRS & VRS regimes	(1) MPI as the product of OTE Change and Technical Change. (2) MPI as the product of PTE Change, SE Change and Technical Change	The decrease in productivity is mainly due to OTE change rather than technological change	IA	Total deposits Personnel expenses Physical capital	Total loans Total income	Malaysia	9 domestic IBs & 3 foreign IBs	2006-2008
(3) There is no significant difference in productivity between foreign and domestic IBs									
Sufian (2009a)	**Adjacent MPI-OO** estimated by solving radial models (i.e., CCR-OO and BCC-OO)	(1) MPI as the product of OTE Change and Technical Change. (2) MPI as the product of PTE Change, SE Change and Technical Change	The dominant source of the decrease in OTE change is managerially related rather than scale-related	IA	Total deposits Personnel expenses Physical capital	Total loans Total income	Malaysia	10 domestic IBs & 4 foreign IBs	2001-2004
Kamarudin et al. (2017)	**Adjacent MPI-OO** (Fare et al., 1992) estimated by solving radial models under VRS and CRS regimes	(1) MPI as the product of OTE Change and Technical Change. (2) MPI as the product of PTE Change, SE Change and Technical Change	The productivity progress is solely attributed to the increase in OTE change	IA	Total deposits Personnel expenses Physical capital	Total loans Investments	Southeast Asian countries (Brunei, Indonesia and Malaysia)	23 domestic IBs & 6 foreign IBs	2006-2014
Panel C: Key empirical findings based on type of modus operandi (Islamic windows vs. full-fledged IBs)									
(1) Islamic windows are more productive than full-fledged IBs									
Sufian (2009a)	**Adjacent MPI-OO** estimated by solving radial models (i.e., CCR-OO and BCC-OO)	(1) MPI as the product of OTE Change and Technical Change. (2) MPI as the product of PTE Change, SE Change and Technical Change	The dominant source of the decrease in OTE change is managerially related rather than scale-related	IA	Total deposits Personnel expenses Physical capital	Total loans Total income	Malaysia	14 IBs including full-fledged IBs and Islamic windows	2001-2004
Alandejani (2014)			The increase in productivity is attributed to OTE change	IA	Deposits & short-term funding Equity Operating expenses	Total loans Other earning assets	GCC countries	16 full-fledged IBs & 18 Islamic windows	2005-2010
Alendejani & Asutay (2017)			Source of productivity progress is OTE change	IA	Deposits & short-term funding Equity Operating expenses	Total loans Other earning assets	GCC countries	16 full-fledged IBs & 18 Islamic windows	2005-2010
(2) Islamic windows are less productive than full-fledged IBs									
Siddique & Rahim (2013)			Productivity growth is attributed to both OTE change (PTE and SE change) and technological change	IA	Total deposits Personnel expenses Physical capital	Loans & advances Investments	Pakistan	5 full-fledged IBs & 5 Islamic windows	2007-2012

Note: IA stands for Intermediation approach. PA stands for Production approach. POA stands for Profit-oriented approach. IBs stands for Islamic banks. CBs stands for Conventional banks. OTE stands for Overall Technical Efficiency. PTE stands for Pure Technical Efficiency. SE stands for Scale Efficiency.

Table 2. Classification of inputs and outputs used in productivity literature on Islamic banking along with their frequency and their % distribution

First level classification	Second level classification	Inputs	Frequency	%	Outputs	Frequency	%
Panel A: Intermediation approach (IA)							
Absolute measures	Balance sheet items	Total deposits	43	25,7%	Total loans	43	33,9%
		Physical capital	33	19,8%	Investments	19	15,0%
		Deposits & short-term funding	10	6,0%	Other earning assets	13	10,2%
		Equity	9	5,4%	Loans & advances to banks	4	3,1%
		Total assets	4	2,4%	Private loans	2	1,6%
		Capital expenses	1	0,6%	Public loans	2	1,6%
					Total demand deposits	2	1,6%
					Off-balance sheet items	2	1,6%
					Net loans	1	0,8%
					NPLs	1	0,8%
					Capital market investment	1	0,8%
					Money market investment	1	0,8%
					Liquid assets	1	0,8%
					Total commercial loans	1	0,8%
					Total earning assets	1	0,8%
	Income statement items	Personnel expenses	41	24,6%	Total income	8	6,3%
		General & administration expenses	6	3,6%	Other operating income	5	3,9%
		Operating expenses	3	1,8%	Interest income	4	3,1%
		Interest expenses	2	1,2%	Operating income	4	3,1%
		Non-interest expenses	2	1,2%	Non-interest income	4	3,1%
		Total expenses	2	1,2%	Net fee & commission income	2	1,6%
		Loan loss provisions (LLPs)	1	0,6%	Total operating income	2	1,6%
		Number of employees	1	0,6%	Investment income	1	0,8%
					Net income	1	0,8%
					Net operating income	1	0,8%
					Non-operating income	1	0,8%
Composite measures	Cost-based measures	Cost of labour	3	1,8%	n.a.		
		Cost of physical capital	3	1,8%	n.a.		
		Cost of deposits	2	1,2%	n.a.		
		Cost of deposits & short-term funding	1	0,6%	n.a.		
	Return-based measures	n.a.			n.a.		
Total		18	167	100,0%	26	127	100,0%
Panel B: Production Approach (PA)							
Absolute measures	Balance sheet items	Physical capital	4	36,4%	Total deposits	4	40,0%
		Equity	2	18,2%	Total loans	4	40,0%
					Investments	1	10,0%
	Income statement items	Personnel expenses	4	36,4%	Total income	1	10,0%
		Interest expenses	1	9,1%			
Total		4	11	100,0%	4	10	100,0%
Panel C: Profit-Oriented Approach (POA)							

First level classification	Second level classification	Inputs	Frequency	%	Outputs	Frequency	%
Panel A: Intermediation approach (IA)							
Absolute measures	Income statement items	Personnel expenses	2	33,3%	Interest income	1	25,0%
		Interest expenses	1	16,7%	Net income	1	25,0%
		Loan loss provisions (LLPs)	1	16,7%	Net interest income	1	25,0%
		Non-interest expenses	1	16,7%	Other operating income	1	25,0%
		Other operating expenses	1	16,7%			
Total			5	6	100,0%	4	4	100,0%

Note: *Cost of labour* is measured either by personnel expenses to total assets or by total expenditures on employees such as salaries, employee benefits and reserves for retirement pay to customer and short-term funding. *Cost of physical capital* is measured either by fixed assets to total assets, or by total expenditures on premises and fixed assets to customer and short-term funds. *Cost of deposits* is measured by total of interest expenses plus other operating expenses to the total deposits. *Cost of deposits & short-term funding* is measured by total non-interest expenses on deposit and non-deposit funds to customer and short-term funding.

Table 3. Classification of the drivers of productivity in the Islamic banking DEA literature along with the percentage of studies that used each variable

First Level Classification	Second Level Classification	Drivers of productivity		Proxy of the driver	% of time use across studies
Internal environment variables	Bank risk variables	Credit risk		Loan loss provisions (LLPs) to total loans	89%
				LLPs to total assets	
				Non-performing loans (NPLs) to total loans	
		Leverage intensity		Total shareholders' equity to total assets	67%
		Total capital adequacy ratio		(Tier 1 capital + Tier 2 capital) to risk weighted assets (RWA)	11%
	Bank probability variables	Return on assets (ROA)		Net income to total assets	56%
		Return on equity (ROE)		Net income to total shareholders' equity	
	Bank liquidity variables	Liquidity		Total loans to total assets	100%
				Loan-to-deposit ratio	
				Cash-to-total-assets ratio	
				Net loans to total assets	
	Bank cost efficiency variables	Management quality		Total non-interest expenses to total assets	89%
				Total non-operating expenses to total assets	
	Bank business model variables	Traditional banking activities		Total loans to total assets (loans intensity)	44%
		Diversification		Total non-operating income to total assets	
	Bank governance variables	Bank ownership	Foreign vs. domestic ownership	A dummy variable that takes a value of "1" for domestic IBs and "0" for foreign IBs	33%
	Bank intrinsic variables	Bank size		The natural logarithm of total assets	89%
		Number of branches		n/a	11%
		Bank market power		The natural logarithm of banks' total deposits	56%
				Bank's deposits to total deposits	
		Bank type (Islamic vs. Conventional)		A dummy variable that takes a value of "1" for IBs and "0" for CBs	22%
		Zakat		A dummy variable that takes a value of 1 if a bank pays Zakat, 0 otherwise	11%
External environment variables	Macroeconomic variables	GDP		The monetary value of all the final goods and services produced in a specific time period	67%
		GDP per capita		GDP of a country divided by its total population	11%
		GDP growth		GDP growth for future GDP estimation and opportunity in business expansion	11%
		Inflation		The annual % change in Consumer Price Index (CPI)	56%
		Unemployment rate		The number of unemployed persons as a percentage of the total number of persons in the labour force	11%
		Exports		Change in the natural logarithm of export value	11%
		Global Financial Crisis of 2007-08		GFC takes a value of 1 in the period of crisis (2007-2008), and 0 otherwise	44%
		Financial market development		Stock market capitalisation-to-GDP-ratio	11%
		Banking sector development		Credit to private sector to GDP	11%
		Currency exchange rate		It is used as an indicator of the international competitiveness and indicates the global position of economy of the country	11%
		Reference interest rate		-	11%

First Level Classification	Second Level Classification	Drivers of productivity		Proxy of the driver	% of time use across studies
	Country governance variables	Voice and accountability		The citizens' participation in selecting their government, freedom of expression, freedom of association and free media.	11%
		Political stability and absence of violence		The stability in the politics but with the likelihood that the government would be destabilised or overthrown by unconstitutional or violent means.	11%
		Government effectiveness		The credibility of the government's commitment to such policies.	11%
		Regulatory quality		The ability of the government to formulate and implement good policies and regulations that permit and promote private sector development.	11%
		Rule of law		Refers to those agents who have confidence in and abide by the rules of society.	11%
		Control of corruption		Controls which public power is exercised for corruption.	11%
	Globalisation variables	Trade globalisation	De facto trade globalisation	It refers to the exchange of goods and services over long distances.	11%
			De jure trade globalisation	It refers to policies that facilitate and promote trade flows between countries.	
		Financial globalisation	De facto financial globalisation	It is measured by capital flows and stocks of foreign assets and liabilities.	11%
			De jure financial globalisation	It measures the openness of a country to international financial flows and investments	
		Interpersonal globalisation	De facto interpersonal globalisation	It captures direct interactions among citizens living in different countries.	11%
			De jure interpersonal globalisation	It refers to policies and resources that enables direct interactions among people living in different countries.	
		Informational globalisation	De facto informational globalisation	It measures the actual flow of ideas, knowledge and images.	11%
			De jure informational globalisation	It refers to the ability to share information across countries.	
		Cultural globalisation	De facto cultural globalisation	It refers to some extent to the domination of U.S. cultural products, measured using the number of McDonald's restaurants.	11%
			De jure cultural globalisation	It refers to openness towards and the ability to understand and adopt foreign cultural influences.	
		Political globalisation	De facto political globalisation	It captures the diffusion of government policies.	11%
			De jure political globalisation	It refers to the ability to engage in international political cooperation.	

Note: Each globalisation indicator is further divided into de facto and de jure globalisation measures. de facto globalization measures actual international flows and activities, de jure globalization measures policies and conditions that, in principle, enable, facilitate and foster flows and activities (Gygli et al., 2019). For further details on definitions of each sub-category of each globalisation indicator, the reader is referred to Gygli et al. (2019), and https://kof.ethz.ch/

Chapter 4
Efficiency Analysis of a Surgery Roadmap Based on Lean Manufacturing Techniques, Simulation, and Data Envelopment Analysis

Leonardo H. Talero-Sarmiento

https://orcid.org/0000-0002-4129-9163

Universidad Autónoma de Bucaramanga, Colombia

Laura Yeraldin Escobar Rodriguez

Universidad Autónoma de Bucaramanga, Colombia

ABSTRACT

This study advances healthcare process optimization, focusing on surgery roadmaps in the healthcare system, a scenario exemplifying optimization challenges due to limited information. This chapter emphasizes enhancing efficiency and resource utilization by employing lean manufacturing, operational research, simulation, data envelopment analysis, and non-dominance analysis. This study discovers 32 correlated patient pathways, showing shared activities and simultaneous multi-route impact from optimization strategies. Instead of merely analyzing pathway performance, the study applies data envelopment analysis to various investment scenarios, providing insights for healthcare decision-makers on improving patient care quality and efficiency. The juxtaposition of data envelopment analysis with a non-dominance algorithm in this mixed-method approach offers a robust framework for addressing healthcare operational challenges, particularly under information scarcity, and promotes continuous process improvement.

DOI: 10.4018/979-8-3693-0255-2.ch004

INTRODUCTION

The field of decision sciences provides invaluable insights into operational efficiency, a concern of urgency in healthcare settings such as surgery roadmaps. A sustainable approach to healthcare necessitates prioritizing efficiency and patient outcomes (N. Jiang & Malkin, 2016; Mehra & Sharma, 2021) due to the increasing complexity and cost of healthcare services and the growing demand for quality care (An et al., 2022). Notably, while clinical decision support tools and electronic health records aim to standardize care and cut costs, clinicians often find them time-consuming (Maniago et al., 2022). Studies using methods like Malmquist-DEA have shown the potential for efficiency analysis in improving both environmental aspects and patient outcomes in healthcare (Pourmahmoud & Bagheri, 2023).

The diverse range of data sources often makes it difficult to carry out crucial efficiency analysis in healthcare (a.k.a., performance analysis in healthcare). The data varies from comprehensive Enterprise Resource Planning systems to simpler spreadsheet records (Rajendran et al., 2023). Challenges arise in various forms: problems with data integration, data quality, privacy concerns, semantic interoperability, analytics complexity, and organizational silos all make it difficult to assess efficiency (Harper & McNair, 2017; Ranchal et al., 2020). Addressing these challenges requires a multifaceted approach that leverages Lean Manufacturing Techniques in healthcare (Nicholas, 2023), Simulation (Fu, 2013), Co-creation activities (Stimmel, 2015), and Data Envelopment Analysis (Cooper, 2013). Lean manufacturing techniques can be utilized to eliminate operational waste and improve patient flow (Kam et al., 2021). Simulation modeling offers a way to prototype and test healthcare processes (Register et al., 2019), while co-creation workshops provide a platform for stakeholder engagement (Azevedo et al., 2017). Lastly, DEA benchmarks technical efficiency in healthcare systems (Stefko et al., 2018).

The chapter aims to outline a strategy for the complex task of estimating efficiency resources in surgery roadmaps. In this approach, we apply Lean techniques for process analysis, simulation for time estimation, co-creation for activity prioritization, and DEA supported by non-dominance analysis for synthesis and comparison. The objective is to provide healthcare decision-makers with an integrative analysis to enhance healthcare delivery efficiency under lack of information.

BACKGROUND

The literature strongly supports the transformative role of Lean Manufacturing, operational research techniques, simulation, and Data Envelopment Analysis (DEA) in boosting healthcare systems. For example, experts recognize Discrete-event simulation (DES) as a crucial tool for tackling dynamic and complex systems in healthcare, frequently used with Lean and Six Sigma methodologies to enhance efficiency metrics (Vázquez-Serrano et al., 2021). Similarly, a systematic review by Ortíz-Barrios and Alfaro-Saíz (2020) highlights the prominence of computer simulation and Lean Manufacturing in solving operational problems in Emergency Departments. Moreover, the integration of Lean tools with advanced technologies like Industry 4.0 has demonstrated improvements in production processes, indicating potential applicability in healthcare settings (Florescu & Barabas, 2022). These methodologies collectively provide a powerful framework for decision-making, quality improvement, and efficiency optimization in healthcare settings.

Lean Manufacturing Techniques in Healthcare

Lean Manufacturing techniques are increasingly adopted by healthcare settings to systematically reduce waste and improve patient flow value Stream Mapping (VSM) emerges as a key technique, which allows for the visualization and analysis of workflows to identify bottlenecks and improvement opportunities (Marin-Garcia et al., 2021). Standard Work establishes task protocols, minimizing variability and boosting efficiency (Patkal & Anasane, 2022). The 5S methodology (Sort, Set-in-order, Shine, Standardize, Sustain) has sharpened focus on environmental factors, enhancing work efficiency and healthcare delivery quality (McDermott et al., 2022). Just-in-Time (JIT streamlines inventory for timely, accurate resources (Sloan et al., 2014). Kaizen fosters a culture of continuous improvement, crucial for healthcare organizations (Flug et al., 2022). Lean Six Sigma, merging Lean and Six Sigma principles, demonstrates effectiveness in reducing process variation and defects (Samanta et al., 2021; Shokri, 2017). These techniques have shown remarkable success in various healthcare settings. These include surgery roadmaps, outpatient clinics, and inpatient pharmacies, thereby significantly enhancing patient care (Cameron & Rangel, 2016; Schonberger, 2018; Sethi et al., 2017; Villa, 2010). The primary objectives and outcomes of these technique implementations are: Shorter length of stay, Reduced lead time, Less time required to perform tasks, Enhanced communication among staff, patients, and families, More time dedicated to care, Shorter distances travelled by professionals, Fewer errors, Better-organized and more visible areas, and Increased and decreased costs (de Barros et al., 2021).

Operational Research Techniques in Healthcare

Operational research (OR) applies advanced analytical methods and mathematical modeling to enhance decision-making and optimize systems. OR develops mathematical models to represent real-world systems, aiming to improve decision-making, efficiency, and performance (Bass et al., 2019). Common methods in OR include simulation, optimization, queueing theory, game theory, statistical analysis, and machine learning (Bagherian et al., 2020). Business, engineering, healthcare, military, and government sectors widely use OR (Vanderbei, 2014). In healthcare, professionals employ OR for appointment scheduling, operating room planning, and optimizing patient flow (Ala & Chen, 2022; Palmer et al., 2018). Operational research techniques effectively tackle healthcare system complexities. For example, Discrete Event Simulation scrutinizes patient flows and resource utilization (ALI & BUTI, 2021; Claudio et al., 2014). Schedulers and planners often use linear and integer programming for resource allocation (Gür & Eren, 2018; Lamé et al., 2023). ARIMA and machine learning models predict healthcare demand and capacity requirements (Claudio et al., 2014; Schaffer et al., 2021; Soyiri & Reidpath, 2013). Queuing theory offers insights for process improvement and capacity planning (Santos et al., 2022). Techniques such as regression analysis and ANOVA have applications ranging from clinical trials to operational analysis (Alenezi et al., 2022; Molcho et al., 2021; Shuwiekh et al., 2022). Decision analysis methods, like decision trees and Markov models, support decision-making under uncertainty (Claudio et al., 2023; Sato & Zouain, 2010). Additionally, the growing application of machine learning provides predictive and classificatory capabilities (Alam et al., 2022). These techniques collectively enable data-driven decision-making in healthcare planning and operations.

Simulation in Healthcare Surgery

Simulation creates a model that represents a real-world system or process. Researchers experiment with this model to understand the system's behavior and make better decisions (Furinghetti et al., 2020). This method enables safe testing of system changes by manipulating the simulation model before implementation ("Advances in Modeling and Simulation," 2022). The common techniques include Discrete event simulation, which models systems as sequences of events over time, like queues or processes ("Modeling and Simulation of Discrete-Event Systems," 2013). Agent-based simulation, capturing interactions between autonomous agents and being applicable to social systems (Bandyopadhyay & Bhattacharya, 2014b). Continuous simulation, modeling continuous systems that change over time using differential equations (Bandyopadhyay & Bhattacharya, 2014a, 2021). Monte Carlo simulation, employing repeated random sampling and statistical analysis (Sarrut et al., 2021). In this context, simulation enables experimentation with systems too complex, dangerous, or resource-intensive to manipulate directly. Ongoing advancements in computing power and algorithms continue to expand simulation's capabilities and applications. The field of surgical education has increasingly utilized simulation, offering a safe environment for training and skill acquisition (Hippe et al., 2020; Keskitalo, 2022; Selzer, 2019). In cardiothoracic surgery, simulation assists in practicing complex procedures, thereby enhancing the quality of surgical interventions (Gauly et al., 2023; Steins & Persson, 2015). For general surgery, simulation training in laparoscopic skills and other procedures helps trainees' transition smoothly to the operating room (Needham et al., 2023). Simulation finds broad implementation, especially in education, due to its cost-effectiveness. An innovative approach emerges when combining simulation with lean principles and process mapping to identify bottlenecks and inefficiencies in healthcare workflows (L. Jiang & Huang, 2023). Such implementations in emergency departments and outpatient clinics have reduced wait times, improved efficiency, and eliminated non-value-added steps (Lee et al., 2015). Lastly, Monte Carlo simulations prove valuable in estimating and optimizing processes in healthcare activities such as surgeries (Agrawal et al., 2022; Luangkesorn & Eren-Doğu, 2016).

Data Envelopment Analysis in Healthcare

Data Envelopment Analysis, a non-parametric technique, emerged to evaluate healthcare system efficiency, offering a comprehensive array of variables for performance measurement (Kohl et al., 2019). This non-parametric technique encapsulates a comprehensive array of variables, establishing it as a pivotal tool for detailed healthcare analysis. For example, in their innovative approach, Gong et al. applied a network DEA model to examine the efficiency of healthcare systems in different Chinese provinces. Their research showed that increased government healthcare spending improved system efficiency (Gong et al., 2019). Similarly, Cylus et al. engaged DEA to construct composite indicators for health system efficiency, thereby facilitating cross-country comparisons (Cylus et al., 2017). The classical DEA model, often referred to as the CCR model (Charnes, Cooper, and Rhodes), employs a linear programming approach to estimate the efficiency of a target DMU. For n DMUs with m inputs x_{ij} and s outputs y_{rj}, the primal problem can be formulated as:

$$max\left(Z\right) = \sum\nolimits_{r=1}^{s} u_r * y_{ro}$$

Subject to:

$$\sum_{i=1}^{I} v_{io} * x_{io} = 1$$

$$\sum_{r=1}^{s} u_r * y_{rj} - \sum_{i=1}^{m} v_i * x_{ij} \leq 0, j = \{1, 2, \ldots, n\}$$

$$u_r \geq 0, r\{1,2,\ldots,s\}$$

$$v_i \geq 0, r=\{1,2,\ldots,m\}$$

Here, u_r and v_i are the weights assigned to the outputs and inputs, respectively. On the other hand, the dual problem for the DEA model is:

$$\min(\theta)$$

Subject to:

$$\theta - \sum_{r=1}^{s} \lambda_r * y_{rj} + \sum_{i=1}^{m} s_i^- * x_{ij} \leq 0, j = \{1, 2, \ldots, n\}$$

$$\sum_{i=1}^{m} s_i^+ * x_{io} - \sum_{r=1}^{s} \lambda_r * y_{ro} = 0, j = \{1, 2, \ldots, n\}$$

$$\lambda_r, s_i^+, s_i^- \geq 0$$

Where θ represents the efficiency score of the target DMU, λr are the dual variables, and s_i^- and s_i^+ are the slack variables for inputs and outputs, respectively. In the primal problem, the objective is to maximize the weighted sum of outputs for a given DMU subject to the weighted sums of all DMUs being less than or equal to one. The weights are obtained in a manner that maximizes this efficiency score. In the dual problem, the objective is to minimize the efficiency score θ. Here, λr can be interpreted as shadow price, and s_i^- and s_i^+ provide insight into how much each input and output needs to be changed to make the DMU efficient.

DEA can serve as a valuable tool in healthcare, but implementing it involves several challenges. A primary issue is the complexity of healthcare systems, making it challenging to select suitable inputs and outputs for DEA modeling. Mirmozaffari et al. highlighted this problem in their study, evaluating hospitals providing stroke care services using an integrated Generalized DEA approach. They stressed the need to include decision-maker preferences for a more accurate model (Mirmozaffari et al., 2021). Similarly, Yousefi Nayer et al. found that factors like hospital size and population coverage significantly affect efficiency scores. This finding underscores the importance of these environmental variables in DEA applications (Yousefi Nayer et al., 2022). Implementing DEA successfully often involves several challenges and barriers, such as:

- **Data Quality and Consistency:** Securing complete, consistent, and high-quality data for evaluation units is the primary challenge. Poor data quality can greatly distort DEA models' efficiency scores, undermining the analysis' integrity (Medina-Borja et al., 2007; Suliman et al., 2019).

- **Model Design:** Choosing suitable inputs, outputs, and performance metrics is crucial and complex in complex sectors like healthcare. The variable selection significantly affects DEA results' reliability and subsequent recommendations (Ichake et al., 2018).

- **Computational Complexity:** The computational complexity of DEA models escalates as the number of variables and units grows. This increase demands significant computational resources and raises the risk of inaccurate results (Medina-Borja et al., 2007).

- **External Factors:** Considering external, uncontrollable variables that affect performance is essential for a comprehensive understanding of efficiency scores, yet it presents its own challenges (Sav, 2013).

- **Interpretation and Contextualization:** While DEA identifies efficient and inefficient units, it doesn't specify the root causes or provide actionable solutions for observed inefficiencies, necessitating further analysis for context and interpretation.

- **Stakeholder Buy-in:** Gaining acceptance from key stakeholders for DEA-derived recommendations often requires significant effort, especially when stakeholders are unfamiliar with the methodology (Jardas Antonić, 2018).

- **Expertise and Software Tools:** The lack of industry-specific DEA expertise and customized software tools further impedes DEA projects' implementation.

- **Cost Constraints:** The high costs of data collection, cleaning, and software can be prohibitive for large-scale implementations, adding complexity to DEA deployment (Medina-Borja et al., 2007).

- **Integration with Existing Systems:** Integrating DEA within an organization's existing processes and systems poses logistical challenges that require careful planning and execution (Jardas Antonić, 2018).

Non-Dominance Algorithms and Efficient Frontiers

We employ non-dominance algorithms in multi-objective optimization to determine Pareto optimal solutions, which excel in multiple objectives (Knowles & Corne, 1999). These algorithms organize solutions into different fronts based on Pareto dominance relationships, with the first front featuring the top-tier solutions (Deb et al., 2002). They find common applications in evolutionary multi-objective optimization algorithms. Key concepts of these algorithms include: Pareto dominance occurs when solution A outperforms solution B, indicating that A is at least equal to, if not superior in, all objectives and excels in at least one. A non-dominated set is a collection of solutions that no other solution outperforms, forming the leading Pareto front (Shao & Ehrgott, 2016). Finally, non-dominated sorting is a technique for organizing solutions into fronts by repeatedly identifying non-dominated sets (Deb & Jain, 2014). Generally, we define non-dominance in relation to Pareto optimality. A solution x attains Pareto optimality if no alternative solution 'x' can improve some objective without degrading another. Mathematically, we consider x non-dominated if no 'x' exists where $f_i(x') \leq f_i(x)$ for all objectives i, and $f_j(x') < f_j(x)$ for at least one objective j. The collection of all such non-dominated solutions constitutes the efficient frontier or Pareto front. This frontier illustrates the trade-offs between objectives, offering a range of optimal solutions. Identifying the efficient frontier is a crucial task in multiobjective optimization. Algorithms like the Non-dominated Sorting Genetic Algorithm (NSGA) (Deb et al., 2002) or the Strength Pareto

Evolutionary Algorithm (SPEA), which iteratively seek to approximate the Pareto front by evolving a population of solutions towards non-dominance (Zitzler & Thiele, 1999).

EFFICIENCY ESTIMATION OF A SURGERY ROADMAP

Problem Statement

In the healthcare sector, particularly within Surgery Departments or pathways for surgical attention, optimally utilizing resources remains a critical challenge. Healthcare first applied Lean methodology, and its potential for improving operational efficiency has been evident in various settings including, but not limited to, Emergency, Oncology, Radiology, Laboratory, HIV services, Intensive Care Unit, Pathology, Pediatrics, Surgery, Anesthesiology, Chronic Services, Maternity Unit, Medicine Dispensation, Orthopedics, Traumatology, Dental Services, Therapy, Nursing, and Support Areas (Marin-Garcia et al., 2021; Vázquez-Serrano et al., 2021). Despite Lean Healthcare's (LH) widespread adoption, several challenges impede its effective implementation, including inadequate resource allocation planning. Moreover, limited data accessibility and transparency, particularly regarding inputs like costs, salaries, capital expenses, etc., constrain model inputs (Chivardi et al., 2023), hindering comprehensive efficiency analyses. A significant research gap exists in integrating Lean principles with advanced simulation techniques in healthcare (Crema & Verbano, 2019). Using DEA models in Lean healthcare faces challenges due to data scarcity and confidentiality constraints (Ngee-Wen et al., 2020). Addressing these gaps is crucial for generating robust solutions that accommodate various stakeholder needs and manage data scarcity. The potential impact of this research includes enhanced resource allocation, more efficient surgery roadmaps, and improved patient care quality. This study aims to develop a strategy to analyze the efficiency of surgery roadmaps through the integration of Lean manufacturing techniques, simulation, design thinking, and DEA, focusing on overcoming data accessibility challenges and ensuring sustainable LH implementation.

Challenges Regarding Efficiency or Performance Estimation in Colombia

The COVID-19 pandemic exacerbated challenges in healthcare operations and surgery, such as financial difficulties, patient safety, and staff well-being (Amer et al., 2022). The COVID-19 pandemic exacerbated challenges in healthcare operations and surgery, such as financial difficulties, patient safety, and staff well-being (Rosenbäck & Svensson, 2023). The healthcare industry in Colombia faces a complex and challenging scenario, characterized by a highly intricate landscape. Fragmentation of the sector, with numerous stakeholders, leads to a lack of standardization, impeding data flow, and insufficient capacity, which further exacerbates the complexity of addressing healthcare challenges in Colombia (Prada et al., 2022; Statista, 2023).

In contrast to existing literature that often concentrates on healthcare costs, resource utilization, or patient outcomes (Dion & Evans, 2023; Paulden et al., 2014), this chapter introduces a holistic approach. It aims to present an iterative analysis framework for assessing the efficiency of surgical roadmaps in Colombia, a healthcare system facing unique challenges and complexities. Despite the value of existing models and techniques like Stochastic Frontier Analysis and Data Envelopment Analysis they often fail to address the complexity and heterogeneity inherent in healthcare settings (Joseph et al., 2020). Hence, a tailored solution that integrates multiple perspectives—from industrial engineering to medical professionals—is essential.

This chapter draws on expertise from various disciplines, including industrial engineers, healthcare providers, and IT professionals, to conduct a comprehensive efficiency analysis. This multi-stage process involves interviews, exploratory data analysis, process simulation, co-creation activities, and DEA for comparing pathways performance. It provides a custom solution for healthcare centers facing challenges in information gathering, like in Colombia, and focuses on co-creation to identify improvement opportunities and validate incremental solutions. In a broader context, the chapter aligns with the book's main theme—'Data Envelopment Analysis (DEA) Methods for Maximizing Efficiency'—by offering a nuanced approach that incorporates DEA but extends beyond its traditional application. It presents a multi-faceted, real-world solution to maximize efficiency in complex healthcare settings, combining lean manufacturing, simulation, co-creation, and DEA to offer a robust analytical tool facing data scarcity challenges. Thus, this chapter significantly contributes to the field.

Methodology

The methodology we designed for this study aims to be comprehensive and integrative, blending academic and practical perspectives. We adopted a mixed-methods approach, incorporating qualitative and quantitative data collection and analysis techniques. In a real health center in Colombia, we implemented these techniques. Owing to confidential agreements, sharing the center's name or using actual data during the DEA analysis is not permissible. Nevertheless, this methodology serves as a versatile framework for gathering diverse strategies to conduct performance efficiency analysis. It invites future researchers or practitioners to explore this concept further and introduce novel variants to the key activities. In the specific case study, our primary aim was to optimize the surgery roadmap for patients by using Decision Sciences methods, such as Exploratory Data Analysis (EDA), simulation techniques, and Data Envelopment Analysis (Figure 1).

1.   Forming a Multidisciplinary Team.

The research starts with the formation of a multidisciplinary team, including academic scholars from the field of decision sciences and professionals from the healthcare sector. The team comprises industrial engineers, doctors, nurses, managers, IT developers, and administrative staff. Their varied expertise guarantees a comprehensive perspective of the healthcare process.

2.   Defining the Patient Surgery Roadmap.

Following the team's assembly, we outline the patient surgery roadmap's scope. This step involves tracking a patient from their entry into the system to their exit from the postoperative unit.

3.   Conducting Exploratory Data Analysis.

The team performs Exploratory Data Analysis (EDA) on existing data to set benchmarks for process times. Using descriptive statistics and graphical presentations, we pinpoint key trends and variations in these times.

Figure 1. Methodology
Source: Own elaboration

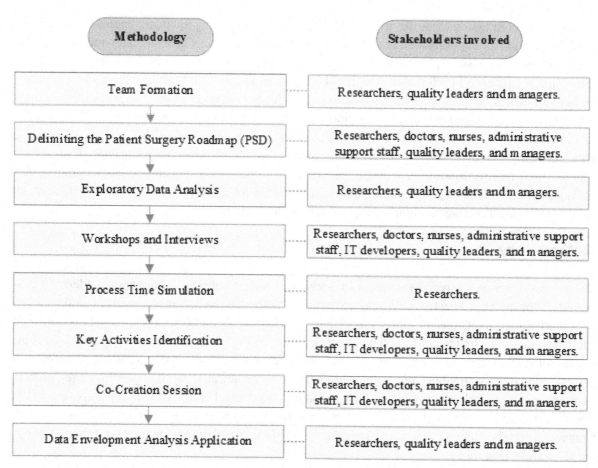

4.   Organizing Workshops and Conducting Interviews.

We organize a series of workshops to clarify surgery processes and interview process chiefs for more accurate activity time estimations. These interviews are crucial for subsequent modeling and simulation.

5.   Simulating Process Times.

We employ a dual-simulation strategy for better accuracy and validation. Initially, Python models process time using triangular distribution functions and conditionals based on various scenarios. Then, we use FlexSim software to further simulate the process and estimate capacity. We compare FlexSim results with the baseline from the EDA. Our research chooses Discrete Event Simulation for its effectiveness in improving and predicting process behavior. It replicates dynamic processes in a computer model, allowing us to assess, measure, and enhance system performance safely and cost-effectively. Furthermore, this approach aligns with Lean Thinking principles (Gabriel et al., 2020) and has shown successful implementation in literature (Hossain et al., 2023).

6.   Identifying Key Activities.

We develop a focused survey to pinpoint critical activities for potential optimization, basing the survey's design on insights from the EDA and simulation stages.

7.   Holding a Co-Creation Session.

During this phase, we conduct a co-creation session to draft a document that prioritizes investments for improving the patient surgery roadmap. This document guides decision-makers in the healthcare sector.

8.   Applying Data Envelopment Analysis.

We employ Data Envelopment Analysis (DEA) to compare expected efficiency levels with the current performance. DEA metrics provide tangible measures for assessing the effectiveness of proposed changes. Additionally, we conduct a complementary efficiency frontier analysis using the Pareto front. This method is effective for identifying incomparable solutions, such as units on the same efficiency frontier (Kvet & Janáček, 2023; Pang et al., 2023)

RESULTS

A diverse team of experts spent a year and a half on collaborative efforts to implement the methodology successfully. This comprehensive approach involved outlining pathways, engaging with key stakeholders, pinpointing essential performance indicators, and rigorously examining data gaps. The team, once formed, held numerous meetings to acquire the necessary data. They carefully selected variables to measure surgical performance effectively. However, they faced a major challenge: the limited information on various surgical pathway activities, except for anesthesiology, surgery, and post-surgery patient transportation. After obtaining the dataset, the team embarked on an extensive exploratory data analysis to identify predictors that affect surgery performance and gather available data for patient characterization. However, the data's breadth meant a vast diversity in the population, from infants to the elderly, with common surgeries such as heart attacks to rare diseases, encompassing patients with private health insurance and those covered by social insurance. After consolidating the dataset and contextualizing the retrieved columns, we began the data analysis.

We used Google Colab in conducting exploratory data analysis, data envelopment analysis, and non-dominance algorithm implementation. We note that its computational environment boasts significant processing capabilities and ample memory allocation. An Intel Xeon CPU, operating at 2.20GHz, serves as the core processing unit. This CPU, known for its reliability and efficiency, is well-suited for data-intensive tasks. It features a substantial 56320 KB cache size, a key factor in enhancing data retrieval speeds, especially when handling the large datasets common in DEA. The system comes equipped with 13.29 GB (13294208 kB) of total memory, with approximately 9.88 GB (9884460 kB) available, indicating plenty of space for data manipulation and storage. This generous memory allocation, combined with a high availability of 12.05 GB (12052364 kB), ensures the smooth handling of large-scale data analyses and minimizes the likelihood of performance bottlenecks. Additionally, the filesystem provides a solid storage capacity of 108 GB, with 81 GB available. This capacity is more than sufficient for storing

Figure 2. EDA process
Source: Own elaboration

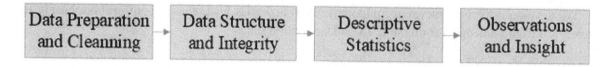

extensive datasets and analysis outputs. The overlay file system, together with other temporary storage allocations (tmpfs), facilitates efficient data handling and temporary data storage during processing.

Exploratory Data Analysis

We conducted Exploratory Data Analysis (Figure 2) to establish a baseline for process times. Our team characterized patients' time before and during surgery using surgery and anesthesia input and output times. The initial steps involved unifying four tables—each corresponding with a different output from SAP because the health center operates in four regions—into a single data frame with congruent variables and columns. We then trimmed the data from 33 to 25 columns to exclude irrelevant or unclear attributes, such as such as expected times, the hour and day of patient admission to the surgery room, surgery start time, and the arrival time of surgeons, nurses, anesthesiologists, townships, and the names of surgeons, anesthesiologists, nurses, etc., resulting in 171,235 entries. Moreover, we converted the column for surgery time from string to float format, enabling numerical analyses. We used a sequence of filters to eliminate non-contributing columns based on specific criteria like lack of pre-surgery availability or irrelevance to surgery time. After rigorously scrutinizing the final data frame, we removed null values to ensure data homogeneity and modeling integrity.

Our comprehensive descriptive exploration yielded significant insights. The mean patient age was approximately 49 years, noting a wide range in patient characteristics including newborns and the elderly. The average duration of all surgeries was 107 minutes, with the longest surgery lasting 1,425 minutes. In terms of categorical data—like surgery type, anesthesia type, and insurance company the analysis uncovered 3,001 distinct surgery types across 86 specialties and identified 85 different anesthesia mixtures. These exploratory findings provide a robust foundation for upcoming predictive modeling. Notably, the average surgery time and patient age could be key variables for further research. The variety in surgery and anesthesia types suggests a complex mix of factors influencing surgery durations, setting the stage for more detailed analyses.

Workshops and Interviews

We organized workshops with stakeholders, including researchers, doctors, nurses, administrative support staff, IT developers, quality leaders, and managers. Additionally, we conducted interviews with process chiefs who oversee different aspects of the surgery process. These consultations had a dual purpose: they clarified the complexities inherent in the surgical processes and provided invaluable qualitative insights essential for this research's subsequent phases. Contrary to initial assumptions, the health center operates not on a singular, standardized surgery patient roadmap but on multiple ones. The workshops and interviews enabled us to model and identify 32 distinct patient pathways through 24 possible activities,

Table 1. General surgery patient activities and pathways identified

Id	Activity	Routes
1	Create order	-
2	Define if the patient is covered by a private health insurance	-
2.1	Request quote	7
2.2	Process authorization of the procedure	7
3	Request surgical turn	14
4	Request the creation of the episode and pre-anesthesia assessment	14
5a	Perform pre-anesthesia assessment	14
5b	Create the benefit in the system by the surgeon	14
6	Is the patient fit for the surgical procedure?	-
6.1	Reschedule the procedure	2
6.2	Perform pre-admission process	12
7	Admit the patient on the day of the procedure	12
8	Make payment of moderator fee, if applicable.	12
9	Enter the surgery service for procedure preparation	12
10	Perform surgical procedure	12
11	Provide care for the patient in recovery	12
12	Discharge the patient from the service	12
13	Is the patient an outpatient?	-
13.1	Deliver orders and indicators for discharge	4
13.2.1	Transfer the patient to the corresponding area: Hospitalization	4
13.2.2	Transfer the patient to the corresponding area: ICU	4
14	Transfer the patient to the exit	4
15a	Perform Invoicing	6

Source: Own elaboration

encompassing all types of surgeries and anesthesia. We could further categorize these pathways into several groups, such as emergency cases (General or ophthalmologic surgery) and patient's health care services (public or private). This identification and categorization of different pathways are crucial for healthcare management, as optimizing shared activities can improve multiple pathways concurrently. Tables 1 and 2 present the identified pathways.

Process Time Simulation

We identified information regarding the capacity and time required for patients' attention in each surgery roadmap as ambiguous during the initial phases of this study. To address this gap, we conducted interviews with process chiefs. They shared their insights on the minimum, average, and maximum time required for each activity within the different pathways. Following the qualitative input, we performed simulations of the activity times using triangular distribution functions, iterating the process 10,000 times using NumPy in Python (Figure 3). Our study revealed that the simulated activity times exceeded

Table 2. Ophthalmologic surgery patient activities and pathways identified

Id	Activity	Routes
1	Patient initial diagnosis and generate procedure orders	12
2	Type of insurance	-
2.1	Request admissions to liquidate the procedure	6
2.2	Provide the patient with the orders for authorization by the insurer	6
3	Schedule depending on the surgical slot and inform the patient of the appointment	12
4	Pre-surgical consultation one day before surgery	12
5	Deliver to the patient the settlement and educational brochure on preparation	12
6	The patient comes on the scheduled appointment day.	-
7	Perform the admission process and installation of the identification bracelet	12
8	Admission of the patient to the transfer service of the identification bracelet	12
9	Receives surgical Care	12
10	Transfer to the recovery and observation area	
10.1	Local anesthesia	4
10.2	Regional anesthesia	4
10.3	General anesthesia	4
10.1	Is the patient discharged?	-
11.1	Give medical and administrative instructions for discharge, remove bracelet.	6
11.2	Refer to the corresponding service	6

Source: Own elaboration

the expectations of the process chiefs. Exploring further, we uncovered that the disparity stemmed from the varying number of patients attended to by different activities simultaneously. To gain a deeper understanding, we employed FlexSim software to model the surgery pathways (Figure 4). By adjusting the capacity parameters for each processor in the model and conducting simulations, we derived accurate estimates of activity capacities. We further corroborated this data with feedback from the process chiefs.

Identification of Key Activities

To pinpoint bottlenecks and enhancement areas, we designed a targeted survey to gather insights on key activities in surgical processes. The survey posed critical questions to understand the following:

- Whether internal or external personnel drive the activity's development.
- The practicality of intervening in the activity.
- The urgency of intervention, rated on a scale from 0 (unnecessary) to 10 (highly necessary).

We gathered data on a specific activity and the involved patient pathways. Process chiefs' responses helped us analyze the data. We calculated the average score for each question, weighted it by the number of pathways involving that activity, and standardized it with range normalization. This approach yielded a comprehensive view, incorporating the prevalence and opinions regarding each activity across path-

Figure 3. Example of path time simulation
Source: Own elaboration using NumPy in Python

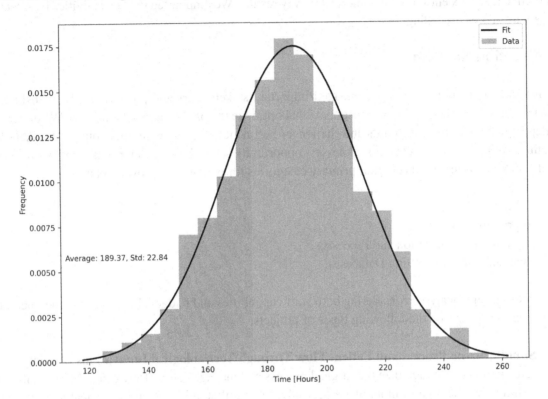

Figure 4. Example of path time simulation
Source: Own elaboration using Flexsim

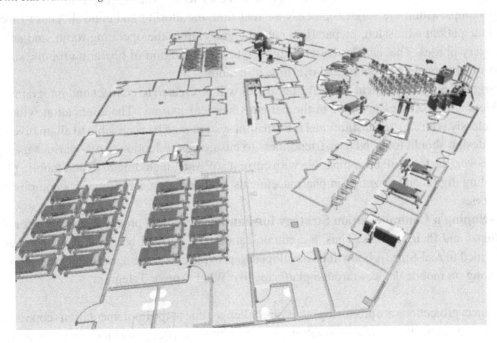

ways. Process chiefs also shared insights on the challenges or ease of optimizing each activity. Their qualitative feedback enriches the numerical survey results. We pinpointed the key activities by selecting those with scores exceeding 75%.

Co-Creation Session

During the co-creation session, we engaged important stakeholders and process chiefs extensively to reach a consensus on prioritizing investments that optimize the patient surgery roadmap. We undertook in-depth analyses of the constraints and challenges pertinent to key activities and convened stakeholder meetings to delve into strengths, weaknesses, opportunities, and barriers. Our dialogues with process chiefs culminated in identifying four primary categories for potential improvements:

- Enhancing Capacity.
- Improving Processes.
- Digitalizing Information and Processes.
- Managing and Integrating Databases.

After thorough analyses considering both staff capabilities and budget allocations for the upcoming fiscal year, we proposed the following types of projects:

1. **Standardizing Process and Patient Flow Through Technological Innovations:** A comprehensive approach to standardize the surgical process and manage patient flow using digital tools. This will involve the organization, planning, and tracking of activities such as surgical area cleaning, medication and device delivery, patient transfers, sterilization, and information systems. Due to their complexity and variability, the goal is to holistically manage each process.

2. **Identifying Critical Points in the Surgical Care Process:** The project aims to determine key timestamps within the surgical process for real-time monitoring and control. These timestamps include patient admission, preparation, entering and exiting the operating room, and subsequent recovery phases. This enables better insights into the utilization of operating rooms, such as occupancy hours, unused hours, and overtime utilization.

3. **Designing a Technological Tool:** A digital tool will be created to connect and integrate all stakeholders and processes involved in the patient's surgical journey. The application will integrate seamlessly with existing institutional information systems and be accessible to all involved parties. The design should focus on user-friendliness to ensure easy adoption across various user groups. Moreover, the tool will be compatible with current software, including SAP and mobile platforms, enabling digital authorization in pharmaceuticals, authorization, and surgery accomplishment by doctors.

4. **Developing a Communication Strategy for Families:** Surgical processes are often stressful for patients and their families. Thus, a communication strategy will be implemented to keep them informed in real-time. A bot will be developed to provide current patient status, offering real-time tracking on mobile devices through platforms like WhatsApp or Telegram.

The project projections are promising but pose challenges due to the implementation scope and budget constraints. Additionally, realizing a solution at its maximum capacity demands years of software development. Therefore, staff and decision-makers in managerial roles, such as Chief Information Officer and Chief Enterprise Officer, must choose one project. This research suggests using DEA to identify the expected number of surgery pathways benefiting from the project execution. To accomplish this, we compare different pathways as units of analysis and assess their current cost, the increase in cost due to the project implementation, and their efficiency. We then determine the number of non-dominance units (cardinality) to contrast with the project's potential for positively impacting more pathways.

Data Envelopment Analysis Application

In the context of surgery pathways sharing critical resources such as beds, medical personnel, and anesthesiologists, it becomes increasingly important to understand the differential impacts of each investment project. In this case, optimizing pathways independently is not feasible due to their shared resources. Instead of focusing on calculating pathway performances (noting that pathways differ in specific details, such as whether a patient arrives on the scheduled appointment day), this study aims to employ Data Envelopment Analysis and multi-objective dominance comparison methods to evaluate surgical pathways' efficiency under the influence of prospective projects. The more pathways that reach the efficient frontier following the anticipated impact of implementing a project, the more relevant the project is for investment. Four cases, each corresponding to a different investment project, were analyzed. These cases were assessed for their impact on pathway efficiency, measured through DEA. This study went beyond evaluating a single efficient frontier by incorporating multi-objective dominance comparison to discern multiple frontiers. Thus, the analysis of units (pathways) to be improved could be applied by frontier instead of by unit. This method helped identify projects that generated more efficient solutions and positively influenced a larger number of pathways. Due to a confidentiality agreement with the health center, the actual data could not be disclosed. However, this section uses an illustrative example with synthetically generated data to approximate the real-world interpretations gleaned from the research. The data frame used for analysis includes the following variables (Table 3 shows the dataset created):

1. **Pathway:** Each pathway identifier (e.g., PW1, PW2, etc.)
2. **Beds:** Number of beds available, modeled using a normal distribution: $N(\mu=500, \sigma=80)$.
3. **Doctor:** Number of doctors, approximated as beds/20.
4. **Nurses:** The number of nurses is calculated as 3 times the number of doctors.
5. **Anesthesiology:** Number of anesthesiologists, approximated as doctors/20.
6. **P1_Cost, P2_Cost, P3_Cost, P4_Cost:** Costs associated with four different projects, also modeled using a normal distribution for each pathway: $N(\mu=100,000, \sigma=1,250)$.
7. 7. **Output:** Calculated output as a function of all input variables and some added noise. This output represents the percentage of surgery patients with satisfactory output.

$$round\left(\frac{\sum inputs}{8 * mean\left(\sum inputs\right)} + 0.3 + N\left(\mu = 0, \sigma = 1\right), 2\right)$$

Table 3. Surgery patient pathways illustrative dataset

PW	B	D	N	A	P1_Cost	P2_Cost	P3_Cost	P4_Cost	Output
PW1	641	32	96	2	100500.20	101223.42	102801.12	102334.45	0.76
PW2	576	28	84	1	99810.80	99870.98	100513.25	100180.05	0.87
PW3	561	28	84	1	100152.09	100554.83	100417.09	101867.60	0.79
PW4	525	26	78	1	98932.38	96808.76	100817.02	101080.55	0.76
PW5	682	34	102	2	98182.04	100057.20	99766.02	101915.97	0.87
PW6	512	25	75	1	100472.70	98890.27	97524.00	99565.11	0.80
PW7	598	29	87	1	101502.97	99515.84	99622.12	98689.31	0.73
PW8	363	18	54	1	102438.47	99362.93	99452.41	98434.01	0.84
PW9	371	18	54	1	99734.07	98880.67	100483.63	99361.49	0.74
PW10	498	24	72	1	100535.41	100083.15	100378.09	99207.10	0.78
PW11	446	22	66	1	99550.56	98983.57	97842.15	100221.78	0.78
PW12	370	18	54	1	100578.48	98865.88	100064.93	100911.36	0.81
PW13	591	29	87	1	98456.47	100502.93	99143.99	98911.50	0.77
PW14	475	23	69	1	100070.21	98543.56	101126.03	100582.08	0.72
PW15	619	30	90	2	102369.86	101473.47	99775.09	98661.56	0.86
PW16	468	23	69	1	101528.06	100260.34	101220.80	100445.46	0.84
PW17	501	25	75	1	102232.34	100158.64	100502.49	102353.94	0.74
PW18	398	19	57	1	101211.75	98533.60	102429.53	99482.98	0.77
PW19	654	32	96	2	101850.64	102334.45	101132.56	98923.47	0.90
PW20	479	23	69	1	101003.07	101184.06	99806.24	100767.60	0.85
PW21	530	26	78	1	98625.75	100372.80	101657.98	99131.79	0.79
PW22	465	23	69	1	102311.58	100840.37	100509.33	99037.60	0.83
PW23	446	22	66	1	100039.79	99205.19	100845.54	100720.74	0.79
PW24	532	26	78	1	98633.67	98135.93	100549.24	100208.34	0.83
PW25	691	34	102	2	101180.60	98858.97	101396.27	98355.12	0.78
PW26	495	24	72	1	102141.68	99069.06	98966.95	99876.93	0.77
PW27	590	29	87	1	98650.09	98565.66	99452.72	99377.46	0.89
PW28	576	28	84	1	100109.44	98468.21	101055.45	98749.73	0.72
PW29	595	29	87	1	100396.18	101151.07	100398.41	101071.04	0.77
PW30	417	20	60	1	100851.99	98995.74	99138.06	99430.58	0.80
PW31	472	23	69	1	98281.31	99195.48	97220.75	100781.54	0.71
PW32	412	20	60	1	100065.21	99075.55	101928.77	98383.93	0.81

PW: Pathway, **B**: Beds, **D**: Doctors, **N**: Weights Inputs Beds, **A**: Anesthesiology
Source: Own elaboration

Data Envelopment Analysis

DEA assesses the efficiency of Decision-Making Units (DMUs) with multiple inputs and outputs. In this analysis, we analyzed 32 pathways as DMUs, with four fixed inputs (Beds, Doctors, Nurses, and Anesthesiology), one dynamic input (the project cost we are comparing), and the percentage of successful surgery patient output as the pathway output (Table 4). DEA represents a non-parametric optimization method, introduced by Charnes, Cooper, and Rhodes in 1978 (Charnes et al., 1978). It constructs a frontier over the given data points using mathematical programming and then compares each DMU's relative efficiency to this frontier to determine its efficiency level. We addressed the problem by employing the packages PuLP in Python (Mitchell et al., 2011).

Function to Solve the Primal DEA Problem

```python
def dea_problem(df, target_firm, inputs, outputs):
    prob = LpProblem("DEA", LpMaximize)
    weights_inputs = LpVariable.dicts("weights_inputs", (i for i in inputs),
lowBound=1e-9)
    weights_outputs = LpVariable.dicts("weights_outputs", (o for o in outputs),
lowBound=1e-9)

    prob += lpSum([weights_outputs[o] * df.loc[target_firm, o] for o in out-
puts])
    prob += lpSum([weights_inputs[i] * df.loc[target_firm, i] for i in in-
puts]) == 1, "Normalized"

    for i, row in df.iterrows():
        prob += lpSum([weights_outputs[o] * row[o] for o in outputs]) <=
lpSum([weights_inputs[i] * row[i] for i in inputs]), f"Efficiency_{i}"

    prob.solve(PULP_CBC_CMD(msg=0, options=["dualTolerance=1e-9"]))

    if LpStatus[prob.status] == 'Optimal':
        efficiency = prob.objective.value()
        return efficiency, {v.name: v.varValue for v in prob.variables()}
    else:
        return None, None
```

Source: Own elaboration using Python

To grasp the complexity of the dea_problem function, we must understand the nature of the DEA problem and the general computational complexity of linear programming algorithms. It's crucial to remember that the actual complexity of solving a DEA problem using linear programming differs significantly based on the problem's specifics, the chosen algorithm, and the implementation details. In this script, weights_inputs and weights_outputs are dictionaries of LP variables. The total number of these variables matches the sum of the number of inputs (n) and the number of outputs (m). Hence, the space required for these variables is proportional to $n+m$. Regarding Constraints: The function introduces one normalization constraint and a series of efficiency constraints, each corresponding to a unit in the DataFrame. With u units (rows) in the DataFrame, the constraint count is $u+1$. Each constraint engages all the weights, making the total space for constraints proportional to $(n+m)\times(u+1)$. Moreover, a loop exists for each unit, and consequently, the results list records the efficiency and weights for every firm. Each list entry is a dictionary comprising $1+n+m$ elements (efficiency score plus the weights). Given u firms, the total space for the results list is proportional to $u\times(1+n+m)$. Combining these aspects, the overall space complexity of the script is primarily influenced by the space needed for the constraints and the results list. We can articulate the space complexity as: $O((n+m)\times(u+1)+u\times(1+n+m))$. Upon simplification, this becomes $O(u\times(n+m))$. This indicates that the space complexity scales linearly with the number of units and the total number of inputs and outputs. This linear relationship is crucial, as it implies that the space required increases directly with the problem's size.

On the other hand, we generally understand the complexity of linear programming problems, such as those the Simplex method or interior-point methods solve, as polynomial in the number of variables and constraints. However, the theoretical worst-case time complexity of the Simplex method is exponential, though it performs efficiently in practice for many problems. Our script uses the COIN-OR Branch and Cut (CBC) solver through the PULP_CBC_CMD interface in PuLP. This tool is primarily for Mixed Integer Programming (MIP) problems, but it also handles LP problems. The complexity analysis for CBC presents several challenges: First, the worst-case time complexity of branch-and-cut algorithms generally scales exponentially, as the number of subproblems can increase exponentially with the integer variables count. Nonetheless, these algorithms often perform significantly better in practice due to the effectiveness of the branching rules, the quality of the cutting planes, and various heuristics. Second, in addressing LP problems (where mip is set to False), CBC acts effectively as an LP solver, using techniques like the Simplex or Primal-Dual methods. Here, its complexity mirrors that of standard LP solvers, which typically demonstrate polynomial-time performance in practice, though they might reach exponential time in the worst cases. Lastly, CBC's efficiency also depends on factors such as the efficacy of the linear algebra routines, the quality of the branching and cutting-plane strategies, and the effectiveness of the presolve and heuristic algorithms.

To estimate the complexity of our script, we developed theoretical scenarios. These scenarios vary the numbers of units (u) from two to 100, the number of inputs (n) from one to 100, and the number of outputs (m) from one to 100, recording the time expended by our script. We then constructed various regression models, encompassing linear, polynomial, and exponential relationships. In these models, we varied the number of predictors from order one (units, inputs, and outputs) to order three, including third-order interactions and the predictors raised to the power of three. We then chose the best models based on the root mean squared error and a comparison of actual versus expected time. The relationship between execution time and the predictors is multiplicative, not additive, as we log the execution time in our regression model. Our final model includes Linear Terms (n,m,u), Interaction Terms ($n\times m$, $n\times u$, $m\times u$), and Squared Terms (n^2,m^2,u^2). To articulate the time complexity, we reversed the logarithm, transforming the linear sum into a product of exponential terms. The complexity can thus be expressed as: $O\left(e^{\left(n+m+u+n\times m+n\times u+m\times u+n^2+m^2+u^2\right)}\right)$. This formula shows that execution time grows exponentially with the number of inputs, outputs, and units, and even more rapidly with their interactions and squared terms. However, this complexity expression is based on an empirical model and may not precisely reflect theoretical complexity. It should be treated as an estimate that reflects observed patterns in our specific dataset.

Non-Dominance in the Efficient Frontier

The concept of non-dominance plays a crucial role in the context of the efficient frontier. It ensures each point on the frontier represents an optimal decision that no other feasible decision can surpass, considering all objectives. For example, in portfolio optimization, each portfolio on the efficient frontier provides the highest expected return for a given risk level. No portfolio in the feasible set can offer more return for the same or lesser risk (Markowitz, H. M., 1952). Non-dominance proves particularly beneficial in multi-objective optimization problems. It allows us to discover a solution set (Pareto set) that exhibits no dominance over each other, thus establishing an efficient frontier in the objective space, known as the Pareto Front (Coello Coello et al., 2007). One benefit of applying non-dominance criteria in building an efficient frontier is its ability to pinpoint truly optimal solutions. However, a drawback of this method is that it yields not a single 'best' solution but a collection of 'equally effective' solutions from which decision-makers must select, guided by their preferences. This concept is notably effective in pinpointing projects that create a multitude of efficient paths.

Function to Identify Efficient Frontiers

```
def identify_efficient_frontiers(df):
    efficient_cols = [col for col in df.columns if col.startswith('Rel_Effi')]
    df['frontier'] = 0
    frontier_counter = 1

    while df['frontier'].eq(0).any():
        for i, row_i in df.iterrows():
            if df.at[i, 'frontier'] != 0:
                continue

            is_efficient = True
            for j, row_j in df.iterrows():
                if i != j and df.at[j, 'frontier'] == 0:

                    if all(row_j[efficient_cols] >= row_i[efficient_cols]) and
any(row_j[efficient_cols] > row_i[efficient_cols]):
                        is_efficient = False
                        break

            if is_efficient:
                df.at[i, 'frontier'] = frontier_counter

        frontier_counter += 1
```

Table 4. DEA coefficient outputs

PW	E	WIA	WIB	WID	WIN	WIC	WO	F
PW1	0.92	0.9999	0.0000	0.0000	0.0000	0.0000	1.1111	4
PW2	0.76	0.0000	0.0000	0.0000	0.0000	0.0000	1.1111	8
PW3	1.00	0.0000	0.0000	0.0107	0.0000	0.0000	1.2048	1
PW4	0.82	0.0000	0.0000	0.0000	0.0033	0.0000	1.1257	4
PW5	0.92	0.9999	0.0000	0.0000	0.0000	0.0000	1.1111	3
PW6	0.90	0.9999	0.0000	0.0000	0.0000	0.0000	1.1111	5
PW7	0.99	0.0000	0.0000	0.0000	0.0034	0.0000	1.1611	1
PW8	0.93	0.0000	0.0000	0.0000	0.0000	0.0000	1.1163	2
PW9	0.87	0.0000	0.0000	0.0000	0.0000	0.0000	1.1033	7
PW10	0.97	0.0000	0.0006	0.0000	0.0000	0.0000	1.1826	1
PW11	0.88	0.9999	0.0000	0.0000	0.0000	0.0000	1.1111	6
PW12	0.89	0.0000	0.0000	0.0000	0.0000	0.0000	1.1184	5
PW13	0.82	0.8283	0.0000	0.0000	0.0030	0.0000	1.1613	3
PW14	0.91	0.8136	0.0000	0.0000	0.0030	0.0000	1.1407	2
PW15	0.95	0.0000	0.0006	0.0000	0.0000	0.0000	1.1832	1
PW16	0.83	0.8358	0.0000	0.0091	0.0000	0.0000	1.1719	2
PW17	0.92	0.0000	0.0000	0.0000	0.0000	0.0000	1.1198	2
PW18	0.80	0.0000	0.0000	0.0000	0.0034	0.0000	1.1611	3
PW19	0.82	0.0000	0.0000	0.0000	0.0000	0.0000	1.1127	4
PW20	0.85	0.7994	0.0000	0.0000	0.0029	0.0000	1.1208	3
PW21	1.00	0.0000	0.0000	0.0000	0.0000	0.0000	1.1111	1
PW22	0.97	0.8136	0.0000	0.0089	0.0000	0.0000	1.1407	1
PW23	0.93	0.0000	0.0000	0.0000	0.0000	0.0000	1.0938	2
PW24	0.80	0.0000	0.0000	0.0000	0.0000	0.0000	1.1111	6
PW25	0.89	0.9999	0.0000	0.0000	0.0000	0.0000	1.1111	5
PW26	0.90	0.0000	0.0000	0.0000	0.0000	0.0000	1.1123	3
PW27	0.90	0.9999	0.0000	0.0000	0.0000	0.0000	1.1111	5
PW28	0.91	0.9999	0.0000	0.0000	0.0000	0.0000	1.1111	4
PW29	0.99	0.7925	0.0000	0.0086	0.0000	0.0000	1.1111	1
PW30	0.88	0.8136	0.0000	0.0089	0.0000	0.0000	1.1407	2
PW31	0.87	0.0000	0.0000	0.0000	0.0000	0.0000	1.1173	6
PW32	0.94	0.0000	0.0000	0.0000	0.0035	0.0000	1.1743	1

PW: Pathway, **E**: Efficiency, **WIA**: Weights Inputs Anesthesiology, **WIB**: Weights Inputs Beds, **WID**: Weights Inputs Doctor, **WIN**: Weights Inputs Nurses, **WIC**: Weights Inputs Project Cost, **WO**: Weights Output, **F**: Frontier

Source: Own elaboration

```
return df
```

Source: Own elaboration using Python

The efficient frontiers function's time complexity is quadratic ($O(n^2)$) relative to the number of rows and linear ($O(m)$) with respect to the efficient columns. This function works best for datasets of moderate size but may show performance issues with extremely large datasets. The space complexity mainly depends on the input Data Frame's size. The time complexity mainly comes from iterating over the rows of the Data Frame. For each row (an $O(n)$ operation where n is the number of rows), the function compares it with other rows yet to be assigned to a frontier. This comparison can also be an $O(n)$ operation in the worst case. The efficient columns are then compared for each row pair, an $O(m)$ operation if m is the number of such columns. Hence, the worst-case time complexity is $O(n^2 \times m)$. However, as the function progresses, rows are marked and excluded from further comparisons, reducing the average comparisons per row. The space complexity considers the input Data Frame, which is $O(n \times m)$ with m representing the total columns. Although an additional column for frontiers slightly increases space requirements, it doesn't alter the overall complexity. Thus, the space complexity remains $O(n \times m)$.

Results of the Project Comparison

We used Data Envelopment Analysis and applied a non-dominance algorithm to four subsets, each corresponding to the expected project cost. This process enabled us to identify four unique solutions, which we then ranked. A ranking of 1 indicates an efficient frontier, while 8 represents the maximum number of frontiers (as shown in Figure 5). After analyzing the number of frontiers, we found that Project 3 had the lowest number of frontiers (4), followed by Project 2 with five frontiers, Project 4 with seven, and finally Project 1 with eight pathways in the efficiency frontier. Since our case includes five inputs, such as the project cost, analyzing the pathways occurs in a five-dimensional space represented by $\mathbb{R}^5$. This multi-dimensionality presents a challenge in graphically representing the efficient frontier without omitting important information. However, Figure 6 displays the 32 pathways by frontier in a two-dimensional space represented by $\mathbb{R}^2$. Typically, frontier 1 appears in the upper right corner of each subplot because our goal is to maximize relative efficiency.

Comparing the DEA primal problem solution with the non-dominance algorithm, we can evaluate the efficiency scores' sensitivity and robustness obtained from each method. The most intriguing comparison involves pathways with a "Frontier" value of 1, which the non-dominance algorithm deems efficient. For instance, pathways PW3, PW7, PW10, PW15, PW21, PW22, PW29, and PW32 demonstrate an efficiency score of 1.0 in this methodology, placing them on the efficient frontier. However, their scores in the DEA model show variation: PW3 and PW21 achieve a perfect score of 1.0, but others, such as PW7, PW10, PW15, PW22, PW29, and PW32, fall short of 1, ranging from 0.94 to 0.99 with one score below 0.94, one at 0.95, two at 0.97, and two at 0.99.

This discrepancy raises a crucial question about the LP-based DEA model's sensitivity. The DEA model derives its efficiency score from a single optimization problem aiming to maximize output for given inputs. This method offers an 'average' efficiency measure, where the weights for each input or output can significantly vary. In contrast, the non-dominance algorithm evaluates multiple objectives, creating a frontier that illustrates various trade-offs. This approach offers a more comprehensive and

Figure 5. Surgery pathways efficiency by project
Source: Own elaboration using seaborn in Python

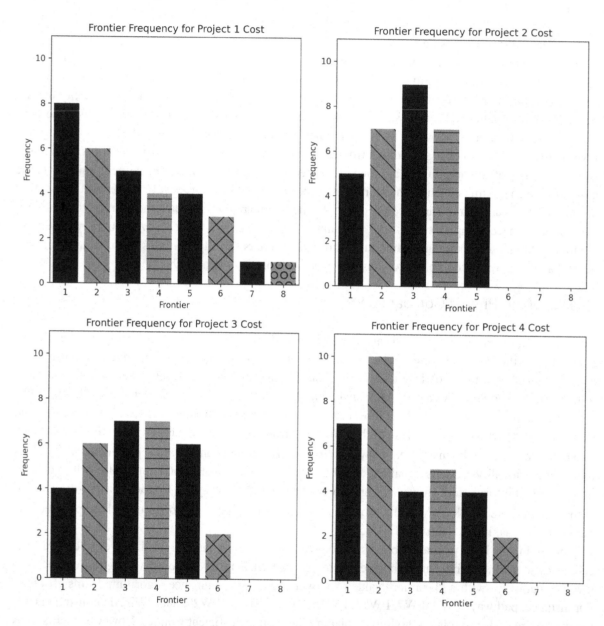

multi-dimensional perspective on efficiency, with each aspect contributing to the overall efficiency frontier. Such an approach might prove more beneficial when balancing multiple criteria. Nevertheless, the DEA model's single score simplifies identifying top-performing pathways for decision-makers.

After identifying efficient pathways, the next step involves suggesting ways to enhance their efficiency further. According to your data, pathways with a "Frontier" value of 2 show efficiency scores below 1, indicating improvement potential. To elevate each pathway's efficiency, implementing tailored strategies based on their specific input-output weights is crucial. Here are some proposed strategies:

Figure 6. Scatterplot of relative efficiency by frontier for Project 1
Source: Own elaboration using seaborn in Python

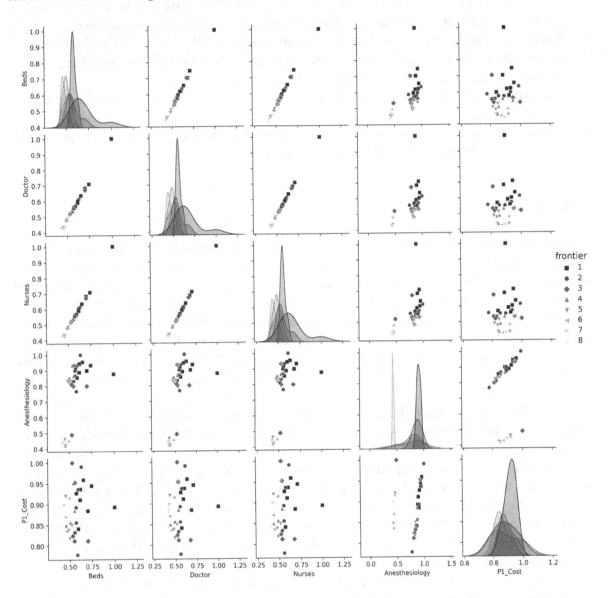

- **PW8** (Efficiency Score: 0.93): After identifying efficient pathways, the next step involves suggesting ways to enhance their efficiency further. According to your data, pathways with a "Frontier" value of 2 show efficiency scores below 1, indicating improvement potential. To elevate each pathway's efficiency, implementing tailored strategies based on their specific input-output weights is crucial. Here are some proposed strategies.

- **PW14** (Efficiency Score: 0.91): Anesthesiology and Nursing carry significant weights of 0.8135844 and 0.0029573738, respectively. Enhancing productivity in these departments through training or technological advancements could improve efficiency. Increasing patient attendance by nurses and anesthesiologists could enhance this pathway's performance.

- **PW16** (Efficiency Score: 0.83): Anesthesiology' and 'Doctor' are crucial, with weights of 0.83583351 and 0.0091147111. Optimizing their schedules and investing in advanced medical equipment could enhance efficiency, reducing the need for specialized professionals.
- **PW17** (Efficiency Score: 0.92): With a significant weight on 'P1_Cost' (1.0177662e-05), strategies similar to PW8 focusing on cost optimization, particularly in 'P1_Cost,' could improve efficiency. Analyzing cost drivers to pinpoint reduction areas is also advisable.
- **PW23** (Efficiency Score: 0.93): The weight on 'P1_Cost' here is 9.9406207e-06. Adopt a strategy similar to PW8.
- **PW30** (Efficiency Score: 0.88): Significant weights on 'Anesthesiology' (0.8135834) and 'Doctor' (0.0088721086) suggest adopting a strategy akin to PW16's.

DISCUSSION

The results of this study differ from previous works, not due to the methodology but to the particularities of the hypothetical case under scrutiny. The applied methodology combines various perspectives and approaches found in the literature, such as Lean Manufacturing Techniques (Nicholas, 2023), Simulation (Fu, 2013), Co-creation activities (Stimmel, 2015), and Data Envelopment Analysis (Cooper, 2013). These diverse methodologies work together to assess efficiency in healthcare systems. Lean techniques, for example, focus on reducing operational waste and enhancing patient flow (Kam et al., 2021), while simulation enables healthcare process prototyping (Register et al., 2019). Co-creation activities incorporate stakeholder engagement (Azevedo et al., 2017) acts as a benchmarking tool for technical efficiency (Stefko et al., 2018).

DEA's relationship with non-dominance analysis clarifies the advantages and limitations of each. While DEA is effective at identifying average efficiencies (Cylus et al., 2017), non-dominance provides a detailed understanding of top alternatives and contextualizes DEA results. The latter aspect tackles a major limitation of DEA: its inability to pinpoint root causes or propose specific solutions for observed inefficiencies, as it struggles to identify subgroups of similar inefficient units. A critical limitation of this work is the assumption of an environment devoid of usual constraints, like budget restrictions and policy issues, a premise established by prior Lean Healthcare and co-creation activities. Although this results in synthetic data due to confidentiality agreements, earlier co-creation efforts and stakeholder involvement yield credible suggestions for relevant inputs and outputs.

Regarding the complexity, the DEA algorithm's execution time grows exponentially with increases in units, inputs, outputs, and especially their interactions and squared terms. This complexity suggests DEA's suitability for datasets of moderate size. DEA measures the average cost needed for a unit to reach efficiency. Its utility lies in continuous improvement and optimal resource allocation, offering a clear efficiency score for each unit, enabling easy comparisons and benchmarking. However, its exponential time complexity reduces its suitability for very large datasets. Conversely, the non-dominance algorithm's time complexity is quadratic regarding rows and linear for columns (inputs and outputs). This complexity implies the algorithm's effectiveness for moderately sized datasets, potentially outperforming DEA with larger datasets. It efficiently identifies similar units in efficiency, creating vital efficient frontiers for decision-making in limited-resource settings. Given its quadratic time complexity, this algorithm might manage larger datasets more effectively than DEA. Although it scales better than DEA, the quadratic complexity still presents challenges for very large datasets. Lastly, it lacks DEA's quantitative insights into the improvements needed for each unit to achieve efficiency.

Noting in this work we do not use pathway times as an efficiency indicator; here, efficiency is synonymous with input performance. Additionally, this work stands out because the units are highly correlated; indeed, they often share a large amount of inputs, so the idea of unit optimization seems insignificant. For this reason, we chose Data Envelopment Analysis for its utility in identifying efficient pathways, especially with expected improvements from a theoretical project. Thus, DEA proved helpful in measuring the theoretical impacts of anticipated projects, aiding decision-makers in selecting the best project to invest in. Moreover, we enhanced DEA for decision-making with shadow prices analysis retrieved in the linear programming model to identify sets of pathways and strategies for improvement. The innovative aspect of this study is using DEA not just to compare existing alternatives but also to evaluate potential investments in projects designed to improve pathways' performance, considering pathways identified in the non-dominance algorithm as equivalent efficient. Hence, the developed framework adapts well to various practical scenarios, including those with different inputs and outputs. Furthermore, the study underscores DEA's implementation challenges and recommends integrating collaborative activities to tackle identified barriers: data quality and consistency (Medina-Borja et al., 2007; Suliman et al., 2019), model design (Ichake et al., 2018), computational complexity (Medina-Borja et al., 2007), external factors (sav, 2013), interpretation and contextualization, stakeholder buy-in (Jardas Antonić, 2018), expertise and software tools, cost constraints (Medina-Borja et al., 2007), and integration with existing systems (Jardas Antonić, 2018).

While conducting the study, we faced the unexpected challenge of unavailable capacity-related data. Nevertheless, we overcame this by conducting stakeholder interviews, simulations, and other validation methods, including Delphi methods. We compared the simulated data with the indicators from the exploratory data analysis and aligned the results with the process chiefs' experiences. It's crucial to note that the study aims to provide a realistic decision-making context, but due to the use of synthetic data, we should consider the results more illustrative than definitive. This limitation underscores the necessity for future research on co-creation's role in modeling quantitative methodologies in operational research and a comparative study between non-dominance and DEA in healthcare settings.

CONCLUSION

We integrated Lean Manufacturing techniques, operational research, simulation, and Data Envelopment Analysis in this study to pinpoint opportunities for improvement in healthcare centers, focusing specifically on surgical pathways that are closely interconnected and part of a singular surgery roadmap. We use DEA as a benchmarking tool to assess average efficiencies and discern the best alternatives through its link with non-dominance analysis. Our study's methodology builds on previous Lean and co-creation activities, allowing us to navigate common hurdles like budget and policy constraints, although we base it on synthetic data. Our comprehensive approach tackles challenges such as data quality, model design, and the complexity of interpreting methodologies and results. Simultaneously, our work proposes new directions for future research in co-creation and operational research methodologies. Our collaborative work with various stakeholders leads to practical strategies for boosting efficiency, with a focus on lowering costs, enhancing staff productivity, and improving resource management. Consequently, our study's framework is flexible and provides a model that can be replicated in diverse healthcare environments.

REFERENCES

(2022). Advances in Modeling and Simulation. InBotev, Z., Keller, A., Lemieux, C., & Tuffin, B. (Eds.), *Advances in Modeling and Simulation*. Springer International Publishing. doi:10.1007/978-3-031-10193-9

Agrawal, V., Zhang, Y., & Sundararaghavan, P. S. (2022). Multi-criteria surgery scheduling optimization using modeling, heuristics, and simulation. *Healthcare Analytics*, 2, 100034. Advance online publication. doi:10.1016/j.health.2022.100034

Ala, A., & Chen, F. (2022). Appointment Scheduling Problem in Complexity Systems of the Healthcare Services: A Comprehensive Review. In Journal of Healthcare Engineering (Vol. 2022). doi:10.1155/2022/5819813

Alam, M. T., Khan, M. A. I., Dola, N. N., Tazin, T., Khan, M. M., Albraikan, A. A., & Almalki, F. A. (2022). Comparative Analysis of Different Efficient Machine Learning Methods for Fetal Health Classification. *Applied Bionics and Biomechanics*, 2022, 1–12. Advance online publication. doi:10.1155/2022/6321884 PMID:35498140

Alenezi, A. M., Thirunavukkarasu, A., Alrasheed, A. K., Alsharari, T. A., Almadhi, K. B. A., Almugharriq, M. M. N., Alshalan, R. A., Alshalan, K. M., Alanazi, A. A. K., & Albayyali, W. S. (2022). Primary Care Physicians' Knowledge, Attitude, and Potential Referral Barriers towards Bariatric Surgery: A Northern Saudi Study. *Medicina (Lithuania), 58*(12). doi:10.3390/medicina58121742

Ali, S. I. M., & Buti, R. H. (2021). Data Mining in Healthcare Sector. *MINAR International Journal of Applied Sciences and Technology, 3*(2), 87–91. doi:10.47832/2717-8234.2-3.11

Amer, Y., Doan, L. T. T., Dania, W. A. P., & Tran, T. T. (2022). Analysis and Improvement in Healthcare Operation Utilizing Automation. *Proceedings - 2022 International Conference on Control, Robotics and Informatics, ICCRI 2022*. 10.1109/ICCRI55461.2022.00022

An, Q., Cheng, Z., Shi, S., & Li, F. (2022). Environmental efficiency of Xiangjiang River in China: A data envelopment analysis cross-efficiency approach. *Industrial Management & Data Systems, 122*(2), 396–418. Advance online publication. doi:10.1108/IMDS-02-2021-0110

Azevedo, C. da S., Sá, M. de C., Cunha, M., Matta, G. C., Miranda, L., & Grabois, V. (2017). Racionalização e construção de sentido na gestão do cuidado: Uma experiência de mudança em um hospital do SUS. *Ciencia & Saude Coletiva, 22*(6), 1991–2002. Advance online publication. doi:10.1590/1413-81232017226.13312016 PMID:28614518

Bagherian, H., Jahanbakhsh, M., & Tavakoli, N. (2020). A review on the use of operational research techniques in the medical records department. *Proceedings of Singapore Healthcare, 29*(1), 42–49. doi:10.1177/2010105819899113

Bandyopadhyay, S., & Bhattacharya, R. (2014a). Discrete and continuous simulation: Theory and practice. In *Discrete and Continuous Simulation*. Theory and Practice. doi:10.1201/b17127

Bandyopadhyay, S., & Bhattacharya, R. (2014b). Simulation with Cellular Automata. In Discrete and Continuous Simulation. doi:10.1201/b17127-20

Bandyopadhyay, S., & Bhattacharya, R. (2021). Simulation with System Dynamics. In Discrete and Continuous Simulation. doi:10.1201/b17127-25

Bass, L. M., Shneider, B. L., Henn, L., Goodrich, N. P., & Magee, J. C. (2019). Clinically Evident Portal Hypertension: An Operational Research Definition for Future Investigations in the Pediatric Population. *Journal of Pediatric Gastroenterology and Nutrition*, *68*(6), 763–767. Advance online publication. doi:10.1097/MPG.0000000000002333 PMID:30908382

Cameron, D. B., & Rangel, S. J. (2016). Quality improvement in pediatric surgery. *Current Opinion in Pediatrics*, *28*(3), 348–355. doi:10.1097/MOP.0000000000000346 PMID:27031660

Charnes, A., Cooper, W. W., & Rhodes, E. (1978). Measuring the efficiency of decision making units. *European Journal of Operational Research*, *2*(6), 429–444. Advance online publication. doi:10.1016/0377-2217(78)90138-8

Chivardi, C., Sosa, A. Z., Galárraga, O., & Sosa-Rubí, S. G. (2023). Efficiency, quality, and management practices in multidisciplinary and traditional diabetes healthcare services in Mexico. *Health Services and Outcomes Research Methodology*. Advance online publication. doi:10.100710742-023-00309-y

Claudio, D., Miller, A., & Huggins, A. (2014). Time series forecasting in an outpatient cancer clinic using common-day clustering. *IIE Transactions on Healthcare Systems Engineering*, *4*(1), 16–26. Advance online publication. doi:10.1080/19488300.2013.879459

Claudio, D., Moyce, S., Albano, T., Ibe, E., Miller, N., & O'Leary, M. (2023). A Markov Chain Model for Mental Health Interventions. *International Journal of Environmental Research and Public Health*, *20*(4), 3525. Advance online publication. doi:10.3390/ijerph20043525 PMID:36834220

Coello Coello, C. A., Lamont, G. B., & Van Veldhuizen, D. A. (2007). Evolutionary Algorithms for Solving Multi-Objective Problems. In *Evolutionary Algorithms for Solving Multi-Objective Problems*. Springer US. doi:10.1007/978-0-387-36797-2

Cooper, W. W. (2013). Data Envelopment Analysis. In Encyclopedia of Operations Research and Management Science (pp. 349–358). Springer US. doi:10.1007/978-1-4419-1153-7_212

Crema, M., & Verbano, C. (2019). *Simulation modelling and lean management in healthcare: first evidences and research agenda*. doi:10.1080/14783363.2019.1572504

Cylus, J., Papanicolas, I., & Smith, P. C. (2017). Using Data Envelopment Analysis to Address the Challenges of Comparing Health System Efficiency. *Global Policy*, *8*(S2), 60–68. Advance online publication. doi:10.1111/1758-5899.12212

de Barros, L. B., Bassi, L. de C., Caldas, L. P., Sarantopoulos, A., Zeferino, E. B. B., Minatogawa, V., & Gasparino, R. C. (2021). Lean Healthcare Tools for Processes Evaluation: An Integrative Review. *International Journal of Environmental Research and Public Health*, *18*(14), 7389. Advance online publication. doi:10.3390/ijerph18147389 PMID:34299840

Deb, K., & Jain, H. (2014). An evolutionary many-objective optimization algorithm using reference-point-based nondominated sorting approach, Part I: Solving problems with box constraints. *IEEE Transactions on Evolutionary Computation, 18*(4), 577–601. Advance online publication. doi:10.1109/TEVC.2013.2281535

Deb, K., Pratap, A., Agarwal, S., & Meyarivan, T. (2002). A fast and elitist multiobjective genetic algorithm: NSGA-II. *IEEE Transactions on Evolutionary Computation, 6*(2), 182–197. doi:10.1109/4235.996017

Dion, H., & Evans, M. (2023). Strategic frameworks for sustainability and corporate governance in healthcare facilities; approaches to energy-efficient hospital management. *Benchmarking*. Advance online publication. doi:10.1108/BIJ-04-2022-0219

Florescu, A., & Barabas, S. (2022). Development Trends of Production Systems through the Integration of Lean Management and Industry 4.0. *Applied Sciences (Basel, Switzerland), 12*(10), 4885. Advance online publication. doi:10.3390/app12104885

Flug, J. A., Stellmaker, J. A., Tollefson, C. D., Comstock, E. M., Buelna, E., Truman, B., Ponce, L., Milosek, A., McCabe, J., & Jokerst, C. E. (2022). Improving Turnaround Time in a Hospital-based CT Division with the Kaizen Method. *Radiographics, 42*(4), E125–E131. Advance online publication. doi:10.1148/rg.210128 PMID:35622490

Fu, M. C. (2013). Simulation Optimization. In Encyclopedia of Operations Research and Management Science (pp. 1418–1423). Springer US. doi:10.1007/978-1-4419-1153-7_958

Furinghetti, M., Lanese, I., & Pavese, A. (2020). Experimental Assessment of the Seismic Response of a Base-Isolated Building Through a Hybrid Simulation Technique. *Frontiers in Built Environment, 6*, 33. Advance online publication. doi:10.3389/fbuil.2020.00033

Gabriel, G. T., Campos, A. T., de Lima Magacho, A., Segismondi, L. C., Vilela, F. F., de Queiroz, J. A., & Montevechi, J. A. B. (2020). Lean thinking by integrating with discrete event simulation and design of experiments: An emergency department expansion. *PeerJ. Computer Science, 6*, e284. Advance online publication. doi:10.7717/peerj-cs.284 PMID:33816935

Gauly, J., Court, R., Currie, G., Seers, K., Clarke, A., Metcalfe, A., Wilson, A., Hazell, M., & Grove, A. L. (2023). Advancing leadership in surgery: a realist review of interventions and strategies to promote evidence-based leadership in healthcare. In Implementation Science (Vol. 18, Issue 1). doi:10.118613012-023-01274-3

Gong, G., Chen, Y., Gao, H., Su, D., & Chang, J. (2019). Has the efficiency of China's healthcare system improved after healthcare reform? A network data envelopment analysis and tobit regression approach. *International Journal of Environmental Research and Public Health, 16*(23), 4847. Advance online publication. doi:10.3390/ijerph16234847 PMID:31810260

Gür, Ş., & Eren, T. (2018). *Application of Operational Research Techniques in Operating Room Scheduling Problems* (Vol. 2018). Literature Overview. In Journal of Healthcare Engineering. doi:10.1155/2018/5341394

Harper, E. M., & McNair, D. (2017). *The Power of Disparate Data Sources for Answering Thorny Questions in Healthcare: Four Case Studies.* doi:10.1007/978-3-319-53300-1_18

Hippe, D. S., Umoren, R. A., McGee, A., Bucher, S. L., & Bresnahan, B. W. (2020). A targeted systematic review of cost analyses for implementation of simulation-based education in healthcare. In SAGE Open Medicine (Vol. 8). doi:10.1177/2050312120913451

Hossain, N. U. I., Lutfi, M., Ahmed, I., & Debusk, H. (2023). Application of systems modeling language (SysML) and discrete event simulation to address patient waiting time issues in healthcare. *Smart Health (Amsterdam, Netherlands)*, 29, 100403. Advance online publication. doi:10.1016/j.smhl.2023.100403

Ichake, S., Gardas, B. B., Kharat, M. G., Raut, R. D., & Choudhury, N. (2018). Evaluation and selection of third party logistics services providers using data envelopment analysis: A sustainable approach. *International Journal of Business Excellence*, *14*(4), 427. Advance online publication. doi:10.1504/IJBEX.2018.10011212

Jardas Antonić, J. (2018). Data Envelopment Analysis in Improving Security Level in Local Government Units. *Balkans Journal of Emerging Trends in Social Sciences*, *1*(1), 59–69. doi:10.31410/Balkans.JETSS.2018.1.1.59-69

Jiang, L., & Huang, Y. L. (2023). Healthcare call center efficiency improvement using a simulation approach to achieve the organization's target. *International Journal of Healthcare Management*, 1–10. Advance online publication. doi:10.1080/20479700.2023.2190250

Jiang, N., & Malkin, B. D. (2016). Use of Lean and CAHPS Surgical Care Survey to Improve Patients' Experiences with Surgical Care. *Otolaryngology - Head and Neck Surgery*, *155*(5), 743–747. doi:10.1177/0194599816657051 PMID:27329420

Joseph, A. L., Kushniruk, A. W., & Borycki, E. M. (2020). Patient journey mapping: Current practices, challenges and future opportunities in healthcare. Knowledge Management & E-Learning. *International Journal (Toronto, Ont.)*, 387–404. Advance online publication. doi:10.34105/j.kmel.2020.12.021

Kam, A. W., Collins, S., Park, T., Mihail, M., Stanaway, F. F., Lewis, N. L., Polya, D., Fraser-Bell, S., Roberts, T. V., & Smith, J. E. H. (2021). Using Lean Six Sigma techniques to improve efficiency in outpatient ophthalmology clinics. *BMC Health Services Research*, *21*(1), 38. Advance online publication. doi:10.118612913-020-06034-3 PMID:33413381

Keskitalo, T. (2022). Pedagogical Practices for Organizing Simulation-Based Healthcare Education. International Journal of Learning. *Teaching and Educational Research*, *21*(4), 80–96. Advance online publication. doi:10.26803/ijlter.21.4.1

Knowles, J., & Corne, D. (1999). The Pareto archived evolution strategy: A new baseline algorithm for Pareto multiobjective optimisation. *Proceedings of the 1999 Congress on Evolutionary Computation, CEC 1999*, 1. 10.1109/CEC.1999.781913

Kohl, S., Schoenfelder, J., Fügener, A., & Brunner, J. O. (2019). The use of Data Envelopment Analysis (DEA) in healthcare with a focus on hospitals. *Health Care Management Science*, *22*(2), 245–286. Advance online publication. doi:10.100710729-018-9436-8 PMID:29478088

Kvet, M., & Janáček, J. (2023). Directed Search for Non-Dominated Emergency Medical System Designs. *Applied Sciences (Basel, Switzerland)*, *13*(8), 4810. Advance online publication. doi:10.3390/app13084810

Lamé, G., Crowe, S., Komashie, A., & Royston, G. (2023). Joining forces: The value of design partnering with operational research to improve healthcare delivery. *Design Science*, *9*, e4. Advance online publication. doi:10.1017/dsj.2023.2

Lee, E. K., Atallah, H. Y., Wright, M. D., Post, E. T., Thomas, C. IV, Wu, D. T., & Haley, L. L. Jr. (2015). Transforming hospital emergency department workflow and patient care. *Interfaces*, *45*(1), 58–82. Advance online publication. doi:10.1287/inte.2014.0788

Luangkesorn, K. L., & Eren-Doğu, Z. F. (2016). Markov Chain Monte Carlo methods for estimating surgery duration. *Journal of Statistical Computation and Simulation*, *86*(2), 262–278. Advance online publication. doi:10.1080/00949655.2015.1004065

Maniago, R., Miao, J., Jou, S., Calip, G. S., Huda, S., Shulman, L. N., Bange, E. M., Singh, A. P., & Davella, C. (2022). Do clinical pathways impede provider workflow: A provider efficiency analysis of time spent using an EHR-embedded clinical decision support tool. *Journal of Clinical Oncology*, *40*(28, suppl), 381–381. doi:10.1200/JCO.2022.40.28_suppl.381

Marin-Garcia, J. A., Vidal-Carreras, P. I., & Garcia-Sabater, J. J. (2021). The Role of Value Stream Mapping in Healthcare Services: A Scoping Review. *International Journal of Environmental Research and Public Health*, *18*(3), 1–25. doi:10.3390/ijerph18030951 PMID:33499116

Markowitz, H. M. (1952). *Portfolio selection.* https://onlinelibrary.wiley.com/doi/10.1111/j.1540-6261.1952.tb01525.x/abstract

McDermott, O., Antony, J., Bhat, S., Jayaraman, R., Rosa, A., Marolla, G., & Parida, R. (2022). Lean Six Sigma in Healthcare: A Systematic Literature Review on Challenges, Organisational Readiness and Critical Success Factors. *Processes (Basel, Switzerland)*, *10*(10), 1945. doi:10.3390/pr10101945

Medina-Borja, A., Pasupathy, K. S., & Triantis, K. (2007). Large-scale data envelopment analysis (DEA) implementation: A strategic performance management approach. *The Journal of the Operational Research Society*, *58*(8), 1084–1098. Advance online publication. doi:10.1057/palgrave.jors.2602200

Mehra, R., & Sharma, M. K. (2021). Measures of Sustainability in Healthcare. *Sustainability Analytics and Modeling*, *1*, 100001. Advance online publication. doi:10.1016/j.samod.2021.100001

Mirmozaffari, M., Shadkam, E., Khalili, S. M., & Yazdani, M. (2021). Developing a Novel Integrated Generalised Data Envelopment Analysis (DEA) to Evaluate Hospitals Providing Stroke Care Services. *Bioengineering (Basel, Switzerland)*, *8*(12), 207. Advance online publication. doi:10.3390/bioengineering8120207 PMID:34940361

Mitchell, S., O'Sullivan, M., & Dunning, I. (2011). *PuLP: A Linear Programming Toolkit for Python.* The University of Auckland.

Modeling and Simulation of Discrete-Event Systems. (2013). *Modeling and Simulation of Discrete-Event Systems.* doi:10.1002/9781118732793

Molcho, M., Gavin, A., & Goodwin, D. (2021). Levels of physical activity and mental health in adolescents in Ireland. *International Journal of Environmental Research and Public Health*, *18*(4), 1713. Advance online publication. doi:10.3390/ijerph18041713 PMID:33578906

Needham, J., Beggs, R., & van de Mortel, T. F. (2023). Supporting learners in prison healthcare work-integrated learning settings through simulation: A cross-sectional study. *BMC Nursing, 22*(1), 322. doi:10.118612912-023-01506-3 PMID:37723488

Ngee-Wen, T., Zailani, S., Aziz, A. A., & Ahmad, R. (2020). Lean public emergency department efficiency evaluation by slack-based measure data envelopment analysis. *Malaysian Journal of Medicine and Health Sciences, 16*(2).

Nicholas, J. (2023). Lean daily management in healthcare: Origins, practices, and associations with lean leadership and lean sustainability. *Total Quality Management & Business Excellence, 34*(11-12), 1526–1552. Advance online publication. doi:10.1080/14783363.2023.2182677

Ortíz-Barrios, M. A., & Alfaro-Saíz, J. J. (2020). Methodological approaches to support process improvement in emergency departments: A systematic review. In International Journal of Environmental Research and Public Health (Vol. 17, Issue 8). doi:10.3390/ijerph17082664

Palmer, R., Fulop, N. J., & Utley, M. (2018). A systematic literature review of operational research methods for modelling patient flow and outcomes within community healthcare and other settings. *Health Systems (Basingstoke, England), 7*(1), 29–50. Advance online publication. doi:10.105741306-017-0024-9 PMID:31214337

Pang, X., Ge, Y. F., Wang, K., Traina, A. J. M., & Wang, H. (2023). Patient assignment optimization in cloud healthcare systems: A distributed genetic algorithm. *Health Information Science and Systems, 11*(1), 30. Advance online publication. doi:10.100713755-023-00230-1 PMID:37397165

Patkal, P. S., & Anasane, S. S. (2022). Implementation of Standard Work in Healthcare Industry. *Proceedings of the International Conference on Industrial Engineering and Operations Management*, 1110–1115. 10.46254/IN02.20220339

Paulden, M., McCabe, C., & Karnon, J. (2014). Achieving allocative efficiency in healthcare: Nice in theory, not so NICE in practice? In PharmacoEconomics (Vol. 32, Issue 4). doi:10.100740273-014-0146-x

Pourmahmoud, J., & Bagheri, N. (2023). Uncertain Malmquist productivity index: An application to evaluate healthcare systems during COVID-19 pandemic. *Socio-Economic Planning Sciences, 87*, 101522. Advance online publication. doi:10.1016/j.seps.2023.101522 PMID:36777893

Prada, S. I., Garcia-Garcia, M. P., & Guzman, J. (2022). COVID-19 response in Colombia: Hits and misses. *Health Policy and Technology, 11*(2), 100621. Advance online publication. doi:10.1016/j.hlpt.2022.100621 PMID:35340774

Rajendran, S., Pan, W., Sabuncu, M. R., Chen, Y., Zhou, J., & Wang, F. (2023). *Patchwork Learning: A Paradigm Towards Integrative Analysis across Diverse Biomedical Data Sources*. Academic Press.

Ranchal, R., Bastide, P., Wang, X., Gkoulalas-Divanis, A., Mehra, M., Bakthavachalam, S., Lei, H., & Mohindra, A. (2020). Disrupting healthcare silos: Addressing data volume, velocity and variety with a cloud-native healthcare data ingestion service. *IEEE Journal of Biomedical and Health Informatics, 24*(11), 3182–3188. Advance online publication. doi:10.1109/JBHI.2020.3001518 PMID:32750932

Register, S., Brown, M., & White, M. L. (2019). Using healthcare simulation in space planning to improve efficiency and effectiveness within the healthcare system. *Health Systems (Basingstoke, England), 8*(3), 184–189. doi:10.1080/20476965.2019.1569482 PMID:31839930

Rosenbäck, R. G., & Svensson, A. (2023). Resilience in keeping the balance between demand and capacity in the COVID-19 pandemic, a case study at a Swedish middle-sized hospital. *BMC Health Services Research, 23*(1), 202. Advance online publication. doi:10.118612913-023-09182-4 PMID:36855122

Samanta, A. K., Varaprasad, G., & Padhy, R. (2021). A systematic review of empirical studies pertaining to Lean, Six Sigma and Lean Six Sigma quality improvement methodologies in paediatrics. *International Journal of Business Excellence, 23*(1), 18–32. doi:10.1504/IJBEX.2021.111936

Santos, A. B., Calado, R. D., Zeferino, A. C. S., & Bourguignon, S. C. (2022). Queuing Theory: Contributions and Applications in the Field of Health Service Management - A Bibliometric Approach. *IFAC-PapersOnLine, 55*(10), 210–214. Advance online publication. doi:10.1016/j.ifacol.2022.09.392

Sarrut, D., Etxebeste, A., Muñoz, E., Krah, N., & Létang, J. M. (2021). Artificial Intelligence for Monte Carlo Simulation in Medical Physics. *Frontiers in Physics (Lausanne), 9*, 738112. Advance online publication. doi:10.3389/fphy.2021.738112

Sato, R. C., & Zouain, D. M. (2010). Markov Models in health care. *Einstein (Sao Paulo, Brazil), 8*(3), 376–379. Advance online publication. doi:10.15901679-45082010rb1567 PMID:26760158

Sav, G. T. (2013). Effects of Financial Source Dependency on Public University Operating Efficiencies: Data Envelopment Single-Stage and Tobit Two-Stage Evaluations. *Revue d'Economie Financiere, 3*, 63–73. https://api.semanticscholar.org/CorpusID:14860400

Schaffer, A. L., Dobbins, T. A., & Pearson, S. A. (2021). Interrupted time series analysis using autoregressive integrated moving average (ARIMA) models: A guide for evaluating large-scale health interventions. *BMC Medical Research Methodology, 21*(1), 58. Advance online publication. doi:10.118612874-021-01235-8 PMID:33752604

Schonberger, R. J. (2018). Reconstituting lean in healthcare: From waste elimination toward 'queueless' patient-focused care. *Business Horizons, 61*(1), 13–22. Advance online publication. doi:10.1016/j.bushor.2017.09.001

Selzer, D. J. (2019). *Overview of Simulation in Surgery*. doi:10.1007/978-3-319-98276-2_2

Sethi, R., Yanamadala, V., Burton, D. C., & Bess, R. S. (2017). Using Lean Process Improvement to Enhance Safety and Value in Orthopaedic Surgery: The Case of Spine Surgery. *The Journal of the American Academy of Orthopaedic Surgeons, 25*(11), e244–e250. doi:10.5435/JAAOS-D-17-00030 PMID:29059115

Shao, L., & Ehrgott, M. (2016). Discrete representation of non-dominated sets in multi-objective linear programming. *European Journal of Operational Research, 255*(3), 687–698. Advance online publication. doi:10.1016/j.ejor.2016.05.001

Shokri, A. (2017). Quantitative analysis of Six Sigma, Lean and Lean Six Sigma research publications in last two decades. *International Journal of Quality & Reliability Management, 34*(5), 598–625. doi:10.1108/IJQRM-07-2015-0096

Shuwiekh, H. A. M., Kira, I. A., Sous, M. S. F., Ashby, J. S., Alhuwailah, A., Baali, S. B. A., Azdaou, C., Oliemat, E. M., & Jamil, H. J. (2022). The differential mental health impact of COVID-19 in Arab countries. *Current Psychology (New Brunswick, N.J.), 41*(8), 5678–5692. Advance online publication. doi:10.100712144-020-01148-7 PMID:33162726

Sloan, T., Fitzgerald, A., Hayes, K. J., Radnor, Z., Robinson, S., & Sohal, A. (2014). Lean in healthcare--history and recent developments. In Journal of health organization and management (Vol. 28, Issue 2). doi:10.1108/JHOM-04-2014-0064

Soyiri, I. N., & Reidpath, D. D. (2013). An overview of health forecasting. In Environmental Health and Preventive Medicine (Vol. 18, Issue 1). doi:10.100712199-012-0294-6

Statista. (2023). *Health Care - Colombia | Statista Market Forecast.* https://es.statista.com/outlook/dmo/ecommerce/beauty-health-personal-household-care/health-care/colombia#revenue

Stefko, R., Gavurova, B., & Kocisova, K. (2018). Healthcare efficiency assessment using DEA analysis in the Slovak Republic. *Health Economics Review, 8*(1), 6. Advance online publication. doi:10.118613561-018-0191-9 PMID:29523981

Steins, K., & Persson, F. (2015). Identifying Factors for Successful Implementation of Simulation Modeling in Healthcare. *International Journal of Privacy and Health Information Management, 3*(1), 1–19. Advance online publication. doi:10.4018/IJPHIM.2015010101

Stimmel, C. L. (2015). Why Design Thinking? In Building Smart Cities (pp. 74–89). Auerbach Publications. doi:10.1201/b18827-11

Suliman, K. R., Rahim, S. A., Ramayah, T., & Degeras, D. K. (2019). Measuring technical efficiency of dry bulk terminal performance using the frontier application of data envelopment analysis: A proposed framework. *Journal of Physics: Conference Series, 1366*(1), 012100. Advance online publication. doi:10.1088/1742-6596/1366/1/012100

Vanderbei, R. J. (2014). *Linear Programming* (Vol. 196). Springer US. doi:10.1007/978-1-4614-7630-6

Vázquez-Serrano, J. I., Peimbert-García, R. E., & Cárdenas-Barrón, L. E. (2021). Discrete-Event Simulation Modeling in Healthcare: A Comprehensive Review. *International Journal of Environmental Research and Public Health, 18*(22), 12262. Advance online publication. doi:10.3390/ijerph182212262 PMID:34832016

Villa, D. (2010). Automation, lean, six sigma: Synergies for improving laboratory efficiency. *Journal of Medical Biochemistry, 29*(4), 339–348. doi:10.2478/v10011-010-0038-3

Yousefi Nayer, M., Fazaeli, A. A., & Hamidi, Y. (2022). Hospital efficiency measurement in the west of Iran: Data envelopment analysis and econometric approach. *Cost Effectiveness and Resource Allocation, 20*(1), 5. Advance online publication. doi:10.118612962-022-00341-8 PMID:35139884

Zitzler, E., & Thiele, L. (1999). Multiobjective evolutionary algorithms: A comparative case study and the strength Pareto approach. *IEEE Transactions on Evolutionary Computation, 3*(4), 257–271. Advance online publication. doi:10.1109/4235.797969

ADDITIONAL READING

Antony, J., Sunder, M. V., Sreedharan, R., Chakraborty, A., & Gunasekaran, A. (2019). A systematic review of Lean in healthcare: A global prospective. *International Journal of Quality & Reliability Management, 36*(8), 1370–1391. doi:10.1108/IJQRM-12-2018-0346

Boyd, D. T., Kronk, L. A., & Boyd, S. C. (2006). Measuring the effects of lean manufacturing systems on financial accounting metrics using data envelopment analysis. *Investment Management and Financial Innovations, 3*(4).

Kohl, S., Schoenfelder, J., Fügener, A., & Brunner, J. O. (2019). The use of Data Envelopment Analysis (DEA) in healthcare with a focus on hospitals. *Health Care Management Science, 22*(2), 245–286. Advance online publication. doi:10.100710729-018-9436-8 PMID:29478088

Koltai, T., Dénes, R. V., & Dénes, Z. (2023). Analysis of the effect of patients' health status on efficiency: Application of data envelopment analysis in healthcare. *Health Services Management Research, 36*(1), 2–9. Advance online publication. doi:10.1177/09514848211065464 PMID:35061548

Mason, S. E., Nicolay, C. R., & Darzi, A. (2015). The use of Lean and Six Sigma methodologies in surgery: A systematic review. *The Surgeon, 13*(2), 91–100. doi:10.1016/j.surge.2014.08.002 PMID:25189692

KEY TERMS AND DEFINITIONS

Co-Creation: A process where multiple stakeholders collaboratively contribute to developing a new solution or service. In healthcare, this concept could involve patients, providers, administrators, relatives, researchers, policy makers, and so on, jointly creating strategies for improved patient care and operational efficiency.

Computational Complexity: The study of the resources a computer requires to solve a specific problem. Analysts often examine this in terms of the problem's size and the time needed to solve a mathematical problem.

Data Envelopment Analysis: A non-parametric method in operations research and economics for measuring the efficiency of decision-making units, like hospitals, pathways, and other resources, by comparing their inputs and outputs. It aids in identifying efficient practices and areas needing improvement at the inputs or outputs to prioritize.

Design-Thinking: An iterative process that aims to understand users, challenge assumptions, and redefine problems to identify alternative strategies and solutions. In healthcare, professionals apply it to enhance patient experiences and service delivery, focusing on user-centered design.

Exploratory Data Analysis: An approach to analyzing data sets to summarize their main characteristics, often employing statistical graphics and other data visualization methods. In healthcare, this method is vital for uncovering trends, patterns, and anomalies in patient or business data.

Lean Healthcare: The application of lean principles and methodologies in healthcare settings, aimed at reducing waste, improving patient care, and enhancing value delivery by optimizing workflows and processes.

Lean Manufacturing Techniques: Methods originally developed in manufacturing to optimize production processes, minimize waste, and boost efficiency. In healthcare, these techniques improve patient flow and reduce operational inefficiencies.

Non-Dominance in Efficient Frontier: A concept in performance measurement where the efficient frontier represents optimal trade-offs between different objectives. In healthcare, it's utilized to pinpoint the most efficient resource usage.

Operational Efficiency: The effectiveness of an organization in using its resources to produce the desired output. In healthcare, this term refers to using medical and administrative resources efficiently to provide high-quality patient care.

Simulation Modeling: A technique for creating a digital model of a real-world system or process. In healthcare, simulation modeling is utilized for analyzing and enhancing patient flow, resource allocation, and process management using computers, simulating real processes without interruptions.

Chapter 5
Synthetic Data Generation:
Methods, Applications, and Multidisciplinary Use Cases

Edlira Martiri

ⓘ https://orcid.org/0000-0002-0684-7590

University of Tirana, Albania

ABSTRACT

This chapter offers a comprehensive examination of contemporary practices in synthetic data generation. Its primary objective is to analyze and synthesize the methodologies, techniques, applications, and challenges associated with synthetic data across diverse scientific disciplines. The motivation behind the use of synthetic data stems from data privacy concerns, limitations in data availability, and the necessity for diverse, representative datasets. This chapter delves into various synthetic data generation methods, such as statistical modeling, generative adversarial networks (GANs), simulation-based techniques, and data envelopment analysis (DEA). It also scrutinizes the evaluation metrics for assessing synthetic data quality and privacy preservation. The chapter highlights applications in healthcare, finance, social sciences, and computer vision, and discusses emerging trends, including deep learning integration and domain adaptation. Researchers, practitioners, and policymakers will gain valuable insights into the state-of-the-art in synthetic data generation.

INTRODUCTION

Synthetic data is a type of artificially generated data designed to replicate the statistical properties of real-world data. It is created using algorithms and simulation models. Synthetic data serves a crucial role in situations where access to real data is limited, restricted due to privacy concerns, or when data is scarce. It has become particularly valuable in training machine learning models, testing systems, and conducting research while ensuring data privacy and compliance with data protection regulations. The concept of synthetic data has evolved significantly over time, progressing from simple statistical methods to advanced AI-driven models. Initially, it was developed to address data scarcity and privacy

DOI: 10.4018/979-8-3693-0255-2.ch005

issues by using statistical sampling and resampling techniques to replicate statistical properties without revealing sensitive information (Rubin, 1993). Over time, complex simulation models, like agent-based modeling, broadened the scope of synthetic data by capturing dynamic interactions and behaviors within datasets (Bonabeau, 2002). These developments had a profound impact on fields such as social sciences and epidemiology. The introduction of Generative Adversarial Networks (GANs) by Goodfellow et al. (2014) represented a major leap forward in synthetic data generation, along with techniques like Variational Autoencoders (Kingma & Welling, 2014), which contributed to creating more realistic and diverse synthetic datasets.

Synthetic data generation has garnered substantial attention as a valuable technique in data-driven research and applications (Assefa et al., 2020; Tyxhari & Martiri, 2022). It offers solutions to challenges associated with limited access to real-world datasets, which may result from privacy concerns, data scarcity, or the need for representative and diverse datasets (Bonnéry et al., 2019). This chapter provides a comprehensive examination of the methodologies, techniques, applications, and challenges related to synthetic data generation across various scientific disciplines.

One primary motivation for using synthetic data is the growing concern for data privacy. Real-world datasets often contain sensitive information about individuals or organizations, making it difficult to share for research purposes (Drechsler et al., 2019). Synthetic data provides a means to generate privacy-preserving substitutes that maintain essential statistical properties while safeguarding individual privacy. Another motivation is addressing data scarcity. In many research domains, obtaining a large and diverse dataset can be time-consuming, expensive, or impractical (Monroe et al., 2018; Bansal et al., 2022). Synthetic data generation techniques enable researchers to create additional data instances, thereby augmenting the available dataset and enabling more comprehensive analyses and model training. Furthermore, synthetic data generation helps ensure the availability of representative and diverse datasets. Real-world datasets can suffer from biases or limited coverage of specific data patterns, potentially impacting the performance and generalization of models trained on such data (Le et al., 2017). Synthetic data can mitigate these issues by creating instances that encompass a broader range of data patterns and ensure a more representative distribution.

Synthetic data is essential for promoting data-driven research across various scientific domains (Drechsler et al., 2019; Bergen et al., 2019). It provides researchers with access to privacy-preserving and diverse datasets, facilitating the development and testing of algorithms, models, and methodologies. Synthetic data allows researchers to explore various scenarios and experiment with data-driven approaches without compromising individual privacy or facing data access limitations. Moreover, synthetic data supports decision-making processes in diverse fields (Monroe et al., 2018; Liu, 2023; Jordon et al., 2022; Hernandez et al., 2022; Martiri, 2022). It offers a simulated environment for testing hypotheses, assessing algorithm performance, and predicting outcomes. In domains such as healthcare, finance, social sciences, and computer vision, synthetic data empowers researchers and practitioners to explore and validate ideas, develop innovative solutions, and make informed decisions based on realistic yet synthetic data instances.

In summary, synthetic data generation has become an indispensable tool for researchers, practitioners, and policymakers. It addresses challenges related to data privacy, scarcity, and representativeness, thereby advancing scientific research, enabling algorithm development, and supporting decision-making processes. In the following sections of this chapter, we will delve into the techniques, evaluation metrics, challenges, applications, and future directions of synthetic data generation. The next section will focus on the practical applications and use cases of synthetic data across different domains. We'll examine how synthetic data addresses data privacy concerns, enhances machine learning model training, aids in anomaly detection and security systems, and fosters data analysis and exploration. Real-world examples will illustrate the pivotal role of synthetic data in revolutionizing industries like healthcare, automotive, finance, and biometric security. Following the exploration of applications, we'll delve into the limitations and challenges of synthetic data. This section will discuss issues related to representativeness, biases, and the generalization of models trained on synthetic data to real-world scenarios. We'll also discuss uncertainties associated with synthetic data and the importance of confidence estimation to make informed decisions based on synthetic data. Ethical considerations and the responsible use of synthetic data will be the focus of the next section, and we will conclude the chapter by discussing future directions and research challenges in the field of synthetic data.

APPROACHES FOR SYNTHETIC DATA GENERATION

Synthetic data generation is a multifaceted field, encompassing a variety of methodologies and techniques designed to produce artificial data instances that emulate the statistical properties and patterns observed in real-world datasets. This section provides an exhaustive exploration of the primary approaches employed in synthetic data generation, including statistical modeling, generative adversarial networks (GANs), and simulation-based techniques. Each of these approaches offers a distinct perspective on how to create synthetic data, and they have found applications in diverse domains ranging from healthcare and finance to computer vision and social sciences.

Statistical Modeling Techniques

Statistical modeling techniques represent a fundamental pillar of synthetic data generation, relying on the art of capturing the underlying statistical properties of a given dataset and leveraging these insights to generate synthetic data that mirrors those properties. A wide array of probability distributions and statistical models are deployed in this process. Let's delve into each technique and offer more comprehensive insights.

Bootstrapping involves the random sampling of observations from the original dataset, often with replacement, thereby retaining the same distributional properties (Goodfellow et al., 2014; Barth et al., 2019). This technique is particularly useful when dealing with datasets that exhibit complex interdependencies between variables. For instance, it is invaluable in preserving intricate relationships within synthetic data, making it indispensable in fields such as econometrics and epidemiology.

Parametric Modeling encompasses the art of fitting parametric models (e.g., Gaussian, exponential) to the original dataset and subsequently generating synthetic instances based on the estimated parameters (Goodfellow et al., 2014; Wood et al., 2021; Snoke et al., 2018). This approach shines when data adheres to specific distributions, and the goal is to generate additional data that faithfully aligns with the distributional characteristics of the original dataset. Applications are manifold, from simulating financial market data to generating realistic biological growth patterns.

Data Augmentation is a technique that introduces random perturbations or transformations to existing data instances, creating additional synthetic data. In image classification tasks, for example, data augmentation techniques like rotation, translation, and scaling are applied to augment the dataset, increasing its diversity (Jaipuria, et al., 2020; Jain et al., 2022). This approach has found widespread use in

Table 1. Statistical modeling techniques for synthetic data generation

Technique	Description
Bootstrapping	Randomly sampling observations from the original dataset with replacement, maintaining the same distributional properties.
Parametric Modeling	Fitting parametric models (e.g., Gaussian, exponential) to the original dataset and generating synthetic instances based on the estimated parameters.
Data Augmentation	Introducing random perturbations or transformations to existing data instances to create additional synthetic instances.
Copula-based Models	Modeling the dependence structure among variables using copulas and generating synthetic instances based on the estimated copula.

computer vision, where generating variations of images aids in the robust training of machine learning models (Alhaija et al., 2018; Zhai et al, 2022).

Copula-based Models are a sophisticated statistical tool for modeling the dependence structure among variables independently of their marginal distributions (Meyer et al., 2021). By estimating the copula function from the original dataset, these models capture the intricate relationships between variables. Subsequently, synthetic instances are generated based on the estimated copula, ensuring the preservation of the underlying dependence structure.

Generative Adversarial Networks (GANs)

Generative Adversarial Networks, or GANs, represent a paradigm shift in synthetic data generation, offering a revolutionary approach to creating synthetic data with remarkable realism (Figueira and Vaz, 2022; Tanaka & Aranha, 2019; Torfi et al., 2022). GANs consist of two neural networks – a generator network and a discriminator network – engaged in a dynamic, adversarial training process. Here, we embark on a more detailed journey into the world of GANs and their various flavors.

Vanilla GAN, which is the foundational architecture, involves training a generator and a discriminator network in an adversarial manner (Goodfellow et al., 2014). The generator's role is to learn to produce synthetic data instances, while the discriminator's role is to differentiate between real and synthetic data (Xu, 2020; Goodfellow et al., 2014). Through an iterative training process, the generator gradually enhances its ability to produce data that is virtually indistinguishable from real data. This vanilla GAN architecture has been pivotal in generating realistic images of human faces, creating lifelike video game environments, and much more.

Conditional GANs, an extension of the GAN framework, introduces the concept of conditioning the generation process on additional input (Mirza et al., 2021). This input could be specific attributes, labels, or any additional information that guides the generation of synthetic data (Xu, 2019). For instance, in image synthesis, a conditional GAN can be trained to generate images conditioned on attributes like age, gender, or pose. This enables the generation of highly customized synthetic data with precise attributes, making it invaluable in domains such as fashion and facial recognition.

CycleGAN, a specialized adaptation of GANs, is engineered for domain translation tasks (Zhu et al., 2017). This means it can transform data from one domain into another while preserving essential features (Liu, et al., 2021). An illustrative example is image-to-image translation, where CycleGAN excels in converting images from one style or season to another. It has found applications in art, photography,

Table 2. Generative adversarial network (GAN) approaches for synthetic data generation

Approach	Description
Vanilla GAN	Basic GAN architecture comprising a generator and discriminator network trained in an adversarial manner.
Conditional GAN	Extending GANs to condition the generation process on additional input, enabling the generation of data conditioned on specific attributes or labels.
CycleGAN	Adapting GANs for domain translation tasks, allowing the generation of synthetic data from one domain that resembles another domain.
Progressive GAN	Progressive training of GANs, starting from low-resolution images and gradually increasing the complexity for high-quality image generation.
StyleGAN	Incorporating style-based synthesis to control the style and attributes of generated images, resulting in high-quality and diverse synthetic data.

and even medical imaging, allowing for remarkable transformations and adaptations (Almahairi et al., 2018; Li et al., 2021; Sandfort et al, 2019).

Progressive GANs are renowned for their ability to generate high-resolution images (Karras et al., 2017). These models deploy a unique training strategy that commences with low-resolution images and gradually amplifies the complexity and resolution of the generated images (Baur et al., 2018; Wu et al., 2022, Zhang et al, 2021). This approach is particularly invaluable in tasks like generating highly detailed images, photorealistic computer-generated imagery (CGI), and realistic video frames (Jeha et al, 2021).

StyleGAN represents a cutting-edge advancement in GAN technology (Karras et al., 2019, Farooq et al., 2023). This flavor of GANs incorporates style-based synthesis, granting fine-grained control over the style and attributes of the generated images. Whether it's generating portraits with specific attributes like age, gender, or hairstyle, or creating diverse and high-quality synthetic data for art and entertainment, StyleGAN has opened up exciting new possibilities in the world of synthetic data generation (Achicanoy et al., 2021).

Simulation-Based Techniques

Simulation-based techniques offer yet another perspective on synthetic data generation. These techniques are rooted in the art of simulating underlying processes or systems that give rise to the observed data. Here, we explore the techniques that fall under this category and provide context through real-world examples.

Agent-Based Modeling delves into simulating the behavior and interactions of autonomous agents to generate synthetic data that represents complex systems. In epidemiology, agent-based models come to life by simulating the spread of infectious diseases within a population (Lombardo et al., 2022). Each individual is modeled as an autonomous agent with specific behaviors, and their interactions lead to realistic disease transmission scenarios, aiding in public health preparedness.

Monte Carlo Simulation is a versatile technique that utilizes random sampling and statistical methods to simulate the behavior of complex systems, subsequently generating synthetic data (Miok et al., 2019; Geier A., 2012). In the realm of finance, Monte Carlo simulations are widely employed to model stock price movements, aiding investors in risk management and financial decision-making.

Discrete Event Simulation takes center stage in modeling discrete events and the flow of entities through a system. In logistics, for example, discrete event simulations help model the movement of

Table 3. Evaluation metrics for similarity and distributional properties

Metric	Description	Sources
Mean and Covariance	Comparing the means and covariances of real and synthetic data to assess the similarity in the first and second moments of the data.	Heine et al, 2023; Fox et al., 2009
Kolmogorov-Smirnov Test	Evaluating the maximum difference between the cumulative distribution functions of real and synthetic data, measuring distributional similarity.	Dankar et al., 2022; Heine et al., 2023; Hittmeier et al., 2019
Jensen-Shannon Divergence	Quantifying the difference between the probability distributions of real and synthetic data, providing a measure of overall distributional similarity.	Nguyen & Vreeken, 2015; Englesson & Azizpour, 2021
Maximum Mean Discrepancy	Computing the difference between the means of real and synthetic data using kernel-based methods, capturing both global and local distributional discrepancies.	Sankaranarayanan, 2018

goods through a supply chain, optimizing operations and minimizing inefficiencies (Chan et al., 2022; Montevechi et al., 2022).

System Dynamics, a more comprehensive technique, delves into modeling the feedback loops and interdependencies within a system (Baressi et al., 2022). In environmental science, these models simulate the intricate interactions between climate, ecosystems, and human activities, offering insights into the impact of environmental policies on a macro scale.

The following section focuses on measures used to assess the quality and utility of synthetic data in comparison to real-world data. We provide insights into the evaluation metrics and benchmarks commonly used to evaluate synthetic data, facilitating comparisons and benchmarking of different synthetic data generation techniques.

EVALUATION METRICS AND BENCHMARKS FOR SYNTHETIC DATA

Evaluating the quality and utility of synthetic data is crucial to ensure its effectiveness in various research and application domains. This section focuses on evaluation metrics and benchmarks commonly used to assess the performance and fidelity of synthetic data compared to real-world data. These metrics provide insights into the similarity, representativeness, and usefulness of synthetic data instances. Furthermore, they facilitate the comparison and benchmarking of different synthetic data generation techniques.

Metrics for Similarity and Distributional Properties

To evaluate the similarity between synthetic and real data, various metrics can be employed (Alaa et al., 2022). These metrics measure the resemblance of statistical properties, distributional characteristics, and higher-order dependencies. Table 1 provides an overview of commonly used metrics for assessing similarity and distributional properties.

Graphical representations, such as histograms, kernel density estimates, or scatter plots, can also be used to visually compare the distributions of real and synthetic data. These visualizations help identify any deviations in the data patterns and provide a qualitative assessment of distributional similarity.

Table 4. Evaluation metrics for model performance and generalization

Metric	Description	Sources
Accuracy	Measuring the classification accuracy of models trained on synthetic data, comparing it to the accuracy on real data	Wang & Zhang, 2018
F1 Score	Evaluating the trade-off between precision and recall for classification tasks, considering both false positives and negatives	Dankar et al., 2022; Alharbi et al., 2020
Mean Squared Error	Assessing the regression performance of models trained on synthetic data by measuring the average squared difference between predicted and actual values	El Emam et al., 2022.
Receiver Operating Characteristic (ROC) Curve	Plotting the true positive rate against the false positive rate to evaluate the performance of binary classifiers trained on synthetic data	Alaa et al., 2022
Precision-Recall Curve	Visualizing the trade-off between precision and recall for different classification thresholds, providing insights into the model's performance on synthetic data	El Emam et al., 2022.

Example: In a financial domain, synthetic financial data can be generated using GANs or statistical modeling techniques. To evaluate the similarity between the synthetic and real financial data, the mean and covariance matrices of key financial variables, such as stock prices or trading volumes, can be compared, the Kolmogorov-Smirnov test can be applied to assess the overall distributional similarity of the financial data.

Metrics for Model Performance and Generalization

Synthetic data should not only mimic the statistical properties of real data but also enable effective model training and generalization. Metrics for assessing the performance and generalization capability of models trained on synthetic data play a vital role in evaluating the usefulness of synthetic data. Table 4 provides an overview of commonly used metrics for evaluating model performance and generalization.

Example: In the healthcare domain, synthetic medical records can be generated to train and evaluate predictive models for disease diagnosis. To assess the performance of the models trained on synthetic data, metrics such as accuracy, F1 score, and receiver operating characteristic (ROC) curves can be employed. These metrics measure the model's ability to correctly classify diseases and identify potential false positives or negatives.

Benchmarks and Comparative Studies

Benchmarks and comparative studies are crucial for assessing the effectiveness of different synthetic data generation techniques (Steinbuss & Bohm, 2021; Pereira & Marcel, 2021). These benchmarks provide standardized datasets, evaluation metrics, and performance baselines, enabling fair comparisons and advancements in the field. Comparative studies often involve multiple synthetic data generation methods applied to the same dataset, with evaluations conducted using various metrics. The results allow researchers to identify strengths, weaknesses, and trade-offs associated with different techniques.

Example: In the field of computer vision, benchmarks like MNIST, CIFAR-10, and ImageNet are commonly used for evaluating the performance of synthetic data generation methods. Multiple synthetic data generation techniques, including GANs, statistical modeling, and simulation-based approaches, can be applied to these benchmarks. Evaluation metrics such as accuracy, mean squared error, or structural similarity index measure the quality of generated images and the performance of models trained on synthetic data.

In addition to quantitative metrics, qualitative evaluations by domain experts or end-users provide valuable insights into the usefulness and usability of synthetic data. User feedback, domain-specific evaluations, and real-world application performance can contribute to a comprehensive assessment of synthetic data quality.

In summary, evaluating synthetic data requires the application of various metrics, graphical comparisons, and benchmarks. These assessments provide quantitative and qualitative insights into the similarity, representativeness, and utility of synthetic data. Additionally, they enable comparative studies to identify the strengths and weaknesses of different synthetic data generation techniques.

INTEGRATION OF SYNTHETIC DATA IN DEA

The integration of synthetic data in Data Envelopment Analysis (DEA) offers a promising avenue to address data availability limitations and privacy concerns while still conducting efficiency analysis (Lychev A., 2023). Synthetic data refers to artificially generated data that closely resembles real-world data in terms of its statistical properties and characteristics. This section explores the concept and significance of integrating synthetic data with DEA, highlighting its potential advantages and applications. The concept of synthetic data involves generating artificial data that captures the essential features and patterns of real data. Synthetic data can be created using various techniques, such as statistical models, machine learning algorithms, or data synthesis methods. In the context of DEA, synthetic data serves as a substitute for real data when access is limited or restricted (Cordero et al., 2013). It allows researchers and analysts to perform efficiency analysis even in situations where actual data may not be readily available.

The integration of synthetic data in DEA offers several benefits and opens up new possibilities for analysis. Firstly, synthetic data provides a means to overcome data availability limitations, particularly in sensitive domains where access to real data is restricted due to privacy concerns or confidentiality requirements (Memari et al., 2014; Whittaker G., 2014). Secondly, synthetic data allows for the augmentation of existing data sets, enabling the exploration of larger and more diverse samples for efficiency analysis. Additionally, synthetic data offers the opportunity to conduct simulated experiments and sensitivity analyses, allowing for a better understanding of the robustness and generalizability of DEA results.

The applications of synthetic data in DEA are diverse and span across various industries and sectors (Kuosmanen et al., 2009). For instance, in healthcare, synthetic data can be used to evaluate the efficiency of healthcare providers when access to actual patient data is restricted (Anderson, 2019). In financial institutions, synthetic data can facilitate the assessment of performance and risk management in scenarios where access to sensitive financial data is limited. Synthetic data can also be employed in evaluating the efficiency of public services, analyzing supply chain operations, or conducting performance benchmarking across different organizations (Banker et al., 1989). The integration of synthetic data in DEA involves replacing or augmenting real data with synthetic data in the input-output matrix used for efficiency analysis. This can be achieved by incorporating the synthetic data into the standard DEA models, such as the CCR (Charnes-Cooper-Rhodes) or BCC (Banker-Charnes-Cooper) models. The synthetic data can be aligned with the same variables and dimensions as the real data, ensuring a comparable analysis.

However, it is crucial to consider the quality and validity of the synthetic data. Validation and verification processes must be implemented to ensure that the synthetic data accurately captures the characteristics and patterns of the real data. Adequate validation techniques, such as goodness-of-fit tests or comparison against known data samples, should be employed to assess the reliability and fidelity of the synthetic data (Wang & Zhang, 2018). Several examples and case studies demonstrate the successful integration of synthetic data in DEA (Fallahpour, et al., 2016). For instance, in healthcare, synthetic data has been used to evaluate the efficiency of hospitals or healthcare systems by generating synthetic patient records that maintain the statistical characteristics of real patient data (Mehrtak et al., 2014; Bowlin et al., 1984). Similarly, in the financial sector, synthetic data has enabled the analysis of efficiency and risk management in banking institutions by simulating realistic financial transaction data (Anderson, 2019).

In conclusion, the integration of synthetic data in DEA provides a valuable approach to address data availability limitations and privacy concerns. By generating artificial data that closely resembles real-world data, researchers and analysts can conduct efficiency analysis even when actual data is inaccessible. The integration of synthetic data offers benefits such as data augmentation, sensitivity analysis, and robustness testing. However, it is essential to validate the quality of synthetic data and ensure its fidelity to real data characteristics. The successful integration of synthetic data in DEA has numerous applications in various domains, allowing for the evaluation of efficiency and performance in scenarios where real data is scarce or sensitive.

APPLICATIONS AND USE CASES OF SYNTHETIC DATA

Synthetic data has found widespread applications across various domains, enabling researchers and practitioners to address data privacy concerns, overcome data scarcity issues, and enhance data-driven decision-making processes. This section highlights some key applications and use cases where synthetic data has been effectively employed.

Data Privacy and Security

In scenarios where sensitive or personally identifiable information (PII) is involved, synthetic data serves as a privacy-preserving solution (Bellovin, 2019. By generating synthetic data that retains the statistical properties and patterns of the original data while obfuscating sensitive information, organizations can share or release data for research, collaboration, or public use without compromising privacy. Synthetic data allows researchers and data scientists to develop and test algorithms, models, and methodologies without accessing the actual sensitive data, ensuring compliance with privacy regulations (Arnold & Neunhoeffer., 2020). _Example_: In the healthcare sector, synthetic medical records can be generated for research purposes while protecting patient privacy. Researchers can use synthetic data to analyze disease prevalence, develop predictive models, and evaluate treatment outcomes without accessing real patient records.

Machine Learning Model Training

real data is scarce or expensive to obtain. Synthetic data generation techniques enable the augmentation of existing datasets, creating larger and more diverse training sets. This process helps improve the model's generalization capabilities, robustness, and performance on unseen data. By incorporating synthetic data, models can learn from a broader range of scenarios and capture variations in the data distribution (Wang et al., 2019). *Example*: In autonomous vehicle development, synthetic data can be used to train computer vision models. Synthetic images and sensor data can simulate various driving scenarios, weather conditions, and rare events, providing a broader training dataset that improves the model's ability to handle real-world situations.

Anomaly Detection and Intrusion Detection Systems

Synthetic data is valuable for developing and evaluating anomaly detection and intrusion detection systems. By generating synthetic data that encompasses normal system behavior and known attack patterns, researchers can create comprehensive datasets for training and testing robust security systems. Synthetic data aids in identifying and mitigating potential vulnerabilities by mimicking real-world data anomalies and cyber threats (Zhang et al., 2018). Example: In cybersecurity, synthetic network traffic data can be generated to simulate normal network behavior, as well as various types of cyberattacks. This synthetic data allows security analysts to develop and evaluate intrusion detection systems for effective threat detection and response (Chen et al, 2019).

Data Analysis and Exploration

Synthetic data serves as a valuable tool for data analysis, exploration, and algorithm development. Researchers and analysts can manipulate synthetic data without the constraints and limitations of real data, enabling them to experiment with different scenarios, test hypotheses, and validate analytical methodologies. Synthetic data fosters innovation and accelerates research in data-driven fields (Drechsler et al, 2019). *Example*: In the field of social sciences, synthetic survey data can be generated to explore trends, conduct simulations, and test statistical models. Researchers can analyze the synthetic data to gain insights into societal patterns, formulate policy recommendations, and understand the impact of different variables on survey outcomes.

Use Cases of Synthetic Data

The utilization of synthetic data across various industries showcases its versatility and crucial role in advancing technology while addressing privacy and security concerns. Here's a detailed look into how synthetic data is being applied in different sectors:

Healthcare

In the healthcare sector, synthetic data is revolutionizing research and development. It plays a pivotal role in enabling the analysis of health trends and the development of treatment strategies while ensuring patient confidentiality is maintained. This is particularly vital given the sensitive nature of medical data. Synthetic datasets mimic the statistical properties of real patient data, allowing researchers to conduct extensive studies without risking privacy breaches. Such applications are crucial in areas like disease detection, drug development, and personalized medicine. The use of synthetic data in healthcare is well-documented by sources like Statice (2022), highlighting its growing importance in the medical field.

Automotive Industry

The automotive industry, especially in the realm of autonomous vehicles, significantly benefits from synthetic data. Companies like Waymo and Tesla leverage synthetic data to train and test the algorithms that drive autonomous vehicles. This training involves creating virtual environments that simulate a wide range of driving conditions, traffic scenarios, and pedestrian interactions, which would be impractical or too risky to replicate in real life. By using synthetic data, these companies can safely and efficiently develop and improve autonomous driving systems. The work of Dosovitskiy et al. (2017) illustrates the profound impact of synthetic data on the development of autonomous driving technology.

Finance

In the financial sector, synthetic data is instrumental in risk modeling and fraud detection. Financial institutions are increasingly relying on synthetic transaction data to train machine learning models for identifying fraudulent activities and assessing credit risk. This approach enhances the security of financial systems without compromising the privacy of customer data. The use of synthetic data allows for the simulation of various financial scenarios and consumer behaviors, leading to more robust and reliable financial models. The research by Huang et al. (2020) provides insights into the extensive applications of synthetic data in finance, from market simulations to credit risk assessment.

Biometric Security

In the field of biometric security, the work of Edlira Martiri on biometric honey templates stands out as a prime example of synthetic data application. Martiri's research focuses on enhancing the security of biometric systems through the generation of synthetic biometric templates, known as honey templates. These templates serve as decoys to protect genuine biometric data from unauthorized access and potential data breaches. By integrating these honey templates into biometric systems, the security and integrity of biometric authentication processes are significantly improved. Martiri et al.'s (2020) research highlights the innovative use of synthetic data in safeguarding biometric information.

The applications of synthetic data in these diverse fields demonstrate its critical role not only in technological advancement but also in addressing key issues like privacy, security, and ethical considerations in data usage.

LIMITATIONS AND CHALLENGES OF SYNTHETIC DATA

While synthetic data offers several advantages, it is important to acknowledge its limitations and challenges. Understanding these limitations helps researchers and practitioners make informed decisions regarding the appropriate use and interpretation of synthetic data.

Representativeness and Bias

One of the main challenges in synthetic data generation is achieving representativeness. Synthetic data may not fully capture the complexities and nuances present in real-world data, leading to potential biases or distortions. It is essential to ensure that the synthetic data generation process accurately represents the underlying population and preserves the statistical properties of interest (Bhanot et al., 2021; Bhanot 2023). Example: When generating synthetic demographic data, special attention must be paid to ensure that the synthesized data accurately reflects the distribution of attributes such as age, gender, ethnicity, and income in the target population. Failure to do so may introduce biases that affect downstream analyses or applications.

Generalization to Unseen Data

Another challenge is the generalization of models trained on synthetic data to real-world, unseen data. While models perform well on synthetic data, their performance may not directly translate to real data due to discrepancies between the synthetic and real distributions. It is crucial to evaluate the model's performance on real data to assess its effectiveness in practical applications (Beery et al., 2020). Example: In natural language processing, models trained on synthetic text data may struggle to generalize to real-world text data due to differences in writing styles, grammatical structures, and contextual nuances. Evaluating the model's performance on real text data is essential to ensure its practical utility.

Uncertainty and Confidence Estimation

Synthetic data generation introduces uncertainties, particularly when extrapolating beyond the range of observed data. It is important to quantify and understand the uncertainties associated with synthetic data and incorporate appropriate confidence estimation techniques to avoid misleading conclusions or decision-making based on synthetic data alone (Martiri & Yang, 2020). Example: In climate modeling, synthetic climate data can be generated to simulate future climate scenarios. However, it is crucial to acknowledge the uncertainties associated with synthetic data when making predictions about extreme weather events or long-term climate patterns.

ETHICAL CONSIDERATIONS AND RESPONSIBLE USE OF SYNTHETIC DATA

The utilization of synthetic data introduces a range of ethical considerations that necessitate responsible practices to ensure its appropriate and fair use. Researchers and practitioners must address these ethical concerns to maintain the integrity and societal impact of their work. Key ethical considerations related to synthetic data encompass data privacy, informed consent, transparency, and potential biases introduced during the data generation process. It is of paramount importance to establish ethical guidelines and frameworks that govern the responsible use of synthetic data (Jordon et al., 2022). *Example*: In the realm of healthcare, when generating synthetic patient data for research purposes, it is imperative to adhere to strict ethical standards to safeguard patient privacy and confidentiality. Respecting the principles of informed consent and ensuring data anonymization are crucial elements in maintaining the privacy rights of patients. Additionally, transparency in the synthetic data generation process, including disclosure of the techniques used and limitations of the generated data, helps build trust and allows stakeholders to make informed decisions.

Furthermore, potential biases embedded within synthetic data generation techniques should be vigilantly addressed. Biases may arise due to the use of biased training data or inherent limitations in the modeling algorithms employed. It is imperative to thoroughly evaluate and mitigate biases to prevent perpetuating unfair or discriminatory practices. Careful attention should be given to balancing representativeness and fairness, ensuring that the synthetic data accurately reflects the diversity and characteristics of the real-world population it aims to represent (Azizi et al., 2021).

FUTURE DIRECTIONS AND RESEARCH CHALLENGES

The field of synthetic data is constantly evolving, and there are numerous avenues for future research and development to enhance its utility and effectiveness. Several key research challenges and directions can be identified, shaping the future of synthetic data generation and utilization.

Advanced Data Generation Techniques

Advancements in data generation techniques are pivotal in improving the quality, diversity, and realism of synthetic data instances. Research should focus on developing novel approaches that leverage hybrid models combining statistical modeling and deep learning techniques. These hybrid models have the potential to capture intricate dependencies and complexities within the data, leading to more accurate and representative synthetic data.

Explainability and Interpretability

Enhancing the explainability and interpretability of synthetic data is crucial to foster trust and facilitate its adoption in decision-making processes. Research efforts should be directed towards developing methods and techniques that provide explanations and justifications for the data generation process. These explanations help users understand and validate the synthetic data instances, ensuring transparency and enabling effective utilization.

Privacy-Preserving Synthetic Data Generation

Further research is essential to address privacy concerns associated with synthetic data generation. The development of privacy-preserving techniques that guarantee the protection of sensitive information while maintaining data utility is a critical area of exploration. Striking the right balance between data privacy and data utility is crucial to ensure the responsible and ethical use of synthetic data in sensitive domains.

Robust Evaluation Metrics and Benchmarks

Continued efforts should be made to develop robust evaluation metrics and benchmarks for synthetic data. These metrics need to capture the intricacies and nuances of various domains, accounting for application-specific requirements and challenges. Establishing standardized evaluation frameworks enables fair comparisons and benchmarking of different synthetic data generation techniques, fostering the advancement of the field.

Fairness and Bias Mitigation

Research endeavors should be dedicated to addressing fairness concerns and mitigating biases in synthetic data generation. Developing methodologies and techniques that actively identify and rectify biases, as well as ensuring fair representation across various demographic groups, is crucial. Striving for fairness and equity in synthetic data is essential for promoting just and unbiased decision-making processes.

In conclusion, the responsible use of synthetic data necessitates addressing ethical considerations and embracing responsible practices. Future research should focus on advancing data generation techniques, enhancing explainability, addressing privacy concerns, and establishing robust evaluation frameworks to maximize the potential of synthetic data in research and applications.

REFERENCES

Achicanoy, H., Chaves, D., & Trujillo, M. (2021). StyleGANs and Transfer Learning for Generating Synthetic Images in Industrial Applications. *Symmetry*, *13*(8), 1497. doi:10.3390ym13081497

Alaa, A., Van Breugel, B., Saveliev, E. S., & van der Schaar, M. (2022, June). How faithful is your synthetic data? sample-level metrics for evaluating and auditing generative models. In *International Conference on Machine Learning* (pp. 290-306). PMLR.

Alhaija, A. H., Mustikovela, S. K., Mescheder, L., Geiger, A., & Rother, C. (2018). Augmented reality meets computer vision: Efficient data generation for urban driving scenes. *International Journal of Computer Vision*, *126*(9), 961–972. doi:10.100711263-018-1070-x

Alharbi, F., Ouarbya, L., & Ward, J. A. (2020, July). Synthetic sensor data for human activity recognition. In *2020 International Joint Conference on Neural Networks (IJCNN)* (pp. 1-9). IEEE. 10.1109/IJCNN48605.2020.9206624

Almahairi, A., Rajeshwar, S., Sordoni, A., Bachman, P., & Courville, A. (2018, July). Augmented cyclegan: Learning many-to-many mappings from unpaired data. In *International conference on machine learning* (pp. 195-204). PMLR.

Anderson, D. S. (2019). Improving data utility with synthetic data: Case studies in finance and healthcare. *Data & Knowledge Engineering*, *23*(5), 67–79.

Arnold, C., & Neunhoeffer, M. (2020). *Really Useful Synthetic Data—A Framework to Evaluate the Quality of Differentially Private Synthetic Data*. arXiv preprint arXiv:2004.07740.

Assefa, S. A., Dervovic, D., Mahfouz, M., Tillman, R. E., Reddy, P., & Veloso, M. (2020, October). Generating synthetic data in finance: opportunities, challenges and pitfalls. In *Proceedings of the First ACM International Conference on AI in Finance* (pp. 1-8). 10.1145/3383455.3422554

Azizi, Z., Zheng, C., Mosquera, L., Pilote, L., & El Emam, K. (2021). Can synthetic data be a proxy for real clinical trial data? A validation study. *BMJ Open*, *11*(4), e043497. doi:10.1136/bmjopen-2020-043497 PMID:33863713

Banker, R. D., Charnes, A., Cooper, W. W., Swarts, J., & Thomas, D. (1989). An introduction to data envelopment analysis with some of its models and their uses. *Research in Governmental and Nonprofit Accounting, 5*(1), 125-163.

Bansal, M. A., Sharma, D. R., & Kathuria, D. M. (2022). A systematic review on data scarcity problem in deep learning: Solution and applications. *ACM Computing Surveys, 54*(10s), 1–29. doi:10.1145/3502287

Baressi Šegota, S., Anđelić, N., Šercer, M., & Meštrić, H. (2022). Dynamics Modeling of Industrial Robotic Manipulators: A Machine Learning Approach Based on Synthetic Data. *Mathematics, 10*(7), 1174. doi:10.3390/math10071174

Barth, R., IJsselmuiden, J., Hemming, J., & Van Henten, E. J. (2019). Synthetic bootstrapping of convolutional neural networks for semantic plant part segmentation. *Computers and Electronics in Agriculture, 161*, 291–304. doi:10.1016/j.compag.2017.11.040

Baur, C., Albarqouni, S., & Navab, N. (2018). Generating highly realistic images of skin lesions with GANs. *OR 2.0 Context-Aware Operating Theaters, Computer Assisted Robotic Endoscopy, Clinical Image-Based Procedures, and Skin Image Analysis: First International Workshop, OR 2.0 2018, 5th International Workshop, CARE 2018, 7th International Workshop, CLIP 2018, Third International Workshop, ISIC 2018, Held in Conjunction with MICCAI 2018, Granada, Spain, September 16 and 20, 2018 Proceedings, 5*, 260–267.

Beery, S., Liu, Y., Morris, D., Piavis, J., Kapoor, A., Joshi, N., ... Perona, P. (2020). Synthetic examples improve generalization for rare classes. In *Proceedings of the IEEE/CVF Winter Conference on Applications of Computer Vision* (pp. 863-873). 10.1109/WACV45572.2020.9093570

Bellovin, S. M., Dutta, P. K., & Reitinger, N. (2019). Privacy and synthetic datasets. *Stan. Tech. L. Rev., 22*, 1.

Bergen, K. J., Johnson, P. A., de Hoop, M. V., & Beroza, G. C. (2019). Machine learning for data-driven discovery in solid Earth geoscience. *Science, 363*(6433), eaau0323. doi:10.1126cience.aau0323 PMID:30898903

Bhanot, K. (2023). *Synthetic Data Generation and Evaluation for Fairness* [Doctoral dissertation]. Rensselaer Polytechnic Institute.

Bhanot, K., Qi, M., Erickson, J. S., Guyon, I., & Bennett, K. P. (2021). The problem of fairness in synthetic healthcare data. *Entropy (Basel, Switzerland), 23*(9), 1165. doi:10.3390/e23091165 PMID:34573790

Bolón-Canedo, V., Sánchez-Maroño, N., & Alonso-Betanzos, A. (2013). A review of feature selection methods on synthetic data. *Knowledge and Information Systems, 34*(3), 483–519. doi:10.100710115-012-0487-8

Bonabeau, E. (2002). Agent-based modeling: Methods and techniques for simulating human systems. *Proceedings of the National Academy of Sciences of the United States of America, 99*(suppl 3), 7280–7287. doi:10.1073/pnas.082080899 PMID:12011407

Bonnéry, D., Feng, Y., Henneberger, A. K., Johnson, T. L., Lachowicz, M., Rose, B. A., Shaw, T., Stapleton, L. M., Woolley, M. E., & Zheng, Y. (2019). The promise and limitations of synthetic data as a strategy to expand access to state-level multi-agency longitudinal data. *Journal of Research on Educational Effectiveness*, *12*(4), 616–647. doi:10.1080/19345747.2019.1631421

Bowlin, W. F., Charnes, A., Cooper, W. W., & Sherman, H. D. (1984). Data envelopment analysis and regression approaches to efficiency estimation and evaluation. *Annals of Operations Research*, *2*(1), 113–138. doi:10.1007/BF01874735

Chan, K. C., Rabaev, M., & Pratama, H. (2022). Generation of synthetic manufacturing datasets for machine learning using discrete-event simulation. *Production & Manufacturing Research, 10*(1), 337-353.10.1080/21693277.2022.2086642

Chen, Z., Zhang, Y., & Kim, H. (2019). Synthetic data generation with confidence estimation. *Journal of Artificial Intelligence Research*, *27*(4), 23–37.

Cordero, J. M., Santín, D., & Sicilia, G. (2013). *Dealing with the endogeneity problem in data envelopment analysis*. Academic Press.

Dankar, F. K., Ibrahim, M. K., & Ismail, L. (2022). A multi-dimensional evaluation of synthetic data generators. *IEEE Access : Practical Innovations, Open Solutions*, *10*, 11147–11158. doi:10.1109/ACCESS.2022.3144765

Dosovitskiy, A. (2017). CARLA: An open urban driving simulator. *Proceedings of the 1st Annual Conference on Robot Learning*.

Drechsler, J., Rieke, N., & Mathiak, K. (2019). *Synthetic data generation for medical imaging*. arXiv preprint arXiv:1912.03408.

El Emam, K., Mosquera, L., Fang, X., & El-Hussuna, A. (2022). Utility metrics for evaluating synthetic health data generation methods: Validation study. *JMIR Medical Informatics*, *10*(4), e35734. doi:10.2196/35734 PMID:35389366

Englesson, E., & Azizpour, H. (2021). Generalized jensen-shannon divergence loss for learning with noisy labels. *Advances in Neural Information Processing Systems*, *34*, 30284–30297.

Fallahpour, A., Olugu, E. U., Musa, S. N., Khezrimotlagh, D., & Wong, K. Y. (2016). An integrated model for green supplier selection under fuzzy environment: Application of data envelopment analysis and genetic programming approach. *Neural Computing & Applications*, *27*(3), 707–725. doi:10.100700521-015-1890-3

Farooq, M. A., Yao, W., Costache, G., & Corcoran, P. (2023). ChildGAN: Large Scale Synthetic Child Facial Data Using Domain Adaptation in StyleGAN. *IEEE Access : Practical Innovations, Open Solutions*, *11*, 108775–108791. doi:10.1109/ACCESS.2023.3321149

Figueira, A., & Vaz, B. (2022). Survey on synthetic data generation, evaluation methods and GANs. *Mathematics*, *10*(15), 2733. doi:10.3390/math10152733

Fox, A., Williams, M., Richardson, A. D., Cameron, D., Gove, J. H., Quaife, T., Ricciuto, D., Reichstein, M., Tomelleri, E., Trudinger, C. M., & Van Wijk, M. T. (2009). The REFLEX project: Comparing different algorithms and implementations for the inversion of a terrestrial ecosystem model against eddy covariance data. *Agricultural and Forest Meteorology, 149*(10), 1597–1615. doi:10.1016/j.agrformet.2009.05.002

Geier, A. (2012). Application of the Swiss fiscal rule to artificial data a Monte Carlo simulation. *Swiss Journal of Economics and Statistics, 148*(1), 37–55. doi:10.1007/BF03399359

Goodfellow, I., Pouget-Abadie, J., Mirza, M., Xu, B., Warde-Farley, D., Ozair, S., . . . Bengio, Y. (2014). Generative adversarial nets. In Advances in neural information processing systems (pp. 2672-2680). Academic Press.

Goodfellow, I. J. (2014). Generative adversarial nets. *Advances in Neural Information Processing Systems, 2672–2680.

Heine, J., Fowler, E. E., Berglund, A., Schell, M. J., & Eschrich, S. (2023). Techniques to produce and evaluate realistic multivariate synthetic data. *Scientific Reports, 13*(1), 12266. doi:10.103841598-023-38832-0 PMID:37507387

Hernandez, M., Epelde, G., Alberdi, A., Cilla, R., & Rankin, D. (2022). Synthetic data generation for tabular health records: A systematic review. *Neurocomputing, 493*, 28–45. doi:10.1016/j.neucom.2022.04.053

Hittmeir, M., Ekelhart, A., & Mayer, R. (2019, August). On the utility of synthetic data: An empirical evaluation on machine learning tasks. In *Proceedings of the 14th International Conference on Availability, Reliability and Security* (pp. 1-6). 10.1145/3339252.3339281

Huang, Z. (2020). Deep learning in finance and banking: A survey. *Artificial Intelligence Review, 53*, 2535–2558.

Jain, S., Seth, G., Paruthi, A., Soni, U., & Kumar, G. (2022). Synthetic data augmentation for surface defect detection and classification using deep learning. *Journal of Intelligent Manufacturing, 33*(4), 1–14. doi:10.100710845-020-01710-x

Jaipuria, N., Zhang, X., Bhasin, R., Arafa, M., Chakravarty, P., Shrivastava, S., ... Murali, V. N. (2020). Deflating dataset bias using synthetic data augmentation. In *Proceedings of the IEEE/CVF Conference on Computer Vision and Pattern Recognition Workshops* (pp. 772-773). 10.1109/CVPRW50498.2020.00394

Jeha, P., Bohlke-Schneider, M., Mercado, P., Kapoor, S., Nirwan, R. S., Flunkert, V., ... Januschowski, T. (2021, October). PSA-GAN: Progressive self attention GANs for synthetic time series. *International Conference on Learning Representations*.

Jordon, J., Szpruch, L., Houssiau, F., Bottarelli, M., Cherubin, G., Maple, C., . . . Weller, A. (2022). *Synthetic Data—what, why and how?* arXiv preprint arXiv:2205.03257.

Karras, T., Aila, T., Laine, S., & Lehtinen, J. (2017). *Progressive growing of GANs for improved quality, stability, and variation.* arXiv preprint arXiv:1710.10196.

Karras, T., Laine, S., & Aila, T. (2019). A style-based generator architecture for generative adversarial networks. In *Proceedings of the IEEE/CVF Conference on Computer Vision and Pattern Recognition* (pp. 4401-4410). 10.1109/CVPR.2019.00453

Kingma, D. P., & Welling, M. (2014). *Auto-Encoding Variational Bayes*. arXiv preprint arXiv:1312.6114.

Kuosmanen, T., Bijsterbosch, N., & Dellink, R. (2009). Environmental cost–benefit analysis of alternative timing strategies in greenhouse gas abatement: A data envelopment analysis approach. *Ecological Economics*, *68*(6), 1633–1642. doi:10.1016/j.ecolecon.2008.07.012

Le, T. A., Baydin, A. G., Zinkov, R., & Wood, F. (2017, May). Using synthetic data to train neural networks is model-based reasoning. In *2017 international joint conference on neural networks (IJCNN)* (pp. 3514-3521). IEEE.

Li, W., & Wang, J. (2021). Residual learning of cycle-GAN for seismic data denoising. *IEEE Access : Practical Innovations, Open Solutions*, *9*, 11585–11597. doi:10.1109/ACCESS.2021.3049479

Liu, J. (2023). *A Synthetic Data-driven Solution for Urban Drinking Water Source Management* [Master's thesis]. NTNU.

Liu, W., Luo, B., & Liu, J. (2021). Synthetic data augmentation using multiscale attention CycleGAN for aircraft detection in remote sensing images. *IEEE Geoscience and Remote Sensing Letters*, *19*, 1–5.

Lombardo, G., Pellegrino, M., & Poggi, A. (2022). Unsupervised Continual Learning From Synthetic Data Generated with Agent-Based Modeling and Simulation: A preliminary experimentation. *CEUR Workshop Proceedings*, *3261*, 1–11.

Lychev, A. V. (2023). Synthetic Data Generation for Data Envelopment Analysis. *Data*, *8*(10), 146. doi:10.3390/data8100146

Martiri, E. (2022). *Honey Templates: a Protection Mechanism for Biometric Systems*. Academic Press.

Martiri, E., & Yang, B. (2020, November). On the predictability of biometric honey templates, based on Bayesian inference. In *2020 the 10th International Conference on Communication and Network Security* (pp. 123-134). 10.1145/3442520.3442532

Mehrtak, M., Yusefzadeh, H., & Jaafaripooyan, E. (2014). Pabon Lasso and Data Envelopment Analysis: A complementary approach to hospital performance measurement. *Global Journal of Health Science*, *6*(4), 107. doi:10.5539/gjhs.v6n4p107 PMID:24999147

Memari, F., Momeni, M., & Ghasemi, A. R. (2014). Synthetic application of data envelopment analysis and balanced scorecard for systems performance Evaluation: A Review In. *International Research Journal of Applied and Basic Sciences*, *8*(10), 1525–1530.

Meyer, D., Nagler, T., & Hogan, R. J. (2021). Copula-based synthetic data augmentation for machine-learning emulators. *Geoscientific Model Development*, *14*(8), 5205–5215. doi:10.5194/gmd-14-5205-2021

Miok, K., Nguyen-Doan, D., Zaharie, D., & Robnik-Šikonja, M. (2019, September). Generating data using Monte Carlo dropout. In *2019 IEEE 15th International Conference on Intelligent Computer Communication and Processing (ICCP)* (pp. 509-515). IEEE. 10.1109/ICCP48234.2019.8959787

Mirza, B., Haroon, D., Khan, B., Padhani, A., & Syed, T. Q. (2021). Deep generative models to counter class imbalance: A model-metric mapping with proportion calibration methodology. *IEEE Access : Practical Innovations, Open Solutions*, *9*, 55879–55897. doi:10.1109/ACCESS.2021.3071389

Monroe, J., Moore, J., & Allen, G. (2018). Synthetic Data for Text. In *Proceedings of the 56th Annual Meeting of the Association for Computational Linguistics (*Volume 1*: Long Papers)* (pp. 501-511). Academic Press.

Nguyen, H. V., & Vreeken, J. (2015). Non-parametric jensen-shannon divergence. *Machine Learning and Knowledge Discovery in Databases: European Conference, ECML PKDD 2015, Porto, Portugal, September 7-11, 2015 Proceedings*, *15*(Part II), 173–189.

Rubin, D. B. (1993). Statistical Disclosure Limitation. *Journal of Official Statistics*, *9*(2), 461–468.

Sandfort, V., Yan, K., Pickhardt, P. J., & Summers, R. M. (2019). Data augmentation using generative adversarial networks (CycleGAN) to improve generalizability in CT segmentation tasks. *Scientific Reports*, *9*(1), 16884. doi:10.103841598-019-52737-x PMID:31729403

Sankaranarayanan, S., Balaji, Y., Jain, A., Lim, S. N., & Chellappa, R. (2018). Learning from synthetic data: Addressing domain shift for semantic segmentation. In *Proceedings of the IEEE conference on computer vision and pattern recognition* (pp. 3752-3761). 10.1109/CVPR.2018.00395

Snoke, J., Raab, G. M., Nowok, B., Dibben, C., & Slavkovic, A. (2018). General and specific utility measures for synthetic data. *Journal of the Royal Statistical Society. Series A, (Statistics in Society)*, *181*(3), 663–688. doi:10.1111/rssa.12358

Statice. (2022). *Types of synthetic data and 4 real-life examples*. Retrieved from https://www.statice.ai

Steinbuss, G., & Böhm, K. (2021). Benchmarking unsupervised outlier detection with realistic synthetic data. *ACM Transactions on Knowledge Discovery from Data (TKDD)*, *15*(4), 1-20. 10.1145/3441453

Tanaka, F. H. K. D. S., & Aranha, C. (2019). *Data augmentation using GANs*. arXiv preprint arXiv:1904.09135.

Torfi, A., Fox, E. A., & Reddy, C. K. (2022). Differentially private synthetic medical data generation using convolutional GANs. *Information Sciences*, *586*, 485–500. doi:10.1016/j.ins.2021.12.018

Tyxhari, G., & Martiri, E. (2022). A systematic review of synthetic data generation methods. *Circular Economy*, 457.

Wang, Q., & Zhang, Y. (2018). Synthetic data in data envelopment analysis for supply chain efficiency evaluation. *International Journal of Production Economics*, *135*(2), 265–276.

WhittakerG. (2014). Creation of Synthetic Microdata for Data Envelopment Analysis Using Nondominated Sorting. SSRN 2499012. doi:10.2139/ssrn.2499012

Wood, E., Baltrušaitis, T., Hewitt, C., Dziadzio, S., Cashman, T. J., & Shotton, J. (2021). Fake it till you make it: face analysis in the wild using synthetic data alone. In *Proceedings of the IEEE/CVF international conference on computer vision* (pp. 3681-3691). 10.1109/ICCV48922.2021.00366

Wu, S., Tang, H., Jing, X. Y., Qian, J., Sebe, N., Yan, Y., & Zhang, Q. (2022). Cross-view panorama image synthesis with progressive attention GANs. *Pattern Recognition*, *131*, 108884. doi:10.1016/j.patcog.2022.108884

Xu, L. (2020). *Synthesizing tabular data using conditional GAN* [Doctoral dissertation]. Massachusetts Institute of Technology.

Xu, L., Skoularidou, M., Cuesta-Infante, A., & Veeramachaneni, K. (2019). Modeling tabular data using conditional gan. *Advances in Neural Information Processing Systems*, 32.

Zhai, G., Narazaki, Y., Wang, S., Shajihan, S. A. V., & Spencer, B. F. Jr. (2022). Synthetic data augmentation for pixel-wise steel fatigue crack identification using fully convolutional networks. *Smart Structures and Systems*, 29(1), 237–250.

Zhang, H., Grimmer, M., Ramachandra, R., Raja, K., & Busch, C. (2021, May). On the applicability of synthetic data for face recognition. In *2021 IEEE International Workshop on Biometrics and Forensics (IWBF)* (pp. 1-6). IEEE. 10.1109/IWBF50991.2021.9465085

Zhu, J. Y., Park, T., Isola, P., & Efros, A. A. (2017). Unpaired image-to-image translation using cycle-consistent adversarial networks. In *Proceedings of the IEEE international conference on computer vision (ICCV)* (pp. 2223-2232). 10.1109/ICCV.2017.244

ADDITIONAL READING

Asghari, S., & Ioannidis, S. (2016). A Bayesian framework for synthetic data generation. In *International Conference on Database Systems for Advanced Applications* (pp. 371-388). Springer.

Böhm, K., Kailing, K., & Kürschner, M. (2018). Synthesizing realistic test data for performance evaluation. *ACM Transactions on Software Engineering and Methodology*, 27(1), 1–37.

Ganju, J., Milanova, A., Saparova, D., & Zhao, J. L. (2016). Data masking techniques for numerical data: A review. *IEEE Access : Practical Innovations, Open Solutions*, 4, 3602–3626.

Kifer, D., Lin, B., & Papadimitriou, S. (1992). Anonymity and information hiding in multiagent systems. In *Proceedings of the Eleventh ACM SIGACT-SIGMOD-SIGART Symposium on Principles of Database Systems* (pp. 213-223).

Li, N., Li, T., & Venkatasubramanian, S. (2007). t-closeness: Privacy beyond k-anonymity and l-diversity. In Data Engineering, 2007. ICDE 2007. IEEE 23rd International Conference on (pp. 106-115). IEEE.

Papenbrock, T., & Pinkwart, N. (2014). Generating synthetic data for improving learning analytics applications. In *European Conference on Technology Enhanced Learning* (pp. 391-404). Springer.

Schnell, R., Bachteler, T., & Reiher, J. (2009). Privacy-preserving record linkage using Bloom filters. *BMC Medical Informatics and Decision Making*, 9(1), 41. doi:10.1186/1472-6947-9-41 PMID:19706187

Ture, F., & Yilmazel, O. (2013). Towards a secure and scalable data anonymization. *Journal of Network and Computer Applications*, 36(3), 996–1013.

KEY TERMS AND DEFINITIONS

Evaluation Metrics and Benchmarks: Quantifiable standards used to assess the performance and quality of synthetic data. Benchmarks are standardized datasets that enable comparisons between different synthetic data generation methods.

Explainability: The degree to which synthetic data generation processes and models can be understood and justified, fostering trust and transparency in their use.

Generalization: The ability of models or algorithms trained on one dataset (synthetic data) to perform well on unseen data, reflecting the model's capacity to apply knowledge learned from the training data to new, real-world scenarios.

Privacy-Preserving Techniques: Methods and strategies used to protect sensitive information in datasets, allowing data sharing and analysis without revealing personal or confidential details.

Representativeness: Indicates how well the synthetic data captures the complexities and nuances of the real-world data it aims to replicate, without introducing biases.

Synthetic Data: Artificially generated data that mimics the statistical properties of real-world data, typically used to protect privacy, overcome data limitations, or improve machine learning models.

Synthetic Data Bias: Systematic errors or inaccuracies in data, often resulting from biased sampling or other data generation methods, that can lead to unfair or misleading conclusions.

Chapter 6
Data Envelopment Analysis–Based Approach for Maximizing Energy Efficiency in Ad Hoc Networks

Muhammed Abiodun Adebimpe
American University of Nigeria, Nigeria

Adeyemi Abel Ajibesin
 https://orcid.org/0000-0001-6518-0231
American University of Nigeria, Nigeria

Franklin Tchakounté
 https://orcid.org/0000-0003-0723-2640
University of Ngaoundere, Cameroon

ABSTRACT

The growth of wireless technology due to global population growth and urbanization has increased internet usage, intensifying network energy demands. Researchers and professionals prioritize energy efficiency to cut costs and reduce emissions, with a focus on wireless networks. This chapter explores energy efficiency's importance, particularly in ad hoc wireless and sensor networks. This study seeks to maintain energy efficiency while maximizing resources like node numbers, using computational methods and data envelopment analysis (DEA) with multicast incremental power (MIP) and coded packet algorithms as DEA inputs. An output-oriented DEA approach enhances network performance by increasing output while maintaining input resources. This research contributes significantly to understanding energy efficiency in wireless networks, providing valuable insights for network administrators and decision-makers, particularly in ad hoc wireless networks.

DOI: 10.4018/979-8-3693-0255-2.ch006

INTRODUCTION

Wireless networks have experienced numerous attention due to the high increase in wireless communication technologies. Globally, the exponential increase in population, high level of development in the urban areas has equally resulted in massive growth in internet usage. This progress has resulted in continuous spike in energy requirement for enterprise and individual network users globally. Researchers, network operators, administrators have been motivated to innovate, review policies and network designs, and evaluate performance of networks (Melki, 2020). Energy efficiency has been seen as a way to reduce energy consumption to meet the development of the increase in demand in wireless networks. Lange et al. (2020) posit that the increase of energy efficiency or economic growth could determine the overall dynamic of energy consumption in the Information and Communication Technology (ICT) sector. For over a decade of ICT emergence, there has been a noticeable increase in energy efficiency (Lange et al., 2020), the energy efficiency research currently is more focused towards wireless applications in the networks. Energy efficiency is hinged on two main factors such as reduction of frequent rise in operational cost and reduction of carbon emission in the network because they are driven by energy (Jahid et al., 2019). Research on energy efficiency is becoming a central focus of research due to the continuous growth in energy demand coupled with incessant surge in the energy price.

The communication sector in the urban areas is one of the most affected in this energy challenge in view of the proliferation of ad hoc wireless and sensor wireless networks (Rashid & Rehmani, 2016; Al-Turjman et al., 2019). After several works have been published on energy efficiency in wireless`s networks. Zhu and Reddi (2013) as well as Zhu et al. (2016) identified that maximization of energy *(energy harvesting)* and minimization of energy consumption has constant benefits in promoting the efficiency of networks. These two research areas are important which are commonly investigated separately. Kyte (2018) reported that we are in the period to rethink and respect energy efficiency because of its worth though it's reforming takes a long period but has huge impact. The forum of "Sustainable Energy for All" encourage every sectors that it possible to achieve energy efficiency with smarter thinking and sustainable approach. Thus, this chapter focuses on maximizing energy to improve performance in wireless networks. Presently, the importance of all wireless networks has gotten wide range of attention for their roles that cut across many fields due to their quality and potential applications in the civil and military environment. All wireless network comprises of many devices known as nodes, configured processor, memory and wireless communication capabilities which communicate through short-range of "ad hoc radio" connections (Čagalj et al., 2005). The advancements, growth and reports in all wireless usage have mandated researchers to devise approaches to evaluate the performance of networks to be energy efficient and super-efficient, hence, our focus to address the energy efficiency by considering the optimization of an energy based on output nodes to assist the network operators to achieve their target and provide efficient networks.

The usefulness of ad hoc networks can be explored at any given circumstances whereby network connectivity is needed temporarily in the absence of wired infrastructure foundation. This type of network does not need infrastructure for the nodes in the network to communicate as the communication is maintained by multi hop transmission (Singh et al., 1999). The emerging type of wireless network known as wireless sensor network merges many features such as sensing, monitoring, communication and computation into a single portable node (Chaal et al., 2017). To support these features, some of the different technology in wireless sensor networks required two major important factors that should be considered such as *Energy efficiency* and *transmission timelines and reliability* to achieve any timely task like monitoring and controlling of applications due to challenge of energy or load on the nodes in industrial sector (Puliafito et al., 2017). Also mesh wireless networks benefit from networking connectivity for identifying and attempting to employ any viable communication path "hopping data" from one node to another node to look for their destination (Chaal et al., 2017). If an emergency happens in a location where a wireless network is required for a limited period, for example, wireless networks must be efficient while also being energy efficient. Čagalj et al. (2005) cited Singh et al. (1999); Wieselthier et al. (2002) that every node has limited energy. Therefore, the energy efficiency of the nodes needed to be considered as an essential criterion when designing in all wireless networks. The optimization of an energy based on output nodes to assist the network operators to achieve their target and provide efficiency networks is one of the keys to network performance.

For communication networks, the impressive level of demanding for network connectivity and data rates is becoming higher and to meet up with the high demand, it requires that all possible resources needed to be used are efficient (Cohen et al., 2020). Wireless networks application and potentials are everywhere around us except we are yet to discover the areas to tap and develop interest. The application of wireless networks in virtual and physical environment as it relates to efficiency cannot be underrated. For instance, the outbreak of the novel coronavirus posed several challenges to every sector of the global economy. In the telecommunication sector for instance, there was an increase in demand for wireless networks which ultimately resulted in high demand for energy by network operators to serve its users. Specifically, the network operators reported that more devices were connected to wireless networks and led to the significant usage of data (CTIA & IEA 2020). In this case, the focus is more concentrated on increasing outputs production than increasing input resources. According to Debela (2020) cited Zhu (2009); Cooper et al., (2006) if an extraordinary pressure of multiple user's demand on service is high, what is relevant and matters most is how to augmenting the outputs for efficiency than contracting the inputs in order to meet or satisfy the demand and avoid energy waste. Therefore, the decision of this chapter in considering output-oriented approach to evaluate the energy efficiency in ad hoc wireless network is to improve performance, which is relevant.

Since 1973, industrialized nations have discovered and realized the significance of being energy efficient (Geller, 2006). Energy efficiency of wireless networks cuts across all major sectors in the world due to the impact of the wireless network technology in human lives, population, health, security, agriculture, military operations, transportation, logistics, banking, and other institutions. No sector or nation would afford to be suboptimal or inefficient. To promote and improve energy efficiency in any sector, sustainable policy, and research are the key to realize the weak areas so that the performance can be optimized for better productivity. This research will consider data envelopment analysis (DEA) method with a focus on output-orientation approach. The previous research on ad hoc wireless networks focused on input orientation approach.

Ad hoc wireless networks are developed to be known as any class of network that are wirelessly deployable and without infrastructure (Ephremides, 2002). Ad hoc is interesting because multiple nodes compete by links. These Wireless multi-hop networks, commonly known as ad hoc networks have been applied in various fields like military, disaster relief communications and emergency (Rajeswari, 2020). Ajibesin et al. (2016) describe energy efficiency as a method of minimizing and limiting energy consumption of the large activities of multicast performed in ad hoc wireless. The researchers implemented an evaluation of the energy efficiency using the linear programming model of DEA for optimization. Ephremides (2002) reviewed the importance of ad hoc wireless network on energy issues such as energy efficiency, energy aware and energy constrained in wireless multicasting. The energy efficiency in wireless networks have been explored to minimize energy with the capacity of the multicasting techniques. To completely optimize wireless network energy, the multicasting techniques have the ability to improve and make the whole system energy efficient.

This research will consider the maximization of energy efficiency in ad hoc wireless networks using combined computational and DEA techniques. This study sources from the research work of Ajibesin et al. (2016) which considered input oriented energy efficiency envelopment model to minimize input resources in ad hoc wireless networks. The research further presented the energy efficiency framework and determined by evaluating the average minimum of energy instead of the expected minimum energy. Compared to the above background, the concern of this research is to address the output oriented approach of energy efficiency using a minimum energy multicasting framework which was applied in ad hoc wireless networks in an input oriented approach. The approach this study intends to adopt will be used to maximize the outputs for optimization performance evaluation for the same networks. It is worthy to note that throughout the world, a lot of people seek energy efficient products in their daily activities. Industries, firms and corporate organizations. There have been many concepts by researchers all over the world to optimize the operation in wireless and wired networks. The wireless networks have the possible requirement to accomplish multicasting (Wieselthier et al., 2002).

Multicasting is a concept technique that is used in the minimum energy framework to reduce energy in wireless and give support to group communications than any other techniques such as unicast and broadcast could provide. Wireless networks consist of nodes that communicate over a medium called wireless channel. All the links in ad hoc networks or multihop radio networks are wireless (Gupta & Kumar, 2000). Wireless channel is naturally a broadcast means, where interference of different nodes from source occurs during transmissions. For wireless links, the quality differs over time and space due to inference, multipath fading, and shadowing. For the conditions of the network, the process of the nodes trying to join and leave the network makes the conditions of the network extremely changing or dynamic as it occurs in an irregular way. When new links are formed and other links disappear, there is a possibility that the routing traffic from one node to another could change frequently. These challenges incited many research work on the design, the analysis, and basic performance scope of ad hoc wireless networks (Setton et al., 2005).

Setton et al. (2005) presented that an ad hoc wireless network is a group of wireless nodes which configure itself to create a network without infrastructure. This means that ad hoc wireless as infrastructureless networks are alternative where a communications infrastructure is costly to install or set up, not easy to deploy and not viable to implement. Ad hoc wireless network potentials are many, such from multihop wireless, to sensor networks, to highway automation, to voice, image, and video communication for disaster areas.

Ad hoc wireless network is a type of network that does not require any fixed infrastructure when communications of device to device are established (Albers, 2010; Ruiz & Bouvry, 2015). The topology of its network primarily comprises a group of radio stations using antennas for communicating signals both in sending and receiving. These two wireless networks, ad hoc and sensor wireless networks have majorly been receiving active attention in research in relation with energy efficient algorithms (Albers, 2010). Many researchers base their focus on how wireless network can be improved better and for this research purpose we are considering ad hoc wireless networks. Ad hoc wireless networks' nature of self-organized, dynamism and decentralized network makes them suitable and applicable to many fields that central nodes are unreliable or not guaranteed. The configuration of these networks are minimal. Its ease of deployment makes it suitable for cases of emergency like battlefield, natural disasters or combat zone for the armed forces (military) (Ruiz & Bouvry, 2015).

Conclusively, like it has been mentioned at the beginning, similar research has been carried out in the past to address the problem of optimization in an ad hoc wireless the work, however, it only considered the one approach input-oriented to determine energy efficiency. This research will examine two minimum energy multicast algorithms such as multicast incremental power (MIP) and coded packets algorithm for energy efficiency in wireless ad hoc networks. The network simulation is considered to generate the nodes that will be used for defining the network to study the energy efficiency. Data Envelopment analysis (DEA) has been growing exponentially in various fields after being introduced, developed and published (in European Journal of Operation research) as a tool to measure efficiency of decision making units and evaluating performance of production (Charnes et al., 1978). DEA is an important linear programming technique and mathematical model, used for evaluating performance and efficiency in different fields which was originated by Charnes, Cooper and Rhodes denoted as (CCR).

The output-oriented approach of DEA will be used to achieve the aim of this research which focuses on how to maximize energy efficiency by increasing the output proportions while input proportion at constant. This chapter is structured into six sections. The introduction has been presented in section one, Section two provides the review of related works and research gap. Section three discusses the research methodology and approach adopted in carrying out the research. Section four analyses and discusses the results. Section five and six provides recommendations and conclusion respectively.

REVIEW OF RELATED WORKS AND RESEARCH GAP

Researchers presented linked studies on Energy Efficiency, DEA, Network Performance Evaluation, Algorithms and methods to improve wireless network performance in the early years. There is a scarcity of research on energy efficiency using a DEA output-oriented methodology to evaluate the performance of ad hoc wireless networks. Below are several literatures relevant to this work. An input oriented DEA has been considered to minimize and be used to evaluate energy efficiency. The researchers considered ad hoc wireless networks to be specific because this chapter is an expansion of research recommendations in order to contribute to the body of knowledge (Ajibesin et al., 2016). Researchers have contributed to academic and industrial perspectives on the challenges of making technology and wireless networks more energy efficient. Some recent journals have presented approaches such as switching strategy, clustering protocol, transmission power controls, vertical handover algorithm and optimization of directional antennas to achieve energy efficient wireless networks (Lim et al., 2019).

In literature in several years back, many researchers have carried out different study on energy efficiency on wireless networks areas such as wireless sensor networks, mesh networks and ad hoc wireless networks due to the development in wireless networking. These authors have explored the minimization of wireless multicast energy efficiency techniques (Blume et al., 2010; Lin et al., 2004; Louhi, 2007). Fang et al. (2010) proposed an Energy-Efficient Cooperative Communication Scheme (EECC) as an augmentation scheme to minimize network performance. EECC is used to improve energy efficiency performance and is very effective for data transmission in wireless sensor networks. El Khediri et al. (2020) proposed an energy efficient algorithm referred to as optimal K means called OK-means, and analyzed the overall energy consumption in the network. The simulated results revealed that the energy consumption in the network can be maximized and balanced optimally in wireless sensor networks compared to other approaches but effectively. The algorithm improves the lifetime of the network. However, the study did not consider the multi-criteria approach and minimization and maximization in terms of efficiency.

The European Commission proclaimed in 2008 that it is critical for ICTs to play a role in improving energy efficiency and lowering the economy's energy intensity (Liu et al., 2017). Blume et al. (2010) presented a study in 2010 that addressed the optimization issue of energy consumption and energy efficiency, and two specific approaches were considered, which were incremental improvements to the systems and a new slate of re-design of changing paradigms. There are two consortium bodies, which are EARTH and the Green Touch Initiative. EARTH (Energy Aware Radio and Network Technologies) was formed in order to address the issue of energy efficiency in order to reduce the energy consumption of mobile networks by 50% and the C02 emissions of ICTs. The EARTH project aims to increase data rate utilization and operating costs (energy) for mobile telecommunications. Also, when EARTH was deployed at the network level, there was a significant increase in energy efficiency. To some extent, tangible progress has been made in the last two decades, but it is not a holistic approach. The results were integrated into a system and validated in a real operation after simulations. Based on the authors' recommendation, there is a need for a holistic approach that will target the whole system for future mobile communication.

Goyal et al. (2020) used DEA techniques to improve the relative efficiency of the 18 selected decision-making units (DMUs) that represented the Information Technology and software service companies. This was used to measure the companies' productivity. Technical efficiencies were also employed to determine benchmarks and production slack. Five companies exhibited higher efficiency. The performance evaluation of Average Overall Technical Efficiency (AOTE), Average Pure Technical Efficiency (APTE) and Average Scale Efficiency (ASE) was estimated to improve the IT service and scale appropriately. Ajibesin et al. (2013) investigated the challenges of energy efficiency in wired and wireless multicasting networks, where they achieved the goal of minimizing the total energy consumption for multicast packets. Energy efficiency were used as measuring system to analyzed two main multicasting algorithms. The performance of these two algorithms was optimized and evaluated using a combination of two methods, such as simulation and the data envelopment analysis (DEA) method. The network effectiveness was determined by the simulation method, while the DEA was used to analyze the network efficiency. The researchers focused on the DEA method. Two kinds of decision making units (DMUs) were assumed for the multicast networks, such as network size and multicast group variables for the random linear network coding (RLNC) and multicast incremental power (MIP) algorithms, respectively. It has been proven that RLNC is better in terms of energy efficiency than MIP performance.

According to Blume et al. (2010) research states that the main optimization problem for energy efficiency of broadcast/multicast routing in wireless networks is how to minimize the total transmission power assigned to all nodes. Globally, the problem is known as one of the major performance challenges facing wireless networking technologies. Linear programming, while assuming coded techniques, is capable of solving the problem of minimum energy multicast in wireless networks (Ajibesin 2018). Ouyang et al. (2020) used the Networked DEA model to analyze the efficiency of network energy and its environment. The DEA model was improved to find inconsistencies between regions of 27 OECD countries, utilizing the Multiplicative function of the efficient frontier to identify efficient DMUs and to aid decision makers in improving the output of inefficient DMUs. The Multiplicative Networked DEA and Slack Based Model SBM methods were also utilized to evaluate the performance of these regional countries and these model results were compared. Ajibesin & Ventura (2015a) researched and developed three models to solve energy efficiency challenges. The models were based on an Input Oriented Data

Envelopment Analysis (DEA) methodology to suitably evaluate the efficiency of multicast energy and also minimize energy transmission in a wireless network without changing the total network performance.

Thasni et al. (2020) used DEA because of its multi-criteria approach to estimating efficiency, to compare the performance of cloud service-based providers using a service management index. This service management index is a useful metric for comparing cloud service providers. The DEA methodology was used to determine the best suitable cloud service based on the rank of the quality of services, in order to assist in selecting the best cloud provider. Thirty cloud service providers were considered and six parameters were used and categorized into three inputs and three outputs. Ajibesin & Ventura (2015b) developed an empirical DEA architecture that incorporates an envelopment model for technical efficiency measures, a slack model for energy projection and an energy gap (EG) for estimating the amount of energy saved. According to the related literature reviewed, the current approaches used to evaluate energy efficient multicast are single metric, which is suitable for evaluating effective performance. Therefore, a single metric is not appropriate for measuring efficiency (Ajibesin et al., 2016).

According to Ajibesin et al. (2014) they developed a new methodological approach to reducing power consumption in wireless sensor networks (WSNs) due to some challenges the existing approach is facing in evaluating power efficiency. The existing methodology was the minimum power multicast (MPM) methodology before the new alternative methodology was developed with the input-oriented Charnes, Cooper, Rhodes (CCR) using data envelopment analysis (DEA) model and multicast incremental power (MIP) algorithm, which can substitute (MPM), because of its efficiency features that the existing one lacks, such as efficiency scores, efficiency references sets (ERS) and Lambdas that could provide more information about the networks to the network administrators. The research further explained and proved how much power could be saved on wireless sensor networks if the WSNs functioned properly (efficiently). In addition, the new model can minimize power consumption without changing the output results. Agajo et al. (2012) uses simulation to study the network performance of wireless networks and optimize the radio parameters to enhance the quality of service. The author's study outcomes maximized the current capacity of the networks to be more efficient and identified the hidden problems that reduce the availability of networks. Recommendations were made on how network operators could utilize the study contribution to reduce operational costs (energy) and improve the overall performance of the network to maintain the satisfaction of users on wireless communication networks.

Ajibesin et al. (2013) implemented DEA methodology to evaluate the performance of wireless networks based on network coding after the throughput benefit has been evaluated. The efficiency of the network was determined by both input and output parameters. In terms of efficiency, the COPE performance was compared to the IEEES02.11. The simulation results showed that COPE outperformed IEEES 20.11. Because COPE and IEEES 20.11 are wireless network coding protocols, the results can be used by network operators when designing a network for maximum efficiency. Ullah et al. (2020) presented a survey which objective was to review the previous techniques, the usage of energy efficiency in smart grids to manage energy consumption, sustain green environment and to improve the economy in smart cities efficiently. The author examined the smart city based challenges with the application of artificial intelligence (AI), deep reinforcement learning (DRL) and machine learning (ML) were explored to create optimal policy for the development of smart city performance.

Gheisari et al. (2019) proposed a new algorithm to improve communication on wireless networks in terms of the quality of service. The approach permits data packet transfer advantages for capacity through routing information, avoidance of network node overcrowding and delay. Then the findings of the evaluation showed that above 10% of unnecessary delays can be avoided through the network using this algorithm, but there is an increase in energy consumption within the network nodes because during the process energy consumption was neglected or not taken into account. Therefore, there is a need to perform more energy efficiency studies in order to minimize and maximize their energy resources in the network node. To the best of my knowledge, there is scanty or no attempt in literature that considers the output-oriented DEA approach to measure performance of energy efficiency in ad hoc wireless networks.

According to a recent study, the energy efficiency model is an appropriate and adequate model for energy minimization in ad hoc wireless networks. The model is called the input oriented CCR/CRS envelopment models that evaluate the energy performance over an effective coded packet model. To the best of my knowledge, there is not much in the literature on evaluating energy efficiency performance using output orientation in wireless networks. Therefore, in order to enhance the performance of the nodes in the network, this study proposes to adopt the output oriented envelopment model to optimize energy in ad hoc wireless networks, as recommended in future work (Ajibesin et al., 2016). This work focuses on an output-oriented approach to energy maximization in ad hoc wireless networks, taking into account technical and scale efficiency to evaluate the network's output resources. This research work also validated the input oriented envelopment model for energy minimization, with the goal of comparing the two approaches to the DEA orientation results if possible.

RESEARCH METHODOLOGY AND APPROACH

In this section, a procedure for the research is explained. It describes the methodology beginning with the minimum energy multicast approach and then the DEA method.

Research Method

In the literature, the evaluation of minimum energy multicast has been evaluated in many studies, as energy efficient algorithms to determine their effectiveness. This study considered a non-parametric approach that relies on a linear programming technique for optimization of ad hoc wireless networks performance. Therefore, the Data Envelopment Analysis framework as shown in *Figure 1* is considered. Figure 1 shows the flowchart of an envelopment model that will be followed in implementing the DEA framework as part of the methodology.

DEA Models and Orientations

There is the possibility of combining the two most common return to scale assumptions, CRS. In the DEA technique, the approach of input oriented and output oriented uses this assumption of return to scale. The type of model to be used depends on what the entities wants to control. The Input orientation model is used to decrease the level of inputs while the outputs are kept at constant. The output orientation is used to increase the level of outputs while the inputs are kept constant (Malana & Malano, 2006; Aldamak & Zolfaghari, 2017). In other words, the input oriented model identifies the minimum level of inputs to be used to produce the current output, while the output oriented model identifies the maximum level of outputs to be produced using the current inputs. The DEA orientation model relies on linear programming as an estimator. Generally, the DEA is known for its output and input orientation model and non-orientation model to measure efficiency. Output oriented is a DEA model that measures the efficiency

Figure 1. Flowchart of envelopment model for implementing the DEA framework

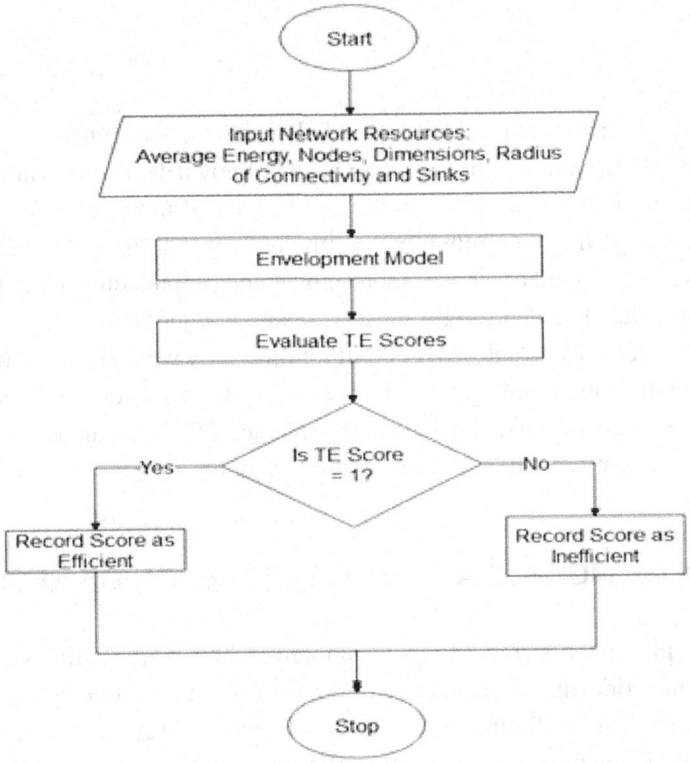

of units relative to their frontier, if they are operating according to best practice or not. Output oriented DEA are more concern in maximization of outputs while inputs are kept constant. The output orientation in DEA is similar to that of the Stochastic Frontier Analysis (SFA), but the DEA is non-parametric and non-econometric, whereas the SFA is parametric and economic. This work focuses on an output-oriented approach with the aim of maximizing the output resources of each ad hoc wireless network.

Output Oriented (ϕ) CCR/CRS Model

This is a mathematical model for the output orientation in an envelopment model with a formulated assumption of constant return to scale (CRS). The objective of this model is to maximize the output using a linear programming approach. This model can augment the outputs with the current given level of inputs such as energy.

$$\phi^* = \phi$$

Subject to

$$\sum\nolimits_{j=1}^{n} \lambda_j x_{ij} \leq x_{i0}; \ i=1,\ldots,m$$

$$\sum_{j=1}^{n}\lambda_{j}y_{rj} \geq \phi y_{r0}; \ r=1,\ldots,s$$

$\lambda j_{\geq}0;(CRS) \ j=1,\ldots,n$ (3.1)

The ϕ denotes that this is an output orientation and also an objective function, $\phi*$ denotes the output efficiency score of DMU0, λj are the weights and important unknown decision variable, j=1,...,n attached to weight to represents the number of DMU, i=1,...,m number of input, xij represents the input in the imaginary constraints, xi0 and yr0 are current target of ith input and rth output of the DMU0 respectively. λ are weights or coefficients assigned to DMUs not to inputs and outputs during the process of optimization. The $\lambda j\geq0$ represents that attached weight must be positive values (non-zero).

Definition: If $\phi* = 1$ then the current DMU output for this study which is the ad hoc wireless network cannot be increased and indicating that at the DMU is at the frontier (efficient). Otherwise If $\phi*>1$, then the DMU fall below the frontier (inefficient) mean the inefficient DMU can augment their input levels to increase output level. Therefore the output orientation model is $\phi*\geq1$.

IMPLEMENTATION OF MODELS AND INTERPRETATION OF RESULTS

The previous section explored the methodology considered for this work. In this section, the implementation of simulated framework (minimum energy multicast algorithms) to evaluate effectiveness of ad hoc wireless networks are briefly discussed. Further, this section discusses the implementation of the output orientation envelopment model to achieve the efficiency performance of ad hoc wireless networks.

All results are evaluated using the proposed energy efficiency models and the result are analyzed.

Implementation of MIP and Coded Packet

This section presents the results of the simulation framework. The results of the MIP and NC previously reported and presented Table 1.

Table 1. Show the results of MIP and NC

Sink	MIPs			NCs		
	20-MIP	30-MIP	40-MIP	20-NC	30-NC	40-NC
2	7.3369	6.80406	6.70263	4.50027	4.1549	3.1439
3	8.19434	7.5984	6.52575	5.46086	5.30356	4.60581
4	8.98436	8.17163	7.48482	6.22791	5.35979	4.75666
5	9.0487	8.62102	7.47209	6.81511	6.07549	4.75814
6	9.48655	9.28325	8.0599	7.32855	6.18796	5.56181
7	10.4696	8.93184	8.36012	7.23365	6.37327	5.58696
8	9.92203	9.54203	8.61111	8.10404	6.5723	6.25809
9	10.7971	9.97383	8.8669	8.81448	7.34824	6.29795
10	10.8188	9.2635	9.00432	8.45438	6.74705	6.30145

Data Collection and Decision-Making Units

Data for this study was obtained through a simulation method (effective performance of two minimum energy multicast algorithms). The dataset is from a coded packet algorithm. The simulated results from the simulation framework will serve as input (54 ad hoc wireless networks) to evaluate the performance of the networks further with a non-parametric and multi-criteria decision approach called the (DEA) envelopment model for energy efficiency. For the 54 DMUs considered as dataset, they have mathematically satisfied the expression stated earlier in the *Concept of Decision-Making Unit (DMU)*. The performance metric confirmed the fairness of the result achieved. The 54 DMU (P = 54), Q = 4, and R = 1; 54 > max {4 x 1, 3 (4+1), that is, 54 > {4, 15}. The findings show that the 54 DMUs of the dataset are greater than the15 DMUs minimum requirements. Therefore, this dataset has satisfied the above conditions.

Analysis of Data and Software

To solve the efficiency of ad hoc wireless networks (DMUs), this research considered an open source DEA solver package called (OSDEA). The OSDEA is open source software that is user friendly, uses linear programming in solving many DEA problems for efficiencies and simple to use for those who are familiar with DEA. The dataset of 54 ad hoc wireless networks was evaluated and configured using DEA packaged tools (orientation type, variables, efficiency and RTS). The OSDEA package was developed to solve different DEA problems using several embedded DEA models. This work considered the implementation of the envelopment model, which is used to evaluate TE. The DEA library includes the linear programming solver (LPsolver) to carry out optimizations on the identified resources. Various types of DEA tools exist. These include the DEAOS online software, Warwick, the DEA program, and the Open Source (OSDEA).

In this chapter, we considered the use of open source software online for the implementation of the data set discussed. The OSDEA is available online. Although it required some level of technicality, specification and installation procedures before it could be used conveniently. However, unlike propriety software, it is freely available and flexible to use. It is particularly recommended for academic research involving frontier analysis such as efficiency evaluation.

Input Variables

- Cost = Average Energy
- Dim = Dimension
- Rad = Radius
- Node = Nodes

Output Variable

- Sink = Sinks

DMUs = 54 Ad hoc Wireless networks

To solve the DEA problem, each of the Ad hoc Wireless networks (DMU), uses four input resources and an output resource simultaneously rather than a single entry in the case of effective evaluation. The DMUs are gathered dataset, from coded packet model which each DMU have various inputs and output and the analysis ranges. The objective here is to optimize, to achieve maximum efficiency of multicast energy in an ad hoc wireless network based on output without affecting its performance establishment. Also, to further identify the efficient and inefficient ad hoc wireless networks, the technical efficiency model and scale efficiency model determine the network size and type of return to scale exhibited. The study combined two energy efficient algorithms and evaluated the performance of the ad hoc wireless network in terms of output. Also, this study validates the efficiency of inputs on the same network for comparison if time permits. This TE will help to determine how inefficient ad hoc wireless networks can be projected to their frontier to improve performance in terms of the output produced. This contributes to the long-term viability of a product or service while the SE will determine the return to scale

Implementation of DEA Steps

This subsection highlights the five major succeeding steps to solve DEA problem through OSDEA:

- *Formulation of DEA Problem* (DEAP) – The first step is to formulate a DEAP. This involves the specific DMUs subject to evaluation and identify the DMUs variables, which are the inputs and outputs. The simulation results serve as the input dataset. The OSDEA tool provides an environment to present a new problem for DEA solver.
- *Import DEA Data* – To import new DEA Problem raw data successfully, the data must observe the rules that satisfy the conditions of OSDEA execution, such as proper data cleaning, and specified formats such as files must be saved in .csv format and data in the file must be numeric or float, file first row should have headers and shouldn't be empty, file first column must contain the DMU names and cannot be left empty, then the raw data set can be imported. Successful imported data will display all the fields of the dataset according to the raw format given in the DEAP. Note that the dataset could be rejected if the rules were not observed in the raw data.
- *Configure the DEA Problem Variables*– This is the next step after DEA problem had been imported, then configure your DEA problem variables by selecting the appropriate variables to and ensure they are correctly configured
- *Configure the DEA Model Type* – This phase allows you to configure the model details (the parameters of the model type), which are very crucial, before the problem can be solved. Also, it ensured that model type selected conforms to the methodology and the objective set in chapter 3. Pay special attention in choosing the orientation that the model is based on from model features e.g. the DEA orientation, efficiency type and returns-to-scale (RTS). The Reset filter option is available if you want to change the selected model type. You don't have to start the whole step afresh.
- *Solve/Reset the DEA Problem – This is the final step; if all of the previous steps, such as data import, variable configuration, and model type configuration before this solution step, were followed correctly, the next step is set, and you are ready to solve the DEA Problem.* The DEA solution can be visualized by expanding the tree of solutions under the pane and selecting the section of interest in the solution. The solution present in the tree are the following objectives technical efficiency scores of each ad hoc wireless network nodes (DMUs), the lambdas, the weights, the slacks, the peer group and projections. Export the solution and save the file in a compatible file format for MS Excel.

Álvarez et al., (2020) current development of the DEA models is that the function can be computed in the MATLAB package as an optimizing technique due to the importance of determining best practice using the frontiers. There are several DEA software application packages, such as Warwick DEA, DEAP (DEA Program), ON-Front, DEAOS (DEA Online Software), "DEAFrontier", "DEA command application in Stata", and OSDEA (Open Source DEA), to mention a few. This chapter uses OSDEA to solve the DEA problem data set received as a result of the simulated framework in order to run the envelopment model. OSDEA is used in this work because it is non-proprietary software that is available for free research. It is user-friendly because of the graphical interface command, the ability to run multiple DEA problems in the pane section, no data set limit, and an easier way to install a linear solver (lpsolve) for the package as required in solving DEA. However, when compared to many other software packages, the results of the DEA problem, which are output-oriented, must be reciprocated. The OSDEA is used to implement the DEA mathematical equations, models, and theorems.

Implementation of CCR/CRS Output-Oriented (CCR_O) Model

In this section, a mathematical model presented using the OSDEA software application. The technical efficiency (TE) scores are extracted from the saved file (exported solution file). The results of the model are analyzed and classified into efficient and inefficient ad hoc wireless networks, because the tool is capable of calculating the technical efficiency of each ad hoc wireless network. The DEA package uses the linear programming integrated within the DEA solver to locate an efficient DMU, and compare its efficiency with other DMUs. The efficient ad hoc wireless networks are those with an efficiency rating of $\phi=1$ (100%). DMUs that are inefficient are greater than 1 $\phi>1$ on efficiency rating. Table 2 presents the efficiency scores report of all DMUs consisting of fifty-four (54) ad hoc wireless networks evaluated by the DEA solver and extracted from the "Objectives" sheet, which is one of the result sheets in the solution exported from the OSDEA software package. Column two of Table 2 shows the objective results but does not conform to the $\phi^*\geq1$ technical efficiency scores of all the DMUs. Then column three of Table 2 presents the results of the technical efficiency ratings (efficient means Yes and inefficient means No) of each DMUs. Columns five and six of Table 2 present the results in general percentages for technical efficiency and technical inefficiency of each DMU under evaluation, respectively. For instance, the most inefficient DMU is DMU10. This interprets that DMU10 could be efficient if the output produced could be augmented by 72.5% without increasing the inputs.

For the result, only four (4) DMUs out of 54 DMUs are identified as efficient with efficiency scores of $\phi=1$ means 100%. These four DMUs (DMU9, DMU18, ₚMU27 and DMU45) are efficient, while other 50 DMUs are identified as inefficient with efficiency scores of $\phi>1$ of greater than 1. For the inefficient DMUs to be efficient, each DMUs must augment their output without affecting the inputs to possibly boost their efficiency scores to be efficient, as presented in Tab*le 2*.

Percentage of inefficient DMUs in column 6 shows that each DMU can reach an efficient frontier (100% efficient). For instance, to be efficient, DMU10, which is the most inefficient DMU as presented in the result, can boost their technical efficiency score by augmenting the output to 72.5% (100 − 27.5) without affecting the inputs. The next inefficient is DMU1. The output to augment is 70% (100 − 30). Similarly, to be efficient, all other remaining inefficient DMUs have percentages of outputs to be augmented as calculated in column six. However, the four (4) DMUs are efficient according to their best practice because they are already on the frontier. No augmentation on number of nodes produced in their networks. Also, there is another model called the *slack model* to confirm and classify the efficiency of

Table 2. Efficiency scores and ratings based on output oriented CCR/CRS Model

DMU Name	Objective Value	Efficient	Efficiency Score	% TE	%TIE
DMU1	0.299912563	No	3.334305	30.0	70.0
DMU2	0.400841406	No	2.494752	40.1	59.9
DMU3	0.492072541	No	2.032221	49.2	50.8
DMU4	0.579887406	No	1.724473	58.0	42.0
DMU5	0.66270102	No	1.508976	66.3	33.7
DMU6	0.78002225	No	1.282015	78.0	22.0
DMU7	0.82426848	No	1.213197	82.4	17.6
DMU8	0.9	No	1.111111	90.0	10.0
DMU9	1	Yes	1	100.0	0.0
DMU10	0.275022435	No	3.636067	27.5	72.5
DMU11	0.395461215	No	2.528693	39.5	60.5
DMU12	0.486574822	No	2.055182	48.7	51.3
DMU13	0.573482391	No	1.743733	57.3	42.7
DMU14	0.670701441	No	1.490976	67.1	32.9
DMU15	0.777649758	No	1.285926	77.8	22.2
DMU16	0.843595512	No	1.185402	84.4	15.6
DMU17	0.9	No	1.111111	90.0	10.0
DMU18	1	Yes	1	100.0	0.0
DMU19	0.303326193	No	3.296781	30.3	69.7
DMU20	0.365214386	No	2.738118	36.5	63.5
DMU21	0.482863666	No	2.070978	48.3	51.7
DMU22	0.54530044	No	1.833851	54.5	45.5
DMU23	0.644580026	No	1.551398	64.5	35.5
DMU24	0.733935619	No	1.362517	73.4	26.6
DMU25	0.817675842	No	1.222979	81.8	18.2
DMU26	0.9	No	1.111111	90.0	10.0
DMU27	1	Yes	1	100.0	0.0
DMU28	0.349318846	No	2.862714	34.9	65.1
DMU29	0.376752369	No	2.654263	37.7	62.3
DMU30	0.468319487	No	2.135294	46.8	53.2
DMU31	0.560772526	No	1.783254	56.1	43.9
DMU32	0.652674313	No	1.532158	65.3	34.7
DMU33	0.698796451	No	1.431032	69.9	30.1
DMU34	0.811986159	No	1.231548	81.2	18.8
DMU35	0.870084707	No	1.149313	87.0	13.0
DMU36	0.967964295	No	1.033096	96.8	3.2
DMU37	0.400868348	No	2.494585	40.1	59.9
DMU38	0.41044572	No	2.436376	41.0	59.0
DMU39	0.529905438	No	1.887129	53.0	47.0
DMU40	0.662175766	No	1.510173	66.2	33.8
DMU41	0.679791291	No	1.47104	68.0	32.0
DMU42	0.789519703	No	1.266593	79.0	21.0

continued on following page

Table 2. Continued

DMU Name	Objective Value	Efficient	Efficiency Score	% TE	%TIE
DMU43	0.805542905	No	1.241399	80.6	19.4
DMU44	0.900500163	No	1.110494	90.1	9.9
DMU45	1	Yes	1	100.0	0.0
DMU46	0.347745829	No	2.875664	34.8	65.2
DMU47	0.438333279	No	2.281369	43.8	56.2
DMU48	0.497345143	No	2.010676	49.7	50.3
DMU49	0.615213762	No	1.625451	61.5	38.5
DMU50	0.693436065	No	1.442094	69.3	30.7
DMU51	0.768271421	No	1.301623	76.8	23.2
DMU52	0.786772363	No	1.271016	78.7	21.3
DMU53	0.885916472	No	1.128775	88.6	11.4
DMU54	0.975856637	No	1.024741	97.6	2.4

Figure 2. Distribution of technical efficiency score scores of 54 ad hoc wireless based on output-oriented CCR/CRS model (non-normalized)

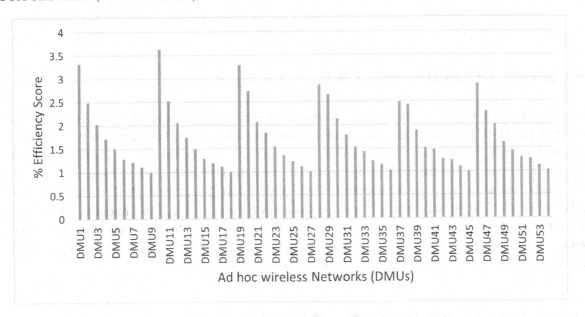

these 4 DMUs further as fully efficient or weakly efficient, but this is not the focus of this chapter. These efficient 4 DMUs could be optimal or sub-optimal in their performance. Note that the slack model can identify how weakly or fully efficient DMUs are. In order to better appreciate the efficiency distribution and visualization, figures 2 and 3 present the efficiency scores against 54 ad hoc wireless networks (DMUs) based on the output oriented CCR/CRS model. It is easy to visualize those efficient DMUs, DMU9, DMU18 DMU27 and DMU45. However, it has been observed that the inefficient DMU54 is very close to the efficient frontier but only requires the augmentation of 2.4% to reach the frontier 100%.

Figure 3. Distribution of technical efficiency scores of 54 ad hoc wireless based on output-oriented CCR/CRS model

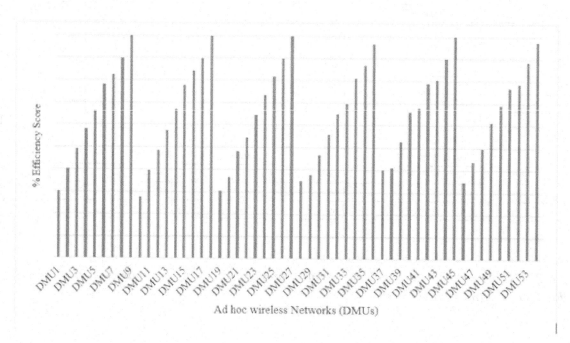

Ranking for Output-Oriented CCR Model (CCR_O)

In this section the ranking of the Output-oriented CCR model (CCR_O) is measured. In the ranking column, any DMUs (ad hoc wireless networks) that scored a technical efficiency score of 100, are efficient. For CCR_O, only four 4 DMUs are efficient and they have been ranked as number 1 out of 54 DMUs. This could assist the network operator to identify the DMUs that are performing better. The ranking is done according to the technical efficiency scores. DMU27, DMU45, DMU9, and DMU18 are all efficient ad hoc wireless networks. Therefore, the network operator or administrator can certainly and confidently rely on the efficiency of these networks. Figure 4 depicts the TE scores against the DMU ranks showing the relation between the TE scores and DMUs ranks, as DMU27 and others are ranked as most efficient, and the DMU10 is ranked as position.

RECOMMENDATIONS AND RESEARCH DIRECTIONS

Network operators, regulators, policymakers, and other researchers who are more concerned with improving the performance of ad hoc wireless networks may consider measuring performance using either the output or input DEA. Also, this study recommends this approach to optimize (maximize) energy efficiency in other wireless networks such as mesh and sensor networks. Furthermore, this study has shown a good step in improving the performance of the network and operating efficiently. This approach in this study is a significant step going forward in achieving the expected efficiency target as a network provider, knowing or realizing how to maximize the nodes with the given energy for instance. In addi-

Figure 4. Ranking of efficiency scores based on output-oriented CCR/CRS model

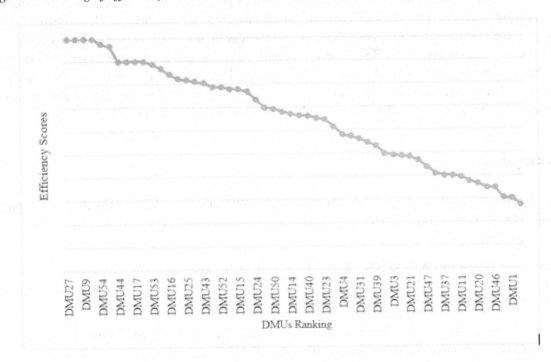

tion, the network provider can decide the efficient DMUs to benchmark based on their efficiency scores and rankings. The network operators would appreciate the idea of best practice in dealing with network issues and making appropriate decisions based on return to scale such as CRS. The outcome of this work provides an alternative way to evaluate the performance of ad hoc wireless networks using Output Oriented DEA. Under the same orientation, there are more models to explore to maximize the sinks in the networks such as the slack models, which may be considered for improving the identified inefficient ad hoc wireless networks and also projecting them to the efficient frontier. Also, the benchmarking model may be explored for establishing the standard in order to improve the inefficient DMUs. Future studies could consider using non oriented DEA (both inputs and outputs can be optimized simultaneously). Super efficiency and application of artificial intelligence are another concept that could be used to expand the idea of energy efficiency of wireless networks.

CONCLUSION

Output oriented DEA for maximizing outputs is indeed a credible approach for efficiency performance. In order to achieve the aim of this study, as an empirical study using two different algorithms were first considered for minimum energy multicast to evaluate the ad hoc wireless networks energy efficiency. An envelopment model was considered to improve and maximize the output produced in an output oriented DEA approach. The DMUs of 54 ad hoc wireless networks were considered for technical efficiency and maximization of outputs resources of the networks. Therefore, in order to appropriately and adequately improve the performance of the network technical efficiency evaluation is inevitable. Technical efficiency (TE) implies that their resource utilization functions properly and that their operation is free of waste of input resources. The TE results have shown that the majority of ad hoc wireless networks need to improve their performance and achieve an efficient frontier in order to be efficient. The CCR model, which is based on assumption of CRS has been explored. It is important to note that this model assumed that when technical efficiency is achieved by a DUM, such a DMU is operating at an optimal scale. The significant of this study was to maximize the use of network resource input by the network administrator to understand how to operate and manage the ad hoc wireless in an efficient manner.

REFERENCES

Agajo, J., Theophilus, A. L., Idigo, V. E., Apkado, K. I., Polytechnic, F., & State, E. (2012). Optimization of Network Performance in Wireless Communication Networks. *Pacific Journal of Science and Technology*, *13*(1), 334–350.

Ajibesin, A., Murgu, A., & Chan, H. A. (2016). *Novel Approaches to Performance Evaluation and Benchmarking for Energy-Efficient Multicast: Empirical Study of Coded Packet Wireless Networks* (Doctoral dissertation)

Ajibesin, A. A. (2018). Efficient Frontier and Benchmarking Models for Energy Multicast in Wireless Network Coding. In *Network Coding*. IntechOpen. doi:10.5772/intechopen.79377

Ajibesin, A. A., Nche, C., Wajiga, G. M., & Odekunle, M. R. (2014). Reducing multicast power consumption in wireless sensor networks nodes. In *2014 IEEE 6th International Conference on Adaptive Science & Technology (ICAST)* (pp. 1-7). IEEE. 10.1109/ICASTECH.2014.7068151

Ajibesin, A. A., & Ventura, N. (2015a). Minimum Energy Multicast in Wireless Networks: Empirical study of coded packet model. *International Journal of Computer Research*, *22*(4), 361.

Ajibesin, A. A., & Ventura, N. (2015b). Gap mechanism for energy efficiency models in wireless multicast networks. *AFRICON*, *2015*, 1–6. Advance online publication. doi:10.1109/AFRCON.2015.7331997

Ajibesin, A. A., Ventura, N., Murgu, A., & Chan, H. (2013). Data envelopment analysis: Efficient technique for measuring performance of wireless network coding protocols. *15th International Conference on Advanced Communication Technology*, 1122–1127.

Al-Turjman, F., Altrjman, C., Din, S., & Paul, A. (2019). Energy monitoring in IoT-based ad hoc networks: An overview. *Computers & Electrical Engineering*, *76*, 133–142. doi:10.1016/j.compeleceng.2019.03.013

Aldamak, A., & Zolfaghari, S. (2017). Review of efficiency ranking methods in data envelopment analysis. *Measurement*, *106*, 161–172. doi:10.1016/j.measurement.2017.04.028

Blume, O., Zeller, D., & Barth, U. (2010). Approaches to energy efficient wireless access networks. *4th International Symposium on Communications, Control and Signal Processing (ISCCSP)*. 10.1109/ISCCSP.2010.5463328

Čagalj, M., Hubaux, J. P., & Enz, C. C. (2005). Energy-efficient broadcasting in all-wireless networks. *Wireless Networks*, *11*(1), 177–188. doi:10.100711276-004-4754-9

Chaal, D., Lyhyaoui, A., & Lehmann, F. (2017, March). Optimization of a modular ad hoc land wireless system via joint Source-Network Coding for correlated sensors. In *ACECS 2017: 4th International Conference on Automation, Control Engineering and Computer Science* (*Vol. 2*, pp. 21-24). International Publisher & CO (IPCO). 10.1007/978-3-319-67910-5_14

Charnes, A., Cooper, W. W., & Rhodes, E. (1978). Measuring the efficiency of decision making units. *European Journal of Operational Research*, *2*(6), 429–444. doi:10.1016/0377-2217(78)90138-8

Cohen, A., Esfahanizadeh, H., Sousa, B., Vilela, J. P., Luís, M., Raposo, D., . . . Médard, M. (2020). *Bringing network coding into SDN: a case-study for highly meshed heterogeneous communications.* arXiv preprint arXiv:2010.00343

Cooper, W. W., Seiford, L. M., & Tone, K. (2006). *Introduction to data envelopment analysis and its uses: With DEA-solver software and references.* Springer Science & Business Media. doi:10.1007/0-387-29122-9

CTIA. (2020, August 25). *2020 Annual Survey Highlights.* https://www.ctia.org/news/report-2020-annual-survey-highlights

Debela, B. K. (2020). *Managing Covid-19 in Africa: A Technical Efficiency Analysis.* /profile/Bacha_Debela/publication/344561594_Managing_Covid-19_in_Africa_A_Technical_Efficiency,Analysis/links/5f804c68458515b7cf72245d/Managing-Covid-19-in-Africa-A-Technical-Efficiency-Analysis

El Khediri, S., Fakhet, W., Moulahi, T., Khan, R., Thaljaoui, A., & Kachouri, A. (2020). Improved node localization using K-means clustering for Wireless Sensor Networks. *Computer Science Review*, *37*, 100284. doi:10.1016/j.cosrev.2020.100284

Ephremides, A. (2002). Energy concerns in wireless networks. *IEEE Wireless Communications*, *9*(4), 48–59. doi:10.1109/MWC.2002.1028877

Fang, W., Liu, F., Yang, F., Shu, L., & Nishio, S. (2010). Energy-efficient cooperative communication for data transmission in wireless sensor networks. *IEEE Transactions on Consumer Electronics*, *56*(4), 2185–2192. doi:10.1109/TCE.2010.5681089

Geller, H., Harrington, P., Rosenfeld, A. H., Tanishima, S., & Unander, F. (2006). Polices for increasing energy efficiency: Thirty years of experience in OECD countries. *Energy Policy*, *34*(5), 556–573. doi:10.1016/j.enpol.2005.11.010

Gheisari, M., Alzubi, J., Zhang, X., Kose, U., & Saucedo, J. A. (2019). A new algorithm for optimization of quality of service in peer to peer wireless mesh networks. *Wireless Networks*, *25*(7), 4445. Advance online publication. doi:10.100711276-019-02016-4

Goyal, S., Sah, A. N., Sharma, R. K., & Puri, J. (2020). Estimating technical efficiencies of Indian IT companies for setting improvement targets for inefficient companies: An empirical analysis with workers' effort as key input. *Work (Reading, Mass.)*, *66*(4), 885–900. doi:10.3233/WOR-203233 PMID:32925144

IEA. (2020, December). *Energy Efficiency 2020.* https://www.iea.org/reports/energy-efficiency-2020

Jahid, A., Islam, M. S., Hossain, M. S., Hossain, M. E., Monju, M. K. H., & Hossain, M. F. (2019). Toward energy efficiency aware renewable energy management in green cellular networks with joint coordination. *IEEE Access : Practical Innovations, Open Solutions, 7*, 75782–75797. doi:10.1109/AC-CESS.2019.2920924

Kyte, R. (2018, March 20). *An Inefficient Truth.* https://www.seforall.org/news/an-inefficient-truth or https://www.euractiv.com/section/energy/opinion/an-inefficient-truth/

Kyte, R. (2018, May 3). Smarter thinking can offer quicker results on global goals of universal energy access. *Sustainable Energy for All.* https://www.seforall.org/press-releases/smarter-thinking-can-offer-quicker-results-on-global-goals-of-universal-energy

Lange, S., Pohl, J., & Santarius, T. (2020). Digitalization and energy consumption. Does ICT reduce energy demand? *Ecological Economics, 176*, 106760. doi:10.1016/j.ecolecon.2020.106760

Louhi, J. T. (2007, September). Energy efficiency of modern cellular base stations. In *INTELEC 07-29th International Telecommunications Energy Conference* (pp. 475-476). IEEE. 10.1109/INTLEC.2007.4448824

Malana, N. M. & Malano, H. M. (2006). Benchmarking productive efficiency of selected wheat areas in Pakistan and India using data envelopment analysis. *Irrigation and Drainage: The Journal of the International Commission on Irrigation and Drainage, 55*(4), 383-394.

Melki, R. (2020). *Designing Physical Layer Security Solutions For Emerging Communication Systems in 5G Networks* [Doctoral dissertation].

Naves, R., Khalife, H., Jakllari, G., Conan, V., & Beylot, A.-L. (2018). A Framework for Evaluating Physical-Layer Network Coding Gains in Multi-hop Wireless Networks. *IEEE Transactions on Mobile Computing*, 1–1. doi:10.1109/TMC.2018.2883429

OSDEA. (2020, March). *OSDEA-GUI.* Retrieved from https://github.com/hub187/opensourcedea-lib.git

Ouyang, W., & Yang, J. (2020). The network energy and environment efficiency analysis of 27 OECD countries: A multiplicative network DEA model. *Energy, 117161.* Advance online publication. doi:10.1016/j.energy.2020.117161

Puliafito, A., Bruneo, D., Distefano, S., & Longo, F. (Eds.). (2017). Lecture Notes in Computer Science *Ad-hoc, Mobile, and Wireless Networks.* doi:10.1007/978-3-319-67910-5

Rajeswari, A. R. (2020). *A Mobile Ad Hoc Network Routing Protocols: A Comparative Study, Recent Trends in Communication Networks, Pinaki Mitra.* IntechOpen. doi:10.5772/intechopen.92550

Rashid, B., & Rehmani, M. H. (2016). Applications of wireless sensor networks for urban areas: A survey. *Journal of Network and Computer Applications, 60*, 192–219. doi:10.1016/j.jnca.2015.09.008

Ruiz, P., & Bouvry, P. (2015). Survey on broadcast algorithms for mobile ad hoc networks. *ACM Computing Surveys, 48*(1), 1–35. doi:10.1145/2786005

Setton, E., Yoo, T., Zhu, X., Goldsmith, A., & Girod, B. (2005). Cross-layer design of ad hoc networks for real-time video streaming. *IEEE Wireless Communications, 12*(4), 59–65. doi:10.1109/MWC.2005.1497859

Singh, S., Raghavendra, C. S., & Stepanek, J. (1999). Power-aware broadcasting in mobile ad hoc networks. *Proceedings of IEEE PIMRC*, *99*, 22–31.

Thasni, T., Kalaiarasan, C., & Venkatesh, K. A. (2020). Cloud Service Selection using DEA based on SMI Attributes. *International Journal of Engineering and Advanced Technology*, *9*(4), 849–855.

Ullah, Z., Al-Turjman, F., Mostarda, L., & Gagliardi, R. (2020). Applications of Artificial Intelligence and Machine learning in smart cities. *Computer Communications*, *154*, 313–323. doi:10.1016/j.comcom.2020.02.069

Wieselthier, J. E., Nguyen, G. D., & Ephremides, A. (2002). Energy-efficient broadcast and multicast trees in wireless networks. *Mobile Networks and Applications*, *7*(6), 481–492. doi:10.1023/A:1020716919751

Zhu, Y., & Reddi, V. J. (2013, February). High-performance and energy-efficient mobile web browsing on big/little systems. In *2013 IEEE 19th International Symposium on High Performance Computer Architecture (HPCA)* (pp. 13-24). IEEE.

Zhu, Z., Chu, Z., Wang, Z., & Lee, I. (2016). Outage constrained robust beamforming for secure broadcasting systems with energy harvesting. *IEEE Transactions on Wireless Communications*, *15*(11), 7610–7620. doi:10.1109/TWC.2016.2605102

ADDITIONAL READING

Cullinane, K., & Wang, T. F. (2006). Data envelopment analysis (DEA) and improving container port efficiency. *Research in Transportation Economics*, *17*, 517–566. doi:10.1016/S0739-8859(06)17023-7

Nikkhah, A., & Van Haute, S. (2020). Energy flow modeling and optimization trends in food supply chain: A mini review. *Current Opinion in Environmental Science & Health*, *13*, 16–22. doi:10.1016/j.coesh.2019.10.001

Yan, Q., Zhao, F., Wang, X., & Balezentis, T. (2021). The Environmental Efficiency Analysis Based on the Three-Step Method for Two-Stage Data Envelopment Analysis. *Energies*, *14*(21), 7028. doi:10.3390/en14217028

Yang, Z., & Wei, X. (2019). The measurement and influences of China's urban total factor energy efficiency under environmental pollution: Based on the game cross-efficiency DEA. *Journal of Cleaner Production*, *209*, 439–450. doi:10.1016/j.jclepro.2018.10.271

Zhao, B., Ren, Y., Gao, D., Xu, L., & Zhang, Y. (2019). Energy utilization efficiency evaluation model of refining unit Based on Contourlet neural network optimized by improved grey optimization algorithm. *Energy*, *185*, 1032–1044. doi:10.1016/j.energy.2019.07.111

KEY TERMS AND DEFINITIONS

Ad Hoc Wireless Networks: A type of wireless network that is formed without central administration or fixed infrastructure. Nodes in these networks communicate directly with each other and can dynamically join or leave the network.

Coded Packet Algorithms: Algorithms used in network communications to encode data packets for efficient transmission, often used to improve the reliability and efficiency of data transfer in wireless networks.

Data Envelopment Analysis (DEA): A performance measurement technique used to evaluate the efficiency of decision-making units (DMUs), such as nodes in a network. It involves comparing the ratios of inputs (like energy) to outputs (like data transferred).

Energy Efficiency: In the context of wireless networks, this refers to the effective use of energy in transmitting and receiving data, aiming to maximize network performance while minimizing energy consumption.

Multicast Incremental Power (MIP): A technique in wireless networks for optimizing the power used in multicast transmissions. It aims to reduce the total power consumption while ensuring reliable data transmission to multiple recipients.

Network Performance: A measure of how effectively a network transmits and receives data. Key factors include speed, reliability, and efficiency.

Optimization: The process of making a system, such as a wireless network, as effective, functional, or efficient as possible. In wireless networks, this often involves maximizing data transmission efficiency while minimizing energy consumption and other costs.

Output-Oriented DEA Approach: In DEA, this approach focuses on maximizing outputs (like data throughput) while keeping inputs (such as energy consumption) constant. It is used to enhance the performance of networks.

Wireless Networks: Communication networks that use wireless data connections for connecting nodes. They include a variety of technologies like Wi-Fi, cellular networks, and ad hoc wireless networks.

Wireless Technology: The technology associated with the transmission of information over distances without the use of wires. In the context of this chapter, it pertains to the devices and methodologies used in constructing and operating wireless networks.

Chapter 7
Efficiency Benchmarking Through Data Envelopment Analysis:
Evaluating Disruptive Technologies in India's Key Sectors

Rajasekhara Mouly Potluri

(iD) https://orcid.org/0000-0002-6935-1373

Kazakh British Technical University, Kazakhstan

Narasimha Rao Vajjhala

(iD) https://orcid.org/0000-0002-8260-2392

University of New York Tirana, Albania

ABSTRACT

In the modern era, disruptive technologies, ranging from artificial intelligence to big data analytics and virtual reality to drone technology, have profoundly impacted India's lifestyles and employment dynamics. This chapter deeply explores these innovations' history, meaning, theory, and significance, focusing mainly on their transformative influence on the Indian industries, health, transport, and energy sectors. Beyond just an exploration, this study employs DEA for efficiency benchmarking, offering a structured assessment of how well these sectors have harnessed the potential of disruptive technologies. The analysis underscores the diverse issues, challenges, and opportunities arising from integrating these technologies and the subsequent shifts in employer-employee relationships and challenges posed to governance. Furthermore, the chapter elaborates on the real-world implementations of these technologies and their broader ramifications, including cost reductions, sustainability, and socially responsible practices in the concerned sectors.

DOI: 10.4018/979-8-3693-0255-2.ch007

INTRODUCTION

In the last two to three decades, technological innovations and upgrades have tremendously changed the way of doing business globally at an abnormal and precise pace. Technology reimagined how people go about their businesses, from automation to artificial intelligence and robotics (Ivanov & Webster, 2019). These technological innovations and upgrades successfully changed the corporate sector's business operations and introduced highly productive business operations, even in the MSMEs. Disruptive technology, often called disruptive innovation, is when a new business model attracts an underserviced market or revenue stream and grows until it supplants incumbent competitors (Von Lohmann, 2017). In simple terms, disruptive technology is an innovation that significantly alters how consumers, industries, or businesses operate. Technology influence is absolutely at an apex level in the lifestyles of the 21st-century public in every part of the globe. It affects almost every aspect of human life, right from the first minute of the day to the last minute. The emergence of the dot.com boom was another technology that boosted the pace of technological innovations on different continents, including in most third-world countries. Technology affects almost every aspect of the manufacturing sector, and uniquely even services, from education, healthcare, transportation, energy, travel, tourism, telecommunications, and retailing, extensively filled with technology-oriented operations (Aheleroff et al., 2021).

In the rapidly evolving technological landscape of the 21st century, disruptive innovations have emerged as pivotal game-changers, redefining the conventional paradigms of business, governance, and daily life (Sewpersadh, 2023). As a vast and diverse country, India presents a unique canvas, where the interplay of traditional systems and modern disruptive technologies paints a picture of contrasts and synergies. Yet, as with every major shift, it becomes imperative to measure, evaluate, and benchmark the efficiency of these transformative forces. How have the sectors truly harnessed the power of disruptive innovations? Have they reached their maximum potential, or is there a latent capacity still waiting to be tapped? And most importantly, in the race to adopt the new, how efficiently have the sectors transitioned? By leveraging DEA, we can understand the relative efficiency of decision-making units (DMUs) in the context of adopting and implementing disruptive technologies (Brum et al., 2023). This chapter endeavors to bridge the gap between technological adoption and its real-world efficiency through a structured examination of sectors like industry, health, transport, and energy.

BACKGROUND

The application of technologies enables global communities to form and share diverse ideas, innovations, and resources more easily with various stakeholders (Harris et al., 2019). Technology has allowed the world population from all walks of life to access different resources. The persistent emergence of multiple technologies is also being used to equip people who need specific backing to enhance their worth and help them avail themselves of opportunities that would otherwise be challenging. Undoubtedly, technology leads to a wholesome life as it is responsible and accountable for advancement in all sectors of the economy, from the core to services. Technology's remarkable evolution in the last two to three decades has intensified the research and development activity in the private and public sectors, led to impressive and novel innovations, and has contributed more than anything to help human lives a life of luxury and convenience (Hänninen et al., 2021). Every field owes its advancement to technology, which undoubtedly reveals the prominence of technology in every aspect of our lives.

In India, the adoption and assimilation of disruptive technologies have been characterized by significant variability across different sectors (Prasad Agrawal, 2023). India has been a fertile ground for the deployment of innovations such as artificial intelligence, big data analytics, virtual reality, and drone technology. These technologies have permeated various sectors, rendering a transformative impact and altering the paradigms of operation, service delivery, and consumer interaction. The industry sector in India, which forms the backbone of the economy, has witnessed a paradigm shift with the incorporation of disruptive technologies. These innovations have facilitated streamlined operations, increased productivity, and fostered the development of new business models. The infusion of technology has not been uniform, however, with some areas leveraging it more effectively than others, thereby necessitating an in-depth analysis to ascertain the extent of efficiency achieved through these technological interventions. Similarly, the health sector has experienced a seismic shift, with disruptive technologies enabling enhanced patient care, diagnostic precision, and operational efficiency. The integration of these innovations has revolutionized healthcare delivery, making healthcare more accessible and personalized (Paul et al., 2021). However, the diverse and expansive landscape of India's healthcare system poses unique challenges, necessitating a nuanced evaluation of technology adoption and its consequential impact (Tiku, 2023).

The transport sector, vital for the connectivity and economic growth of the diverse and geographically vast nation, has also been at the forefront of adopting disruptive technologies (Sargam et al., 2023). These innovations have enabled the development of smart and sustainable transportation solutions, addressing the multifarious challenges posed by the increasing demand for mobility and urbanization. However, the heterogeneous nature of India's transportation infrastructure demands a meticulous assessment of the efficiency and effectiveness of technology implementation. Furthermore, the energy sector, critical for fueling India's growing economy and addressing the energy needs of its burgeoning population, has seen significant advancements with the adoption of disruptive technologies. These innovations have paved the way for sustainable and efficient energy solutions, enabling the diversification of energy sources and enhancing grid reliability. In a country marked by varied energy requirements and consumption patterns, assessing the efficiency of technology adoption becomes imperative. The introduction and incorporation of disruptive technologies in these key sectors have brought forth a spectrum of opportunities, challenges, and implications. While these innovations have the potential to drive unprecedented growth and development, their integration also poses challenges to governance, necessitating a re-evaluation of regulatory frameworks, policies, and ethical considerations. The shifts in employer-employee relationships, brought about by the automation and digitization of tasks, have further underscored the need for adaptive strategies and policies to address the evolving employment dynamics (Napierala & Kvetan, 2023).

DEA offers a robust framework for evaluating the relative efficiency of different units or sectors in adopting and harnessing disruptive technologies (Chachuli et al., 2021). Through this analytical approach, this study aims to benchmark the efficiency of technology adoption across India's key sectors, thereby providing insights into the areas of improvement, potential enhancements, and strategies for optimized technology integration. By exploring deep into the historical evolution, theoretical underpinnings, and practical implementations of these disruptive technologies, this chapter aims to provide a comprehensive and nuanced perspective on the transformative influence of these innovations on India's socio-economic landscape.

In advancing technology, extensive development of innovations taken up by Prof. Clayton Christensen and his collaborators identified four types of innovations. These are sustaining, evolutionary, revolutionary (discontinuous but sustaining), and finally, disruptive innovations, which create a new market or enter at the bottommost of a current market by delivering a different set of values, which ultimately (and unexpectedly) overtakes incumbents (Christensen & Raynor, 2013). Disruptive innovation refers to the process of renovating an expensive or highly erudite product, offering, or service into one that is more naive, greener, more reasonably priced, and available to a broader population. Companies and their think tanks must keenly and continuously identify the technological innovations in their respective fields and plan to develop plans, programs, and strategies with a proper budget to dump those innovations into their companies. Otherwise, there will be a risk of obsolescence of their products and services, leading to the risk of closure of their units. Companies' investments in millions or billions of dollars are not meant for short-term purposes; almost all businesses' investments are exclusive with long-term orientation only (Xia & Chen, 2023). That, too, no company in the world depends only on one business. These companies always want to maintain yesterday's has-beens and tomorrow's breadwinners.

Companies must consistently observe industry changes when technologies or markets change for the kind of planned expansion and diversification (both related and unrelated). The onus is more on the shoulders of the top management of these established companies in these situations because of their aggressive investment patterns in the technologies crucial to maintaining their current customers. Suppose any company fails to make the technological investments that future customers demand. In that case, they will make a drastic decision to shift from your company to other competitors in the segment. The primary reason is that leading companies yield unique of the most prevalent and valued managing views; they stay adjacent to their customers. Customers exert exceptional power in commanding a company's investments. Concerning sophisticated technology introductions, customers have hesitated because they fear losing their money in the product or technology failure (Park & Zhang, 2022). The fundamental reason is that customers, particularly in developing and underdeveloped countries, are ready to purchase new products with technological advancements but not too new. Another reason, in this case, customers are also afraid of these technological innovations to address their needs, wants, and aspirations effectively. Even with these kinds of fear factors, disruptive innovations, and technologies are showing novel ways for the corporate sectors of the entire world to pave the way to introduce these, especially to win the hearts of the markets.

Through this book chapter, the researchers highlight the comprehensive influence of all these disruptive technologies in India's industries, health, transport, and energy sectors, with examples that keep socially responsible actions in mind. While explaining the effect of these disruptive technologies' influence on the said sectors, remember the reciprocal benefits to both companies and consumers. Furthermore, the researchers intend to comprehensively discuss the possibility of implementing these technologies and consider the technologies' impact on the public related to lowering the prices, augmented customer benefits, sustainability, and socially responsible actions of the innovators. The researchers also propose elaborately discussing these technologies' pros and cons on different stakeholders of the selected sectors like industries, health, transport, and energy.

DISRUPTIVE TECHNOLOGY: HISTORY, MEANING, AND THEORY

The term disruptive technology was initially coined by Professor Clayton Christensen of Harvard University Business School in 1995 through his research on the disk drive industry and further enunciated in his book "The Innovator's Dilemma" in 1997 (Christensen, 2013). In the Innovator's Solution, Prof. Clayton replaced the term with disruptive innovation. The sensational article titled "Disruptive Technologies: Catching the Wave" by Prof. Clayton M. Christensen, with the co-authorship of Prof. Joseph Bower, first identified the term disruptive technology (Bower & Christensen, 1996). The article highlighted and reiterated that managing officials who cause the sponsoring or buying choices in circles and the research community, chiefly in authority for introducing the disruptive direction to the consumer markets. In his other sensational book, "The Innovator's Dilemma," Prof. Christensen explored the case of the disk drive industry and the excavating and earth-moving sectors. Prof. Christensen substituted the term disruptive technology with disruptive innovation because he acknowledged that most technologies are not fundamentally disruptive or sustaining in character (Christensen & Raynor, 2013). He explained the dynamic forces of "business model innovation" in his HBR article "Reinventing Your Business Model" (Christensen et al., 2013). The disruptive technology concept maintains a long tradition of identifying the revolutionary scientific shift in the research of invention by economic experts and its completion by its management at a corporate or policy level. According to Christensen, disruptive innovation is misleading when it refers to the derivate or prompt value of the marketplace performance of the product or service rather than the integral or sum over the histories of the product's market behavior (Christensen et al., 2013).

Disruptive technology is any innovation that radically changes how consumers, businesses, and industries operate (Choi et al., 2022). When first developed, disruptive technologies initiate a new market and institute their value network. These technologies enter an established market but profoundly change how business is handled, and needs are met. These technologies comprehensively substitute their antecedents by presenting outstanding, exceptional progressive benefits that confidently provide multiple benefits to many stakeholders. Disruptive technology entering an existing market can make everyday items or processes obsolete. In its report, McKinsey Global Institute stressed that disruptive technology advances would transform life, business, and the global economy by identifying twelve technologies that might drive immense monetary conversions and disruptions in the future (Srinivasan & Eden, 2021). These twelve disruptive technologies include mobile Internet, automation of knowledge work, IoT, cloud, advanced robotics, autonomous and near-autonomous vehicles, next-generation genomics, energy storage, 3-D printing, advanced materials, refined oil and gas exploration and recovery, and renewable energy. Conventionally, the wheel, the light bulb, and the cell phone are three classic examples of disruptive technologies. At the time, these sensational innovations caused a profound break with previous patterns, bringing about significant changes in the lifestyles of the global population.

The theory of disruptive innovation expounds on the phenomenon by which an innovation alters an existing market or sector by establishing easiness, accessibility, openness, and affordability, where obstacles and high expenditure are the conditions (Sampat et al., 2023). In the beginning, disruptive innovation is modeled in a niche market that may look repellant or insignificant to industry incumbents. Still, ultimately, the new product or idea entirely redefines the industry. Disruptive technology is an innovation that significantly alters how consumers, industries, or businesses operate (Jin & Shin, 2020). It moves away from the systems or habits it substitutes because it has recognizably superior features. For instance, e-commerce, online news sites, ride-sharing apps, and GPS systems are classic examples of disruptive technology. The report from this renowned consultancy stressed that applying these technologies together may potentially have a lucrative impact between USD 14 trillion and $33 trillion a year in 2025 (Martin & Riordan, 2020).

Conversely, the corporate sector and its leaders are at the forefront of commercializing new technologies that don't primarily experience the functional demands of most consumers and plead only to minor or developing markets. To continue at the apex level, the managing cadre should initially be able to spot the technologies that fall into this category. To pursue these technologies, managers must safeguard them from the processes and incentives pitched concerning serving mainstream customers. The only way is to create organizations entirely independent of mainstream business. It's vital to recall that distraction is a constructive intensity. Disruptive originations are not revolutionary knowledge that makes good products better; instead, they are originations that make products and services more welcoming and reasonable, thereby making them presented to a much larger market. Disruption transpires when demonstrated companies overlook new technologies that gobble up customers at the low end of a market until it is too late to stop the disrupters from moving upmarket and accomplishing the incumbent's best customers (Flavin & Flavin, 2020). Disruption is not only a threat for large, slower-moving companies. It can also be a more significant threat to small and medium-sized firms because they will likely have less capital to shield them from losing customers if they are the disruption targets. The best defensive measure against disruption is anticipating the future and cannibalizing your core business faster than your rivals.

EVALUATING DISRUPTIVE TECHNOLOGIES IN INDIA'S KEY SECTORS

Application of DEA in Disruptive Technologies in Industries

DEA can be applied to assess the impact and efficiency of Industry 4.0 technologies like IoT, robotics, and 3D printing in the manufacturing sector (Yıldırım et al., 2020). By evaluating parameters like production costs, downtime, and product quality, DEA can identify areas for improvement and guide the adoption of the most efficient technologies. In agriculture sector industries, DEA can be utilized to evaluate the efficiency of AI-based crop monitoring, precision farming, and drone technology (Sah et al., 2021). By analyzing input and output variables such as cost, resource utilization, and yield, DEA helps in identifying the most efficient technologies and practices, thereby guiding investments and policy formulation in the sector. In retail, DEA can be applied to assess the efficiency of AR/VR, AI, and blockchain in enhancing the shopping experience and managing supply chains (Rowan et al., 2022). By analyzing sales, customer engagement, and inventory management, DEA can guide retailers in adopting efficient technologies and practices.

The industrial sector from all continents always tries to produce different products that most accurately satisfy the needs and wants of the widely scattered markets with additional requirements. In this process, industries often attempt to design principal activities (inbound logistics, operations, outbound logistics, marketing and sales, and services) to produce a perfect value chain along with support activities (technology, firm infrastructure, human resources management, and procurement system) with a motive to receive an expected margin from the targeted markets. Since the 1800s, the world has experienced three industrial revolutions. First, a disruptive new technology powered the current industry 4.0, revolutionizing the automation, monitoring, and analysis of supply chains through intelligent technology. Contemporary Industry 4.0 is confidently fueled by the Industrial Internet of Things and cyber-physical systems- intelligent, autonomous systems that use computer-based algorithms to monitor and control physical things like machinery, robots, and vehicles (Munirathinam, 2020). Ultimately, Industry 4.0 is a significant part of any company's digital transformation (Teichert, 2019).

Industry 4.0 is built on nine technological pillars that are most disruptive in nature. These technologies or innovations bridge the gap between the physical and digital worlds and make intelligent and autonomous systems, viz., big data and artificial intelligence analytics, horizontal and vertical integration, cloud computing, augmented reality, industrial Internet of things, additive manufacturing/3D printing, autonomous robots, simulation or digital twins, and cybersecurity. The discussed Industry 4.0 disruptive technologies offer multiple benefits to the industry: intelligent products, assets, factories, and empowered people. Companies from different parts of the globe are experiencing lucrative advantages like profound developments in productivity and computerization, resiliency, and swiftness no matter what the market or economy brings, and the confidence to explore new business models and seize opportunities rapidly, with green and sustainable solutions without sacrificing profitability. Even with these advantages, companies must think about upskilling their existing human resources, which will be an uphill task because of the newness of these disruptive technologies.

Several companies have taken up the value chain analysis to understand where opportunities for improvement lie. The incessant conducting of a value chain analysis prompts these companies to consider how each step adds or subtracts value from your final product or service. In the value chain analysis, companies can first identify various activities where chances are there to improve in the primary activities based on which companies can develop plans, programs, policies, strategies, and budgets (Riahi Dorcheh et al., 2021). Whatever the type of technology, ease of use and usefulness of the technology, corporate needs, and social acceptance are the critical reasons for the approval of technology. Therefore, technologies or innovations influence major industries and small and medium enterprises (SMEs) (Borah et al., 2022). The corporate sector confidently believes that persistent value chain analysis (both primary and support activities) proliferates the value deliverables to the market; in turn, a chance of getting the expected margins would be possible. With this backdrop, digital disruption has occurred in recent decades impressively and extraordinarily changed the way of doing business/industries in most sectors and led to the introduction of novel digital technologies and business models on existing goods, services, systems, and structures. However, this shift from the conventional application of technology to the present digital formats takes time, and the impact of digital technologies is increasing exponentially. With the introduction of particularly disruptive technology or innovations, businesses can competently establish in their respective markets and have a massive opportunity to enter into new markets or take advantage to displace significant competitors in an established landscape by defining and redefining their competitive advantage. Starting as a company in 1997 by Reed Hastings and Marc Randolph in Scotts Valley, California, initially supplying DVD mailouts, the American media company Netflix is a classic example of the world's leading entertainment services, with 231 million paid memberships in over 190 countries offering a cost-effective and convenient product to an area of the market that was previously overlooked (Randolph, 2019).

Sensational disruptive technologies include e-commerce, online news sites, online banking and company sites, ride-sharing apps, and GPS systems, just like automobiles, electricity service, and television in their times (Valavanidis, 2020). Through e-commerce, every product and service is available virtually via the Internet. Without moving from their homes, customers can purchase any product, from consumer to industrial products. E-commerce successfully in most countries replaced physical retailing, and this trend was slowly increasing and identified a drastic hike in e-commerce in the last three years of the pandemic (Potluri & Thomas, 2023). The primary reason for this is digital disruption, so preferences and comfort have switched to buying practically anything online. It has been demonstrated to be a boon for retailers caught between well-funded competitors and a highly uncertain market. Digital transformation always continues in the life of a retailer who keeps their business up to date. All these developments are only with the proliferation of the Internet, smartphones, liberalization, privatization, and globalization (LPG). E-commerce business has witnessed a lot of new trends around digital transformation and disruption in the context of the current and upcoming mega-market for the segment. These e-commerce trends are data-driven commerce, augmented reality (AR) disrupting the way customers shop, the primary source of revenue for an increasing number of brick-and-mortar retailers e-commerce, increasing reliance on non-traditional payment methods, and personalized products (Langer & Mukherjee, 2023). Technology and innovation will drive the e-commerce revolution in most parts of the world, including India. Notably, India is at the cusp of an e-commerce revolution. Even though e-commerce has existed in India for over a decade or two, in recent years, only has identified an appropriate ecosystem or platform due to internet access, significant penetration of smartphones, and robust investment have driven the growth of this industry and if the current projections are continuing in the same trend. The industry players who can adjust and transform in the face of these changes in e-commerce will be in a better position for success. India has set an aspiring target of expanding into a $1 trillion digital economy by 2025 (Dubey et al., 2023). The driving force toward this economic growth will come from several industry sectors, many of which are already in the progressed stages of digitalization. These sectors include IT, IT-enabled services, electronics, telecom, e-commerce, financial services, the Internet of Things (IoT), and media and entertainment (Kumar et al., 2022). Finally, Indian organizations in every sector, with careful analysis of their value chain, confidently provide better value than their competing counterparts by introducing diverse disruptive technologies we discussed in the early parts of the book chapter.

Application of DEA in Disruptive Technologies in the Health Sector

India's health sector is diverse and evolving, making it a pertinent field for the introduction of innovative solutions to address its unique challenges. DEA is used to evaluate the efficiency of telemedicine services by comparing input resources such as costs, technology, and healthcare professionals against outputs like patient satisfaction, accessibility, and health outcomes (Kontodimopoulos et al., 2006). This analysis helps in identifying the most efficient telemedicine platforms and guides resource allocation to improve healthcare delivery, especially in remote areas. DEA assesses the effectiveness and efficiency of AI-based diagnostic and treatment tools. By analyzing inputs like cost, data accuracy, and time against outputs like diagnosis accuracy, treatment success rates, and patient outcomes, DEA helps in identifying the most efficient AI-based solutions and optimizing their implementation (Fallahpour et al., 2016). DEA evaluates the application of blockchain technology in ensuring data security, traceability, and interoperability in healthcare. By comparing resource inputs against outcomes like data breach rates, information exchange efficiency, and patient satisfaction, DEA assists in benchmarking blockchain applications and guiding their optimal utilization. Electronic Health Records are pivotal in streamlining healthcare data management. DEA is used to assess the efficiency of EHR systems by analyzing the resources used and the outcomes achieved, such as data accuracy, accessibility, and impact on healthcare delivery (Cowie et al., 2017). This helps in identifying areas for improvement and optimizing the use of EHRs. DEA is instrumental in evaluating the efficiency of wearable health technologies like fitness trackers and health monitors. By comparing input variables like cost, user engagement, and technology against health outcomes and user satisfaction, DEA helps in optimizing the development and use of wearable health technology. Remote patient monitoring tools are essential in chronic disease management. DEA compares the inputs such as costs, technology, and healthcare personnel against outputs like patient health outcomes, readmission rates, and patient satisfaction to identify the most efficient remote monitoring tools and guide their implementation. DEA is used to evaluate the efficiency of personalized medicine approaches by analyzing input resources and resulting health outcomes. This analysis is vital in identifying the most effective personalized medicine strategies and optimizing their application to enhance patient care.

India's healthcare sector has become more centered on innovations and technology over the past two decades, and 80% of healthcare systems aim to increase their investment in digital healthcare tools in the coming five years (Lee & Yoon, 2021). The country's healthcare sector encompasses hospitals, medical devices, clinical trials, outsourcing, telemedicine, medical tourism, health insurance, and medical equipment. The healthcare delivery system in India is labeled into two major components – public and private. India's competitive advantage is kept in its large pool of well-trained medical professionals. India is also cost-competitive compared to its peers in Asia and Western countries (Mohanan, 2021). The cost of surgery in India is about one-tenth of that in the US or Western Europe. In the healthcare sector, disruption often shifts care from hospitals to clinics, office settings, and even into patients' homes. Telemedicine is the most obvious example. The process matches the clinician's skill level with the difficulty of the medical problem. Persistent innovation is no stranger to the healthcare sector in India. The world has witnessed the success story of the Indian healthcare sector by inventing and offering Covid-19 vaccinations most effectively and efficiently (Walia et al., 2023). New therapies, medical devices, and healthcare management practices are consistently implemented. Disruptive innovations source revolutionary change and often result in new leaders in the field. They downturn the predictable way of doing things to such an extent that they have a ripple effect throughout the healthcare industry.

The following disruptive innovations in healthcare in India are positioned on technology, customer-centric care, and third-party advancements. Undoubtedly, technology is the enormous driver of many disruptive innovations in healthcare since every healthcare viewpoint depends on some form of technology. Any new technology could shake up healthcare, from wearables and mobile phone apps to big data and artificial intelligence (AI) use in diagnosis (Wahid et al., 2023). Nowadays, consumers take charge of their health journey, employing the data collected from their smartwatches, Fitbits, and mobile phone fitness apps. Doctors can use the data picked from these wearables to make treatment decisions (Baig et al., 2017). However, the substantial amount of confidential information garnered by these apps has indicated legal and ethical concerns over data privacy. Disruptive technologies or innovations like artificial intelligence (AI) applications can manage patient intake, scheduling, and billing, along with other Chatbots answering patient questions (Xu et al., 2021). With innate language processing capacities, AI can pool and explore survey responses. AI may enhance its use to reduce healthcare costs and let doctors and staff focus on patient care. Healthcare leaders and management staff must know about database management and patient privacy issues. Blockchain is a database technology that applies encryption and supplementary security measures to store data and link it to enhance security and usability. This innovation enables many aspects of healthcare, including patient records, supply and distribution, and research. Tech start-ups have entered the healthcare sector with blockchain applications that have transformed how providers manipulate medical data. The Indian healthcare sector also effectively implements another disruptive technology, i.e., the Internet of Things, which collects data from wearable devices, thermometers, smartwatches, and various other consumer devices and then uses the same data to discover disease clusters and provide care to patients more effectively. Cloud services, also known as cloud computing, permit patients' data files to be saved on the Internet without needing external storage equipment and risk of any theft or loss of data (Rosenthal et al., 2010). This disruptive technology signifies excellent benefits for healthcare providers and companies because it allows users to enjoy management tools from anywhere worldwide by connecting from their devices. Like the above technology-centered care, disruptive technologies are also valuable for providing consumer-centered care with some combination of aspects like the consumerization of healthcare; the patient-healthcare provider relationship has also experienced sweeping change.

In this field of commitment to saving the lives of the public, the combination of technology in general and disruptive technology in particular, along with public policy, has transformed how patients access the required healthcare services with constant interaction with the service providers. The healthcare sector, both in the public and private sectors, must maintain the vast data related to patient care since adopting the Consumer Protection Act 2019 (Math et al., 2019). However, the massive amount of EHR data goes far beyond patient health records and can be used to conduct research, improve care, build AI applications, and create new business opportunities. Therefore, healthcare providers must be aware of EHR security issues. Even in the most recent outburst of Covid-19, disruptive technologies include high-tech and emerging technologies such as artificial intelligence, Industry 4.0, Internet of Medical Things (IoMT), big data, virtual reality (VR), drone technology and autonomous robots, 5G, and blockchain to offer digital transformation (Mondal & Mitra, 2022), research and development, and service delivery. Disruptive technologies are vital for Industry 4.0 developments and proposed a framework that uses disruptive technologies for Covid-19 analysis (Abdel-Basset et al., 2021). The suggested framework restricts the spread of Covid-19 outbreaks, ensures the safety of the healthcare teams, and maintains patients' physical and psychological healthcare conditions. The development patterns of disruptive technologies for environmental monitoring are studied and anticipated to aid in promoting India's environmental monitoring and protection (Gupta, 1995).

Application of DEA in Disruptive Technologies in Transportation Sector

Transport is vital to economic growth, creating jobs, linking people to essential services such as healthcare and education, and ensuring trade and network extension (Sokolov et al., 2019). However, in many developing countries, the advantages are not being grasped. Thanks to the governments in India, which has primarily succeeded in establishing all-weather transportation facilities from the top to bottom of the country. Transportation is a rudimentary infrastructure, and its progress indicates the country's development. The transport sector's improvement and reforms augment freight and passengers' dynamicity in almost all regions in India (Niu et al., 2023). Transport is critical because it facilitates trade between people and places, essential for developing civilizations. India's transport system encompasses several distinct modes and services, notably railways, roads, road transport, ports, inland water transport, coastal shipping, airports, and airlines.

Transportation enables communication, trade, exchange, etc., between societies, which is significant for its development (Mora et al., 2021). It contributes to developing economic, social, political, and cultural fields of civilization and helps to better their conditions. Transportation converts a means to carry necessary raw materials from raw material providers to factories where it is used to produce goods. Transportation helps to bring stability to the prices of different commodities. It helps relocate goods from more supplied places to scarcely provided areas. Transportation creates time and place utilities for goods and services produced by manufacturers and marketers.

In India, the transport sector plays a pivotal role in connecting diverse regions and supporting economic development. The incorporation of disruptive technologies is intended to enhance connectivity, improve service efficiency, and meet the rising demand for transportation services. DEA is instrumental in evaluating these technologies, ensuring they are optimally efficient and effectively addressing the sector's unique challenges. DEA can be used to assess the operational and environmental efficiency of electric vehicles in comparison to traditional fuel vehicles (Chen et al., 2012). By analyzing inputs such as energy consumption, costs, and maintenance against outputs like emissions, travel distance, and user satisfaction, DEA aids in guiding policies and investments towards sustainable transport solutions (Choudhury et al., 2018). In India, the advent of autonomous vehicles holds the promise of reducing traffic congestion and accidents. DEA evaluates the efficiency of autonomous vehicles by considering inputs like technology, fuel, and maintenance, and comparing them against outputs such as travel time, safety, and passenger satisfaction. This assists in optimizing the integration of autonomous vehicles within India's diverse transportation landscape.

DEA is employed to assess the efficiency of Intelligent Traffic Management Systems (ITMS) in mitigating traffic congestion and enhancing road safety (Tabatabai & Tabatabai, 2024). By evaluating the resources invested and the resultant improvement in traffic flow and reduction in accidents, DEA helps in optimizing the deployment of ITMS across urban centers in India. DEA can benchmark the efficiency of emerging technologies like Hyperloop (Pinho, 2017). By analyzing the inputs like investment costs, energy consumption, and operational expenses against outputs such as speed, passenger throughput, and safety, DEA can guide decision-makers in evaluating the feasibility and scalability of Hyperloop technology in India. The efficiency of drone delivery systems for transporting goods, especially in remote and inaccessible regions, can be assessed using DEA. By comparing input variables like energy consumption, operational costs, and technology against output variables like delivery time, reach, and reliability, DEA provides insights into optimizing drone delivery services. DEA is instrumental in evaluating the efficiency of ride-sharing platforms in India (Cantzler et al., 2020). By analyzing inputs such as fleet size, technology, and operational costs against outputs like passenger satisfaction, ride availability, and environmental impact, DEA helps in enhancing the operational efficiency of ride-sharing services. Given the significance of the railway network in India, DEA is used to assess technologies aimed at optimizing train schedules, reducing delays, and enhancing passenger services. By evaluating input resources and resultant service improvements, DEA assists in optimizing technology deployment across the rail network.

European Bank for Reconstruction and Development (EBRD) is working persistently to support the promotion of innovative new technology, specifically in the transport sector in the economies where the bank operates, to improve competitiveness and provide demonstration effects (Shields, 2020). The following four disruptive technologies are highly effective, influence the transport sector, and lead revolutionary changes, which provide lucrative benefits to service providers and their customers. The main applications of these technologies in transportation emphasize demand forecasting and optimization, resulting in improved traffic management, asset management, travel planning, and operation of autonomous vehicles (AVs) (Gomes Correia & Ferreira, 2023). The significant challenge in developing the recognized disruptive technologies and their applications will be their productive integration into new business and governance models, maximizing their collective benefits to sustain the end goal.

The four applications of the disruptive technologies that transform the Indian transport sector in the following areas: i) Traffic management using intelligent transport systems (ITS) – by means of new technologies to envisage future traffic demand more precisely and augment road networks thus, providing a wide range of social and economic benefits, including reduced congestion and pollution, enhanced safety and travel experiences for all road users (Iyer, 2021); ii) Personal travel planning and public transport – examining accessible information on travel demand and travel patterns of the population to enable the optimization of planning, programming, and operation of public transport systems, as well as improving personal journey planning for the public (Oviedo et al., 2020); iii) Autonomous and connected vehicles for mobility – developing applications for AVs that can contribute to increased safety, a better user experience, economic savings, and reductions in congestion by facilitating car sharing and "mobility as a service" (Maas) (Alyavina et al., 2022); iv) Unmanned aerial vehicles/drones for monitoring - expending technology to transfigure the way we undertake asset management, maintenance and inspections (bridges, tunnels and construction sites) and offering an efficient means to deliver packages (logistics) (Aabid et al., 2022).

These technology application areas were evaluated in the circumstance of their contribution to the following policy objectives: (1) transport efficiency, (2) safety and security, (3) environment and climate change, and (4) socioeconomics. From the analysis of these policy objectives, we concluded that the technology application areas that have the most profound (disruption) potential impacts were new smart mobility (AVs/MaaS and drones) and intelligent transport systems (ITS), each requiring and leveraging different digital technologies. The vital challenge in improving the recognized digital technologies and their applications will be successfully integrating the business and governance models for new mobility technologies, services, and systems. The following challenges significantly influence the Indian transport sector. a) Harmonizing established and new policies transmitted to the legal framework for using and operationalizing such technologies; b) Accelerating pragmatic and data sharing; c) Endorsing vehicle-to-infrastructure (V2I) and vehicle-to-vehicle (V2V) communication; d) Safeguarding data security and tackling risk sharing/accountability concerns; e) Recognizing necessities for facilitating necessary enabling "public" infrastructure and forms of economic regulation to empower extensive acceptance; f) Emerging cost-benefit analysis methodologies and the subsidiary indication base to encourage adoption; g) Introducing diagnostic work and evolving state-of-the-art operating replicas; h) Rising unified mobility systems; i) Sharing data and digital infrastructure; j) Supportive capacity-building, education, and awareness-raising.

Application of DEA in the Disruptive Technologies in Energy Sector

Disruptive innovation in the energy sector permits electric generation foundations to state extra power to supply energy swiftly and at a higher capacity, all gratitude to grid integration technologies. Such innovation essentially incorporates green renewable energy's transmission, distribution, and grounding. The world energy sector is incessantly pushing itself toward digital business transformation to empower its operations to provide quality and the required quantity of energy to the customers' community. The Indian energy sector started its efforts by making better decisions to initiate a digital journey for its energy-transition plans and leverage its customer-centric approach to drive deeper customer connections and loyalty (Mukherjee & Janssen, 2023). In keeping with the ever-evolving energy landscape of India, extensive disruptive technologies have been introduced and based on which an expected degree of quantity and quality of energy persistently supplying to the world's second-largest market.

In India, the energy sector is a focal point of innovation and development, given the country's growing energy needs and the government's emphasis on sustainable solutions. The application of DEA in evaluating disruptive technologies in this sector is vital for optimizing resource utilization, ensuring sustainability, and meeting the diverse energy demands efficiently (Zeng et al., 2020). DEA is instrumental in assessing the efficiency of renewable energy technologies like solar, wind, and bioenergy. By analyzing inputs such as installation costs, maintenance, and land use against outputs like energy generation, emission reduction, and reliability, DEA helps in identifying the most efficient renewable energy solutions and guides investments and policy decisions (Rostami et al., 2022). Energy storage solutions like batteries and pumped hydro storage are crucial for managing energy supply and demand.

DEA evaluates these technologies by comparing input resources and operational costs against outputs such as storage capacity, discharge duration, and reliability, thereby aiding in the optimization of energy storage infrastructure (Arriola et al., 2022). Smart grids play a pivotal role in enhancing the reliability and efficiency of energy distribution. DEA is used to benchmark smart grid technologies by analyzing inputs like technology, infrastructure, and operational costs against outcomes like energy loss reduction, reliability improvement, and integration of renewable energy, which guides the development and deployment of smart grids across India.

Microgrids are essential for providing energy access in remote and off-grid areas in India. DEA assesses the efficiency of microgrid solutions by comparing the investment, operational costs, and technology against the achieved energy access, reliability, and sustainability, which helps in optimizing microgrid deployments and addressing energy access challenges (Babazadeh et al., 2016). DEA is applied to evaluate technologies aimed at enhancing energy efficiency in industries and buildings. By analyzing the investment, technology, and maintenance against the achieved energy savings, emission reductions, and cost savings, DEA helps in identifying and promoting the most efficient energy conservation solutions. Demand response solutions are critical for managing peak energy demand. DEA evaluates these solutions by comparing the technology, infrastructure, and operational inputs against outcomes like peak demand reduction, cost savings, and grid stability, thereby guiding the implementation of demand response strategies effectively. DEA assesses the efficiency of waste-to-energy technologies by analyzing inputs such as waste processing, technology, and operational costs against outputs like energy generation, waste reduction, and environmental impact (Albores et al., 2016). This helps in promoting sustainable waste management and energy generation practices. DEA can be used to assess the operational efficiency of nuclear power plants by analyzing inputs like fuel usage, operational costs, and safety measures against outputs like energy generation, safety records, and environmental impact (Goto et al., 2014). This assists in optimizing nuclear energy production and ensuring its safe and sustainable use.

Disruptive technologies developed in the energy sector rapidly transform the global energy scene. In brief, a technology that creates new business models that disrupt traditional ones is called disruptive technology (Bughin et al., 2010). Such disruptive technology in the energy sector can spur a transformation in technological capacities, digital transformation, cost, and the business model itself. Identifying the impact of disruptive innovations on diverse energy sectors is critical and obligatory, as it will give disruptors the push they need to move forward. Disruptive energy resolutions are mounting because they are mandatory, and the sooner this fact is realized, the more advanced the sector can experience. Primarily, the industrial and environmental policy furnished enormous favor and deep space for renewable energy to exist. Even though consumer-level proposals such as net metering and feed-in tariffs have been bundled with real incentives to encourage the adoption of such industry among consumers. For instance, even among financial reserves, giants like the USA and China still enjoyed the fruits of accelerating innovation and developing clean, dependable, and affordable energy (Arunachalam & Fleischer, 2008).

Even in India, extensive efforts have been initiated by the energy sector, along with all types of governments (Central, State, and Local), to introduce disruptive technologies/innovations to meet the escalating trend of energy requirements of the country beyond the conventional towards green energy which is affordable to meet the pocket strength of the developing country India. All through history, technology has obtained a strange inclination to transform whole industries within the blink of an eye. When it does, new prospects arise as swiftly as obsolete methods are eclipsed. Today's energy sector from India is no exception, though the interests are much higher as rising CO2 levels make accepting renewable energy a pressing global challenge. Developments in home energy management, energy storage, connectivity, and grid technology are blurring up the old business models of practicalities and suppliers and profoundly reordering their relationship with customers. In the meantime, digital technology inventions in big-data analysis, the Internet of Things (IoT), and artificial intelligence are authorizing the development of new ways to improve energy efficiency and security, as well as new services. The Future Bridge (2022) highlighted the following five disruptive technologies: a) wireless energy transmission for the EV charging infrastructure, b) perovskite solar cells are easy-to-synthesize materials that can convert sunlight to electricity with efficiencies of over 30% and would cost much less than traditional silicon solar cells in the coming years, c) passive cooling technology requires only sunlight and can drastically reduce electricity consumption and cost, d) solid-state batteries as an alternative solution to lithium-ion batteries' deficiencies of flammability, low energy density, and slow charging speed, solid-state batteries provide a safe and scalable option, and e) methane pyrolysis for hydrogen production.

The most prominent energy disruptive solutions like artificial intelligence, big data, integrating grids, intricate photovoltaics, and robotics in the reputed international telecoms business magazine "Inside Telecom," a young digital news platform specializing in tech and telecoms (Ahmad et al., 2021). Artificial intelligence (AI) developed one of the energetic forces for computing departments in high-energy infrastructures, enabling you to anticipate energy consumption. AI even allows the analytical protection of renewable energy methods (Bedi et al., 2022). This technology paved the way for intricate automated analysis tools to identify and create a digital map to resolve technical issues. Artificial intelligence also acknowledges Internet of Things (IoT) functions that reckon grid capacity levels. Concerning integrating grids, disruptive innovation in the energy sector permits electric generation foundations to have extra power to disperse energy rapidly and at a higher capacity, all merit grid integration technologies. Such invention principally includes the transmission, distribution, and grounding of green renewable energy. It functions via a complicated network of wires with a fully programmable setup. Grid integration was a disruptive solution that used microcontroller-based components to crack frequency and voltage fluctuation. Regarding intricate photovoltaics, solar power energy is more popular due to its simple adaptation innovations, specifically solar panels. Some solar solutions suppliers initiate thin-film cells to lower costs and weight and foster mobility, elasticity, and integration. This shows that the sunlight absorption in the cells will be catalyzed and even feasible at substantial volumes. Furthermore, companies are obtaining breakthrough ways to employ solar power utilizing mirrors and lenses. Related to robotics, this disruptive technology in the energy sector seems like a science-fiction movie.

Automated machines ensure fluid operations of the whole power generation plant (Yang et al., 2022). Robot-based autonomous operations and maintenance (O&M) occur via drones carrying on inspections. Risky and monotonous labor is now in the robotic hands of these futuristic workers. Drones use phased array ultrasonic imaging to recognize damage to enormous wind turbines abruptly; drones monitor and spot monitors evident weaknesses dreadful for the human eye to notice (Makhdoom et al., 2022). Robotics is not uniquely a thing for giants like the USA and China. Developing nations have invested in these tech solutions in recent years to get a breakthrough for their energy sector. The Indian energy sector has been enjoying critical benefits like better electrification, more intelligent infrastructures, and the advancement of electrification for decades. This technology will catalyze the worldwide shift to renewable green energy, a step toward a greener or planet-friendly energy resource for safe and secure humanity. Throughout the globe, energy companies are on the verge of unprecedented impediments, and dynamic customer expectations are also expanding exponentially. Firms are forced to operate, maintain, and keep their systems up to date. Tomorrow is beginning today, and if electric companies and leaders do not want to prioritize the benefit of our planet, then the entire world is in deep, muddy water.

FUTURE RESEARCH DIRECTIONS

Future researchers could consider conducting a comparative study of the efficiency of disruptive technology adoption across different countries, focusing on the variances and the driving factors behind these differences. There is also a need for conducting a study employing a longitudinal approach, assessing the progress of technology adoption and efficiency over time, providing insights into the evolving trends and the long-term impacts of disruptive technologies on different sectors. While this study touched on shifts in employer-employee relationships, a more in-depth exploration of how disruptive technologies are affecting job creation, job displacement, skill requirements, and labor market dynamics is needed. A sector-specific deep dive, focusing on individual sectors like health, transport, or energy, can provide detailed insights and nuanced understanding of the unique challenges and opportunities within each sector. There is also a need for integrating other benchmarking techniques alongside DEA, such as Stochastic Frontier Analysis (SFA) or Balanced Scorecard (BSC), offering a more holistic and robust analysis of efficiency.

Further research can be directed towards understanding the specific governance challenges arising from the integration of disruptive technologies and proposing frameworks to address these challenges. The inclusion and assessment of emerging and future disruptive technologies, not covered in the current study, can keep future researchers in this rapidly evolving technological landscape. An exploration into the societal and environmental impacts of the adoption of disruptive technologies in key sectors is also needed to provide a balanced view of their benefits and potential drawbacks. An in-depth analysis of the existing policies governing disruptive technologies, their effectiveness, and gaps, along with actionable policy recommendations, can be valuable for stakeholders and policymakers. Future researchers could also consider conducting detailed case studies of organizations that have successfully adopted and harnessed disruptive technologies which can offer practical insights and lessons learned for others in the field.

CONCLUSION

Disruptive technology is more than an innovation in today's economy. It is a probability of outperforming the existing completion and getting better. Therefore, it is a must to introduce sophisticated technology into the organization by expecting reciprocal benefits from both companies and customers. Inviting technology, in general, and disruptive technologies, in particular, empowers businesses and their way of doing things to satisfy different stakeholders by overcoming various risks and staying afloat in the competitive environment. The corporate world continuously designs plans, policies, programs, procedures, and budgets to flourish in the highly competitive existing business world. Therefore, businesses must adopt the culture of investing in disruptive innovations. In the last two to three decades, particularly in India, the corporate sector intensified its efforts to embrace the culture of investing in disruptive technologies. The role of business leaders is quite crucial. First, they must update their organizational strategies in the face of continuously evolving technologies. Disruptive innovations will be the game changer shortly, particularly in the developing and underdeveloped world. The bottom line is that disruption is all about trial and error, as that's the way innovations take birth. These innovations and technologies benefit multinational organizations or businesses and are highly lucrative even to micro, small, and medium enterprises (MSMEs). To survive and stay long-term, companies and their think tanks must be transparent and flexible enough to embrace disruptive innovations. The application of disruptive technologies in Indian industries, healthcare sector, transport, and energy sectors in the last decade or two has been more extensive with the developments of artificial intelligence, big data analysis, augmented reality, virtual reality, drone technology, Internet of Things (IoT), and Internet of Medical Things (IoMT) along with e-commerce, and the astonishing Global Positioning System (GPS). These sensational disruptive technologies have been tremendously changing the lives of the Indian public.

ACKNOWLEDGMENT

This research received no specific grant from any funding agency in the public, commercial, or not-for-profit sectors.

REFERENCES

Aabid, A., Parveez, B., Parveen, N., Khan, S. A., & Shabbir, O. (2022). A Case Study of Unmanned Aerial Vehicle (Drone) Technology and Its Applications in the COVID-19 Pandemic. *J. Mech. Eng. Res. Dev*, *45*, 70–77.

Abdel-Basset, M., Chang, V., & Nabeeh, N. A. (2021). An intelligent framework using disruptive technologies for COVID-19 analysis. *Technological Forecasting and Social Change*, *163*, 120431. doi:10.1016/j.techfore.2020.120431 PMID:33162617

Aheleroff, S., Mostashiri, N., Xu, X., & Zhong, R. Y. (2021). Mass personalisation as a service in industry 4.0: A resilient response case study. *Advanced Engineering Informatics*, *50*, 101438. doi:10.1016/j.aei.2021.101438

Ahmad, T., Zhang, D., Huang, C., Zhang, H., Dai, N., Song, Y., & Chen, H. (2021). Artificial intelligence in sustainable energy industry: Status Quo, challenges and opportunities. *Journal of Cleaner Production*, *289*, 125834. doi:10.1016/j.jclepro.2021.125834

Albores, P., Petridis, K., & Dey, P. (2016). Analysing efficiency of waste to energy systems: Using data envelopment analysis in municipal solid waste management. *Procedia Environmental Sciences*, *35*, 265–278. doi:10.1016/j.proenv.2016.07.007

Alyavina, E., Nikitas, A., & Njoya, E. T. (2022). Mobility as a service (MaaS): A thematic map of challenges and opportunities. *Research in Transportation Business & Management*, *43*, 100783. doi:10.1016/j.rtbm.2022.100783

Arriola, E. R., Ubando, A. T., & Chen, W. H. (2022). A bibliometric review on the application of fuzzy optimization to sustainable energy technologies. *International Journal of Energy Research*, *46*(1), 6–27. doi:10.1002/er.5729

Arunachalam, V., & Fleischer, E. (2008). The global energy landscape and materials innovation. *MRS Bulletin*, *33*(4), 264–288. doi:10.1557/mrs2008.61

Babazadeh, E., Jannati Oskuee, M. R., Pourmahmoud, J., & Najafi-Ravadanegh, S. (2016). Optimal Planning of Smart Distribution Network Based on Efficiency Evaluation Using Data Envelopment Analysis. *International Journal on Electrical Engineering & Informatics*, 8(1), 45–61. doi:10.15676/ijeei.2016.8.1.4

Baig, M. M., GholamHosseini, H., Moqeem, A. A., Mirza, F., & Lindén, M. (2017). A systematic review of wearable patient monitoring systems–current challenges and opportunities for clinical adoption. *Journal of Medical Systems*, 41(7), 1–9. doi:10.100710916-017-0760-1 PMID:28631139

Bedi, P., Goyal, S., Rajawat, A. S., Shaw, R. N., & Ghosh, A. (2022). Application of AI/IoT for smart renewable energy management in smart cities. *AI and IoT for Smart City Applications*, 115-138.

Borah, S., Kama, C., Rakshit, S., & Vajjhala, N. R. (2022). Applications of Artificial Intelligence in Small-and Medium-Sized Enterprises (SMEs). In *Cognitive Informatics and Soft Computing: Proceeding of CISC 2021* (pp. 717-726). Springer.

Bower, J. L., & Christensen, C. M. (1996). Disruptive technologies: Catching the wave. *Journal of Product Innovation Management*, 1(13), 75–76.

Brum, C. P., & de Faria Corrêa, R. G., de J. Pacheco, D. A., Nepomuceno, T. C. C., de Oliveira, A. L. R., & Marsola, K. B. (2023). Efficiency analysis of inland waterway locks in maritime transportation systems: Practical, economic and policy implications. *Maritime Policy & Management*, 1–24. doi:10.1080/03088839.2023.2252431

Bughin, J., Chui, M., & Manyika, J. (2010). Clouds, big data, and smart assets: Ten tech-enabled business trends to watch. *The McKinsey Quarterly*, 56(1), 75–86.

Cantzler, J., Creutzig, F., Ayargarnchanakul, E., Javaid, A., Wong, L., & Haas, W. (2020). Saving resources and the climate? A systematic review of the circular economy and its mitigation potential. *Environmental Research Letters*, 15(12), 123001. doi:10.1088/1748-9326/abbeb7

Chachuli, F. S. M., Ludin, N. A., Jedi, M. A. M., & Hamid, N. H. (2021). Transition of renewable energy policies in Malaysia: Benchmarking with data envelopment analysis. *Renewable & Sustainable Energy Reviews*, 150, 111456. doi:10.1016/j.rser.2021.111456

Chen, C., Zhu, J., Yu, J.-Y., & Noori, H. (2012). A new methodology for evaluating sustainable product design performance with two-stage network data envelopment analysis. *European Journal of Operational Research*, 221(2), 348–359. doi:10.1016/j.ejor.2012.03.043

Choi, T. M., Kumar, S., Yue, X., & Chan, H. L. (2022). Disruptive technologies and operations management in the Industry 4.0 era and beyond. *Production and Operations Management*, 31(1), 9–31. doi:10.1111/poms.13622

Choudhury, N., Raut, R. D., Gardas, B. B., Kharat, M. G., & Ichake, S. (2018). Evaluation and selection of third party logistics services providers using data envelopment analysis: A sustainable approach. *International Journal of Business Excellence*, 14(4), 427–453. doi:10.1504/IJBEX.2018.090311

Christensen, C., & Raynor, M. (2013). *The innovator's solution: Creating and sustaining successful growth*. Harvard Business Review Press.

Christensen, C., Raynor, M. E., & McDonald, R. (2013). *Disruptive innovation*. Harvard Business Review Brighton.

Christensen, C. M. (2013). *The innovator's dilemma: when new technologies cause great firms to fail*. Harvard Business Review Press.

Cowie, M. R., Blomster, J. I., Curtis, L. H., Duclaux, S., Ford, I., Fritz, F., Goldman, S., Janmohamed, S., Kreuzer, J., Leenay, M., Michel, A., Ong, S., Pell, J. P., Southworth, M. R., Stough, W. G., Thoenes, M., Zannad, F., & Zalewski, A. (2017). Electronic health records to facilitate clinical research. *Clinical Research in Cardiology; Official Journal of the German Cardiac Society, 106*(1), 1–9. doi:10.100700392-016-1025-6 PMID:27557678

Dubey, B., Agrawal, S., & Sharma, A. K. (2023). India's Renewable Energy Portfolio: An Investigation of the Untapped Potential of RE, Policies, and Incentives Favoring Energy Security in the Country. *Energies, 16*(14), 5491. doi:10.3390/en16145491

Fallahpour, A., Olugu, E. U., Musa, S. N., Khezrimotlagh, D., & Wong, K. Y. (2016). An integrated model for green supplier selection under fuzzy environment: Application of data envelopment analysis and genetic programming approach. *Neural Computing & Applications, 27*(3), 707–725. doi:10.100700521-015-1890-3

Flavin, M., & Flavin, M. (2020). Conclusion: Switch It Off, Switch It on Again—Reimagining Technology-Enhanced Learning in Higher Education. *Re-imagining Technology Enhanced Learning: Critical Perspectives on Disruptive Innovation*, 145-200.

Gomes Correia, M., & Ferreira, A. (2023). Road Asset Management and the Vehicles of the Future: An Overview, Opportunities, and Challenges. *International Journal of Intelligent Transportation Systems Research*, 1-18.

Goto, M., Otsuka, A., & Sueyoshi, T. (2014). DEA (Data Envelopment Analysis) assessment of operational and environmental efficiencies on Japanese regional industries. *Energy, 66*, 535–549. doi:10.1016/j.energy.2013.12.020

Gupta, M. C. (1995). Environmental management and its impact on the operations function. *International Journal of Operations & Production Management, 15*(8), 34–51. doi:10.1108/01443579510094071

Hänninen, M., Kwan, S. K., & Mitronen, L. (2021). From the store to omnichannel retail: Looking back over three decades of research. *International Review of Retail, Distribution and Consumer Research, 31*(1), 1–35. doi:10.1080/09593969.2020.1833961

Harris, P. A., Taylor, R., Minor, B. L., Elliott, V., Fernandez, M., O'Neal, L., McLeod, L., Delacqua, G., Delacqua, F., Kirby, J., & Duda, S. N. (2019). The REDCap consortium: Building an international community of software platform partners. *Journal of Biomedical Informatics, 95*, 103208. doi:10.1016/j.jbi.2019.103208 PMID:31078660

Ivanov, S., & Webster, C. (2019). Conceptual framework of the use of robots, artificial intelligence and service automation in travel, tourism, and hospitality companies. *Robots, artificial intelligence, and service automation in travel, tourism and hospitality*, 7-37.

Iyer, L. S. (2021). AI enabled applications towards intelligent transportation. *Transportation Engineering*, *5*, 100083. doi:10.1016/j.treng.2021.100083

Jin, B. E., & Shin, D. C. (2020). Changing the game to compete: Innovations in the fashion retail industry from the disruptive business model. *Business Horizons*, *63*(3), 301–311. doi:10.1016/j.bushor.2020.01.004

Kontodimopoulos, N., Nanos, P., & Niakas, D. (2006). Balancing efficiency of health services and equity of access in remote areas in Greece. *Health Policy (Amsterdam)*, *76*(1), 49–57. doi:10.1016/j.healthpol.2005.04.006 PMID:15927299

Kumar, D., Singh, R. K., Mishra, R., & Wamba, S. F. (2022). Applications of the internet of things for optimizing warehousing and logistics operations: A systematic literature review and future research directions. *Computers & Industrial Engineering*, *171*, 108455. doi:10.1016/j.cie.2022.108455

Langer, A., & Mukherjee, A. (2023). *Developing a Path to Data Dominance: Strategies for Digital Data-Centric Enterprises*. Springer Nature. doi:10.1007/978-3-031-26401-6

Lee, D., & Yoon, S. N. (2021). Application of artificial intelligence-based technologies in the healthcare industry: Opportunities and challenges. *International Journal of Environmental Research and Public Health*, *18*(1), 271. doi:10.3390/ijerph18010271 PMID:33401373

Makhdoom, I., Lipman, J., Abolhasan, M., & Challen, D. (2022). Science and Technology Parks: A futuristic approach. *IEEE Access : Practical Innovations, Open Solutions*, *10*, 31981–32021. doi:10.1109/ACCESS.2022.3159798

Martin, S., & Riordan, R. (2020). *Capital Mobilization Plan for a Canadian Low-Carbon Economy*. Institute for Sustainable Finance, Queen's University. https://smith. queensu. ca/centres/isf/pdfs/ISF-CapitalMobil izationPlan. pdf

Math, S. B., Basavaraju, V., Harihara, S. N., Gowda, G. S., Manjunatha, N., Kumar, C. N., & Gowda, M. (2019). Mental Healthcare Act 2017–aspiration to action. *Indian Journal of Psychiatry*, *61*(Suppl 4), S660. doi:10.4103/psychiatry.IndianJPsychiatry_188_19 PMID:31040454

Mohanan, P. (2021). Cardiological Society of India: Cardiological Society of India. *AsiaIntervention*, *7*(2), 76. doi:10.4244/AIJV7I2A16 PMID:34913009

Mondal, S., & Mitra, P. (2022). The Role of Emerging Technologies to Fight Against COVID-19 Pandemic: An Exploratory Review. *Transactions of the Indian National Academy of Engineering : an International Journal of Engineering and Technology*, *7*(1), 157–174. doi:10.100741403-022-00322-6 PMID:35837009

Mora, H., Mendoza-Tello, J. C., Varela-Guzmán, E. G., & Szymanski, J. (2021). Blockchain technologies to address smart city and society challenges. *Computers in Human Behavior*, *122*, 106854. doi:10.1016/j.chb.2021.106854

Mukherjee, J., & Janssen, M. C. (2023). *Recreating the Power Grid: Navigating Technological and Organizational Changes*. Taylor & Francis.

Munirathinam, S. (2020). Industry 4.0: Industrial internet of things (IIOT). *Advances in Computers*, *117*, 129–164. doi:10.1016/bs.adcom.2019.10.010

Napierala, J., & Kvetan, V. (2023). Changing job skills in a changing world. In *Handbook of Computational Social Science for Policy* (pp. 243–259). Springer International Publishing Cham. doi:10.1007/978-3-031-16624-2_13

Niu, Y., Li, X., Zhang, J., Deng, X., & Chang, Y. (2023). Efficiency of railway transport: A comparative analysis for 16 countries. *Transport Policy*, *141*, 42–53. doi:10.1016/j.tranpol.2023.07.007

Oviedo, D., Granada, I., & Perez-Jaramillo, D. (2020). Ridesourcing and travel demand: Potential effects of transportation network companies in Bogotá. *Sustainability (Basel)*, *12*(5), 1732. doi:10.3390u12051732

Park, H. J., & Zhang, Y. (2022). Technology readiness and technology paradox of unmanned convenience store users. *Journal of Retailing and Consumer Services*, *65*, 102523. doi:10.1016/j.jretconser.2021.102523

Paul, S., Riffat, M., Yasir, A., Mahim, M. N., Sharnali, B. Y., Naheen, I. T., Rahman, A., & Kulkarni, A. (2021). Industry 4.0 applications for medical/healthcare services. *Journal of Sensor and Actuator Networks*, *10*(3), 43. doi:10.3390/jsan10030043

Pinho, B. A. (2017). *The global airline industry: an assessment of the impact of low-cost carriers on the technical efficiency of full-service airlines.* ISCTE-Instituto Universitario de Lisboa.

Potluri, R. M., & Thomas, S. J. (2023). Trends in E-Commerce During COVID-19: A Case of UAE. In Advancing SMEs Toward E-Commerce Policies for Sustainability (pp. 235-247). IGI Global.

Prasad Agrawal, K. (2023). Towards adoption of Generative AI in organizational settings. *Journal of Computer Information Systems*, 1–16. doi:10.1080/08874417.2023.2240744

Randolph, M. (2019). That will never work: The birth of Netflix and the amazing life of an idea. Hachette UK.

Riahi Dorcheh, F., Razavi Hajiagha, S. H., Rahbari, M., Jafari-Sadeghi, V., & Amoozad Mahdiraji, H. (2021). Identification, analysis and improvement of red meat supply chain strategies considering the impact of COVID-19 pandemic: A hybrid SWOT-QSPM approach in an emerging economy. *British Food Journal*, *123*(12), 4194–4223. doi:10.1108/BFJ-09-2020-0865

Rosenthal, A., Mork, P., Li, M. H., Stanford, J., Koester, D., & Reynolds, P. (2010). Cloud computing: A new business paradigm for biomedical information sharing. *Journal of Biomedical Informatics*, *43*(2), 342–353. doi:10.1016/j.jbi.2009.08.014 PMID:19715773

Rostami, F., Kis, Z., Koppelaar, R., Jiménez, L., & Pozo, C. (2022). Comparative sustainability study of energy storage technologies using data envelopment analysis. *Energy Storage Materials*, *48*, 412–438. doi:10.1016/j.ensm.2022.03.026

Rowan, N. J., Murray, N., Qiao, Y., O'Neill, E., Clifford, E., Barceló, D., & Power, D. M. (2022). Digital transformation of peatland eco-innovations ('Paludiculture'): Enabling a paradigm shift towards the real-time sustainable production of 'green-friendly' products and services. *The Science of the Total Environment*, *838*, 156328. doi:10.1016/j.scitotenv.2022.156328 PMID:35649452

Sah, B., Gupta, R., & Bani-Hani, D. (2021). Analysis of barriers to implement drone logistics. *International Journal of Logistics*, *24*(6), 531–550. doi:10.1080/13675567.2020.1782862

Sampat, B., Mogaji, E., & Nguyen, N. P. (2023). The dark side of FinTech in financial services: A qualitative enquiry into FinTech developers' perspective. *International Journal of Bank Marketing*. Advance online publication. doi:10.1108/IJBM-07-2022-0328

Sargam, S., Gupta, R., Sharma, R., & Jain, K. (2023). Adoption of 5G in developing economies: A supply side perspective from India. *Telematics and Informatics, 84*, 102034. doi:10.1016/j.tele.2023.102034

Sewpersadh, N. S. (2023). Disruptive business value models in the digital era. *Journal of Innovation and Entrepreneurship, 12*(1), 1–27. doi:10.118613731-022-00252-1 PMID:36686335

Shields, S. (2020). The EBRD, fail forward neoliberalism and the construction of the European periphery. *Economic and Labour Relations Review, 31*(2), 230–248. doi:10.1177/1035304620916652

Sokolov, A., Veselitskaya, N., Carabias, V., & Yildirim, O. (2019). Scenario-based identification of key factors for smart cities development policies. *Technological Forecasting and Social Change, 148*, 119729. doi:10.1016/j.techfore.2019.119729

Srinivasan, N., & Eden, L. (2021). Going digital multinationals: Navigating economic and social imperatives in a post-pandemic world. *Journal of International Business Policy, 4*(2), 228–243. doi:10.105742214-021-00108-7

Tabatabai, S. M., & Tabatabai, F. A.-S. (2024). Integrating Inverse Data Envelopment Analysis and Machine Learning for Enhanced Road Transport Safety in Iran. *Journal of Soft Computing in Civil Engineering, 8*(1), 141–160.

Teichert, R. (2019). Digital transformation maturity: A systematic review of literature. *Acta Universitatis Agriculturae et Silviculturae Mendelianae Brunensis, 67*(6), 1673–1687. doi:10.11118/actaun201967061673

Tiku, S. (2023). *AI-Induced Labor Market Shifts and Aging Workforce Dynamics: A Cross-National Study of Corporate Strategic Responses in Japan, USA, and India*. Academic Press.

Valavanidis, A. (2020). *Artificial Intelligence (AI)*. Applications.

Von Lohmann, F. (2017). Fair use as innovation policy. In *Copyright Law* (pp. 169–205). Routledge. doi:10.4324/9781315095400-6

Wahid, M. A., Bukhari, S. H. R., Daud, A., Awan, S. E., & Raja, M. A. Z. (2023). COVICT: An IoT based architecture for COVID-19 detection and contact tracing. *Journal of Ambient Intelligence and Humanized Computing, 14*(6), 7381–7398. doi:10.100712652-022-04446-z PMID:36281429

Walia, K., Mendelson, M., Kang, G., Venkatasubramanian, R., Sinha, R., Vijay, S., Veeraraghavan, B., Basnyat, B., Rodrigues, C., Bansal, N., Ray, P., Mathur, P., Gopalakrishnan, R., & Ohri, V. C. (2023). How can lessons from the COVID-19 pandemic enhance antimicrobial resistance surveillance and stewardship? *The Lancet. Infectious Diseases, 23*(8), e301–e309. doi:10.1016/S1473-3099(23)00124-X PMID:37290476

Xia, Y., & Chen, M. (2023). The Janus face of stateness: China's development-oriented equity investments in Africa. *World Development, 162*, 106133. doi:10.1016/j.worlddev.2022.106133

Xu, L., Sanders, L., Li, K., & Chow, J. C. (2021). Chatbot for health care and oncology applications using artificial intelligence and machine learning: Systematic review. *JMIR Cancer, 7*(4), e27850. doi:10.2196/27850 PMID:34847056

Yang, B., Yang, S., Lv, Z., Wang, F., & Olofsson, T. (2022). Application of digital twins and metaverse in the field of fluid machinery pumps and fans: A review. *Sensors (Basel), 22*(23), 9294. doi:10.339022239294 PMID:36501994

Yıldırım, M., Yıldız, M. S., & Durak, İ. (2020). Industry 4.0 performances of OECD countries: a data envelope analysis. *İşletme Araştırmaları Dergisi, 12*(3), 2788-2798.

Zeng, Y., Guo, W., Wang, H., & Zhang, F. (2020). A two-stage evaluation and optimization method for renewable energy development based on data envelopment analysis. *Applied Energy, 262*, 114363. doi:10.1016/j.apenergy.2019.114363

ADDITIONAL READING

Bansal, R. (2019). Efficiency evaluation of Indian oil and gas sector: data envelopment analysis. *International Journal of Emerging Markets, 14*(2), 362-378.

Joshi, P. V., & Bhalerao, M. J. (2011). Efficiency evaluation of banking sector in India based on data envelopment analysis. *Indian Journal of Commerce and Management Studies, 2*(3), 31–42.

Mitra Debnath, R., & Shankar, R. (2008). Benchmarking telecommunication service in India: An application of data envelopment analysis. *Benchmarking, 15*(5), 584–598. doi:10.1108/14635770810903169

Seth, H., Chadha, S., & Sharma, S. (2021). Benchmarking the efficiency model for working capital management: Data envelopment analysis approach. *International Journal of Productivity and Performance Management, 70*(7), 1528–1560. doi:10.1108/IJPPM-10-2019-0484

Tamatam, R., Dutta, P., Dutta, G., & Lessmann, S. (2019). Efficiency analysis of Indian banking industry over the period 2008–2017 using data envelopment analysis. *Benchmarking, 26*(8), 2417–2442. doi:10.1108/BIJ-12-2018-0422

KEY TERMS AND DEFINITIONS

Artificial Intelligence (AI): A branch of computer science focused on creating intelligent agents capable of performing tasks that typically require human intelligence, such as learning, reasoning, problem-solving, and perception.

Big Data Analytics: The process of collecting, organizing, and analyzing large datasets to discover patterns, correlations, and other insights, typically using advanced computational methods and algorithms.

Data Envelopment Analysis (DEA): A non-parametric method in operations research and economics for measuring the efficiency of decision-making units (DMUs) through input and output comparison.

Disruptive Technologies: Innovations that significantly alter or replace existing technologies, often leading to a paradigm shift in industry structures, consumer behaviors, or market dynamics.

Efficiency Benchmarking: A method for comparing the performance efficiency of different entities or processes, typically with the aim of identifying best practices, setting performance standards, and improving operational efficiency.

Governance: The processes, structures, and organizational traditions that determine how power is exercised, how stakeholders have their say, how decisions are made, and how decision-makers are held to account.

Sustainability: A principle that involves meeting the needs of the present without compromising the ability of future generations to meet their own needs, typically encompassing environmental, social, and economic dimensions.

Virtual Reality (VR): A computer-generated simulation of a three-dimensional environment that can be interacted with in a seemingly real or physical way by a person using special electronic equipment.

Chapter 8
Data Envelopment Analysis for Improving the Microgrid Operations

Uetutiza C. C. Kuzatjike
Namibia University of Science and Technology, Namibia

K. S. Sastry Musti
 https://orcid.org/0000-0003-4384-7933
Namibia University of Science and Technology, Namibia

ABSTRACT

Microgrid configurations provide a reliable and sustainable energy supply to off-grid settlements. Various energy sources, including renewable and non-renewables, are currently used to power the microgrids. Scheduling these energy resources and managing the microgrids can be challenging due to various constraints. Data envelopment analysis (DEA) is one of the well-known solution methodologies that can be effectively used for energy management studies. This chapter applies a multi-objective DEA to the energy management of a typical rural, remote micro-grid supplied by a solar plant and diesel generator sets. The methodology utilizes the DEA algorithm to identify microgrid optimal configurations by considering technical, environmental, and economic factors. The Tsumkwe rural region of Namibia is considered for studying the DEA application and analysis. The study evaluated the energy system's performance under varying efficiencies, fuel consumptions, and generator capacities.

INTRODUCTION

A good number of countries are still struggling to provide affordable energy access to their population, particularly those living in rural areas. Rural electrification is a very challenging task as socioeconomic conditions are entirely different from those that exist in typical urban areas. Some of the issues with rural communities are, but not limited to lesser prospects for the utilities to earn more revenues, lower energy requirements, economic hardships of the communities, and higher investment requirements for standard

DOI: 10.4018/979-8-3693-0255-2.ch008

power grid infrastructure etc. However, several studies found that the provision of modern energy services have a positive correlation with enhancing human development opportunities, improvement in quality of life, reduced crime rates, improved health, and increased opportunities for small businesses. Mini and micro-grids powered specifically by solar and wind energy plants have been suggested by various researchers and even several such grids have been established in different parts of the world to serve rural communities. However, electricity demand increases with time and the need for uninterrupted power generation and supply arises. Energy management in small scale mini or micro-grids can be challenging and this chapter tries to address that very problem.

Modern power grids are fed by different energy plants such as solar, wind and even diesel generators. The loads are typically located in different geographical locations and several power system components (also known as power apparatus) exist, besides transmission and distribution networks. The major functions of energy management in smart grids are - Planning and operation of energy production, Economic energy dispatch and storage, and Improvement of overall system efficiency. These three tasks require data acquisition, computation, and timely control.

Data acquisition is typically done by SCADA systems, however rural grids may not enjoy such support due to various reasons as explained above. Most of the control apparatus can function automatically to manage the load side aspects. Short-term and long-term generation scheduling, energy dispatch and energy storage management are the tasks that need to be addressed carefully through a series of studies and simulations. These tasks require optimization to maximize benefits as well. Data Envelopment Analysis is one of the well-known and currently trending solutions that can be effectively used for energy management studies. This chapter applies the DEA to energy management of a typical rural, remote micro-grid that is supplied by a solar and a diesel generator set.

BACKGROUND

It is always challenging to supply electricity to remote areas due to various technical and socio-economic reasons. Several researchers have reported on the challenges associated with rural electrification (Matheus & Musti, 2023; Chiguvare, 2019). Demand in the rural areas can be too low and thus utilities may not be able to invest in the standard power grid infrastructure due to lesser prospects of financial returns (Sastry, 2023). Small scale generating units are typically used to power the microgrids as the overall demand is generally less (Musti, 2020). Typically, solar PV plants and diesel generator sets are popular choices. Solar energy costs have been drastically reducing over the years and diesel generator sets are very simple to manage and are generally reliable. However, solar energy is usually available for 5 or 6 hours only during the day and thus diesel generator sets, and battery banks need to be used for the remaining duration.

On the other hand, users in remote areas are now encouraged through the green energy policies in various parts of the world to use solar water heaters (Sastry, 2023; Musti & Kapali 2021). Such changes in energy usages and the usual load changes result in dynamically varying energy demand profiles (Sastry, 2020). Thus, scheduling of the generation resources can be challenging due to varying operating conditions. Over the years, several authors have studied the problem of generator scheduling problems to meet the varying load conditions. DEA method is a non-parametric method that can be used empirically to determine the best possible solutions to a problem that has different constraints. One of the major steps in DEA methodology is to determine the DMU. Then the relative efficiency of each of the DMUs is determined by calculating the ratio of weighted outputs to weighted inputs, while ensuring the same ratios for all DMUs.

DMUs that obtain an efficiency rating of one are considered fully efficient, whereas an efficiency score lower than one implies inefficiency. Since the DEA solution involves various stages of computations, the overall methodology requires the use of computer programming to deal with application of logic, constraints and the data involved. The main objective of DEA is to identify the DMU with the highest ratio of weighted outputs to weighted inputs. The impartial nature of DEA allows for a fair efficiency measure. Babazadeh (2016) applied a novel capacitor bank and distributed generators (DG) allocation method. This method accounted for several objective constraints for the analysis of economic and technical microgrid parameters. These functions included reduced emissions, power loss, and voltage stability. With the use of an intelligent algorithm, the location and sizing of equipment was found. DEA analysis was then applied to identify the most efficient sizing and location of the capacitor bank configuration.

The DEA model can be analyzed using input or output orientation. In the input-oriented analysis, the efficiency score measures how efficiently a DMU uses its inputs to generate outputs. It focuses on identifying ways to reduce inputs while maintaining or improving outputs. Conversely, in output-oriented analysis, the goal is to maximize outputs given a certain level of inputs. The focus lies in increasing outputs while keeping inputs constant or minimizing them (Chachuli, 2020). For this study, an input-oriented analysis was employed for all efficiency analyses. By utilizing the multi-criteria DEA model and input-oriented analysis, this research aimed to comprehensively evaluate the techno-economic and environmental efficiency of different hybrid off-grid DMUs. This approach allowed for a holistic understanding of how efficiently each microgrid utilized its resources and contributed to sustainable energy solutions.

Two traditional DEA models, the Banker, Charnes, and Cooper (BCC) and Charnes, Cooper, and Rhodes (CCR) models, were used in this study. The BCC model employs the radial measure approach, considering both input and output variables simultaneously and assuming Variable Returns to Scale (VRS). This implies that changes in inputs are not directly proportional to changes in outputs. The BCC model provides two efficiency measures: pure technical efficiency, comparing DMUs with compatible scale sizes, and scale efficiency, demonstrating the impact of scale size on efficiency. On the other hand, the CCR model uses the multiplier approach, assuming Constant Returns to Scale (CRS), where growth in inputs is directly proportional to growth in outputs. Unlike the BCC model, the CCR model does not differentiate between scale efficiency and pure technical efficiency (Mirmozaffari, 2021).

Due to its non-parametric analysis method, DEA does not make any assumptions regarding the data. Thus, allowing for the analysis of varied inputs and outputs. Additionally, multiple DMUs, input and output parameters can be assessed in one go. This is particularly useful when comparing the efficiency of large-scale scenarios. Notably, DEA simplifies the analysis process by eliminating the need to assign weights to inputs and outputs. Various analysis models such as CRS VRS & Slack-Based model can be selected by researchers based on the requirements of their study. From the above, it is clear that the energy management problem in smart grids is varying in nature with several constraints; and that DEA is a potential solving methodology. This chapter tries to apply DEA for the energy resource scheduling for varying demand conditions in a typical microgrid. The organization of the content in this chapter is as follows. Next section presents a comprehensive literature review and then identifies the objectives, followed by a detailed methodology for applying DEA and two case studies.

LITERATURE REVIEW

Meng (2019) has applied DEA to the problem of generation scheduling of a smart grid. The efficiency of four distributed power generation parks in northern China was tested. The operating evaluation was done using CPLEX and DEA. The efficiency indicators were split into three categories: energy efficiency, service level and economic efficiency. The analysis deduced that, by utilizing multi-energy optimal allocation, an increase of the primary energy utilization rate and the terminal energy utilization rate can be achieved. Enhancing the effectiveness of converting multiple energy sources proved to be crucial to improving the operational capability of multi-energy micro-grids (Meng,2019). Ewertowska's (2017) thesis introduced innovative techniques for evaluating Life Cycle Assessment (LCA) metrics and conducting uncertainty analysis to measure a system's environmental performance. To assess the sustainability of a system, the Pedigree matrix, Monte Carlo Simulation, and DEA were utilized, in conjunction with life cycle assessment. The study facilitated the analysis of the leading European countries and their energy sector. Several environmental impacts associated with the production of 1 kWh were used to determine the environmental efficiency of these countries. Out of the 26 countries, 7 displayed poor environmental efficiency in their energy sector. For these countries, adjustments in their energy mixes were identified to improve environmental efficiency.

The cement industry is a significant contributor to greenhouse gas emissions, prompting leaders in the field and policymakers alike to assess and improve their environmental impact. To evaluate the eco-friendliness of 22 Iranian cement companies, Mirmozaffari utilized DEA and machine learning algorithms. The study also conducted a comparison of three analysis models, namely the CCR, BCC, and additive models. The machine learning algorithm was used to calculate the Malmquist Productivity Index (MPI). The findings demonstrated that the additive model was superior to both the CCR and BCC input-oriented and output-oriented models in determining Eco-efficiency (Mirmozaffari, 2021).

Dogan and Tugcu (2015) conducted a study utilizing the input-oriented DEA model based on CCR. The aim of the study was to calculate the technical efficiency scores of G-20 countries in electricity production between 1990 and 2011. China and Russia were the top performers in terms of energy efficiency, whereas the European Union and France were inefficient in four of the five analyzed periods. Additionally, the study concluded that transitioning from a mono polar to a multi polar energy sector significantly improves energy production efficiency. Nkiriki and Ustun (2016) conducted a study to explore policies related to minigrid projects in Sub-Saharan Africa (SSA). Policy guidelines for rural electrification were then made in the form of a policy toolkit. The study investigated the advantages of renewable energy (RE) minigrids in decentralized systems and analyzed the challenges of attracting private sector participation. The policy toolkit was developed to mitigate uncertainties and risks and to increase profitability of minigrids for rural electrification. The study found that the lack of specific policies and regulations for minigrid development made Tsumkwe project in Namibia economically unfeasible. This can largely be attributed to the unclear ownership and upkeep responsibility of the minigrid that took place at the time of publication. The analysis has shown that a well-defined minigrid plant policy is essential to ensure economic feasibility. Based on the study, a private-public partnership with community involvement was found to be the most sustainable and economically viable solution.

Other notable research contributions along with their findings are summarized in Table 1.

It can be derived from the literature, that the use of DEA extends to a wide range of applications, encompassing energy efficiency and technical efficiency evaluation. This analytical tool not only enables the identification of both efficient and inefficient parameters. Thus, guiding them towards achieving

Table 1. Literature summary

Author(s) and Year	Scope	Application Area	Study Purpose	Results
Martin -Gamboa, Iribarren & Dufour (2018)	20 NGCC power plants located in Spain	Eco efficiency	Proposed a combined DEA & LCA method to evaluate NGCC plant efficiency from 2010–2015	One plant was environmentally efficient, and the overall scores were above 60%.
Song, Li, Zhang, He, Tao, (2015)	34 coal-fired power units in China	Energy efficiency	Analysis of the utilization efficiency of coal-fired power plants	Slack analysis concluded that an average electricity saving potential of 19.95 MWh for 14 power units.
Aldieri, Gatto & Vinci (2022)	148 developing and transition economies	Energy resilience	Identify opportunities for innovation in transition economies using DEA and Tobit	Zambia and Zimbabwe displayed high-efficiency scores in their energy sector.
Toshiyuki & Goto (2019)	10 countries worldwide	Energy efficiency	Comparison of different thermal power station efficiencies with consideration of transmission congestion	Solar thermal power stations from the U.S are the most efficient.
Hemapala, Herath, Gnana & Swathika (2019)	Western Province, Sri Lanka	Technical efficiency	Efficiency evaluation of 32 medium voltage feeders	14 out of 32 feeders were efficient. Relevant targets were set to aid the inefficient feeders in gaining efficiency.
Xu, You, Li & Shao (2020)	Worldwide	DEA literature review	Evaluation of various DEA models used in literature	By evolving DEA from a static model to a dynamic model, efficiency evaluation has been greatly improved over the years.
Mardani, Balezentis, Saman & Khoshnaa (2018)	Worldwide	DEA literature review	Overview of DEA application in the energy and environmental industry	An extensive review of DEA and their uses in different sectors was made.

their efficiency targets. The conclusions derived from conducting a DEA study hold immense value for engineers as they strive to enhance their environmental and technical efficiency while implementing measures to reduce costs. Moreover, employing dynamic models in conjunction with DEA can offer more comprehensive and detailed evaluations. The protection of AC systems is often overlooked in the design of minigrids. In a study by Simeon Chowdhury (2020), the absence of a coordinated over current protection system was identified in the Tsumkwe minigrid. The maximum fault current was determined using the IEC 60909 method, and DigSILENT's short circuit calculation tool was used to conduct the study.

The simulation results revealed that the micro-grid protection system was exposed to varying fault currents, depending on the rotational and static generators. The thermal fuses and traditional circuit breakers used in the minigrid showed long fault clearing times and inconsistent coordination among protection devices. Minigrid electrification systems in Tsumkwe faced technical challenges, including generator breakdowns, poorly maintained PV modules, defective batteries, and loose battery terminals. This is primarily due to inadequate monitoring and a lack of local technicians. This highlights the potential for significant power distribution losses if technical capacity is not improved to meet rising energy demands. Boamah, (2019) recommended measures to address these issues, including enhanced facility monitoring, on-site training, generator spare kits, and damaged PV module replacement. These examples from Namibia demonstrate that the effectiveness of solar PV systems in achieving equitable, development-focused, and low-carbon energy futures depends on community characteristics, technical expertise, settlement patterns, and infrastructure distribution.

In 2019, Chiguvare conducted a study to investigate the impact of the minigrid on the Tsumkwe community's perception of energy access and energy poverty. A total of 47 households were interviewed for this study. The study used various data collection methods, including questionnaires, key informant interviews, focus group discussions, and direct observations. The study found that the provision of modern energy services has a positive correlation with enhancing human development opportunities. Access to electricity has contributed to an improvement in the quality of life for the Tsumkwe community, with reduced crime rates, improved health and increased small business opportunities. Residents feel much safer at night due to the presence of streetlights at night. The provision of electricity has enabled residents to global news and media. Electricity has also enhanced food preservation, enabled fresh food access, and supported local businesses. The community's access to electricity aligns with the World Bank's five-tier energy access classification, falling within tiers 3 and 4, indicating reliable, affordable, and convenient electricity access, with over 80% having electricity for more than 22 hours. However, there is a lack of discussion on the environmental impact of the minigrid, particularly the negative effects of diesel generator operation.

From the above, a good number of authors have reported on various challenges with the minigrids. However, minigrids just as the conventional high voltage power grids; do face several operational challenges especially when it comes to the energy management. Such challenges can only be addressed with solution methodologies that can inherently consider various constraints and there is a huge gap in the literature on use of innovative techniques to obtain satisfactory solutions. This study aims to address this research gap by applying the DEA to identify the most techno-economic and environmentally efficient configuration for the minigrid. Thus, the major objectives of this chapter are:

1. To develop a multi-objective DEA framework that integrates technical, environmental, and economic criteria, allowing for a comprehensive evaluation of microgrid configurations.
2. To evaluate the most techno-economic and environmentally efficient configuration
3. To perform sensitivity analyses on key parameters, such as system efficiency and generator capacity, to understand their impact on the overall efficiency and performance of sustainable microgrid configurations.
4. To provide insights and guidelines for policymakers, energy planners, and stakeholders in selecting and designing sustainable microgrid solutions that meet the energy needs of off-grid settlements while ensuring environmental stewardship and economic feasibility.

METHODOLOGY

This section discusses the methodology employed to evaluate the efficiency of microgrids using Data Envelopment Analysis. The methodology is presented as a structured process, outlined step by step in a flow diagram in Figure 1 for clarity and reproducibility. By following this comprehensive methodology, we ensure a rigorous and systematic approach to assessing microgrid performance.

Performing a DEA analysis requires a myriad of data and technical specifications. Data on energy demand patterns of the off-grid settlement, renewable available energy resources, fuel consumption of diesel generators, capital costs of equipment, operation and maintenance expenses, and other relevant parameters were obtained from the GKSD-330 INC ATS datasheet, IRENA (2022). The technical, environmental, and economic parameters are shown in Tables 3 to 5. The ratings of the system components

Figure 1. Methodology flowchart

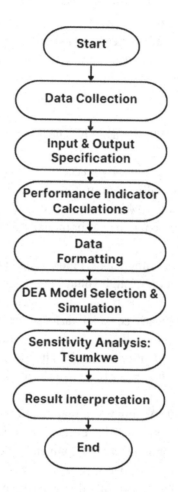

and the load profile were provided by a representative from Cenored, ensuring the reliability of the data. Tsumkwe's load profile is divided into essential and non-essential loads. The former is comprised of the two schools, water bore hole, clinic, and the police station, whilst the latter is comprised of domestic and commercial loads. A study conducted by Zongwe (2017) deduced that the average daily load is 1,763kWh/day, with the domestic load constituting about 88% of the energy load. The block diagram for the minigrid is illustrated in Figure 2.

Minigrid Specifications

The technical specifications of the grid are as follows:

- 3 MWh lead-acid battery bank
- 300 kWp solar PV system (1302 panels)
- 180kW 3-phase inverter/ charger installation (36 units)
- 2 diesel generator sets each rated at 300kVA.

Figure 2. Minigrid block diagram

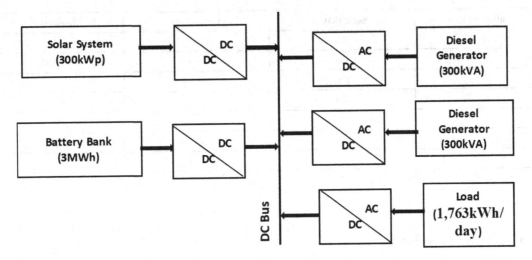

To meet the settlement's energy demands, several microgrid configurations were proposed, with each DMU representing a unique system configuration. The different DMUs to be tested and their operating hours are depicted in Table 2. Then the inputs and outputs relevant to evaluating the efficiency of the hybrid micro-grid system configuration were determined. For the sake of keeping this paper's focus on DEA, the various performance indicator calculations were omitted.

The DEA models in this study were formulated based on the equations derived from Song's seminal work in 2015.

CCR model:

min θk

   s.t.

$$\theta_k x_{ik} \geq \sum\nolimits_{j=1}^{n} \lambda_j x_{ij}, i = 1,...,m \tag{1}$$

$$y_{rk} \leq \sum\nolimits_{j=1}^{n} \lambda_j y_{rj}, r = 1,...,s$$

λj$_\geq$0, $\forall$i,j,r

BCC model:

Table 2. Microgrid configurations

Configuration	Solar (kW)	Wind (kW)	Diesel (kW)
A	300	0	510
B	300	100	510
C	100	0	765
D	500	300	0
E	400	200	255
F	600	400	255
G	0	200	510

Table 3. Technical indicators

Technical	Input	Outputs		
DMU	Capacity (kW)	Energy Generation (kWh)	Efficiency (%)	Supply/Demand
DMU A	810	1416	44.30	0.70
DMU B	910	1480	48.00	0.73
DMU C	865	2648	44.30	1.31
DMU D	800	2216	50.67	1.10
DMU E	855	1868	48.00	0.92
DMU F	1255	3700	48.00	1.83
DMU G	710	1760	57.33	0.87

Table 5. Economic indicators

Economic	Inputs			Output
DMU	Capital Investment (U$D)	Operation & Maintenance (U$D)	Diesel Fuel Cost (U$D)	LCOE (U$D)
DMU A	454247	10025	517	1715
DMU B	513247	11825	258	1007
DMU C	219021	1012	1744	5349
DMU D	837500	12450	0	425
DMU E	675374	927	129	721
DMU F	1057574	18557	3888	1777
DMU G	175947	9395	775	2511

Table 4. Environmental indicators

Environmental	Inputs			Outputs	
DMU	Fuel Used (l)	Solar Panel Area (m^2)	Wind Turbines	Emissions ($kgCO_2$)	Renewable Energy (%)
DMU A	493	5820	0	1843	22.72
DMU B	247	5820	10	996	36.84
DMU C	1480	1940	0	5184	6.11
DMU D	0.00	9700	30	203	100.00
DMU E	123	7760	20	604	66.00
DMU F	740	5820	40	1585	77.73
DMU G	492	0	20	1734	36.65

min θk

s.t.

$$\theta_k x_{ik} \geq \sum_{j=1}^{n} \lambda_j x_{ij}, i = 1,...,m \qquad (2)$$

$$y_{rk} \leq \sum_{j=1}^{n} \lambda_j y_{rj}, r = 1,...,s$$

$$\sum_{j=1}^{n} \lambda_j = 1$$

λj$_\geq$0, $\forall$i,j,r

The notation used in this study is as follows: θk represents the efficiency score of DMU k.xi_k and xi$_j$ denote the input i for DMU k and DMU j respectively whilst yr$_j$ and yr$_k$ denote the amount of output r for DMU j and DMU k respectively. The input and output weight of DMU j is denoted by λj. The sub-script k *d*enotes the DMU under evaluation, while the subscripts r,*j a*nd i *r*epresent the serial numbers of the outputs in the set of r=*1*,...,s, the serial numbers of the DMUs in the set of j=*1*,...,n *a*nd the serial numbers of the inputs in the set of i=*1*,...,m *a*nd respectively.

To make the microgrid data suitable for the DEA model, two significant modifications were implemented. First, to comply with the positivity requirement of basic DEA models and handle negative or zero data values, a positive constant of 10 was added to all inputs and outputs showing zero values. Second, since undesirable outputs, like greenhouse gas emissions, are not directly incorporated in the standard DEA framework, a transformation was applied by using their reciprocals to enable an accurate efficiency analysis. Both these adaptations were employed for both the environmental and economic efficiency analyses, as proposed by Sarkis in 2002.The techno-economic and environmental analysis was then performed using R software. With all analysis methods, the main limitation of DEA lies in the data variation sensitivity. Variations in data, inputs, and outputs as well as selected scale efficiency may lead to different efficiency results. As such, it is vital to perform sensitivity analysis on results. This provides a clearer picture on the impact of data variation. Although the analysis provides efficiency scores, no explanation is given for the results. It is up to the operator to correctly interpret results.

To test the robustness of the DEA, a sensitivity analysis was conducted. The diesel generator capacity, as well as the efficiency rating for the various energy sources was varied. To demonstrate the reliability of DEA as an effective tool for optimizing microgrid configurations, a case study was undertaken. In a previous study, Iqbal and Siddiqui (2017) employed the HOMER software to identify the optimal microgrid configuration for Aligarh Muslim University (AMU) in India. The dataset from their study served as the basis for conducting a DEA analysis, aimed at assessing whether this optimization method could yield results comparable to tried and tested software like HOMER while providing equally meaningful insights.

Various data representations were considered, by taking cues from existing literature trends. Martin-Gamboa (2018) used tabular representation of DMUs in a table format and presented the ranked Eco-efficiency of power plants using a bar graph. The analysis was conducted over a 5-year period, and efficiency was compared with operating hours in a scatter plot. Song (2015) utilized the Nyquist plot to demonstrate the DEA approach for determining technical, purely technical, and scale efficiency for both the BCC and CCR models. The paper also employed a line graph to represent the efficiency values of 34 coal-fired power plants using the BCC and CCR models. Input and output parameters were presented in tabular form, while various scatter plots illustrated the linear relationships between CCR efficiency and the net calorific value of coal, the load factor, and capacity factor.

In a different domain outside the energy sector, Mirmozaffari (2021) represented the average Eco-efficiency of 22 cement plants over a 5-year period using a bar graph. The results were displayed for the BCC, CCR, and Malmquist Productivity Index (MPI). Additionally, the study computed the accuracy of several DEA algorithms using different analysis tools, resulting in varying accuracy ratings for each tool. Ziaee (2017) employed DEA to estimate the power interruption costs of industrial businesses, utilizing histograms and line graphs to illustrate the interruption costs and their relation to efficiency. Considering the diverse methods utilized in these previous studies, the decision was made to utilize bar graphs, tables, and line graphs as data assessment of the techno-economic and environmental efficiency of various hybrid off-grid DMUs will be effectively conveyed.

CASE STUDIES AND RESULTS

The methodology described earlier is applied to two different cases to study the effectiveness of data envelopment. The DEA model was constructed using R software, which is a versatile programming environment for statistical computing and graphics. Developed by Ross Ihaka and Robert Gentleman in 1993, R is an open-source language and is commonly utilized in data analysis and statistical applications. Its well-developed and integrated tools for data analysis make it a popular choice for researchers (Simplilearn, 2023). R offers a range of resources for DEA analysis, providing users with flexibility and customization options in data processing, model specification, and analysis procedures. Being an open-source language, R is freely available for use, making it a cost-effective alternative to commercial software like HOMER.

Appropriate grid configurations were considered for both case studies. The first case study revolves around the Tsumkwe rural region of Namibia. The "x" and "y" terms in the frontier plots represent inputs and outputs respectively. The second case study revolves around a typical microgrid analysis presented by Iqbal and Siddiqui (2017). However, their work did not use DEA, instead the HOMER software was used to analyze various configurations of a microgrid at Aligarh Muslim University (AMU) in India.

Case Study 1: Tsumkwe Minigrid

The technical efficiency analysis unveiled that only two DMUs attained CRS efficiency, while three DMUs exhibited VRS efficiency. The efficiency frontier graphically portrays the performance of the analyzed DMUs, with those lying on the frontier showcasing the most effective utilization of inputs to produce outputs in comparison to other DMUs. As depicted in Fig. 3, DMUs F, C, and G attained a perfect VRS efficiency score of 1, while DMU D showed notable proximity to achieving efficiency. Upon closer examination of Table 6 and Table 2, the efficiency scores of the DEA analysis reveal a logical pattern. DMU G has a capacity of 710 kW, while the lowest rated DMUs A and B have a capacity of 810kW and 910 kW. Albeit the two DMUs have a greater capacity, DMU G generates more energy, generating 344kWh more than DMU A. DMU G also outperforms DMU A and B in terms of efficiency and supply to demand ratio. As such, it is evident that DMU G can better maximize its output, while having the lowest input of all other DMUs.

In the examination of environmental efficiency, it was observed that all DMUs achieved a perfect VRS efficiency score. However, when evaluating CRS efficiency, only two DMUs attained perfect scores. Despite all DMUs exhibiting perfect efficiency scores, Fig. 4 illustrates that not all of them lie on the efficiency frontier. This can be attributed to the fact that the DMUs on the frontier utilize their inputs so effectively that they set a benchmark for the overall data set efficiency, effectively shifting the frontier

Figure 3. Technical efficiency frontier plot

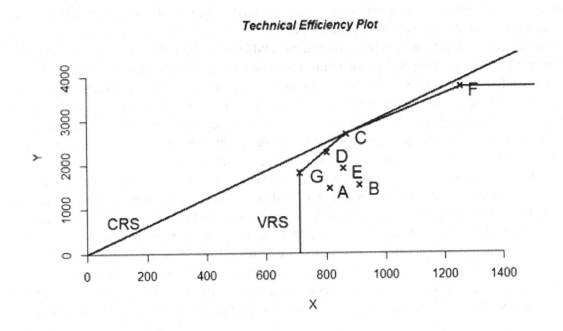

Figure 4. Environmental efficiency frontier plot

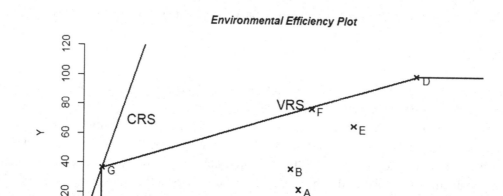

position to a more optimal point. Taking DMU C as an example, its low renewable energy penetration and large generator usage (765 kW) lead to higher greenhouse gas emissions and fuel consumption. Consequently, the CRS efficiency rating of 0.272, as opposed to the VRS efficiency of 1, provides a more accurate representation of the microgrid's environmental impact. It is easy to understand why DMU D is environmentally efficient. It has a renewable energy penetration of 100%, thus no fuel consumption and the lowest CO_2 emissions. DMU E on the other hand, has the second lowest fuel consumption but fails to achieve efficiency, with a rating of 0.88. However, DMU G obtained an efficiency score of one, albeit having a higher fuel consumption. This can be attributed to the lack of a solar system in DMU G, which enables this configuration to occupy less land.

Regarding economic efficiency, it was observed that DMUs A and F exhibited inefficient VRS scores of 0.880 and 0.546, respectively, indicating room for improvement in their cost-effectiveness. In the CRS efficiency analysis, only DMUs E and D obtained perfect efficiency scores, signifying their optimal utilization of resources in the production process. Remarkably, these two DMUs also boast the highest renewable energy penetration, which sheds light on the cost-effectiveness of incorporating renewable energy sources as alternatives to expensive nonrenewable energy generation systems. This is further cemented by DMU C's low efficiency score of 0.3815, the second lowest rating. It can thus be deduced that high fuel costs make this configuration economically unfeasible. With a supply to demand ratio of 1.83, DMU F has the largest capacity. Nonetheless, DMU F is largely oversized compared to its counter parts and this is evident in its classification as the least efficient configuration, as reflected by an efficiency score of 0.1897. Both the base case A and DMU F were unable to obtain a VRS score of one. The economic efficiency plot depicted in Fig. 5 further illustrates the variations in economic performance among the DMUs. Table 6. summarizes the techno-economic and environmental efficiency scores.

The findings from this study reveal a distinct contrast between the two efficiency models: CRS and VRS. Generally, CRS efficiency scores are lower than VRS efficiency scores, which can be attributed

Figure 5. Economic efficiency frontier plot

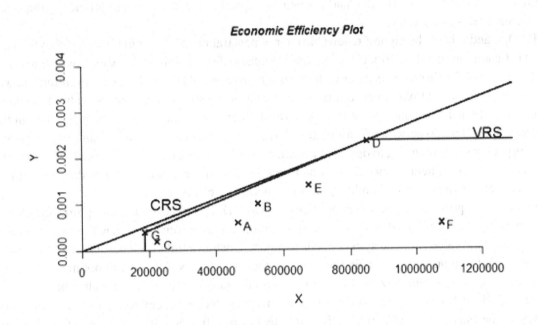

to the inherent disparities in their underlying assumptions and modeling methodologies. The CRS efficiency model operates on the assumption that all DMUs function optimally at a fixed scale, allowing for proportional adjustments of inputs and outputs while preserving efficiency. Essentially, the CRS model assumes that there are no economies of scale in the production process. On the other hand, the VRS efficiency model permits variable returns to scale, meaning that the efficiency of DMUs can vary as they operate at different scales. VRS takes into account the potential existence of economies of scale, which can positively or negatively impact efficiency as the scale of operations changes. When comparing CRS and VRS efficiency scores, several factors contribute to CRS scores being consistently lower. Firstly, in real-world applications, many DMUs may not operate precisely at the optimal scale due to various constraints such as limited resources, market conditions, or technological limitations. As a result, CRS

Table 6. CRS & VRS efficiency results

DMU	Technical		Environmental		Economic		Total Efficiency	
	CRS	VRS	CRS	VRS	CRS	VRS	CRS	VRS
DMU A	0.6943	0.8765	0.9088	1.0000	0.4574	0.8803	0.6869	0.9189
DMU B	0.6549	0.7802	0.7368	1.0000	0.6895	1.0000	0.6937	0.9271
DMU C	1.0000	1.0000	0.2718	1.0000	0.3815	1.0000	0.5511	1.0000
DMU D	0.9897	0.9908	1.0000	1.0000	1.0000	1.0000	0.9976	0.9969
DMU E	0.8086	0.8525	0.88	1.0000	1.0000	1.0000	0.8962	0.9508
DMU F	0.9631	1.0000	0.8429	1.0000	0.1897	0.5461	0.6652	0.8487
DMU G	1.0000	1.0000	1.0000	1.0000	0.8062	1.0000	0.9335	1.0000

efficiency scores may underestimate the true efficiency of DMUs in practical scenarios. Therefore, the VRS model proves to be more flexible and realistic in capturing the variations in efficiency that arise from different scales of operation.

DMU D, F and E have the highest renewable energy penetration as shown in Fig 6, but they're technically inefficient, this can be attributed to the intermittency of solar and wind systems, which refers to their inherent variability in energy generation based on environmental factors. Unlike conventional power sources, such as fossil fuel-based generators, solar panels and wind turbines rely on natural elements like sunlight and wind to produce electricity. As a result, their energy output fluctuates throughout the day and season, leading to periods of both high and low energy generation. The variability of solar and wind energy makes it challenging to optimize the microgrid's efficiency using traditional DEA models. The inclusion of intermittent energy sources adds complexity to the analysis, and finding an optimal balance between efficiency and reliability becomes much more challenging.

R software also provides target indicators that can assist DMUs in achieving an optimal efficiency score. In inefficient input-oriented models, the output parameters remain unchanged, while the input target values represent the values that the system needs to adjust to achieve full efficiency. On the other hand, for efficient DMUs, input values remain the same, as they are already operating at optimal efficiency. For this analysis, base system A was selected to perform the target analysis. The results obtained from the target analysis reveal specific adjustments needed to achieve technical, environmental, and economic efficiency in the microgrid configuration. To attain technical efficiency, it is suggested to reduce the system capacity from 810 kW to 563.079kW, with only a slight decrease in energy generation from 1416 kWh to 1415 kWh. For optimal environmental efficiency, the DEA analysis indicates the necessity of reducing fuel consumption to 227.2l, along with decreasing the solar panel area from 5830m^2 to 2206m^2. Regarding economic efficiency, certain target changes are required to improve cost-effectiveness. The

Figure 6. Renewable energy penetration

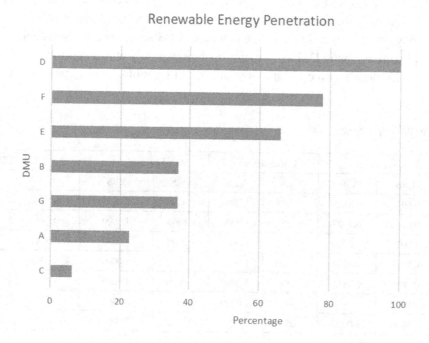

capital investment should be reduced from U$D 454247.12 to U$D 207771.3, while the operation & maintenance cost needs to decrease from U$D 10024.71 to U$D 3088. Additionally, the diesel fuel cost should be lowered from U$D 516.83 to U$D 478.95.

However, it is essential to acknowledge that implementing these target values may pose challenges due to various constraints and technical demands. The DEA analysis highlights that the current use of diesel generators is neither environmentally nor economically efficient for the settlement, as indicated by the data from Tsumkwe. These findings underscore the significance of exploring alternative and sustainable energy solutions to optimize the microgrid's performance, reduce environmental impact, and enhance economic viability. Decision-makers can use these insights to design and implement more efficient and eco-friendlier microgrid configurations, aligning with the settlement's energy needs and promoting long-term sustainability. Based on CRS efficiency scores, DMU D emerges as the top-performing microgrid with an overall efficiency score of 0.9976. Following closely is DMU G, which also shows promising efficiency. However, considering the intermittent nature of renewable energy sources, it is prudent to include at least one diesel emergency backup generator in the microgrid configuration. In this regard, DMU G with an efficiency score of 0.9335 becomes a strong contender. It is important to note that the evaluation was conducted assuming all systems were yet to be implemented due to data constraints, which limited the availability of real-world data. However, given the extensive investments already made in the existing solar panels, it would be unwise to completely remove them from the system. Therefore, an optimal solution would involve integrating the existing power infrastructure to improve the demand/supply ratio while addressing financial, environmental, and technical constraints. Based on these considerations, DMU E emerges as the most viable option with an efficiency score of 0.8962. By incorporating the existing power infrastructure, this configuration strikes a balance between efficiency and practicality, ensuring the effective utilization of resources and meeting the energy needs of the settlement in a sustainable and cost-effective manner.

Sensitivity Analysis

In the energy sector, sensitivity analyses hold significant importance as they allow us to understand the potential impact of small changes on the overall efficiency and performance of energy systems. This understanding facilitates better decision-making and resource management, ensuring the optimization of energy resources and operational effectiveness in the dynamic and evolving energy landscape. The DEA analysis, combined with R software's target analysis, proves to be a valuable tool for DMUs seeking to improve their efficiency scores. However, it is essential to consider the practical limitations and feasibility of achieving the target values in real-world scenarios during implementation.

The sensitivity analysis conducted in this study sheds light on the effects of variations in generator capacity and system efficiencies on the DEA efficiency scores and microgrid configurations. For the technical efficiency indicators, the system efficiencies of the solar and wind systems were adjusted from their ideal values of 0.2 and 0.59 to 0.15 and 0.3, respectively. The resulting efficiency scores for each DMU were visualized in Fig.7. Notably, DMU A's efficiency improved from 0.6943 to 0.8055, confirming the target value analysis that indicated a reduced capacity would enhance the system's efficiency. Conversely, the remaining inefficient DMUs experienced a decrease in efficiency, with DMU F suffering the most significant decline of 0.31. For the environmental and economic indicators, the sensitivity analysis involved reducing the generator capacity from 100% to 75%, leading to decreased fuel usage from 61.2 l/h to 42 l/h. This was illustrated in Fig. 8. These changes resulted in increased environmental

Figure 7. Technical efficiency comparison

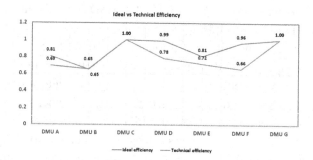

Figure 8. Generator capacity comparison

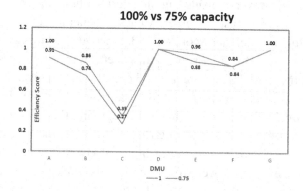

efficiency for the inefficient DMUs. However, they had no influence on economic efficiency due to the lack of financial data. For the economic aspect, it was assumed that the decreased generator capacity would have the most significant impact on fuel usage costs, as such the impact on other economic indicators were assumed to be negligible.

Overall, the sensitivity analysis demonstrates that changes in generator capacity and system efficiencies can have varying impacts on the efficiency scores of microgrid configurations. While some DMUs may experience efficiency improvements, others may face declines. These findings highlight the importance of considering technical, environmental, and economic parameters in the design and optimization of microgrid configurations to achieve optimal performance and resource utilization. Such insights can inform decision-making processes and promote the implementation of efficient and sustainable microgrid systems.

Case Study 2: Aligarh Muslim University

To reduce emissions and reliance on non-renewable resources, Iqbal and Siddiqui (2017) proposed the implementation of a microgrid at Aligarh Muslim University (AMU) in India. The study's main objective was to establish an optimized and dependable power system that would decrease the university's dependence on the national grid. To achieve this, a comprehensive HOMER analysis was conducted. Several microgrid configurations of varying sizes were simulated. The study encompassed a total of six

Figure 9. Frontier efficiency plot

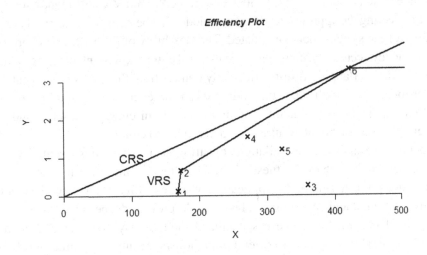

distinct cases: Case one featured a microgrid exclusively powered by diesel generators and the second relied solely on the national grid for power. Case three comprised a combination of wind and photovoltaic configurations. Cases four and five incorporated wind and PV systems, respectively, alongside the national grid. Finally, case six integrated the national grid with PV and wind energy sources.

Analysis from Iqbal and Siddiqui (2017), clearly indicates that cases four through six outperformed the others, with case six emerging as the most optimal configuration. The study's conclusion emphasized that the most favorable outcomes arise from an energy mix involving solar, the national grid, and wind energy. As such, the first microgrid configuration was identified as the poorest performing microgrid due to its high emissions and electricity costs. This finding was further corroborated by a DEA, which assigned case one the lowest efficiency rating of 0.17, closely followed by case three with an efficiency score of 0.18. In contrast, cases four and six both achieved a perfect efficiency score of one using the CCR analysis model. The microgrid solely supplied by the national grid demonstrated an efficiency rating of 0.99, highlighting the usefulness of grid integration, particularly in urban settings. The frontier efficiency plot is illustrated in Figure 9. It is important to note that certain factors, such as load shedding, were not considered in the analysis. Case four outperformed case five, with respective ratings of 1 and 0.83. This may be attributed to the relatively lower efficiency of solar systems, thus requiring more panels to generate energy comparable to wind systems.

DISCUSSION AND PROSPECTS FOR FURTHER WORK

DMUs A and F can focus on optimizing resource allocation and operational strategies to improve their cost-effectiveness. Meanwhile, the success of DMUs E and D in achieving satisfactory efficiency scores while incorporating higher renewable energy penetration exemplifies the advantages of sustainable practices in reducing energy costs and environmental impact. Based on the results, DMU D and G emerged as top-performing microgrids. However, considering the existing infrastructure in Tsumkwe, DMU E appears to be the more feasible and practical alternative. The multivariate DEA analysis employed in this study has demonstrated its value in the energy sector, providing valuable information for decision-making and resource management. The disparities between CRS and VRS efficiency scores emphasize the significance of selecting the appropriate efficiency model that best fits the specific characteristics and operational realities of the systems being evaluated. The flexibility of the VRS model proves beneficial in representing efficiency accurately, considering real-world complexities and offering valuable insights for various sectors. The overlapping results effectively demonstrate that DEA is a potent analysis tool, standing shoulder-to-shoulder with other methods used in the energy sector and beyond. Embracing these powerful tools equips us to navigate the complexities of our energy landscape and empowers us to forge a brighter and more sustainable future for generations to come.

To delve deeper into the analysis, the availability of sufficient data becomes essential. Obtaining more extensive datasets can enhance the robustness of the DEA results, allowing for more comprehensive and reliable conclusions. Furthermore, the application of more advanced DEA models, tailored to perform in-depth environmental and economic analyses, could provide deeper insights into the microgrid configurations' overall performance. These specialized models may consider additional indicators, such as social and sustainability factors, to offer a more holistic evaluation of microgrid efficiency. To further expand the sensitivity analysis, it would be valuable to test microgrid configuration efficiencies at different times of the day. This approach could shed light on the impact of renewable energy resource intermittency on grid efficiency, offering valuable information on how to optimize energy storage and management strategies. This approach can also help identify which microgrid configurations are the most feasible and easily implementable to apply into the utility grid, considering practical limitations and technical constraints.

By embracing renewable energy sources, optimizing resource allocation, and considering both VRS and CRS efficiency measures, decision-makers can unveil opportunities to enhance overall microgrid performance and ensure a greener and more sustainable energy landscape. These findings underscore the importance of adopting cost-effective and environmentally friendly solutions in the energy sector, meeting future energy demands while minimizing our carbon footprint. Additionally, exploring the dynamic nature of microgrid efficiency over extended periods could provide valuable insights into the system's performance under various conditions and seasonal changes. Long-term studies could identify trends and patterns that may not be apparent in short-term assessments, leading to more informed decisions for sustainable energy planning. These efforts can contribute to informed decision-making, promoting sustainable energy solutions, and addressing the challenges of energy supply in off-grid settlements and beyond. The second case study highlights the effectiveness of DEA analysis, demonstrating its validity in producing results consistent with established software such as HOMER. The findings illustrate the importance of utilizing an integrated approach that incorporates multiple energy sources to achieve sustainable and efficient microgrid configurations, especially in urban areas.

CONCLUSION

The DEA analysis has provided valuable insights into the technical, environmental, and economic efficiencies of different microgrid configurations in Tsumkwe. The study highlights the importance of carefully evaluating both the efficiency scores and real-world constraints to make informed decisions regarding the most suitable microgrid configurations for the specific context. The findings outline the importance of sustainable energy solutions in remote areas. DEA's non-parametric nature and R software's flexibility enable a comprehensive evaluation of diverse parameters and decision-making units. The reliability of DEA results in the energy sector was verified with a case study. This case study effectively demonstrates the validity of DEA analysis, yielding results consistent with established software like HOMER. These outcomes emphasize the importance of adopting an integrated approach that combines multiple energy sources to create sustainable and efficient microgrid configurations. This is particularly crucial in urban areas where microgrids can significantly enhance energy access, reduce costs, and minimize environmental impact. The findings also indicate that there is significant potential for enhancing economic efficiency by embracing more sustainable energy options. In conclusion, the fusion of DEA, target analysis, and sensitivity analyses presents a powerful and all-encompassing approach for evaluating and optimizing microgrid configurations. This study's significance extends beyond the engineering community. It offers valuable insights for researchers and policymakers alike to address energy access challenges. By optimizing microgrid configurations, stakeholders can play a pivotal role in achieving Sustainable Development Goals, fostering green energy adoption, and driving positive change in underserved regions.

REFERENCES

Aldieri, L., Gatto, A., & Vinci, C. (2022). Is there any room for renewable energy innovation in developing and transition economies? Data envelopment analysis of energy behaviour and resilience data. *Resources, Conservation and Recycling, 186*, 106587. Advance online publication. doi:10.1016/j.resconrec.2022.106587

Babazadeh, E., Oskuee, M.R., Pourmahmoud, J., & Najafi-Ravadanegh, S. (2016). *Optimal Planning of Smart Distribution Network Based on Efficiency Evaluation Using Data Envelopment Analysis*. Academic Press.

Boamah, F. (2019). Desirable or debatable? Putting Africa's decentralised solar energy futures in context. *Energy Research & Social Science, 62*, 101390. Advance online publication. doi:10.1016/j.erss.2019.101390

Chiguvare, T.M. (2019). *An evaluation of human development through renewable energy provision in an offgrid Tsumkwe settlement area of Otjozondjupa region in Namibia*. Academic Press.

Dogan, N. O., & Tugcu, C. T. (2015). Energy Efficiency in Electricity Production: A Data Envelopment Analysis (DEA) Approach for the G-20 Countries. *International Journal of Energy Economics and Policy, 5*(1), 246–252.

Ewertowska, A. (2017). *Systematic tools based on data envelopment analysis for the life cycle sustainability evaluation of technologies*. Universitat Rovira Virgili. https://www.tesisenred.net/handle/10803/457128

Hemapala, K., Herath, H. M., & Swathika, O. V. (2019). Benchmarking medium voltage feeders using data envelopment analysis: A case study. *Telkomnika, 17*(3), 1547. Advance online publication. doi:10.12928/telkomnika.v17i3.9288

Ileka, H., Zongwe, D., & Reuther, K. (2017). Rural Electrification with Hybrid Minigrids: Finding an Efficient and Durable Ownership Model. *The Law Reform and Development Commission of Namibia*, *25*, 351–382.

Iqbal, F., & Siddiqui, A. (2017). Optimal configuration analysis for a campus microgrid—A case study. *Protection and Control of Modern Power Systems*, *2*(1), 23. Advance online publication. doi:10.118641601-017-0055-z

IRENA. (2022). *Renewable Power Generation Costs in 2021.* International Renewable Energy Agency. Available online_https://www.irena.org/publications/2022/Jul/Renewable-Power-Generation-Costs-in-2021

Mardani, A., Streimikiene, D., Balezentis, T., Saman, M., Nor, K., & Khoshnava, S. (2018). Data Envelopment Analysis in Energy and Environmental Economics: An Overview of the State-of-the-Art and Recent Development Trends. *Energies, 11*(8). . doi:10.3390/en11082002

Martín-Gamboa, M., Iribarren, D., & Dufour, J. (2017). Environmental impact efficiency of natural gas combined cycle power plants: A combined life cycle assessment and dynamic data envelopment analysis approach. *The Science of the Total Environment*, *615*, 29–37. doi:10.1016/j.scitotenv.2017.09.243 PMID:28963894

Matheus, M. N., & Sastry Musti, K. S. (2023), Design and Simulation of a Floating Solar Power Plant for Goreagab Dam, Namibia. In Human Agro-Energy Optimization for Business and Industry. IGI Global. doi:10.4018/978-1-6684-4118-3.ch001

Meng, L., & Yi, L., & Li, W. (2019). The Empirical Research of Multi-energy Micro grid Operation Efficiency Based on DEA Method. *IOP Conference Series: Earth and Environmental Science.* 10.1088/1755-1315/300/4/042071

Mirmozaffari, M., Shadkam, E., Khalili, S. M., Kabirifar, K., Yazdani, R., & Asgari Gashteroodkhani, T. (2021). A novel artificial intelligent approach: Comparison of machine learning tools and algorithms based on optimization DEA Malmquist productivity index for eco-efficiency evaluation. *International Journal of Energy Sector Management*, *15*(3), 523–550. doi:10.1108/IJESM-02-2020-0003

Musti, K. S. S. (2020). Quantification of Demand Response in Smart Grids. *IEEE International Conference INDISCON*, 278-282. 10.1109/INDISCON50162.2020.00063

Musti, K. S. S., & Kapali, D. (2021). *Digital Transformation of SMEs in the Energy Sector to Survive in a Post-COVID-19 Era. In Handbook of Research on Strategies and Interventions to Mitigate COVID-19 Impact on SMEs*. IGI Global. doi:10.4018/978-1-7998-7436-2.ch009

Nkiriki, J., & Ustun, T. S. (2017). *Minigrid policy directions for decentralized smart energy models in Sub-Saharan Africa. In IEEE PES Innovative Smart Grid Technologies Conference Europe*. ISGT-Europe. doi:10.1109/ISGTEurope.2017.8260217

Pitra, G. M., & Musti, K. S. S. (2021). Duck Curve with Renewable Energies and Storage Technologies. *13th International Conference on Computational Intelligence and Communication Networks (CICN)*, 66-71. 10.1109/CICN51697.2021.9574671

Sastry, M. K. S. (2007). Integrated Outage Management System: An effective solution for power utilities to address customer grievances. *International Journal of Electronic Customer Relationship Management*, *1*(1), 30–40. doi:10.1504/IJECRM.2007.014424

Sastry, M. K. S., & Van der Merwe, M. (2022). *A Novel MS Excel Tool for Multi-Criteria Decision Analysis in Energy Systems*. IGI-Global. doi:10.4018/978-1-6684-4012-4.ch003

Sastry Musti, K. S. (2023). Multicriteria Decision Analysis for Sustainable Green Financing in Energy Sector. In *Green Finance Instruments, FinTech, and Investment Strategies. Sustainable Finance*. Springer. doi:10.1007/978-3-031-29031-2_1

Simeon, A., & Chowdhury, S. (2020). *Protection Challenges in a Stand-alone Microgrid: Case Study of Tsumkwe Microgrid*. . doi:10.1109/PowerAfrica49420.2020.9219972

Simplilearn. (2023). *What is R: Overview, its Applications and what is R used for?* Available online, https://www.simplilearn.com/what-is-r-article

Song, C., Li, M., Zhang, F., He, Y., & Tao, W. (2015). A data envelopment analysis for energy efficiency of coal-fired power units in China. *Energy Conversion and Management*, *102*, 121–130. doi:10.1016/j.enconman.2014.12.062

Toshiyuki, S., & Goto, M. (2019). Comparison among Three Groups of Solar Thermal Power Stations by Data Envelopment Analysis. *Energies*, *12*(13), 2454. Advance online publication. doi:10.3390/en12132454

Xu, T., You, J., Li, H., & Shao, L. (2020). Energy Efficiency Evaluation Based on Data Envelopment Analysis: A Literature Review. *Energies, 13*(14), 3548. doi:10.3390/en13143548

Ziaee, O., & Falahati, B. (2017). *A data envelopment analysis (DEA)-based model for power interruption cost estimation for industrial companies. In IEEE Power & Energy Society Innovative Smart Grid Technologies Conference*. ISGT. doi:10.1109/ISGT.2017.8086058

ADDITIONAL READING

Geng, Z., Dong, J., Han, Y., & Zhu, Q. (2017). Energy and environment `efficiency analysis based on an improved environment DEA cross-model: Case study of complex chemical processes. *Applied Energy*, *205*, 465–476. doi:10.1016/j.apenergy.2017.07.132

Li, L., Lei, Y., Pan, D., & Si, C. (2016). Research on Sustainable Development of Resource-Based Cities Based on the DEA Approach: A Case Study of Jiaozuo, China. *Mathematical Problems in Engineering*, *2016*, 1–10. Advance online publication. doi:10.1155/2016/5024837

Nguyen, T.-L., Nguyen, P.-H., Pham, H.-A., Nguyen, T.-G., Nguyen, D.-T., Tran, T.-H., Le, H.-C., et al. (2022). A Novel Integrating Data Envelopment Analysis and Spherical Fuzzy MCDM Approach for Sustainable Supplier Selection in Steel Industry. *Mathematics, 10*(11), 1897. . doi:10.3390/math10111897

Shadkam, E. (2022). A Novel Two-Phase Algorithm for a Centralized Production Planning Problem by Symmetric Weighted DEA Approach: A Case Study in Energy Efficiency. *European Journal of Industrial Engineering*, *16*(1), 10043239. Advance online publication. doi:10.1504/EJIE.2022.10043239

Soheilirad, S., Govindan, K., Mardani, A., Zavadskas, E. K., Nilashi, M., & Zakuan, N. (2018). Application of data envelopment analysis models in supply chain management: A systematic review and meta-analysis. *Annals of Operations Research*, *271*(2), 915–969. doi:10.100710479-017-2605-1

Wei, Z., Wang, X., Qi, T., & Wu, X. (2018). Transmission Cost Allocation Based on Data Envelopment Analysis and Cooperative Game Method. *Electric Power Components and Systems*, *46*(2), 208–217. doi:10.1080/15325008.2018.1444113

Zhu, J. (2015). *Data Envelopment Analysis: A Handbook of Models and Methods*. doi:10.1007/978-1-4899-7553-9

KEY TERMS AND DEFINITIONS

Data Envelopment Analysis (DEA): A mathematical technique for assessing the relative efficiency of multiple decision-making units (DMUs) by comparing their input and output performance. The best performing DMUs can be identified and a benchmark for inefficient units is set to improve their performance.

Efficiency Rating: A numerical measure or ratio that evaluates how effectively a particular configuration of a Decision Making Unit (DMU) transforms inputs into desired outputs. Efficiency scores vary between 0 and 1, with higher values signifying superior performance.

Energy Mix: The combination of different energy sources, such as solar, wind, grid power, and fossil fuels, used to meet energy demands efficiently and sustainably.

Green Energy: Energy derived from renewable and environmentally friendly sources, such as solar, wind, hydroelectric, and geothermal power. Green energy is often characterized by its reduced carbon footprint and lower environmental impact compared to fossil fuels, making it a key component of sustainable energy systems.

Rural Electrification: The process of providing electrical power to remote or sparsely populated areas that are often located far from centralized power generation facilities. The goal of rural electrification is to improve the quality of life and promote economic development in underserved rural communities by ensuring access to electricity.

Sustainable Energy Systems: Energy systems that prioritize the utilization of renewable and eco-friendly energy sources to meet present energy requirements while ensuring the capacity of future generations to fulfill their energy needs. Sustainable energy systems aim to lower emissions of greenhouse gases and mitigate other ecological consequences.

Chapter 9
Advancing Supply Chain Efficiency and Sustainability:
A Comprehensive Review of Data Envelopment Analysis Applications

Natasha Cecilia Edeh

https://orcid.org/0000-0001-9627-7001

American University of Nigeria, Nigeria

ABSTRACT

This chapter investigates data envelopment analysis (DEA) in the context of supply chain management. DEA, a non-parametric method for assessing productive efficiency with many inputs and outputs, has considerably impacted research and practical implementation. It enables performance analysis across organizations with complicated input-output interactions. DEA provides user-friendly and customizable criterion weighting, simplifies analysis by eliminating the need for production function calculation, and delivers comprehensive efficiency measurements. This chapter examines existing research on the use of DEA in supply chains to assess present practices, recent breakthroughs, and techniques critically. This chapter addresses the central research question, "What are the latest advancements and methodologies in applying DEA to the supply chain?" The findings of this study add to the understanding of current practices at the confluence of DEA and supply chain management, which is critical in today's complex corporate context.

INTRODUCTION

A non-parametric way of measuring the productive efficiency of procedures with many inputs and outputs is called data envelopment analysis (Liu et al., 2013). Since its inception in 1978, the contemporary version of Data Envelopment Analysis (DEA) has significantly contributed to advancements in both research and practical implementation (Sıcakyuz, 2023). DEA is a way of analyzing the performance traits of various organizations where multiple inputs and outputs make comparisons more difficult. It

DOI: 10.4018/979-8-3693-0255-2.ch009

is essentially a linear programming methodology (Mahmoudi et al., 2020). With this approach, various inputs and outputs are combined and transformed into a single efficiency indicator. This method first establishes an "efficient frontier" made up of a group of DMUs that demonstrate best practices, and then it gives the efficiency level to other non-frontier units based on how close they are to the efficient frontier (Fotova Čiković & Lozić, 2022; Liu et al., 2013).

The Data Envelopment Analysis (DEA) method has several benefits. First off, it gives criteria weights automatically, improving the effectiveness of the ranking process. Second, DEA makes the analysis simpler by doing away with the need to estimate a production function and its corresponding assumptions. Thirdly, it evaluates each observation against an efficient border that has been optimized, giving a thorough efficiency measurement. Additionally, DEA is renowned for being straightforward and user-friendly, enabling reliable decision-making based on actual data. Finally, it provides flexibility by simultaneously supporting a range of inputs, outputs, and measurement criteria (Rezaei & Adressi, 2015).

According to research, the DEA approach is primarily applied in the following five research fields: agriculture, finance, supply chains, transportation, and public policy. An important part of ensuring the smooth and effective operation of supply chain processes is played by industrial engineering, a specialized branch of engineering. It includes a broad range of methods, strategies, and guidelines targeted at streamlining operations, boosting output, and eventually strengthening supply chain networks' overall performance and competitiveness. Industrial engineering is a crucial part of contemporary supply chain management because of its multidimensional approach, which includes elements like logistics, quality assurance, operations management, and resource allocation (Fotova Čiković & Lozić, 2022).

The overarching objective of this chapter is to conduct a comprehensive review and analysis of existing research papers within the realm of Data Envelopment Analysis (DEA) and its application in the context of supply chains. By scrutinizing these papers, we aim to present a precise and critical assessment of the current state of practices in this field. This endeavor seeks to shed light on the latest advancements, methodologies, and insights derived from the body of literature by asking the question, what are the latest advancements and methodologies in applying DEA to supply chain management in current literature? And ultimately offering a valuable contribution to the understanding and evaluation of contemporary practices at the intersection of DEA and supply chain management.

BACKGROUND

The modern business landscape is characterized by complex interdependencies among various stakeholders, including merchants, manufacturers, suppliers, and retailers, all intricately woven together to form the supply chain. This intricate network functions as a combined flow of resources and materials, as highlighted in the works of (Dutta et al., 2022; Huang, 2018; Saputri et al., 2019). The performance of individual companies within this supply chain is not isolated but rather contingent upon the effectiveness of collaboration among its participants, thereby directly impacting the overall performance of the entire supply chain, as underscored by (Soheilirad et al., 2018). In today's fiercely competitive business environment, where customer satisfaction is paramount, companies recognize the paramount importance of overseeing their supply chains. This recognition has grown exponentially in recent decades as businesses strive not only to attain but also to sustain their competitive edge. Consequently, the quest for methods to assess and optimize supply chain performance has led to the development of various techniques that offer diverse perspectives on effectiveness, as elaborated upon by (Ramezankhani et al., 2018).

Among the multitude of methodologies available, Data Envelopment Analysis (DEA) has emerged as one of the most prevalent tools employed for evaluating the performance and efficiency of supply chains, as evidenced by the works of (Dutta et al., 2022; Sihotang et al., 2022; Soheilirad et al., 2018). DEA offers a rigorous analytical framework that enables organizations to quantify their performance in relation to industry benchmarks and best practices. Its versatility allows for the assessment of multiple facets of supply chain operations, making it a preferred choice for businesses striving to enhance their supply chain effectiveness.

REVIEW OF LITERATURE OF DEA AND SUPPLY CHAIN

In-depth studies of DEA in supply chain have been published over the years. A study by Babazadeh et al., (2017) starts by explaining global challenges and how these challenges have prompted policymakers and development practitioners to find sustainable solutions in the area of bioenergy. This study focuses particularly on biodiesel production. The study presents an integrated hybrid approach that combines DEA with mathematical programming techniques to design a biodiesel supply chain network in Iran utilizing two potential feedstocks, waste cooking oil (WCO) and Jatropha Curcas L. (JCL), which were viewed as promising and long-term sources. There are two basic stages to the process:

- Evaluation of JCL's farming areas: In this phase, JCL agriculture regions are assessed using a unified DEA (UDEA) model based on meteorological and sociological factors.
- Network design for the biodiesel supply chain: Locations that in the first phase received the appropriate efficiency scores are taken into consideration as potential candidate locations for JCL cultivation in the second phase. The number, locations, and capacities of JCL cultivation centers, JCL seed and WCO collection centers, bio-refineries, and distribution centers are all optimized using a mathematical programming model. The results show the usefulness and efficiency of this strategy in supporting policymakers in making strategic and tactical decisions related to biodiesel supply chain planning. The proposed approach is implemented in Iran over a planning horizon of 10 years. In essence, it provides a methodical and data-driven way to deal with the complex issues related to supply chain management and biodiesel production in the context of sustainability and environmental concerns.

A literature study by Soheilirad et al., (2018) showed the importance of supply chain management in optimizing information, financial flow, and products to meet the requirements of consumers in an efficient and cost-effective manner to increase the profitability of the supply chain. The authors also highlighted the fact that DEA is a strong mathematical tool used in the evaluation of supply chain management. The study also emphasized the lack of systematic literature evaluations and categorizations of studies in this area, even though several DEA models have been presented for measuring and evaluating supply chain management. The researchers used well-known databases like Web of Science and Scopus, as well as the systematic and meta-analysis technique known as "PRISMA", to fill this gap. Following their review, the researchers examined 75 articles that had been published between 1996 and 2016 and were taken from 35 scholarly international journals and conferences. They sought to offer a thorough overview of DEA models used in supply chain management evaluation. The publications were sorted according to several factors, such as the authors' names, publication dates, methods employed, application domains, countries of origin, scope, DEA-related goals, research gaps, contributions made, outcomes, and the journals or conferences where they were presented. The results of the survey showed that several topics were more frequently studied than others, including supplier selection, supply chain effectiveness, and sustainable supply chains. In addition, the evaluation concluded that DEA has potential as a tool for evaluating supply chain management in the future, particularly when evaluating the production link between inputs and outputs.

Another literature study by Dutta et al., (2022) discussed the pivotal role of purchasing in supply chain management and its impact on the competitive advantage of a firm. This study further stated that purchasing managers utilize multi-criteria decision-making tools to address issues like decisions related to supplier selection, evaluation, and performance. The authors state that the focus of their paper is on DEA which has gained widespread use for supplier evaluation. The report provided a thorough analysis of 161 articles that have been written about the use of DEA in supplier selection that have been published since 2000. The Scopus database served as the source for these articles. The study is trailblazing work that can help DEA practitioners in the purchasing function because it fills a vacuum in the body of knowledge by offering a thorough review of this subject. Some important trends were shown by the examination of the articles under consideration. First off, there has been an increasing emphasis on sustainability and green supply chains in recent years, signaling a shift in supplier selection priorities. Second, a noteworthy development in resolving the difficulties of supplier selection has been the use of hybrid approaches, which integrate DEA with other techniques. Based on input criteria, application areas, and case studies from the entire industry, the article further divides DEA approaches into categories. These classifications provide fast insights into the varied applications of DEA in supplier selection across several sectors and industries, serving as useful references for academics and buying managers.

This paper by Badiezadeh et al., (2018) discusses the growing importance of assessing the effectiveness of sustainable supply chain management (SSCM) in the current environment, gaining interest from both researchers and practitioners. The research suggested Data Envelopment Analysis (DEA) as a suitable tool for evaluating SSCM performance, particularly when working with Big Data, to address this issue. The research especially focuses on Network DEA (NDEA), which can determine efficiency in multi-stage processes under the DEA framework. The originality of this study comes in the creation of a NDEA model that evaluates both optimistic and pessimistic efficiency, giving performance a more complete picture. It is significant because this model can consider unwanted results, which are important in sustainability assessments. The model is also built to rank supply networks according to their efficiency ratings. Decision-makers can gain important insights from this ranking tool to pinpoint problem areas and optimize supply chain operations. A case study is offered in the paper to verify the viability of the suggested paradigm. This practical example shows how the model may be used to evaluate the effectiveness of supply networks and offers proof of its usefulness.

This study filled a critical gap in earlier studies on the supply networks for tourism. Although earlier research had emphasized the need for collaboration and coordination in tourism supply chains, it had mostly concentrated on assessing the performance of individual departments or elements within a particular tourism supply chain. The study's main goal was to develop a hybrid Network Data Envelopment Analysis (DEA) model that could evaluate the performance of supply chains for the tourism industry both as a whole and by division. This DEA model differed from earlier network models in that it considered various input kinds. It used mathematical programming to measure variable and semifixed inputs under radial and nonradial assumptions, resulting in a more complex assessment of supply chain efficiency. The hybrid Network DEA model's capacity to assess the total effectiveness of tourist supply chains distinguished it from earlier models that concentrated on components. The study evaluated the efficiency of China's tourist supply chains across 30 locations to validate the model. The study's empirical findings provided useful information that might be used to guide supply chain management strategies for the tourism industry (Huang, 2018).

The use of Data Envelopment Analysis (DEA) in the context of Supply Chain Management (SCM) was examined in this research through a bibliometric analysis. The goal of the study was to look at DEA-related research trends in SCM from 2000 to 2023. The Web of Science database (WoS) served as the data source for this investigation, and the VOS viewer software was used for detailed mapping and visualization of pertinent articles. In this bibliometric analysis, the vast body of literature spanning the application of DEA in SCM on a global scale was carefully reviewed and synthesized. A thorough analysis of the use of DEA in the field of supply chain management (SCM) was provided by the analysis of 352 academic papers that were distributed in prestigious journals. The year of publication, the country(ies) of the author(s), the area(s) of focus, the journals of publication, and the content of the studies were just a few of the factors used to categorize the articles. This methodical classification procedure provided insight into the changing DEA landscape in SCM research. The most important finding of this study is the enormous potential of DEA as a useful evaluation tool for future research, especially in addressing sustainability issues in the SCM sector. A deeper understanding of the role played by DEA in influencing SCM research and practice is made possible by the thorough analysis and mapping of research trends offered in this paper (Sıcakyuz, 2023).

In this study, the emphasis was on evaluating company performance through the prism of financial measures, especially those generated from internal accounting data. The investigation adopted a novel approach by looking at business value and its relationship to operational supply chain (SC) performance from the perspective of financial markets. This strategy made it possible to investigate the contributions of profitability (earns) and asset utilization (turns) to a firm's overall worth. This was accomplished by the study using data envelopment analysis (DEA) on a large dataset that included listed US corporations from the years 2007 to 2015, spanning across 13 manufacturing industries. The major goal was to provide information about how the financial crisis of 2008–2009 affected operational SC performance. Several interesting results from the study were found: Internal accounting revealed a negative association between earnings and turnover, classifying industries as having "high earnings/low turnover" or "low earnings/high turnover." When compared to their capacity to use asset utilization for value generation, manufacturing companies tended to be less effective at converting earnings into firm value. Since 2007, which was the final year before the financial crisis, value-based supply chain management strategies have become less effective, according to the report, particularly in manufacturing industries. It's interesting to note that, up until 2015, despite this drop, the stock markets' general increase in firm value was able to offset these difficulties (Hahn et al., 2021).

The article emphasized the need to measure supply chain (SC) efficiency for managers and decision-makers. The authors suggested a Network Data Envelopment Analysis (NDEA) model that reflected the underlying structure of networks during efficiency assessments to achieve this goal. The ratio between the two contained essential information for administrative decision-making in many real-world circumstances where data on inputs and outputs was readily available. However, ratio data presented challenges for conventional Data Envelopment Analysis (DEA) models. To address this issue, the study presented NDEA-R models (also known as NDEA-R) for the evaluation of SC performance. The suggested models considered a supply chain's internal organization and the connections between its many sections. To describe the nature of these linkages, two essential hypotheses—free-links and fixed-links—were taken into consideration. A case study comprising the assessment of the supply chain performance of 19 hospitals in Iran over a six-month period served to illustrate the applicability of the NDEA-R models. Sensitivity analysis was used in the study to evaluate the effects of the supply chain connectivity assumptions that were made. The findings showed that the decision-making units' (DMUs') overall efficiency scores under the fixed-link assumption were either higher or equal to those of the DMUs' under the free-link assumption. This implied that the proposed models successfully addressed the issue of pseudo-inefficiency scores and underestimating efficiency, improving the accuracy of SC efficiency assessments (Gerami et al., 2023).

The vulnerability to quick and unexpected changes in the business environment, as well as the financial ramifications of such disruptions, have grown more obvious in today's complex supply chain landscape. Resilience offers a way to lessen supply chain vulnerabilities as a strategic planning strategy in the case of disruptions. This study identifies a complete collection of 16 resilience enablers following a thorough review of the literature on resilient supply chains. The questionnaire that was sent out to more than 150 specialists and staff members involved in a real-world example involving an Iranian automotive supply chain was built based on these identified enablers. The report's conclusions, which are based on a case study of the Iranian automotive supply chain, highlight the need to improve resilience enablers, especially those that have the biggest effects on supply chain performance. By doing this, businesses can successfully lessen their susceptibility to supply chain interruptions. The framework that this paper proposes may find widespread practical use in a variety of supply chains (Yazdanparast et al., 2021).

For successful supply chain management, which aims to maximize business operations' efficiency, the use of a performance measurement system was regarded as a crucial prerequisite. Due to demands from many stakeholders, there has been an increase in interest in integrating sustainability practice assessment into supply chain operations in recent years. The sustainability paradigm places a strong emphasis on the need to strike a balance between social, environmental, and economic factors. The three main goals of this paper's analysis of supply chain activities were to maximize financial gains, reduce negative environmental effects, and satisfy societal expectations. The study proposed a multi-stage data envelopment analysis (DEA) model designed to evaluate the sustainability of a network of interconnected business partners to establish a thorough framework for assessing the success of such operations. Two case studies were used to put the suggested mathematical paradigm into practice. One case study was about the manufacturing industry, and the other was about the banking industry. These case studies provided real-world examples of how the model could be used to evaluate the sustainability of supply chain activities that took into account economic, environmental, and social factors (Tajbakhsh & Hassini, 2015).

Particularly when they placed a focus on efficient operations, supply chains were frequently susceptible to unanticipated disruptions. Recognizing this weakness, increasing attention has been placed on improving supply chain resilience (SCR) to better handle shocks and boost competitiveness. The methodology for measuring resilience across different supply chain network (SCN) designs was introduced in this research, considering several significant elements. The study used data envelopment analysis (DEA) to distinguish between the best-practice and worse-performing SCN configurations from a range of possibilities to achieve this. This method made it possible to determine how much a configuration's resilience may be improved. The use of the concept was shown through a case study involving E1, a Korean company that manufactures liquefied petroleum gas (LPG). Topological and operational measures were included among the factors considered when evaluating resilience. The analysis's findings suggested that in order to improve its overall resilience, the LPG supply chain in the case study could gain from an increase in the quantity and capacity of supply nodes within its network (Pourhejazy et al., 2017).

This study's goal was to present a brand-new Data Envelopment Analysis (DEA) model with two stochastic stages that were created to assess supply chain sustainability. Two-stage DEA models consider the supply chain's intermediate goods, in contrast to standard DEA models, which often regard each decision-making unit as a black box. The main contribution of this study is the construction of a two-stage DEA model in a centralized setting while taking into account the inclusion of stochastic data, which introduces uncertainty into the analysis. A case study was used to demonstrate the efficacy and applicability of the suggested technique, highlighting its potential use in determining and strengthening the sustainability of supply chains in real-world situations (Izadikhah & Farzipoor Saen, 2023).

Establishing an efficient, sustainable supply chain necessitated the selection of sustainable suppliers, which frequently required decisions based on many criteria. The application of Data Envelopment Analysis (DEA) models proved a useful strategy for assessing sustainable suppliers. For ranking decision-making units (DMUs), a variety of DEA models were available that could be used to choose the best sustainable providers. This paper modifies context-dependent DEA models to propose a unique DEA model for rating DMUs, specifically suppliers. The proposed method, which offered a new viewpoint on DEA-based supplier ranking, was founded on the ideas of attractiveness and advancement for each supplier. Notably, this technique could rank both efficient and inefficient suppliers equally. A case study was provided to demonstrate the usefulness of the suggested approach. The approach was used in the study to identify the Sazeh Gostare Saipa Company's most environmentally friendly suppliers. The outcomes selected Hydraulic Structures Engineering Services as the most sustainable provider out of the fourteen active suppliers taken into account (Izadikhah & Farzipoor Saen, 2020).

To assess the sustainability of supply networks, this research introduced a dynamic network data envelopment analysis (DNDEA) model that could handle interval data. This was especially important because it was possible for the manufacturing technology's convexity constraint to be broken in many real-world situations. A DNDEA model was created based on the free disposal hull (FDH) technique to address this problem. The development of a DNDEA free disposal hull (FDH) model within the SCOR framework was first done in this research, which is noteworthy. To solve the issue of supply chains that could otherwise be deemed unsustainable, the model was created to reliably produce finite efficiency scores for evaluating the sustainability of supply chains. The model additionally provided a useful method for determining benchmarks that might be applied to improve the sustainability of these supply networks. A case study in the print industry was done to validate the suggested model, and the results showed that the model is effective at determining supply chain sustainability and that it has the potential to direct improvements in unsustainable supply chains (Ebrahimi et al., 2021).

The issue of sustainability has become of utmost importance in the field of supply chain management (SCM). Numerous studies have examined the selection of sustainable suppliers in recent years, giving various techniques for doing so in both deterministic and fuzzy situations. Reviewing the study literature reveals that fuzzy-based studies have drawn decision-makers' attention more frequently due to their improved accuracy and data gathering precision. This paper's main goal was to present an innovative triangular fuzzy model for sustainable supplier selection (SSS) in the supply chain. The capabilities of the model were demonstrated by looking at a real-world SSS situation within Iran Khodro Company (IKCO). Three automobile industry professionals reviewed this case, and the decision criteria were chosen after conducting a thorough assessment of the available research and consulting other experts. According to the assessment's findings, ISACO Parts Supply Company was the study's most environmentally friendly provider (Amiri et al., 2021).

In recent years, governments and social organizations in Iran have implemented mandates aimed at resolving environmental and socioeconomic challenges. Simultaneously, the capacity to respond efficiently to supply chain disruptions has proven critical in saving many organizations from going bankrupt or shutting down completely. As a result, the operational integration of sustainability and resilience ideas has become a necessity for business supply chains. This is critical for their survival in a highly competitive and continuously changing market environment. This research describes a revolutionary dynamic network data envelopment analysis (DEA) framework intended to be used as a comprehensive performance management system. It evaluates the performance of a supply chain dynamically, considering both sustainability and resilience across time. A hybrid strategy that combines Quality Function Deployment (QFD) with Decision Making Trial and Evaluation Laboratory (DEMATEL) supplements the suggested model. This hybrid method finds the most important sustainability and resilience elements, which are then incorporated into the data envelopment analysis model. The proposed framework was applied to the car manufacturing sector to demonstrate its capabilities and efficacy. This practical application highlighted the model's ability to monitor and manage supply chain performance completely, with a focus on sustainability and resilience (Ramezankhani et al., 2018)

Many of the studies suggest novel approaches and models, such as hybrid DEA techniques, to address complicated supply chain management concerns. These approaches frequently combine DEA with other mathematical or statistical tools to improve the robustness of the analyses. Several publications contain real-world case studies that demonstrate the actual applicability of the proposed DEA models in various industries, such as biodiesel production, tourism, automotive, and manufacturing. The evaluated papers place a particular emphasis on sustainability. DEA is being used to assess sustainable supply chain practices, suggesting a growing awareness of environmental concerns and the need for sustainable supply chain solutions. Some studies incorporate numerous criteria into DEA models, such as economic, environmental, and social variables, resulting in a holistic evaluation framework for supply chain sustainability. The publications that were assessed emphasized the significance of data-driven decision-making in supply chain management. DEA helps organizations make strategic and tactical decisions based on quantitative analysis, resulting in increased overall efficiency.

Some articles lack a thorough contextualization of the sectors under consideration. A more extensive discussion of the unique difficulties confronting the industries in question could improve the research's usefulness. The success of DEA models is dependent on the assumptions made during their development. Some studies may not properly evaluate the sensitivity of their models to various assumptions, which may have an impact on the dependability of the conclusions. Comparative evaluations of alternative DEA models or DEA and other evaluation methodologies are frequently absent. Such comparisons could provide useful information on the advantages and disadvantages of DEA compared to other techniques. For DEA assessments, data quality and availability are critical. Some articles fail to examine the limitations of data quality in depth, which is critical for recognizing potential biases in the results. While the publications highlight unique approaches, several do not go into detail about theoretical issues. A more thorough theoretical framework could improve understanding of the approaches used and their implications for supply chain management theory.

METHODOLOGY

This chapter will employ a scoping review. A scoping review tries to accomplish several goals, including the identification of knowledge gaps, mapping the volume of literature that is currently available, demystifying complicated ideas, and investigating research methods. Additionally, prior to performing systematic reviews, scoping studies can be used to ensure that inclusion criteria are adequate and to hone possible research questions (Lingard & Colquhoun, 2022; Munn et al., 2018; Pham et al., 2014). In addition to the exploratory nature of this chapter, another important finding in the body of prior literature served as the motivation for choosing a scoping review rather than a systematic review. Data Envelopment Analysis (DEA) and supply chain management have been the subject of several studies, most of which have primarily used systematic review techniques or other research methods. This study forges a unique path within the research domain by choosing a scoping review approach. This study stands out among numerous others in the field that haven't used scoping reviews. This decision not only highlights the novelty of the study but also exemplifies the fresh viewpoint that this chapter seeks to present. In essence, the decision to use a scoping review methodology not only fits with the exploratory goals of this chapter but also gives the research a layer of distinctiveness that distinguishes it from other systematic reviews and adds to the body of knowledge on DEA and supply chain management.

Data for this study was gathered from Google Scholar and Science Direct. Based on a preliminary analysis of the relevant literature, certain keywords were created. Terms like "data envelopment analysis" and "supply chain" are among them. These terms were then paired with the search terms "DEA and supply chain," "Application of DEA in supply chain," and "Application of DEA in supply chain management." The number of articles collected was 97. The year range applied was from 2015 to 2023. The full list of research articles was curated using a methodical process to separate the relevant articles from the irrelevant ones. A set of inclusion and exclusion criteria was used in the selection process to identify papers that matched the main study subject. This included papers that specifically examined supply chain performance using DEA as well as those that looked at DEA's efficiency analysis in relation to supply chain management. A two-stage procedure was used to omit articles that did not satisfy these inclusion requirements to assure objectivity and accuracy. This careful process ensures that the chosen articles are directly related to the main points and goals of this study.

The article selection process consisted of two distinct stages to ensure precision. Prior to doing a second round of abstract analysis, subjects and keywords were carefully inspected to determine their significance. Due to these strict criteria, the author was only able to choose 20 articles, which served as the foundation for the initial review. The reference lists of these 20 publications were carefully scrutinized to extend the focus of the study in order to find more papers that were relevant to the topic of investigation. None of the references from these 20 papers, nevertheless, matched the author's area of interest. Then, each of the 20 chosen articles was carefully examined. The goal was to identify recurrent patterns, investigate the methodology used, investigate applied theories, and hone in on crucial results to help this study's setting receive a thorough investigation.

RESULTS

The 20 articles were thoroughly analyzed, and some interesting themes were found. Firstly, of the 20 articles that were analyzed, 55% were studies carried out in Iran, while 20% of these articles were published in

Figure 1. Graphical illustration of papers and country of publication

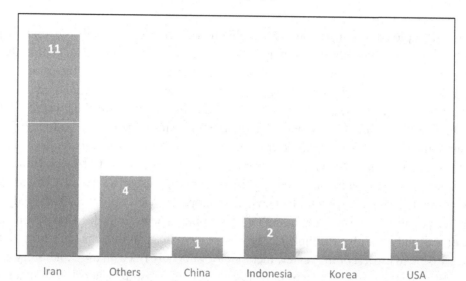

Figure 2. Year of publication of articles

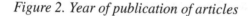

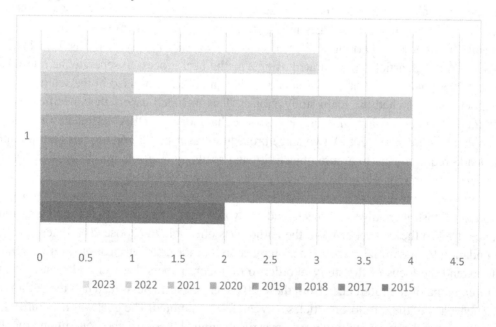

other countries. 105 of these articles were from Indonesia, while the US and Korea each had one article contributing 5% each to the total. Figure 1 below shows a graphical representation of these statistics.

The selected articles for this study were sourced from the years 2015 to 2023, as illustrated in Figure 2 below. The distribution of publications by year revealed certain trends, with the years 2017, 2018, and 2021 witnessing the highest number of publications.

Figure 3. Focus areas of analyzed articles

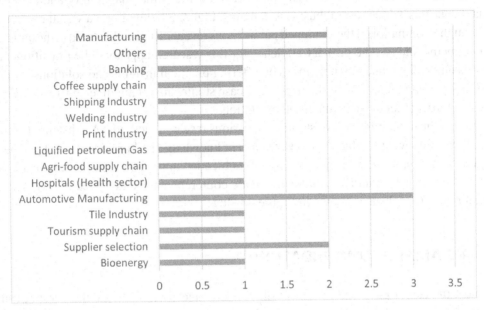

Figure 4. Methodologies employed in the selected 20 articles

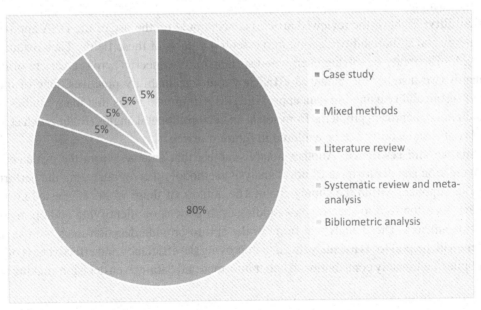

The analysis of the examined publications highlights the diversity of these research subject areas, which span a wide range of businesses and shed light on diverse sectors within the supply chain domain. Automotive manufacturing and other manufacturing segments emerged as the most prominent topics of research among these sectors. Researchers have focused their efforts on these industries in order to bring useful insights and answers to the unique issues and opportunities they present in the field of supply chain management. This focus on many industries illustrates the adaptability and applicability of supply chain concepts across several business domains. Figure 3 below gives a visual representation.

The thorough examination of the examined publications reveals a noticeable trend in the target audience and research methodology. The primary audience for this research appears to be practitioners, including managers and policymakers, with a focus on offering practical insights and solutions for real-world applications. Approximately 80% of the papers are case studies involving diverse firms and industries, indicating a significant focus on actual implementation.

Furthermore, the remaining 20% of studies use various research methods. A substantial chunk (15%) consists of literature reviews, which synthesize current knowledge and provide critical perspectives on the issue. Furthermore, a lesser proportion (5%) uses blended approaches, combining features such as questionnaires, interviews, and case studies to create comprehensive and varied knowledge. A visual representation of this analysis is shown in Figure 4 below.

SOLUTIONS AND RECOMMENDATIONS

For this study, the author proposed to answer the research question: What are the latest advancements and methodologies in applying DEA to supply chains in the current literature? The author conducted a literature review in order to answer the research question. This section will discuss some themes that show the advancements in applying DEA to the supply chain. This section will also propose solutions and recommendations.

Sustainability: Eight of the reviewed articles concentrated on the use of the DEA approach in the fields of energy and sustainability, delving into essential aspects of these fields. These examples demonstrate DEA's flexibility in solving energy and sustainability concerns across a variety of industries, giving quantitative insights for enhanced efficiency and sustainability practices. One of the authors approached sustainability using big data approach. This author also notes that many studies on supply chain sustainability approach problems from social and environmental angles (Badiezadeh et al., 2018). Other angles of sustainability can be explored in future research.

Performance and resilience: Another notable subject that emerged from the evaluated publications is the creation and deployment of novel analysis methodologies for analyzing the performance of enterprises or suppliers within the supply chain. The authors of these works suggested novel models and approaches customized to specific case studies, with a focus on identifying and optimizing input and output parameters. These analytical frameworks aim to provide decision-makers in supply chain management with helpful tools for analyzing and improving the efficiency and effectiveness of organizations or suppliers, ultimately contributing to better informed and data-driven decision-making processes.

FUTURE RESEARCH DIRECTIONS

Given the regional concentration of DEA studies in the Middle East and Asia, as well as the prevailing emphasis on supply chain sustainability across several industries, future research can strategically expand and diversify in the following ways: Using DEA, conduct a global comparative analysis of supply chain performance, focusing on regional differences and their impact on efficiency and sustainability. To stimulate cross-sector learning, investigate the transferability of sustainability practices and efficiency solutions across industries. Investigate supply chain resilience and risk management, particularly in high-risk locations, and use DEA models to discover mitigation solutions. Examine the impact of government policies on supply chain performance and sustainability, especially in regions with changing regulatory environments. Continue to conduct detailed case studies to highlight best practices and lessons learned for practitioners and policymakers. Examine the impact of emerging technologies on improving supply chain sustainability and efficiency, with an emphasis on DEA-based assessments.

CONCLUSION

Finally, Data Envelopment Analysis (DEA) has emerged as a significant non-parametric method for measuring organizational efficiency and performance, notably in the complicated arena of supply chain management. This approach, which has grown greatly since its debut in 1978, provides various advantages, such as automatic criterion weight determination, ease of analysis, and thorough efficiency assessments. DEA has been used in a variety of study domains, with a particular emphasis on agriculture, finance, supply networks, transportation, and public policy. The modern corporate landscape is defined by sophisticated supply chain networks in which stakeholder participation is critical for success. In this scenario, DEA is critical in analyzing and optimizing supply chain performance. Its adaptability allows for a multifaceted review of supply chain operations, making it a preferred choice for firms looking to boost their competitiveness. This scoping study has provided significant insights into the most recent breakthroughs and approaches for applying DEA to supply chain management. It has shown various subject areas, like sustainability and resilience, where DEA has been used with amazing efficiency. Furthermore, the study emphasized the practical nature of this research, with a particular emphasis on case studies and their relevance to practitioners, managers, and policymakers.

Future research in this field could investigate global comparative analyses of supply chain performance, cross-sector learning and transferability of sustainability practices, supply chain resilience and risk management, government influence, and the impact of emerging technologies on supply chain sustainability and efficiency. These guidelines can help us gain a better grasp of DEA's relevance and efficacy in dealing with the challenges and opportunities of modern supply chain management. Overall, the incorporation of DEA into supply chain management has proven to be a great asset for organizations looking to optimize their operations, improve sustainability, and adapt to a constantly changing business context. As supply networks become more complicated, DEA is a valuable tool for making educated decisions and improving performance.

REFERENCES

Amiri, M., Hashemi-Tabatabaei, M., Ghahremanloo, M., Keshavarz-Ghorabaee, M., Zavadskas, E. K., & Banaitis, A. (2021). A new fuzzy BWM approach for evaluating and selecting a sustainable supplier in supply chain management. *International Journal of Sustainable Development and World Ecology*, *28*(2), 125–142. doi:10.1080/13504509.2020.1793424

Babazadeh, R., Razmi, J., Rabbani, M., & Pishvaee, M. S. (2017). An integrated data envelopment analysis–mathematical programming approach to strategic biodiesel supply chain network design problem. *Journal of Cleaner Production, 147,* 694–707. doi:10.1016/j.jclepro.2015.09.038

Badiezadeh, T., Saen, R. F., & Samavati, T. (2018). Assessing sustainability of supply chains by double frontier network DEA: A big data approach. *Computers & Operations Research, 98,* 284–290. doi:10.1016/j.cor.2017.06.003

Dutta, P., Jaikumar, B., & Arora, M. S. (2022). Applications of data envelopment analysis in supplier selection between 2000 and 2020: A literature review. *Annals of Operations Research, 315*(2), 1399–1454. doi:10.100710479-021-03931-6

Ebrahimi, F., Saen, R. F., & Karimi, B. (2021). Assessing the sustainability of supply chains by dynamic network data envelopment analysis: A SCOR-based framework. *Environmental Science and Pollution Research International, 28*(45), 64039–64067. doi:10.100711356-021-12810-3 PMID:33893584

Fotova Čiković, K., & Lozić, J. (2022). Application of Data Envelopment Analysis (DEA) in Information and Communication Technologies. *Tehnički Glasnik, 16*(1), 129–134. doi:10.31803/tg-20210906103816

Gerami, J., Kiani Mavi, R., Farzipoor Saen, R., & Kiani Mavi, N. (2023). A novel network DEA-R model for evaluating hospital services supply chain performance. *Annals of Operations Research, 324*(1–2), 1041–1066. doi:10.100710479-020-03755-w

Hahn, G. J., Brandenburg, M., & Becker, J. (2021). Valuing supply chain performance within and across manufacturing industries: A DEA-based approach. *International Journal of Production Economics, 240,* 108203. doi:10.1016/j.ijpe.2021.108203

Huang, C. (2018). Assessing the performance of tourism supply chains by using the hybrid network data envelopment analysis model. *Tourism Management, 65,* 303–316. doi:10.1016/j.tourman.2017.10.013

Izadikhah, M., & Farzipoor Saen, R. (2020). Ranking sustainable suppliers by context-dependent data envelopment analysis. *Annals of Operations Research, 293*(2), 607–637. doi:10.100710479-019-03370-4

Izadikhah, M., & Farzipoor Saen, R. (2023). Developing a linear stochastic two-stage data envelopment analysis model for evaluating sustainability of supply chains: A case study in welding industry. *Annals of Operations Research, 322*(1), 195–215. doi:10.100710479-021-04160-7

Lingard, L., & Colquhoun, H. (2022). The story behind the synthesis: Writing an effective introduction to your scoping review. *Perspectives on Medical Education, 11*(5), 1–6. doi:10.1007/S40037-022-00719-7 PMID:35960445

Liu, J. S., Lu, L. Y. Y., Lu, W.-M., & Lin, B. J. Y. (2013). Data envelopment analysis 1978–2010: A citation-based literature survey. *Omega, 41*(1), 3–15. doi:10.1016/j.omega.2010.12.006

Mahmoudi, R., Emrouznejad, A., Shetab-Boushehri, S.-N., & Hejazi, S. R. (2020). The origins, development and future directions of data envelopment analysis approach in transportation systems. *Socio-Economic Planning Sciences, 69,* 100672. doi:10.1016/j.seps.2018.11.009

Munn, Z., Peters, M. D. J., Stern, C., Tufanaru, C., McArthur, A., & Aromataris, E. (2018). Systematic review or scoping review? Guidance for authors when choosing between a systematic or scoping review approach. *BMC Medical Research Methodology*, *18*(1), 143. doi:10.118612874-018-0611-x PMID:30453902

Pham, M. T., Rajić, A., Greig, J. D., Sargeant, J. M., Papadopoulos, A., & McEwen, S. A. (2014). A scoping review of scoping reviews: Advancing the approach and enhancing the consistency. *Research Synthesis Methods*, *5*(4), 371–385. doi:10.1002/jrsm.1123 PMID:26052958

Pourhejazy, P., Kwon, O., Chang, Y.-T., & Park, H. (2017). Evaluating Resiliency of Supply Chain Network: A Data Envelopment Analysis Approach. *Sustainability (Basel)*, *9*(2), 255. doi:10.3390u9020255

Ramezankhani, M. J., Torabi, S. A., & Vahidi, F. (2018). Supply chain performance measurement and evaluation: A mixed sustainability and resilience approach. *Computers & Industrial Engineering*, *126*, 531–548. doi:10.1016/j.cie.2018.09.054

Rezaei, A. H., & Adressi, A. (n.d.). *Supply Chain Performance Evaluation Using Data Envelopment Analysis*. Academic Press.

Saputri, V., Sutopo, W., Hisjam, M., & Ma'aram, A. (2019). Sustainable Agri-Food Supply Chain Performance Measurement Model for GMO and Non-GMO Using Data Envelopment Analysis Method. *Applied Sciences (Basel, Switzerland)*, *9*(6), 1199. doi:10.3390/app9061199

Sıcakyuz, C. (2023). Bibliometric Analysis of Data Envelopment Analysis in Supply Chain Management. *Journal of Operational and Strategic Analytics*, *1*(1), 14–24. doi:10.56578/josa010103

Sihotang, H. T., Marsoit, P. T., & Ortizan, K. G. (2022). *Data envelopment analysis for stochastic production and supply chain planning*. Academic Press.

Soheilirad, S., Govindan, K., Mardani, A., Zavadskas, E. K., Nilashi, M., & Zakuan, N. (2018). Application of data envelopment analysis models in supply chain management: A systematic review and meta-analysis. *Annals of Operations Research*, *271*(2), 915–969. doi:10.100710479-017-2605-1

Tajbakhsh, A., & Hassini, E. (2015). A data envelopment analysis approach to evaluate sustainability in supply chain networks. *Journal of Cleaner Production*, *105*, 74–85. doi:10.1016/j.jclepro.2014.07.054

Yazdanparast, R., Tavakkoli-Moghaddam, R., Heidari, R., & Aliabadi, L. (2021). A hybrid Z-number data envelopment analysis and neural network for assessment of supply chain resilience: A case study. *Central European Journal of Operations Research*, *29*(2), 611–631. doi:10.100710100-018-0596-x

ADDITIONAL READING

Lee, K. H., & Saen, R. F. (2012). Measuring corporate sustainability management: A data envelopment analysis approach. *International Journal of Production Economics*, *140*(1), 219–226. doi:10.1016/j.ijpe.2011.08.024

Mardani, A., Zavadskas, E. K., Streimikiene, D., Jusoh, A., & Khoshnoudi, M. (2017). A comprehensive review of data envelopment analysis (DEA) approach in energy efficiency. *Renewable & Sustainable Energy Reviews*, *70*, 1298–1322. doi:10.1016/j.rser.2016.12.030

Mirhedayatian, S. M., Azadi, M., & Saen, R. F. (2014). A novel network data envelopment analysis model for evaluating green supply chain management. *International Journal of Production Economics*, *147*, 544–554. doi:10.1016/j.ijpe.2013.02.009

Sihotang, H. T., Marsoit, P. T., & Ortizan, K. G. (2022). Data envelopment analysis for stochastic production and supply chain planning. *International Journal of Enterprise Modelling*, *16*(3), 115–124.

Zhou, H., Yang, Y., Chen, Y., & Zhu, J. (2018). Data envelopment analysis application in sustainability: The origins, development and future directions. *European Journal of Operational Research*, *264*(1), 1–16. doi:10.1016/j.ejor.2017.06.023

KEY TERMS AND DEFINITIONS

Data Envelopment Analysis (DEA): A non-parametric method used to evaluate the efficiency of different decision-making units, such as organizations or businesses, by comparing multiple inputs and outputs.

Efficiency: In the context of supply chain management, it refers to the effectiveness with which resources are used to produce outputs. High efficiency means achieving maximum output with minimum input.

Performance: The measurement of how well an organization, such as a supply chain, achieves its objectives and goals. Performance in supply chains can include metrics like delivery speed, cost reduction, and sustainability.

Productive Efficiency: A state where a system, such as a supply chain, cannot produce more of one good without producing less of another, given fixed inputs. DEA is used to measure this efficiency.

Resilience: The ability of a supply chain to effectively respond to and recover from disruptions, such as natural disasters or market changes. This includes adaptability and flexibility in operations.

Supply Chain: A network between a company and its suppliers to produce and distribute a specific product to the final buyer. It includes all processes involved in the production and distribution of goods.

Supply Chain Management (SCM): The management of the flow of goods and services, involving the movement and storage of raw materials, work-in-process inventory, and finished goods from the point of origin to the point of consumption.

Sustainability: In supply chain context, it refers to conducting operations in a way that is environmentally friendly, socially responsible, and economically viable over the long term.

Chapter 10
Efficiency Assessment and Optimization in Renewable Energy Systems Using Data Envelopment Analysis

Tarun Kumar Vashishth
ⓘ https://orcid.org/0000-0001-9916-9575
IIMT University, India

Vikas Sharma
ⓘ https://orcid.org/0000-0001-8173-4548
IIMT University, India

Kewal Krishan Sharma
IIMT University, India

Bhupendra Kumar
IIMT University, India

Rajneesh Panwar
IIMT University, India

Sachin Chaudhary
ⓘ https://orcid.org/0000-0002-8415-0043
IIMT University, India

ABSTRACT

Renewable energy systems have gained significant attention in recent years due to their potential to mitigate climate change and reduce reliance on fossil fuels. However, ensuring the efficient utilization of resources and optimizing the performance of these systems remain critical challenges. This chapter focuses on applying data envelopment analysis (DEA) as a valuable tool for assessing and optimizing the efficiency of renewable energy systems in various scientific, information technology, and engineering contexts. The chapter overviews DEA principles, methodologies, and models and explores its specific application in renewable energy systems. The integration of DEA with other analytical tools, such as life cycle assessment (LCA) and optimization techniques, is also examined. The chapter highlights data availability and quality challenges and identifies future research directions in DEA for renewable energy systems.

DOI: 10.4018/979-8-3693-0255-2.ch010

INTRODUCTION

Renewable energy systems are at the forefront of the global transition to sustainable and environmentally responsible energy sources. As the world grapples with climate change and the depletion of traditional fossil fuels, the efficiency of renewable energy systems becomes paramount. This chapter provides an in-depth exploration of efficiency assessment and optimization within the realm of renewable energy systems, with a particular focus on the application of Data Envelopment Analysis (DEA). The background and significance of efficiency assessment in renewable energy systems lie in the urgent need for sustainable and environmentally responsible energy sources in the face of climate change and the depletion of traditional fossil fuels. As the world grapples with the dire consequences of global warming, the transition to renewable energy systems becomes paramount.

BACKGROUND

The burning of fossil fuels for energy generation is a major contributor to greenhouse gas emissions, leading to global warming and its associated consequences, including extreme weather events, rising sea levels, and loss of biodiversity. Traditional fossil fuels such as coal, oil, and natural gas are finite resources. As they become scarcer, their prices rise, and their extraction becomes environmentally damaging and economically unsustainable. Renewable energy systems, such as solar, wind, hydro, and geothermal power, offer a sustainable and clean alternative. These sources are virtually inexhaustible and produce little to no greenhouse gas emissions during energy generation.

Figure 1. Renewable energy systems

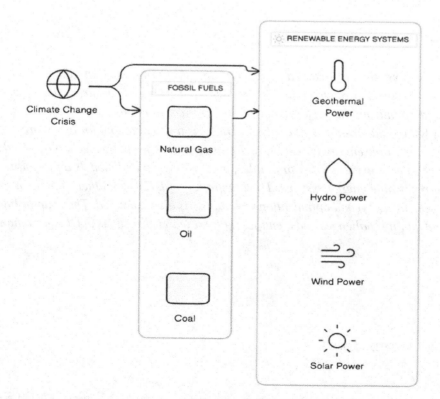

The efficient operation of renewable energy systems (see Figure 1) is critical for their effectiveness and widespread adoption. Maximizing efficiency ensures that these systems produce the most energy from available resources, reducing waste and improving their economic viability. Efficiency assessment helps in directing resources, investments, and incentives toward the most efficient technologies and practices within the renewable energy sector. This allocation ensures that investments yield the best returns in terms of energy production. Assessing and optimizing the efficiency of renewable energy systems aligns with international sustainability goals, including the United Nations' Sustainable Development Goals. It promotes responsible resource use, environmental stewardship, and the mitigation of climate change. Efficient renewable energy systems are not only environmentally friendly but also economically competitive with traditional fossil fuels. This competitiveness is crucial for the long-term affordability of clean energy. Renewable energy systems contribute to energy security by diversifying energy sources, reducing dependence on fossil fuel imports, and enhancing a nation's resilience to energy supply disruptions.

DEA plays a crucial role in evaluating and optimizing renewable energy systems by providing a comprehensive framework for assessing their efficiency and identifying areas for improvement. DEA allows for the quantification of efficiency in renewable energy systems. It assesses how effectively these systems convert inputs, such as sunlight, wind, or water, into useful energy output. Efficiency scores provide a clear picture of how well a system is performing relative to its peers. By comparing the performance of various renewable energy systems, DEA helps identify best practices and benchmarks. It pinpoints which technologies or operational strategies are the most efficient, enabling others to learn from and replicate their success. DEA assists in the allocation of limited resources, such as funding, manpower, and land, to maximize energy output. Decision-makers can use DEA results to prioritize investments in the most efficient technologies or geographic locations. It evaluates the operational efficiency of renewable energy facilities, including power plants and solar arrays. DEA can identify bottlenecks or areas where improvements in processes or maintenance are needed to enhance efficiency. DEA provides insights into how to optimize renewable energy systems. By analyzing the relationships between inputs and outputs, it offers guidance on the ideal mix of resources, equipment, and operational procedures to achieve maximum efficiency.

DEA can track the impact of technological advancements on efficiency over time. It helps assess whether new technologies, such as more efficient solar panels or advanced wind turbines, are delivering the expected gains in performance. In addition to efficiency, DEA can incorporate environmental and sustainability indicators into its analysis. This allows for a more holistic evaluation of renewable energy systems that considers not only energy production but also environmental impact. Governments and regulatory bodies can use DEA results to inform policy development. For instance, subsidies or incentives can be directed toward technologies or projects that demonstrate the potential for improved efficiency. DEA promotes a culture of continuous improvement in the renewable energy sector. Regular assessments encourage operators and organizations to seek ways to enhance efficiency, reduce waste, and increase energy generation. Organizations that achieve higher efficiency scores through DEA analysis gain a competitive advantage in the renewable energy market. They can position themselves as leaders in sustainability and attract investors and customers concerned about environmental impact. DEA serves as a powerful tool for decision-makers, researchers, and stakeholders in the renewable energy sector, facilitating the transition to cleaner, more efficient, and sustainable energy systems.

LITERATURE REVIEW

Zeng et al. (2020) developed a comprehensive model aimed at maximizing overall efficiency, enabling the optimization of proportions among various renewable energy resources. Jiang et al. (2021) introduced an evaluation index system for assessing green technology innovation efficiency within renewable energy enterprises. They employed dynamic DEA, factoring in undesirable output, to measure this efficiency and identified opportunities for improvement in underperforming enterprises. Seyed Hashem Mousavi-Avval and Shahin Rafiee (2011) focused on analyzing the energy consumption patterns in canola production within Iran's Golestan province. They utilized a non-parametric DEA approach to evaluate the technical and scale efficiency of producers. Additionally, the study identified inefficiencies in energy usage among farmers and proposed potential energy-saving measures for various inputs.

José Ramón San Cristóbal (2011) employs a Multiple Criteria Data Envelopment Analysis (MCDEA) model to assess the efficiency of 13 different Renewable Energy technologies. Martín-Gamboa et al. (2017) explore the integration of life cycle (LC) approaches with DEA to conduct sustainability assessments of energy systems. Chachuli et al. (2020) offer a comprehensive analysis of renewable energy performance utilizing DEA (see Figure 2), shedding light on the varying trajectories of renewable energy development across countries. Mardani et al. (2017) conducted a comprehensive review and synthesis of various DEA models applied globally to address energy efficiency challenges.

Song et al. (2012) investigated to assess the theoretical and practical foundations of environmental policy analysis, aiming to identify areas for future research directions. Li et al. (2020) conducted a study that offers valuable insights to designers and construction managers, aiding them in identifying optimal solutions for retrofitting building envelopes to achieve energy-efficient building operations. Han et al. (2020) proposed an innovative approach that combines DEA with cross-model integrated interpretative structural modeling and analytic hierarchy process. This approach is designed for energy efficiency evaluation and optimization modeling.

Hesampour et al. (2022) aim to enhance date production efficiency through input reduction using both parametric and non-parametric methods, while also assessing energy consumption and economic metrics in Iran's Khuzestan region. The study critically addresses the need for optimization in date palm production. Kouaissah and Hocine (2022) introduce XOR-DEA, a novel research direction within the DEA paradigm, specifically designed to address decision-making challenges associated with XOR input/output data. This paper critically delves into the need for specialized techniques in such scenarios.

Overview of Data Envelopment Analysis (DEA)

DEA, a powerful analytical tool used for evaluating and optimizing the efficiency of various entities, including those in the renewable energy sector. DEA is a non-parametric approach that assesses the relative performance of multiple decision-making units (DMUs) by comparing their input-output relationships (see Figure 3). In this overview, we delve into the fundamental principles, methodologies, and applications of DEA, setting the stage for its relevance in the context of renewable energy systems. DEA is a powerful and versatile quantitative technique used for assessing the relative efficiency and performance of multiple entities, often referred to as Decision-Making Units (DMUs). It has gained significant importance in various fields, including economics, finance, healthcare, and renewable energy systems. In this section, we delve into the fundamental principles and methodology that underlie DEA.

Figure 2. Data envelopment analysis (DEA) plays a crucial role in evaluating and optimizing renewable energy systems

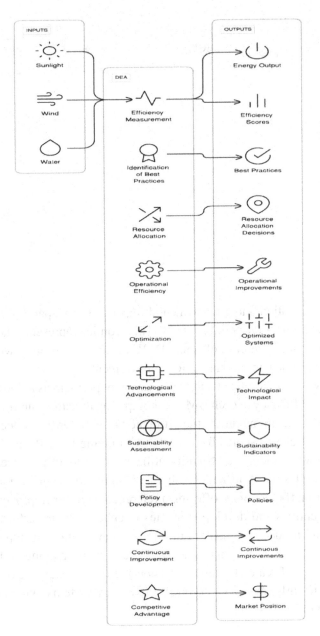

DEA is a non-parametric method used to evaluate the efficiency of DMUs by comparing their input-output relationships. It aims to identify the most efficient DMUs that can serve as benchmarks for others. This is particularly useful when dealing with complex systems, such as renewable energy projects, where multiple inputs and outputs need evaluation. DEA requires selecting appropriate input and output variables that best represent the entities under scrutiny. For renewable energy systems, these variables may include inputs like available sunlight, wind speed, and financial investments, as well as

Figure 3. Data envelopment analysis (DEA)

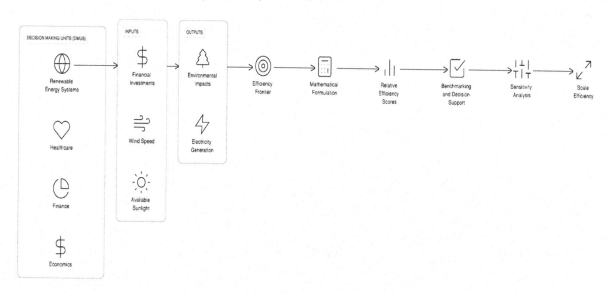

outputs like electricity generation and environmental impacts. DEA operates based on the concept of an efficiency frontier or production possibility set. This frontier represents the maximum achievable output for a given set of inputs. The most efficient DMUs lie on this frontier, while others fall below it. The goal is to identify inefficiencies and areas for improvement.

DEA mathematically formulates the efficiency assessment problem as a linear programming model. This model quantifies the efficiency of each DMU by comparing its actual outputs to a linear combination of the inputs. The model seeks to maximize the efficiency of each DMU subject to certain constraints. DEA produces relative efficiency scores for each DMU, ranging from 0 (inefficient) to 1 (efficient). These scores indicate how efficiently each entity utilizes its inputs to produce outputs, making them comparable across all DMUs. DEA provides valuable insights for decision-makers. Efficient DMUs serve as benchmarks for inefficient ones, offering a reference point for improvement. Decision-makers can identify inefficient entities and develop strategies to enhance their performance. DEA allows for sensitivity analysis, enabling decision-makers to explore how changes in input and output variables impact efficiency scores. This aids in scenario analysis and decision-making under different conditions. DEA addresses the concept of scale efficiency, considering the optimal size or scale of operations for each DMU. This is particularly important in renewable energy systems, where the scale of operations can significantly impact efficiency.

DEA Models and Variations Suitable for Renewable Energy Systems

DEA offers several models and variations tailored to specific contexts, including renewable energy systems. These models provide versatile tools for assessing and optimizing the efficiency of renewable energy projects. In this section, we explore some DEA models and their adaptations relevant to the renewable energy domain. The CCR model is the fundamental DEA model, assessing the relative efficiency of DMUs by comparing their input-output relationships. It assumes constant returns to scale (CRS), meaning that a proportional increase in inputs leads to a proportional increase in outputs. The CCR model is commonly used in renewable energy efficiency assessments. It can evaluate how efficiently different energy projects convert inputs (e.g., sunlight, wind, financial investments) into outputs (e.g., electricity generation, environmental benefits).

Unlike the CCR model, the BCC model allows for variable returns to scale (VRS). This means that it accommodates cases where input-output relationships may not exhibit proportional scaling. Renewable energy systems often operate under conditions where scale efficiencies vary. The BCC model is well-suited to assess and compare projects with differing scales and resource utilization. The super-efficiency model is used to identify DMUs that are not only efficient but also outperform their peers. These DMUs operate at the highest levels of efficiency within the dataset. In renewable energy, it's valuable to identify projects that excel in terms of efficiency and performance. The super-efficiency model can pinpoint best practices and serve as benchmarks for others.

DEA window analysis assesses efficiency over time, allowing for the evaluation of dynamic processes. It considers changes in efficiency as inputs and outputs fluctuate. Renewable energy systems often face variable conditions (e.g., seasonal changes, weather patterns). DEA window analysis can capture how efficiently projects adapt to these dynamics. Environmental DEA (EDEA) extends traditional DEA models by considering environmental impacts as an additional output variable. It evaluates the eco-efficiency of projects. Given the environmental benefits associated with renewable energy, EDEA is valuable for assessing not only the economic but also the environmental efficiency of renewable projects. Network DEA evaluates the efficiency of interconnected entities, such as power grids or integrated renewable energy systems. It accounts for shared resources and dependencies. Renewable energy often involves multiple interconnected components, including generation, storage, and distribution. Network DEA can optimize the efficiency of these integrated systems. These DEA models and variations offer a robust toolkit for evaluating and optimizing the efficiency of renewable energy systems. Depending on the specific objectives and characteristics of a project, one or more of these models can be applied to provide valuable insights for decision-makers in the renewable energy sector.

DEA Efficiency Scores and Interpretation

Efficiency scores generated through DEA play a crucial role in assessing the performance and optimization potential of renewable energy systems. In this section, we delve into the computation and interpretation of DEA efficiency scores. DEA calculates efficiency scores for each Decision Making Unit (DMU), representing renewable energy projects or entities. These scores indicate how efficiently a DMU utilizes its inputs to produce outputs. The process involves linear programming and can be summarized as follows:

- Normalization: DEA starts by normalizing input and output data. This ensures that all variables are measured on a common scale, typically between 0 and 1.
- Formulation of the DEA Model: Depending on the specific DEA model chosen (e.g., CCR, BCC, super-efficiency), linear equations are formulated to assess the efficiency of each DMU. These equations represent the optimization problem DEA solves.
- Efficiency Score Calculation: By solving the optimization problem, DEA assigns an efficiency score to each DMU. The scores range from 0 to 1, where 1 represents perfect efficiency, and values below 1 indicate relative inefficiency.

Interpretation of DEA Efficiency Scores

Interpreting DEA efficiency scores is essential for making informed decisions and optimizing renewable energy systems. Here's how to interpret these scores effectively:

a. Efficient DMUs (Score = 1):
   ○ DMUs with an efficiency score of 1 are considered fully efficient. They represent the best practices within the dataset, achieving the highest level of output for a given set of inputs.
   ○ These DMUs can serve as benchmarks for others, showcasing what is theoretically attainable with the available resources.

b. Inefficient DMUs (Score < 1):
   ○ DMUs with scores below 1 are deemed inefficient. They are not utilizing their inputs optimally to produce outputs.
   ○ The efficiency score indicates the proportion of potential output that the DMU is currently achieving. For example, a score of 0.75 suggests that the DMU is achieving 75% of its potential output given its inputs.

c. Potential for Improvement:
   ○ Inefficient DMUs present an opportunity for improvement. Decision-makers can explore ways to enhance the utilization of inputs or reduce resource consumption to move closer to full efficiency.
   ○ DEA identifies the most critical input(s) limiting efficiency, providing guidance for optimization efforts.

d. Use in Decision-Making:
   ○ Efficiency scores guide resource allocation and decision-making. Projects or entities with lower scores may require adjustments or investment to improve their efficiency.
   ○ Decision-makers can prioritize interventions based on the magnitude of inefficiency and the potential for cost savings or performance enhancement.

e. Dynamic Efficiency Analysis:
   ○ DEA efficiency scores can be analyzed over time using techniques like window analysis. This assesses how efficiency changes as inputs and outputs fluctuate, offering insights into dynamic performance.

f. Environmental Efficiency:
   ○ In the context of renewable energy, environmental DEA (EDEA) can be used to assess both economic and environmental efficiency. It evaluates how efficiently DMUs generate outputs while considering their environmental impacts.

In summary, DEA efficiency scores provide a quantitative basis for evaluating and optimizing renewable energy systems. They enable decision-makers to identify inefficiencies, prioritize improvement efforts, and benchmark performance against the best in the field. By interpreting these scores effectively, organizations can make informed decisions to enhance their contributions to sustainable energy production.

Figure 4. Application of data envelopment analysis (DEA) in renewable energy systems

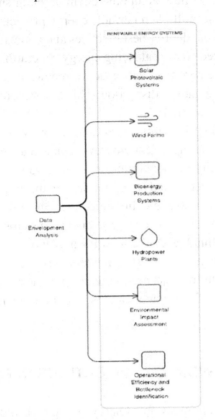

APPLICATION OF DEA IN RENEWABLE ENERGY SYSTEMS

The application of DEA in renewable energy systems is instrumental in evaluating and optimizing their efficiency (see Figure 4). DEA, a powerful mathematical technique, enables the assessment of the relative performance of different renewable energy projects, highlighting areas for improvement and resource allocation. In this section, we explore several key applications of DEA in the renewable energy sector.

Solar PV systems are a cornerstone of renewable energy production. DEA can assess the efficiency of these systems by considering factors such as capital investment, maintenance costs, energy generation, and environmental impact. It helps identify the most efficient PV systems and informs decision-making for optimizing resource allocation. Wind farms are significant contributors to clean energy generation. DEA evaluates the efficiency of wind farms by analyzing factors like capital expenditure, turbine specifications, operational costs, and electricity production. This assessment guides wind farm operators in enhancing performance while minimizing resource consumption. Bioenergy production involves multiple processes, from biomass collection to energy conversion. DEA assesses the efficiency of bioenergy systems by considering inputs like biomass type, collection costs, conversion technologies, and outputs such as energy yield and economic viability. It aids in optimizing the bioenergy supply chain for sustainability.

Hydropower is a reliable and renewable energy source. DEA can optimize the efficiency of hydropower plants by evaluating inputs such as water availability, infrastructure expenses, and maintenance costs, along with outputs like electricity generation and environmental impact. This optimization ensures efficient energy production while maintaining environmental sustainability. DEA enables the benchmarking of performance across multiple renewable energy projects. By comparing the efficiency of various initiatives, stakeholders can identify best practices and allocate resources more effectively to achieve higher efficiency and reduced costs. Balancing energy generation with environmental concerns is critical. DEA helps evaluate the environmental impact of renewable energy projects by considering factors like emissions, land use, and habitat disruption. This assessment supports the development of environmentally sustainable energy solutions.

DEA identifies operational bottlenecks within renewable energy systems. By pinpointing areas with suboptimal efficiency, operators can implement improvements that enhance overall system performance and productivity. Sustainability is a key criterion for renewable energy projects. DEA assesses whether these projects meet environmental and economic sustainability goals. It ensures that renewable energy initiatives align with long-term sustainability objectives. In summary, DEA plays a pivotal role in assessing and optimizing the efficiency of renewable energy systems. Its applications span various aspects, from evaluating specific technologies like solar PV and wind farms to assessing environmental impacts and sustainability. By leveraging DEA, stakeholders in the renewable energy sector can make data-driven decisions that contribute to a cleaner, more sustainable energy future. In the subsequent sections, we delve deeper into each of these applications, providing insights into their methodologies and real-world examples.

CASE STUDIES AND REAL-WORLD APPLICATIONS IN RENEWABLE ENERGY

The real-world applications of DEA in renewable energy systems have demonstrated its effectiveness in evaluating and optimizing the efficiency of various projects. In this section, we present case studies and practical examples that highlight the value of DEA in the renewable energy sector.

Case Study 1: Solar PV Efficiency Assessment

Objective: To assess the efficiency of multiple solar photovoltaic (PV) installations in a region.

Methodology: DEA was employed to evaluate the relative efficiency of different PV systems based on their energy output, initial investment, maintenance costs, and environmental impact. The analysis revealed the most efficient PV installations.

Outcome: By identifying the most efficient PV systems, local authorities allocated resources for scaling up these installations. This led to increased solar energy generation while optimizing costs and minimizing the environmental footprint.

Case Study 2: Wind Farm Performance Evaluation

Objective: To improve the operational efficiency of a wind farm.

Methodology: DEA was utilized to assess the performance of individual wind turbines within the farm. Factors considered included turbine specifications, maintenance expenditures, energy generation, and land use.

Outcome: The analysis identified underperforming turbines and specific maintenance needs. By addressing these issues, the wind farm increased its energy output while reducing operational costs.

Case Study 3: Bioenergy Supply Chain Optimization

Objective: To optimize the efficiency of a bioenergy supply chain, from biomass collection to energy conversion.

Methodology: DEA assessed the efficiency of each stage in the supply chain, considering factors such as biomass collection costs, transportation efficiency, conversion yields, and energy output.

Outcome: The analysis revealed inefficiencies in biomass collection and transportation. Implementing recommendations improved the overall supply chain efficiency and increased bioenergy production.

Case Study 4: Hydropower Plant Optimization

Objective: To optimize the operational efficiency of a hydropower plant.

Methodology: DEA analyzed the inputs (water availability, infrastructure costs, maintenance) and outputs (electricity generation, environmental impact) of the plant to identify areas for improvement.

Outcome: By addressing maintenance bottlenecks and optimizing water resource allocation, the hydropower plant achieved higher energy generation and reduced its environmental impact.

Case Study 5: Sustainability Evaluation of a Renewable Energy Project

Objective: To assess the sustainability of a large-scale renewable energy project.

Methodology: DEA considered economic, environmental, and social sustainability criteria to evaluate the project's performance over time. Factors included cost-effectiveness, emissions reduction, and community impact.

Outcome: The sustainability assessment informed project stakeholders about areas needing improvement. It resulted in adjustments to project management practices, enhancing long-term sustainability.

Case Study 6: Benchmarking Renewable Energy Projects

Objective: To benchmark the performance of various renewable energy projects within a region.

Methodology: DEA compared the efficiency of multiple projects, including solar, wind, and bioenergy initiatives, based on their inputs and outputs.

Outcome: Benchmarking allowed policymakers to identify top-performing projects and allocate funding more efficiently. It encouraged healthy competition among project operators, leading to overall sectoral growth.

These case studies exemplify how DEA has been applied effectively in renewable energy systems, leading to improved efficiency, reduced costs, and enhanced sustainability. By adopting DEA methodologies and lessons from these real-world applications, stakeholders can make informed decisions to accelerate the transition to clean and sustainable energy sources. In the subsequent sections, we delve into specific DEA models and techniques tailored to each renewable energy sector.

Integration of DEA With Other Analytical Tools

In the quest for efficient and sustainable renewable energy systems, the integration of DEA with other analytical tools has proven to be a powerful approach. This section explores three key aspects of combining DEA with complementary techniques to enhance the evaluation and optimization of renewable energy systems.

Combining DEA With Life Cycle Assessment (LCA) for Sustainable Energy Systems

Objective: To assess the sustainability and environmental impact of renewable energy projects.

Approach: The integration of DEA with Life Cycle Assessment (LCA) provides a holistic view of the environmental, economic, and social dimensions of renewable energy systems. DEA evaluates the operational efficiency, while LCA analyzes the entire life cycle, from resource extraction to disposal (see Figure 5).

Benefits:

- **Comprehensive Sustainability Assessment:** By combining DEA's operational efficiency assessment with LCA's life cycle perspective, decision-makers gain a comprehensive understanding of the sustainability of renewable energy projects.
- **Environmental Impact Identification:** LCA identifies environmental impacts at every stage of a renewable energy system's life cycle. It helps pinpoint areas where improvements can reduce negative environmental effects.
- **Informed Decision-Making:** This synergy guides the selection of renewable energy projects that not only operate efficiently but also align with environmental and social sustainability goals.
- **Optimized Resource Allocation:** By considering life cycle impacts, resource allocation decisions can be optimized to minimize environmental harm while maximizing efficiency.
- **Policy Alignment:** The integrated approach supports policymakers in developing regulations and incentives that promote both efficiency and sustainability in renewable energy.

Challenges:

- **Data Complexity:** LCA requires extensive data on resource use, emissions, and environmental impacts, which can be challenging to collect and manage.
- **Interdisciplinary Collaboration:** Effective integration demands collaboration between experts in DEA, LCA, and renewable energy, which can be logistically complex.
- **Subjectivity:** LCA involves subjective choices, such as selecting impact categories and defining system boundaries, which can influence results.
- **Complexity Trade-Off:** Balancing operational efficiency and sustainability objectives may lead to trade-offs that require careful consideration.

Incorporating Life Cycle Assessment into DEA enhances decision-making by accounting for the broader environmental and societal impacts of renewable energy systems. It empowers stakeholders to pursue sustainable solutions that efficiently harness renewable resources while minimizing their overall ecological footprint.

Synergy of DEA and Optimization Techniques in Renewable Energy Planning

Objective: To enhance decision-making in renewable energy planning and resource allocation.

Approach: The synergy of DEA with optimization techniques creates a powerful framework for optimizing the performance of renewable energy systems. DEA assesses current efficiency, while optimizations algorithms help identify the optimal resource allocation for improved efficiency (see Figure 6).

Benefits:

- **Efficiency Improvement:** DEA identifies underperforming aspects of renewable energy systems, which optimization techniques can address by suggesting resource allocation changes.
- **Cost Reduction:** Optimization algorithms can minimize costs, such as operation and maintenance expenses, while maintaining or improving efficiency.
- **Resource Allocation:** Synergy helps allocate resources effectively, balancing various factors, including energy output, costs, and environmental impact.
- **Risk Mitigation:** DEA and optimization techniques can simulate different scenarios to identify and mitigate risks associated with renewable energy projects.
- **Real-time Decision Support:** The combination allows for real-time monitoring and adjustment of renewable energy systems to adapt to changing conditions.

Challenges:

- **Complex Models:** Developing integrated DEA-optimization models can be complex, requiring expertise in both fields.
- **Data Availability:** Reliable data is essential for accurate modeling, and data availability can be a constraint in some cases.
- **Interdisciplinary Collaboration:** Collaboration between experts in renewable energy, operations research, and DEA is necessary but may pose challenges.
- **Model Validation:** Ensuring the models accurately represent real-world systems is crucial for trustworthy results.

The synergy of DEA and optimization techniques empowers renewable energy planners to make data-driven decisions that improve system efficiency, reduce costs, and enhance sustainability. By optimizing resource allocation and operation, renewable energy projects can maximize their positive impact while minimizing waste and inefficiency. This approach is vital for achieving a sustainable and clean energy future.

Incorporating Uncertainty and Sensitivity Analysis in DEA-Based Assessments

Objective: To enhance the robustness and reliability of DEA by incorporating uncertainty and sensitivity analysis into renewable energy assessments.

Approach: Uncertainty and sensitivity analysis in DEA involves evaluating the impact of variations in input and output data on efficiency scores and decision-making. In the context of renewable energy systems, this means accounting for uncertainties in factors like energy production, costs, and environmental impacts.

Benefits:

Figure 5. Data envelopment analysis (DEA) with other analytical tools

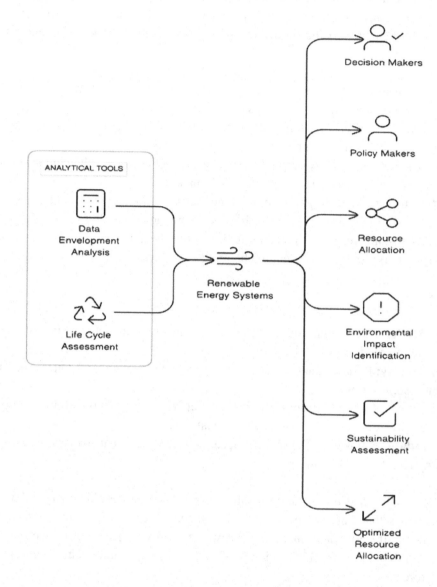

- **Robust Decision-Making:** Uncertainty analysis helps assess how variations in data affect DEA results, allowing decision-makers to account for potential fluctuations in renewable energy system performance.
- **Risk Assessment:** Identifying sensitive inputs or outputs reveals which factors have the most significant impact on efficiency scores, highlighting potential areas of risk in renewable energy projects.
- **Optimization under Uncertainty:** Combining uncertainty analysis with optimization techniques enables decision-makers to make resource allocation decisions that are resilient to uncertainties.
- **Improved Planning:** Sensitivity analysis identifies critical parameters, guiding planners in focusing resources on the most influential aspects of renewable energy projects.

Figure 6. Synergy of DEA and optimization techniques in renewable energy planning

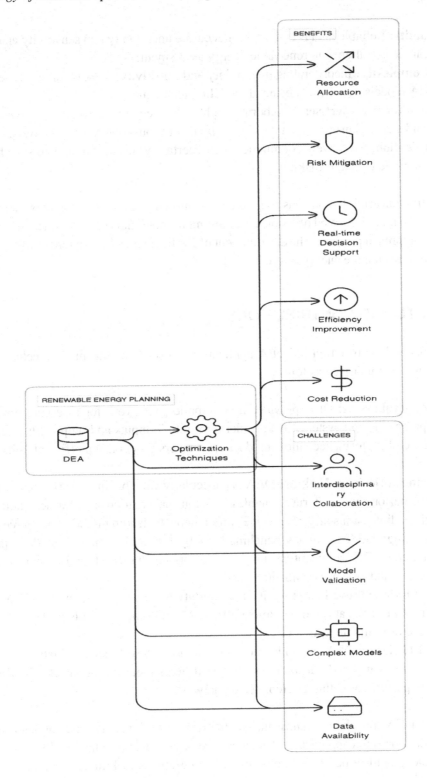

Challenges:

- **Data Quality:** Reliable data is essential for accurate uncertainty and sensitivity analysis, but data quality can be a challenge in renewable energy assessments.
- **Model Complexity:** Incorporating uncertainty and sensitivity analysis can increase the complexity of DEA models, requiring advanced modeling techniques.
- **Interdisciplinary Expertise:** Collaborative efforts between DEA experts, renewable energy specialists, and statisticians may be needed to implement robust uncertainty analysis.
- **Communication:** Effectively communicating uncertainty-related findings to stakeholders is crucial for informed decision-making.

By integrating uncertainty and sensitivity analysis into DEA-based assessments, renewable energy planners can make more informed decisions, accounting for potential risks and variations in system performance. This approach promotes the development of resilient and adaptive renewable energy systems, contributing to a sustainable energy future.

KEY INSIGHTS AND CONTRIBUTIONS

The key insights and contributions of DEA applications in science, information technology (IT), and engineering can be summarized as follows:

a. **Efficiency Evaluation:** DEA provides a systematic framework for assessing the efficiency of entities, processes, and systems by considering multiple inputs and outputs. It offers a quantitative measure of performance, allowing decision-makers to identify inefficient units and areas for improvement.

b. **Multi-Criteria Decision-Making:** DEA is particularly valuable in scenarios with multiple, often conflicting, performance criteria. It enables decision-makers to make informed choices by considering various dimensions of performance simultaneously, leading to better resource allocation.

c. **Benchmarking:** DEA facilitates benchmarking by comparing entities to their peers or best-performing units. This comparative analysis helps organizations set realistic performance targets, track progress, and enhance competitiveness.

d. **Resource Optimization:** In sectors like transportation, logistics, and energy, DEA assists in optimizing resource allocation to maximize efficiency and output. It aids in determining the most effective use of available resources.

e. **Network Efficiency:** DEA has applications in evaluating the efficiency of network-based systems, such as supply chains and telecommunications. It helps identify bottlenecks, inefficiencies, and areas for improvement within interconnected networks.

In summary, DEA contributes significantly to the fields of science, IT, and engineering by offering a quantitative, data-oriented approach to efficiency assessment and optimization. Its adaptability, ability to handle complex, multi-dimensional problems, and integration capabilities make it a valuable tool for improving decision-making and resource management across a wide range of domains.

Importance of DEA in Optimizing Renewable Energy Systems

DEA plays a crucial role in optimizing renewable energy systems for several reasons. DEA provides a systematic and data-driven approach to assess the efficiency of renewable energy systems. By identifying inefficient components or processes, it helps optimize resource utilization, enhancing overall system efficiency. In the renewable energy sector, efficient resource allocation is vital. DEA assists in determining how to allocate resources such as land, capital, and labor to maximize energy output while minimizing waste. Renewable energy technologies are continually evolving. DEA can be used to evaluate the efficiency of different technologies, making it easier to decide which ones to adopt or invest in for optimal energy generation. DEA helps identify areas of inefficiency that may be driving up costs. By addressing these inefficiencies, renewable energy projects can reduce operating expenses and become more cost competitive. As sustainability becomes a central concern, DEA can assess the environmental efficiency of renewable energy systems. This evaluation ensures that energy generation is environmentally friendly and aligns with sustainability goals. DEA enables benchmarking against the most efficient systems or competitors. This comparison helps set performance targets and provides insights into best practices that can be adopted for optimization. In some regions, renewable energy projects must meet specific efficiency standards to qualify for incentives or comply with regulations. DEA helps ensure that these standards are met.

CHALLENGES AND FUTURE DIRECTIONS

Efficiency assessment using DEA is a powerful tool for evaluating the performance of renewable energy systems. However, it is not without limitations and potential biases that must be considered. Here, we outline some of the key limitations and potential biases associated with DEA-based efficiency assessment in the context of renewable energy systems. DEA is highly sensitive to the quality and accuracy of input and output data. Inaccurate or incomplete data can lead to erroneous efficiency scores. Rigorous data validation and cleansing processes are essential to ensure that input and output data accurately represent the performance of renewable energy systems.

DEA is sensitive to the scale of input and output variables. Inconsistencies in the units of measurement or the range of values can affect efficiency scores. Researchers must carefully preprocess data to normalize scales, reducing the impact of scale sensitivity. Different scaling methods and robustness checks can also be employed. The selection of inputs and outputs for DEA models can introduce bias. Inappropriate choices may not fully capture the complexity of renewable energy systems. Researchers should engage domain experts and stakeholders to carefully choose relevant inputs and outputs that align with the specific goals of the assessment. DEA assumes that observed inefficiencies are solely due to the system's performance. It does not account for external factors or uncontrollable variables that may influence efficiency. Sensitivity analysis can help assess the impact of external factors and provide insights into the robustness of efficiency scores.

DEA benchmarks systems against each other, potentially leading to relative efficiency scores. Benchmarking against the best-performing system may not represent an achievable target for all systems. Researchers can use frontier shift and target setting techniques to set more realistic benchmarks that account for external factors and operational constraints. DEA is a powerful method for evaluating the efficiency of renewable energy systems. However, DEA applications often face challenges related to data availability and data quality. Addressing these issues is crucial to ensure the accuracy and reliability of DEA-based assessments in the context of renewable energy.

Renewable energy projects may have limited historical data, especially for emerging technologies. The strategies include collecting data over time to build a more comprehensive dataset, even if it requires several years of observations. Also, collaborating with renewable energy projects, utilities, or government agencies to access relevant data sources is another important strategy. Another strategy could be implementing advanced sensor technology to gather real-time data, which can enhance the dataset.

Inaccurate or incomplete data can lead to biased results. Implementing rigorous data validation and cleaning procedures to identify and rectify errors or outliers is essential. Engaging domain experts to review and verify data quality, especially when dealing with complex variables is an important strategy. Maintaining clear documentation of data sources, pre-processing steps, and any data transformations applied is also required.

A key data availability challenge is missing data points which can disrupt the analysis. One of the strategies to address this challenge is using statistical methods or machine learning techniques for imputing missing data points. Another strategy is to assess the impact of missing data on DEA results through sensitivity analysis.

Selecting relevant inputs and outputs is critical for accurate assessments. One of the strategies to ensure this is by consulting with experts to determine the most meaningful variables for assessing renewable energy system efficiency. Another strategy could be conducting exploratory data analysis to identify relationships and correlations among variables. Another key data quality challenge is inconsistent scales or units that can affect DEA results. The strategies include normalizing data to a common scale to mitigate scale-related biases. Another strategy is to perform sensitivity analysis to assess the impact of different scaling methods.

Future Trends and Emerging Research Areas in DEA for Renewable Energy Systems

DEA continues to evolve as a valuable tool for assessing and optimizing the efficiency of renewable energy systems (see Figure 7). As the renewable energy sector grows and faces new challenges, several future trends and emerging research areas in DEA for renewable energy systems are expected. The integration of machine learning techniques with DEA is likely to become more prevalent. ML models can help in predicting efficiency scores, identifying influential factors, and enhancing the accuracy of DEA-based assessments. A key emerging research area is developing models that predict renewable energy system efficiency based on historical data and external factors. Also, using ML for anomaly detection to identify and address unusual patterns in efficiency data is another emerging research direction. Another interesting area will be to explore novel hybrid models that combine the strengths of both DEA and ML for more robust assessments.

With increasing emphasis on sustainability, future research will focus on integrating environmental and sustainability metrics into DEA models for renewable energy systems. An emerging research direction is to combine DEA with LCA to assess the environmental impact of renewable energy projects. Another emerging research trend is to develop models that consider the trade-off between economic efficiency and sustainability goals. Multi-objective optimization using DEA is expected to gain traction. It allows decision-makers to simultaneously optimize multiple conflicting objectives, such as cost, environmental impact, and social acceptance. An emerging research direction in this area is to explore Pareto-efficient

Figure 7. Future trends and emerging research areas in DEA for renewable energy systems

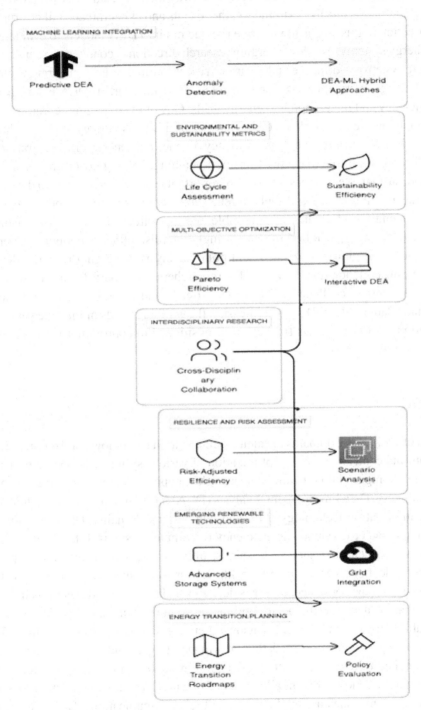

solutions that balance competing objectives. Another emerging research direction is developing interactive decision support systems that allow decision-makers to explore trade-offs and make informed choices.

As renewable energy systems become integral to energy infrastructure, assessing their resilience and vulnerability to external factors like extreme weather events and cyber threats will be crucial. An emerging research direction in this area is to integrate risk factors into DEA models to evaluate the resilience of renewable energy systems. Another emerging research direction is conducting scenario-based assessments to evaluate system performance under various risk scenarios. As emerging renewable technologies (e.g., advanced energy storage, next-generation solar) enter the market, DEA research will expand to assess their efficiency and integration into energy grids. One of the emerging research directions in this area involves applying DEA to evaluate the efficiency of advanced energy storage solutions. Another important research direction is to assess the efficiency of renewable energy grid integration technologies.

DEA will play a pivotal role in energy transition planning, helping governments and organizations transition to more sustainable energy systems. An important research direction is to develop DEA-based roadmaps for transitioning from fossil fuels to renewable energy sources. Another important research direction is evaluating the efficiency of renewable energy policies and incentives using DEA. DEA research in renewable energy will become increasingly interdisciplinary, involving experts from fields such as economics, environmental science, and policy analysis. Emerging research directions in this area include fostering collaboration between DEA researchers and experts from diverse fields to address complex renewable energy challenges. These future trends and emerging research areas demonstrate the versatility and adaptability of DEA in addressing the evolving needs of the renewable energy sector. Researchers and practitioners in this field are well-positioned to contribute to a more sustainable and efficient global energy landscape.

CONCLUSION

The application of DEA in the domains of science, information technology, and engineering has yielded valuable insights and contributed to the optimization of various systems. This chapter has explored the significance of DEA, highlighting its role as a versatile and powerful tool for evaluating and enhancing efficiency. In summary, Data Envelopment Analysis (DEA) has found diverse and valuable applications across science, information technology (IT), and engineering domains. DEA provides a systematic and data-driven approach to evaluate the efficiency of complex systems. It has been used to assess the performance of various entities, such as hospitals, universities, and manufacturing plants, enabling decision-makers to identify areas for improvement. DEA is well-suited for scenarios involving multiple criteria or dimensions of performance. It allows decision-makers to consider various inputs and outputs simultaneously, making it a powerful tool for optimizing systems with multiple objectives. One of DEA's strengths is its ability to benchmark entities against their peers or best-performing units. This comparative analysis helps organizations set realistic performance targets and improve their competitiveness. DEA has been applied to optimize resource allocation in contexts like transportation and logistics. It helps in determining the most efficient allocation of resources to maximize output or service quality. In network-based systems, such as supply chains and telecommunications, DEA aids in assessing the efficiency of interconnected components. It helps identify bottlenecks and areas where improvements can enhance overall network performance. In an era of sustainability, DEA has been extended to evaluate the environmental efficiency of processes and systems. It assists in assessing how efficiently resources are used to minimize environmental impact. DEA's reliance on quantitative data aligns with the growing trend of data-driven decision-making. It provides objective insights based on empirical data, reducing subjectivity in decision processes. DEA transcends disciplinary boundaries, finding applications in diverse fields ranging from healthcare and education to finance and agriculture. Its adaptability makes it a versatile tool for assessing and optimizing efficiency. DEA can be integrated with other analytical tools, such as life cycle assessment (LCA) and optimization techniques, to enhance the depth and breadth of analysis. This integration enables more comprehensive decision support. Overall, DEA stands as a valuable methodology for performance evaluation and optimization in science, IT, and engineering. Its wide-ranging applications underscore its flexibility and relevance in addressing complex challenges across various domains. As data availability and computational capabilities continue to grow, DEA is poised to play an increasingly influential role in aiding decision-makers in their pursuit of efficiency and sustainability.

REFERENCES

Han, Y., Zhou, R., Geng, Z., Bai, J., Ma, B., & Fan, J. (2020). A novel data envelopment analysis cross-model integrating interpretative structural model and analytic hierarchy process for energy efficiency evaluation and optimization modeling: Application to ethylene industries. *Journal of Cleaner Production, 246*, 118965. doi:10.1016/j.jclepro.2019.118965

Hesampour, R., Hassani, M., Hanafiah, M. M., & Heidarbeigi, K. (2022). Technical efficiency, sensitivity analysis and economic assessment applying data envelopment analysis approach: A case study of date production in Khuzestan State of Iran. *Journal of the Saudi Society of Agricultural Sciences, 21*(3), 197–207. doi:10.1016/j.jssas.2021.08.003

Jiang, T., Ji, P., Shi, Y., Ye, Z., & Jin, Q. (2021). Efficiency assessment of green technology innovation of renewable energy enterprises in China: A dynamic data envelopment analysis considering undesirable output. *Clean Technologies and Environmental Policy, 23*(5), 1509–1519. doi:10.100710098-021-02044-9

Kouaissah, N., & Hocine, A. (2022). XOR data envelopment analysis and its application to renewable energy sector. *Expert Systems with Applications, 207*, 118044. doi:10.1016/j.eswa.2022.118044

Li, H. X., Li, Y., Jiang, B., Zhang, L., Wu, X., & Lin, J. (2020). Energy performance optimisation of building envelope retrofit through integrated orthogonal arrays with data envelopment analysis. *Renewable Energy, 149*, 1414–1423. doi:10.1016/j.renene.2019.10.143

Mardani, A., Zavadskas, E. K., Streimikiene, D., Jusoh, A., & Khoshnoudi, M. (2017). A comprehensive review of data envelopment analysis (DEA) approach in energy efficiency. *Renewable & Sustainable Energy Reviews, 70*, 1298–1322. doi:10.1016/j.rser.2016.12.030

Martín-Gamboa, M., Iribarren, D., García-Gusano, D., & Dufour, J. (2017). A review of life-cycle approaches coupled with data envelopment analysis within multi-criteria decision analysis for sustainability assessment of energy systems. *Journal of Cleaner Production, 150*, 164–174. doi:10.1016/j.jclepro.2017.03.017

Mohd Chachuli, F. S., Ahmad Ludin, N., Mat, S., & Sopian, K. (2020). Renewable energy performance evaluation studies using the data envelopment analysis (DEA): A systematic review. *Journal of Renewable and Sustainable Energy, 12*(6), 062701. Advance online publication. doi:10.1063/5.0024750

Mousavi-Avval, S. H., Rafiee, S., Jafari, A., & Mohammadi, A. (2011). Improving energy use efficiency of canola production using data envelopment analysis (DEA) approach. *Energy*, *36*(5), 2765–2772. doi:10.1016/j.energy.2011.02.016

San Cristóbal, J. R. (2011). A multi criteria data envelopment analysis model to evaluate the efficiency of the Renewable Energy technologies. *Renewable Energy*, *36*(10), 2742–2746. doi:10.1016/j.renene.2011.03.008

Song, M., An, Q., Zhang, W., Wang, Z., & Wu, J. (2012). Environmental efficiency evaluation based on data envelopment analysis: A review. *Renewable & Sustainable Energy Reviews*, *16*(7), 4465–4469. doi:10.1016/j.rser.2012.04.052

Zeng, Y., Guo, W., Wang, H., & Zhang, F. (2020). A two-stage evaluation and optimization method for renewable energy development based on data envelopment analysis. *Applied Energy*, *262*, 114363. doi:10.1016/j.apenergy.2019.114363

KEY TERMS AND DEFINITIONS

Data Envelopment Analysis (DEA): DEA is a quantitative method used for evaluating the relative efficiency and performance of decision-making units, such as organizations, processes, or systems. It assesses how well these units convert multiple inputs into outputs and identifies areas for improvement by comparing them to efficient peers or benchmarks. DEA is particularly useful for optimizing resource allocation and enhancing efficiency in various sectors, including finance, healthcare, and renewable energy.

Decision-Making Units (DMUs): DMUs are entities or organizations that are subject to evaluation and comparison in Data Envelopment Analysis (DEA). These units can represent various entities like companies, institutions, or departments, and they are assessed based on their input and output parameters to determine their relative efficiency and performance. DEA helps identify DMUs that are operating efficiently and those that may need improvements in resource utilization or productivity.

Life Cycle Assessment (LCA): LCA is a systematic and comprehensive method for evaluating the environmental impacts of a product, process, or service throughout its entire life cycle, from raw material extraction to disposal. LCA quantifies the environmental aspects, including resource use, emissions, and energy consumption, to support more sustainable decision-making and reduce the environmental footprint of products and systems.

Machine Learning (ML): ML is a subset of artificial intelligence (AI) that focuses on developing algorithms and statistical models enabling computer systems to improve their performance on a specific task through learning from data and experiences. ML algorithms enable computers to identify patterns, make predictions, and improve their decision-making without being explicitly programmed for each task. It finds applications in various fields, including data analysis, pattern recognition, natural language processing, and autonomous systems.

Photovoltaic (PV): PV refers to the technology that converts sunlight into electricity using semiconductor materials, typically silicon solar cells. When exposed to sunlight, these cells generate a direct electrical current, making PV systems a clean and renewable source of energy commonly used in solar panels for electricity generation.

Chapter 11
Data Envelopment Analysis in Healthcare Management:
Overview of the Latest Trends

Narasimha Rao Vajjhala
 https://orcid.org/0000-0002-8260-2392
University of New York Tirana, Albania

Philip Eappen
 https://orcid.org/0000-0002-8120-8449
Cape Breton University, Canada

ABSTRACT

This chapter explores the applications, contributions, limitations, and challenges of data envelopment analysis (DEA) in healthcare management. DEA, a non-parametric method used for evaluating the efficiency of decision-making units, has found extensive applications in healthcare sectors such as hospital management, nursing, and outpatient services. The review consolidates findings from a broad range of studies, highlighting DEA's significant contributions to efficiency measurement, benchmarking, resource allocation and optimization, and performance evaluation. However, despite DEA's robust applications, the chapter also identifies several limitations and challenges, including the selection of inputs and outputs, sensitivity to outliers, inability to handle statistical noise, lack of inherent uncertainty measures, homogeneity assumption, and the static nature of traditional DEA models. These challenges underscore the need for further research and methodological advancements in applying DEA in healthcare management.

INTRODUCTION

Data Envelopment Analysis (DEA) is a non-parametric method used in operations research and economics for the estimation of production frontiers (Koengkan et al., 2022). It is used to empirically measure productive efficiency of decision-making units (DMUs), which can be businesses, organizations, or parts of organizations (Nepomuceno et al., 2023). DEA was first proposed by Charnes, Cooper, and Rhodes

DOI: 10.4018/979-8-3693-0255-2.ch011

in 1978 (Charnes et al., 1978), and it has been widely used in many different fields such as healthcare, transportation, finance, and more. This method is particularly useful when the production process involves multiple inputs and outputs, which is difficult to handle in traditional statistical techniques. The key concept of DEA is the efficiency score, which is calculated by comparing the DMU's performance to a best practice frontier that is constructed from the data (Horta et al., 2013). The best practice frontier is essentially the envelope of the most efficient DMUs. If a DMU is on the frontier, it is considered as efficient (efficiency score equals to 1) and if it is below the frontier, it is considered as inefficient (efficiency score less than 1) (Jahed et al., 2015; Jiang et al., 2020). The further a DMU is from the frontier, the lower its efficiency score.

The modern healthcare landscape is increasingly complex and requires innovative solutions to balance efficiency, effectiveness, and quality of care. In this demanding environment, DEA has emerged as a pivotal tool, offering a unique perspective on operational efficiency and resource utilization. In healthcare management, DEA's focus on efficiency takes on profound importance. With finite resources and ever-growing demands, healthcare organizations are continually challenged to deliver high-quality care without over-utilizing resources. DEA provides an analytical framework to understand how well healthcare entities are converting inputs (such as staff hours, medical equipment, and funds) into desired outputs (like patient satisfaction, recovery rates, and overall health outcomes) (Kohl et al., 2019). The application of DEA in healthcare has led to significant insights into the workings of different healthcare settings (Tompkins et al., 2017). From assessing the performance of individual healthcare providers to understanding the efficiency of entire healthcare systems, DEA offers a nuanced and flexible approach that accommodates the multifaceted nature of medical care.

Beyond its analytical capabilities, DEA fosters a culture of continuous improvement. By benchmarking against the most efficient units, healthcare providers can learn from best practices, implement changes, and monitor progress over time. This iterative process supports data-driven decision-making and encourages healthcare organizations to strive for excellence in both efficiency and quality of care. However, it is essential to recognize that DEA is not without limitations and challenges. The next section provides a background for this study followed by the review of literature, solutions, findings, as well as recommendations for future research.

BACKGROUND

DEA is a multifaceted tool with broad applications and numerous benefits. DEA is flexible, non-parametric in nature and can handle complex multi-input and multi-output systems making it an invaluable asset in various fields. From healthcare and education to finance and manufacturing, DEA continues to offer insightful analyses, guiding efficiency improvements, and strategic decision-making across diverse landscapes (Azadi et al., 2021; Pang & Gai, 2022). The core of DEA involves assessing multiple inputs and outputs to evaluate the relative efficiency of DMUs. Inputs are the resources consumed by the DMU, and outputs are the products or services produced. DMUs are entities responsible for converting inputs into outputs, which can range from organizations to individual processes within a system. DEA identifies an efficiency frontier that represents the best-performing DMUs. Any DMUs falling below this frontier are considered relatively inefficient. DEA can model constant returns to scale (CRS) where output increases proportionately with input, or variable returns to scale (VRS), where the relationship between input and output is non-linear. DEA can focus on either input-orientation (minimizing inputs for a given output level) or output-orientation (maximizing outputs for a given input level).

Universities, schools, and educational systems use DEA to assess the use of resources like faculty, funds, and facilities to produce outcomes like student success, research publications, etc. (Cossani et al., 2022; Obadić & Aristovnik, 2011). DEA helps in evaluating the efficiency of financial institutions, including banks, insurance companies, and investment firms (Mahmoudabadi & Emrouznejad, 2019; Omrani et al., 2022). In manufacturing, DEA can analyze production processes to find the most efficient production methods, considering factors like labor, material costs, and energy usage. Government and public service organizations employ DEA to understand the effectiveness of various programs and initiatives (Kumar & Gulati, 2009; Seol et al., 2008). From airlines to public transport, DEA has been used to analyze efficiency regarding fuel consumption, labor, fleet utilization, and other factors (Caulfield et al., 2013; Jain & Natarajan, 2015; Yu et al., 2019).

DEA can handle multiple inputs and outputs, making it applicable across diverse sectors and complex systems. Unlike parametric methods, DEA doesn't require a specific functional form for the relationship between inputs and outputs, enhancing its adaptability. DEA identifies best-performing units, allowing others to learn from and emulate best practices. DEA can focus on either minimizing inputs or maximizing outputs, aligning with organizational goals and strategies. DEA provides detailed insights that guide decision-making, resource allocation, and strategic planning. DEA can be combined with other techniques like stochastic frontier analysis (SFA) and analytic hierarchy process (AHP) to create hybrid models, enhancing its utility (Fu et al., 2011; Gharizadeh Beiragh et al., 2020).

REVIEW OF LITERATURE

Current Applications of DEA in Hospital Management

The literature review on current applications of DEA in hospital management reveals a broad range of studies that explore the efficiency and performance of hospitals across various dimensions. One of the most common uses of DEA in hospital management is to assess the relative efficiency of hospitals (Kocisova et al., 2018; Kohl et al., 2019; Li & Dong, 2015; Vitezic et al., 2016). Inputs typically include resources like the number of doctors, nurses, beds, and medical equipment, while outputs can include the number of patients treated, patient satisfaction scores, and various health outcomes. DEA computes an efficiency score for each hospital by comparing its performance to a 'best practice' frontier created from the data (Zarrin et al., 2022). This allows managers to identify top-performing hospitals and learn from their practices. DEA also facilitates benchmarking by identifying peer hospitals for each inefficient hospital (Medarević & Vuković, 2021). These peer hospitals operate on the efficiency frontier and have similar input-output structures to the inefficient hospital. By learning from these peer hospitals, the inefficient hospital can potentially improve its performance.

DEA can inform resource allocation decisions by identifying sources of inefficiency (Alatawi et al., 2020). For instance, DEA can help managers understand whether a hospital is overusing certain resources (input excess) or under-producing given the resources it has (output shortfall) (Habib & Shahwan, 2020). This can guide managers in reallocating resources to achieve better performance. DEA can be used to evaluate the impacts of policy changes on hospital performance. For instance, researchers have used DEA to study the effects of healthcare reforms on hospital efficiency. This can provide valuable insights for policymakers. DEA models can be extended to track the performance of hospitals over time, allowing managers to evaluate the effectiveness of their improvement initiatives.

The use of DEA can assist hospital administrators and health policymakers in discovering inefficiencies, allowing them to make more informed decisions (Alatawi et al., 2020). An investigation conducted in Saudi Arabia revealed that the number of full-time physicians was a partially more significant reason for inefficiency than the other components, with an average excess of 22.4% from an input standpoint. Other labor variables that indicated a surplus in usage were the number of nurses and allied health staff, as well as the excess number of hospital beds (capital variable). To be efficient, hospitals are required to increase the number of outpatients and hospitalized inpatient services by 12.2% and 14.2%, respectively, according to the findings of the analysis (Alatawi et al., 2020).

For instance, a study by Chitnis and Mishra (2019) analyzed the efficiency of 25 Indian private hospitals using an output-oriented CCR model. The results show seven hospitals as the most efficient ones using DEA in the first stage and identified a positive correlation between patient satisfaction and efficiency. In another study, Ghasemi et al. (2021) determined the factors affecting operating rooms' (ORs) efficiency and evaluate the performance and ranking of operating rooms in 10 of Tehran's largest hospitals using input-oriented CCR (CCR-I), output-oriented CCR (CCR-O), input-output oriented CCR (CCR_IO) and AP models. Both industrialized and developing nations have made substantial use of DEA in a variety of medical settings. To evaluate the efficacy of nursing home care throughout the Netherlands, applied DEA carried out research (Kooreman, 1994). A further investigation found that, when compared to their national equivalents, fewer than 10% of Turkish acute general hospitals were running effectively (Ersoy et al., 1997).

Several studies have employed DEA to benchmark hospitals and identify best practices (Alatawi et al., 2020; Habib & Shahwan, 2020; Li & Dong, 2015). This helps hospitals understand their performance relative to their peers and improve their practices. Kamel and Mousa (2021) measured and evaluated the operational efficiency of 26 isolation hospitals in Egypt during the COVID-19 pandemic, as well as identified the most important inputs affecting their efficiency employing an input-oriented BCC model. They found out that of 26 isolation hospitals, only 4 were found efficient according to CCR model and 12 out of 26 hospitals achieved efficiency under the BCC model. Ghaziyani et al. (2019) presented data from an Iranian hospital, in North region of Iran in years 2010 and 2019 using an output-oriented BCC model. This study compares the performance of different parts of the hospital over the years and helps in improving hospital performance. Some studies have explored the impact of technology adoption on hospital efficiency (Chen et al., 2022; Panwar et al., 2022). These studies typically consider technology-related variables as inputs in DEA models and evaluate their effects on efficiency. For example, a study by Lee et al. (2022) examined the effect of Electronic Health Records (EHR) implementation on hospital efficiency. They found that EHR implementing hospitals outperformed non-EHR implementing hospitals in operational efficiency, profitability, and quality.

DEA has also been used to guide resource allocation and decision-making in hospitals (Peixoto et al., 2020). These studies typically employ DEA to evaluate the optimal allocation of resources like staff, beds, or budget to improve efficiency and performance (Alatawi et al., 2020; Kamel & Mousa, 2021; Ngobeni et al., 2020). For instance, a study by Ahmed et al. (2019) used the output-oriented DEA approach to estimate the technical efficiency of the health systems in Asian countries. The findings of the study demonstrate that about 91.3% of the studied Asian countries were inefficient with respect to using healthcare system resources, and most of the efficient countries belonged to the high-income group and only one country belonged to the lower middle-income group.

Similarly, analysis using DEA discovered that increasing the number of physician practices in the United States did not enhance their efficiency, and efficient practices appeared to handle each input efficiently (Shahhoseini et al., 2011). The DEA was used to calculate the overall spending of Kenya's state hospitals and health centers. DEA calculated the average TE in the Irish hospital sector and highlighted the diversity in TE values between institutions. Studies have also revealed a significant degree of purely technical and scale inefficiency in Namibian district hospitals (Shahhoseini et al., 2011). Similarly, another research that targeted a total of 66 observations from 2010 through 2015 looked at the technical effectiveness of 11 public hospitals in the West Bank of the Palestinian Territories. Input-oriented DEA models were employed to collect nationally representative data from the official yearly health reports and estimate efficiency ratings. They utilized Tobit regression to identify contextual variables whose influence on inefficient performance is statistically significant to elucidate performance further. Despite a 4% rise in efficiency mean scores between 2010 and 2015, the results indicate potential resource consumption savings of 14.5% without a decrease in the number of services offered (Sultan & Crispim, 2018).

Some studies have explored the impact of environmental and socioeconomic factors on hospital efficiency using DEA (Liu et al., 2022). A study by Liu et al. (2022) used panel data from 31 provinces and cities in China from 2008 to 2019 to estimate efficiency of pediatric health services and analyze the influential factors influencing the efficiency of pediatric services. The findings of this study indicate that there is a significant redundancy and disparity in the resources invested in pediatric services, and optimization of the economic, technological, and professional environment will continue to influence pediatric service efficiency.

Current Applications of DEA in Nursing

DEA's ability to handle multiple inputs and outputs simultaneously makes it a suitable tool for assessing the efficiency of nursing units or services (Ni Luasa et al., 2018). Nursing services are critical in healthcare and involve multiple inputs and outputs. The inputs could include the number of nursing staff, their qualifications, and working hours, while outputs can include patient outcomes, patient satisfaction, and care quality measures (Osman et al., 2011). DEA has been used to assess the efficiency of nursing units by comparing each unit's performance with an efficiency frontier formed from the most efficient units (Mark et al., 2009). DEA provides a method for benchmarking, by identifying the most efficient nursing units that serve as a reference point for less efficient units (Sherman & Zhu, 2006). The comparison allows the less efficient units to understand potential areas for improvement.

DEA can be used to make informed decisions about resource allocation in nursing (O'Donnell & Nguyen, 2011). For example, it can help managers understand whether certain resources are over- or under-utilized and guide resource redistribution to enhance efficiency. DEA was used in research to assess relative nursing care quality efficiency in U.S. nursing homes and to identify organizational elements that contribute to care quality efficiency across 50 states. Adequate nurse staffing has been identified as a critical component in enhancing nursing home care quality. The study showed that nursing care efficiency evaluation is critical to manage expenses and provide efficient quality nursing care to patients (Min et al., 2016). DEA can be used to compare the efficiency of nursing services across different healthcare facilities (Stefko et al., 2018). This can offer valuable insights for policymakers and administrators in identifying best practices and promoting system-wide improvements. By incorporating a temporal aspect into DEA models, researchers and managers can track the performance of nursing units over time. This allows for the evaluation of the effectiveness of various interventions and changes in practices.

Current Applications of DEA in Outpatient Services

DEA has been increasingly used in the context of outpatient services within healthcare management (Hofmarcher et al., 2002). Its ability to account for multiple inputs and outputs simultaneously makes it particularly well-suited for assessing the efficiency of outpatient departments or clinics. One of the key applications of DEA in outpatient services is to assess the relative efficiency of different outpatient departments or clinics (Mirmozaffari & Kamal, 2023). Input might include resources like the number of physicians, nurses, or other staff, as well as equipment and facility expenses. Outputs could encompass the number of patients served, patient satisfaction scores, quality of care measures, or health outcomes. By comparing each outpatient service's performance to an efficiency frontier established from the data, DEA generates an efficiency score that can be used to gauge relative performance. DEA allows for benchmarking by identifying the most efficient outpatient services that can serve as a reference or a "benchmark" for less efficient services (Marinho & Araújo, 2021). The inefficient outpatient services can then study these benchmarks to understand and emulate the practices that contribute to their high efficiency.

DEA can guide decisions about resource allocation in outpatient services (Yaya et al., 2020). For instance, it can help managers identify whether certain resources are over- or under-utilized, and accordingly adjust resource distribution to enhance efficiency. The primary cause for high wait times has been determined as insufficient employee availability, together with congestion and a changeable arrival pattern of walk-in patients in a study using the DEA model (Safdar et al., 2020). The DEA model presented the "required" number of people for various wait durations, demonstrating queue build-up. DEA has been used to evaluate the impacts of policy changes on the efficiency of outpatient services. For example, researchers have employed DEA to study the effects of health insurance reforms or new clinical guidelines on outpatient efficiency. DEA can be used to monitor the performance of outpatient services over time. By incorporating a temporal dimension into DEA models, it allows for the evaluation of the impacts of various interventions or changes in practices.

Challenges of Using DEA in Healthcare Management

DEA's results are heavily dependent on the selection of inputs and outputs (Gerami, 2019). If important inputs or outputs are omitted, the DEA model can yield misleading results. This issue is particularly challenging in healthcare, where it can be difficult to quantify all relevant aspects of care (Mohanta et al., 2023). DEA is sensitive to outliers in the data. A single outlier can significantly influence the efficiency frontier and thus the efficiency scores of all units (Yilmaz et al., 2022). DEA assumes that all deviations from the efficiency frontier are due to inefficiency, ignoring the possibility of statistical noise or random error (Liu et al., 2023). This could lead to an overestimation of inefficiency. Traditional DEA models do not provide measures of uncertainty or confidence intervals around efficiency scores. This could potentially lead to overconfidence in the results (Aparicio et al., 2021). DEA assumes homogeneity among decision-making units (Chen et al., 2022). This may not hold in the healthcare context where organizations can be vastly different in terms of size, specialization, patient demographics, etc. A potential drawback of DEA is the comparative evaluation of units with extremely wide size variances. This flaw has the potential to mislead the analysis's results. DEA analysis does not address quality data, and the input and output employed are simply quantitative in nature. Nonetheless, quality indicators have not been routinely employed to assess the efficiency of healthcare services (Zavras et al., 2002). The DEA method's lack of statistical features makes it unable to take measurement mistakes into account when estimating efficiency, which is one of its main shortcomings. Because the efficient units determine the efficient and thus the efficiency scores of those units under this frontier, DEA is highly susceptible to faulty data (Mitropoulos et al., 2015). Traditional DEA models are static and do not consider the temporal dimension. While there are extensions of DEA that can handle longitudinal data, they are more complex and less commonly used (Mulder & Hamaker, 2021). While DEA can identify less efficient units, it does not offer specific guidance on how to improve efficiency. Further analysis is usually required to understand the specific practices that lead to superior performance in the benchmark units.

METHODOLOGY

The purpose of this systematic literature exploration is to assess the existing body of work on DEA in healthcare management and provide insights into its trends, applications, and future directions. The search strategy for this study included a search for relevant articles using several electronic databases, including PubMed, Scopus, Web of Science, ScienceDirect, and Google Scholar. The search terms included various combinations of "data envelopment analysis", "DEA", "healthcare management", "efficiency measurement", "performance evaluation", and "healthcare systems". Several criteria were applied for the search, including only articles published in peer-reviewed journals or conference proceedings between 2015 and June 2023 written in English and focusing on the application of DEA in healthcare management. Articles that were excluded included reviews, editorials, or non-empirical works that were not related to healthcare management and did not apply DEA in their analysis. After conducting the initial search and eliminating duplicates, titles and abstracts were screened for relevance according to the inclusion and exclusion criteria. Full-text articles were then examined for eligibility following which data extraction was performed systematically using a predefined template. The information was extracted from each included study included the author(s) and year of publication, country of study, sample size and time of analysis, DEA model, as well as application area within healthcare management along with the key findings and conclusions. The extracted data were synthesized and analyzed using a thematic approach following which the themes were identified based on the recurring topics and trends found in the literature. Within each theme, the results and conclusions of the studies were synthesized and compared, considering the heterogeneity of the studies in terms of variables, DEA models, and application areas. To identify the research trends in the application of DEA in healthcare management, a bibliometric analysis was conducted. This involved analyzing the publication years, geographic distribution, application areas, and the impact of articles. Citation counts were then retrieved from Google Scholar to determine the most influential articles in the field. This systematic approach ensured comprehensive coverage of the literature on DEA in healthcare management and provided a foundation for understanding the current state of research, identifying gaps, and suggesting future research directions. In this exploratory review, a total of 623 articles were initially identified through the literature search. After the screening process and removing duplicates, 83 articles were deemed eligible for full-text review. Following the full-text review, 41 articles were finally included in the analysis, providing a comprehensive overview of the applications of machine learning in SMEs, as well as the associated challenges and opportunities.

SOLUTIONS AND RECOMMENDATIONS

The frequencies and percentages of the key trends identified in this study are presented in Table 1. Integrated approaches are one of the key trends identified as shown in Table 1. As healthcare management becomes increasingly complex, there is a trend of integrating DEA with other analytical tools or methodologies to address multifaceted issues. For instance, several studies combined DEA with machine learning or AI techniques refining efficiency evaluations and predicting future performance trends. Another trend identified from this study was the emergence of patient-centric models. With the increased emphasis on patient-centered care in the healthcare industry, there is a shift in DEA applications that prioritize patient outcomes, satisfaction, and quality of care, rather than just operational efficiency. Virtual and telehealth evaluations were also identified as a key trend in this study. Given the rapid rise of telehealth, especially post the COVID-19 pandemic, DEA is increasingly used to measure the efficiency and effectiveness of virtual healthcare services, comparing them with traditional in-person services. The fourth key trend identified in this study is sustainability and resource optimization as with the global emphasis on sustainability, DEA applications in healthcare are trending towards evaluating the efficient use of resources, waste management, and environmental impact, ensuring that healthcare institutions are sustainable in their operations. The last key trend identified in this study was the benchmarking and establishment of best practices, because as the healthcare institutions are more keenly focused on achieving best practices and setting industry standards, the use of DEA for benchmarking institutions against top performers and identifying best practices is a prevailing trend. This involves cross-country or regional comparisons to derive global best practices.

Table 1. Frequencies and percentages of key trends

Themes (Trends)	Frequency	Percentage
Integrated Approaches	15	36.58%
Integrated Approaches	11	26.82%
Virtual and Telehealth Evaluations	7	17.07%
Sustainability and Resource Optimization	5	12.19%
Benchmarking and Best Practices	3	7.31%

As shown in Table 2, efficiency measurement emerged as a key application of DEA in healthcare management accounting for 26.82% and is pivotal within the healthcare sector. DEA's non-parametric method becomes instrumental in gauging the efficiency of various decision-making units within healthcare settings, such as hospitals, clinics, and nursing units. The prominence of this theme accentuates DEA's vital role in optimizing healthcare delivery by scrutinizing and enhancing the utility of resources and processes.

The second key application of DEA in healthcare sector with 24.39% is benchmarking. This finding aligns with DEA's intrinsic capability to compare the performance and practices of healthcare units against industry benchmarks or peer entities. This application is paramount in identifying performance gaps, promoting best practices, and fostering continuous improvement in healthcare delivery. Resource

Table 2. Frequencies and percentages of key applications

Themes (Applications)	Frequency	Percentage
Efficiency Measurement	11	26.82%
Benchmarking	10	24.39%
Resource Allocation and Optimization	9	21.95%
Performance Evaluation for Healthcare Professionals	6	14.6%
Outpatient Service Evaluation	5	12.20%

allocation and optimization, representing 21.95% emerged as the third key application, underscoring the necessity for prudent management of resources within healthcare settings. DEA plays a crucial role in strategizing the distribution and utilization of available resources, thereby contributing to the enhancement of operational efficiency and the attainment of healthcare objectives. DEA's application in performance evaluation for healthcare professionals, accounting for 14.6% emerged as the fourth key application of DEA in healthcare. This finding indicates its significance in assessing and optimizing the contributions of healthcare staff. By evaluating the performance of healthcare professionals, DEA aids in ensuring adherence to quality standards, enhancing healthcare outcomes, and fostering professional development. Lastly, outpatient service evaluation, constituting 12.20%, signifies DEA's role in appraising the quality and efficacy of outpatient services. This application is integral for maintaining high standards of patient care, ensuring patient satisfaction, and refining service delivery in outpatient settings.

FUTURE RESEARCH DIRECTIONS

Given the inherent limitations of DEA, such as the sensitivity to outliers and the inability to handle statistical noise, further research is needed to develop and test methods to overcome these issues. For instance, hybrid models combining DEA with other approaches, like stochastic frontier analysis (SFA) or artificial neural networks (ANNs), may be explored. Traditional DEA models are static and do not consider the temporal dimension of data. Future research could explore the use of dynamic DEA models in healthcare management, which consider intertemporal relationships of inputs and outputs. A significant challenge in applying DEA to healthcare is the incorporation of quality measures. Future studies can focus on developing robust ways to integrate quality indicators in the DEA framework, thus providing a more holistic view of healthcare efficiency.

This review reveals that DEA has been applied in various countries. However, cross-country comparative studies are still scarce. Future research could use DEA to compare the efficiency of healthcare systems across different countries, which could provide valuable policy insights. DEA applications in specific healthcare settings, such as mental health services, elderly care, or palliative care, are underrepresented. Future research could delve deeper into these areas, providing more nuanced insights into efficiency and performance. While this review focused on academic literature, there is a need for research on the practical aspects of DEA implementation in healthcare management, including staff training and the integration of DEA results into decision-making processes. By addressing these areas, future research can continue to advance our understanding of the role and potential of DEA in healthcare management, ultimately contributing to the improvement of healthcare delivery and outcomes.

CONCLUSION

In conclusion, this systematic literature exploration reveals that DEA has been extensively employed in healthcare management, particularly in the assessment of efficiency, benchmarking, decision-making, and technology adoption. Studies have considered a diverse range of input and output variables, including hospital size, staff numbers, patient throughput, and patient satisfaction, offering nuanced insights into the complex relationships between resources and performance. A significant finding from our review is that hospital efficiency varies considerably across studies, indicating that there is no one-size-fits-all approach to enhancing efficiency in healthcare management. Various factors such as regional economic development, healthcare policies, and technology adoption have been identified as key determinants of efficiency. Additionally, the adoption of advanced technologies, particularly EHR systems, has been observed to have a positive impact on hospital efficiency. These findings underscore the need for hospitals to adopt a tailored approach to improving efficiency, considering their specific context and available resources.

Furthermore, this chapter highlights the importance of benchmarking and best practices in enhancing hospital performance. By identifying hospitals that outperform their peers, DEA can help identify potential best practices and areas for improvement. However, it is essential to note that DEA does not provide a comprehensive assessment of performance, as it only focuses on relative efficiency. Therefore, it should be used in conjunction with other performance metrics and tools. It is also evident from our review that optimal resource allocation plays a crucial role in enhancing hospital performance. DEA has been used to guide resource allocation decisions, considering factors like health expenditure and the number of healthcare workers. These studies suggest that allocating resources more efficiently can lead to improved life expectancy and quality of life.

Finally, this systematic literature exploration identifies several research gaps and directions for future studies. There is a need for more research on the impact of technology on hospital efficiency, as well as studies exploring the influence of environmental and socioeconomic factors. Additionally, future studies should consider employing other performance metrics and tools in conjunction with DEA to provide a more comprehensive assessment of performance in healthcare management. In summary, DEA has been a valuable tool for assessing efficiency and performance in healthcare management. This review provides a solid foundation for future research, offering insights into the factors that drive hospital efficiency and performance, as well as directions for improvement.

ACKNOWLEDGMENT

This research received no specific grant from any funding agency in the public, commercial, or not-for-profit sectors.

REFERENCES

Ahmed, S., Hasan, M. Z., MacLennan, M., Dorin, F., Ahmed, M. W., Hasan, M. M., Hasan, S. M., Islam, M. T., & Khan, J. A. (2019). Measuring the efficiency of health systems in Asia: A data envelopment analysis. *BMJ Open*, *9*(3), e022155. doi:10.1136/bmjopen-2018-022155 PMID:30918028

Alatawi, A. D., Niessen, L. W., & Khan, J. A. (2020). Efficiency evaluation of public hospitals in Saudi Arabia: An application of data envelopment analysis. *BMJ Open*, *10*(1), e031924. doi:10.1136/bmjopen-2019-031924 PMID:31932390

Aparicio, J., Cordero, J. M., & Ortiz, L. (2021). Efficiency analysis with educational data: How to deal with plausible values from international large-scale assessments. *Mathematics*, *9*(13), 1579. doi:10.3390/math9131579

Azadi, M., Moghaddas, Z., Farzipoor Saen, R., & Hussain, F. K. (2021). Financing manufacturers for investing in Industry 4.0 technologies: Internal financing vs. External financing. *International Journal of Production Research*, 1–17. doi:10.1080/00207543.2021.1912431

Caulfield, B., Bailey, D., & Mullarkey, S. (2013). Using data envelopment analysis as a public transport project appraisal tool. *Transport Policy*, *29*, 74–85. doi:10.1016/j.tranpol.2013.04.006

Charnes, A., Cooper, W. W., & Rhodes, E. (1978). A data envelopment analysis approach to evaluation of the program follow through experiment in US public school education. Management Sciences Research Group, Graduate School of Industrial….

Chen, K.-C., Lin, S.-Y., & Yu, M.-M. (2022). Exploring the efficiency of hospital and pharmacy utilizations in Taiwan: An application of dynamic network data envelopment analysis. *Socio-Economic Planning Sciences*, *84*, 101424. doi:10.1016/j.seps.2022.101424

Chitnis, A., & Mishra, D. K. (2019). Performance efficiency of Indian private hospitals using data envelopment analysis and super-efficiency DEA. *Journal of Health Management*, *21*(2), 279–293. doi:10.1177/0972063419835120

Cossani, G., Codoceo, L., Cáceres, H., & Tabilo, J. (2022). Technical efficiency in Chile's higher education system: A comparison of rankings and accreditation. *Evaluation and Program Planning*, *92*, 102058. doi:10.1016/j.evalprogplan.2022.102058 PMID:35525093

Ersoy, K., Kavuncubasi, S., Ozcan, Y. A., & Harris, J. M. II. (1997). Technical efficiencies of Turkish hospitals: DEA approach. *Journal of Medical Systems*, *21*(2), 67–74. doi:10.1023/A:1022801222540 PMID:9297615

Fu, H.-P., Chu, K.-K., Chao, P., Lee, H.-H., & Liao, Y.-C. (2011). Using fuzzy AHP and VIKOR for benchmarking analysis in the hotel industry. *Service Industries Journal*, *31*(14), 2373–2389. doi:10.1080/02642069.2010.503874

Gerami, J. (2019). An interactive procedure to improve estimate of value efficiency in DEA. *Expert Systems with Applications*, *137*, 29–45. doi:10.1016/j.eswa.2019.06.061

Gharizadeh Beiragh, R., Alizadeh, R., Shafiei Kaleibari, S., Cavallaro, F., Zolfani, S. H., Bausys, R., & Mardani, A. (2020). An integrated multi-criteria decision making model for sustainability performance assessment for insurance companies. *Sustainability (Basel)*, *12*(3), 789. doi:10.3390u12030789

Ghasemi, S., Aghsami, A., & Rabbani, M. (2021). Data envelopment analysis for estimate efficiency and ranking operating rooms: a case study. *International Journal of Research in Industrial Engineering*, *10*(1), 67-86.

Ghaziyani, K., Ejlaly, B., & Bagheri, S. (2019). Evaluation of the efficiency by DEA a case study of hospital. *International Journal of Research in Industrial Engineering, 8*(3), 283-293.

Habib, A. M., & Shahwan, T. M. (2020). Measuring the operational and financial efficiency using a Malmquist data envelopment analysis: A case of Egyptian hospitals. *Benchmarking, 27*(9), 2521–2536. doi:10.1108/BIJ-01-2020-0041

Hofmarcher, M. M., Paterson, I., & Riedel, M. (2002). Measuring hospital efficiency in Austria–a DEA approach. *Health Care Management Science, 5*(1), 7–14. doi:10.1023/A:1013292801100 PMID:11860081

Horta, I., Camanho, A., Johnes, J., & Johnes, G. (2013). Performance trends in the construction industry worldwide: An overview of the turn of the century. *Journal of Productivity Analysis, 39*(1), 89–99. doi:10.100711123-012-0276-0

Jahed, R., Amirteimoori, A., & Azizi, H. (2015). Performance measurement of decision-making units under uncertainty conditions: An approach based on double frontier analysis. *Measurement, 69*, 264–279. doi:10.1016/j.measurement.2015.03.014

Jain, R. K., & Natarajan, R. (2015). A DEA study of airlines in India. *Asia Pacific Management Review, 20*(4), 285–292. doi:10.1016/j.apmrv.2015.03.004

Jiang, H., Hua, M., Zhang, J., Cheng, P., Ye, Z., Huang, M., & Jin, Q. (2020). Sustainability efficiency assessment of wastewater treatment plants in China: A data envelopment analysis based on cluster benchmarking. *Journal of Cleaner Production, 244*, 118729. doi:10.1016/j.jclepro.2019.118729

Kamel, M. A., & Mousa, M. E.-S. (2021). Measuring operational efficiency of isolation hospitals during COVID-19 pandemic using data envelopment analysis: A case of Egypt. *Benchmarking, 28*(7), 2178–2201. doi:10.1108/BIJ-09-2020-0481

Kocisova, K., Hass-Symotiuk, M., & Kludacz-Alessandri, M. (2018). *Use of the DEA method to verify the performance model for hospitals.* Academic Press.

Koengkan, M., Fuinhas, J. A., Kazemzadeh, E., Osmani, F., Alavijeh, N. K., Auza, A., & Teixeira, M. (2022). Measuring the economic efficiency performance in Latin American and Caribbean countries: An empirical evidence from stochastic production frontier and data envelopment analysis. *International Economics, 169*, 43-54. https://doi.org/https://doi.org/10.1016/j.inteco.2021.11.004

Kohl, S., Schoenfelder, J., Fügener, A., & Brunner, J. O. (2019). The use of Data Envelopment Analysis (DEA) in healthcare with a focus on hospitals. *Health Care Management Science, 22*(2), 245–286. doi:10.100710729-018-9436-8 PMID:29478088

Kooreman, P. (1994). Nursing home care in The Netherlands: A nonparametric efficiency analysis. *Journal of Health Economics, 13*(3), 301–316. doi:10.1016/0167-6296(94)90029-9 PMID:10138856

Kumar, S., & Gulati, R. (2009). Measuring efficiency, effectiveness and performance of Indian public sector banks. *International Journal of Productivity and Performance Management, 59*(1), 51–74. doi:10.1108/17410401011006112

Lee, C. C., Kim, Y., Choi, J. H., & Porter, E. (2022). Does Electronic Health Record Systems Implementation Impact Hospital Efficiency, Profitability, and Quality? *Journal of Applied Business & Economics, 24*(2).

Li, H., & Dong, S. (2015). Measuring and benchmarking technical efficiency of public hospitals in Tianjin, China: A bootstrap–data envelopment analysis approach. *INQUIRY: The Journal of Health Care Organization, Provision, and Financing, 52*, 0046958015605487. PMID:26396090

Liu, F., Li, L., Ye, B., & Qin, Q. (2023). A novel stochastic semi-parametric frontier-based three-stage DEA window model to evaluate China's industrial green economic efficiency. *Energy Economics, 119*, 106566. doi:10.1016/j.eneco.2023.106566

Liu, H., Wu, W., & Yao, P. (2022). A study on the efficiency of pediatric healthcare services and its influencing factors in China——estimation of a three-stage DEA model based on provincial-level data. *Socio-Economic Planning Sciences, 84*, 101315. doi:10.1016/j.seps.2022.101315

Mahmoudabadi, M. Z., & Emrouznejad, A. (2019). Comprehensive performance evaluation of banking branches: A three-stage slacks-based measure (SBM) data envelopment analysis. *International Review of Economics & Finance, 64*, 359–376. doi:10.1016/j.iref.2019.08.001

Marinho, A., & Araújo, C. A. S. (2021). Using data envelopment analysis and the bootstrap method to evaluate organ transplantation efficiency in Brazil. *Health Care Management Science, 24*(3), 569–581. doi:10.100710729-021-09552-6 PMID:33730290

Mark, B. A., Jones, C. B., Lindley, L., & Ozcan, Y. A. (2009). An examination of technical efficiency, quality, and patient safety in acute care nursing units. *Policy, Politics & Nursing Practice, 10*(3), 180–186. doi:10.1177/1527154409346322 PMID:20008398

Medarević, A., & Vuković, D. (2021). Efficiency and productivity of public hospitals in Serbia using DEA-malmquist model and tobit regression model, 2015–2019. *International Journal of Environmental Research and Public Health, 18*(23), 12475. doi:10.3390/ijerph182312475 PMID:34886202

Min, A., Park, C. G., & Scott, L. D. (2016). An examination of nursing care quality efficiency in US nursing homes: Using data envelopment analysis. *Western Journal of Nursing Research, 38*(10), 1387–1388. doi:10.1177/0193945916658196 PMID:27655090

Mirmozaffari, M., & Kamal, N. (2023). The Application of Data Envelopment Analysis to Emergency Departments and Management of Emergency Conditions: A Narrative Review. *Healthcare*.

Mohanta, K. K., Sharanappa, D. S., & Aggarwal, A. (2023). A novel modified Khatter's approach for solving Neutrosophic Data Envelopment Analysis. *Croatian Operational Research Review, 14*(1), 15–28. doi:10.17535/crorr.2023.0002

Mulder, J. D., & Hamaker, E. L. (2021). Three extensions of the random intercept cross-lagged panel model. *Structural Equation Modeling, 28*(4), 638–648. doi:10.1080/10705511.2020.1784738

Nepomuceno, T. C. C., Costa, A. P. C. S., & Daraio, C. (2023). Theoretical and Empirical Advances in the Assessment of Productive Efficiency since the introduction of DEA: A Bibliometric Analysis. *International Journal of Operational Research, 46*(4), 505–549. doi:10.1504/IJOR.2023.129960

Ngobeni, V., Breitenbach, M. C., & Aye, G. C. (2020). Technical efficiency of provincial public healthcare in South Africa. *Cost Effectiveness and Resource Allocation*, *18*(1), 1–19. doi:10.118612962-020-0199-y PMID:32002018

Ni Luasa, S., Dineen, D., & Zieba, M. (2018). Technical and scale efficiency in public and private Irish nursing homes–a bootstrap DEA approach. *Health Care Management Science*, *21*(3), 326–347. doi:10.100710729-016-9389-8 PMID:27787751

O'Donnell, C., & Nguyen, K. (2011). *Review of efficiency measurement methodologies to inform hospital resource allocation decisions in NSW: a rapid review*. Sax Institute.

Obadić, A., & Aristovnik, A. (2011). Relative efficiency of higher education in Croatia and Slovenia: An international comparison. *Amfiteatru Economic Journal*, *13*(30), 362–376.

Omrani, H., Emrouznejad, A., Shamsi, M., & Fahimi, P. (2022). Evaluation of insurance companies considering uncertainty: A multi-objective network data envelopment analysis model with negative data and undesirable outputs. *Socio-Economic Planning Sciences*, *82*, 101306. doi:10.1016/j.seps.2022.101306

Osman, I. H., Berbary, L. N., Sidani, Y., Al-Ayoubi, B., & Emrouznejad, A. (2011). Data envelopment analysis model for the appraisal and relative performance evaluation of nurses at an intensive care unit. *Journal of Medical Systems*, *35*(5), 1039–1062. doi:10.100710916-010-9570-4 PMID:20734223

Pang, C., & Gai, Y. (2022). Research on efficiency in financing of small and medium companies based on DEA method. *Discrete Dynamics in Nature and Society*, *2022*, 2022. doi:10.1155/2022/4914151

Panwar, A., Olfati, M., Pant, M., & Snasel, V. (2022). A review on the 40 years of existence of data envelopment analysis models: Historic development and current trends. *Archives of Computational Methods in Engineering*, *29*(7), 5397–5426. doi:10.100711831-022-09770-3 PMID:35702633

Peixoto, M. G. M., Musetti, M. A., & de Mendonça, M. C. A. (2020). Performance management in hospital organizations from the perspective of Principal Component Analysis and Data Envelopment Analysis: The case of Federal University Hospitals in Brazil. *Computers & Industrial Engineering*, *150*, 106873. doi:10.1016/j.cie.2020.106873

Safdar, K. A., Emrouznejad, A., & Dey, P. K. (2020). An optimized queue management system to improve patient flow in the absence of appointment system. *International Journal of Health Care Quality Assurance*, *33*(7/8), 477–494. doi:10.1108/IJHCQA-03-2020-0052 PMID:33179461

Seol, H., Lee, H., Kim, S., & Park, Y. (2008). The impact of information technology on organizational efficiency in public services: A DEA-based DT approach. *The Journal of the Operational Research Society*, *59*(2), 231–238. doi:10.1057/palgrave.jors.2602453

Shahhoseini, R., Tofighi, S., Jaafaripooyan, E., & Safiaryan, R. (2011). Efficiency measurement in developing countries: Application of data envelopment analysis for Iranian hospitals. *Health Services Management Research*, *24*(2), 75–80. doi:10.1258/hsmr.2010.010017 PMID:21471577

Sherman, H. D., & Zhu, J. (2006). Benchmarking with quality-adjusted DEA (Q-DEA) to seek lower-cost high-quality service: Evidence from a US bank application. *Annals of Operations Research*, *145*(1), 301–319. doi:10.100710479-006-0037-4

Stefko, R., Gavurova, B., & Kocisova, K. (2018). Healthcare efficiency assessment using DEA analysis in the Slovak Republic. *Health Economics Review*, *8*(1), 1–12. doi:10.118613561-018-0191-9 PMID:29523981

Sultan, W. I., & Crispim, J. (2018). Measuring the efficiency of Palestinian public hospitals during 2010–2015: An application of a two-stage DEA method. *BMC Health Services Research*, *18*(1), 1–17. doi:10.118612913-018-3228-1 PMID:29843732

Tompkins, D. A., Hobelmann, J. G., & Compton, P. (2017). Providing chronic pain management in the "Fifth Vital Sign" Era: Historical and treatment perspectives on a modern-day medical dilemma. *Drug and Alcohol Dependence*, *173*, S11–S21. doi:10.1016/j.drugalcdep.2016.12.002 PMID:28363315

Vitezic, N., Segota, A., & Setnikar Cankar, S. (2016). Measuring the efficiency of public health services by DEA. *Int'l Pub. Admin. Rev.*, *14*, 27.

Yaya, S., Xi, C., Xiaoyang, Z., & Meixia, Z. (2020). Evaluating the efficiency of China's healthcare service: A weighted DEA-game theory in a competitive environment. *Journal of Cleaner Production*, *270*, 122431. doi:10.1016/j.jclepro.2020.122431

Yilmaz, M. K., Kusakci, A. O., Aksoy, M., & Hacioglu, U. (2022). The evaluation of operational efficiencies of Turkish airports: An integrated spherical fuzzy AHP/DEA approach. *Applied Soft Computing*, *119*, 108620. doi:10.1016/j.asoc.2022.108620

Yu, H., Zhang, Y., Zhang, A., Wang, K., & Cui, Q. (2019). A comparative study of airline efficiency in China and India: A dynamic network DEA approach. *Research in Transportation Economics*, *76*, 100746. doi:10.1016/j.retrec.2019.100746

Zarrin, M., Schoenfelder, J., & Brunner, J. O. (2022). Homogeneity and best practice analyses in hospital performance management: An analytical framework. *Health Care Management Science*, *25*(3), 406–425. doi:10.100710729-022-09590-8 PMID:35192085

Zavras, A. I., Tsakos, G., Economou, C., & Kyriopoulos, J. (2002). Using DEA to evaluate efficiency and formulate policy within a Greek national primary health care network. *Journal of Medical Systems*, *26*(4), 285–292. doi:10.1023/A:1015860318972 PMID:12118812

ADDITIONAL READING

Čiković, F., Katerina, I. M., & Lozić, J. (2022). Application of data envelopment analysis (DEA) in the selection of sustainable suppliers: A review and bibliometric analysis. *Sustainability (Basel)*, *14*(11), 6672. doi:10.3390u14116672

Kohl, S., Schoenfelder, J., Fügener, A., & Brunner, J. O. (2019). The use of Data Envelopment Analysis (DEA) in healthcare with a focus on hospitals. *Health Care Management Science*, *22*(2), 245–286. doi:10.100710729-018-9436-8 PMID:29478088

Narayanan, E., Ismail, W. R., & Mustafa, Z. (2022). A data-envelopment analysis-based systematic review of the literature on innovation performance. *Heliyon*, *8*(12), e11925. doi:10.1016/j.heliyon.2022.e11925 PMID:36506397

Panwar, A., Olfati, M., Pant, M., & Snasel, V. (2022). A review on the 40 years of existence of data envelopment analysis models: Historic development and current trends. *Archives of Computational Methods in Engineering*, *29*(7), 5397–5426. doi:10.100711831-022-09770-3 PMID:35702633

Zhang, R., Wei, Q., Li, A., & Chen, S. (2022). A new intermediate network data envelopment analysis model for evaluating China's sustainability. *Journal of Cleaner Production*, *356*, 131845. doi:10.1016/j.jclepro.2022.131845

KEY TERMS AND DEFINITIONS

Benchmarking: The process of comparing one's performance metrics with those of similar organizations to identify best practices and areas for improvement.

Data Envelopment Analysis (DEA): A non-parametric method used to assess the relative efficiency of decision-making units (DMUs), such as hospitals or healthcare systems, by comparing the ratio of inputs to outputs.

Efficiency: The ability to achieve desired outcomes with the least amount of resources. In the context of healthcare, it refers to the ability of a hospital or healthcare system to deliver high-quality care with optimal resource utilization.

Electronic Health Records (EHR): Digital versions of patients' medical histories, including information such as diagnoses, treatment plans, and medications. The adoption of EHR systems can impact hospital efficiency and patient care.

Input-Oriented DEA Model: A DEA model that seeks to minimize inputs while maintaining a given level of outputs. This approach is used when the focus is on reducing resource usage.

Output-Oriented DEA Model: A DEA model that seeks to maximize outputs while keeping inputs constant. This approach is used when the goal is to increase service levels or performance.

Performance Metrics: Quantitative measures used to assess the performance of organizations, such as hospitals or healthcare systems. Common performance metrics in healthcare include patient satisfaction, treatment outcomes, and resource utilization.

Resource Allocation: The process of distributing resources, such as staff, budget, or equipment, among various units or departments within an organization. Effective resource allocation is crucial for optimizing efficiency and performance in healthcare management.

Systematic Literature Exploration: A comprehensive and structured approach to reviewing and synthesizing the existing body of literature on a specific topic. It involves identifying, selecting, and analyzing relevant studies to draw conclusions and identify research gaps.

Variables: In the context of DEA, variables refer to the inputs and outputs used in the analysis. Inputs represent the resources used by a hospital or healthcare system, while outputs represent the outcomes or services provided.

Chapter 12
Exploring Productivity by Evaluating ISP Efficiency in Nigeria's Telecommunications Sector

Adeyemi Abel Ajibesin
https://orcid.org/0000-0001-6518-0231
American University of Nigeria, Nigeria

Yakub Akinmoyede
American University of Nigeria, Nigeria

Senthil Kumar Thangavel
https://orcid.org/0000-0001-8160-7223
Amrita School of Computing, Amrita Vishwa Vidyapeetham, India

Ridwan Salahudeen
https://orcid.org/0009-0000-1097-0906
Caritas Institute of Higher Education, Hong Kong

ABSTRACT

The digital divide in Africa, particularly Nigeria, has raised concerns about the efficiency of internet service providers (ISPs) in providing quality services to their subscribers. This research focuses on evaluating the efficiencies of the major ISPs in Nigeria, including MTN, Glo, Airtel, and 9mobile, using data envelopment analysis (DEA). The study examines vital efficiency metrics such as internet speed, cost of data, years of existence, and subscriber base over five years from 2015 to 2019. The results reveal varying levels of efficiency among ISPs, with MTN consistently ranking as the most efficient. These findings have implications for improving the quality of internet services and promoting healthy competition within the Nigerian telecommunications industry. The study also highlights the importance of considering multiple parameters in assessing ISP efficiency, shedding light on areas for future research and regulatory interventions by the Nigeria Communications Commission.

DOI: 10.4018/979-8-3693-0255-2.ch012

INTRODUCTION

The use of the internet to gain competitive advantage has become a key infrastructure issue amongst organizations in the fast-globalizing environment. However, a good and secure network is the essential component on which any organization is relied as there would possibly be an attack that can be seen in most of the communications. Bharadwaj et.al (2021) stated that detection of these attacks like Denial of Service (DoS) is prominent in the field of communication. Authentication of the right user is another prominent aspect in the field of communication. In recent times, cloud-based technologies also have gained popularity in the process of authentication. To prevent intruders, an additional layer of security is transformed by the model that is developed by Senthil Kumar Thangavel et.al (2014) for user authentication. The overarching means of business transactions now depend largely on connectivity, knowledge, and information (Pavic, Koh, Simpson, & Padmore, 2007). It is noted by Pradhan, Arvin, and Norman (2015) that technological infrastructures such as the internet, mobile phones, broadband, and telephone networks have made it possible for individuals, groups, businesses, and government to share information that beats the initial limitation of speed, scale, and scope of exchange. Transactions over the internet have helped in exposing individuals and organizations to communicate faster and meet up with global competitiveness. Internet services utilization and commercialization has become more widespread throughout the world, the use and adoption of novel internet-enabled services can generate new business opportunities and various benefits. More so, there is an increasing consciousness of the necessity to take in profit through investment in information technological tools.

Currently, the internet revolutions have swept across many organizations around the globe, particularly, Nigeria has an internet penetration of about 113.3 billion subscribers in 2019 and projected to reach 187.8 by 2023 (Statista, 2019). To this end, it is germane to posit that the availability of functional and efficient internet service is a sine-qua-non for any country that wishes to compete in today's global economy. Umezuruike, Oludele, Kuyoro, and Izang (2015) revealed that the International Telecommunication Union (ITU) predicted that in 2014, there will be almost 3 billion Internet users, two-thirds of these subscribers would come from the developing world, and the number of mobile-broadband subscriptions will reach 2.3 billion globally by end of 2014. Fifty-five percent of these subscriptions are expected to be in the developing world, this confirms that internet technologies would continue to be the key drivers of the information society. The liberalization of the Telecommunication industry by the Nigerian Government in 2001 has led to an exponential growth in the number of subscribers to mobile phone services and data services provided by internet service providers (Ononiwu, Akinwole, Agubor, & Onojo, 2016). This liberalization brought several operators into the industry thus leading to fierce competition and thus giving the users group the prerogative of making choices as to internet service providers to patronize. Therefore, the quality of service and efficiency of these service providers become important to both the regulatory body and the public.

The surge in both calls and data services in Nigeria have challenged Telecommunication operators to improve their services in the last decade, progressing from analog to digital system that can handle the growing needs in a cost-efficient, effective, fast, and reliable manner. This progress was driven by high demand for good quality service, high spectral efficiency, standardization, and new services from both customers and regulatory bodies (Ozovehe & Usman, 2015). While celebrating the increasing proliferation of information communication technology across Africa and the quantum of contexts in which information technology solutions have been applied, the question that stakeholders, researchers, and policymakers need to ask is, how efficient are the internet service providers because they determine the gains that can be derived from a given information technology solution. This thought brings about the need to assess the activities of internet service providers who are the point of connection between the end-users and the internet. Critical to achieving efficiency is the need for the internet services provider to be able to exchange traffic and cooperate towards ensuring sustained connectivity on internet networks. In all, Quality of Service (QoS) must not be compromised so that the quality of voice, video, and packet transfers within the internet is beneficial to the end-users.

There are efficiency parameters that matter to users and regulators, these variables include cost-efficiency, effectiveness, speed, reliability, quality service, high spectral efficiency, standardization are otherwise referred to as the metrics that customers generally seek for adopting a particular service provider. Zhu (2014) stressed that data envelopment analysis uses Mathematical programming techniques and models to evaluate performance. It helps in estimating the efficiencies of different operators under the context of multiple performance metrics. To this end, this study intends to evaluate the efficiency of internet service providers in Nigeria using Data Envelopment Analysis to meet the internet needs of individuals, corporate organizations and government establishment, and other critical stakeholders in Nigeria. This chapter is structured into six sections. The introduction has been presented in section one; Section two provides the background of the study. Section three discusses the research methodology and approach adopted in carrying out the research. Section four analyses and discusses the results. Section five and six provide recommendations and conclusion respectively.

BACKGROUND

This section presents the study background and reviews some conceptual and theoretical dimensions that bolster the understanding of internet service provider efficiencies in Nigeria. Some of the concepts reviewed are the conceptual clarification of internet and internet service providers, the related study conducted on internet service efficiencies, the performance of Mobile internet service performance, the concept of organizational efficiencies and DEA roles, ISP functions and liabilities within Nigeria and subscribers' preferences concerning internet services as well as data envelopment analysis.

Conceptual Clarifications of Internet and Internet Service Providers

The internet has become a buzzword because it is a common terminology that is recognized in every facet of human endeavor, its emergence has had a transformative effect on the way things are done today. Selby and Bawa (2018) stressed that the internet refers to a global network of computers which combines several of the smaller network thereby facilitating the sharing of information and enhancing communication among people, entity, and organization around the world. As a credible platform that integrates other platforms, the internet connects thousands of computers using a protocol suite called Transmission Control Protocol/Internet Protocol (TCP/IP) that is connected to millions of devices. Today, the internet has expanded to the point where users can access countless services on the internet platform.

As the world continues to experience the visible impact of the internet, the internet infrastructure and intermediaries have also continued to expand, and such expansion facilitates the increasing impact of the internet on every aspect of human endeavors. The expansion cuts across scaling of internet services and improving the scope of services which contributes to integrating many users and enhancing the speed of access. This expansion is however not without challenges; organizations experience dynamic changes because some organizations continue to expand their infrastructure to continue providing the same services while others develop complex infrastructure to provide diverse services. These intermediaries that serve as the link between users and the World Wide Web are addressed as internet service providers (ISPs), a universal terminology that refers to the providers of internet services in a different geographical context. Notwithstanding, the terminology of internet service providers is confusing because it does not demarcate between host providers, access providers, and other platforms.

The conceptualization of internet service providers following the framework of Saadat and Soltanifar (2014) describes organizations that provide internet access services; they allow subscribers to access the internet through an active data connection that operates based on physical transport infrastructure. Through this access, Internet users can access content and a broad range of information services on the Internet. This also includes the capacity to publish and distribute electronic materials on the digital platform. In this regard, Internet service providers operate on a local, national, or regional scale, depending on the available infrastructure and backbone support of the organization.

Historically, it was known that the first semblance of ISPs was introduced in the United States of America, these ISPs are America Online (AOL) and CompuServe (Usman, 2018). These earlier known ISPs were not full in terms of functionality, but content providers who offer narrow Internet access. Organization for Economic Co-operation and Development (OECD) classification has added to the list of ISPs who have a wide range of operations across different geographical areas to include: Yahoo, Google, Free Fr, Verizon, Internet Initiative Japan, Comcast, NTT, BT, Vodafone, Orange, T-Mobile, and MTN. OECD further classified ISP as an entity that offers services such as; Web portal services, and a Proxy server (Farano, 2012). From the above, ISPs by an instance of serving as intermediaries between the web and the users provide huge functions, therefore they are also saddled with some liabilities in terms of efficiency of services as well as verifiable online content.

Functions of Internet Service Providers

Internet Service Providers are rapidly evolving in scale, nature, and scope and are poised to provide an increasing number of services to users. The function expected of the Internet user community is dynamic and is increasing in scope. Saadat and Soltanifar (2014) posited that ISPs provide local, regional coverage for clients, and may also provide backbone services for other Internet service providers. Internet service providers have telecommunication equipment and network access required for internet connection. They sometimes provide other services beyond Internet access, such as web design, hosting, and consulting services to networking software and hardware companies. Usman (2018) deduced that since ISPs is the conduit between users and the World Wide Web and coordinates command and request between users of the Internet, the following ISP's functions have been outlined from the technical point of view. These are the provision of access to the Internet for users, hosting, and processing of data services for content providers, caching services, provision of searching services, the maintenance of web portals, and peering services.

ISP Regulations in Nigeria

The regulation of the internet comes under the concept of internet governance. Governance of the Internet is a complex activity around the world and no one entity regulates the internet activities. The World Summit on Information Society (WSIS) in 2006, defined Internet governance as activities undertaken by the governments, the private sector and general society in the combined roles of formulating principles, norms, rules, and decision-making procedures in the development, application, and use of the Internet. Usman (2018) the regulations of the Internet and the Internet providers in Nigeria are collaboratively undertaken by various departments of the Government, these varied department efforts are coordinated by the Nigeria Communication Commission (NCC). Some important objective of the Commission is to ensure the provision of modern, reliable, efficient, affordable, and easily accessible communications services to the widest range of people throughout Nigeria. Their functions also include the formulation of Internet policies and industry codes developed to address issues peculiar to Nigeria and International best practices that conflict with existing national laws. The Commission is also bolstered by the cybercrime act under section 40 of the Nigerian constitution. The Cybercrime Act imposes a legal duty on ISP to collaborate with security agencies in cases of violation of internet use and perpetuation of illegality on the internet. The NCC was formally constituted in the year 2003 as an independent Regulatory Authority for the Telecommunications industry in Nigeria. The Commission has many oversight functions among which is licensing and regulations, technology regulations, creating an enabling environment for competition among operators as well as ensuring the provision of qualitative and efficient telecommunications services throughout the country (Nigerian Communications Commission, 2020).

Related Study on Internet Service Providers Efficiencies

Internet technology is in continuous transition in terms of evolving sophistication of the technology in use. In the beginning when communication over the Internet became a possibility people were awestruck about the technology. Nowadays, efficiency matters because of the realization of the immense utility woven into technology. Consequently, studies that unravel the current efficiencies with a view of making an inroad to more of the potential are being conducted. Kuboye, Alese, and Imasuen (2012) revealed that the reason for efficiency measurement is that the world is fast becoming a global village, and the necessary technology that incubates this revolution is access to the Internet technology and other competitive information technologies that would allow easy hook-up with customers. Towards this end, the Internet has become a key driver for businesses to achieve business advantage and hence the reason for the various spotlight on its efficiencies. Furthermore, Nigam, Thakur, Sethi, and Singh (2012) studied on how to benchmark the Indian Telecommunication and Internet Service Providers for relative efficiencies using data envelopment analysis. The DEA was used to perform comparative efficiencies of mobile telecommunication firms. Similarly, Galadanci and Abdullahi (2018) conducted a study to assess the performance analysis of the G.S.M network within Kano metropolis. Key Performance Indicators set by NCC were used to evaluate the performance of GSM networks. The result of the study revealed that four carriers could not meet the minimum threshold set by NCC for Call Setup Success Rate (CSSR), Handover Success Rate (HOSR) and call blocking.

Papadimitriou and Prachalias (2009) conducted a study on the use of data envelopment analysis to evaluate the marketing cost of global Telecommunication Operators to uncover their productive factors. Sample of about eighteen companies was used along with their revenues as the outputs. The inputs considered were marketing expenses, traffic of mobile telephony, number of staff, investments, and traffic of fixed telephony. The study revealed and recommended that there should be a reduction in expenses for efficiency to be achieved. Ononiwu et al. (2016) evaluated the effectiveness of mobile network operators in Nigeria using key performance indicators in Owerri Township. The four major mobile network operators such as Airtel, Glo, MTN, and Etisalat are used as a case study. The result of the research showed that mobile network operators in Nigeria are yet to meet the requirements specifications in terms of efficiency set by Nigeria communication commission considering the variables observed. However, Etisalat is said to have a better performance compared to other mobile operators. Moreover, their study recommended using multiple parameters to establish a valid efficiency or inefficiency measurement among Mobile Network Operators (MNOs).

Research Gap

From the analysis of the relevant and recent literature on the nature of Internet service efficiency in Nigeria using data envelopment analysis, the following gaps were identified, and this formed the basis for this study:

a)   There are noticeable dominant researches conducted on Internet service providers (Galadanci and Abdullahi, 2018; Iosifidis et al., 2017; Mugo, 2013; Selby and Bawa, 2018). Few of these studies concentrated on efficiency evaluation of different ISP. Studies such as (Iosifidis et al., 2017; Selby and Bawa, 2018) discussed efficiency, but Iosifidis (2017) concentrated on resources sharing in Hong Kong, and Selby and Bawa (2018) were centered on higher education in Ghana. Therefore, the efficiency of ISP in Nigeria was noted as a gap to be covered.

b)   Existing research has also failed to address the efficiency issues of the operations of Internet service providers. In the research of George, Lin, Jianwei, and Leandros (2016) for instance, the focus of the study was limited to the nature of access to the internet over the mobile network architecture, but nothing was said with specific reference to internet service provider efficiency in delivering required service over the mobile network window. Other research especially that of Farnaz and Mohammad (2014) looked at the role of Internet service providers in providing Internet services to customers, but the research failed to explore the efficiency of the ISP in the context of providing such services. Even Shaibu (2013) explored similar research on the responsibilities of ISP towards security but this as like others did not address the gap of efficiency.

Several models were used in previous research, the Network Simulation Model (Lewis and Anthony, 2018), the Systems Model (George et al, 2016), Stackelberg Game Model (Ramy and Richard, 2015), the Falger Theory (Farnaz and Mohammad, 2014), Stahl-Rubein model (Paul, Bridger and Padmanabhan, 2011) and the Quality-of-Service Model (Guan, 2000). Implicitly, only a few research especially that of Meher, Bulbul, and Khaled (2013) were based on the SERVQUAL Model which is quite effective and globally recognized in the discourse on the efficiency of internet services. While the SERVQUAL model would help in the consideration of service quality, DEA is considered in this work to better analyze the quantitative data for technical efficiency.

RESEARCH METHODOLOGY AND APPROACH

This section discusses a procedure for carrying out the research. The procedures discussed include the research design, method of data collection, the efficiency metrics used, the DEA tools, and the analysis of the data using the DEA model.

Research Design and DEA Flowchart

This study considered a non-Parametric method that relies on a linear programming technique for efficiency evaluation of ISP performance. This technique evaluates the efficiency of ISPs by comparing the input and output resources. DEA has been applied in numerous studies since its inception. It has been used to test the technical efficiency in the education sector, manufacturing, banking, economics, and telecommunications (Aldamak & Zolfaghari, 2016).

Figure 1 is the schematic process flow of data envelopment analysis that is depicted to reflect the efficiency measurement of ISPs. The first stage is to design ISP efficiency problems based on DEA efficiency notions and then categorize each variable into DMU. In this study, four variables with three inputs and one output were evaluated. The identified data for the ISPs, which is their DMUs, is supplied to the DEA solver, and then the metrics and model parameters, including the assumptions, are configured. Each DMU's technical efficiency (TE) score is evaluated by the solver. For classifications, the DMU values are compared to the absolute value 1. DMUs equal to one are considered efficient, whereas those fewer than one is considered inefficient.

Figure 1. DEA methodology for ISP's efficiency

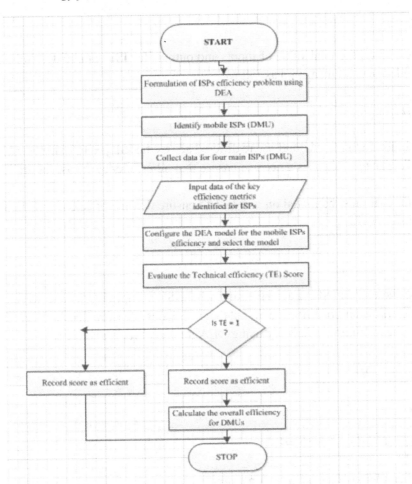

Model Selection

Efficiency benchmarking employs different models that are based on linear programming techniques. Among them, the DEA model is one of the most effective and commonly used (Ajibesin, Ventura, Chan & Murgu, 2014). There are two popular models in DEA simulation; these are CCR and BCC models. This study focuses on CCR model that exhibits constant returns to scale (CRS), In the case of CRS, it is assumed that an increase in the number of inputs consumed would lead to a proportional increase in the number of outputs produced. Under CRS, the sum of the output bundles of the entities called decision-making units (DMUs) is producible from the sum of the corresponding input bundles simulated in the model. Going by this adopted DEA model, there is a need to determine the relative efficiency of k number of ISPS using DEA model. The DEA model derivations is shown below:

Assuming each ISP j produces m different types of outputs, using n different types of inputs. Let X_j be an (n x 1) vector consisting of inputs of ISP_j. Similarly, let Y_j be an m x1 vector of ISP_j's output factors. Each input and output can be assigned. Let U_j denote an n x 1 vector of different resources of ISP_j and V_j be an m x 1 vector of implicit cost for outputs. From an economic perspective, these resources should be positive.

Therefore,

$$Uj, Vj > 0 \tag{1}$$

With these resources, the total value of inputs and outputs for ISP_j can be determined. Then the efficiency K of the ISP_j can be measured as follows

$$\eta = (VjYj)/(UjXj) \tag{2}$$

It, therefore, holds that vector U_j and V_j are differed across the ISP j = 1, k, due to varied opportunity cost for each ISP. Likewise, there is a need to ensure that all efficiency measures are in the range less than or equal to 1.

The constraints that must be meted on any ISP_j to ensure that the efficiency of the ISP is less than or equal to 1 is:

$$(VjYj) < (UjXj) \tag{3}$$

Thus, to know how other ISPs are performing when ISP_j's implicit resourse were used during the time to determine efficiency for ISPj, It is noted that efficiency measure does not exceed 1.

To determine the maximum efficiency using DEA for each ISP_j is given as:

$$\text{Maximize } (V'jYj)/(U'jXj), \tag{4}$$

Therefore,

$$\text{Subject to: } (V'jYj)/(U'jXj) < 1 \text{ for } k = 1, k. \tag{5}$$

Thus, applied conditions for non-zero constraints (1).

These conditions ensure that none of the ISP efficiency is more than 100%. Also, if the objective function is less than 1, then in comparison to ISP_j, one or more of the ISP, denoted by constraints in equation (5) is producing more output using the same level of inputs, or producing the same level of output using less input, or both. Such a result would show that ISP_j is relatively inefficient compared to other ISPs. This maximization problem of (3) subject to (1) and (5) is a nonlinear programming problem. Transforming maximization problems into linear programing using Charnes et al. (1978) model based on a constant return to scale adopted in this study, it holds that:

$$\text{Max } (V'jYj) \tag{6}$$

Subject to:

$$-V'jYj + U'jXj > 0 \text{ for j} = 1, \text{k} \tag{7}$$

$$UjXj = 1 \tag{8}$$

$$Uj, Vj > \varepsilon \tag{9}$$

Where ε is a small positive number

Formulation of linear programing problem consisting of equations (6) to (9) constitutes the basic DEA technique. This maximization problem is solved for each ISP. The ISP which has objective functions value equal to 1 is considered efficient, while those less than 1 are deemed relatively inefficient. Moreover, two methods are usually considered in the measurement of efficiency. It could be measured by using an input or output-oriented approach. This study uses an input-oriented approach because it focuses on the optimization of resources used to obtain better output, in other words it can translate inefficient factors into efficient factors since the inputs are observed during optimization (João-Carlos et al., 2013). The input approach shows that an inefficient unit can be made efficient by minimizing the number of inputs used while the number of outputs produced remains constant.

Research Approach and Software Used

This research uses a quantitative research method. The quantitative research method derives its input from statistical and numerical data. This study involves the analysis of ISP data to describe a phenomenon that is used to evaluate efficiency. There are two approaches to evaluate efficiency: the constant return to scale (CRS) and the variable return to scale (VRS). This research considers the CRS approach in addition to the envelopment model. This study formulated the DEA model to compare the five years of each of the major ISPS in Nigeria. The result analysis showed the efficient and inefficient ISPs and their ranking based on performance. Twenty Decision Making Units (DMU) were formed based on the number of years considered and the number of variables that served as customer and NCC regulations. The software used for this study is the DEA package called (OSDEA). It is an open-source software that is freely available and could calculate efficiency using linear programming. The OSDEA application is designed to solve multiple DEA problems therefore it has different inbuilt models for different problems.

The technical efficiency (TE) in OSDEA is well configured and well suited DEA tool. It is particularly recommended for different areas of academic research involving efficiency evaluation.

Data Collection, Performance Metrics and Decision-Making Units

This study used data obtained from secondary sources. The dataset was sourced from NCC database (www.ncc.gov.ng) and the respective websites of each mobile ISP used as a case study for this research, broadband speed checker, and Nigerianstat.gov. The duration for data considered was 2015 to 2019, which is 5 years period. This available data is enough to formulate the DEA model of each ISP. In terms of metrics, the NCC has some set of guidelines for Internet service operators and provided a benchmark to measure the performance of ISPs in Nigeria. Different metrics were codified in the annual questionnaire sent to the ISPs annually with a view to obtaining the performances of each operator; some of this information is published on the NCC website. More so, there is some additional information that is available on the ISP's website. This study used the NCC metrics to establish the variables necessary for this study. The indices that pertain to Internet services that were creatively crafted out are: number of data subscriber of each operator, bandwidth or internet speed of the operator, reputation of each operator which was related to the number of years of establishment in Nigeria, the cost of data. These variables were classified as input and output as follows:

Input variables

i.   Bandwidth or Internet speed per download
ii. Cost per megabyte of data
iii. Reputation/number of years of existence of the operator

Output variables
Number of internet subscriber/Customer base

The decision-making units (DMUs) for this research are the four major mobile ISPs in Nigeria Airtel, Glo, 9mobile, and MTN. According to the rule of DEA simulations, to achieve a more acceptable DEA result that can be generalized from the model, a basic requirement for the number of DMUs selection must be followed. This rule states that the DMU must exceed two times the number of indexes (input and output). Charnes, Cooper, & Rhodes (1978) opined that a rough rule of thumb has the following relationships: $X > \max \{Y \times Z, 3(Y + Z)\}$, where X is the number of DMUs, Y is the number of inputs and Z is the number of outputs. As a result, the data set that was considered for this work consists of 20 DMU (X = 20), Y = 3, and Z = 1. Mathematically, $X > \max \{3 \times 1, 3(3+1)\}$, that is, $X > \{3, 12\}$. In other words, 20 DMU is greater than 12 DMU minimum requirements. Thus, the data set satisfied the above conditions.

RESULTS, ANALYSIS, AND DISCUSSION

This section showed the results of the analysis simulated using OSDEA. The statistical data analyzed results of the DEA model for each of the ISPs. This study used operations data from four major ISPs that are providing Internet services in Nigeria.

Table 1. Average internet download speed

	Speed / Year					Average
	2015	**2016**	**2017**	**2018**	**2019**	
MTN	6.93	48.65	13.8	13.8	8.73	18.32
GLOBACOM	10.7	1.89	34.94	19.12	2.4	13.81
9MOBILE	2.01	8.9	7.57	3.84	5.31	5.52
AIRTEL	21	0.37	16.04	16.04	28.45	16.32

Effective Performance of ISPs

Effectiveness could be referred to as the extent to which the outputs of ISPs achieve the stated objectives of that service. The literature has shown that existing approaches employed by NCC to evaluate the performance of mobile operators are done using a single variable per time, such as Internet speed and cost of download per megabyte. Using this method, it would be difficult to evaluate the efficiency of ISPs. Therefore, this section first demonstrates the effective performance of ISPs that is currently being considered by the NCC. Parameters and data to establish forthwith on how true efficiency evaluation was obtained. However, the analysis of the existing methods was done to serve as a source of data for the proposed DEA method. Below are the existing data and metrics of performance evaluation.

Average Internet Downloads Speed (Mbps)

Internet speed refers to the speed at which electronic content travels from the World Wide Web to a particular computer, tablet, or smartphone. The speed of the Internet is measured in megabits per second (Mbps). The average internet speed comprised of download (downlink) speeds and upload (uplink). Download speed refers to the rate that digital data is transferred from the Internet to a device, while upload speed is the rate that online data is transferred from an electronic device to the Internet. This parameter is very important to subscribers who use the services to engage with online documents and as such the NCC uses this parameter to rate the effectiveness of a given ISP. NCC expects that the average Internet speed by providers is optimized to ensure better online for subscribers. Table 1 presents the effective Internet speed performance of four operators namely MTN, GLO, Airtel, and 9mobile over five years of operation. Figure 2 shows the graphical representation of the average Internet speed of the data in Table 1. The table showed that the performance of each operator has not been consistent over the years, while Airtel had the highest internet speed in 2015, MTN was highest in 2016, whereas in 2017 and 2018 Globacom had the highest internet speed and in 2019 Airtel internet speed was the highest.

Cost of Data per Megabyte

The cost of data is the rate at which subscribers pay in Naira for a given megabyte of download. While the Internet speed is desirable by subscribers, they all want an Internet speed that is also affordable. NCC advocates an affordable cost of data for subscribers. Table 2 presents the cost of data per megabyte of four operators over five years of operation. Figure 3 shows the graphical representation of the average

Figure 2. Effective performance of the four ISPs based on internet speed

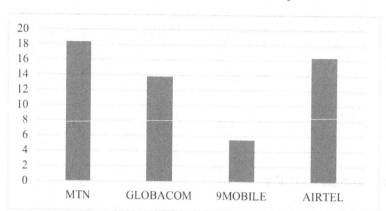

Table 2. Cost of data per megabyte

	Average Cost of Data (NAIRA/MB)					Average
	2015	**2016**	**2017**	**2018**	**2019**	
MTN	4.6	4.7	4.7	1.4	1.11	3.302
GLOBACOM	4.6	4.7	3	0.8	0.7	2.76
9MOBILE	3.3	0.6	1.4	1.32	0.73	1.46
AIRTEL	1.7	1.4	0.76	0.7	0.9	1.092

cost of data per megabyte in Table 2. The figure shows that MTN has the highest average performance followed by GLOBACOM while AIRTEL has the least.

Number of Internet Subscriber

Each ISP used as a case study in this research has customers who patronize their products and services. This study used the number of subscribers as an output criterion; this is because if the services, such as the price of data, internet speed, and reputation is properly construed in a better light by customers,

Figure 3. Cost of data by the ISPs

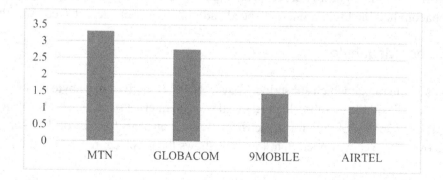

Table 3. Internet Subscribers base for ISPs

	Internet Subscribers				
	2015	**2016**	**2017**	**2018**	**2019**
MTN	39,924,737	32,974,177	36,069,597	41,678,804	65,707,899
GLOBACOM	25,082,066	26,628,065	26,997,178	28,084,948	47,265,628
9MOBILE	15,189,788	13,338,839	11,338,839	9,919,820	15,605,255
AIRTEL	16,835,952	19,363,545	23,985,203	29,757,791	47,921,891

it should have a corresponding effect of the number of subscribers base they have obtained. Therefore, the number of internet subscribers an ISP has is predicted to be the evaluator of the services. Table 3 presents the number of Internet subscribers of each operator over five years of operation. Figure 4 shows the graphical representation of the average number of Internet subscribers in Table 3. The figure shows that MTN has the highest average performance followed by GLOBACOM while AIRTEL has the least.

Efficiency Performance of Internet ISPs Using DEA

This section focusses on the efficiency measurement of the four ISPs using the DEA, the quantitative evaluation of the ISP was done based on the technical efficiency (TE) known as productivity of the four ISPs in Nigeria and to classify them based on their efficiency rating. To evaluate the TE of Internet service providers, this study has developed an envelopment model presented in the methodology. The study considered input oriented CCR/CRS approach. The model determines the degree of efficiency for ISP against the best-practice (efficient) and suggests how the inefficient operators could attain efficiency so that they are productive.

Analysis of Data for DMUs

The major contribution of this study is the evaluation of efficiency performance of the ISPs based on the frontier analysis of the DEA technique. The first step is the analysis and transformation of data obtained from NCC dataset into the DMUs. The metrics are classified into inputs and outputs. One

Figure 4. Internet subscribers of four ISPs

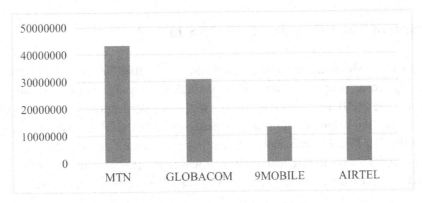

Table 4. ISP dataset based on four DMUs

DMUs	Output	Input		
	Internet Subscribers	Cost of Data (Naira/MB)	Average Download Speed (Mbps)	Years of Existence
MTN 2015	39924737	4.6	6.93	14
GLOBACOM 2015	25082066	4.6	10.7	12
9MOBILE 2015	15189788	3.3	2.01	7
AIRTEL 2015	16835952	1.7	21	14
MTN 2016	32974177	4.7	48.65	15
GLOBACOM 2016	26628065	4.7	1.89	13
9MOBILE 2016	13338839	0.6	8.9	8
AIRTEL 2016	19363545	1.4	0.37	15
MTN 2017	36069597	4.7	13.8	16
GLOBACOM 2017	26997178	3	34.94	14
9MOBILE 2017	11338839	1.4	7.57	9
AIRTEL 2017	23985203	0.76	16.04	16
MTN 2018	41678804	1.4	13.8	17
GLOBACOM 2018	28084948	0.8	19.12	15
9MOBILE 2018	9919820	1.32	3.84	10
AIRTEL 2018	29757791	0.7	16.04	17
MTN 2019	65707899	1.11	8.73	18
GLOBACOM 2019	47265628	0.7	2.4	16
9MOBILE 2019	15605255	0.73	5.31	11
AIRTEL 2019	47921891	0.9	28.45	18

of the unique characteristics of frontier analysis is the consideration for all the variables and how they impact the entire operation of ISPs. These variables were carefully examined, then classified into inputs and outputs for the DEA solver. Unlike the existing NCC method, which considered the evaluation of variables separately with the aim to achieve operation effectiveness, the DEA method combined all the variables to achieve efficiency of operation. Thus, this study seeks to measure the efficiency of ISPs using the DUMs presented in Table 4.

Implementation of Input-Oriented CCR/CRS Model

In this section, a CCR/CSR model presented in section 3 is applied here using the OSDEA tool. The technical efficiency scores are processed from the variables input. The outputs of the model are classified into efficient and inefficient ISPs because the tool can calculate the technical efficiency of each ISP. The DEA tool uses the linear programming embedded within the DEA solver to locate efficient ISP in comparison with other ISP. The efficient ISPs are those with an efficiency rating of $\Theta = 1$. The inefficient DMUs are identified by an efficiency rating of less than 1 ($\Theta < 1$). Table 5 presents the efficiency scores of all DMUs comprising four ISPs evaluated by the DEA solver. Each efficiency ranking is done

Table 5. Efficiency score of ISPs based on CCR model

	Efficiency Score Based on CCR/CRS Model					Average
	2015	**2016**	**2017**	**2018**	**2019**	
MTN	0.781212084	0.602195672	0.617555838	0.671616336	1	0.734516
GLOBACOM	0.572581068	0.708059316	0.528256997	0.562842467	1	0.674348
9MOBILE	0.669915481	0.45675464	0.345128643	0.288325087	0.389130709	0.429851
AIRTEL	0.329431078	1	0.483596552	0.629586282	0.832755371	0.655074

in comparison with each other ISPS according to the years and the results of technical efficiency scores of all the ISPs are shown according to years. From Table 5, in the year 2015, none of the ISPs attained the threshold of $\Theta = 1$. That means the ISPs were inefficient based on the technical efficiency ratings of the DEA solver. However, looking at the value of the ratings critically, MTN has the highest rating since 0.78 in 2015 than any other ISPs.

This was followed by 9mobile, Globacom, and Airtel. From Table 5, in the year 2016, Airtel had a decisive efficiency rating of 1. Globacom was next in the efficiency rating followed by MTN and then 9mobile. In 2017 and 2018 none of the ISP achieved the threshold efficiency rating of $\Theta = 1$. In 2019, MTN and Globacom had decisive efficient values of 1. Table 5 presented the average efficient performance of each ISPs with the MTN being the highest followed by GLOBACOM and AIRTEL while 9MOBILE is the least. Figure 5 shows the corresponding efficient performance of each ISPs.

The efficiency rating of each of the ISP's is cumulatively computed to further understand which of the ISP had the highest efficiency rating. Therefore, figure 6 confirmed the efficiency performance of the ISPs presented in Table 5.

Figure 5. Visualization of the efficiencies of the ISPs based on the CCR/CRS model

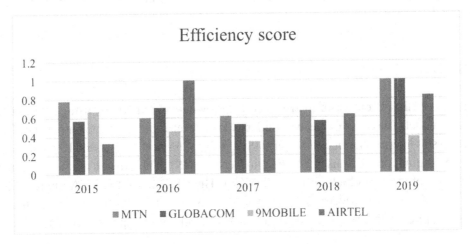

Figure 6. Visualization of cumulative efficiency of ISPs

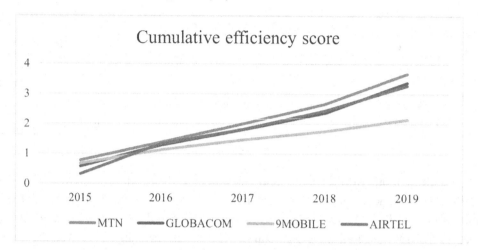

RECOMMENDATIONS AND RESEARCH DIRECTIONS

This study proffers the following suggestions: Internet service governance and regulators such as NCC should consider efficiency performance as a measure for evaluating and advising ISP in Nigeria. The study presented a new and better way to rank ISPs in Nigeria based on efficiency as oppose effective evaluation. This study recommends that NCC should consider using frontier analysis tools such as DEA for the performance evaluation of the ISP with a view of uncovering opportunities for better patronage.

The parameters used in building the DEA model unravel the flashpoint for ISP to compete favorably with their competitors and have a good market share. This was because the CCR/CRS model posits that subscribers are likely to increase when customers' perceived parameters like internet speed, reputation, and data cost in a positive light. While the data used for this study are from secondary sources, future work involving DEA in ISP efficiency may intend to collect primary data from subscribers to compare the disparity of both in the data and the results from the models. ISP may also provide more data to improve the number of data and variables used. DEA, which is a quantitative method, could be used to benchmark other ISPs in other counties and information system performance with a view to popularizing the method in information system research. Furthermore, other DEA models could be used, and results compared.

CONCLUSION

This study evaluated the efficiency of Internet service providers in Nigeria by using a data envelopment analysis (DEA) model. The study model was built based on three inputs and one output. The DEA model was designed to suit Internet Service Providers (ISPs) using Charnes Cooper and Rhodes Model (CCR) technique with assumption of Constant Return to Scale (CRS). This model was used to measure the relative efficiency of Decision Making Units (DMUs). The adoption of the DEA model allows for the evaluation of the ISP and the performance parameters that are essential for the ISP. This linear programming approach applied in this research allows all values for all the ISPs and their respective parameters to be simultaneously simulated in the OSDEA solver. The data were sourced from NCC, ISP, broadband speed checker, and Nigerian statistics websites considering the period of five years, which is 2015 to 2019. The result of the DEA model based on data used and the model applied revealed variant performance efficiency for the selected ISPs. The efficiencies of the ISPs were not consistent with yearly simulations. But cumulatively, the CCR/CRS model revealed that MTN had the highest efficiency within the five years, followed by Globacom, Airtel, and then 9mobile respectively. The adoption of DEA method provides concrete evidence that the DEA technique can unravel technical efficiency among the ISPs and in the Telecommunication industry generally. This approach would help competitors to compare their efficiency to others operating in the same economic space. It would also help them to understand what variable(s) account for the strengths and weakness of their competitors based on the line efficiency metrics applied in this study.

REFERENCES

Adegoriola, A., & Isa, M. (2018). The Problem of Infrastructure on E-Commerce, Small and Medium Enterprises in Nigeria. *Journal of Economics and Sustainable Development, 9*(4).

Adom, D., Joe, A., & Hussein, E. (2018). Theoretical and Conceptual Framework: Mandatory Ingredients of a Quality Research. *International Journal of Scientific Research, 7*(1).

Ajibesin, A. A., Ventura, N., Murgu, A., & Chan, H. A. (2014). Data envelopment analysis with slacks model for energy efficient multicast over coded packet wireless networks. *IET Science, Measurement &amp. IET Science, Measurement & Technology, 8*(6), 408–419. doi:10.1049/iet-smt.2013.0195

Aleke, B., Ojiako, U., & Wainwright, D. W. (2011). ICT adoption in developing countries: Perspectives from small-scale agribusinesses. *Journal of Enterprise Information Management, 24*(1), 68–84. Advance online publication. doi:10.1108/17410391111097438

Aliev, I. M. (2008). A model for the selection of internet service providers. *Automatic Control and Computer Sciences, 42*(5), 249–254. doi:10.3103/S0146411608050039

Apulu, I., & Ige, E. (2011). Are Nigeria Smes Effectively Utilizing Ict? *International Journal of Business and Management, 6*(6), 207–214. doi:10.5539/ijbm.v6n6p207

Avgerou, C. (2003). The Link between ICT and Economic Growth in the Discourse of Development. In M. Korpela, R. Montealegre, & A. Poulymenakou (Eds.), *Organizational Information Systems in the Context of Globalization: IFIP TC8 & TC9 / WG8.2 & WG9.4 Working Conference on Information Systems Perspectives and Challenges in the Context of Globalization June 15–17, 2003, Athens, Greece* (pp. 373–386). Springer US. 10.1007/978-0-387-35695-2_23

Barr, N. (2004). Higher Education Funding. *Oxford Review of Economic Policy, 20*(2), 264–283. doi:10.1093/oxrep/grh015

Beckinsale, M., Levy, M., & Powell, P. (2006). Exploring Internet Adoption Drivers in SMEs. *Electronic Markets, 16*(4), 361–370. doi:10.1080/10196780600999841

Bharadwaj, M., Aditya Reddy, M., Senthil Kumar, T., & Vajipayajula, S. (2022). Detection of DoS and DDoS Attacks Using Hidden Markov Model. In Inventive Communication and Computational Technologies. *Proceedings of ICICCT, 2021*, 979–992.

Brown, D. H., Lockett, N., & Schubert, P. (2005). Preface to the Focus Theme Section 'SMEs and E-Business.'. *Electronic Markets*, 15(2), 76–78. doi:10.1080/10196780500083720

Bruni, A., & Teli, M. (2007). Reassembling the Social: An Introduction to Actor Network Theory. *Management Learning*, 38(1), 121–125. doi:10.1177/1350507607073032

Carroll, N., Whellan, E., & Richardson, I. (2012). Service Science – an Actor Network Theory Approach. *International Journal of Actor-Network Theory and Technological Innovation*, 4(3), 52–70. doi:10.4018/jantti.2012070105

Chitekedza, I. (2015). *Efficiency evaluation of South Africa tertiary education institutions using data envelopment analysis* [Masters Thesis]. Nelson Mandela Metropolitan University.

Cook, W. D., Tone, K., & Zhu, J. (2014). Data envelopment analysis: Prior to choosing a model. *Omega*, 44, 1–4. doi:10.1016/j.omega.2013.09.004

Cooper, W. W., Seiford, L. M., & Zhu, J. (2011). Handbook on Data Envelopment Analysis. Springer Science & Business Media.

Cooper, W. W., Seiford, L., & Zhu, J. (2011). Data Envelopment Analysis: History, Models, and Interpretations. In *Handbook on Data envelopment analysis*. Elsevier. doi:10.1007/978-1-4419-6151-8_1

Dahunsi, F. M., & Akinlabi, A. A. (2019). Measuring mobile broadband performance in Nigeria: 2G and 3G. *Nigerian Journal of Technology*, 38(2), 422. doi:10.4314/njt.v38i2.19

Eke, H. (2011). *Digitizing resources for University of Nigeria repository: Process and challenges*. Webology. http://www.webology.org/2011/v8n1/a85.html

Emrouznejad, A., Parker, B. R., & Tavares, G. (2008). Evaluation of research in efficiency and productivity: A survey and analysis of the first 30 years of scholarly literature in DEA. *Socio-Economic Planning Sciences*, 42(3), 151–157. doi:10.1016/j.seps.2007.07.002

Farano, B. (2012). Internet intermediaries' liability for copyright and trademark infringement: Reconciling the EU and US Approaches. *Transatlantic Technology Law Forum Working Papers, 14*.

Federal Communications Commission (FCC). (2014). *Types of Broadband Connections*. Federal Communications Commission. https://www.fcc.gov/general/types-broadband-connections

Forsund, F. (2001). Categorical variables in DEA. *International Centre for Economic Working Paper*, 1–18.

Galadanci, G. S., & Abdullahi, S. (2018). Performance Analysis of GSM Networks inKano Metropolis ofNigeria. *American Journal of Engineering Research (AJER)2018American Journal of Engineering Research*, 7(5), 69–79.

Ghobakhloo, M., Sabouri, M. S., Hong, T. S., & Zulkifli, N. (2011). Information Technology Adoption in Small and Medium-sized Enterprises; An Appraisal of Two Decades Literature. *Interdisciplinary Journal of Research in Business*, *1*(7), 53–80.

Government of Nigeria. (2013). *Nigeria's National Broadband Plan 2013 - 2018*. Government of Nigeria. https://www.researchictafrica.net>national broadband plan 2013-2018.pdf

Grant, C., & Osanloo, A. (2016). Understanding, Selecting, and Integrating a Theoretical Framework in Dissertation Research. *Administrative Issues Journal: Connecting Education, Practice and Research*, 12–22.

Harper, J. (2005). Do ISPs have a duty to protect the world?: Against ISP Liability. *Telecommunications and Technology*, *28*, 30.

Ifeonu, R. O. (2014). *Investigating the Impact of Technology Trust on the Acceptance of Mobile Banking Technonlgy Within Nigeria* [Doctoral thesis]. University of Huddersfield.

Ihua, U. (2010). Local Content Policy and SMEs Sector Promotion: The Nigerian Oil Industry Experience. *International Journal of Business and Management*, *5*(5), 3–14. doi:10.5539/ijbm.v5n5p3

Iosifidis, G., Gao, L., Huang, J., & Tassiulas, L. (2017). Efficient and Fair Collaborative Mobile Internet Access. *IEEE/ACM Transactions on Networking*, *25*(3), 1386–1400. doi:10.1109/TNET.2016.2638939

Irefin, I., Abdul-Azeez, I., & Tijani, A. (2012). Aninvestigative Studyof the Factors Affecting the Adoptionof Information and Communication Technology in Small and Medium Scale Enterprises in Nigeria. *Australian Journal of Business and Management Research, 5*(5), 1–9.

João-Carlos, J. C. C. B., Angulo Meza, L., da Silveira, J. Q., & Gomes, E. G. (2013). About negative efficiencies in Cross Evaluation BCC input oriented models. *European Journal of Operational Research*, *229*(3), 732–737. doi:10.1016/j.ejor.2013.02.020

Joshi, P. (2019). *Understand the Similarity of Internet Service Providers via Peer-to-Peer User Interest Analysis* [Masters Thesis]. University of Minnesota.

Kuboye, B., Alese, B., & Imasuen, F. (2012). A Twin Approach to Internet Service Provision in Sparse Rural Community in Nigeria. *International Journal of Networks and Communications*, *2*(5), 132–137. doi:10.5923/j.ijnc.20120205.06

Kuboye, B. M. (2017). Evaluation of Broadband Network Performance in Nigeria. *International Journal of Communications, Network and Systems Sciences*, *10*(09), 199–207. doi:10.4236/ijcns.2017.109011

Kumbhakar, S. C., Wang, H.-J., & Horncastle, A. P. (2015). *A Practitioner's Guide to Stochastic Frontier Analysis Using Stata*. Cambridge University Press. doi:10.1017/CBO9781139342070

Lawal, L. S., Ahmed-Rufai, T., Chatwin, C. R., & Young, R. C. D. (2013). Delivery of broadband services to SubSaharan Africa via Nigerian communications satellite. *International Journal of Information and Computer Science*, *2*(5), 77–88.

Maghsoodi, A., Saghaei, A., & Hafezalkotob, A. (2019). Service quality measurement model integrating an extended SERVQUAL model and a hybrid decision support system. *European Research on Management and Business Economics*, 25(3), 151–164. doi:10.1016/j.iedeen.2019.04.004

Mugo, M. (2013). Determinants of Service Quality among the Internet Service Providers in Kenya. *Journal of Business Management and Corporate Affairs*, 2(2), 19–29.

Nigam, V., Thakur, T., Sethi, V. K., & Singh, R. P. (2012). Benchmarking of Indian mobile telecom operators using DEA with sensitivity analysis. *Benchmarking*, 19(2), 219–238. Advance online publication. doi:10.1108/14635771211224545

Nigerian Communications Commission. (2018). *Nigerian Communications Commission Stakeholder Information*. Nigerian Communications Commission. https://www.ncc.gov.ng/stakeholder/statistics-reports/industry-overview#view-graphs-tables

Nigerian Communications Commission. (2020). *Who We Are*. https://www.ncc.gov.ng/the-ncc/who-we-are

Nissi, E., & Rapposelli, A. (2010). A Data Envelopment Analysis of Italian Courts Efficiency. *Italian Journal of Applied Statistics*, 22(2), 12.

O'Sullivan, A., & Sheffrin, A. (2003). *Economics: Principles and actions*. Prentice hall.

Olise, M., Anigbogu, T., Edoko, T., & Okoli, M. (2014). Determinants of ICT Adoption for Improved SME's Performance in Anambra State, Nigeria. *American International Journal of Contemporary Research*, 4(7), 163–176.

Ononiwu, G., Akinwole, B., Agubor, C., & Onojo, J. (2016). Performance Evaluation of Major Mobile network operators in Owerri metropolis of Nigeria. *International Journal of Engineering Technologies in Computational and Applied Sciences*, 18(1), 6–13.

Oyatoye, E. O., Adebiyi, S. O., & Amole, B. B. (2015). Evaluating Subscribers Preference for Service Attributes of Mobile Telecommunication in Nigeria Using Analytic Hierarchy Process (ahp). *International Journal of the Analytic Hierarchy Process*, 7(2), 171–187. doi:10.13033/ijahp.v7i2.299

Ozovehe, A., & Usman, A. U. (2015). Performance Analysis of Gsm Networks in Minna Metropolis of Nigeria. *Nigerian Journal of Technology*, 34(2), 359-367. https://doi.org/ doi:10.4314/njt.v34i2.21

Pasquale, F. A. (2010). *Trusting (and Verifying) Online Intermediaries' Policing (SSRN Scholarly Paper ID 1762236)*. Social Science Research Network. https://papers.ssrn.com/abstract=1762236

Pavic, S., Koh, S. C. L., Simpson, M., & Padmore, J. (2007). Could e-business create a competitive advantage in UK SMEs? *Benchmarking*, 14(3), 320–351. doi:10.1108/14635770710753112

Popoola, J. J. (2009). Investigation on Quality of Service Provided by Third Tier Internet Service Providers in Nigeria: Akure Cybercafés as case study. *International Journal on Computer Science and Engineering*, 1(3), 186–191.

Pradhan, R. P., Arvin, M. B., & Norman, N. R. (2015). The dynamics of information and communications technologies infrastructure, economic growth, and financial development: Evidence from Asian countries. *Technology in Society*, 42, 135–149. doi:10.1016/j.techsoc.2015.04.002

Pradhan, S., Patel, G., & Olfati, M. (2019). Integrationa and Application of Analytic Hierarchy Process with Data Envelopment Analysis - a Literature Review. *International Journal of Analytic Hierarchy Process, 11*(2), 228–268. doi:10.13033/ijahp.v11i2.632

Saadat, F., & Soltanifar, M. (2014). *The Role of Internet Service Providers (ISPS) in Encouraging Customers to Use Their Internet Services in Iran*. Academic Press.

Selby, L. M., & Bawa, A. (2018). Optimizing an Efficient Use of Internet Bandwidth for Higher Learning Institutions in Ghana. *International Journal of Scientific Research in Computer Science*i, *Engineering and Information Technology, 3*(8), 50–65. doi:10.32628/CSEIT183819

Senthil Kumar, T., Suresh, A., & Karumathil, A. (2014). Improvised classification model for cloud based authentication using keystroke dynamics. In *Frontier and Innovation in Future Computing and Communications* (pp. 885–893). Springer Netherlands. doi:10.1007/978-94-017-8798-7_97

Smith, A., Rupp, W., & Motley, D. (2013). Corporate reputation as strategic competitive advantage of manufacturing and service-based firms: Multi-industry case study. *International Journal of Services and Operations Management, 14*(2), 131–156. doi:10.1504/IJSOM.2013.051826

Umezuruike, C., & Oludele, A. (2015). Broadband Internet Penetration in Nigeria: A Review. *International Journal of Research Studies in Computer Science and Engineering, 2*(1), 1–7.

Usman, H. (2018). *The Nature and Extent of Internet Service Providers' (ISPs) Liability in the European Union: Lessons for Nigerian Regulators* (*SSRN* Scholarly Paper ID 3204377). Social Science Research Network. https://papers.ssrn.com/abstract=3204377

Venkatesh, V., Morris, M. G., Davis, G. B., & Davis, F. D. (2003). User Acceptance of Information Technology: Toward a Unified View. *MIS Quarterly, 27*(3), 425–478. doi:10.2307/30036540

Waehama, W., McGrath, M., Korthaus, A., & Fong, M. (2014). ICT Adoption and the UTAUT Model. *International Journal of Information Technology : an Official Journal of Bharati Vidyapeeth's Institute of Computer Applications and Management, 8*.

Williams, M. D., Rana, N. P., & Dwivedi, Y. K. (2015). The unified theory of acceptance and use of technology (UTAUT): A literature review. *Journal of Enterprise Information Management, 28*(3), 443–488. Advance online publication. doi:10.1108/JEIM-09-2014-0088

Zhu, J. (2014). *Quantitative Models for Performance Evaluation and Benchmarking: Data Envelopment Analysis with Spreadsheets*. Springer.

ADDITIONAL READING

Chen, C. M. (2019). Evaluating the efficiency change and productivity progress of the top global telecom operators since OTT's prevalence. *Telecommunications Policy, 43*(7), 101805. doi:10.1016/j.telpol.2019.01.004

Nepomuceno, T. C. C., Costa, A. P. C. S., & Daraio, C. (2023). Theoretical and Empirical Advances in the Assessment of Productive Efficiency since the introduction of DEA: A Bibliometric Analysis. *International Journal of Operational Research*, *46*(4), 505–549. doi:10.1504/IJOR.2023.129960

Pramod, V. R., & Banwet, D. K. (2012). Benchmarking Indian telecom service providers: A data envelopment analysis. *International Journal of Electronic Finance*, *6*(3-4), 268–284. doi:10.1504/IJEF.2012.051169

Serrano-Cinca, C., Fuertes-Callén, Y., & Mar-Molinero, C. (2005). Measuring DEA efficiency in Internet companies. *Decision Support Systems*, *38*(4), 557–573. doi:10.1016/j.dss.2003.08.004

Tsai, H. C., Chen, C. M., & Tzeng, G. H. (2006). The comparative productivity efficiency for global telecoms. *International Journal of Production Economics*, *103*(2), 509–526. doi:10.1016/j.ijpe.2005.11.001

KEY TERMS AND DEFINITIONS

Data Envelopment Analysis (DEA): A performance measurement method used to evaluate the efficiency of organizations or decision-making units, such as ISPs, by comparing multiple inputs and outputs.

Digital Divide: The gap between demographics and regions that have access to modern information and communications technology, and those that don't or have restricted access.

Efficiency: In the context of ISPs, it refers to the ability to provide high-quality internet services using the least amount of resources, such as cost and infrastructure.

Internet Service Providers (ISPs): Companies that provide services for accessing, using, or participating on the internet. Key players in the telecommunications sector.

MTN: A major telecommunications company in Nigeria and several other African countries, known for providing a range of services including internet connectivity.

Nigeria Communications Commission (NCC): The regulatory authority for the Nigerian telecommunications industry, responsible for overseeing ISPs and ensuring fair competition and quality service.

Subscriber Base: The number of active subscribers or users that an ISP has, often used as a metric to gauge the company's market reach and scale of operations.

Telecommunications: The transmission of information by various types of technologies over wire, radio, optical, or other electromagnetic systems.

Chapter 13
Comparison of Cost and Profit Efficiencies of Indian Public Sector Banks in the Post–Reform Period

Vipul Gupta
https://orcid.org/0000-0002-1920-7314
DIT University, India

ABSTRACT

The chapter aims to analyze and compare the cost and profit efficiency of public sector banks (PSBs) in India after the post-banking sector reforms of 1991. The data was gathered and analyzed from 1995 to 2017, i.e., from the post-liberalization period until the significant State Bank of India merger in 2017. Average profit efficiency (PE) and cost efficiency (CE) scores were analyzed year-wise for each PSB in India. The distribution and median of efficiency scores in two sub-periods were also assessed using non-parametric Friedman's two-way ANOVA and Wilcoxon signed-rank test. The results revealed profit inefficiencies among PSBs in the selected period. Over the whole period, PE is less than the CE scores. The findings also revealed wide variations across public sector banks from 1995 to 2017. Moreover, the PE of PSBs has declined since the banking sector reform in 1991 in India.

INTRODUCTION

A bank is an institution licensed by the government to lend money and accepts deposits from the citizens of the country. Banks are the life blood of an economy and being the life blood of the economy, banks make huge contributions towards GDP growth of the country, infrastructure spending and tap rural areas. The banking sector channelizes the savings of public into productive ventures. The ability of the banking sector to channel funds also impacts their efficiency and performance. The banking sector in India was needed to be strengthened after achieving freedom from Britishers in 1947. The partition of India during 1947 influenced the whole economy with drastic impact on banking sector. This had also ended the

DOI: 10.4018/979-8-3693-0255-2.ch013

laissez faire of financial regime in the country. With the advent of various Industrial Policy Resolutions after independence, the government evolved in various other sectors of the economy including banking and finance. The Banking Regulation Act 1949 was also formed, which imparted the powers of control and supervision of all the banks to Reserve Bank of India (RBI) established in 1935.

In the modern era, responsibility of banks is paramount towards sustainable development because of their diverse financial services. It creates a multiplier effect on the whole economy with long-term sustainability in the culture of today. Banks are responsible for the smooth functioning of money and capital markets in an economy. The banks also possess the responsibility towards society which supports them by purchasing their products and services (Carroll, 2008; Gupta, 2021). To attain development, the country should have a sound financial system that supports the economy as well as society (Kumar and Gulati, 2009). Therefore, banks are crucial to the nation's social and economic well-being. The banking sector in India experienced a major transformation following Narshimham Committee recommendations in 1991 and 1998 respectively. The structure of banking in India comprises of cooperative banks and Scheduled Commercial Banks (SCBs). The SCBs are further divided into Public Sector Banks (PSBs), Private Sector Banks, Foreign Banks, and Regional Rural Banks. While the cooperative banks were established for the cooperation principle and controlled and owned by the members. The public owner-ship of banks was accomplished in three consecutive phases in 1955, 1969, and 1980 respectively and recognized as PSBs.

Public Sector Banks

The PSBs were emanated by the ruling Britishers in India from three Presidency Banks namely Bengal (1809), Bombay (1840) and Madras (1843). These banks were merged to form the Imperial Bank of India in the year 1921 during first World War. After gaining independence from the Britishers the Impe-rial Bank was named as State Bank of India (SBI). The SBI's associates were formed with the rulers of different states namely Patiala, Bikaner, Jaipur, Indore, Saurashtra, Hyderabad, Mysore, and Travancore in the year 1957. The PSBs became Twenty-seven with the merger of New Bank with Punjab National Bank. The Reserve Bank of India and Ministry of Finance both regulates the functioning of PSBs in India. PSBs are the banks in which the majority of stake is held by the government of India. PSBs are listed in stock exchanges and leveraged by the government to fulfil he social obligations for an economy. PSBs were regulated from both the Reserve Bank of India (RBI) and the Ministry of Finance. PSBs in India had many branches with a considerable rural presence provides largest employment opportunities to the citizens of the country.

BACKGROUND

Being the backbone of the economy as government banks, PSBs have greater social responsibility than other businesses because their financial services create multiplier effect on the whole economy and drive long term sustainability. An economy's efficiency is correlated with the effectiveness of the financial system (Kumar & Gulati, 2008). In Indian economy, the PSBs are facing efficiency crunch and were being merged or privatized. The post COVID 19 situation also intensified the operation problems among PSBs. Moreover, the mandatory social responsibility norms of PSBs marked a burden on banks apart from rising NPAs. It is now necessary to estimate (in)efficiency of each PSBs and investigate potential areas for development. Additionally, it is crucial to determine the efficiency of PSBs because of their declining performance.

Considering this, Data Envelopment Analysis (DEA) is used in the current study to analyze the Cost Efficiency (CE) and Profit Efficiency (PE) of PSBs in India. There are several factors that constitutes Indian Public Sector banking sector as an appealing case study:

(i) It classifies "best practices" and "worst practices" implicated from calculated efficiency scores and helps to enhance the performance of PSBs in India,

(ii) It helps the policymakers of an economy to investigate the dynamics of efficiency based on owner-ship of banks.

Additionally, there is limited literature available on the measurement and examination of CE and PE of PSBs in India, though there has been extensive literature on measuring technical efficiency of commercial banks over the past decades. The relevant literature mostly focuses on measuring and analyzing the profitability of banks using financial ratios. These financial ratios encounter drawbacks in the context of measuring competitive advantage and lack coverage of all dimensions of firms.

REVIEW OF PAST STUDIES

A review of literature in the context of the measurement and determinants of efficiencies in the banking sector is depicted in Table 1.

Based on study of literature on the banking sector in India it has been identified that many studies are available on measuring and analyzing profitability ratios of banks, but few studies are available on measuring and analyzing CE and PE of banks. The available studies on the CE and PE of banks is a blend of PSBs, Private Sector Banks and Foreign banks with limited focus on specific sector efficiency. Hence this study considered the efficiency analysis of PSBs in India using Data Envelopment Analysis (DEA) approach.

Data Envelopment Analysis

The non-parametric frontier method of linear programming is used in DEA. Farrell (1957) initiated productivity measurement with inputs and outputs. The frontier approach of DEA states the maximum efficiency for each selected unit in comparison to the best frontier. The Decision-Making Units (DMUs) constructed through DEA lie on the frontier which is efficient or get enveloped in that frontier. DMUs situated on the efficient frontier have the score 1 and DMUs enveloped under the frontier having scores between 0 and 1. The application of DEA on the data demand the following steps as:

1. The inputs and outputs of DMUs (Banks) are chosen in the first stage.
2. The second stage includes an estimation of efficiency scores for DMUs by dividing outputs (weighted sum) with inputs (weighted sum).

Table 1. A review of literature in the context of the measurement and determinants of efficiencies in the banking sector

Authors	Locale	Time Period	Major Findings
Isik and Hassan (2002)	Turkey	Years - 1992, 1996 and 1998	1.The banks had an average Cost of 90% and Profit Efficiency of 84%. 2. Turkish banks were more effective in managing costs.
Maudos et al. (2002)	Transition Countries	1993 to 1996	1. Banks demonstrated high-Cost Efficiency and a low Profit Efficiency, confirming that the inefficiencies were on the income side. 2. Portugal and the United Kingdom had the highest earnings while having the lowest cost efficiency.
Maudos and Pastor (2003)	Spain	1985 to 1996	1. Savings and Commercial Banks scored 90.9% and 80.2%, respectively, for cost effectiveness. 2. Commercial banks' average profit efficiency was 66.5%, while saving banks' average profit efficiency was 47.2%. 3. Savings banks had a score of 34.7%, compared to 52.9% for commercial banks in the alternative profit efficiency category.
Das et al. (2005)	India	1996 to 2003	1. Most banks received good cost-efficiency rankings, according to the results. 2. The profit efficiency of PVBs, FBs, and PSBs increased from 2001 to 2003.
Kasram and Yildirim (2006)	Europe	1995 to 2002	1. The foreign banks had an average cost-efficiency score of 0.207%. 2. The least cost inefficiency was depicted as 17.4% in Estonia. 3. The Czech Republic had the greatest cost-efficiency rate (21.3%). 4. The most profitable nations throughout the research period were Lithuania and the Czech Republic.
Semih Yildirim and Philippatos (2007)	Europe	1993 to 2000	1. Banks' cost efficiency, as determined by DFA, varied between 45% and 66%. 2. According to the SFA data, the cost efficiency for the 12 CEE nations was 77% on average. 3. Poland and Slovenia were the most productive nations.
Ariff and Can (2008)	China	1995 to 2004	1. The banks had a lower profit efficiency than cost efficiency in China. 2. The cost efficiency of the Chinese banks was 79.8% and profit efficiency was 50.5%. 3. The commercial banks jointly operated were the most efficient banks and the PSBs were the inefficient in China.
Kamaruddin et al. (2008)	Islamic Countries	1998 to 2004	1. All banks scored 69.5% for cost efficiency and 62% for profit efficiency. 2. Domestic banks scored higher for cost efficiency than foreign banks, with a score of 70.8% against 63.6%. 3. Domestic Islamic banks' profit efficiency was 73.7%, compared to 57.9% for foreign Islamic banks.
Das and Ghosh (2009)	India	1992 to 2004	1. The Indian banks had a profit efficiency below 50% in the selected period. 2. The PSBs had better Profit Efficiency in comparison to other banks in India.
Ghosh (2009)	India	1992 to 2004	1. From the year 1992 to 2004, PSBs had cost efficiency scores of more than 85%. 2. The profit efficiency of banks lie between 40.04% and 70.63% in most of the years. 3. The profitability efficiency of PSBs was higher as compared to other banks.
Ray and Das (2010)	India	1996 to 2003	1. State Bank of India and its associates were more cost efficient than other banks. 2. Private banks performed the least efficiently in terms of profit efficiency rankings, whereas State banks did the best.
Jayaraman and Srinivasan (2019)	India	2004 to 2013	1. The cost and profit efficiency of the selected banks were correlated in the study period. The results also revealed that if the banks were cost efficient, they were also profit efficient. 2. The profit efficiency was the best measure for separating performing banks from non-performing banks in India.
Kamaruddin (2019)	Malaysia	2006 to 2015	1. The revenue efficiency of domestic banks in Malaysia is lower than foreign banks due to the higher differences between cost and profit efficiencies of banks in Malaysia. 2. The findings suggested that higher revenue efficiency can improve the profit efficiency of banks in Malaysia.
Thaker et al. (2021)	India	2008-2018	1. The cost efficiency of PSBs was lower as compared to private sector banks. 2. The profit efficiency of PSBs was higher as compared to other banks in the country
Rakshit (2022)	India	1997 to 2017	1. The higher level of efficiencies (cost, revenue and profit) among banks were witnessed in India. 2. PSBs were cost efficient in comparison to other banks.

Cost Efficiency

Cost Efficiency (CE) is the banks' closeness of the costs to the best practice frontier with given outputs. The objective function and input prices are necessary for the computation of cost efficiency as shown in Figure 1.

The bank employs X1 and X2 as inputs to create Y, as shown in the illustration. Additionally, the production frontier of the bank y = f (X1, X2), which displayed consistent returns to scale, served as a

Figure 1. Cost-efficiency

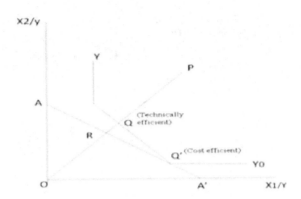

representation of the efficient unit isoquant YYo. The bank will be technically effective if the company employs YYO output because:

(OR/OP) = (OR/OQ) X (OQ/OP)

Mathematically,
subject to

x_i free,

Whereas yi is the output vector, and wi is the input price vector for bank (i), it is connected to all other banks by a linear combination. The constant returns to scale technique states that no further input is required beyond the ideal input combination vector xi under CRS. The minimum and observed costs wi'xi of bank (i) are contrasted to ascertain the minimal cost wi'xi CRS. It results in the following cost effectiveness: $WiXi^{CRS} / WiXi = CEi^{CRS}$

Profit Efficiency

Profit Efficiency (PE) is witnessed with the closeness of bank to the standard frontier (bank) under prevailing conditions. The PE is calculated by dividing maximum profits with actual profits as depicted in Figure 2.

Figure 2 reveals that OQ curve depicts the production possibility frontier. Point (A) depicts the combination of input and output of Bank A with (x_A, y_A) at actual level. The profits earned by Bank A are depicted as $\pi = q_A y_A - w_A x_A$. The inputs and outputs combinations of Bank B with x*and y*, inputs and outputs is Π^* revealing the maximum normalized profits. The maximum profit line can be reached by bank A is iso-profit line intersecting EF at which profits equal Bank B as:

$$\Pi^* = q_A y^*_A - w_A x^*_A = q_B y_B - w_B x_B.$$

A non-oriented DEA model was used to estimate the efficiencies allowing both an increase and the decrease in inputs and outputs with the prevailing market prices in an economy. Let us suppose, n num-

Figure 2. Profit efficiency (diagrammatic)

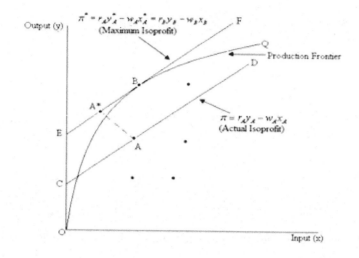

ber of banks in an economy (B =1,....c) producing the vector of s outputs O=($o_1,....,o_s$) sold at price p= ($p_1...,q_p$) vector is utilized for i inputs. Fare et al. (1997) and Fare and Grosskopf (1997) computed profit efficiency with the help of linear programming equations as follows:

$$\text{Max} \sum_{r=1}^{s} q_{ry_{ra}}^{a} - \sum_{i=1}^{c} p_i^a x_{ia}^D$$

With respect to:

$$\sum_{j=1}^{c} \lambda_B x_{iB}^D \le x_{ia}^D , i = 1,.....,c$$

$$\sum_{j=1}^{c} \lambda_B x_{KB}^{QF} \le x_{ka}^{QF} , k=1,......1$$

$$\sum_{j=1}^{c} \lambda_B y_{rB}^1 \le y_{ro}, r =1......s$$

$$x_{ia} \ge x_{ia}^D$$

$$y_{ro} \le y_{ro}$$

$$\lambda B \ge 0,$$

B = 1...., c

The maximum profits can be computed as $\sum_{r=1}^{s} q_r^a y_{ra} - \sum_{r=1}^{s} p_i^a x_{ia}$. The PE of Bank "a" is then determined by dividing the actual profit by the maximum standard bank profit. The calculated PE scores have a maximum value of 1 and are likewise bound above that value. The profit efficiency falls within the range of $(-\infty, 1)$. There is also the possibility of low-profit efficiency with negative values.

INPUTS AND OUTPUTS SELECTION

Researchers, scholars, and academicians mostly get confused in choosing the appropriate inputs and outputs to measure banking efficiency (Gulati, 2008). Humphrey (1985) discussed two approaches to select the inputs and outputs of banks: (i) the production approach and (ii) the intermediation approach. Deposits and loans (number of accounts) were considered as an output under the production model, which designated DMU (bank) as a service provider to the customer of banks. On the other hand, the physical capital and its cost as inputs of banks. The intermediation approach specified DMU as a producer of assets which utilizes deposits of customers in producing assets of banks. As a result of this methodology, banks provide intermediation services by calculating outputs in monetary terms and total costs that include interest payments and operational expenditures (Sealey and Lindley, 1977). Except for how the operations of banks are specified, both methods apply the conventional microeconomic theory to the banking sector in general. According to the empirical research for Banks, the inputs and outputs of the current study are processed utilizing a modified form of the intermediation technique rather than the production strategy. The input and output vectors are described as follows:

The variables included in the input vector are:

1. Fixed assets: capital (in millions of rupees)
2. Bank labor: total number of workers
3. Bank Loanable Funds: Deposits and Borrowings (in Millions of Rupees)

The variable included in the output vector are:

1. Advances of loans by banks: advances to Indian borrowers (term loans, discounted and bought bills, cash credits, etc.) as well as advances to foreigners (Rupee millions)
2. Investments of banks: investments made in India (in government securities as well as other securities that have been allowed, etc.) and investments made abroad (Rupee millions)
3. Income other than interest income: commissions, exchange, brokerage, and other types of revenue; net profits or losses from the sale of real estate and other assets; other receipts; and net exchange operations profits (in millions of Rupees)
4. Equity in terms of capital (quasi-fixed input variable): capital plus reserves of banks (Rupee millions)

Prices for the following inputs were included:

1. The price of capital (including lights, taxes, rent, stationery, printing, depreciation on its assets, insurance, repairs, and maintenance), divided by the amount of capital.
2. The price of bank employees: Payment to labor divided by total labor yields.
3. The price of loanable funds given by banks is calculated as follows: loanable funds divided by the sum of interest on deposits plus interest on borrowing from other institutions and the RBI.

Prices for the following outputs are included:

1. Price of loans advanced by banks: (interest/discount on bills/advances) divided by total advances.
2. Investment Price: (Income from Investments) divided by total investments.
3. Non-interest income's price is one (when seen as a constant).
4. The price of equity is one assumed to be constant.

The variable non-interest income refers to net earnings of a bank through lending money and investing in both non-government and government instruments. The non-interest income refers to the money that banks make from items not visible in their balance sheet viz. commission, exchange, and brokerage. To account for changes in production services provided by PSBs in addition to their conventional banking, non-interest income is considered when calculating efficiency scores. The sample size of the research influences DEA computed efficiency results; hence the chapter's sample size was chosen as a general rule of thumb based on the pertinent literature. The research identified the guidelines as follows (Cooper et al., 2007):

N must be greater than equal to max $\{a \times b; 3(a + b)\}$,
where:

n = DMUs (number)
a = inputs (number)
b = outputs (number)

The current research considered $a = 3$ and $b = 2$ and DMUs $n = 27$ which exceeded the desirable size of the sample suggested by rule of thumb (Avikiran, 1999b).

A year wise and bank wise profit efficiency scores of PSBs in India for the period 1994 to 2017 was analyzed using inputs and outputs. The entire period was further divided into two sub periods, 1995 to 2004 till the priority sector lending and financial inclusion reforms in the banking sector in 2005. The second sub period was from 2005 to 2017 till the major merger of State Bank of India and its associates in the year 2017. The data for the research related to inputs and outputs in the current research is collected from the website of RBI. The nominal data collected from RBI was deflated to produce the real numbers. The study utilized real values using the implicit GDP price deflator at factor cost (base 2014 -2015=100) for all the variables selected in the study except workers of banks. Following the literature specifically the studies of Denizer et al. (2007), Kumar and Gulati (2009), and Kumar and Gulati (2011) the selected input and output variables for efficiency calculations were normalized by dividing them with number of branches of each bank for each year using deflator. The data was normalized by the researchers to lessen the random noise resulting from measurement error in the chosen inputs and outputs.

RESULTS AND DISCUSSION

The chapter utilizes separate bank-wise efficiency frontiers of every year in line with the studies of Pasiorus et al. (2007) and Kyj and Isik (2008). Calculating a distinct yearly border has two advantages, according to Isik and Hassan (2002): (i) It is more appropriate than establishing a rigid multi-year limit for PSBs since it is adaptable. ii) By enabling an efficient bank to become inefficient in a subsequent year, it reduces the issue of random mistakes in DEA. It is predicated on the idea that data errors do not remain constant throughout time. Additionally, since they are influenced by widespread technological improvement in the business, efficiency estimates obtained from the grand frontier are frequently inflated. It is thus considered that year-wise computation efficiency frontiers are more reliable and accurate than the grand frontier efficiency model. The results and discussions of two sub- periods are discussed as follows:

Table 2. Cost efficiency scores 1995-2004 of PSBs

DMU	1995	1996	1997	1998	1999	2000	2001	2002	2003	2004
B1	1.000	1.000	1.884	-16.380	1.540	-1.200	2.056	-1.001	2.431	34.605
B2	1.000	1.000	1.000	1.000	1.000	1.000	1.000	2.418	1.347	0.467
B3	1.000	1.000	1.000	1.067	1.302	-2.683	1.498	4.652	1.856	6.994
B4	1.186	1.518	1.000	1.000	1.000	-2.649	1.000	1.000	1.000	1.000
B5	1.000	1.000	1.156	1.415	1.363	1.444	1.760	28.095	1.763	2.106
B6	1.000	1.810	1.506	18.892	1.490	-1.020	1.848	-3.588	1.450	3.442
B7	1.251	-6.955	1.000	-0.393	1.437	-1.098	2.111	-0.868	7.317	-9.680
B8	1.000	1.000	1.000	1.000	1.000	1.000	1.000	1.000	1.000	1.000
B9	1.000	4.687	1.000	1.000	1.000	1.000	1.450	2.863	1.543	1.000
B10	1.000	2.813	1.471	1.000	1.000	-0.736	1.000	-0.411	1.000	1.000
B11	1.000	3.573	1.561	-2.369	1.586	-1.090	1.918	-1.924	2.258	-97.401
B12	1.000	1.000	1.000	1.000	1.000	1.000	1.000	1.000	1.000	1.000
B13	1.160	-2.956	1.250	1.342	1.365	15.665	1.736	-2.006	1.652	1.000
B14	1.363	-1.160	1.831	-1.545	1.572	-1.163	1.841	-1.190	2.784	-8.490
B15	1.000	1.000	1.000	1.000	1.000	1.000	1.417	1.000	1.216	1.000
B16	1.000	1.000	1.000	1.000	1.000	1.000	1.000	1.000	1.000	1.000
B17	1.000	1.000	1.000	1.506	1.311	1.000	1.645	6.064	1.309	1.600
B18	1.000	1.000	1.000	1.000	1.000	1.000	1.000	1.000	1.000	1.000
B19	1.000	1.000	1.000	1.000	1.000	1.000	1.000	1.000	1.000	2.262
B20	1.000	1.000	1.263	1.000	1.000	1.000	1.000	1.000	1.000	1.019
B21	1.134	1.000	1.000	1.000	1.000	1.000	1.000	1.000	1.000	1.000
B22	1.000	1.000	1.000	1.000	1.000	1.000	1.000	1.369	1.000	1.000
B23	1.000	1.000	1.769	-1.710	1.660	-2.230	1.965	-1.016	2.940	-3.538
B24	1.000	-0.556	1.941	-0.423	1.000	-3.745	1.233	-0.482	3.508	-7.954
B25	1.000	-2.099	1.485	-0.863	1.526	-1.626	1.617	31.998	1.583	5.419
B26	1.000	1.000	1.000	1.000	1.000	1.000	1.000	1.000	1.000	1.000
B27	1.312	1.000	2.728	-0.460	1.598	-1.004	1.996	-2.598	2.198	3.466

Table 2 depicts CE Scores 1995-2004 of PSBs. Among all the PSBs after banking sector reforms (1991) in India B1 (Allahabad Bank), B5 (Bank of Maharashtra), B9 (Dena Bank), B13 (Punjab and Sindh Bank), B14 (Punjab National Bank), B23 (Syndicate Bank), B25 (Union Bank of India) and B27(Vijaya Bank) was never cost-efficient banks or on the efficient frontier in the selected period by attaining the efficient score of 1.0. The banks B3 (Bank of Baroda), B6 (Canara Bank), B4 (Central Bank of India), B11 (Indian Overseas Bank) were on the efficient frontier and was cost efficient in one year in the selected range after reforms whereas other banks were cost efficient in one or more years in the selected range. The bank B17 (State Bank of India) and B8 (Corporation Bank) attained the CE score of 1.0 most of the years.

Table 3. Cost efficiency scores 2005-2017 of PSBs

DMU	2005	2006	2007	2008	2009	2010	2011	2012	2013	2014	2015	2016	2017
B1	0.435	0.895	0.776	0.788	0.962	0.933	0.927	0.490	0.516	1.000	0.955	0.911	1.000
B2	1.000	0.971	0.928	0.896	0.970	1.000	1.000	0.455	0.714	0.979	0.974	0.990	0.859
B3	0.510	0.906	0.784	0.826	0.994	0.861	0.957	0.439	0.554	0.966	0.952	0.874	0.798
B4	0.436	0.905	0.866	0.808	1.000	0.848	0.914	0.387	0.465	0.966	0.969	0.846	0.759
B5	0.606	0.966	0.736	0.463	0.945	0.848	0.847	0.475	0.442	0.949	0.964	0.966	0.408
B6	0.580	0.985	0.761	0.792	0.937	0.881	0.947	0.411	0.487	0.919	0.900	0.889	0.781
B7	0.455	0.923	0.686	0.579	0.930	0.830	0.865	0.365	0.418	0.897	0.925	0.905	0.663
B8	0.930	1.000	0.959	0.888	1.000	1.000	1.000	0.570	0.769	1.000	1.000	0.957	0.923
B9	0.456	0.938	0.868	0.832	0.877	0.840	0.917	0.445	0.477	0.940	0.897	0.920	0.666
B10	0.981	0.974	0.936	1.000	1.000	1.000	1.000	0.423	0.494	1.000	0.991	0.966	0.839
B11	0.535	0.928	0.751	0.742	0.943	0.875	0.904	0.395	0.412	0.938	0.905	0.906	0.461
B12	0.542	1.000	0.947	0.860	1.000	0.940	1.000	0.446	0.530	1.000	0.979	0.979	0.753
B13	0.791	0.882	0.743	0.759	0.948	0.218	0.954	0.452	0.424	0.943	0.956	0.961	0.790
B14	0.572	0.840	0.799	0.747	0.953	0.894	0.921	0.444	0.496	0.978	0.953	0.922	0.722
B15	0.930	0.931	0.875	0.928	1.000	0.839	0.972	0.449	0.705	1.000	1.000	1.000	0
B16	0.696	1.000	1.000	0.897	1.000	0.927	0.974	0.424	0.568	0.975	1.000	1.000	0
B17	0.678	1.000	1.000	1.000	1.000	1.000	1.000	1.000	1.000	1.000	1.000	1.000	1.000
B18	0.671	1.000	0.848	0.882	1.000	0.904	0	0	0	0	0	0	0
B19	0.974	1.000	0.959	1.000	0.915	0.835	0.929	0.329	1.000	0.921	0.912	0.896	0
B20	0.709	1.000	0.858	0.813	0.980	0.880	0.973	0.380	0.571	0.955	0.991	0.917	0
B21	0.601	0.919	0.688	0.675	0	0	0	0	0	0	0	0	0
B22	0.732	1.000	0.876	0.794	1.000	0.875	0.973	0.447	0.615	0.958	0.974	0.990	0
B23	0.492	0.916	0.702	1.000	0.913	0.793	0.959	0.369	0.466	0.987	0.964	0.900	0.792
B24	0.394	0.917	0.737	0.572	0.903	0.946	0.909	0.379	0.442	0.947	0.946	0.913	0.742
B25	1.000	0.953	0.753	0.723	0.888	0.875	0.928	0.400	0.479	0.953	0.985	0.955	0.830
B26	0.458	0.529	0.467	0.554	0.920	0.990	0.893	0.405	0.450	1.000	0.921	0.907	0.935
B27	0.561	0.947	0.759	0.648	0.920	0.911	0.977	0.445	0.505	0.941	0.974	0.946	0.946

Table 3 depicts CE Scores 2005-2017 of PSBs. The banks B5 (Bank of Maharashtra), B6 (Canara Bank), B7 (Central Bank of India), B9 (Dena Bank), B12 (Punjab and Sindh Bank), B13 (Punjab National Bank), B11 (Indian Overseas Bank), B24 (UCO Bank) and B27 (Vijaya Bank) had never touched the cost-efficient frontier and attained the score of 1.0 in the specified range. The banks B4 (Bank of India), B25 (Union Bank of India), B26 (United Bank of India) was on the efficient frontier in one year in the selected range after reforms whereas other banks were on the efficient frontier or cost efficient in one or more years in the selected range. The banks B17 (State Bank of India) and B8 (Corporation Bank) attained the cost-efficient score of 1.0 most of the years.

Average Cost Efficiency

Table 4 depicts the major findings of average CE scores from 1995-2017. The relative mean CE scores were relatively high in the first subperiod. In this period, the majority of PSBs are located near to the benchmark cost frontier. Between 1995 and 2004, the average cost-inefficiency of PSBs was determined to be under 9%. The majority of PSBs are far from the benchmark cost frontier in the second subperiod with low level of relative mean cost efficiency scores. During 2012, it was discovered that average cost-inefficiency of PSBs was below 60%; by 2013 and it had decreased below 40%. It depicted that PSBs in India operated at lower technical and allocative efficiency. As a result, PSBs were unable to regulate the input-mix to satisfy their conflicting needs and to prevent underutilization of resources. In other words, PSBs in India exhibited both relatively high levels of technical and allocative efficiency. As a result, PSBs had effectively regulated the wastage and underutilization of input resources and, to a large part, selected the right input-mix when balancing opposing demands. As a result, PSBs can regulate the input-mix in relation to their conflicting needs and control the underutilization of resources.

Table 5 depicts PE Scores 1995-2004 of PSBs. After Liberalization, Privatization and Globalization reforms in the financial sector, almost all the PSBs in the selected range attained the profit efficient score of 1.0 in most of the years from 1995 to 2004 in India. The banks were also found under the efficient frontier or away from it with the negative values indicating profit inefficiency for B7 (Central Bank of India), B14 (Punjab National Bank), B24 (UCO Bank) and most of the inefficiencies were witnessed in the year 2000. Among all the PSBs B17 (State Bank of India) attained the PE score of 1.0 in all the years in the range.

Table 6 depicts PE Scores 2005-2017 of PSBs. The efficiency calculation was away from the efficient frontiers for B1 (Allahabad Bank) and B7 (Central Bank of India) had efficiency scores of less than 1.0 in the specified range of periods but attained the score 1.0 in one year. The efficiency scores of all the PSBs declined in the selected range after 2005 and specifically after the financial crisis in the year 2008. Among all the PSBs B17 (State Bank of India) attained the PE score of 1.0 in all the years in the range. The efficiency results also depict the negative values indicating profit inefficiency in the year 2009 after the global financial crisis of 2008.

Average Profit Efficiency

The efficiency scores are discussed in Table 7. The PE scores from 1995 to 2017 are shown by year in Table 7. Wide variations across public sector banks are suggested by profit efficiency scores. Particularly, in the first subperiod PSBs were inside the efficient profit frontier, except for 2004, when PSBs were profit inefficient. Profit efficiency of PSBs was greater than 100% in 1995, 1997, 1999, 2001, 2002 and

Table 4. Average cost efficiency from 1995 to 2017

Years	Cost Efficiency	
	Average	STDEV
1995	0.973524	0.045732
1996	0.943135	0.058869
1997	0.936965	0.062343
1998	0.940859	0.058275
1999	0.92371	0.074809
2000	0.92125	0.081264
2001	0.919341	0.069787
2002	0.908859	0.068654
2003	0.923209	0.067881
2004	0.921734	0.067022
2005	0.656557	0.197237
2006	0.934214	0.092313
2007	0.817076	0.119531
2008	0.794987	0.14441
2009	0.922103	0.188494
2010	0.842357	0.22155
2011	0.875601	0.255742
2012	0.41563	0.169325
2013	0.518423	0.215859
2014	0.893012	0.258994
2015	0.888364	0.257997
2016	0.867196	0.253407
2017	0.580235	0.373912
Average	0.839928	0.147974
Grand Mean		
Entire Period (1995-2017)	0.839928	0.147974
First Sub-Period (1995-2005)	0.931258	0.065464
Second Sub-Period (2005-2017)	0.769674	0.211444

2003. Furthermore, the impact of 1991 reforms were evident in the convergence of PSBs performance during the first subperiod came from a significant and consistent standard deviation in terms of PE. The second subperiod revealed notable variations across PSBs in PE scores. The global financial crisis of 2008 made banks profit inefficient during 2008-2011 and banks were situated inside the benchmark frontier. The performance of banks was very close to the benchmark as PSBs battled to reduce input

Table 5. Computation of profit efficiency scores from the year 1995 to 2004

DMU	1995	1996	1997	1998	1999	2000	2001	2002	2003	2004
B1	1.000	1.000	1.884	-16.380	1.540	-1.200	2.056	-1.001	2.431	-34.605
B2	1.000	1.000	1.000	1.000	1.000	1.000	1.000	2.418	1.347	0.467
B3	1.000	1.000	1.000	1.067	1.302	-2.683	1.498	4.652	1.856	6.994
B4	1.186	1.518	1.000	1.000	1.000	-2.649	1.000	1.000	1.000	1.000
B5	1.000	1.000	1.156	1.415	1.363	1.444	1.760	28.095	1.763	2.106
B6	1.000	1.810	1.506	18.892	1.490	-1.020	1.848	-3.588	1.450	3.442
B7	1.251	-6.955	1.000	-0.393	1.437	-1.098	2.111	-0.868	7.317	-9.680
B8	1.000	1.000	1.000	1.000	1.000	1.000	1.000	1.000	1.000	1.000
B9	1.000	4.687	1.000	1.000	1.000	1.000	1.450	2.863	1.543	1.000
B10	1.000	2.813	1.471	1.000	1.000	-0.736	1.000	-0.411	1.000	1.000
B11	1.000	3.573	1.561	-2.369	1.586	-1.090	1.918	-1.924	2.258	-97.401
B12	1.000	1.000	1.000	1.000	1.000	1.000	1.000	1.000	1.000	1.000
B13	1.160	-2.956	1.250	1.342	1.365	15.665	1.736	-2.006	1.652	1.000
B14	1.363	-1.160	1.831	-1.545	1.572	-1.163	1.841	-1.190	2.784	-8.490
B15	1.000	1.000	1.000	1.000	1.000	1.000	1.417	1.000	1.216	1.000
B16	1.000	1.000	1.000	1.000	1.000	1.000	1.000	1.000	1.000	1.000
B17	1.000	1.000	1.000	1.506	1.311	1.000	1.645	6.064	1.309	1.600
B18	1.000	1.000	1.000	1.000	1.000	1.000	1.000	1.000	1.000	1.000
B19	1.000	1.000	1.000	1.000	1.000	1.000	1.000	1.000	1.000	2.262
B20	1.000	1.000	1.263	1.000	1.000	1.000	1.000	1.000	1.000	1.019
B21	1.134	1.000	1.000	1.000	1.000	1.000	1.000	1.000	1.000	1.000
B22	1.000	1.000	1.000	1.000	1.000	1.000	1.000	1.369	1.000	1.000
B23	1.000	1.000	1.769	-1.710	1.660	-2.230	1.965	-1.016	2.940	-3.538
B24	1.000	-0.556	1.941	-0.423	1.000	-3.745	1.233	-0.482	3.508	-7.954
B25	1.000	-2.099	1.485	-0.863	1.526	-1.626	1.617	31.998	1.583	5.419
B26	1.000	1.000	1.000	1.000	1.000	1.000	1.000	1.000	1.000	1.000
B27	1.312	1.000	2.728	-0.460	1.598	-1.004	1.996	-2.598	2.198	3.466

resource waste and underutilization and, to a significant extent, succeeded in choosing the proper input mix in response to competing demands in the second half of the subperiod.

These results pointed to both a decline in market dominance in price fixing and an inconsistency in the quality of bank output as shown by changes in input prices. Standard deviations that were high and remained constant showed that the second-generation reforms brought about convergence. These results were consistent with research that show banks to be inefficient in making a profit (Maudos & Pastor, 2003). Fluctuations factor prices in the policy environment, the interbank fluctuations in the output-mix play a significant impact in the PSBs' ability to determine their input prices. This gives a lot of opportunities for increased profitability and productivity through careful credit management, investment selection, and investment mix. The findings are consistent with the study of Humphrey's (1998) which

Table 6. Computation of profit efficiency scores from the year 2005 to 2017

DMU	2005	2006	2007	2008	2009	2010	2011	2012	2013	2014	2015	2016	2017
B1	-5.843	-5.843	-5.843	-5.843	-5.843	-5.843	-5.843	-5.843	-5.843	-5.843	-5.843	-5.843	-5.843
B2	-5.843	-5.843	-5.843	-5.843	-5.843	-5.843	-5.843	1.000	1.000	0.794	1.000	1.000	0.734
B3	-2.494	-11.529	-1.949	1.000	1.000	0.536	1.000	1.000	1.000	1.000	1.000	1.000	1.000
B4	-13.767	-18.190	-7.244	-1.577	1.000	0.139	0.329	0.406	0.605	1.000	1.000	0.540	0.830
B5	1.703	1.000	-8.219	-1.048	1.000	-0.752	-0.118	0.084	0.338	0.285	1.000	1.000	0.199
B6	2.391	1.000	-4.600	19.325	-45.859	0.118	0.625	0.368	0.562	0.632	0.522	0.469	0.616
B7	-2.010	1.708	-2.542	-1.138	-3.704	-0.549	-0.040	-0.003	0.216	0.170	0.228	0.213	0.302
B8	1.000	1.000	1.000	1.000	1.000	1.000	1.000	1.000	1.000	1.000	1.000	1.000	1.000
B9	-8.117	1.000	-4.002	-1.498	-2.949	-0.771	0.206	0.176	0.313	0.507	0.345	0.282	0.572
B10	1.000	1.000	1.873	1.000	1.000	1.000	1.000	0.780	0.924	1.000	1.000	1.000	1.000
B11	-4.869	1.807	-5.478	-7.593	-13.812	-0.457	0.223	0.128	0.280	0.513	0.261	0.263	0.596
B12	1.000	1.000	1.000	1.000	1.000	1.000	1.000	1.000	1.000	1.000	1.000	1.000	0.601
B13	1.000	1.000	-3.415	-0.421	-10.261	-0.124	0.390	-0.094	0.148	0.247	0.413	0.591	0.597
B14	37.654	-1.392	-1.206	-0.492	-15.335	0.474	0.531	0.390	0.623	0.881	0.766	0.644	0.889
B15	1.000	1.981	1.000	1.554	1.000	-2.593	1.000	0.369	1.000	1.000	1.000	1.000	0
B16	1.000	1.000	1.000	1.000	1.000	-0.774	1.000	0.124	0.621	0.446	1.000	1.000	0
B17	1.000	1.000	1.000	1.000	1.000	1.000	1.000	1.000	1.000	1.000	1.000	1.000	1.000
B18	1.000	1.000	1.523	1.000	1.000	9.177	0	0	0	0	0	0	0
B19	1.000	1.000	1.000	1.000	-5.322	-0.013	1.000	0.216	1.000	0.437	0.447	0.445	0
B20	1.000	1.000	1.000	1.000	1.000	5.622	0.012	-0.001	-0.042	0.341	1.000	0.492	0
B21	1.956	2.462	-4.631	-10.188	0	0	0	0	0	0	0	0	0
B22	1.000	1.000	1.685	1.000	1.000	-2.158	1.000	-0.180	-0.304	-0.489	0.142	1.000	0
B23	13.462	-6.788	-10.461	1.000	6.905	-1.931	1.000	-0.082	0.159	1.000	0.323	0.102	0.484
B24	-9.529	4.888	-23.116	-7.456	-61.803	-2.567	-0.035	-0.040	0.110	0.410	0.533	1.000	0.442
B25	1.000	14.131	-24.553	-3.892	-1.592	0.130	0.573	0.330	0.509	0.417	1.000	1.000	0.748
B26	-0.573	-0.919	-0.264	-0.767	-2.406	1.000	0.325	0.166	0.212	1.000	1.000	0.207	1.000
B27	3.428	1.636	5.797	1.000	5.277	-2.709	1.000	0.040	0.063	-0.119	1.000	0.327	0.327

found that (Cost) X-inefficiency is a significant issue for underperformance of financial institutions. The lower profit efficiency is the reflection of inefficiency among PSBs in India.

COMPARISON OF COST AND PROFIT EFFICIENCY

The efficiencies of PSBs for the entire period (1995 to 2017) is divided into two subperiods 1995 to 2004 (the period following the liberalization and globalization reforms) and 2005 to 2017 (the period following the social control norms in 2005 till the major merger of SBI in 2017). The analysis also

Table 7. Average profit scores from 1995 to 2017

Years	Profit Efficiency	
	Average	STDEV
1995	1.052116	0.106927
1996	0.654617	2.119865
1997	1.290545	0.431345
1998	0.521411	5.004949
1999	1.212886	0.254964
2000	0.365339	3.399725
2001	1.410815	0.419761
2002	2.680589	8.170099
2003	1.783569	1.307785
2004	-1.98831	20.51905
2005	0.72402	8.922474
2006	-0.32934	5.661657
2007	3.352322	37.51186
2008	-0.55103	5.14506
2009	-5.5758	14.97337
2010	-0.21811	2.906925
2011	0.086449	1.76028
2012	0.086392	1.247211
2013	0.240496	1.281369
2014	0.319589	1.300667
2015	0.449491	1.30924
2016	0.397496	1.300129
2017	0.262754	1.275583
Grand Mean		
Entire Period (1995-2017)	0.357753	5.492621
First Sub-Period (1995-2005)	0.898358	4.173447
Second Sub-Period (2005-2017)	-0.0581	6.507371

reveals that PE is less than CE scores in both the subperiods, but PE is much lower in the second sub period as depicted in figures 3 and 4.

Hypotheses Testing

The two non-parametric hypothesis testing tools viz. Wilcoxon Signed rank test and Friedman Annova were applied to verify the hypotheses. Friedman's tests show changes in the distribution of the two specified

Figure 3. Graphical comparison of profit and cost efficiency from 1995 to 2004

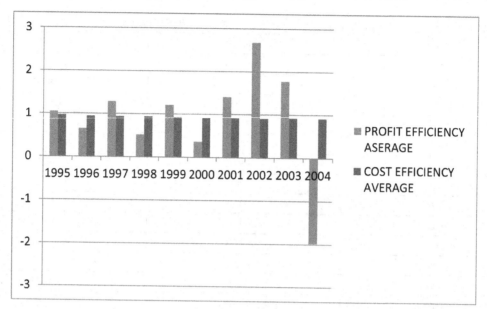

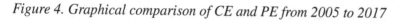

Figure 4. Graphical comparison of CE and PE from 2005 to 2017

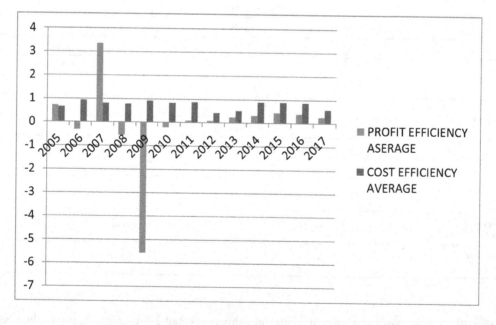

periods, whereas Wilcoxon's tests record the difference in medians between the two periods. In addition, the median efficiency score from 1995 to 2004 is identical to the median efficiency score from 2005 to 2017 (i.e., 0). The distribution of efficiency values from 1995 to 2004 is also identical to the distribution of efficiency values from 2004 to2017. The results of both the non-parametric hypothesis testing is 00, which rejects null hypothesis i.e. the cost and profit efficiency of banks in two sub periods is similar.

CONCLUSION

Most of the available literature on the efficiency of banks studied technological efficiency of banks and rejected the notion of potential inefficiencies on the cost and revenue sides. The research that is currently available on profit efficiency points to a higher level of inefficiency in profit than in cost. In the context of this chapter, profit as well as cost-effectiveness were examined using a non-parametric framework from 1995 to 2017 of PSBs in India. The period was further divided into two sub periods from 1995-2004 and 2005 -2017. The results show the substantial inefficiency of PSBs over costs and profits. The PE is inferior to CE in the selected time and there are significant differences in the distribution and median of the CE and PE in the two sub periods i.e., from 1995 to 2004 and 2005 to 2017 rejected the null hypothesis. The results also show that wide variations were witnessed across Public Sector Banks from 1995 to 2017. Moreover, the PE is declining for PSBs in comparison to the CE. PSBs should run efficiently so that they are not a drag on the government's budgetary resources. They should deliver value to the government which provides them with their capital. Banks should raise their return on assets, widen net interest margins, improve the quality of their assets by reducing their NPAs and reduce the cost of deposits to increase their profit efficiency. Additionally, the inefficiency in banks needs to be identified which could relate to lack of technological and managerial knowledge, employment of untrained employees, and underdeveloped socioeconomic environment etc. Banks should rejuvenate the banking models with the period of change to enhance the profit efficiency and reduce costs. Consequently, the government can utilize these assets to fund its social objectives. It can also use some of that money to incentivize the banks to be socially responsible without impacting their profits. The future research can be carried out combining the parametric and non -parametric approach. In this context future studies shall be performed by analyzing the interaction between profitability and Efficiency of banks.

REFERENCES

Andersen, P., & Petersen, N. C. (1993). A procedure for ranking efficient units in data envelopment analysis. *Management Science*, *39*(10), 1261–1265. doi:10.1287/mnsc.39.10.1261

Arbelo, A., Arbelo-Pérez, M., & Pérez-Gómez, P. (2020). Profit efficiency as a measure of performance and frontier models: a resource-based view. *BRQ Business Research Quarterly*.

Ariff, M., & Can, L. (2009). IMF bank-restructuring efficiency outcomes: Evidence from East Asia. *Journal of Financial Services Research*, *35*(2), 167–187. doi:10.100710693-008-0047-2

Athanassoglou, S. (2016). Revisiting worst-case DEA for composite indicators. *Social Indicators Research*, *128*(3), 1259–1272. doi:10.100711205-015-1078-3

Avkiran, N. K. (1999a). An Application Reference for Data Envelopment Analysis: Helping the Novice Researcher. *International Journal of Bank Marketing*, *17*(5), 206–220. doi:10.1108/02652329910292675

Avkiran, N. K. (2006). Productivity Analysis in the Services Sector with Data Envelopment Analysis (3rd ed.). University of Queensland Business School, The University of Queensland. doi:10.2139srn.2627576

Banker, R. D. (1984). Estimating Most Productive Scale Size using Data Envelopment Analysis. *European Journal of Operational Research*, *17*(1), 35–44. doi:10.1016/0377-2217(84)90006-7

Berger, A., & Humphrey, D. (1997). Efficiency of Financial Institutions: International Survey and Directions for Future Research. *European Journal of Operational Research, 98*(2), 175–212. doi:10.1016/S0377-2217(96)00342-6

Berger, A., Hunter, W., & Timme, S. (1993). The efficiency of financial institutions: A review and preview of research past, present and future. *Journal of Banking & Finance, 17*(2–3), 221–249. doi:10.1016/0378-4266(93)90030-H

Berger, A., & Mester, L. (1997). Inside the black box: What explains differences in the efficiency of financial institutions? *Journal of Banking & Finance, 21*(7), 895–947. doi:10.1016/S0378-4266(97)00010-1

Berger, A. N., & Humphrey, D. B. (1997). Efficiency of financial institutions: International survey and directions for future research. *European Journal of Operational Research, 98*(2), 175–212. doi:10.1016/S0377-2217(96)00342-6

Bhanawat, S. S., & Kothari, S. (2013). Impact of banking sector reforms on profitability of banking industry in India. *Pacific Business Review International, 6*, 60–65.

Casu, B., & Girardone, C. (2002). A Comparative Study of the Cost Efficiency of Italian Bank Conglomerates. *Managerial Finance, 28*(9), 3–23. doi:10.1108/03074350210768031

Casu, B., & Girardone, C. (2002). A comparative study of the cost efficiency of Italian bank conglomerates. *Managerial Finance, 28*(2), 3–23. doi:10.1108/03074350210768031

Casu, B., & Molyneux, P. (2001). *Efficiency in European banking.* John Wiley & Sons Ltd.

Charnes, A., Cooper, W. W., Lewin, A. Y., & Seiford, L. M. (1994). *Data Envelopment Analysis: Theory, Methodology and Applications.* Kluwer Academic Publishers. doi:10.1007/978-94-011-0637-5

Charnes, A., Cooper, W. W., & Rhodes, E. (1978). Measuring the efficiency of decision making units. *European Journal of Operational Research, 2*(6), 429–444. doi:10.1016/0377-2217(78)90138-8

Chatterjee, B., & Sinha, R. P. (2006). Cost efficiency and commercial bank lending: Some empirical results. *The Indian Economic Journal, 54*(1), 145–165. doi:10.1177/0019466220060109

Cherchye, L., Moesen, W., & Van Puyenbroeck, T. (2004). Legitimately diverse, yet comparable: On synthesizing social inclusion performance in the EU. *Journal of Common Market Studies, 42*(5), 919–955. doi:10.1111/j.0021-9886.2004.00535.x

Coelli, T. J., Prasada Rao, D. S., O'Donnell, C. J., & Battese, G. E. (2005). An Introduction to Efficiency and Productivity Analysis (2nd ed.). Springer Science + Business Media.

Cooper, W. W., Seiford, L. M., & Tone, K. (2007). Data Envelopment Analysis: A Comprehensive Text with Models, Applications, References and DEA-Solver Software (2nd ed.). Springer Science + Business Media.

Das, A. (1997a). Measurement of productive efficiency and its decomposition in Indian banking firms. *The Asian Economic Review, 39*(3), 422–439.

Das, A. (2000). Efficiency of Public Sector Banks: An Application of Data Envelopment Analysis Model. Prajnan. *Journal of Social and Management Sciences, 28*(1), 119–131.

Das, A., & Ghosh, S. (2009). Financial deregulation and profit efficiency: A nonparametric analysis of Indian banks. *Journal of Economics and Business, 61*(6), 509–528. doi:10.1016/j.jeconbus.2009.07.003

Das, A., Nag, A., & Ray, S. C. (2005). Liberalization, ownership and efficiency in Indian banking: A non-parametric analysis. *Economic and Political Weekly, 40*(12), 1190–1197.

Debasish, S. S. (2006). Efficiency performance in Indian banking-use of data envelopment analysis. *Global Business Review, 7*(2), 325–333. doi:10.1177/097215090600700209

Gazi, M. A. I., Alam, M. S., Hossain, G. M. A., Islam, S. M. N., Rahman, M. K., Nahiduzzaman, M., & Hossain, A. I. (2021). Determinants of Profitability in Banking Sector: Empirical Evidence from Bangladesh. *Universal Journal of Accounting and Finance, 9*(6), 1377–1386. doi:10.13189/ujaf.2021.090616

Gupta, V. (2021). Composite Non-Paramertric CSR index for public sector banks of India. *PalArch's Journal of Archaeology of Egypt/Egyptology, 18*(8), 1589-1607.

Humphrey, D. B. (1985). Costs and Scale Economies in Bank Intermediation. In R. C. Aspinwall & R. A. Eisenbeis (Eds.), *Handbook for Banking Strategy* (pp. 745–783). John Wiley and Sons.

Isik, I., & Hassan, M. K. (2002). Technical, scale and allocative efficiencies of Turkish banking industry. *Journal of Banking & Finance, 26*(4), 719–766. doi:10.1016/S0378-4266(01)00167-4

Jayaraman, A. R., & Srinivasan, M. R. (2019). Determinants of Indian banks efficiency: A two-stage approach. *International Journal of Operational Research, 36*(2), 270–291. doi:10.1504/IJOR.2019.102414

Kamaruddin, B. H., Safab, M. S., & Mohd, R. (2008). Assessing production efficiency of Islamic banks and conventional bank Islamic windows in Malaysia. *International Journal of Business and Management Science, 1*(1), 31–48.

Kamaruddin, F., Sufian, F., Nassir, A. M., Anwar, N. A. M., & Hussain, H. I. (2019). Bank efficiency in Malaysia a DEA approach. *Journal of Central Banking Theory and Practice.*

Kumar, S. (2008). An analysis of efficiency-profitability relationship in Indian public sector banks. *Global Business Review, 9*(1), 115–129. doi:10.1177/097215090700900108

Kumar, S., & Gulati, R. (2008). Evaluation of technical efficiency and ranking of public sector banks in India: An analysis from cross-sectional perspective. *International Journal of Productivity and Performance Management, 57*(7), 540–568. doi:10.1108/17410400810904029

Kumar, S., & Gulati, R. (2009). Did Efficiency of Indian public sector banks converge with banking reforms? *International Review of Economics, 56*(1), 47–84. doi:10.100712232-008-0057-2

Kumar, S., & Gulati, R. (2010). Measuring efficiency, effectiveness and performance of Indian public sector banks. *International Journal of Productivity and Performance Management.*

Kumar, S., & Gulati, R. (2014). *Deregulation and efficiency of Indian banks.* Academic Press.

Kumar, S., & Gulati, R. (2016). Assessing the impact of the global financial crisis on the profit efficiency of Indian banks. *Economic Modelling, 58,* 167–181. doi:10.1016/j.econmod.2016.05.029

Kumar, S., & Verma, S. (2003). Technical efficiency, benchmarks and targets: A case study of Indian public sector banks. *Prajnan: Journal of Social and Management Sciences, 31*(4), 275–300.

Maudos, J., & Pastor, J. M. (2003). Cost and profit efficiency in the Spanish banking sector (1985–1996): A non-parametric approach. *Applied Financial Economics, 13*(1), 1–12. doi:10.1080/09603100110086087

Maudos, J., Pastor, J. M., Perez, F., & Quesada, J. (2002). Cost and profit efficiency in European banks. *Journal of International Financial Markets, Institutions and Money, 12*(1), 33–58. doi:10.1016/S1042-4431(01)00051-8

Mester, I. J., Nakamura, I. I., & Renault, M. (1998). *Checking accounts and bank monitoring*. Working Paper No. 98-125, Federal Reserve Bank of Philadelphia.

Mistry, D., Savani, V., & Vidyanagar, V. 2015. A Comparative Study of the Profitability Performance in the Banking Sector Evidence from Indian Private Sector Bank. *XVI Annual Conference Proceedings*, 346–60.

Pasiouras, F., Sifodaskalakis, E., & Zopounidis, C. (2007). *Estimating and analyzing the cost efficiency of Greek cooperative banks: an application of two-stage data envelopment analysis*. Working Paper Series 2007.12, University of Bath, School of Management, Bath, UK.

Puyenbroeck, T. (2018). On the output orientation of the benefit-of-the-doubt-model. *Social Indicators Research, 139*(2), 415–431. doi:10.100711205-017-1734-x

Ray, S. C. (2004). *Data Envelopment Analysis: Theory and Techniques for Economics and Operations Research*. Cambridge University Press. doi:10.1017/CBO9780511606731

Ray, S. C., & Das, A. (2010). Distribution of cost and profit efficiency: Evidence from Indian banking. *European Journal of Operational Research, 201*(1), 297–307. doi:10.1016/j.ejor.2009.02.030

Sealey, C. W. Jr, & Lindley, J. T. (1977). Inputs, Outputs, and a Theory of Production and Cost at Depository Financial Institutions. *The Journal of Finance, 32*(4), 1251–1266. doi:10.1111/j.1540-6261.1977.tb03324.x

Seiford, L. M., & Thrall, R. M. (1990). Recent developments in DEA: The mathematical programming approach to frontier analysis. *Journal of Econometrics, 46*(1–2), 7–38. doi:10.1016/0304-4076(90)90045-U

Semih Yildirim, H., & Philippatos, G. C. (2007). Efficiency of banks: Recent evidence from the transition economies of Europe, 1993–2000. *European Journal of Finance, 13*(2), 123–143. doi:10.1080/13518470600763687

Sensarma, R. (2005). Cost and profit efficiency of Indian banks during 1986–2003: A stochastic frontier analysis. *Economic and Political Weekly, 40*(12), 1198–1208.

Siems, T. F., & Clark, J. A. (1997). Rethinking Bank Efficiency and Regulation: How Off-balance Sheet Activities Make a Difference. *Financial Industry Studies, 3*(2), 1–11.

Singh, S., & Das, S. (2018). Impact of post-merger and acquisition activities on the financial performance of banks: A study of Indian private sector and public sector banks. *Revista Espacios Magazine, 39*, 25.

Soni, R. (2012). Managerial efficiency-Key driver towards the profitability of Indian commercial banks in turbulent time. *International Journal of Applied Research and Studies, 1*.

Srivastava, A., & Jain, V. (2006). Efficiency of banks in India: A DEA approach. *Review of Professional Management, 4*(2), 31–38.

Sufian, F. (2006). The Efficiency of Non-Bank Financial Institutions: Empirical Evidence from Malaysia. *International Research Journal of Finance and Economics, 1*(6), 49–65.

Sufian, F., & Majid, M. A. (2007a). Singapore Banking Efficiency and its Relation to Stock Returns: A DEA Window Analysis Approach. *International Journal of Business Studies, 15*(1), 83–106.

Sufian, F., & Majid, M. A. (2007b). Deregulation, consolidation and banks efficiency in Singapore: Evidence from event study window approach and Tobit analysis. *International Review of Economics, 54*(2), 261–283. doi:10.100712232-007-0017-2

Sun, H., Rabbani, M. R., Ahmad, N., Sial, M. S., Cheng, G., Zia-Ud-Din, M., & Fu, Q. (2020). CSR, co-creation and green consumer loyalty: Are green banking initiatives important? A moderated mediation approach from an emerging economy. *Sustainability (Basel), 12*(24), 10688. doi:10.3390u122410688

Sun, S. (2002). Measuring the relative efficiency of police precincts using data envelopment analysis. *Socio-Economic Planning Sciences, 36*(1), 51–71. doi:10.1016/S0038-0121(01)00010-6

Thaker, K., Charles, V., Pant, A., & Gherman, T. (2022). A DEA and random forest regression approach to studying bank efficiency and corporate governance. *The Journal of the Operational Research Society, 73*(6), 1258–1277. doi:10.1080/01605682.2021.1907239

Thanassoulis, E., Witte, K. D., Johnes, J., Karagiannis, J. G., & Portela, C. S. (2016). Applications of data envelopment analysis in education, In Data Envelopment Analysis: A Handbook of Empirical Studies and Application. Springer Science and Business Media.

Thumma, C. (2020). Impact of Operating efficiency of public sector banks on its profitability in India. *Indian Journal of Commerce and Management Studies, 8*, 54–62.

Tofallis, C. (2001). Combining two approaches to efficiency assessment. *The Journal of the Operational Research Society, 52*(11), 1225–1231. doi:10.1057/palgrave.jors.2601231

Wank, P. F., Barros, C., & Emrouznejad, A. (2015). Assessing Productive Efficiency of Banks Using integrated Fuzzy-DEA and bootstrapping: A Case of Mozambican Banks. *European Journal of Operational Research, 249*(1), 378–389. doi:10.1016/j.ejor.2015.10.018

Widiarto, I., & Emrouznejad, A. (2015). Social and financial efficiency of Islamic microfinance institutions: A Data Envelopment Analysis application. *Socio-Economic Planning Sciences, 50*(1), 1–17. doi:10.1016/j.seps.2014.12.001

Zhu, J. (2003). *Quantitative Models for Performance Evaluation and Benchmarking: Data Envelopment Analysis with Spreadsheets and DEA Excel Solver*. Kluwer Academic Publishers. doi:10.1007/978-1-4757-4246-6

ADDITIONAL READING

Chattopadhyay, S. K. (2019). Post-reform Development of Banking Sector in India. *Indian Economy: Reforms and Development: Essays in Honour of Manoj Kumar Sanyal*, 209-251.

Joshi, P. V., & Bhalerao, M. J. (2011). Efficiency evaluation of banking sector in India based on data envelopment analysis. *Indian Journal of Commerce and Management Studies*, 2(3), 31–42.

Rajput, N., & Gupta, M. (2011). Efficiency of public sector banks operating in India: Post-reforms period analysis. *Afro-Asian Journal of Finance and Accounting*, 2(4), 349–368. doi:10.1504/AAJFA.2011.043869

Singh, O., & Bansal, S. (2017). An analysis of revenue maximising efficiency of public sector banks in the post-reforms period. *Journal of Central Banking Theory and Practice*, 6(1), 111–125. doi:10.1515/jcbtp-2017-0006

Tanwar, J., Seth, H., Vaish, A. K., & Rao, N. V. M. (2020). Revisiting the efficiency of Indian banking sector: An analysis of comparative models through data envelopment analysis. *Indian Journal of Finance and Banking*, 4(1), 92–108. doi:10.46281/ijfb.v4i1.585

KEY TERMS AND DEFINITIONS

Conventional Microeconomic Theory: A conventional premise of microeconomic theory reveals that demand and supply of commodities are adjusted through quantities.

Cost Efficiency: This term states the closeness of banks' costs to the best practice frontier with given outputs.

Data Envelopment Analysis: DEA states the non-parametric frontier method of linear programming.

Friedman's Tests: These tests show changes in the distribution between the two periods.

Intermediation approach: This approach specified DMU as a producer of assets which utilizes deposits of customers in producing assets of banks.

Production Approach: This approach states that the deposits and loans (number of accounts) of banks were considered as an output and the physical capital and its cost as inputs of banks.

Profit Efficiency: This term states the closeness of banks' profit to the standard frontier (bank) under prevailing conditions.

Public Sector Banks: These are the banks in which the majority of stake is held by the government of India.

Wilcoxon's Tests: These tests show the differences in medians between the two periods.

Chapter 14
Impact of Mergers and Acquisitions on Shareholder Wealth in Indian Banks:
A Data Envelopment Analysis Approach

Trilochan Jena
Birla Global University, India

Pradipta Kumar Sanyal
iD https://orcid.org/0000-0002-4459-3894
Birla Global University, India

- Sreekumar
iD https://orcid.org/0000-0002-6534-896X
Rourkela Institute of Management Studies, India

ABSTRACT

In today's changing business environment characterized by complexity and volatility, the Indian banking sector is witnessing tough competition from national and multinational players. In this study, the authors studied the Indian bank mergers between 2006 and 2018 to measure the impact of mergers and acquisitions (M&A) on efficiency in financial performance. A sample of four Indian banks—State Bank of India, Bank of Baroda, HDFC Bank, and Kotak Mahindra Bank—was selected based on market capitalization. This chapter evaluated five years of pre- and post-merger financial efficiency to measure the impact of M&A on efficiency in financial performance. The authors considered seven critical variables impacting the performance of Indian banks for the study. The non-parametric technique data envelopment analysis (DEA) is used for efficiency measurement over the period. The study shows that mergers and acquisitions positively impact the enhancement of financial efficiency.

DOI: 10.4018/979-8-3693-0255-2.ch014

INTRODUCTION

All the business houses accommodate operations with changes which are only constant in today's economic scenario. The objectives of profit maximization or cost minimization have become direct proportional to the growth of the business. The competitive global world has adopted Merger and Acquisition (M&A) as a corporate strategy to survive and experience growth. Inorganic growth, expansion, diversification and restructuring of corporate sectors are the outcomes of M&A. Synergistic impact originated by M&A increases efficiencies to achieve the target strategy. In recent times, M&A has become an important instrument all over the world to lift the financial and economic status of a nation providing synergy to companies to face the challenges of increased worldwide competition and rapid growth of markets (Distler, 2018). Synergy to experience growth in term of sales, expansions in operations, enhancement of market share, reduction of cut-throat competition and overall cost of production, wealth, and profit maximization lead to consolidation of business resulted through mergers and acquisitions which have been taking momentum since 1991 in India. There are multiple reasons, motives, economic forces, and institutional factors that can be taken together or in isolation, which influence corporate decisions to engage in M&A (Khemani, 1991). Mergers and Acquisitions in banking sectors in India have rapidly taken momentum as it is witnessed in 2017 when State Bank of India acquired most of the public sector banks which subsequently forced other public sectors banks Like Punjab National Bank and Bank of Baroda to adopt the same strategy to face the challenges. Mergers and acquisitions help the banks to achieve significant growth in their day-to-day operations, help in minimizing their expenses to a considerable extent and reduces its competition as merger eliminates competitors from the banking industry. The main objectives of instigating the Banks through mergers and acquisitions is to plan for gaining 'cost efficiency' by improving performance to result in maximizing profit by eliminating tough competition.

Indian Banking system started its journey in 1770 when Bank of Hindustan started its operation to help colonial government for effecting fund transfer. Subsequently, Bank of Bombay in 1840, Bank of Calcutta in 1840 and Bank of Madras in 1843 got established under the charter of British East India company. First bank mergers took place in India in 1921 when all these four banks merged and formulated Imperial Bank of India. The concept of nationalization of bank came in 1955 when Imperial Bank of India was nationalized on 1st July 1955 with the name of State Bank of India along with its 8 associate banks. Government of India nationalized 14 banks on 19th July 1969 and 6 banks on 15th April 1980. The year 1991 is reckoned as the year of industrial development in India when Indian Government initiated the liberalization policy and started issuing licenses to private banks which resulted massive growth in Indian banking sector. Mergers and Acquisitions in banking sectors in India taken the momentum with the recommendation of Narasimha Committee in 1988 for Mergers among the strong banks (Rajamani & Ramkrishnan, 2015). Reserve Bank of India (RBI) always plays the role to protect the interest of depositors and rescue the banks from liquidation with preventive measures to abstain banks from unfair practices. To achieve this, RBI recommends forced or hostile mergers to merge weak banks with strong banks. On the contrary, friendly, or voluntary mergers are also recommended by the RBI to have synergistical impact on market dynamics, business diversification, economies of scale, strong credit rating, minimization of costs and enhancement of efficiency effectively (Madan Lal Singla, 2015).

In most of the studies it is found that the primary objective of M&A is to generate synergy, the general meaning of which is efficiency. Curiosity emerges in the mind of researchers to know whether M&A has been maximizing efficiency for the business to achieve the most desired objectives. A KPMG survey in London found that 53% of mergers and acquisitions destroy shareholder value (Brewis, 2000).

In this paper we have tried to use the Data Envelopment Analysis (DEA) as a technique to measure and analyze the impact of mergers and acquisitions in maximizing efficiency to create value for the business and wealth for the shareholders. We found in most of the studies, researchers have used Event Study Methodology to assess the impact of mergers and acquisitions for value creation examining the returns to shareholders in the period close to announcement of merger. There are four techniques used to measure the impact of mergers and acquisitions on the growth of business and shareholders wealth (Bruner, 2002). These four techniques are event study, accounting study, clinical study, and survey of executives. Event study is ex-Ante study used to assess the shareholders return comparing AAR (Average Abnormal Return) with AR (Average Return) that arises on market price volatility of shares close to the period of mergers announcement. An accounting study, which is also called ex-post study used to assess the impact of mergers and acquisitions on value creation by examining the financial performance of acquiring firm before and after the acquisition. In the survey of executives, information collected from the sample of executives through a standard questionnaire and analysis is based on their opinion about mergers. Clinical study is in-depth analysis and inductive research which examines the effectiveness of mergers analyzing information deriving from field interview and knowledgeable observers. In this paper, we have studied the impact of M&A on value creation for growth of business and shareholders wealth analyzing the financial performance by using DEA as a methodology. The objectives of this study include measuring the efficiency in long term financial performance of acquiring banks under merger in Indian banking industry and evaluating and comparing the pre-merger and post-merger financial efficiency of acquiring banks.

OVERVIEW OF MERGER AND ACQUISITION IN INDIA

Second World War put the platform for Merger and Acquisition deals to become effective for transformation of industrial sector in India. Inflationary situation which was witnessed during war period motivated many Indian businessmen to accumulate income by earning high profit, dividend, and black money (Kothari, 1967). There was hectic activity in stock exchange caused by huge infiltration of businessmen into the market. Craziness to acquire control over the management of established and reputed companies, adopting the practices of acquiring shares in the open market and swapping the managing agency right became a common issue in the post second world war period. Adopting the practices of acquiring shares and managing agency rights, large numbers of business houses passed on to the hands of prominent industrial houses in the country (Kothari, 1967). In the event of independence, most of the British managing agency houses and individual industrial undertaking transferred their ownership at a very lucrative price to Indian businessmen. During that time, prominent Indian business houses acquired the control over insurance companies to utilize their fund to acquire the substantial holdings in other companies. Most of the British corporates are taken by the Indian companies having huge cash flow with cash payment as free cash flow generates more profit since profit cannot be profitably re-invested in the business (Jensen, 1986; Ghosh, 2001). Besides, prominent business houses started banks and investment companies to accelerate the motive to acquire control over the established business in the country.

Early post-war period is known to be the genesis of Mergers and Acquisitions as many mergers took place in the industries of jute, sugar, textiles, banking, insurance, electricity, and tea plantation. However, anti-government policies of the 1960s and 1970s actively became a deterrent for mergers and acquisitions. The restriction was imposed mostly for horizontal and vertical combinations to neutralize the concentration of economic power for the common interest of the people whereas conglomerate combinations were freely undertaken. Even the government encouraged mergers of sick industrial units. Formation of Life Insurance Corporation and Nationalization of life Insurance Business in 1956 is the outcome of the mergers of 243 insurance companies and similar development in the General Insurance Business and National Textiles Corporation has been witnessed through M&A (Kar, 2004). Many researchers have found in their studies that vertical and horizontal mergers generate more profit and perform better than unrelated conglomerate mergers (Moeller Schlingemann & Stulz, 1980; Sudarsanam, 2003).

The importance of M&As has undergone a sea change when Indian economy became liberalized in 1991. The Indian laws governing M&As were amended which provided the way for the large business and foreign companies to adopt M&As as a growth strategy. M&As as a growth strategy has been adopted by several prominent business houses like Manu Chhabria, Vijay Mallya, and R.P. Goenka Group for growth and expansion in eighties. Mallya's United Breweries (UB) is the outcome of M&As. RPG group is resulted by taking over the business of Dunlop, Ceat, Philips Carbon Black and Gramophone India. Hindustan Lever Limited (HLL) adopted M&As as a growth strategy in the post liberalization period. Ajay Piramal group is entirely resulted by M&As deals. Murugappa group in southern part of India is built by M&As acquiring EID Parry, Coromandel Fertilizer, Sterling Abrasive etc. Some other companies whose growth has been witnessed through M&As are Ranbaxy Laboratory Ltd, Sun pharmaceuticals Company, Reliance Group, Tata group, Birla group and many more. During this decade, there have been mergers and acquisitions massively taking place in sector of Indian industry including banking sector in India.

Evolution of Mergers and Acquisitions in Indian Banking Industry

The year 1921 is the earmark for M&A in Indian banking industry when Bank of Hindustan, Bank of Bombay, Bank of Calcutta and Bank of Madras merged and formulated Imperial Bank of India. Subsequently on 1st July 1955, Imperial bank of India was nationalized and renamed as State Bank of India with its eight associate banks. Operational and distributional efficiency of commercial banks in India have always been an issue and government of India in consultation with RBI appointed several committees to bring suggestion on structural change. In this regard, some important committees formed are Banking Commissions in 1972 under the chairmanship of R.G. Saraiya, in 1976 under the chairmanship of Manubhai Shah and in 1978 under the chairmanship of James S. Raj. All these three committees emphasized on restructuring of Indian banking system to improve credit delivery and recommended that there would be three to four large banks at all India level and other should operate in regional level. Narasimha Committee's recommendation in 1988 opened a space to adopt M&A as a tool for growth and development by the Indian banking industry when the committee suggested that strong banks should go for mergers, both in the public and private sectors and even with financial institution and NBFCs (Rajamani & Ramakrishnan, 2015).

The growth of banking sector in India is witnessed from the year 1991 when economic policy was reformed, and government of India framed liberalized policy for industrial growth. During pre-reform period, government adopted the route of forced merger u/s 45(1) of Banking Regulation Act,1949. Under this scheme, weak banks are pointed out on the basis of NPA and bad loans. Strong banks are asked to prepare scheme of merger and weak banks get merged with a strong bank with settlement of claims to different parties who do not want to continue with a strong bank after merger. All most all bank mergers taken place during pre-reform period fall in the category of forced merger and thirteen (13) bank mergers in India are forced mergers out of the bank mergers taken place during post-reform period (Source: RBI publication).

Indian banking industry is at cut-throat competition. Emergence of many private banks and penetration of foreign banks into Indian market, massive bank mergers are witnessed during the last decade. Voluntary mergers are taking place in Indian banking industry to achieve the objective of expansion, diversification and synergistical impact on overall growth. Recently voluntary mergers are adopted as growth strategy as it is evidenced from the study that forced mergers have destroyed wealth of acquiring banks (Chong et al., 2006). In post-reform period, first forced merger took place in 1993 when Punjab National Bank taken up the New Bank of India, followed by Bank of Karad with Bank of India (1994), Kashinath Seth Bank with SBI (1995), Punjab Co-operative bank with Oriental Bank of Commerce (1996), Bari Doab Bank Ltd with Oriental Bank of Commerce (1997), Bareilly Corp Bank Ltd with Bank of Baroda (1999) and Sikkim Bank Ltd with Bank of India (1999), Banaras State Bank Ltd with Bank of Baroda (2002), Nedungadi Bank Ltd with Punjab National Bank (2003), South Gujarat Local area Bank with Bank of Baroda (2004), Global Trust Bank with oriental Bank of Commerce (2004), Ganesh Bank of Kurandwad with Federal Bank (2006), United western Bank with Industrial development Bank of India (2006). (Source: RBI publication).

Voluntary Bank mergers in India taken its momentum from the year 2000 when HDFC Bank Ltd acquired Times Bank Ltd followed by Bank of Madura with ICICI bank (2001), ICICI Ltd with ICICI bank (2002), IDBI with IDBI Bank Ltd (2004), Centurion Bank with Bank of Punjab (2005), Lord Krishna Bank with Centurion Bank (2006), Sangli Bank with ICICI bank (2006), Bharat Overseas Bank with Indian Overseas Bank (2007). (Source: RBI Publication). Besides, many voluntary bank mergers are taken place in 2017 when SBI taken over most of the public sector banks which puts the challenge for other banks to adopt the strategy of M&A to ensure survival and growth.

Legal Framework for Merger and Acquisition in India

Both acquirer and target firms design their structure and carry out the M&A transaction on mutual understanding. However, for the enforcement of transactions of M&A in the court of law, each of the parties must ensure that certain predefined rules and regulations are followed. The legal framework plays the vital role to ensure that the interest of different interested parties is not badly affected due to M&A deal. Before 1991, Indian market for M&A was not much opened, as a result very few numbers of mergers and acquisitions deals were announced by Indian business houses. There are various laws which were controlling M&A activities before economic reforms are Companies Act,1956, Income Tax Act,1961, Monopolies and Restrictive Trade practice Act, 1969, Sick Industrial Companies (Special Provisions) Act, 1985 and Industrial (Development and Regulation) Act, 1951. Government liberalized many legal provisions after economic reforms to promote M&A activities. Details guidelines have been framed by RBI which need to be complied by foreign companies to make investment in India through M&A by Foreign Direct Investment (FDI). Securities and Exchange Board of India (SEBI) is established in 1992 to act as nodal authority for regulating M&A activities of listed companies. SEBI (Substantial Acquisition of Shares and Takeovers) Regulation, 2011 is framed to regulate acquisition of shares and voting rights in listed companies.

Recent developments are the adoption of IFRS (International Financial Reporting Standards) by the companies. IFRS is globally accepted as a financial reporting framework for companies which compels the companies to disclose all material financial information to the public. This improves transparency and accounting quality of both acquiring and acquired firms. IFRS reduces overvaluation of acquiring and acquired firms which results in a reduction of risk for both firms under merger. Cash-offer and stock-offer deals are properly evaluated computing swap ratio by the adoption of IFRS by the companies. Adoption of IFRS is a significant event to make M&A activities more transparent to protect the interest of shareholders and public having interest in the business consolidation.

Activities of Mergers and acquisitions of Indian banking entities are governed by the Banking Regulation Act, 1949. Section 44A specifies that approval of two-thirds of the shareholders of both acquiring and acquired bank is necessary for banks to merge. After getting the approval from the shareholders of both banks, the scheme of merger is sent to RBI for approval. Section 45 empowers the RBI to apply to the Central Government for suspension of operating activities of banking company and for passing an order of moratorium. During moratorium period, RBI must ensure that the interest of the public, depositors, and interest of whole banking system, is not getting affected and thereafter RBI prepares a scheme for the reconstruction of the banking system by way of mergers and acquisitions. Section 234 of Companies Act,2013 states that RBI permission is mandatory for the banks going voluntary mergers with NBFC. After RBI approval, M&A deals materialized after such plan is approved by the National Company Law Tribunal. Besides, the Competition Act, 2002 also regulates M&A activities taking place in the banking sector to restrict anti-competitive practices. However, mergers of nationalized banks in 2017 did not comply with the requirement of law as government was to ensure quick consolidation of Public Sectors Banks.

Impact of Merger and Acquisition on Indian Economy

Mergers and Acquisitions (M&As) are accepted universally as a tool for the overall growth and expansion of an economy. The synergistical impact of M&As motivates the company to go for merger at the tough time. Greater market share and cost efficiency are the main outcomes of M&As as this strategy reduces competition with a monopolistic market view. Weaker business houses integrate their business with stronger ones and create synergy in their overall production at minimum cost achieved through economies of scale. M&As saves the weaker company from liquidation as it is better to be with another, rather than to be vanished completely. M&A deals makes Indian economy massive in its scale and inspires the business houses with stronger financial base to invest in sector such as textile, agriculture, education, clothing, technology, and automobiles. Good mergers boost the economy of a country, promoting employment, R&D, capital flow, increased return to shareholders and countless opportunities of growth. However, there are critics who emphasizes that horizontal mergers may be a route for unemployment when the transferee company manages the operation with is existing labor force. Besides, mergers and acquisitions may create a monopoly market, thereby exploiting consumer mass charging more price which may lead to hyperinflation. However, these limitations can be overruled with adequate law as have already been framed to regulate M&As activities.

LITERATURE REVIEW

Mergers and Acquisitions (M&A) are the inorganic growth strategies widely used around the world for business consolidation and restructuring. A prominent number of studies in corporate finance and strategic management have given the focus on the motives for M&A transactions. Different motives of M&A have different effects on shareholders' wealth. Many research studies have been carried out in the field of M&A. Most of the studies were conducted on the motive of M&A deals during 1970 to 1980 and proved different hypotheses on market power, synergy, managerial efficiency, economy of scale, production, and productivity enhancement (Chevalier & Redor, 2008). Study conducted on the determinants of M&A by Vyas *et al.* (2012), Erdogan (2012) and Ismaili (2011) identified factors like company size, age of company, leverage, culture, profitability, deal value, management control, operating activities, tax implication and microeconomic conditions affects the M&A performance. Studies conducted by Alshwer *et al.* (2011), Andre and Ben (2009), Ray (2010) and DePamphilis (2010) found that payment, method adopted by the acquiring company to discharge purchase consideration, play a very crucial role to shareholders' wealth gain and business growth. Patel & Shah (2016) pointed out in their study that M&As deal will enhance the efficiency of acquiring bank if the M&A activities are agreed to be carried out in structured manner after detail investigation made into the fundamental analysis of the company. Verma &Rathore (2018) in their research paper made a comparative study on bank mergers making an extensive literature review of 22 papers out of 82. It is found in their study that Indian research is not constructive to meet the international standard in terms of methodology and the results found out on efficiency measurement need to be studied further. Agarwal, Vichore & Gup (2019) studied to evaluate the effectiveness of mergers in commercial banks in India. A comparative analysis is made by them among SBI, ICICI bank, HDFC bank and Kotak Mahindra Bank between pre and post mergers using sample pair-t test and found the M&A has significant positive impact in private sector banks as compared to public sector banks. Mousumi & Sarit (2021) measure the effects of mergers and acquisitions on the stock price and financial performance of the acquirer banks considering 28 bank mergers which are registered in NSE. Using event study Du Point analysis, it is found that M&As failed to show any significant on post-merger period due to negative reaction of market. Agarwal & Garg (2022) studied the impact of mergers and acquisitions on accounting-based performance of acquiring firms in India considering 68 mergers during the year 2007-08 to 2011-12. Analyzing the liquidity, profitability, and solvency with 3years pre and post mergers using comparative study and sample – t test, they found in their study that liquidity and profitability position has significant positive impact but failed to have significant impact on solvency. Going through various literature based on efficiency measurement impacted by mergers and acquisitions, we found efficiency measurement using the DEA approach is not properly addressed. Considering the massive growth of Mergers and Acquisitions in Indian Banking Sector, some of the concerned literatures are reviewed to measure and understand the impact of M&A on the value of the business and shareholders wealth using Data Envelopment Analysis Approach (DEA) as highlighted under.

Amin and Boamah (2023) defined different types of strategic alliance collaborations and partnership between different decision-making units (DMUs). They developed the DEA model to guide partners how to redistribute their inputs and outputs that could improve their performance. They found in their study that the companies could get benefits through strategic alliance. They also tried to apply the DEA method to highlight the advantage of banking companies.

Chiu et al. (2020) examined the technical efficiencies of 14 financial holding banks in Taiwan from 2015 to 2019 using DEA. They used the Resample Slack-Based Measure and Merger potential Gain model and used the concept of premerger evaluation to analyze technical efficiency. They found positive and post-merger efficiency gains and suggested that there would be no guarantee for efficiency gains for the holding company after the merger.

Tanwar et al. (2020) examined the efficiency of Indian banking sector using DEA approach. They made a comparative study among public, private and foreign banks. The sample of 17 public sector banks, 18 private sector banks and 15 foreign banks for the period from 2009 to 2019 are considered for the study. They found that all the Indian banks fall short of efficiency and performance of Indian banks is sensitive to input and output variables. They studied only the internal factors of the bank to measure efficiency.

Naveen and Boateng (2020) conducted a study on measuring performance improvement after mergers. The researchers conclude that even though merger brings on board enormous benefits to companies involved. These companies should not expect a drastic automatic improvement in performance after the merger.

Shah., Wu and Korotkov (2019) evaluated the performance and productivity of sustainable banks and tried to explore the practical issues by providing supportive documents. They employed DEA and MPI to evaluate sustainable bank performance and productivity for 9 years. They found that sustainable banks are more efficient and productive and suggested that the productivity of both sustainable and non-sustainable banks greatly influenced by internal and external factors respectively.

Henriques et al. (2018) conducted a study to evaluate bank efficiency in Brazilian banking sector from the period from 2012 to 2016 with DEA. They took the sample of 37 Brazilian banks by using the intermediation approach. They tried to find out the causes of bank inefficiencies and suggested how inefficiency can be made efficient. Both CRR and BCC models are applied, and they concluded that the efficiency of the sector could be increased by adopting policies which will lead to an increase in the participation of smallest bank in the sector.

Henriques et al. (2018) conducted a study to evaluate bank efficiency in Brazilian banking sector from the period from 2012 to 2016 with DEA. They took the sample of 37 Brazilian banks by using the intermediation approach. They tried to find out the causes of bank inefficiencies and suggested how inefficiency can be made efficient. Both CRR and BCC models are applied, and they concluded that the efficiency of the sector could be increased by adopting policies which will lead to an increase in the participation of smallest bank in the sector.

Rahman, Lambkin and Hussain (2016) tried to measure the post-merger marketing efficiency of US commercial banking industry. They investigated through empirical study of 20 M&A deals using the Data Envelopment Analysis (DEA) to measure the efficiency employing two input and two output variables. They found that merger and acquisitions transactions created a positive effect on the marketing efficiency of the combined firm irrespective of size.

Lee and Johnson (2015) used the concept of effective production and effectiveness to measure the effect of sales on operational performance. They used the Malmquist Productivity Index (MPI) to measure the sales effects as the difference between the production function associated with efficiency and sales-truncated production associated with effectiveness. They made an empirical study on US airline and conducted productive change analysis. The outcomes of the study demonstrate the concept of effectiveness and quantifies the effect taking sales as output.

Singla (2015) conducted a study on measuring the growth Indian banking sector resulted from mergers and acquisitions occurred between 2000 and 2006. He found that the Merger and Acquisition is the useful tool for growth and expansion in the Indian banking sector. It is helpful for the survival of weak banks by merging into larger bank but no guarantee to enhance the profitability, liquidity, efficiency, and capital base.

Gandhi and Shankar (2014) analyzed the economic efficiencies of selected Indian retailers using Data Envelopment analysis (DEA), Malmquist Productivity Index (MPI) and Bootstrapped Tobit Regression and found that five retail firms out of eighteen retail firms are efficient under CRR model of DEA and seven out of eighteen are efficient under the BCC model of DEA. They suggested that the DEA model produces robust results as compared to any other models.

Jayaraman, Srinivasan and Arunachalam (2014) examined the impact and efficiency of Indian banks followed by mergers and acquisitions with the use of DEA. The study was conducted comparing the efficiency of merged banks three years before and after the merger. To validate the efficiency, they compared the efficiency of merged banks with the efficiency of non-merged banks. Efficient frontier is used for interval estimation. They found with DEA that the technical efficiency of banks reduces immediately after a merger but after three years it gets improved. They also found that the effect of mergers and acquisitions on profitability and operational cost of the merged bank are not significant.

Halkos and Salamouris (2004) measured and examined the efficiency in performance of the Greek banking sector using DEA methodology interpreting several suggested efficiency ratios for the period from 1997 to 1999. They made input-output analysis as well as simple ratio analysis. They suggested that the DEA can be used as an alternative or complement to ratio analysis for the organizational performance evaluation. They found in their study that higher the size of asset leads to higher efficiency in performance.

Research Gap

From the literature review, following research gaps are worth noting:

(i) Efficiency measurement resulted by mergers and acquisitions in Indian banking industry, is not adequately addressed using Data Envelopment Analysis Approach in Indian context.
(ii) There are very few studies which analyses pre-merger and post-merger condition using DEA with reference to financial performance and shareholder's wealth of Indian banking sector.
(iii) Pre and post long period comparison of combined bank performance on mergers and acquisitions is not properly analyzed with application of DEA approach.

DATA AND METHODOLOGY

In this study, researchers took the sample size of 4 Indian bank mergers took place from the year 2006 to 2018, based on market capitalization. In this study, the researchers took sample size 4 as merger cases happened between the year 2006 to 2018. The sample units are State Bank of India, Bank of Baroda, HDFC Bank and Kotak Mahindra Bank are selected for the study. Researcher critically analyzed 5 years pre- merger and post-merger performance of the selected public and private banks in India, with the help of financial ratios viz, Net profit margin ratio, Asset Yield, Return on Equity, Return on Assets, Earning per Share, Dividend per share and profit per share. Researchers used secondary data and calculated efficiency using Data Envelopment Analysis (DEA). On literature the seven important parameters impacting the banking performance was identified. For analysis purposes the variables are classified into two categories viz. input and output. The details of classifications are shown below.

DEA has been gaining importance since 1978 for efficiency measurement in management, to clearly understand the past accomplishment of a business and for planning the future development. DEA is widely recognized as an effective technique for measurement of relative efficiency of a set of Decision-Making Units (DMUs) that apply multiple inputs to produce multiple outputs with many theoretical developments and practical applications (Charnes & Cooper, 1984). The DMU is the homogeneous entity responsible for the conversion of inputs into outputs. A matrix with inputs, outputs, and complementary elements of the sample of DMUs are required for carrying out the DEA study. After the formulation of DEA model in accordance with a set of features such as matrix and orientation, the matrix is implemented in the model to be solved. Therefore, Data Envelopment Analysis emerged as a suitable method to measure sustainability. It is a non-parametric method that is used for the assessment of the technical efficiency of DMUs relative to one another where technical efficiency can be defined as a measure of how well a DMU can transform inputs into outputs.

The DEA methodology has got universal applicability which can be used for measuring efficiency and performance. Researchers find it a friendly user technique since it is easy to apply and analyze the outcomes. DEA methodology introduced by Abraham Charnes and colleagues estimates an efficiency frontier by considering the best performance observations (extreme points) which "envelop" the remaining observations using mathematical programming techniques. The concept of efficiency can be defined as a ratio of produced outputs to the used inputs:

$$Efficiency = \frac{Output}{Input} \tag{1}$$

So that an inefficient unit can become efficient by expanding products (output) keeping the same level of used resources, or by reducing the used resources keep the same production level, or by a combination of both.

Considering $j = 1, 2, 3, . m$ Decision Making Units (DMUs) using $x_i \,|\, i = 1, 2, 3, ., n$ inputs to produce $y_r \,|\, r = 1, 2, 3, .,$ outputs and prices (multipliers) v_i and u_r associated with those inputs and outputs, we can also formalize the efficiency expression in (1) as the ratio of weighted outputs to weighted inputs:

For our study we have used the variable return to scale (VRS) model with output orientation. The Banker, Charnes, and Cooper (1984) BCC model is developed with a production frontier that has variable returns to scale. The model is as shown below.

The basic BCC model formulation (dual problem/envelopment form):

$$Min\theta - \varepsilon \left(\sum_{i=1}^{m} s_i^- + \sum_{r=1}^{s} s_r^+ \right)$$

Subject to:

$$\sum_{j=1}^{n} \lambda_j x_{ij} + s_i^- = \theta x_{i0} \ (i=1, \ldots\ldots\ldots, m)$$

Table 1. List of banks with market capitalization and net worth as on 31.03.2020

SN	Banks Name	Year of M&A	Net worth as 0n 31.03.2020	Market Cap
	Banks after Mergers & Acquisitions (M&A) in India			
1	State Bank of India	2017	2.32 Lakhs Crores	$33.55 Billion
2	Punjab National Bank	2019	0.62 Lakhs Crores	$04.73 Billion
3	Bank of Baroda	2018	0.72 Lakhs Crores	$04.88 Billion
4	Canara Bank	2019	0.39 Lakhs Crores	$02.90 Billion
5	Indian Bank	2019	0.22 Lakhs Crores	$01.32 Billion
6	Union Bank of India	2019	0.34 Lakhs Crores	$02.76 Billion
7	HDFC Bank	2008	1.71 Lakhs Crores	$107.70 Billion
8	ICICI Bank	2010	1.16 Lakhs Crores	$50.29 Billion
9	IDBI Bank	2006	0.34 Lakhs Crores	$04.57 Billion
10	IDFC First Bank	2018	0.15 Lakhs Crores	$02.87 Billion
11	Kotak Mahindra Bank	2014	0.49 Lakhs Crores	$54.04 Billion

$$\sum_{j=1}^{n} \lambda_j y_{rj} - s_r^+ = y_{r0} \ (r=1, \ldots\ldots\ldots, s) \tag{3}$$

$$\lambda_j \geq 0 \ (j=1, \ldots\ldots\ldots, n)$$

$$\sum_{j=1}^{n} \lambda_j = 1$$

As a result, we have an efficiency score θ which varies from 0 to 1 designating the efficiency for each decision-making unit. This approach forms a convex hull of intersecting planes. These planes envelop the data points more tightly than the constant returns to scale (CRS) conical hull. As a result, the variable returns to scale (VRS) approach provides technical efficiency (TE) scores that are greater than or equal to scores obtained from the CRS approach (Coelli, Rao & Battese, 1998).

Financial Statement Analysis

Along with the DEA approach, different financial ratios are used for the study. The ratios used are net profit margin ratio, Earning Per Share (EPS), Return on Equity (ROE), Return on Assets (ROA), asset yield ratio, dividend per share and profit per share. These ratios are computed from the financial statements of the banks under study. Researchers conducted this study to measure the impact of mergers on efficiency enhancement on financial performance of acquiring banks in the post-merger period. For this objective, the hypothesis that is taken is there is no change in efficiency in the financial performance of anchor bank in post-merger period as compared to pre-merger period. Table 1 shows a list of banks with market capitalization in 2020.

Table 2. Description list of Indian bank mergers from 2006-2018

SN	Anchor Banks	Merged Banks	Date of Merger	Headquarters	Taglines
1	Federal Bank	Ganesh Bank of Kurandwad	09.01.2006	Kerala	Your perfect Banking Partner
2	IDBI Ltd	United Western Bank	03.10.2006	Mumbai	Banking for all. Aao Sochein Bada Bank Aisa dost Jaisa
3	Indian Overseas Bank	Bharat Overseas Bank	31.03.2007	Chennai	Good people to grow with
4	ICICI Bank Ltd	Sangli Bank	19.04.2007	Mumbai	Hum hai na and Khayal Apka
5	HDFC Bank Ltd	Centurian Bank of Punjab	23.03.2008	Mumbai	We understand your world
6	State Bank of India	State Bank of Saurashtra	13.08.2008	Mumbai	Suraksha aur Bharosa Dono
7	ICICI Ltd	Bank of Rajasthan Ltd	23.05.2010	Mumbai	Khayal Apka
8	Kotak Mahindra Bank	ING Vyasa Bank	20.04.2014	Mumbai	Let's make money simple.
9	State Bank of India	#Five Associates and one other PSU	01.04.2017	Mumbai	Let's make money simple.
10	Bank of Baroda	Dena Bank & Vijaya Bank	31.12. 2018	Vadodara	India's International Bank

State Bank of Patiala, State Bank of Bikaner &Jaipur, State Bank of Travancore, State Bank of Hyderabad, State Bank of Mysore & Bhartiya Mahila Bank

Table 2 provides the description list of all the bank mergers that took place in India during the period 2006-2018.

Dataset for the Indian Banks

Table 3 presents the financial indicators of the State Bank of India during 2017. Table 4 presents the financial indicators of the Bank of Baroda during 2018. Table 5 presents the financial indicators of the HDFC during 2008. Table 6 presents the financial indicators of the Kotak Mahindra Bank during 2014.

Table 3. Financial indicators of State Bank of India

State Bank of India (DOA: 01.04.2017)	T-5	T-4	T-3	T-2	T-1		T+1	T+2	T+3	T+4	T+5
Net Profit Margin	9.69	10.39	7.03	7.49	5.19	4.97	-2.47	-0.25	4.79	6.61	10.02
EPS	184.3	210.0	15.68	17.55	12.98	13.43	-7.67	0.97	16.23	22.87	35.49
ROA	0.88	0.90	0.61	0.64	0.42	0.39	-0.19	-0.02	0.37	0.45	0.64
ROE	13.95	14.26	9.21	10.20	6.90	5.57	-2.99	-0.32	6.24	8.04	11.31
Asset Yield	12.28	11.44	11.27	11.72	11.18	11.17	11.40	11.11	11.07	10.82	10.08
Dividend per share	35.00	41.50	30.00	35.47	26.00	26.44	0.00	0.00	0.00	40.00	71.00
Profit/Share	174.4	206.2	145.88	175.49	128.18	131.49	-73.36	-7.82	162.34	228.70	354.93

Table 4. Financial indicators of Bank of Baroda

Bank of Baroda (DOA: 31.12.2018)	T-5	T-4	T-3	T-2	T-1	T-0	T+1	T+2	T+3	T+4	T+5
Net Pr0fit Margin	10.30	6.99	5.86	-7.32	2.36	-21.60	-17.00	0.53	2.16	3.96	2.58
EPS	139.52	93.91	16.91	-20.82	6.45	-55.39	-30.94	0.62	2.08	3.16	2.28
ROA	10.30	6.99	5.86	-7.32	2.36	-21.60	-17.00	0.53	2.16	3.96	2.58
ROE	1343.16	923.19	825.42	-1012.02	311.29	-2224.71	-1083.34	24.95	96.47	156.98	113.85
Asset Yield	8.99	8.03	7.88	7.37	6.81	6.58	6.97	6.82	6.85	6.07	6.16
Dividend/share	27.00	10.00	16.93	0.00	0.00	0.00	0.00	0.00	0.00	3.20	3.25
Profit/Share	134.32	92.32	82.54	-101.20	31.13	-222.47	-108.33	2.49	9.65	15.70	11.38

Table 5. Financial indicators of HDFC Bank

HDFC Bank (DOA: 30.05.2008)	T-5	T-4	T-3	T-2	T-1	T-0	T+1	T+2	T+3	T+4	T+5
Net Pr0fit Margin	12.07	12.33	13.71	14.75	14.39	50.68	17.83	18.32	18.08	19.02	21.30
EPS	17	22.11	28.49	35.47	42.15	48.84	57.18	67.76	78.65	48.01	56.58
ROA	1.73	1.72	1.68	1.53	1.42	1.73	1.68	1.64	1.69	1.72	1.78
ROE	40.11	45.10	41.77	37.90	33.33	42.55	42.56	47.19	41.24	44.14	43.50
Asset Yield	13.26	13.58	14.63	13.96	12.46	12.96	12.50	12.19	12.08	11.55	10.67
Dividend/ share	40	34.3	27.5	21.5	16.5	47.5	55	65	75	25	65
Profit/Share	88.09	73.40	58.30	44.82	34.09	105.71	124.88	136.00	163.47	202.80	224.93

Table 6. Financial indicators of Kotak Mahindra Bank

Kotak Mahindra (DOM:20.04.14)	T-5	T-4	T-3	T-2	T-1	T-0	T+1	T+2	T+3	T+4	T+5
Net Pr0fit Margin	16.46	15.16	14.79	14.78	15.88	11.00	16.11	17.16	17.04	18.41	21.56
EPS	11.35	14.69	18.31	19.62	24.20	11.42	18.57	21.54	25.52	30.88	35.17
ROA	1.61	1.65	1.63	1.72	1.76	1.09	1.59	1.54	1.56	1.65	1.82
ROE	222.07	292.99	364.51	390.10	483.19	227.85	370.63	428.65	509.79	621.75	702.87
Asset Yield	8.56	9.77	9.93	10.38	9.45	9.06	8.69	7.78	7.94	7.74	7.29
Dividend/share	0.04	0.03	0.03	0.03	0.02	0.04	0.02	0.02	0.02	0.01	0.01
Profit/Share	22.21	29.30	36.45	39.01	48.32	22.78	37.06	42.87	50.98	62.18	70.29

(T-0 represents merger year, T-1 to T-5 represent five years pre-merger period and T+1 to T+5 represent five years post-merger period)

Empirical Analysis of Selected Indian Banks

State Bank of India (SBI)

Table 7 shows the descriptive statistics of State Bank of India. It's interesting to note that the dividend per share varies from zero to Rs.71/- with an average value of Rs.27.76. The minimum value of profit per share is in the negative.

Table 7. Statistics on input/output data (SBI)

	EPS	ROA	ROE	Asset Yield	Dividend per Share	Profit Per Share
Max	210.06	0.900551	14.26421	12.27801313	71.00004482	354.9288484
Min	-7.67	-0.18952	-2.98795	10.07537148	0	-73.36407234
Average	47.44545	0.46157	7.488428	11.23114373	27.76512298	147.862785
SD	71.56819	0.318966	5.126292	0.518728211	20.54240776	108.0127616

Table 8 shows the correlation between the variables under study. It is observed that return on asset and return on equity is highly correlated, followed by return on equity and profit per share. The variable asset yield and profit per share has a low degree of negative correlation.

Table 8. Correlation between variables

	EPS	ROA	ROE	Asset Yield	Dividend per Share	Profit per Share
EPS	1	0.722796	0.707514	0.467817111	0.364702093	0.330634943
ROA	0.722796	1	0.99522	0.218440598	0.725850614	0.780416647
ROE	0.707514	0.99522	1	0.154496578	0.761543075	0.826191623
Asset Yield	0.467817	0.218441	0.154497	1	-0.31626321	-0.383947421
Dividend per share	0.364702	0.725851	0.761543	-0.31626321	1	0.871186255
Profit Per Share	0.330635	0.780417	0.826192	-0.383947421	0.871186255	1

Table 9 indicates that the efficiency score of SBI is 1 in 6 years i.e., 2015 to 2022 and in rest of the year's efficiency score ranges between 0.95 – 0.49.

Figure-1 shows that the efficiency score of SBI during far 3years out of 5 years prior to merger was below 1 but was increasing. However, before 2 years near to merger, the efficiency score became 1 which indicates the impact of pre-merger announcement increasing the bank's performance efficiency.

Figure-2 showing post-meger efficiency score indicates that the bank's performance is satisfactory after merger as the efficiency score is maintained at 1 for all the 5 years after merger.

Table 9. Efficiency score of State Bank of India

No.	Year	Eff. Score	Rank	1/Score
1	2012	0.492962	9	2.028555435
2	2013	0.58451	8	1.710835112
3	2014	0.952563	7	1.049798988
4	2015	1	1	1
5	2016	1	1	1
6	2017	1	1	1
9	2020	1	1	1
10	2021	1	1	1
11	2022	1	1	1

Figure 1. Pre-merger efficiency score of the State Bank of India

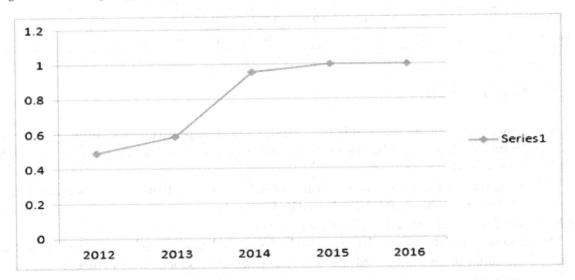

Figure 2. Post-merger efficiency scope of the State Bank of India

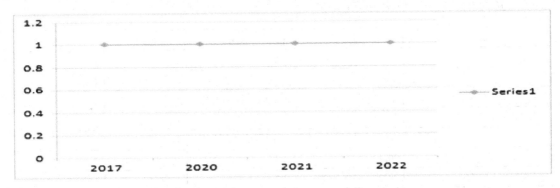

Table 10. Statistics on input/output data (BoB)

	EPS	ROA	ROE	Asset Yield	Dividend per Share	Profit per Share
Max	139.52	10.296567	1343.161	8.994679584	27.0003112	134.3160664
Min	-55.39	-21.595544	-2224.71	6.07295431	0	-222.4705222
Average	14.34364	-1.0151831	-47.7052	7.140218277	5.489195726	-4.770522247
SD	52.9391	9.6280477	981.844	0.829176498	8.554782672	98.18439871

Table 11. Correlation between variables

	EPS	ROA	ROE	Asset Yield	Dividend per Share	Profit per Share
EPS	1	0.760788	0.833175	0.782301572	0.831827215	0.833174693
ROA	0.760788	1	0.964839	0.393967143	0.584518568	0.964839428
ROE	0.833175	0.9648394	1	0.525151691	0.684302942	1
Asset Yield	0.782302	0.3939671	0.525152	1	0.831735586	0.525151691
Dividend per share	0.831827	0.5845186	0.684303	0.831735586	1	0.684302942
Profit Per Share	0.833175	0.9648394	1	0.525151691	0.684302942	1

Bank of Baroda (BoB)

Table 10 shows the descriptive statics of Bank of Baroda. Dividend per share varies from 0 to 27 with average dividend per share 5.48. where as, profit per share varies from minimum – 222.47 to maximum 134.31 with average -4. 77.

Table-11 shows the correlation between variables of BoB under study. It shows the perfect correlation exists between profit per share and ROE, followed by ROA and profit per share. It is observed from the table that variables under study are possitively correlated.

The efficiency score during pre-merger period of 5 years is 3 times in the year 2013, 2014 and in 2017 and and during post-merger period of five the efficiency score is found at 1 two times in 2021 and 2022. This indicates that the efficiency in performance is same before and after the merger.

Table 12. Efficiency score of Bank of Baroda

No.	DMU	Score	Rank	1/Score
1	2013	1	1	1
2	2014	1	1	1
3	2015	0.001287	1	1
5	2017	1	1	1
8	2020	0.2057592	1	1
9	2021	1	1	1
10	2022	1	1	1
11	2023	0.7929435	1	1

Figure 3. Pre-merger efficiency of the Bank of Baroda

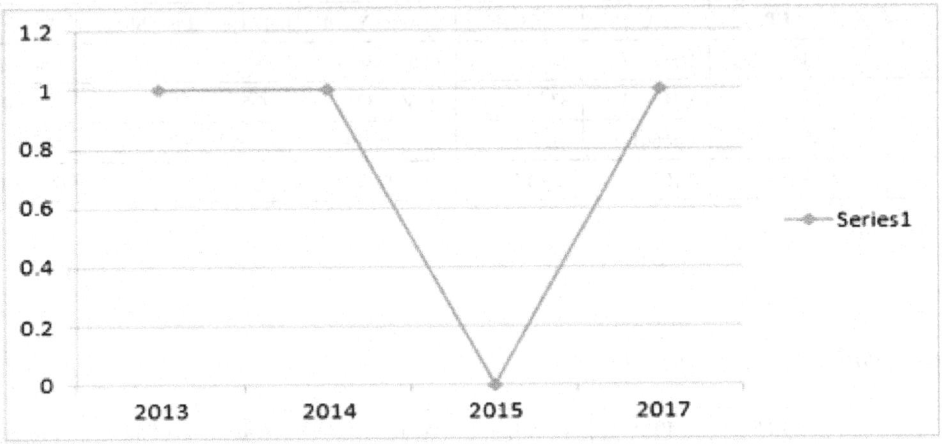

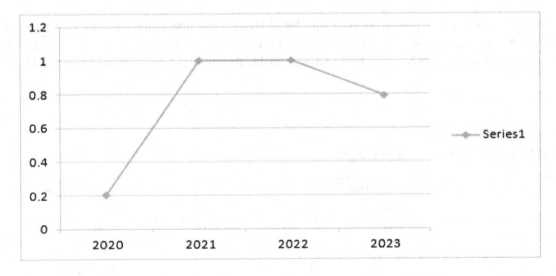

Figure-3 shows that the efficiency score of Bank of baroda is 'v' shape in nature in pre-merger period which indicates the efficiency score is increasing and decreasing at same rate.

Figure 4 shows the efficiency score during post-merger period is increasing to 1 level and remains

Figure 4. Graph showing post-merger efficiency score of the Bank of Baroda

same for one year and than slightly decreases.

HDFC Bank

Table 13 shows the descriptive statistics of HDFC bank. It shows profit per share varies from minimum Rs.34.08 to maximum Rs.224.92 with average Rs 114.22. Dividend per share varies from minimum Rs 16.5 to maximum Rs 75 with average Rs 42.93. It is interesting to observe that there is little variation between minimum and maximum of ROA.

Table 13. Statistics on input/output data

	EPS	ROA	ROE	Asset Yield	Dividend per Share	Profit per Share
Max	78.65	1.781273	47.18535	14.62738878	75	224.9263053
Min	17	1.415671	33.33114	10.66863719	16.5	34.08865969
Average	45.65818	1.666614	41.76233	12.7121419	42.93636364	114.2264481
SD	18.16917	0.100544	3.561559	1.072272394	18.99675918	60.22613045

Table 14. Correlation between variables

	EPS	ROA	ROE	Asset Yield	Dividend per Share	Profit per Share
EPS	1	0.051499	0.247874	-0.653321177	0.727332356	0.604573404
ROA	0.051499	1	0.75651	-0.235877789	0.533955516	0.635588395
ROE	0.247874	0.75651	1	-0.22544044	0.52838131	0.570976987
Asset Yield	-0.65332	-0.23588	-0.22544	1	-0.519148526	-0.843013492
Dividend per share	0.727332	0.533956	0.528381	-0.519148526	1	0.627837354
Profit Per Share	0.604573	0.635588	0.570977	-0.843013492	0.627837354	1

Table 14 shows the correlation between variable of HDFC bank under study. It shows the strong and positive correlation exists between Dividend per share and EPS followed by profit per share and EPS. It is seen negative correlation between EPS and asset yield, also dividend per share and asset yield.

Table 15. Efficiency Score of HDFC Bank

No.	DMU	Score	Rank	1/Score
1	2003	1	1	1
2	2004	0.802493	10	1.246117507
3	2005	0.660147	11	1.51481382
4	2006	0.805119	9	1.242051809
5	2007	0.999893	6	1.000107494
6	2008	0.806845	8	1.239395095
7	2009	0.99975	7	1.000249928
8	2010	1	1	1
9	2011	1	1	1
10	2012	1	1	1
11	2013	1	1	1

Figure 5. Pre-merger efficiency of the HDFC Bank

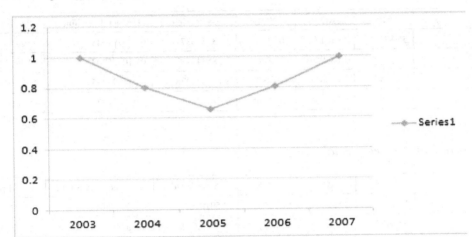

Figure 6. Post-merger efficiency of the HDFC Bank

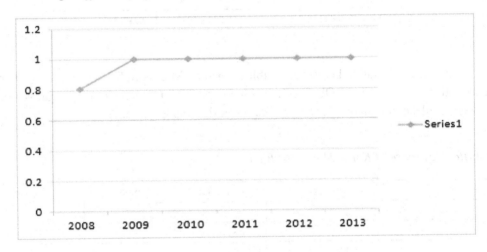

Table 15 shows the efficiency score is 1 four times after merger in 2010, 2011, 2012 and 2013 and the score is less than 1 during pre-merger period. This indicates the efficiency in performance after merger is increased in HDFC bank.

Figure 5 shows the efficiency during pre-merger is flater 'V' shape which indicates the performance is just at average or less than average.

Figure 6 shows that the efficiency of HDFC bank during post- merger has been increased.

Kotak Mahindra Bank

Table 16 shows the descriptive statistics of variables under study. It is seen that profit per share varies from minimum 22.20 to max 70.28 whereas dividend per share varies from minimum 0,01 to max 0.04.

Table 16. Statistics on input/output data

	EPS	ROA	ROE	Asset Yield	Dividend per Share	Profit per Share
Max	35.17	1.816179	702.866	10.37626371	0.039771545	70.28660235
Min	11.35	1.086956	222.066	7.285348882	0.010365203	22.2066008
Average	21.02455	1.600614	419.4907	8.779263976	0.024093285	41.94907076
SD	7.19292	0.180966	145.0665	0.974692114	0.00958162	14.50664851

Table 17. Correlation between variables

	EPS	ROA	ROE	Asset Yield	Dividend per Share	Profit per Share
EPS	1	0.569394	0.999934	-0.59104628	-0.955428049	0.999934381
ROA	0.569394	1	0.56472	-0.028528091	-0.557765154	0.564719566
ROE	0.999934	0.56472	1	-0.590526242	-0.95515973	1
Asset Yield	-0.59105	-0.02853	-0.59053	1	0.591958759	-0.590526242
Dividend per share	-0.95543	-0.55777	-0.95516	0.591958759	1	-0.95515973
Profit Per Share	0.999934	0.56472	1	-0.590526242	-0.95515973	1

Table 17 shows the correlation between variables of Kotak Mahindra Bank under study. Perfect and positive correlation exist between ROE, Profit per share and EPS. On the contrary, negative correlation exists between dividend per share and other variables besides asset yield.

Table 18. Efficiency score of Kotak Mahindra Bank

No.	DMU	Score	Rank	1/Score
1	2009	1	1	1
2	2010	0.862851	1	1
3	2011	0.712281	1	1
4	2012	0.658406	1	1
5	2013	0.462443	1	1
6	2014	0.137139	1	1
7	2015	0.287709	1	1
8	2016	0.341584	1	1
9	2017	0.537547	1	1
10	2018	1	1	1

Table 18 shows that the efficiency score of Kotak Mahindra Bank is found 1 once in pre-merger period in 2009 and once during post-merger period in 2018. In the rest years the score ranges between 0.86 – 0.13.

Figure 7. Pre-merger efficiency of the Kotak Mahindra Bank

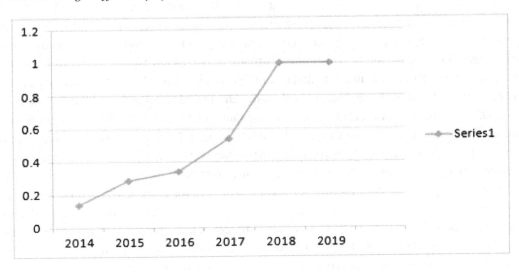

Figure 7 shows that the efficiency score decreased during the pre-merger period of Kotak Mahindra bank.

Figure 8. Post-merger efficiency of the Kotak Mahindra Bank

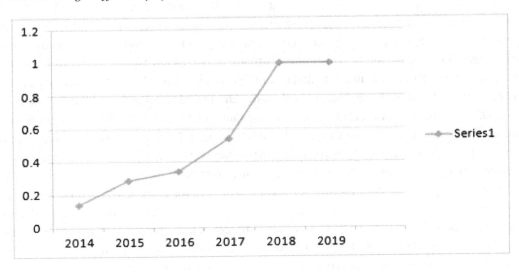

Figure 8 shows that the efficiency score of Kotak Mahindra Bank is increasing during post-merger period.

DISCUSSION OF RESULTS

Table 9 indicates that the efficiency score of SBI is 1 in 2 years during per-merger period and remains at 1 all the years during post-merger period and in rest of the year's efficiency scores ranges between

0.95 - 0.49. The graph shows that the efficiency score of SBI increased continuously in all the 5 years during pre-merger merger period. However, the graph shows that the efficiency score of SBI is flat in nature in the post-merger period which indicates the efficiency remains tag net during all the years after merger. Financial efficiency of State Bank of India after merger has been enhanced as compared to pre-merger period.

Table 12 indicates that the efficiency score of Bank of Baroda is 1 in 3 years out of 5 years during per-merger period and the score is maintained at1 in 2 years out of 5 years during post-merger period and in remaining years the score is ranging between 0.79 – 0.01. The graph shows that the efficiency score of Kotak Mahindra Bank is 'v' shape in nature in pre-merger period. At first the efficiency score decreased, and then the efficiency score increased in 2017. The graph shows that the efficiency score of Bank of Baroda is showing an increasing trend. First it is decreasing in 2020 and increasing in 2021, remain same in 2022 and slightly decreasing in 2023. Therefore, overall financial efficiency is found good and satisfactory.

Table 15 shows the efficiency score is 1 four times after merger in 2010, 2011, 2012 and 2013 and in rest of the year the score is ranging between 0.99 – 0.66. The graph shows the efficiency during pre-merger is flater 'V' shape which indicates the performance is just at average or less than average. However, the graph shows the efficiency remains constant in all the years during post-merger period. This shows that the financial efficiency of HDFC bank has been increased after merger and the the financial performance is positively significant. Table 18 reflects the efficiency score of Kotak Mahindra Bank and found the score is 1 in one year during pre-merger and the score is found 1 in one year during post-merger in 2008 and 2019 respectively and in rest of the year the score is ranging between 0.86 – 0.13. The pre-merger efficiency score graph shows the continuous decreasing of efficiency during all the 5 years before merger and post-merger graph shows the efficiency score is rising all the years during post-merger period under study. This indicates that the merger has had the effect of increasing the financial efficiency of Kotak Mahindra Bank. Overall findings in this study are the efficiency in financial performance during the post-merger period is showing an upward trend in the all the four banks under the study. The post-merger period efficiency score is found positive, and the efficiency graph indicates the efficiency score increases during the period after the merger. Now, it is evident from the study that Indian banking sector is influenced positively and efficiency in financial performance increases during post-merger period. The sample size taken is only four Indian bank mergers and period of study is 10 years comprising 5 years for both pre-merger and post-merger for comparative study. The efficiency score of the selected 4 Indian Bank will be more in post-merger period, if the time span for the analysis is taken for long period i.e., 10 years or more as after merger, it takes time for the firm to adopt the new environment and compete with the market. Besides, for validation of result found, a comparative study with non-merged banks on financial efficiency is not supported in this study.

CONCLUSION

For the study data was collected from financial statement of the selected Indian Merged Bank of 10 years (i.e., five-year pre-merger and five-year post-merger). After that the data was analysis by using DEA model to find the efficiency score of given inputs and outputs of bank's pre-merger and post-merger data. From the above tables and graphs, we have observed that the SBI's financial efficiency as compared to pre-merger has been increased but remains tag net after merger. Bank of Baroda has made an overall improvement in efficiency after the merger. HDFC bank has witnessed an enhancement in financial efficiency after the merger as compared to the volatile nature of efficiency change during the pre-merger period under the study. From the study, we found the Kotak Mahindra Bank has made an eye souring improvement in financial efficiency. Kotak Mahindra Bank made a U-turn about efficiency enhancement from decreasing trend in pre-merger period to increasing trend in post-merger period. From the analysis and interpretation, it is justified to address that Merger and Acquisition impacts positively on enhancement of financial efficiency in Indian banking sector.

REFERENCES

Agarwal, P., & Garg, S. (2022). Impact of Mergers and Acquisitions on Accounting – based Performance of Acquiring firms in India. *Global Business Review*, *23*(1), 218–236. doi:10.1177/0972150919852009

Agarwal, R., Vichore, S., & Gup, M. (2019). The effect of mergers and acquisitions on the performance of commercial banks in India. *The Management Quest*, *2*(2), 15–31.

Amin, G. R., & Boamah, M. I. (2023). Modelling business partnership: A data envelopment analysis approach. *European Journal of Operational Research*, *305*(1), 329–337. doi:10.1016/j.ejor.2022.05.036

Andre, P., & Ben – Amar, W. (2009). Control threat and means of Payment: Evidence from Canadian mergers and acquisitions. *The Journal of Economic Perspectives*, *59*(2), 118–135.

Banker, R. D., Charnes, A., & Cooper, W. W. (1984). Some models for estimating technical and scale inefficiencies in data envelopment analysis. *Management Science*, *30*(9), 1078–1092. doi:10.1287/mnsc.30.9.1078

Brewis, J. (2000). Most M&A deals fail to add value. *Corporate Finance*, *182*(8), 124–139.

Bruner, R. F. (2002). Does M&A pay? A survey of evidence from the decision-maker. *Journal of Applied Finance (JAF)*, *12*(1), 48–68.

Charnes, A., & Cooper, W. W. (1984). The non-Archimedean CRR ratio for efficiency analysis: A rejoinder to Boyd and Fare. *European Journal of Operational Research*, *15*(3), 333–334. doi:10.1016/0377-2217(84)90102-4

Chevalier, A., & Redor, E. (2008). *The choice of payment method in mergers and acquisitions. Handbook of Financial Engineering*. Springer.

Chiu, Y., Lin, T., Chang, T., Lin, Y., & Chiu, S. (2020). Pre-valuating efficiency gains from potential mergers and acquisitions in the financial industry with the resample past-present-future data envelopment analysis approach. *MDE. Managerial and Decision Economics*, *42*(2), 369–384. doi:10.1002/mde.3241

Chong, B.-S., Liu, M.-H., & Tan, K.-H. (2006). The Wealth Effect of Forced Bank Mergers and Cronyism. *Journal of Banking & Finance*, *30*(11), 3215–3233. doi:10.1016/j.jbankfin.2005.12.004

Coelli, T., Rao, D., & Battese, G. (1998). An introduction to efficiency and productivity analysis. Kluwer Academic Publisher group.

DePamphilis, D. M. (2010). *Mergers, Acquisitions and Restructuring Activities* (5th ed.). Academic press.

Distler, J. (2018). *Acquisitions by Emerging Multinational Corporations*. Springer Gabler. doi:10.1007/978-3-658-19112-2

Erdogan, A. I. (2012). The determinants of mergers and acquisitions: Evidence from Turkey. *International Journal of Economics and Finance, 27*(2), 149–176. doi:10.5539/ijef.v4n4p72

Gandhi, A., & Shankar, R. (2014). Efficient measurement of Indian retailers using Data envelopment Analysis. *International Journal of Retail & Distribution Management, 42*(6), 500–520. doi:10.1108/IJRDM-10-2012-0094

Ghosh, A. (2001). Does operating performance really improve following corporate acquisitions? *Journal of Corporate Finance, 7*(3), 151–178. doi:10.1016/S0929-1199(01)00018-9

Halkos, G. E., & Salamouris, D. S. (2004). Efficiency measurement of the GREEK commercial banks with the use of financial ratios: A data envelopment analysis approach. *Management Accounting Research, 15*(2), 201–224. doi:10.1016/j.mar.2004.02.001

Henriques, C., Sobreiro, V. A., Kimura, H., & Mariano, E. B. (2018). Efficiency in the Brazilian banking system using data envelopment analysis. *Future Business Journal, 4*(2), 157–178. doi:10.1016/j.fbj.2018.05.001

Ismali, A., & Krause, A. (2010). Determinants of the method of payment in mergers and acquisitions. *The Quarterly Review of Economics and Finance, 50*(4), 471–484. doi:10.1016/j.qref.2010.06.003

Jayaraman, A.R., Srivasan, M.R., & Arunachalam, R. (2014). Impact of mergers and acquisition on the efficiency of Indian banks: a pre-post analysis using data envelopment analysis. *Journal of Financial Service Management, 7*(1), 1-18.

Jensen, M. C. (1986). Agency cost of free cash flow, corporate finance, and takeovers. *The American Economic Review, 76*(2), 5–50.

Kar, R.N. (2004). *Me4rgers and Acquisitions in India: Background, Implications and Emerging Issues*. Charted Secretary.

Khemani, R. S. (1991). *Recent Trends in Merger and Acquisition Activity in Canada and Selected Countries*. Paper presented at the Investment Canada Conference, Corporate Globalization through Mergers and Acquisitions, Toronto, Canada.

Kothari, R. (1967). Political Change of 1967. *Economic and Political Weekly, 6*(3/5), 231–250.

Lee, C., & Johnson, A. L. (2015). Effective production: Measuring of the sales effect using data envelopment analysis. *Annals of Operations Research, 235*(1), 453–486. doi:10.100710479-015-1932-3

Moeller, S. B., Schlingemann, F. P., & Stulz, R. M. (2004). Firm Size and the gain from acquisitions. *Journal of Financial Economics, 73*(2), 201–228. doi:10.1016/j.jfineco.2003.07.002

Mousumi, B., & Sarit, B. (2021). Mergers and Acquisition and Value Creation: A Banking Industry Perspective. *IUP Journal of Accounting Research and Audit Practices, 20*(4), 32–46.

Patel, R., & Shah, D. (2016). Mergers and Acquisitions – The game of profit and Loss: A study on Indian banking sector. Journal of Arts. *Science and Commerce, 8*(3), 92–110.

Rahman, A., Lambkin, M., & Hussain, D. (2016). Value Creation and appropriation following M&A: A data envelopment analysis. *Journal of Business Research, 69*(12), 5628–5635. doi:10.1016/j.jbusres.2016.03.070

Rajamani, M., & Ramakrishnan, P. R. (2015). A Study on Impact of Merger of Centurian Bank of Punjab on the Financial Performance of HDFC Bank. *IOSR Journal Of Humanities And Social Science, 20*(5), 28–31.

Shah, A. A., Wu, D., & Korotkov, V. (2019). Are Sustainable Banks Efficient and Productive? A data Envelopment Analysis and Malmquist Productivity Index Analysis. *Sustainability (Basel), 11*(8), 2398. doi:10.3390u11082398

Singla, M. L. (2015). Merger and Acquisition in Indian Banking Industry. *International Journal of Research in Management, 662*(4), 77–94.

Sudarsanam, S. (2003). *Creating value from mergers and acquisitions: The Challenges: An integrated and international perspective.* Pearson Education.

Tanwar, J., Seth, H., Vaish, A. K., & Rao, N. V. M. (2020). Revisiting the efficiency of Indian banking sector: An analysis of comparative models through data envelopment analysis. *Indian Journal of Finance and Banking, 4*(1), 92–108. doi:10.46281/ijfb.v4i1.585

Verma, R., & Rathore, J. S. (2018). Mergers and Acquisitions (M&As) in the banking sector: A comparative study of the Indian and International literature. Journal of banking. *Information Technology Management, 15*(1), 22–36.

Vyas, V., Narayanan, K., & Ramanathan, A. (2012). Determinants of mergers and acquisitions in Indian pharmaceuticals industry. *Eurasian Journal of Business and Economics, 5*(9), 79–102.

Zhu, J. (2003). Quantitative models for performance evaluation and benchmarking. Kluwer Academic Publishers Group.

ADDITIONAL READING

Chaudhary, G. M., Shah, S. Z. A., & Hashmi, S. H. (2016). Impact of mergers & acquisitions upon banking efficiency in Pakistan: A Data Envelopment Analysis Approach. *Journal of Business Studies Quarterly, 8*(1), 46.

Jayaraman, A. R., Srinivasan, M. R., & Arunachalam, R. (2014). Impact of merger and acquisition on the efficiency of Indian banks: A pre-post analysis using data envelopment analysis. *International Journal of Financial Services Management, 7*(1), 1–18. doi:10.1504/IJFSM.2014.062287

Nandy, D. (2012). Efficiency study of Indian public sector banks–an application of data envelopment analysis and cluster analysis. *International Journal of Business Performance Management, 13*(3-4), 312–329. doi:10.1504/IJBPM.2012.047298

Shobhana, V. K., & Deepa, N. (2012). Impact of Mergers and Acquisitions on the Shareholder Wealth of the Select Acquirer Banks in India: An Event Study Approach. *IUP Journal of bank. Management, 11*(2).

Singh, P. K., & Thaker, K. (2020). Profit efficiency and determinants of Indian banks; A truncated bootstrap and data envelopment analysis. *Cogent Economics & Finance, 8*(1), 1724242. doi:10.1080/2 3322039.2020.1724242

KEY TERMS AND DEFINITIONS

Data Envelopment Analysis (DEA): A method used to assess the efficiency and productivity of decision-making units, like banks, by comparing various input and output factors.

Financial Efficiency: The effectiveness with which a bank or financial institution manages its resources to maximize profits and minimize costs.

HDFC Bank: A major Indian banking and financial services company known for its significant presence in the Indian banking sector.

Indian Banking Sector: The network of banking institutions operating in India, comprising a mix of public sector, private sector, and foreign banks.

Kotak Mahindra Bank: An Indian private sector bank recognized for its innovative banking practices and significant role in the Indian banking landscape.

Market Capitalization: The total market value of a company's shares of stock. It is used as a measure of corporate size and health in the financial industry.

Mergers and Acquisitions (M&A): Business activities where companies are combined or purchased to consolidate market presence and enhance operational efficiency.

Non-Parametric Techniques: Statistical methods that do not assume a specific data distribution, often used in diverse research areas for more flexible analysis.

Performance Measurement: The process of evaluating the effectiveness and efficiency of a company's operations, typically involving financial and operational indicators.

State Bank of India: The largest public sector bank in India, playing a key role in the Indian banking system and known for its extensive reach and services.

Compilation of References

Aabid, A., Parveez, B., Parveen, N., Khan, S. A., & Shabbir, O. (2022). A Case Study of Unmanned Aerial Vehicle (Drone) Technology and Its Applications in the COVID-19 Pandemic. *J. Mech. Eng. Res. Dev*, *45*, 70–77.

Abbas, M., Hammad, R. S., Elshahat, M. F., & Azid, T. (2015). Efficiency, productivity and Islamic banks: An application of DEA and Malmquist index. *Humanomics*, *31*(1), 118–131. doi:10.1108/H-03-2013-0022

Abdel-Basset, M., Chang, V., & Nabeeh, N. A. (2021). An intelligent framework using disruptive technologies for COVID-19 analysis. *Technological Forecasting and Social Change*, *163*, 120431. doi:10.1016/j.techfore.2020.120431 PMID:33162617

Abduh, M., Hasan, S. M., & Pananjung, A. G. (2013). Efficiency and Performance of Islamic Banks in Bangladesh. *Journal of Islamic Banking and Finance*, *30*(2), 94–106.

Abdul-Wahab, A.-H., & Haron, R. (2017). Efficiency of Qatari banking industry: An empirical investigation. *International Journal of Bank Marketing. Unit*, *07*, 1–5.

Abu-Alkheil, A. M., Burghof, H. P., & Khan, W. A. (2012). Comparison of efficiency and productivity changes of Islamic and conventional banks: Evidence from Europe and Muslim-Majority countries? *Journal of Applied Business Research*, *28*(6), 1385–1412. doi:10.19030/jabr.v28i6.7351

Achicanoy, H., Chaves, D., & Trujillo, M. (2021). StyleGANs and Transfer Learning for Generating Synthetic Images in Industrial Applications. *Symmetry*, *13*(8), 1497. doi:10.3390ym13081497

Ada, A. A., & Dalkılıç, N. (2014). Efficiency Analysis in Islamic Banks: A Study for Malaysia and Turkey. *BDDK Bankacılık ve Finansal Piyasalar*, *8*(1), 9–33.

Adegoriola, A., & Isa, M. (2018). The Problem of Infrastructure on E-Commerce, Small and Medium Enterprises in Nigeria. *Journal of Economics and Sustainable Development*, *9*(4).

Adom, D., Joe, A., & Hussein, E. (2018). Theoretical and Conceptual Framework: Mandatory Ingredients of a Quality Research. *International Journal of Scientific Research*, *7*(1).

Afiatun, P., & Wiryono, S. (2010). Efficiency and Productivity of Indonesian Islamic Banking. *Journal of Technology Management*, *9*(3), 264–278.

Agajo, J., Theophilus, A. L., Idigo, V. E., Apkado, K. I., Polytechnic, F., & State, E. (2012). Optimization of Network Performance in Wireless Communication Networks. *Pacific Journal of Science and Technology*, *13*(1), 334–350.

Agarwal, P., & Garg, S. (2022). Impact of Mergers and Acquisitions on Accounting – based Performance of Acquiring firms in India. *Global Business Review*, *23*(1), 218–236. doi:10.1177/0972150919852009

Agarwal, R., Vichore, S., & Gup, M. (2019). The effect of mergers and acquisitions on the performance of commercial banks in India. *The Management Quest, 2*(2), 15–31.

Agrawal, V., Zhang, Y., & Sundararaghavan, P. S. (2022). Multi-criteria surgery scheduling optimization using modeling, heuristics, and simulation. *Healthcare Analytics, 2*, 100034. Advance online publication. doi:10.1016/j.health.2022.100034

Aheleroff, S., Mostashiri, N., Xu, X., & Zhong, R. Y. (2021). Mass personalisation as a service in industry 4.0: A resilient response case study. *Advanced Engineering Informatics, 50*, 101438. doi:10.1016/j.aei.2021.101438

Ahmad, T., Zhang, D., Huang, C., Zhang, H., Dai, N., Song, Y., & Chen, H. (2021). Artificial intelligence in sustainable energy industry: Status Quo, challenges and opportunities. *Journal of Cleaner Production, 289*, 125834. doi:10.1016/j.jclepro.2021.125834

Ahmed, S., Hasan, M. Z., MacLennan, M., Dorin, F., Ahmed, M. W., Hasan, M. M., Hasan, S. M., Islam, M. T., & Khan, J. A. (2019). Measuring the efficiency of health systems in Asia: A data envelopment analysis. *BMJ Open, 9*(3), e022155. doi:10.1136/bmjopen-2018-022155 PMID:30918028

Aisyah, S., & Hosen, M. N. (2018). Total Factor Productivity and Efficiency Analysis on Islamic Banks in Indonesia. *Jurnal Keuangan Dan Perbankan, 22*(1), 137–147. doi:10.26905/jkdp.v22i1.1333

Ajibesin, A. A., Nche, C., Wajiga, G. M., & Odekunle, M. R. (2014). Reducing multicast power consumption in wireless sensor networks nodes. In *2014 IEEE 6th International Conference on Adaptive Science & Technology (ICAST)* (pp. 1-7). IEEE. 10.1109/ICASTECH.2014.7068151

Ajibesin, A. A., Ventura, N., Murgu, A., & Chan, H. (2013). Data envelopment analysis: Efficient technique for measuring performance of wireless network coding protocols. *15th International Conference on Advanced Communication Technology*, 1122–1127.

Ajibesin, A., Murgu, A., & Chan, H. A. (2016). *Novel Approaches to Performance Evaluation and Benchmarking for Energy-Efficient Multicast: Empirical Study of Coded Packet Wireless Networks* (Doctoral dissertation)

Ajibesin, A. A. (2018). Efficient Frontier and Benchmarking Models for Energy Multicast in Wireless Network Coding. In *Network Coding*. IntechOpen. doi:10.5772/intechopen.79377

Ajibesin, A. A., & Ventura, N. (2015a). Minimum Energy Multicast in Wireless Networks: Empirical study of coded packet model. *International Journal of Computer Research, 22*(4), 361.

Ajibesin, A. A., & Ventura, N. (2015b). Gap mechanism for energy efficiency models in wireless multicast networks. *AFRICON, 2015*, 1–6. Advance online publication. doi:10.1109/AFRCON.2015.7331997

Ajibesin, A. A., Ventura, N., Murgu, A., & Chan, H. A. (2014). Data envelopment analysis with slacks model for energy efficient multicast over coded packet wireless networks. *IET Science, Measurement &amp. IET Science, Measurement & Technology, 8*(6), 408–419. doi:10.1049/iet-smt.2013.0195

Ajija, S. R., Yasin, M. Z., & Albra, R. (2017). Indonesian Banking Efficiency: Transmission to the Financial Stability Confronting ASEAN Economic Community. *Jurnal Ekonomi Pembangunan, 18*(2), 183. doi:10.23917/jep.v18i2.5095

Ala, A., & Chen, F. (2022). Appointment Scheduling Problem in Complexity Systems of the Healthcare Services: A Comprehensive Review. In Journal of Healthcare Engineering (Vol. 2022). doi:10.1155/2022/5819813

Alaa, A., Van Breugel, B., Saveliev, E. S., & van der Schaar, M. (2022, June). How faithful is your synthetic data? sample-level metrics for evaluating and auditing generative models. In *International Conference on Machine Learning* (pp. 290-306). PMLR.

Alam, M. T., Khan, M. A. I., Dola, N. N., Tazin, T., Khan, M. M., Albraikan, A. A., & Almalki, F. A. (2022). Comparative Analysis of Different Efficient Machine Learning Methods for Fetal Health Classification. *Applied Bionics and Biomechanics*, *2022*, 1–12. Advance online publication. doi:10.1155/2022/6321884 PMID:35498140

Alam, N. (2013). Impact of banking regulation on risk and efficiency in Islamic banking. *Journal of Financial Reporting and Accounting*, *11*(1), 29–50. doi:10.1108/JFRA-03-2013-0010

Alandejani, M. (2014). *Efficiency, Survival, and Non-Performing Loans in Islamic and Conventional Banking in the GCC. Durham Theses*. Durham University.

Alatawi, A. D., Niessen, L. W., & Khan, J. A. (2020). Efficiency evaluation of public hospitals in Saudi Arabia: An application of data envelopment analysis. *BMJ Open*, *10*(1), e031924. doi:10.1136/bmjopen-2019-031924 PMID:31932390

Albores, P., Petridis, K., & Dey, P. (2016). Analysing efficiency of waste to energy systems: Using data envelopment analysis in municipal solid waste management. *Procedia Environmental Sciences*, *35*, 265–278. doi:10.1016/j.proenv.2016.07.007

Aldamak, A., & Zolfaghari, S. (2017). Review of efficiency ranking methods in data envelopment analysis. *Measurement*, *106*, 161–172. doi:10.1016/j.measurement.2017.04.028

Aldieri, L., Gatto, A., & Vinci, C. (2022). Is there any room for renewable energy innovation in developing and transition economies? Data envelopment analysis of energy behaviour and resilience data. *Resources, Conservation and Recycling*, *186*, 106587. Advance online publication. doi:10.1016/j.resconrec.2022.106587

Aleke, B., Ojiako, U., & Wainwright, D. W. (2011). ICT adoption in developing countries: Perspectives from small-scale agribusinesses. *Journal of Enterprise Information Management*, *24*(1), 68–84. Advance online publication. doi:10.1108/17410391111097438

Alendejani, M., & Asutay, M. (2017). Determining the Efficiency of Islamic and Conventional Commercial Banks in the GCC. In *Islamic Finance* (Vol. 3, pp. 11–50). Performance and Efficiency. doi:10.2307/j.ctt1df4hbd.4

Alenezi, A. M., Thirunavukkarasu, A., Alrasheed, A. K., Alsharari, T. A., Almadhi, K. B. A., Almugharriq, M. M. N., Alshalan, R. A., Alshalan, K. M., Alanazi, A. A. K., & Albayyali, W. S. (2022). Primary Care Physicians' Knowledge, Attitude, and Potential Referral Barriers towards Bariatric Surgery: A Northern Saudi Study. *Medicina (Lithuania)*, *58*(12). doi:10.3390/medicina58121742

Alexakis, C., Izzeldin, M., Johnes, J., & Pappas, V. (2019). Performance and Productivity in Islamic and Conventional Banks: Evidence from the Global Financial Crisis. *Economic Modelling*, *79*, 1–14. Advance online publication. doi:10.1016/j.econmod.2018.09.030

Alhaija, A. H., Mustikovela, S. K., Mescheder, L., Geiger, A., & Rother, C. (2018). Augmented reality meets computer vision: Efficient data generation for urban driving scenes. *International Journal of Computer Vision*, *126*(9), 961–972. doi:10.100711263-018-1070-x

Alharbi, F., Ouarbya, L., & Ward, J. A. (2020, July). Synthetic sensor data for human activity recognition. In *2020 International Joint Conference on Neural Networks (IJCNN)* (pp. 1-9). IEEE. 10.1109/IJCNN48605.2020.9206624

Alhassan, A. L., & Biekpe, N. (2015). Explaining Bank Productivity in Ghana. *MDE. Managerial and Decision Economics*, *37*(8), 563–573. doi:10.1002/mde.2748

Ali, S. I. M., & Buti, R. H. (2021). Data Mining in Healthcare Sector. *MINAR International Journal of Applied Sciences and Technology*, *3*(2), 87–91. doi:10.47832/2717-8234.2-3.11

Aliev, I. M. (2008). A model for the selection of internet service providers. *Automatic Control and Computer Sciences*, *42*(5), 249–254. doi:10.3103/S0146411608050039

Almahairi, A., Rajeshwar, S., Sordoni, A., Bachman, P., & Courville, A. (2018, July). Augmented cyclegan: Learning many-to-many mappings from unpaired data. In *International conference on machine learning* (pp. 195-204). PMLR.

Al-Muharrami, S. (2007). The causes of productivity change in GCC banking industry. *International Journal of Productivity and Performance Management, 56*(8), 731–743. doi:10.1108/17410400710833029

Alpay, S., & Hassan, M. K. (2007). A Comparative Efficiency Analysis of Interest Free Financial Institutions and Conventional Banks: A Case Study on Turkey. *Working Paper, 0714*, 1–18.

Alsharif, M., Md Nassir, A., Kamarudin, F., & Zariyawati, M. A. (2019). The productivity of GCC Islamic and conventional banks after Basel III announcement. *Journal of Islamic Accounting and Business Research, 10*(5), 770–792. doi:10.1108/JIABR-04-2017-0050

Al-Turjman, F., Altrjman, C., Din, S., & Paul, A. (2019). Energy monitoring in IoT-based ad hoc networks: An overview. *Computers & Electrical Engineering, 76*, 133–142. doi:10.1016/j.compeleceng.2019.03.013

Alyavina, E., Nikitas, A., & Njoya, E. T. (2022). Mobility as a service (MaaS): A thematic map of challenges and opportunities. *Research in Transportation Business & Management, 43*, 100783. doi:10.1016/j.rtbm.2022.100783

Amer, Y., Doan, L. T. T., Dania, W. A. P., & Tran, T. T. (2022). Analysis and Improvement in Healthcare Operation Utilizing Automation. *Proceedings - 2022 International Conference on Control, Robotics and Informatics, ICCRI 2022.* 10.1109/ICCRI55461.2022.00022

Amin, G. R., & Boamah, M. I. (2023). Modelling business partnership: A data envelopment analysis approach. *European Journal of Operational Research, 305*(1), 329–337. doi:10.1016/j.ejor.2022.05.036

Amiri, M., Hashemi-Tabatabaei, M., Ghahremanloo, M., Keshavarz-Ghorabaee, M., Zavadskas, E. K., & Banaitis, A. (2021). A new fuzzy BWM approach for evaluating and selecting a sustainable supplier in supply chain management. *International Journal of Sustainable Development and World Ecology, 28*(2), 125–142. doi:10.1080/13504509.2020.1793424

Andersen, P., & Petersen, N. C. (1993). A procedure for ranking efficient units in data envelopment analysis. *Management Science, 39*(10), 1261–1265. doi:10.1287/mnsc.39.10.1261

Anderson, D. S. (2019). Improving data utility with synthetic data: Case studies in finance and healthcare. *Data & Knowledge Engineering, 23*(5), 67–79.

Andre, P., & Ben – Amar, W. (2009). Control threat and means of Payment: Evidence from Canadian mergers and acquisitions. *The Journal of Economic Perspectives, 59*(2), 118–135.

An, Q., Cheng, Z., Shi, S., & Li, F. (2022). Environmental efficiency of Xiangjiang River in China: A data envelopment analysis cross-efficiency approach. *Industrial Management & Data Systems, 122*(2), 396–418. Advance online publication. doi:10.1108/IMDS-02-2021-0110

Aparicio, J., Cordero, J. M., & Ortiz, L. (2021). Efficiency analysis with educational data: How to deal with plausible values from international large-scale assessments. *Mathematics, 9*(13), 1579. doi:10.3390/math9131579

Apulu, I., & Ige, E. (2011). Are Nigeria Smes Effectively Utilizing Ict? *International Journal of Business and Management, 6*(6), 207–214. doi:10.5539/ijbm.v6n6p207

Ara, S. (2016). Comparison between conventional banking and islamic banking in terms of x-efficiency using data envelopment analysis and malmquist productivity index analysis. *Proceedings of the 14th International Conference of DEA.*

Arazmuradov, A., Martini, G., & Scotti, D. (2014). Determinants of total factor productivity in former Soviet Union economies: A stochastic frontier approach. *Economic Systems*, *38*(1), 115–135. doi:10.1016/j.ecosys.2013.07.007

Arbelo, A., Arbelo-Pérez, M., & Pérez-Gómez, P. (2020). Profit efficiency as a measure of performance and frontier models: a resource-based view. *BRQ Business Research Quarterly*.

Ariff, M., & Can, L. (2009). IMF bank-restructuring efficiency outcomes: Evidence from East Asia. *Journal of Financial Services Research*, *35*(2), 167–187. doi:10.100710693-008-0047-2

Arjomandi, A., Harvie, C., & Valadkhani, A. (2012). An empirical analysis of Iran's banking performance. *Studies in Economics and Finance*, *29*(4), 287–300. doi:10.1108/10867371211266928

Arnold, C., & Neunhoeffer, M. (2020). *Really Useful Synthetic Data—A Framework to Evaluate the Quality of Differentially Private Synthetic Data*. arXiv preprint arXiv:2004.07740.

Arriola, E. R., Ubando, A. T., & Chen, W. H. (2022). A bibliometric review on the application of fuzzy optimization to sustainable energy technologies. *International Journal of Energy Research*, *46*(1), 6–27. doi:10.1002/er.5729

Arrow, K. J., Chenery, H. B., Minhas, B. S., & Solow, R. M. (1961). Capital labor substitution and economic efficiency. *The Review of Economics and Statistics*, *18*(4), 225–250. doi:10.2307/1927286

Arunachalam, V., & Fleischer, E. (2008). The global energy landscape and materials innovation. *MRS Bulletin*, *33*(4), 264–288. doi:10.1557/mrs2008.61

Aschauer, D. A. (1989). Is public expenditure productive? *Journal of Monetary Economics*, *23*(2), 177–200. doi:10.1016/0304-3932(89)90047-0

Aschauer, D. A. (2000). Public capital and economic growth: Issues of quantity, finance, and efficiency. *Economic Development and Cultural Change*, *48*(2), 391–406. doi:10.1086/452464

Assefa, S. A., Dervovic, D., Mahfouz, M., Tillman, R. E., Reddy, P., & Veloso, M. (2020, October). Generating synthetic data in finance: opportunities, challenges and pitfalls. In *Proceedings of the First ACM International Conference on AI in Finance* (pp. 1-8). 10.1145/3383455.3422554

Athanassoglou, S. (2016). Revisiting worst-case DEA for composite indicators. *Social Indicators Research*, *128*(3), 1259–1272. doi:10.100711205-015-1078-3

Athari, S. A., Irani, F., & Hadood, A. A. (2023). Country risk factors and banking sector stability: Do countries' income and risk-level matter? Evidence from global study. *Heliyon*, *10*(9), e20398. doi:10.1016/j.heliyon.2023.e20398 PMID:37780769

Avgerou, C. (2003). The Link between ICT and Economic Growth in the Discourse of Development. In M. Korpela, R. Montealegre, & A. Poulymenakou (Eds.), *Organizational Information Systems in the Context of Globalization: IFIP TC8 & TC9 / WG8.2 & WG9.4 Working Conference on Information Systems Perspectives and Challenges in the Context of Globalization June 15–17, 2003, Athens, Greece* (pp. 373–386). Springer US. 10.1007/978-0-387-35695-2_23

Avkiran, N. K. (2006). Productivity Analysis in the Services Sector with Data Envelopment Analysis (3rd ed.). University of Queensland Business School, The University of Queensland. doi:10.2139srn.2627576

Avkiran, N. K. (1999a). An Application Reference for Data Envelopment Analysis: Helping the Novice Researcher. *International Journal of Bank Marketing*, *17*(5), 206–220. doi:10.1108/02652329910292675

Azadi, M., Moghaddas, Z., Farzipoor Saen, R., & Hussain, F. K. (2021). Financing manufacturers for investing in Industry 4.0 technologies: Internal financing vs. External financing. *International Journal of Production Research*, 1–17. doi:10.1080/00207543.2021.1912431

Azad, M. A. K., Munisamy, S., Masum, A. K. M., Saona, P., & Wanke, P. (2017). Bank efficiency in Malaysia: A use of Malmquist meta-frontier analysis. *Eurasian Business Review*, 7(2), 287–311. doi:10.100740821-016-0054-4

Azevedo, C. da S., Sá, M. de C., Cunha, M., Matta, G. C., Miranda, L., & Grabois, V. (2017). Racionalização e construção de sentido na gestão do cuidado: Uma experiência de mudança em um hospital do SUS. *Ciencia & Saude Coletiva*, 22(6), 1991–2002. Advance online publication. doi:10.1590/1413-81232017226.13312016 PMID:28614518

Azizi, Z., Zheng, C., Mosquera, L., Pilote, L., & El Emam, K. (2021). Can synthetic data be a proxy for real clinical trial data? A validation study. *BMJ Open*, 11(4), e043497. doi:10.1136/bmjopen-2020-043497 PMID:33863713

Azzam, A., & Rettab, B. (2020). Comparative TFP Growth Between GCC Conventional and Islamic Banks Before and After the 2008 Financial Crisis. *The Singapore Economic Review*. Advance online publication. doi:10.1142/S0217590820420047

Babazadeh, E., Oskuee, M.R., Pourmahmoud, J., & Najafi-Ravadanegh, S. (2016). *Optimal Planning of Smart Distribution Network Based on Efficiency Evaluation Using Data Envelopment Analysis*. Academic Press.

Babazadeh, E., Jannati Oskuee, M. R., Pourmahmoud, J., & Najafi-Ravadanegh, S. (2016). Optimal Planning of Smart Distribution Network Based on Efficiency Evaluation Using Data Envelopment Analysis. *International Journal on Electrical Engineering & Informatics*, 8(1), 45–61. doi:10.15676/ijeei.2016.8.1.4

Babazadeh, R., Razmi, J., Rabbani, M., & Pishvaee, M. S. (2017). An integrated data envelopment analysis–mathematical programming approach to strategic biodiesel supply chain network design problem. *Journal of Cleaner Production*, 147, 694–707. doi:10.1016/j.jclepro.2015.09.038

Badiezadeh, T., Saen, R. F., & Samavati, T. (2018). Assessing sustainability of supply chains by double frontier network DEA: A big data approach. *Computers & Operations Research*, 98, 284–290. doi:10.1016/j.cor.2017.06.003

Bagherian, H., Jahanbakhsh, M., & Tavakoli, N. (2020). A review on the use of operational research techniques in the medical records department. *Proceedings of Singapore Healthcare*, 29(1), 42–49. doi:10.1177/2010105819899113

Bahrini, R. (2015). Productivity of MENA Islamic banks: A bootstrapped Malmquist index approach. *International Journal of Islamic and Middle Eastern Finance and Management*, 8(4), 508–528. doi:10.1108/IMEFM-11-2014-0114

Baig, M. M., GholamHosseini, H., Moqeem, A. A., Mirza, F., & Lindén, M. (2017). A systematic review of wearable patient monitoring systems–current challenges and opportunities for clinical adoption. *Journal of Medical Systems*, 41(7), 1–9. doi:10.100710916-017-0760-1 PMID:28631139

Bandyopadhyay, S., & Bhattacharya, R. (2014b). Simulation with Cellular Automata. In Discrete and Continuous Simulation. doi:10.1201/b17127-20

Bandyopadhyay, S., & Bhattacharya, R. (2021). Simulation with System Dynamics. In Discrete and Continuous Simulation. doi:10.1201/b17127-25

Bandyopadhyay, S., & Bhattacharya, R. (2014a). Discrete and continuous simulation: Theory and practice. In *Discrete and Continuous Simulation*. Theory and Practice. doi:10.1201/b17127

Banker, R. D., Charnes, A., Cooper, W. W., Swarts, J., & Thomas, D. (1989). An introduction to data envelopment analysis with some of its models and their uses. *Research in Governmental and Nonprofit Accounting*, 5(1), 125-163.

Banker, R. D. (1984). Estimating Most Productive Scale Size using Data Envelopment Analysis. *European Journal of Operational Research*, *17*(1), 35–44. doi:10.1016/0377-2217(84)90006-7

Banker, R. D., Charnes, A., & Cooper, W. W. (1984). Some models for estimating technical and scale inefficiencies in data envelopment analysis. *Management Science*, *30*(9), 1078–1092. doi:10.1287/mnsc.30.9.1078

Bansal, M. A., Sharma, D. R., & Kathuria, D. M. (2022). A systematic review on data scarcity problem in deep learning: Solution and applications. *ACM Computing Surveys*, *54*(10s), 1–29. doi:10.1145/3502287

Baressi Šegota, S., Anđelić, N., Šercer, M., & Meštrić, H. (2022). Dynamics Modeling of Industrial Robotic Manipulators: A Machine Learning Approach Based on Synthetic Data. *Mathematics*, *10*(7), 1174. doi:10.3390/math10071174

Barr, N. (2004). Higher Education Funding. *Oxford Review of Economic Policy*, *20*(2), 264–283. doi:10.1093/oxrep/grh015

Barth, R., IJsselmuiden, J., Hemming, J., & Van Henten, E. J. (2019). Synthetic bootstrapping of convolutional neural networks for semantic plant part segmentation. *Computers and Electronics in Agriculture*, *161*, 291–304. doi:10.1016/j.compag.2017.11.040

Basri, M. F., Muhamat, A. A., & Jaafar, M. N. (2018). The efficiency of Islamic banks in Malaysia: Based on DEA and Malmquist productivity index. *Journal of Emerging Economies and Islamic Research*, *6*(3), 15. doi:10.24191/jeeir.v6i3.8784

Bass, L. M., Shneider, B. L., Henn, L., Goodrich, N. P., & Magee, J. C. (2019). Clinically Evident Portal Hypertension: An Operational Research Definition for Future Investigations in the Pediatric Population. *Journal of Pediatric Gastroenterology and Nutrition*, *68*(6), 763–767. Advance online publication. doi:10.1097/MPG.0000000000002333 PMID:30908382

Baumol, W.J. (1994). Multivariate growth patterns: contagion and common forces as possible sources of convergence. *Convergence of productivity*, 62-85.

Baumol, W. J. (1986). Productivity growth, convergence, and welfare: What the long run data show. *The American Economic Review*, 1072–1085.

Baur, C., Albarqouni, S., & Navab, N. (2018). Generating highly realistic images of skin lesions with GANs. *OR 2.0 Context-Aware Operating Theaters, Computer Assisted Robotic Endoscopy, Clinical Image-Based Procedures, and Skin Image Analysis: First International Workshop, OR 2.0 2018, 5th International Workshop, CARE 2018, 7th International Workshop, CLIP 2018, Third International Workshop, ISIC 2018, Held in Conjunction with MICCAI 2018, Granada, Spain, September 16 and 20, 2018 Proceedings*, *5*, 260–267.

BBB. (2023). *Customer Reviews and Business Profile for Walden University*. Arlington, VA: Better Business Bureau (BBB). https://www.bbb.org/us/mn/minneapolis/profile/college-and-university/walden-university-llc-0704-5722

Beckinsale, M., Levy, M., & Powell, P. (2006). Exploring Internet Adoption Drivers in SMEs. *Electronic Markets*, *16*(4), 361–370. doi:10.1080/10196780600999841

Beck, T., Demirgüç-Kunt, A., & Levine, R. (2006). Bank supervision and corruption in lending. *Journal of Monetary Economics*, *53*(8), 2131–2163. doi:10.1016/j.jmoneco.2005.10.014

Beck, T., Demirgüç-Kunt, A., & Merrouche, O. (2013). Islamic vs. conventional banking: Business model, efficiency and stability. *Journal of Banking & Finance*, *37*(2), 433–447. doi:10.1016/j.jbankfin.2012.09.016

Bedi, P., Goyal, S., Rajawat, A. S., Shaw, R. N., & Ghosh, A. (2022). Application of AI/IoT for smart renewable energy management in smart cities. *AI and IoT for Smart City Applications*, 115-138.

Beery, S., Liu, Y., Morris, D., Piavis, J., Kapoor, A., Joshi, N., ... Perona, P. (2020). Synthetic examples improve generalization for rare classes. In *Proceedings of the IEEE/CVF Winter Conference on Applications of Computer Vision* (pp. 863-873). 10.1109/WACV45572.2020.9093570

Bellovin, S. M., Dutta, P. K., & Reitinger, N. (2019). Privacy and synthetic datasets. *Stan. Tech. L. Rev.*, *22*, 1.

Bergen, K. J., Johnson, P. A., de Hoop, M. V., & Beroza, G. C. (2019). Machine learning for data-driven discovery in solid Earth geoscience. *Science*, *363*(6433), eaau0323. doi:10.1126cience.aau0323 PMID:30898903

Berger, A. N., Cummins, J. D. D., Weiss, M. A., & Zi, H. (2000). Conglomeration Versus Strategic Focus: Evidence from the Insurance Industry. SSRN *Electronic Journal*. doi:10.2139/ssrn.174810

Berger, A. N., & DeYoung, R. (1997). Problem loans and cost efficiency in commercial banks. *Journal of Banking & Finance*, *21*(6), 849–870. doi:10.1016/S0378-4266(97)00003-4

Berger, A. N., DeYoung, R., Genay, H., & Udell, G. F. (2000). Globalization of Financial Institutions: Evidence from Cross-Border Banking Performance. *Brookings-Wharton Papers on Financial Service*, *3*(1), 23–120. doi:10.1353/pfs.2000.0001

Berger, A. N., & Mester, L. J. (2003). Explaining the dramatic changes in performance of US banks: Technological change, deregulation, and dynamic changes in competition. *Journal of Financial Intermediation*, *12*(1), 57–95. doi:10.1016/S1042-9573(02)00006-2

Berger, A., & Humphrey, D. (1997). Efficiency of Financial Institutions: International Survey and Directions for Future Research. *European Journal of Operational Research*, *98*(2), 175–212. doi:10.1016/S0377-2217(96)00342-6

Berger, A., Hunter, W., & Timme, S. (1993). The efficiency of financial institutions: A review and preview of research past, present and future. *Journal of Banking & Finance*, *17*(2–3), 221–249. doi:10.1016/0378-4266(93)90030-H

Berger, A., & Mester, L. (1997). Inside the black box: What explains differences in the efficiency of financial institutions? *Journal of Banking & Finance*, *21*(7), 895–947. doi:10.1016/S0378-4266(97)00010-1

Bhanawat, S. S., & Kothari, S. (2013). Impact of banking sector reforms on profitability of banking industry in India. *Pacific Business Review International*, *6*, 60–65.

Bhanot, K. (2023). *Synthetic Data Generation and Evaluation for Fairness* [Doctoral dissertation]. Rensselaer Polytechnic Institute.

Bhanot, K., Qi, M., Erickson, J. S., Guyon, I., & Bennett, K. P. (2021). The problem of fairness in synthetic healthcare data. *Entropy (Basel, Switzerland)*, *23*(9), 1165. doi:10.3390/e23091165 PMID:34573790

Bharadwaj, M., Aditya Reddy, M., Senthil Kumar, T., & Vajipayajula, S. (2022). Detection of DoS and DDoS Attacks Using Hidden Markov Model. In Inventive Communication and Computational Technologies. *Proceedings of ICICCT*, *2021*, 979–992.

Bhatia, V., Basu, S., Mitra, S. K., & Dash, P. (2018). *A review of bank efficiency and productivity*. OPSEARCH., doi:10.100712597-018-0332-2

Bitar, M., Naceur, S. B., Ayadi, R., & Walker, T. (2020). Basel Compliance and Financial Stability: Evidence from Islamic Banks. *Journal of Financial Services Research*, *60*(1), 81–134. doi:10.100710693-020-00337-6

Bjurek, H. (1996). The Malmquist Total Factor Productivity Index. *The Scandinavian Journal of Economics*, *98*(2), 303–313. doi:10.2307/3440861

Blume, O., Zeller, D., & Barth, U. (2010). Approaches to energy efficient wireless access networks. *4th International Symposium on Communications, Control and Signal Processing (ISCCSP).* 10.1109/ISCCSP.2010.5463328

Boamah, F. (2019). Desirable or debatable? Putting Africa's decentralised solar energy futures in context. *Energy Research & Social Science, 62*, 101390. Advance online publication. doi:10.1016/j.erss.2019.101390

Bolón-Canedo, V., Sánchez-Maroño, N., & Alonso-Betanzos, A. (2013). A review of feature selection methods on synthetic data. *Knowledge and Information Systems, 34*(3), 483–519. doi:10.100710115-012-0487-8

Bonabeau, E. (2002). Agent-based modeling: Methods and techniques for simulating human systems. *Proceedings of the National Academy of Sciences of the United States of America, 99*(suppl 3), 7280–7287. doi:10.1073/pnas.082080899 PMID:12011407

Bonnéry, D., Feng, Y., Henneberger, A. K., Johnson, T. L., Lachowicz, M., Rose, B. A., Shaw, T., Stapleton, L. M., Woolley, M. E., & Zheng, Y. (2019). The promise and limitations of synthetic data as a strategy to expand access to state-level multi-agency longitudinal data. *Journal of Research on Educational Effectiveness, 12*(4), 616–647. doi:10.1080/19345747.2019.1631421

Boopen, S. (2006). Transport infrastructure and economic growth: Evidence from Africa using dynamic panel estimates. *The Empirical Economics Letters, 5*(1), 37–52.

Borah, S., Kama, C., Rakshit, S., & Vajjhala, N. R. (2022). Applications of Artificial Intelligence in Small-and Medium-Sized Enterprises (SMEs). In *Cognitive Informatics and Soft Computing: Proceeding of CISC 2021* (pp. 717-726). Springer.

Bourkhis, K., & Nabi, M. S. (2013). Islamic and Conventional Banks' Soundness during the 2007-2008 Financial Crisis. *Review of Financial Economics, 22*(2), 68–77. doi:10.1016/j.rfe.2013.01.001

Bower, J. L., & Christensen, C. M. (1996). Disruptive technologies: Catching the wave. *Journal of Product Innovation Management, 1*(13), 75–76.

Bowlin, W. F., Charnes, A., Cooper, W. W., & Sherman, H. D. (1984). Data envelopment analysis and regression approaches to efficiency estimation and evaluation. *Annals of Operations Research, 2*(1), 113–138. doi:10.1007/BF01874735

Boyacioglu, M. A., & Şahin, İ. E. (2014). A Comparison of the Financial Efficiencies of Commercial Banks and Participation Banks: The Case of Turkey. *11th International Academic Conference*, Reykjavik, 7–26.

Brewis, J. (2000). Most M&A deals fail to add value. *Corporate Finance, 182*(8), 124–139.

Brown, D. H., Lockett, N., & Schubert, P. (2005). Preface to the Focus Theme Section 'SMEs and E-Business.'. *Electronic Markets, 15*(2), 76–78. doi:10.1080/10196780500083720

Brum, C. P., & de Faria Corrêa, R. G., de J. Pacheco, D. A., Nepomuceno, T. C. C., de Oliveira, A. L. R., & Marsola, K. B. (2023). Efficiency analysis of inland waterway locks in maritime transportation systems: Practical, economic and policy implications. *Maritime Policy & Management*, 1–24. doi:10.1080/03088839.2023.2252431

Bruner, R. F. (2002). Does M&A pay? A survey of evidence from the decision-maker. *Journal of Applied Finance (JAF), 12*(1), 48–68.

Bruni, A., & Teli, M. (2007). Reassembling the Social: An Introduction to Actor Network Theory. *Management Learning, 38*(1), 121–125. doi:10.1177/1350507607073032

Bughin, J., Chui, M., & Manyika, J. (2010). Clouds, big data, and smart assets: Ten tech-enabled business trends to watch. *The McKinsey Quarterly, 56*(1), 75–86.

Bushara, M. O., Aziz, Y. A., & Hussain, A. I. (2018). The sources of productivity change in Yemen Islamic banks: An application of Malmquist productivity index. *International Journal of Financial Management and Economics*, *1*(1), 39–45. doi:10.33545/26179210.2018.v1.i1a.8

Čagalj, M., Hubaux, J. P., & Enz, C. C. (2005). Energy-efficient broadcasting in all-wireless networks. *Wireless Networks*, *11*(1), 177–188. doi:10.100711276-004-4754-9

Cameron, D. B., & Rangel, S. J. (2016). Quality improvement in pediatric surgery. *Current Opinion in Pediatrics*, *28*(3), 348–355. doi:10.1097/MOP.0000000000000346 PMID:27031660

Campo, J., & Mendoza, H. (2018). Public expenditure and economic growth: A regional analysis for Colombia, 1984-2012. *Lecturas de Economía*, *88*, 77–108.

Canning, D., & Pedroni, P. (2004). *The Effect of Infrastructure on Long-Run Economic Growth* (Department of Economics Working Papers 2004-04). Department of Economics, Williams College. Available at: https://web.williams.edu/Economics/wp/pedroniinfrastructure.pdf

Cantzler, J., Creutzig, F., Ayargarnchanakul, E., Javaid, A., Wong, L., & Haas, W. (2020). Saving resources and the climate? A systematic review of the circular economy and its mitigation potential. *Environmental Research Letters*, *15*(12), 123001. doi:10.1088/1748-9326/abbeb7

Carroll, N., Whellan, E., & Richardson, I. (2012). Service Science – an Actor Network Theory Approach. *International Journal of Actor-Network Theory and Technological Innovation*, *4*(3), 52–70. doi:10.4018/jantti.2012070105

Casetext. (2017). *Latonya Thornhill v. Walden University and Laureate Education*. Ohio District Court. https://casetext.com/case/thornhill-v-walden-univ-llc-1

Casu, B., & Girardone, C. (2002). A Comparative Study of the Cost Efficiency of Italian Bank Conglomerates. *Managerial Finance*, *28*(9), 3–23. doi:10.1108/03074350210768031

Casu, B., & Molyneux, P. (2001). *Efficiency in European banking*. John Wiley & Sons Ltd.

Caulfield, B., Bailey, D., & Mullarkey, S. (2013). Using data envelopment analysis as a public transport project appraisal tool. *Transport Policy*, *29*, 74–85. doi:10.1016/j.tranpol.2013.04.006

Chaal, D., Lyhyaoui, A., & Lehmann, F. (2017, March). Optimization of a modular ad hoc land wireless system via joint Source-Network Coding for correlated sensors. In *ACECS 2017: 4th International Conference on Automation, Control Engineering and Computer Science* (Vol. 2, pp. 21-24). International Publisher & CO (IPCO). 10.1007/978-3-319-67910-5_14

Chachuli, F. S. M., Ludin, N. A., Jedi, M. A. M., & Hamid, N. H. (2021). Transition of renewable energy policies in Malaysia: Benchmarking with data envelopment analysis. *Renewable & Sustainable Energy Reviews*, *150*, 111456. doi:10.1016/j.rser.2021.111456

Chan, K. C., Rabaev, M., & Pratama, H. (2022). Generation of synthetic manufacturing datasets for machine learning using discrete-event simulation. *Production & Manufacturing Research*, *10*(1), 337-353. 10.1080/21693277.2022.2086642

Chapra, M. U. (2011). The Global Financial Crisis: Can Islamic Finance Help? *Islamic Economics and Finance*, 135–142. doi:10.1057/9780230361133_5

Chapra, U. M., (2008). The Global Financial Crisis - Economic Challenges and Prospects for Islamic Finance. *ICR Journal*, *1*(2).

Charnes, A., Cooper, W. W., & Rhodes, E. (1978). A data envelopment analysis approach to evaluation of the program follow through experiment in US public school education. Management Sciences Research Group, Graduate School of Industrial....

Charnes, A., & Cooper, W. W. (1984). The non-Archimedean CRR ratio for efficiency analysis: A rejoinder to Boyd and Fare. *European Journal of Operational Research, 15*(3), 333–334. doi:10.1016/0377-2217(84)90102-4

Charnes, A., Cooper, W. W., Lewin, A. Y., & Seiford, L. M. (1994). *Data Envelopment Analysis: Theory, Methodology and Applications*. Kluwer Academic Publishers. doi:10.1007/978-94-011-0637-5

Charnes, A., Cooper, W. W., & Rhodes, E. (1978). Measuring the efficiency of decision making units. *European Journal of Operational Research, 2*(6), 429–444. doi:10.1016/0377-2217(78)90138-8

Chatterjee, B., & Sinha, R. P. (2006). Cost efficiency and commercial bank lending: Some empirical results. *The Indian Economic Journal, 54*(1), 145–165. doi:10.1177/0019466220060109

Chen, C., Zhu, J., Yu, J.-Y., & Noori, H. (2012). A new methodology for evaluating sustainable product design performance with two-stage network data envelopment analysis. *European Journal of Operational Research, 221*(2), 348–359. doi:10.1016/j.ejor.2012.03.043

Chen, K.-C., Lin, S.-Y., & Yu, M.-M. (2022). Exploring the efficiency of hospital and pharmacy utilizations in Taiwan: An application of dynamic network data envelopment analysis. *Socio-Economic Planning Sciences, 84*, 101424. doi:10.1016/j.seps.2022.101424

Chen, Z., Zhang, Y., & Kim, H. (2019). Synthetic data generation with confidence estimation. *Journal of Artificial Intelligence Research, 27*(4), 23–37.

Cherchye, L., Moesen, W., & Van Puyenbroeck, T. (2004). Legitimately diverse, yet comparable: On synthesizing social inclusion performance in the EU. *Journal of Common Market Studies, 42*(5), 919–955. doi:10.1111/j.0021-9886.2004.00535.x

Chevalier, A., & Redor, E. (2008). *The choice of payment method in mergers and acquisitions. Handbook of Financial Engineering*. Springer.

Chiguvare, T.M. (2019). *An evaluation of human development through renewable energy provision in an offgrid Tsumkwe settlement area of Otjozondjupa region in Namibia*. Academic Press.

Chitekedza, I. (2015). *Efficiency evaluation of South Africa tertiary education institutions using data envelopment analysis* [Masters Thesis]. Nelson Mandela Metropolitan University.

Chitnis, A., & Mishra, D. K. (2019). Performance efficiency of Indian private hospitals using data envelopment analysis and super-efficiency DEA. *Journal of Health Management, 21*(2), 279–293. doi:10.1177/0972063419835120

Chiu, Y., Lin, T., Chang, T., Lin, Y., & Chiu, S. (2020). Pre-valuating efficiency gains from potential mergers and acquisitions in the financial industry with the resample past-present-future data envelopment analysis approach. *MDE. Managerial and Decision Economics, 42*(2), 369–384. doi:10.1002/mde.3241

Chivardi, C., Sosa, A. Z., Galárraga, O., & Sosa-Rubí, S. G. (2023). Efficiency, quality, and management practices in multidisciplinary and traditional diabetes healthcare services in Mexico. *Health Services and Outcomes Research Methodology*. Advance online publication. doi:10.100710742-023-00309-y

Choi, T. M., Kumar, S., Yue, X., & Chan, H. L. (2022). Disruptive technologies and operations management in the Industry 4.0 era and beyond. *Production and Operations Management, 31*(1), 9–31. doi:10.1111/poms.13622

Chong, B.-S., Liu, M.-H., & Tan, K.-H. (2006). The Wealth Effect of Forced Bank Mergers and Cronyism. *Journal of Banking & Finance, 30*(11), 3215–3233. doi:10.1016/j.jbankfin.2005.12.004

Chortareas, G. E., Girardone, C., & Ventouri, A. (2012). Bank supervision, regulation, and efficiency: Evidence from the European Union. *Journal of Financial Stability, 8*(4), 292–302. doi:10.1016/j.jfs.2011.12.001

Choudhri, E. U., & Hakura, D. S. (2000). International Trade and Productivity Growth: Exploring the Sectoral Effects for Developing Countries. *IMF Staff Papers, 47*(1), 1–2. doi:10.2307/3867624

Chowdhury, M. A. M., & Haron, R. (2021). The efficiency of Islamic Banks in the Southeast Asia (SEA) Region. *Future Business Journal, 7*(16), 1–16. doi:10.118643093-021-00062-z

Christensen, C. M. (2013). *The innovator's dilemma: when new technologies cause great firms to fail.* Harvard Business Review Press.

Christensen, C., & Raynor, M. (2013). *The innovator's solution: Creating and sustaining successful growth.* Harvard Business Review Press.

Christensen, C., Raynor, M. E., & McDonald, R. (2013). *Disruptive innovation.* Harvard Business Review Brighton.

ClassAction. (2016). *Jennifer Wright, Kelli Callahan, Janet Harrison, Pete Holubz, and Kelly Gardiner (class action) v. Walden University and Laureate Education*, 1-145. District Court of Minnesota. https://www.classaction.org/news/walden-university-laureate-education-inc-hit-with

Claudio, D., Miller, A., & Huggins, A. (2014). Time series forecasting in an outpatient cancer clinic using common-day clustering. *IIE Transactions on Healthcare Systems Engineering, 4*(1), 16–26. Advance online publication. doi:10.1080/19488300.2013.879459

Claudio, D., Moyce, S., Albano, T., Ibe, E., Miller, N., & O'Leary, M. (2023). A Markov Chain Model for Mental Health Interventions. *International Journal of Environmental Research and Public Health, 20*(4), 3525. Advance online publication. doi:10.3390/ijerph20043525 PMID:36834220

Coelli, T. J., Prasada Rao, D. S., O'Donnell, C. J., & Battese, G. E. (2005). An Introduction to Efficiency and Productivity Analysis (2nd ed.). Springer Science + Business Media.

Coelli, T., Rao, D., & Battese, G. (1998). An introduction to efficiency and productivity analysis. Kluwer Academic Publisher group.

Coello Coello, C. A., Lamont, G. B., & Van Veldhuizen, D. A. (2007). Evolutionary Algorithms for Solving Multi-Objective Problems. In *Evolutionary Algorithms for Solving Multi-Objective Problems.* Springer US. doi:10.1007/978-0-387-36797-2

Cohen, A., Esfahanizadeh, H., Sousa, B., Vilela, J. P., Luís, M., Raposo, D., . . . Médard, M. (2020). *Bringing network coding into SDN: a case-study for highly meshed heterogeneous communications.* arXiv preprint arXiv:2010.00343

Cook, W. D., Tone, K., & Zhu, J. (2014). Data envelopment analysis: Prior to choosing a model. *Omega, 44*, 1–4. doi:10.1016/j.omega.2013.09.004

Cooper, W. W. (2013). Data Envelopment Analysis. In Encyclopedia of Operations Research and Management Science (pp. 349–358). Springer US. doi:10.1007/978-1-4419-1153-7_212

Cooper, W. W., Seiford, L. M., & Tone, K. (2007). Data Envelopment Analysis: A Comprehensive Text with Models, Applications, References and DEA-Solver Software (2nd ed.). Springer Science + Business Media.

Cooper, W. W., Seiford, L. M., & Zhu, J. (2011). Handbook on Data Envelopment Analysis. Springer Science & Business Media.

Cooper, W. W., Seiford, L. M., & Tone, K. (2006). *Introduction to data envelopment analysis and its uses: With DEA-solver software and references.* Springer Science & Business Media. doi:10.1007/0-387-29122-9

Cooper, W. W., Seiford, L., & Zhu, J. (2011). Data Envelopment Analysis: History, Models, and Interpretations. In *Handbook on Data envelopment analysis.* Elsevier. doi:10.1007/978-1-4419-6151-8_1

Cordero, J. M., Santín, D., & Sicilia, G. (2013). *Dealing with the endogeneity problem in data envelopment analysis.* Academic Press.

Cossani, G., Codoceo, L., Cáceres, H., & Tabilo, J. (2022). Technical efficiency in Chile's higher education system: A comparison of rankings and accreditation. *Evaluation and Program Planning, 92,* 102058. doi:10.1016/j.evalprogplan.2022.102058 PMID:35525093

Cowie, M. R., Blomster, J. I., Curtis, L. H., Duclaux, S., Ford, I., Fritz, F., Goldman, S., Janmohamed, S., Kreuzer, J., Leenay, M., Michel, A., Ong, S., Pell, J. P., Southworth, M. R., Stough, W. G., Thoenes, M., Zannad, F., & Zalewski, A. (2017). Electronic health records to facilitate clinical research. *Clinical Research in Cardiology; Official Journal of the German Cardiac Society, 106*(1), 1–9. doi:10.100700392-016-1025-6 PMID:27557678

Crema, M., & Verbano, C. (2019). *Simulation modelling and lean management in healthcare: first evidences and research agenda.* doi:10.1080/14783363.2019.1572504

CTIA. (2020, August 25). *2020 Annual Survey Highlights.* https://www.ctia.org/news/report-2020-annual-survey-highlights

Cylus, J., Papanicolas, I., & Smith, P. C. (2017). Using Data Envelopment Analysis to Address the Challenges of Comparing Health System Efficiency. *Global Policy, 8*(S2), 60–68. Advance online publication. doi:10.1111/1758-5899.12212

Dahunsi, F. M., & Akinlabi, A. A. (2019). Measuring mobile broadband performance in Nigeria: 2G and 3G. *Nigerian Journal of Technology, 38*(2), 422. doi:10.4314/njt.v38i2.19

Dankar, F. K., Ibrahim, M. K., & Ismail, L. (2022). A multi-dimensional evaluation of synthetic data generators. *IEEE Access : Practical Innovations, Open Solutions, 10,* 11147–11158. doi:10.1109/ACCESS.2022.3144765

Das, A. (1997a). Measurement of productive efficiency and its decomposition in Indian banking firms. *The Asian Economic Review, 39*(3), 422–439.

Das, A. (2000). Efficiency of Public Sector Banks: An Application of Data Envelopment Analysis Model. Prajnan. *Journal of Social and Management Sciences, 28*(1), 119–131.

Das, A., & Ghosh, S. (2009). Financial deregulation and profit efficiency: A nonparametric analysis of Indian banks. *Journal of Economics and Business, 61*(6), 509–528. doi:10.1016/j.jeconbus.2009.07.003

Das, A., Nag, A., & Ray, S. C. (2005). Liberalization, ownership and efficiency in Indian banking: A non-parametric analysis. *Economic and Political Weekly, 40*(12), 1190–1197.

de Barros, L. B., Bassi, L. de C., Caldas, L. P., Sarantopoulos, A., Zeferino, E. B. B., Minatogawa, V., & Gasparino, R. C. (2021). Lean Healthcare Tools for Processes Evaluation: An Integrative Review. *International Journal of Environmental Research and Public Health, 18*(14), 7389. Advance online publication. doi:10.3390/ijerph18147389 PMID:34299840

Debasish, S. S. (2006). Efficiency performance in Indian banking-use of data envelopment analysis. *Global Business Review, 7*(2), 325–333. doi:10.1177/097215090600700209

Debela, B. K. (2020). *Managing Covid-19 in Africa: A Technical Efficiency Analysis.* /profile/Bacha_Debela/publication/344561594_Managing_Covid-19_in_Africa_A_Technical_Efficiency,Analysis/links/5f804c68458515b7cf72245d/Managing-Covid-19-in-Africa-A-Technical-Efficiency-Analysis

Deb, K., & Jain, H. (2014). An evolutionary many-objective optimization algorithm using reference-point-based nondominated sorting approach, Part I: Solving problems with box constraints. *IEEE Transactions on Evolutionary Computation, 18*(4), 577–601. Advance online publication. doi:10.1109/TEVC.2013.2281535

Deb, K., Pratap, A., Agarwal, S., & Meyarivan, T. (2002). A fast and elitist multiobjective genetic algorithm: NSGA-II. *IEEE Transactions on Evolutionary Computation, 6*(2), 182–197. doi:10.1109/4235.996017

Debreu, G. (1951). The Coefficient of Resource Utilization. *Econometrica, 19*(3), 273–292. doi:10.2307/1906814

DePamphilis, D. M. (2010). *Mergers, Acquisitions and Restructuring Activities* (5th ed.). Academic press.

Dion, H., & Evans, M. (2023). Strategic frameworks for sustainability and corporate governance in healthcare facilities; approaches to energy-efficient hospital management. *Benchmarking.* Advance online publication. doi:10.1108/BIJ-04-2022-0219

Distler, J. (2018). *Acquisitions by Emerging Multinational Corporations.* Springer Gabler. doi:10.1007/978-3-658-19112-2

Diyoke, K., Yusuf, A., & Demirbas, E. (2017). Government expenditure and economic growth in lower middle income countries in Sub-Saharan Africa: An empirical investigation. *Asian Journal of Economics. Business and Accounting, 5*(4), 1–11.

Dogan, N. O., & Tugcu, C. T. (2015). Energy Efficiency in Electricity Production: A Data Envelopment Analysis (DEA) Approach for the G-20 Countries. *International Journal of Energy Economics and Policy, 5*(1), 246–252.

Dosovitskiy, A. (2017). CARLA: An open urban driving simulator. *Proceedings of the 1st Annual Conference on Robot Learning.*

Drechsler, J., Rieke, N., & Mathiak, K. (2019). *Synthetic data generation for medical imaging.* arXiv preprint arXiv:1912.03408.

Dreher, A. (2006). Does globalization affect growth? Evidence from a new index of globalization. *Applied Economics, 38*(10), 1091–1110. doi:10.1080/00036840500392078

Dubey, B., Agrawal, S., & Sharma, A. K. (2023). India's Renewable Energy Portfolio: An Investigation of the Untapped Potential of RE, Policies, and Incentives Favoring Energy Security in the Country. *Energies, 16*(14), 5491. doi:10.3390/en16145491

Dutta, P., Jaikumar, B., & Arora, M. S. (2022). Applications of data envelopment analysis in supplier selection between 2000 and 2020: A literature review. *Annals of Operations Research, 315*(2), 1399–1454. doi:10.100710479-021-03931-6

Ebrahimi, F., Saen, R. F., & Karimi, B. (2021). Assessing the sustainability of supply chains by dynamic network data envelopment analysis: A SCOR-based framework. *Environmental Science and Pollution Research International, 28*(45), 64039–64067. doi:10.100711356-021-12810-3 PMID:33893584

Eke, H. (2011). *Digitizing resources for University of Nigeria repository: Process and challenges.* Webology. http://www.webology.org/2011/v8n1/a85.html

El Emam, K., Mosquera, L., Fang, X., & El-Hussuna, A. (2022). Utility metrics for evaluating synthetic health data generation methods: Validation study. *JMIR Medical Informatics, 10*(4), e35734. doi:10.2196/35734 PMID:35389366

El Khediri, S., Fakhet, W., Moulahi, T., Khan, R., Thaljaoui, A., & Kachouri, A. (2020). Improved node localization using K-means clustering for Wireless Sensor Networks. *Computer Science Review, 37*, 100284. doi:10.1016/j.cosrev.2020.100284

Emrouznejad, A., Parker, B. R., & Tavares, G. (2008). Evaluation of research in efficiency and productivity: A survey and analysis of the first 30 years of scholarly literature in DEA. *Socio-Economic Planning Sciences, 42*(3), 151–157. doi:10.1016/j.seps.2007.07.002

Emrouznejad, A., & Yang, G. L. (2018). A Survey And Analysis Of The First 40 Years Of Scholarly Literature In DEA: 1978-2016. *Socio-Economic Planning Sciences, 61*(1), 4–8. doi:10.1016/j.seps.2017.01.008

Englesson, E., & Azizpour, H. (2021). Generalized jensen-shannon divergence loss for learning with noisy labels. *Advances in Neural Information Processing Systems, 34*, 30284–30297.

Ephremides, A. (2002). Energy concerns in wireless networks. *IEEE Wireless Communications, 9*(4), 48–59. doi:10.1109/MWC.2002.1028877

Erdogan, A. I. (2012). The determinants of mergers and acquisitions: Evidence from Turkey. *International Journal of Economics and Finance, 27*(2), 149–176. doi:10.5539/ijef.v4n4p72

Ersoy, K., Kavuncubasi, S., Ozcan, Y. A., & Harris, J. M. II. (1997). Technical efficiencies of Turkish hospitals: DEA approach. *Journal of Medical Systems, 21*(2), 67–74. doi:10.1023/A:1022801222540 PMID:9297615

Ewertowska, A. (2017). *Systematic tools based on data envelopment analysis for the life cycle sustainability evaluation of technologies.* Universitat Rovira Virgili. https://www.tesisenred.net/handle/10803/457128

Fallahpour, A., Olugu, E. U., Musa, S. N., Khezrimotlagh, D., & Wong, K. Y. (2016). An integrated model for green supplier selection under fuzzy environment: Application of data envelopment analysis and genetic programming approach. *Neural Computing & Applications, 27*(3), 707–725. doi:10.100700521-015-1890-3

Fang, W., Liu, F., Yang, F., Shu, L., & Nishio, S. (2010). Energy-efficient cooperative communication for data transmission in wireless sensor networks. *IEEE Transactions on Consumer Electronics, 56*(4), 2185–2192. doi:10.1109/TCE.2010.5681089

Farano, B. (2012). Internet intermediaries' liability for copyright and trademark infringement: Reconciling the EU and US Approaches. *Transatlantic Technology Law Forum Working Papers, 14*.

Fare, R., Grosskopf, S., Lindgren, B., & Roos, P. (1992). Productivity Changes in Swedish Pharmacies 1980-1989: A Non-Parametric Malmquist Approach. *Journal of Productivity Analysis, 3*, 85–101. doi:10.1007/BF00158770

Fare, R., Grosskopf, S., Norris, M., & Zhang, Z. (1994). Productivity growth, technical progress, and efficiency change in industrialized countries. *The American Economic Review*, 66–83.

Farooq, M. A., Yao, W., Costache, G., & Corcoran, P. (2023). ChildGAN: Large Scale Synthetic Child Facial Data Using Domain Adaptation in StyleGAN. *IEEE Access : Practical Innovations, Open Solutions, 11*, 108775–108791. doi:10.1109/ACCESS.2023.3321149

Farrell, M. J. (1957). The measurement of productive efficiency. *Journal of the Royal Statistical Society. Series A (General), 120*(3), 253–281. doi:10.2307/2343100

Faruk, U., Disman, D., & Nugraha, N. (2017). Efficiency and Productivity Growth Analysis of the Islamic Banking in Indonesia: Data Envelopment Analysis and Malmquist Productivity Index Approach. *1st International Conference on Islamic Economics, Business, and Philanthropy*, 213–218. 10.5220/0007079502130218

Federal Communications Commission (FCC). (2014). *Types of Broadband Connections*. Federal Communications Commission. https://www.fcc.gov/general/types-broadband-connections

Figueira, A., & Vaz, B. (2022). Survey on synthetic data generation, evaluation methods and GANs. *Mathematics, 10*(15), 2733. doi:10.3390/math10152733

Firmansyah, I. (2018). Measuring of Islamic Banking Productivity in Indonesia Using Malmquist Index. *International Conference on Life, Innovation, Change, and Knowledge, 203,* 251–254. 10.2991/iclick-18.2019.51

Flavin, M., & Flavin, M. (2020). Conclusion: Switch It Off, Switch It on Again—Reimagining Technology-Enhanced Learning in Higher Education. *Re-imagining Technology Enhanced Learning: Critical Perspectives on Disruptive Innovation,* 145-200.

Florescu, A., & Barabas, S. (2022). Development Trends of Production Systems through the Integration of Lean Management and Industry 4.0. *Applied Sciences (Basel, Switzerland), 12*(10), 4885. Advance online publication. doi:10.3390/app12104885

Flug, J. A., Stellmaker, J. A., Tollefson, C. D., Comstock, E. M., Buelna, E., Truman, B., Ponce, L., Milosek, A., McCabe, J., & Jokerst, C. E. (2022). Improving Turnaround Time in a Hospital-based CT Division with the Kaizen Method. *Radiographics, 42*(4), E125–E131. Advance online publication. doi:10.1148/rg.210128 PMID:35622490

Forsund, F. (2001). Categorical variables in DEA. *International Centre for Economic Working Paper,* 1–18.

Fotova Čiković, K., & Lozić, J. (2022). Application of Data Envelopment Analysis (DEA) in Information and Communication Technologies. *Tehnički Glasnik, 16*(1), 129–134. doi:10.31803/tg-20210906103816

Fox, A., Williams, M., Richardson, A. D., Cameron, D., Gove, J. H., Quaife, T., Ricciuto, D., Reichstein, M., Tomelleri, E., Trudinger, C. M., & Van Wijk, M. T. (2009). The REFLEX project: Comparing different algorithms and implementations for the inversion of a terrestrial ecosystem model against eddy covariance data. *Agricultural and Forest Meteorology, 149*(10), 1597–1615. doi:10.1016/j.agrformet.2009.05.002

Fu, M. C. (2013). Simulation Optimization. In Encyclopedia of Operations Research and Management Science (pp. 1418–1423). Springer US. doi:10.1007/978-1-4419-1153-7_958

Fu, H.-P., Chu, K.-K., Chao, P., Lee, H.-H., & Liao, Y.-C. (2011). Using fuzzy AHP and VIKOR for benchmarking analysis in the hotel industry. *Service Industries Journal, 31*(14), 2373–2389. doi:10.1080/02642069.2010.503874

Furinghetti, M., Lanese, I., & Pavese, A. (2020). Experimental Assessment of the Seismic Response of a Base-Isolated Building Through a Hybrid Simulation Technique. *Frontiers in Built Environment, 6,* 33. Advance online publication. doi:10.3389/fbuil.2020.00033

Gabriel, G. T., Campos, A. T., de Lima Magacho, A., Segismondi, L. C., Vilela, F. F., de Queiroz, J. A., & Montevechi, J. A. B. (2020). Lean thinking by integrating with discrete event simulation and design of experiments: An emergency department expansion. *PeerJ. Computer Science, 6,* e284. Advance online publication. doi:10.7717/peerj-cs.284 PMID:33816935

Galadanci, G. S., & Abdullahi, S. (2018). Performance Analysis of GSM Networks inKano Metropolis ofNigeria. *American Journal of Engineering Research (AJER)2018American Journal of Engineering Research, 7*(5), 69–79.

Gandhi, A., & Shankar, R. (2014). Efficient measurement of Indian retailers using Data envelopment Analysis. *International Journal of Retail & Distribution Management, 42*(6), 500–520. doi:10.1108/IJRDM-10-2012-0094

Ganouati, J., & Essid, H. (2017). The sources of productivity change and efficiency in Islamic banking: Application of Malmquist productivity index. *The Central European Review of Economics and Management, 1*(4), 35–67. doi:10.29015/cerem.555

Garcia-Milà, T., McGuire, T. J., & Porter, R. H. (1996). The effect of public capital in state-level production functions reconsidered. *The Review of Economics and Statistics, 78*(1), 177–180. doi:10.2307/2109857

Gauly, J., Court, R., Currie, G., Seers, K., Clarke, A., Metcalfe, A., Wilson, A., Hazell, M., & Grove, A. L. (2023). Advancing leadership in surgery: a realist review of interventions and strategies to promote evidence-based leadership in healthcare. In Implementation Science (Vol. 18, Issue 1). doi:10.118613012-023-01274-3

Gazi, M. A. I., Alam, M. S., Hossain, G. M. A., Islam, S. M. N., Rahman, M. K., Nahiduzzaman, M., & Hossain, A. I. (2021). Determinants of Profitability in Banking Sector: Empirical Evidence from Bangladesh. *Universal Journal of Accounting and Finance, 9*(6), 1377–1386. doi:10.13189/ujaf.2021.090616

Geier, A. (2012). Application of the Swiss fiscal rule to artificial data a Monte Carlo simulation. *Swiss Journal of Economics and Statistics, 148*(1), 37–55. doi:10.1007/BF03399359

Geller, H., Harrington, P., Rosenfeld, A. H., Tanishima, S., & Unander, F. (2006). Polices for increasing energy efficiency: Thirty years of experience in OECD countries. *Energy Policy, 34*(5), 556–573. doi:10.1016/j.enpol.2005.11.010

Gerami, J. (2019). An interactive procedure to improve estimate of value efficiency in DEA. *Expert Systems with Applications, 137*, 29–45. doi:10.1016/j.eswa.2019.06.061

Gerami, J., Kiani Mavi, R., Farzipoor Saen, R., & Kiani Mavi, N. (2023). A novel network DEA-R model for evaluating hospital services supply chain performance. *Annals of Operations Research, 324*(1–2), 1041–1066. doi:10.100710479-020-03755-w

Gharizadeh Beiragh, R., Alizadeh, R., Shafiei Kaleibari, S., Cavallaro, F., Zolfani, S. H., Bausys, R., & Mardani, A. (2020). An integrated multi-criteria decision making model for sustainability performance assessment for insurance companies. *Sustainability (Basel), 12*(3), 789. doi:10.3390u12030789

Ghasemi, S., Aghsami, A., & Rabbani, M. (2021). Data envelopment analysis for estimate efficiency and ranking operating rooms: a case study. *International Journal of Research in Industrial Engineering, 10*(1), 67-86.

Ghaziyani, K., Ejlaly, B., & Bagheri, S. (2019). Evaluation of the efficiency by DEA a case study of hospital. *International Journal of Research in Industrial Engineering, 8*(3), 283-293.

Gheisari, M., Alzubi, J., Zhang, X., Kose, U., & Saucedo, J. A. (2019). A new algorithm for optimization of quality of service in peer to peer wireless mesh networks. *Wireless Networks, 25*(7), 4445. Advance online publication. doi:10.100711276-019-02016-4

Ghobakhloo, M., Sabouri, M. S., Hong, T. S., & Zulkifli, N. (2011). Information Technology Adoption in Small and Medium-sized Enterprises; An Appraisal of Two Decades Literature. *Interdisciplinary Journal of Research in Business, 1*(7), 53–80.

Ghosh, A. (2001). Does operating performance really improve following corporate acquisitions? *Journal of Corporate Finance, 7*(3), 151–178. doi:10.1016/S0929-1199(01)00018-9

Gomes Correia, M., & Ferreira, A. (2023). Road Asset Management and the Vehicles of the Future: An Overview, Opportunities, and Challenges. *International Journal of Intelligent Transportation Systems Research*, 1-18.

Gong, G., Chen, Y., Gao, H., Su, D., & Chang, J. (2019). Has the efficiency of China's healthcare system improved after healthcare reform? A network data envelopment analysis and tobit regression approach. *International Journal of Environmental Research and Public Health, 16*(23), 4847. Advance online publication. doi:10.3390/ijerph16234847 PMID:31810260

Goodfellow, I., Pouget-Abadie, J., Mirza, M., Xu, B., Warde-Farley, D., Ozair, S., . . . Bengio, Y. (2014). Generative adversarial nets. In Advances in neural information processing systems (pp. 2672-2680). Academic Press.

Goodfellow, I. J. (2014). Generative adversarial nets. *Advances in Neural Information Processing Systems*, 2672–2680.

Goto, M., Otsuka, A., & Sueyoshi, T. (2014). DEA (Data Envelopment Analysis) assessment of operational and environmental efficiencies on Japanese regional industries. *Energy*, *66*, 535–549. doi:10.1016/j.energy.2013.12.020

Government of Nigeria. (2013). *Nigeria's National Broadband Plan 2013 - 2018*. Government of Nigeria. https://www.researchictafrica.net>national broadband plan 2013-2018.pdf

Goyal, S., Sah, A. N., Sharma, R. K., & Puri, J. (2020). Estimating technical efficiencies of Indian IT companies for setting improvement targets for inefficient companies: An empirical analysis with workers' effort as key input. *Work (Reading, Mass.)*, *66*(4), 885–900. doi:10.3233/WOR-203233 PMID:32925144

Grant, C., & Osanloo, A. (2016). Understanding, Selecting, and Integrating a Theoretical Framework in Dissertation Research. *Administrative Issues Journal: Connecting Education, Practice and Research*, 12–22.

Green, E. L. (2022, April 8). Lawsuit Charges For-Profit University Preyed on Black and Female Students. *NY Times*. https://www.nytimes.com/2022/04/08/us/politics/walden-university-lawsuit.html

Griffith, R., Redding, S. J., & Van Reenen, J. M. (2000). Mapping the two Faces of R&D: Productivity Growth in a Panel of OECD Industries. *SSRN*, *86*(4), 442–448. doi:10.2139srn.229400

Gupta, V. (2021). Composite Non-Paramertric CSR index for public sector banks of India. *PalArch's Journal of Archaeology of Egypt/Egyptology*, *18*(8), 1589-1607.

Gupta, M. C. (1995). Environmental management and its impact on the operations function. *International Journal of Operations & Production Management*, *15*(8), 34–51. doi:10.1108/01443579510094071

Gür, Ş., & Eren, T. (2018). *Application of Operational Research Techniques in Operating Room Scheduling Problems* (Vol. 2018). Literature Overview. In Journal of Healthcare Engineering. doi:10.1155/2018/5341394

Gygli, S., Haelg, F., Potrafke, N., & Sturm, J.-E. (2019). The KOF Globalisation Index – revisited. *The Review of International Organizations*, *14*(3), 543–574. Advance online publication. doi:10.100711558-019-09344-2

Habib, A. M., & Shahwan, T. M. (2020). Measuring the operational and financial efficiency using a Malmquist data envelopment analysis: A case of Egyptian hospitals. *Benchmarking*, *27*(9), 2521–2536. doi:10.1108/BIJ-01-2020-0041

Hadad, M. D., Hall, M. J. B., Kenjegaliev, K. A., Santoso, W., & Simper, R. (2011). Productivity changes and risk management in Indonesian banking: A Malmquist analysis. *Applied Financial Economics*, *21*(12), 847–861. doi:10.1080/09603107.2010.537636

Hadi, F. S. A., & Saad, N. M. (2010). An analysis on the efficiency of the Malaysian Islamic banking industry: Domestic vs. foreign. *Review of Islamic Economics*, *14*(1), 27–47.

Hahn, G. J., Brandenburg, M., & Becker, J. (2021). Valuing supply chain performance within and across manufacturing industries: A DEA-based approach. *International Journal of Production Economics*, *240*, 108203. doi:10.1016/j.ijpe.2021.108203

Halkos, G. E., & Salamouris, D. S. (2004). Efficiency measurement of the GREEK commercial banks with the use of financial ratios: A data envelopment analysis approach. *Management Accounting Research*, *15*(2), 201–224. doi:10.1016/j.mar.2004.02.001

Hänninen, M., Kwan, S. K., & Mitronen, L. (2021). From the store to omnichannel retail: Looking back over three decades of research. *International Review of Retail, Distribution and Consumer Research, 31*(1), 1–35. doi:10.1080/0 9593969.2020.1833961

Han, Y., Zhou, R., Geng, Z., Bai, J., Ma, B., & Fan, J. (2020). A novel data envelopment analysis cross-model integrating interpretative structural model and analytic hierarchy process for energy efficiency evaluation and optimization modeling: Application to ethylene industries. *Journal of Cleaner Production, 246*, 118965. doi:10.1016/j.jclepro.2019.118965

Harper, E. M., & McNair, D. (2017). *The Power of Disparate Data Sources for Answering Thorny Questions in Healthcare: Four Case Studies.* doi:10.1007/978-3-319-53300-1_18

Harper, J. (2005). Do ISPs have a duty to protect the world?: Against ISP Liability. *Telecommunications and Technology, 28*, 30.

Harris, P. A., Taylor, R., Minor, B. L., Elliott, V., Fernandez, M., O'Neal, L., McLeod, L., Delacqua, G., Delacqua, F., Kirby, J., & Duda, S. N. (2019). The REDCap consortium: Building an international community of software platform partners. *Journal of Biomedical Informatics, 95*, 103208. doi:10.1016/j.jbi.2019.103208 PMID:31078660

Hassan, M. K. (2006). The X-Efficiency in Islamic Banks. *Islamic Economic Studies, 13*(2), 49–78.

Heine, J., Fowler, E. E., Berglund, A., Schell, M. J., & Eschrich, S. (2023). Techniques to produce and evaluate realistic multivariate synthetic data. *Scientific Reports, 13*(1), 12266. doi:10.103841598-023-38832-0 PMID:37507387

Hemapala, K., Herath, H. M., & Swathika, O. V. (2019). Benchmarking medium voltage feeders using data envelopment analysis: A case study. *Telkomnika, 17*(3), 1547. Advance online publication. doi:10.12928/telkomnika.v17i3.9288

Henriques, C., Sobreiro, V. A., Kimura, H., & Mariano, E. B. (2018). Efficiency in the Brazilian banking system using data envelopment analysis. *Future Business Journal, 4*(2), 157–178. doi:10.1016/j.fbj.2018.05.001

Hernandez, M., Epelde, G., Alberdi, A., Cilla, R., & Rankin, D. (2022). Synthetic data generation for tabular health records: A systematic review. *Neurocomputing, 493*, 28–45. doi:10.1016/j.neucom.2022.04.053

Hesampour, R., Hassani, M., Hanafiah, M. M., & Heidarbeigi, K. (2022). Technical efficiency, sensitivity analysis and economic assessment applying data envelopment analysis approach: A case study of date production in Khuzestan State of Iran. *Journal of the Saudi Society of Agricultural Sciences, 21*(3), 197–207. doi:10.1016/j.jssas.2021.08.003

Hippe, D. S., Umoren, R. A., McGee, A., Bucher, S. L., & Bresnahan, B. W. (2020). A targeted systematic review of cost analyses for implementation of simulation-based education in healthcare. In SAGE Open Medicine (Vol. 8). doi:10.1177/2050312120913451

Hittmeir, M., Ekelhart, A., & Mayer, R. (2019, August). On the utility of synthetic data: An empirical evaluation on machine learning tasks. In *Proceedings of the 14th International Conference on Availability, Reliability and Security* (pp. 1-6). 10.1145/3339252.3339281

Hofmarcher, M. M., Paterson, I., & Riedel, M. (2002). Measuring hospital efficiency in Austria–a DEA approach. *Health Care Management Science, 5*(1), 7–14. doi:10.1023/A:1013292801100 PMID:11860081

Holtz-Eakin, D., & Schwartz, A. E. (1995). Spatial productivity spillovers from public infrastructure: Evidence from state highways. *International Tax and Public Finance, 12*(4), 459–468.

Horta, I., Camanho, A., Johnes, J., & Johnes, G. (2013). Performance trends in the construction industry worldwide: An overview of the turn of the century. *Journal of Productivity Analysis, 39*(1), 89–99. doi:10.100711123-012-0276-0

Ho, S. Y., & Iyke, B. N. (2020). The determinants of economic growth in Ghana: New empirical evidence. *Global Business Review*, *21*(3), 626–644. doi:10.1177/0972150918779282

Hossain, N. U. I., Lutfi, M., Ahmed, I., & Debusk, H. (2023). Application of systems modeling language (SysML) and discrete event simulation to address patient waiting time issues in healthcare. *Smart Health (Amsterdam, Netherlands)*, *29*, 100403. Advance online publication. doi:10.1016/j.smhl.2023.100403

Huang, C. (2018). Assessing the performance of tourism supply chains by using the hybrid network data envelopment analysis model. *Tourism Management*, *65*, 303–316. doi:10.1016/j.tourman.2017.10.013

Huang, Z. (2020). Deep learning in finance and banking: A survey. *Artificial Intelligence Review*, *53*, 2535–2558.

Humphrey, D. B. (1985). Costs and Scale Economies in Bank Intermediation. In R. C. Aspinwall & R. A. Eisenbeis (Eds.), *Handbook for Banking Strategy* (pp. 745–783). John Wiley and Sons.

Ichake, S., Gardas, B. B., Kharat, M. G., Raut, R. D., & Choudhury, N. (2018). Evaluation and selection of third party logistics services providers using data envelopment analysis: A sustainable approach. *International Journal of Business Excellence*, *14*(4), 427. Advance online publication. doi:10.1504/IJBEX.2018.10011212

Iddouch, K., El Badraoui, K., & Ouenniche, J. (2023). Landscape of research on the efficiency profiles of Islamic banks using DEA: Survey, classification and critical analysis of the literature. *International Journal of Business*, *28*(3), 1–46. Advance online publication. doi:10.55802/IJB.028(3).004

IEA. (2020, December). *Energy Efficiency 2020*. https://www.iea.org/reports/energy-efficiency-2020

Ifeonu, R. O. (2014). *Investigating the Impact of Technology Trust on the Acceptance of Mobile Banking Technonlgy Within Nigeria* [Doctoral thesis]. University of Huddersfield.

Ihua, U. (2010). Local Content Policy and SMEs Sector Promotion: The Nigerian Oil Industry Experience. *International Journal of Business and Management*, *5*(5), 3–14. doi:10.5539/ijbm.v5n5p3

Ileka, H., Zongwe, D., & Reuther, K. (2017). Rural Electrification with Hybrid Minigrids: Finding an Efficient and Durable Ownership Model. *The Law Reform and Development Commission of Namibia*, *25*, 351–382.

Imam, P., & Kpodar, K. (2016). Islamic banking: Good for growth? *Economic Modelling*, *59*, 387–401. doi:10.1016/j.econmod.2016.08.004

Iosifidis, G., Gao, L., Huang, J., & Tassiulas, L. (2017). Efficient and Fair Collaborative Mobile Internet Access. *IEEE/ACM Transactions on Networking*, *25*(3), 1386–1400. doi:10.1109/TNET.2016.2638939

Iqbal, F., & Siddiqui, A. (2017). Optimal configuration analysis for a campus microgrid—A case study. *Protection and Control of Modern Power Systems*, *2*(1), 23. Advance online publication. doi:10.118641601-017-0055-z

Irefin, I., Abdul-Azeez, I., & Tijani, A. (2012). Aninvestigative Studyof the Factors Affecting the Adoptionof Information and Communication Technology in Small and Medium Scale Enterprises in Nigeria. *Australian Journal of Business and Management Research, 5*(5), 1–9.

IRENA. (2022). *Renewable Power Generation Costs in 2021*. International Renewable Energy Agency. Available online_https://www.irena.org/publications/2022/Jul/Renewable-Power-Generation-Costs-in-2021

Isik, I., Kulali, I., & Agcayazi-Yilmaz, B. (2016). Total Factor Productivity Change in the Middle East Banking: The Case of Jordanian Banks at the Turn of the Millennium. *International Journal of Research in Business and Social Science, 5*(3), 1–29. doi:10.20525/ijrbs.v5i3.296

Isik, I., & Hassan, M. K. (2002). Technical, scale and allocative efficiencies of Turkish banking industry. *Journal of Banking & Finance, 26*(4), 719–766. doi:10.1016/S0378-4266(01)00167-4

Ismail, F., & Rahim, R. A. (2013). Productivity of Islamic and Conventional Banks of Malaysia: An Empirical Analysis. *The IUP Journal of Telecommunications, 12*(3), 7–20.

Ismali, A., & Krause, A. (2010). Determinants of the method of payment in mergers and acquisitions. *The Quarterly Review of Economics and Finance, 50*(4), 471–484. doi:10.1016/j.qref.2010.06.003

Ivanov, S., & Webster, C. (2019). Conceptual framework of the use of robots, artificial intelligence and service automation in travel, tourism, and hospitality companies. *Robots, artificial intelligence, and service automation in travel, tourism and hospitality*, 7-37.

Iyer, L. S. (2021). AI enabled applications towards intelligent transportation. *Transportation Engineering, 5*, 100083. doi:10.1016/j.treng.2021.100083

Izadikhah, M., & Farzipoor Saen, R. (2020). Ranking sustainable suppliers by context-dependent data envelopment analysis. *Annals of Operations Research, 293*(2), 607–637. doi:10.100710479-019-03370-4

Izadikhah, M., & Farzipoor Saen, R. (2023). Developing a linear stochastic two-stage data envelopment analysis model for evaluating sustainability of supply chains: A case study in welding industry. *Annals of Operations Research, 322*(1), 195–215. doi:10.100710479-021-04160-7

Jahan, N. (2019). Productivity Analysis of Commercial Banks of Bangladesh: A Malmquist Productivity Index Approach. *International Journal of Economics and Financial Issues, 9*(1), 108–115.

Jahed, R., Amirteimoori, A., & Azizi, H. (2015). Performance measurement of decision-making units under uncertainty conditions: An approach based on double frontier analysis. *Measurement, 69*, 264–279. doi:10.1016/j.measurement.2015.03.014

Jahid, A., Islam, M. S., Hossain, M. S., Hossain, M. E., Monju, M. K. H., & Hossain, M. F. (2019). Toward energy efficiency aware renewable energy management in green cellular networks with joint coordination. *IEEE Access : Practical Innovations, Open Solutions, 7*, 75782–75797. doi:10.1109/ACCESS.2019.2920924

Jain, R. K., & Natarajan, R. (2015). A DEA study of airlines in India. *Asia Pacific Management Review, 20*(4), 285–292. doi:10.1016/j.apmrv.2015.03.004

Jain, S., Seth, G., Paruthi, A., Soni, U., & Kumar, G. (2022). Synthetic data augmentation for surface defect detection and classification using deep learning. *Journal of Intelligent Manufacturing, 33*(4), 1–14. doi:10.100710845-020-01710-x

Jaipuria, N., Zhang, X., Bhasin, R., Arafa, M., Chakravarty, P., Shrivastava, S., ... Murali, V. N. (2020). Deflating dataset bias using synthetic data augmentation. In *Proceedings of the IEEE/CVF Conference on Computer Vision and Pattern Recognition Workshops* (pp. 772-773). 10.1109/CVPRW50498.2020.00394

Jalilian, H., Kirkpatrick, C., & Parker, D. (2007). The Impact of Regulation on Economic Growth in Developing Countries: A Cross-Country Analysis. *World Development, 35*(1), 87–103. doi:10.1016/j.worlddev.2006.09.005

Jardas Antonić, J. (2018). Data Envelopment Analysis in Improving Security Level in Local Government Units. *Balkans Journal of Emerging Trends in Social Sciences, 1*(1), 59–69. doi:10.31410/Balkans.JETSS.2018.1.1.59-69

Jayaraman, A.R., Srivasan, M.R., & Arunachalam, R. (2014). Impact of mergers and acquisition on the efficiency of Indian banks: a pre-post analysis using data envelopment analysis. *Journal of Financial Service Management, 7*(1), 1-18.

Jayaraman, A. R., & Srinivasan, M. R. (2019). Determinants of Indian banks efficiency: A two-stage approach. *International Journal of Operational Research*, 36(2), 270–291. doi:10.1504/IJOR.2019.102414

Jeha, P., Bohlke-Schneider, M., Mercado, P., Kapoor, S., Nirwan, R. S., Flunkert, V., ... Januschowski, T. (2021, October). PSA-GAN: Progressive self attention GANs for synthetic time series. *International Conference on Learning Representations*.

Jensen, M. C. (1986). Agency Cost of Free Cash Flow, Corporate Finance, and Takeovers. *SSRN*, 76(2), 323–329. doi:10.2139srn.99580

Jensen, M. C. (1986). Agency cost of free cash flow, corporate finance, and takeovers. *The American Economic Review*, 76(2), 5–50.

Jiang, H., Hua, M., Zhang, J., Cheng, P., Ye, Z., Huang, M., & Jin, Q. (2020). Sustainability efficiency assessment of wastewater treatment plants in China: A data envelopment analysis based on cluster benchmarking. *Journal of Cleaner Production*, 244, 118729. doi:10.1016/j.jclepro.2019.118729

Jiang, L., & Huang, Y. L. (2023). Healthcare call center efficiency improvement using a simulation approach to achieve the organization's target. *International Journal of Healthcare Management*, 1–10. Advance online publication. doi:10.1080/20479700.2023.2190250

Jiang, N., & Malkin, B. D. (2016). Use of Lean and CAHPS Surgical Care Survey to Improve Patients' Experiences with Surgical Care. *Otolaryngology - Head and Neck Surgery*, 155(5), 743–747. doi:10.1177/0194599816657051 PMID:27329420

Jiang, T., Ji, P., Shi, Y., Ye, Z., & Jin, Q. (2021). Efficiency assessment of green technology innovation of renewable energy enterprises in China: A dynamic data envelopment analysis considering undesirable output. *Clean Technologies and Environmental Policy*, 23(5), 1509–1519. doi:10.100710098-021-02044-9

Jin, B. E., & Shin, D. C. (2020). Changing the game to compete: Innovations in the fashion retail industry from the disruptive business model. *Business Horizons*, 63(3), 301–311. doi:10.1016/j.bushor.2020.01.004

João-Carlos, J. C. C. B., Angulo Meza, L., da Silveira, J. Q., & Gomes, E. G. (2013). About negative efficiencies in Cross Evaluation BCC input oriented models. *European Journal of Operational Research*, 229(3), 732–737. doi:10.1016/j.ejor.2013.02.020

Johnes, J., Izzeldin, M., & Pappas, V. (2009). *The efficiency of Islamic and conventional banks in the Gulf Cooperation Council (GCC) countries: An analysis using financial ratios and data envelopment analysis*. Working Paper.

Johnes, J., Izzeldin, M., & Pappas, V. (2014). Efficiency in Islamic and Conventional Banks: Evidence from the Gulf Cooperation Council Countries. SSRN *Electronic Journal*, 1–36. doi:10.2139/ssrn.2411974

Jokipii, T., & Monnin, P. (2013). The impact of banking sector stability on the real economy. *Journal of International Money and Finance*, 32, 1–16. doi:10.1016/j.jimonfin.2012.02.008

Jordon, J., Szpruch, L., Houssiau, F., Bottarelli, M., Cherubin, G., Maple, C., ... Weller, A. (2022). *Synthetic Data—what, why and how?* arXiv preprint arXiv:2205.03257.

Joseph, A. L., Kushniruk, A. W., & Borycki, E. M. (2020). Patient journey mapping: Current practices, challenges and future opportunities in healthcare. Knowledge Management & E-Learning. *International Journal (Toronto, Ont.)*, 387–404. Advance online publication. doi:10.34105/j.kmel.2020.12.021

Joshi, P. (2019). *Understand the Similarity of Internet Service Providers via Peer-to-Peer User Interest Analysis* [Masters Thesis]. University of Minnesota.

Jubilee, R. V. W., Kamarudin, F., Latiff, A. R. A., Hussain, H. I., & Tan, K. M. (2021a). Do Islamic versus conventional banks progress or regress in productivity level? *Future Business Journal*, 7(1), 22. Advance online publication. doi:10.118643093-021-00065-w

Jubilee, R. V. W., Razman, A., & Latiff, A. (2021b). (in press). Does globalisation have an impact on dual banking system productivity in selected Southeast Asian banking industry? *Asia-Pacific Journal of Business Administration*. Advance online publication. doi:10.1108/APJBA-09-2020-0343

Justia. (2011). *Yolanda Rene Travis, Leah Zitter, and Abbie Goldbas v. Walden University and Laureate Education.* https://cases.justia.com/federal/district-courts/maryland/mddce/1:2015cv00235/304055/304033/304050.pdf?ts=1446286879

Justia. (2022), *Kevin Morris et al., VS Rutgers-Newark University, et al.* [Court Case]. New Jersey Superior Court, Appellate Division. https://law.justia.com/cases/new-jersey/appellate-division-published/2022/a-0582-21.html

Kalyvitis, S., & Vella, E. (2011). Public capital maintenance, decentralization, and US productivity growth. *Public Finance Review*, 39(6), 784–809. doi:10.1177/1091142111422439

Kam, A. W., Collins, S., Park, T., Mihail, M., Stanaway, F. F., Lewis, N. L., Polya, D., Fraser-Bell, S., Roberts, T. V., & Smith, J. E. H. (2021). Using Lean Six Sigma techniques to improve efficiency in outpatient ophthalmology clinics. *BMC Health Services Research*, 21(1), 38. Advance online publication. doi:10.118612913-020-06034-3 PMID:33413381

Kamaruddin, F., Sufian, F., Nassir, A. M., Anwar, N. A. M., & Hussain, H. I. (2019). Bank efficiency in Malaysia a DEA approach. *Journal of Central Banking Theory and Practice*.

Kamaruddin, B. H., Safab, M. S., & Mohd, R. (2008). Assessing production efficiency of Islamic banks and conventional bank Islamic windows in Malaysia. *International Journal of Business and Management Science*, 1(1), 31–48.

Kamarudin, F., Hue, C. Z., Sufian, F., & Mohamad Anwar, N. A. (2017). Does productivity of Islamic banks endure progress or regress? Empirical evidence using data envelopment analysis-based Malmquist Productivity Index. *Humanomics*, 33(1), 84–118. doi:10.1108/H-08-2016-0059

Kamarudin, F., Mohamad Anwar, N. A., Md. Nassir, A., Sufian, F., Tan, K. M., & Iqbal Hussain, H. (2022). Does country governance and bank productivity Nexus matters? *Journal of Islamic Marketing*, 13(2), 329–380. doi:10.1108/JIMA-05-2019-0109

Kamarudin, F., Sufian, F., & Nassir, A. M. (2016). Global financial crisis, ownership and bank profit efficiency in the Bangladesh's state owned and private commercial banks. *Contaduría y Administración*, 61(4), 705–745. doi:10.1016/j.cya.2016.07.006

Kamel, M. A., & Mousa, M. E.-S. (2021). Measuring operational efficiency of isolation hospitals during COVID-19 pandemic using data envelopment analysis: A case of Egypt. *Benchmarking*, 28(7), 2178–2201. doi:10.1108/BIJ-09-2020-0481

Kao, C. (2010). Malmquist productivity index based on common-weights DEA: The case of Taiwan forests after reorganization. *Omega*, 38(6), 484–491. doi:10.1016/j.omega.2009.12.005

Kar, R.N. (2004). *Me4rgers and Acquisitions in India: Background, Implications and Emerging Issues.* Charted Secretary.

Karanlioglu, G., & Musajeva, S. (2017). *Comparison of Efficiency and Productivity between Islamic Banks in the GCC region A quantitative study using DEA and Malmquist index.* Academic Press.

Karras, T., Aila, T., Laine, S., & Lehtinen, J. (2017). *Progressive growing of GANs for improved quality, stability, and variation.* arXiv preprint arXiv:1710.10196.

Karras, T., Laine, S., & Aila, T. (2019). A style-based generator architecture for generative adversarial networks. In *Proceedings of the IEEE/CVF Conference on Computer Vision and Pattern Recognition* (pp. 4401-4410). 10.1109/CVPR.2019.00453

Kerstens, K., & de Woestyn, I. V. (2014). Comparing Malmquist and Hicks–Moorsteen productivity indices: Exploring the impact of unbalanced vs. balanced panel data. *European Journal of Operational Research, 233*(4), 749–758. doi:10.1016/j.ejor.2013.09.009

Keskitalo, T. (2022). Pedagogical Practices for Organizing Simulation-Based Healthcare Education. International Journal of Learning. *Teaching and Educational Research, 21*(4), 80–96. Advance online publication. doi:10.26803/ijlter.21.4.1

Khanal, S., & Bhatta, B. P. (2017). Evaluating Efficiency of Personnel in Nepalese Commercial Banks. *International Advances in Economic Research, 23*(4), 379–394. doi:10.100711294-017-9654-8

Khan, M. I., & Shah, I. A. (2015). Cost Efficiency and Total Factor Productivity of Islamic and Conventional Banks in Pakistan. *Research Journal of Finance and Accounting, 6*(5), 135–146.

Khemani, R. S. (1991). *Recent Trends in Merger and Acquisition Activity in Canada and Selected Countries.* Paper presented at the Investment Canada Conference, Corporate Globalization through Mergers and Acquisitions, Toronto, Canada.

Khoveyni, M., & Eslami, R. (2022). Merging two-stage series network structures: A DEA-based approach Merging two-stage series network structures: A DEA-based approach. *OR-Spektrum, 44*(1), 273–302. doi:10.100700291-021-00653-w

Kingma, D. P., & Welling, M. (2014). *Auto-Encoding Variational Bayes.* arXiv preprint arXiv:1312.6114.

Knowles, J., & Corne, D. (1999). The Pareto archived evolution strategy: A new baseline algorithm for Pareto multiobjective optimisation. *Proceedings of the 1999 Congress on Evolutionary Computation, CEC 1999, 1.* 10.1109/CEC.1999.781913

Kocisova, K., Hass-Symotiuk, M., & Kludacz-Alessandri, M. (2018). *Use of the DEA method to verify the performance model for hospitals.* Academic Press.

Koengkan, M., Fuinhas, J. A., Kazemzadeh, E., Osmani, F., Alavijeh, N. K., Auza, A., & Teixeira, M. (2022). Measuring the economic efficiency performance in Latin American and Caribbean countries: An empirical evidence from stochastic production frontier and data envelopment analysis. *International Economics, 169*, 43-54. https://doi.org/https://doi.org/10.1016/j.inteco.2021.11.004

Kohl, S., Schoenfelder, J., Fügener, A., & Brunner, J. O. (2019). The use of Data Envelopment Analysis (DEA) in healthcare with a focus on hospitals. *Health Care Management Science, 22*(2), 245–286. Advance online publication. doi:10.100710729-018-9436-8 PMID:29478088

Kontodimopoulos, N., Nanos, P., & Niakas, D. (2006). Balancing efficiency of health services and equity of access in remote areas in Greece. *Health Policy (Amsterdam), 76*(1), 49–57. doi:10.1016/j.healthpol.2005.04.006 PMID:15927299

Koopmans, T. C. (1951). An Analysis of Production as an Efficient Combination of Activities. In T. C. Koopmans (Ed.), *Activity Analysis of Production and Allocation.* NY: Cowles Commission for Research in Economics. https://www.scirp.org/%28S%28351jmbntvnsjt1aadkposzje%29%29/reference/referencespapers.aspx?referenceid=3107432

Kooreman, P. (1994). Nursing home care in The Netherlands: A nonparametric efficiency analysis. *Journal of Health Economics, 13*(3), 301–316. doi:10.1016/0167-6296(94)90029-9 PMID:10138856

Kosmidou, K. (2008). The determinants of banks' profits in Greece during the period of EU financial integration. *Managerial Finance*, *34*(3), 146–159. doi:10.1108/03074350810848036

Kothari, R. (1967). Political Change of 1967. *Economic and Political Weekly*, *6*(3/5), 231–250.

Kouaissah, N., & Hocine, A. (2022). XOR data envelopment analysis and its application to renewable energy sector. *Expert Systems with Applications*, *207*, 118044. doi:10.1016/j.eswa.2022.118044

Kuboye, B. M. (2017). Evaluation of Broadband Network Performance in Nigeria. *International Journal of Communications, Network and Systems Sciences*, *10*(09), 199–207. doi:10.4236/ijcns.2017.109011

Kuboye, B., Alese, B., & Imasuen, F. (2012). A Twin Approach to Internet Service Provision in Sparse Rural Community in Nigeria. *International Journal of Networks and Communications*, *2*(5), 132–137. doi:10.5923/j.ijnc.20120205.06

Kumar, S., & Gulati, R. (2014). *Deregulation and efficiency of Indian banks*. Academic Press.

Kumar, D., Singh, R. K., Mishra, R., & Wamba, S. F. (2022). Applications of the internet of things for optimizing warehousing and logistics operations: A systematic literature review and future research directions. *Computers & Industrial Engineering*, *171*, 108455. doi:10.1016/j.cie.2022.108455

Kumar, S. (2008). An analysis of efficiency-profitability relationship in Indian public sector banks. *Global Business Review*, *9*(1), 115–129. doi:10.1177/097215090700900108

Kumar, S., & Gulati, R. (2008). Evaluation of technical efficiency and ranking of public sector banks in India: An analysis from cross-sectional perspective. *International Journal of Productivity and Performance Management*, *57*(7), 540–568. doi:10.1108/17410400810904029

Kumar, S., & Gulati, R. (2009). Did Efficiency of Indian public sector banks converge with banking reforms? *International Review of Economics*, *56*(1), 47–84. doi:10.100712232-008-0057-2

Kumar, S., & Gulati, R. (2009). Measuring efficiency, effectiveness and performance of Indian public sector banks. *International Journal of Productivity and Performance Management*, *59*(1), 51–74. doi:10.1108/17410401011006112

Kumar, S., & Gulati, R. (2016). Assessing the impact of the global financial crisis on the profit efficiency of Indian banks. *Economic Modelling*, *58*, 167–181. doi:10.1016/j.econmod.2016.05.029

Kumar, S., & Verma, S. (2003). Technical efficiency, benchmarks and targets: A case study of Indian public sector banks. *Prajnan: Journal of Social and Management Sciences*, *31*(4), 275–300.

Kumbhakar, S. C., Wang, H.-J., & Horncastle, A. P. (2015). *A Practitioner's Guide to Stochastic Frontier Analysis Using Stata*. Cambridge University Press. doi:10.1017/CBO9781139342070

Kuosmanen, T., Bijsterbosch, N., & Dellink, R. (2009). Environmental cost–benefit analysis of alternative timing strategies in greenhouse gas abatement: A data envelopment analysis approach. *Ecological Economics*, *68*(6), 1633–1642. doi:10.1016/j.ecolecon.2008.07.012

Kvet, M., & Janáček, J. (2023). Directed Search for Non-Dominated Emergency Medical System Designs. *Applied Sciences (Basel, Switzerland)*, *13*(8), 4810. Advance online publication. doi:10.3390/app13084810

Kyte, R. (2018, March 20). *An Inefficient Truth*. https://www.seforall.org/news/an-inefficient-truth or https://www.euractiv.com/section/energy/opinion/an-inefficient-truth/

Kyte, R. (2018, May 3). Smarter thinking can offer quicker results on global goals of universal energy access. *Sustainable Energy for All*. https://www.seforall.org/press-releases/smarter-thinking-can-offer-quicker-results-on-global-goals-of-universal-energy

Lamé, G., Crowe, S., Komashie, A., & Royston, G. (2023). Joining forces: The value of design partnering with operational research to improve healthcare delivery. *Design Science*, *9*, e4. Advance online publication. doi:10.1017/dsj.2023.2

Langer, A., & Mukherjee, A. (2023). *Developing a Path to Data Dominance: Strategies for Digital Data-Centric Enterprises*. Springer Nature. doi:10.1007/978-3-031-26401-6

Lange, S., Pohl, J., & Santarius, T. (2020). Digitalization and energy consumption. Does ICT reduce energy demand? *Ecological Economics*, *176*, 106760. doi:10.1016/j.ecolecon.2020.106760

Lawal, L. S., Ahmed-Rufai, T., Chatwin, C. R., & Young, R. C. D. (2013). Delivery of broadband services to SubSaharan Africa via Nigerian communications satellite. *International Journal of Information and Computer Science*, *2*(5), 77–88.

Le, T. A., Baydin, A. G., Zinkov, R., & Wood, F. (2017, May). Using synthetic data to train neural networks is model-based reasoning. In *2017 international joint conference on neural networks (IJCNN)* (pp. 3514-3521). IEEE.

Lee, C. C., Kim, Y., Choi, J. H., & Porter, E. (2022). Does Electronic Health Record Systems Implementation Impact Hospital Efficiency, Profitability, and Quality? *Journal of Applied Business & Economics*, *24*(2).

Lee, C., & Johnson, A. L. (2015). Effective production: Measuring of the sales effect using data envelopment analysis. *Annals of Operations Research*, *235*(1), 453–486. doi:10.100710479-015-1932-3

Lee, D., & Yoon, S. N. (2021). Application of artificial intelligence-based technologies in the healthcare industry: Opportunities and challenges. *International Journal of Environmental Research and Public Health*, *18*(1), 271. doi:10.3390/ijerph18010271 PMID:33401373

Lee, E. K., Atallah, H. Y., Wright, M. D., Post, E. T., Thomas, C. IV, Wu, D. T., & Haley, L. L. Jr. (2015). Transforming hospital emergency department workflow and patient care. *Interfaces*, *45*(1), 58–82. Advance online publication. doi:10.1287/inte.2014.0788

Leimbach, M., Kriegler, E., Roming, N., & Schwanitz, J. (2017). Future growth patterns of world regions – A GDP scenario approach. *Global Environmental Change*, *42*, 215–225. doi:10.1016/j.gloenvcha.2015.02.005

Liang, L., Cook, W. D., & Zhu, J. (2008). DEA models for two-stage processes: Game approach and efficiency decomposition. *Naval Research Logistics*, *55*(7), 643–653. doi:10.1002/nav.20308

Li, H. X., Li, Y., Jiang, B., Zhang, L., Wu, X., & Lin, J. (2020). Energy performance optimisation of building envelope retrofit through integrated orthogonal arrays with data envelopment analysis. *Renewable Energy*, *149*, 1414–1423. doi:10.1016/j.renene.2019.10.143

Li, H., & Dong, S. (2015). Measuring and benchmarking technical efficiency of public hospitals in Tianjin, China: A bootstrap–data envelopment analysis approach. *INQUIRY: The Journal of Health Care Organization, Provision, and Financing*, *52*, 0046958015605487. PMID:26396090

Lingard, L., & Colquhoun, H. (2022). The story behind the synthesis: Writing an effective introduction to your scoping review. *Perspectives on Medical Education*, *11*(5), 1–6. doi:10.1007/S40037-022-00719-7 PMID:35960445

Lithgart, J. E., & Suarez, R. M. (2011). The productivity of public capital: a meta-analysis. In W. Jonkhoff & W. Manshanden (Eds.), *Infrastructure Productivity Evaluation* (pp. 5–32). Springer.

Liu, J. (2023). *A Synthetic Data-driven Solution for Urban Drinking Water Source Management* [Master's thesis]. NTNU.

Liu, F., Li, L., Ye, B., & Qin, Q. (2023). A novel stochastic semi-parametric frontier-based three-stage DEA window model to evaluate China's industrial green economic efficiency. *Energy Economics*, *119*, 106566. doi:10.1016/j.eneco.2023.106566

Liu, H., Wu, W., & Yao, P. (2022). A study on the efficiency of pediatric healthcare services and its influencing factors in China——estimation of a three-stage DEA model based on provincial-level data. *Socio-Economic Planning Sciences*, *84*, 101315. doi:10.1016/j.seps.2022.101315

Liu, J. S., Lu, L. Y. Y., Lu, W.-M., & Lin, B. J. Y. (2013). Data envelopment analysis 1978–2010: A citation-based literature survey. *Omega*, *41*(1), 3–15. doi:10.1016/j.omega.2010.12.006

Liu, W., Luo, B., & Liu, J. (2021). Synthetic data augmentation using multiscale attention CycleGAN for aircraft detection in remote sensing images. *IEEE Geoscience and Remote Sensing Letters*, *19*, 1–5.

Li, W., & Wang, J. (2021). Residual learning of cycle-GAN for seismic data denoising. *IEEE Access : Practical Innovations, Open Solutions*, *9*, 11585–11597. doi:10.1109/ACCESS.2021.3049479

Llorens, V., Martín-Oliver, A., & Salas-Fumas, V. (2020). Productivity, competition and bank restructuring process. *SERIEs*, *11*(3), 313–340. doi:10.100713209-020-00214-4

Lombardo, G., Pellegrino, M., & Poggi, A. (2022). Unsupervised Continual Learning From Synthetic Data Generated with Agent-Based Modeling and Simulation: A preliminary experimentation. *CEUR Workshop Proceedings*, *3261*, 1–11.

Lotfi, F. H., Ebrahimnejad, A., Vaez-Ghasemi, M., & Moghaddas, Z. (2020). *Data Envelopment Analysis with R Ebook*. Springer. doi:10.1007/978-3-030-24277-0

Louhi, J. T. (2007, September). Energy efficiency of modern cellular base stations. In *INTELEC 07-29th International Telecommunications Energy Conference* (pp. 475-476). IEEE. 10.1109/INTLEC.2007.4448824

Luangkesorn, K. L., & Eren-Doğu, Z. F. (2016). Markov Chain Monte Carlo methods for estimating surgery duration. *Journal of Statistical Computation and Simulation*, *86*(2), 262–278. Advance online publication. doi:10.1080/00949655.2015.1004065

Lychev, A. V. (2023). Synthetic Data Generation for Data Envelopment Analysis. *Data*, *8*(10), 146. doi:10.3390/data8100146

Maghsoodi, A., Saghaei, A., & Hafezalkotob, A. (2019). Service quality measurement model integrating an extended SERVQUAL model and a hybrid decision support system. *European Research on Management and Business Economics*, *25*(3), 151–164. doi:10.1016/j.iedeen.2019.04.004

Mahmoudabadi, M. Z., & Emrouznejad, A. (2019). Comprehensive performance evaluation of banking branches: A three-stage slacks-based measure (SBM) data envelopment analysis. *International Review of Economics & Finance*, *64*, 359–376. doi:10.1016/j.iref.2019.08.001

Mahmoudi, R., Emrouznejad, A., Shetab-Boushehri, S.-N., & Hejazi, S. R. (2020). The origins, development and future directions of data envelopment analysis approach in transportation systems. *Socio-Economic Planning Sciences*, *69*, 100672. doi:10.1016/j.seps.2018.11.009

Makhdoom, I., Lipman, J., Abolhasan, M., & Challen, D. (2022). Science and Technology Parks: A futuristic approach. *IEEE Access : Practical Innovations, Open Solutions*, *10*, 31981–32021. doi:10.1109/ACCESS.2022.3159798

Malana, N. M. & Malano, H. M. (2006). Benchmarking productive efficiency of selected wheat areas in Pakistan and India using data envelopment analysis. *Irrigation and Drainage: The Journal of the International Commission on Irrigation and Drainage, 55*(4), 383-394.

Maniago, R., Miao, J., Jou, S., Calip, G. S., Huda, S., Shulman, L. N., Bange, E. M., Singh, A. P., & Davella, C. (2022). Do clinical pathways impede provider workflow: A provider efficiency analysis of time spent using an EHR-embedded clinical decision support tool. *Journal of Clinical Oncology*, *40*(28, suppl), 381–381. doi:10.1200/JCO.2022.40.28_suppl.381

Mardani, A., Streimikiene, D., Balezentis, T., Saman, M., Nor, K., & Khoshnava, S. (2018). Data Envelopment Analysis in Energy and Environmental Economics: An Overview of the State-of-the-Art and Recent Development Trends. *Energies*, *11*(8). . doi:10.3390/en11082002

Mardani, A., Zavadskas, E. K., Streimikiene, D., Jusoh, A., & Khoshnoudi, M. (2017). A comprehensive review of data envelopment analysis (DEA) approach in energy efficiency. *Renewable & Sustainable Energy Reviews*, *70*, 1298–1322. doi:10.1016/j.rser.2016.12.030

Marin-Garcia, J. A., Vidal-Carreras, P. I., & Garcia-Sabater, J. J. (2021). The Role of Value Stream Mapping in Healthcare Services: A Scoping Review. *International Journal of Environmental Research and Public Health*, *18*(3), 1–25. doi:10.3390/ijerph18030951 PMID:33499116

Marinho, A., & Araújo, C. A. S. (2021). Using data envelopment analysis and the bootstrap method to evaluate organ transplantation efficiency in Brazil. *Health Care Management Science*, *24*(3), 569–581. doi:10.100710729-021-09552-6 PMID:33730290

Mark, B. A., Jones, C. B., Lindley, L., & Ozcan, Y. A. (2009). An examination of technical efficiency, quality, and patient safety in acute care nursing units. *Policy, Politics & Nursing Practice*, *10*(3), 180–186. doi:10.1177/1527154409346322 PMID:20008398

Markowitz, H. M. (1952). *Portfolio selection.* https://onlinelibrary.wiley.com/doi/10.1111/j.1540-6261.1952.tb01525.x/abstract

Martin, S., & Riordan, R. (2020). *Capital Mobilization Plan for a Canadian Low-Carbon Economy.* Institute for Sustainable Finance, Queen's University. https://smith. queensu. ca/centres/isf/pdfs/ISF-CapitalMobilizationPlan. pdf

Martín-Gamboa, M., Iribarren, D., & Dufour, J. (2017). Environmental impact efficiency of natural gas combined cycle power plants: A combined life cycle assessment and dynamic data envelopment analysis approach. *The Science of the Total Environment*, *615*, 29–37. doi:10.1016/j.scitotenv.2017.09.243 PMID:28963894

Martín-Gamboa, M., Iribarren, D., García-Gusano, D., & Dufour, J. (2017). A review of life-cycle approaches coupled with data envelopment analysis within multi-criteria decision analysis for sustainability assessment of energy systems. *Journal of Cleaner Production*, *150*, 164–174. doi:10.1016/j.jclepro.2017.03.017

Martiri, E. (2022). *Honey Templates: a Protection Mechanism for Biometric Systems.* Academic Press.

Martiri, E., & Yang, B. (2020, November). On the predictability of biometric honey templates, based on Bayesian inference. In *2020 the 10th International Conference on Communication and Network Security* (pp. 123-134). 10.1145/3442520.3442532

Matheus, M. N., & Sastry Musti, K. S. (2023), Design and Simulation of a Floating Solar Power Plant for Goreagab Dam, Namibia. In Human Agro-Energy Optimization for Business and Industry. IGI Global. doi:10.4018/978-1-6684-4118-3.ch001

Math, S. B., Basavaraju, V., Harihara, S. N., Gowda, G. S., Manjunatha, N., Kumar, C. N., & Gowda, M. (2019). Mental Healthcare Act 2017–aspiration to action. *Indian Journal of Psychiatry*, *61*(Suppl 4), S660. doi:10.4103/psychiatry.IndianJPsychiatry_188_19 PMID:31040454

Maudos, J., & Pastor, J. M. (2003). Cost and profit efficiency in the Spanish banking sector (1985–1996): A non-parametric approach. *Applied Financial Economics, 13*(1), 1–12. doi:10.1080/09603100110086087

Maudos, J., Pastor, J. M., Perez, F., & Quesada, J. (2002). Cost and profit efficiency in European banks. *Journal of International Financial Markets, Institutions and Money, 12*(1), 33–58. doi:10.1016/S1042-4431(01)00051-8

McDermott, O., Antony, J., Bhat, S., Jayaraman, R., Rosa, A., Marolla, G., & Parida, R. (2022). Lean Six Sigma in Healthcare: A Systematic Literature Review on Challenges, Organisational Readiness and Critical Success Factors. *Processes (Basel, Switzerland), 10*(10), 1945. doi:10.3390/pr10101945

Medarević, A., & Vuković, D. (2021). Efficiency and productivity of public hospitals in Serbia using DEA-malmquist model and tobit regression model, 2015–2019. *International Journal of Environmental Research and Public Health, 18*(23), 12475. doi:10.3390/ijerph182312475 PMID:34886202

Medina-Borja, A., Pasupathy, K. S., & Triantis, K. (2007). Large-scale data envelopment analysis (DEA) implementation: A strategic performance management approach. *The Journal of the Operational Research Society, 58*(8), 1084–1098. Advance online publication. doi:10.1057/palgrave.jors.2602200

Mehra, R., & Sharma, M. K. (2021). Measures of Sustainability in Healthcare. *Sustainability Analytics and Modeling, 1*, 100001. Advance online publication. doi:10.1016/j.samod.2021.100001

Mehrtak, M., Yusefzadeh, H., & Jaafaripooyan, E. (2014). Pabon Lasso and Data Envelopment Analysis: A complementary approach to hospital performance measurement. *Global Journal of Health Science, 6*(4), 107. doi:10.5539/gjhs.v6n4p107 PMID:24999147

Melki, R. (2020). *Designing Physical Layer Security Solutions For Emerging Communication Systems in 5G Networks* [Doctoral dissertation].

Memari, F., Momeni, M., & Ghasemi, A. R. (2014). Synthetic application of data envelopment analysis and balanced scorecard for systems performance Evaluation: A Review In. *International Research Journal of Applied and Basic Sciences, 8*(10), 1525–1530.

Meng, L., & Yi, L., & Li, W. (2019). The Empirical Research of Multi-energy Micro grid Operation Efficiency Based on DEA Method. *IOP Conference Series: Earth and Environmental Science.* 10.1088/1755-1315/300/4/042071

Mester, I. J., Nakamura, I. I., & Renault, M. (1998). *Checking accounts and bank monitoring.* Working Paper No. 98-125, Federal Reserve Bank of Philadelphia.

Meyer, D., Nagler, T., & Hogan, R. J. (2021). Copula-based synthetic data augmentation for machine-learning emulators. *Geoscientific Model Development, 14*(8), 5205–5215. doi:10.5194/gmd-14-5205-2021

Min, A., Park, C. G., & Scott, L. D. (2016). An examination of nursing care quality efficiency in US nursing homes: Using data envelopment analysis. *Western Journal of Nursing Research, 38*(10), 1387–1388. doi:10.1177/0193945916658196 PMID:27655090

Miok, K., Nguyen-Doan, D., Zaharie, D., & Robnik-Šikonja, M. (2019, September). Generating data using Monte Carlo dropout. In *2019 IEEE 15th International Conference on Intelligent Computer Communication and Processing (ICCP)* (pp. 509-515). IEEE. 10.1109/ICCP48234.2019.8959787

Mirmozaffari, M., & Kamal, N. (2023). The Application of Data Envelopment Analysis to Emergency Departments and Management of Emergency Conditions: A Narrative Review. *Healthcare.*

Mirmozaffari, M., Shadkam, E., Khalili, S. M., Kabirifar, K., Yazdani, R., & Asgari Gashteroodkhani, T. (2021). A novel artificial intelligent approach: Comparison of machine learning tools and algorithms based on optimization DEA Malmquist productivity index for eco-efficiency evaluation. *International Journal of Energy Sector Management*, *15*(3), 523–550. doi:10.1108/IJESM-02-2020-0003

Mirmozaffari, M., Shadkam, E., Khalili, S. M., & Yazdani, M. (2021). Developing a Novel Integrated Generalised Data Envelopment Analysis (DEA) to Evaluate Hospitals Providing Stroke Care Services. *Bioengineering (Basel, Switzerland)*, *8*(12), 207. Advance online publication. doi:10.3390/bioengineering8120207 PMID:34940361

Mirza, B., Haroon, D., Khan, B., Padhani, A., & Syed, T. Q. (2021). Deep generative models to counter class imbalance: A model-metric mapping with proportion calibration methodology. *IEEE Access : Practical Innovations, Open Solutions*, *9*, 55879–55897. doi:10.1109/ACCESS.2021.3071389

Mistry, D., Savani, V., & Vidyanagar, V. 2015. A Comparative Study of the Profitability Performance in the Banking Sector Evidence from Indian Private Sector Bank. *XVI Annual Conference Proceedings*, 346–60.

Mitchell, S., O'Sullivan, M., & Dunning, I. (2011). *PuLP: A Linear Programming Toolkit for Python*. The University of Auckland.

Mobarek, A., & Kalonov, A. (2014). Comparative performance analysis between conventional and Islamic banks: Empirical evidence from OIC countries. *Applied Economics*, *46*(3), 253–270. doi:10.1080/00036846.2013.839863

Modeling and Simulation of Discrete-Event Systems. (2013). *Modeling and Simulation of Discrete-Event Systems*. doi:10.1002/9781118732793

Moeller, S. B., Schlingemann, F. P., & Stulz, R. M. (2004). Firm Size and the gain from acquisitions. *Journal of Financial Economics*, *73*(2), 201–228. doi:10.1016/j.jfineco.2003.07.002

Mohanan, P. (2021). Cardiological Society of India: Cardiological Society of India. *AsiaIntervention*, *7*(2), 76. doi:10.4244/AIJV7I2A16 PMID:34913009

Mohanta, K. K., Sharanappa, D. S., & Aggarwal, A. (2023). A novel modified Khatter's approach for solving Neutrosophic Data Envelopment Analysis. *Croatian Operational Research Review*, *14*(1), 15–28. doi:10.17535/crorr.2023.0002

Mohd Chachuli, F. S., Ahmad Ludin, N., Mat, S., & Sopian, K. (2020). Renewable energy performance evaluation studies using the data envelopment analysis (DEA): A systematic review. *Journal of Renewable and Sustainable Energy*, *12*(6), 062701. Advance online publication. doi:10.1063/5.0024750

Molcho, M., Gavin, A., & Goodwin, D. (2021). Levels of physical activity and mental health in adolescents in Ireland. *International Journal of Environmental Research and Public Health*, *18*(4), 1713. Advance online publication. doi:10.3390/ijerph18041713 PMID:33578906

Mollah, S., Hassan, M. K., Al Farooque, O., & Mobarek, A. (2016). The governance, risk-taking, and performance of Islamic banks. *Journal of Financial Services Research*, *51*(2), 195–219. doi:10.100710693-016-0245-2

Mondal, S., & Mitra, P. (2022). The Role of Emerging Technologies to Fight Against COVID-19 Pandemic: An Exploratory Review. *Transactions of the Indian National Academy of Engineering : an International Journal of Engineering and Technology*, *7*(1), 157–174. doi:10.100741403-022-00322-6 PMID:35837009

Monroe, J., Moore, J., & Allen, G. (2018). Synthetic Data for Text. In *Proceedings of the 56th Annual Meeting of the Association for Computational Linguistics (Volume 1: Long Papers)* (pp. 501-511). Academic Press.

Mora, H., Mendoza-Tello, J. C., Varela-Guzmán, E. G., & Szymanski, J. (2021). Blockchain technologies to address smart city and society challenges. *Computers in Human Behavior*, *122*, 106854. doi:10.1016/j.chb.2021.106854

Mousavi-Avval, S. H., Rafiee, S., Jafari, A., & Mohammadi, A. (2011). Improving energy use efficiency of canola production using data envelopment analysis (DEA) approach. *Energy*, *36*(5), 2765–2772. doi:10.1016/j.energy.2011.02.016

Mousumi, B., & Sarit, B. (2021). Mergers and Acquisition and Value Creation: A Banking Industry Perspective. *IUP Journal of Accounting Research and Audit Practices*, *20*(4), 32–46.

Mugo, M. (2013). Determinants of Service Quality among the Internet Service Providers in Kenya. *Journal of Business Management and Corporate Affairs*, *2*(2), 19–29.

Mukherjee, J., & Janssen, M. C. (2023). *Recreating the Power Grid: Navigating Technological and Organizational Changes*. Taylor & Francis.

Mulder, J. D., & Hamaker, E. L. (2021). Three extensions of the random intercept cross-lagged panel model. *Structural Equation Modeling*, *28*(4), 638–648. doi:10.1080/10705511.2020.1784738

Munirathinam, S. (2020). Industry 4.0: Industrial internet of things (IIOT). *Advances in Computers*, *117*, 129–164. doi:10.1016/bs.adcom.2019.10.010

Munnell, A. H. (1990). Why has productivity growth declined? Productivity and public investment. *New England Economic Review*, 3–22.

Munnell, A. H., & Cook, L. M. (1990). How does public infrastructure affect regional economic performance? *New England Economic Review*, 11–33.

Munn, Z., Peters, M. D. J., Stern, C., Tufanaru, C., McArthur, A., & Aromataris, E. (2018). Systematic review or scoping review? Guidance for authors when choosing between a systematic or scoping review approach. *BMC Medical Research Methodology*, *18*(1), 143. doi:10.118612874-018-0611-x PMID:30453902

Murova, O., & Khan, A. (2017). Public investments, productivity and economic growth: A cross-state study of selected public expenditures in the United States. *International Journal of Productivity and Performance Management*, *66*(2), 251–265. doi:10.1108/IJPPM-12-2015-0190

Musti, K. S. S. (2020). Quantification of Demand Response in Smart Grids. *IEEE International Conference INDISCON*, 278-282. 10.1109/INDISCON50162.2020.00063

Musti, K. S. S., & Kapali, D. (2021). *Digital Transformation of SMEs in the Energy Sector to Survive in a Post-COVID-19 Era. In Handbook of Research on Strategies and Interventions to Mitigate COVID-19 Impact on SMEs*. IGI Global. doi:10.4018/978-1-7998-7436-2.ch009

Myers, S. C. (1977). Determinants of corporate borrowing. *Journal of Financial Economics*, *5*(2), 147–175. doi:10.1016/0304-405X(77)90015-0

Napierala, J., & Kvetan, V. (2023). Changing job skills in a changing world. In *Handbook of Computational Social Science for Policy* (pp. 243–259). Springer International Publishing Cham. doi:10.1007/978-3-031-16624-2_13

Nartey, A. B., Osei, K. A., & Sarpong-Kumankoma, E. (2019). Bank productivity in Africa. *International Journal of Productivity and Performance Management*, *69*(9), 1973–1997. doi:10.1108/IJPPM-09-2018-0328

Naves, R., Khalife, H., Jakllari, G., Conan, V., & Beylot, A.-L. (2018). A Framework for Evaluating Physical-Layer Network Coding Gains in Multi-hop Wireless Networks. *IEEE Transactions on Mobile Computing*, 1–1. doi:10.1109/TMC.2018.2883429

Needham, J., Beggs, R., & van de Mortel, T. F. (2023). Supporting learners in prison healthcare work-integrated learning settings through simulation: A cross-sectional study. *BMC Nursing*, 22(1), 322. doi:10.118612912-023-01506-3 PMID:37723488

Nepomuceno, T. C. C., Costa, A. P. C. S., & Daraio, C. (2023). Theoretical and Empirical Advances in the Assessment of Productive Efficiency since the introduction of DEA: A Bibliometric Analysis. *International Journal of Operational Research*, 46(4), 505–549. doi:10.1504/IJOR.2023.129960

Ngee-Wen, T., Zailani, S., Aziz, A. A., & Ahmad, R. (2020). Lean public emergency department efficiency evaluation by slack-based measure data envelopment analysis. *Malaysian Journal of Medicine and Health Sciences*, 16(2).

Ngobeni, V., Breitenbach, M. C., & Aye, G. C. (2020). Technical efficiency of provincial public healthcare in South Africa. *Cost Effectiveness and Resource Allocation*, 18(1), 1–19. doi:10.118612962-020-0199-y PMID:32002018

Nguyen, H. V., & Vreeken, J. (2015). Non-parametric jensen-shannon divergence. *Machine Learning and Knowledge Discovery in Databases: European Conference, ECML PKDD 2015, Porto, Portugal, September 7-11, 2015 Proceedings*, 15(Part II), 173–189.

Ni Luasa, S., Dineen, D., & Zieba, M. (2018). Technical and scale efficiency in public and private Irish nursing homes–a bootstrap DEA approach. *Health Care Management Science*, 21(3), 326–347. doi:10.100710729-016-9389-8 PMID:27787751

Nicholas, J. (2023). Lean daily management in healthcare: Origins, practices, and associations with lean leadership and lean sustainability. *Total Quality Management & Business Excellence*, 34(11-12), 1526–1552. Advance online publication. doi:10.1080/14783363.2023.2182677

Nigam, V., Thakur, T., Sethi, V. K., & Singh, R. P. (2012). Benchmarking of Indian mobile telecom operators using DEA with sensitivity analysis. *Benchmarking*, 19(2), 219–238. Advance online publication. doi:10.1108/14635771211224545

Nigerian Communications Commission. (2018). *Nigerian Communications Commission Stakeholder Information*. Nigerian Communications Commission. https://www.ncc.gov.ng/stakeholder/statistics-reports/industry-overview#view-graphs-tables

Nigerian Communications Commission. (2020). *Who We Are*. https://www.ncc.gov.ng/the-ncc/who-we-are

Nissi, E., & Rapposelli, A. (2010). A Data Envelopment Analysis of Italian Courts Efficiency. *Italian Journal of Applied Statistics*, 22(2), 12.

Niu, Y., Li, X., Zhang, J., Deng, X., & Chang, Y. (2023). Efficiency of railway transport: A comparative analysis for 16 countries. *Transport Policy*, 141, 42–53. doi:10.1016/j.tranpol.2023.07.007

Nkiriki, J., & Ustun, T. S. (2017). *Minigrid policy directions for decentralized smart energy models in Sub-Saharan Africa. In IEEE PES Innovative Smart Grid Technologies Conference Europe*. ISGT-Europe. doi:10.1109/ISGTEurope.2017.8260217

Nugrohowati, R. N. I., Fakhrunnas, F., & Haron, R. (2020). Examining Technological and Productivity Change in the Islamic Banking Industry. *Pertanika Journal of Social Science & Humanities*, 28(4), 3355–3374. doi:10.47836/pjssh.28.4.47

O'Donnell, C., & Nguyen, K. (2011). *Review of efficiency measurement methodologies to inform hospital resource allocation decisions in NSW: a rapid review*. Sax Institute.

O'Sullivan, A., & Sheffrin, A. (2003). *Economics: Principles and actions*. Prentice hall.

Obadić, A., & Aristovnik, A. (2011). Relative efficiency of higher education in Croatia and Slovenia: An international comparison. *Amfiteatru Economic Journal*, *13*(30), 362–376.

Octrina, F., & Mariam, A. G. S. (2021). Productivity of Islamic Banking in Indonesia. *Jurnal Perspektif Pembiayaan Dan Pembangunan Daerah*, *9*(1), 19–28. doi:10.22437/ppd.v9i1.11041

Olise, M., Anigbogu, T., Edoko, T., & Okoli, M. (2014). Determinants of ICT Adoption for Improved SME's Performance in Anambra State, Nigeria. *American International Journal of Contemporary Research*, *4*(7), 163–176.

Omar, M. A., Abd. Majid, M. S., & Rulindo, R. (2006). Efficiency and Productivity Performance of the National Private Banks in Indonesia. *Gadjah Mada International Journal of Business*, *9*(1), 1. doi:10.22146/gamaijb.5603

Omrani, H., Emrouznejad, A., Shamsi, M., & Fahimi, P. (2022). Evaluation of insurance companies considering uncertainty: A multi-objective network data envelopment analysis model with negative data and undesirable outputs. *Socio-Economic Planning Sciences*, *82*, 101306. doi:10.1016/j.seps.2022.101306

Ononiwu, G., Akinwole, B., Agubor, C., & Onojo, J. (2016). Performance Evaluation of Major Mobile network operators in Owerri metropolis of Nigeria. *International Journal of Engineering Technologies in Computational and Applied Sciences*, *18*(1), 6–13.

Onour, I. A., & Abdalla, A. M. A. (2011). Efficiency of Islamic Banks in Sudan: A non-parametric Approach. *Journal of Islamic Economics. Banking and Finance*, *7*(4), 79–92.

Ortíz-Barrios, M. A., & Alfaro-Saíz, J. J. (2020). Methodological approaches to support process improvement in emergency departments: A systematic review. In International Journal of Environmental Research and Public Health (Vol. 17, Issue 8). doi:10.3390/ijerph17082664

OSDEA. (2020, March). *OSDEA-GUI*. Retrieved from https://github.com/hub187/opensourcedea-lib.git

Osman, I. H., Berbary, L. N., Sidani, Y., Al-Ayoubi, B., & Emrouznejad, A. (2011). Data envelopment analysis model for the appraisal and relative performance evaluation of nurses at an intensive care unit. *Journal of Medical Systems*, *35*(5), 1039–1062. doi:10.100710916-010-9570-4 PMID:20734223

Otaviya, S. A., & Rani, L. N. (2020). Productivity and its Determinants in Islamic Banks: Evidence from Indonesia. *Journal of Islamic Monetary Economics and Finance*, *6*(1), 189–212. doi:10.21098/jimf.v6i1.1146

Othman, A., Kari, F., & Hamdan, R. (2013). A Comparative Analysis of the Co-operative, Islamic and Conventional Banks in Malaysia. *American Journal of Economics*, *3*(5C), 184–190. doi:10.5923/c.economics.201301.31

Ouyang, W., & Yang, J. (2020). The network energy and environment efficiency analysis of 27 OECD countries: A multiplicative network DEA model. *Energy*, *117161*. Advance online publication. doi:10.1016/j.energy.2020.117161

Oviedo, D., Granada, I., & Perez-Jaramillo, D. (2020). Ridesourcing and travel demand: Potential effects of transportation network companies in Bogotá. *Sustainability (Basel)*, *12*(5), 1732. doi:10.3390u12051732

Oyatoye, E. O., Adebiyi, S. O., & Amole, B. B. (2015). Evaluating Subscribers Preference for Service Attributes of Mobile Telecommunication in Nigeria Using Analytic Hierarchy Process (ahp). *International Journal of the Analytic Hierarchy Process*, *7*(2), 171–187. doi:10.13033/ijahp.v7i2.299

Ozbugday, F. C., Tirgil, A., & Kose, E. G. (2019). Efficiency changes in long-term care in OECD countries: A non-parametric Malmquist Index approach. *Socio-Economic Planning Sciences*, *100733*. Advance online publication. doi:10.1016/j.seps.2019.100733

Ozovehe, A., & Usman, A. U. (2015). Performance Analysis of Gsm Networks in Minna Metropolis of Nigeria. *Nigerian Journal of Technology, 34*(2), 359-367. https://doi.org/ doi:10.4314/njt.v34i2.21

Palmer, R., Fulop, N. J., & Utley, M. (2018). A systematic literature review of operational research methods for modelling patient flow and outcomes within community healthcare and other settings. *Health Systems (Basingstoke, England), 7*(1), 29–50. Advance online publication. doi:10.105741306-017-0024-9 PMID:31214337

Pambuko, Z. B., Usman, N., & Andriyani, L. (2019). Spin-off and Social Funds' Productivity of Islamic Banking Industry in Indonesia. *1st International Conference on Progressive Civil Society (IConProCS 2019), 317*, 7–10. 10.2991/iconprocs-19.2019.2

Pang, C., & Gai, Y. (2022). Research on efficiency in financing of small and medium companies based on DEA method. *Discrete Dynamics in Nature and Society, 2022*, 2022. doi:10.1155/2022/4914151

Pang, X., Ge, Y. F., Wang, K., Traina, A. J. M., & Wang, H. (2023). Patient assignment optimization in cloud healthcare systems: A distributed genetic algorithm. *Health Information Science and Systems, 11*(1), 30. Advance online publication. doi:10.100713755-023-00230-1 PMID:37397165

Panwar, A., Olfati, M., Pant, M., & Snasel, V. (2022). A review on the 40 years of existence of data envelopment analysis models: Historic development and current trends. *Archives of Computational Methods in Engineering, 29*(7), 5397–5426. doi:10.100711831-022-09770-3 PMID:35702633

Paradi, J. C., Vela, S. A., & Zhu, H. (2010). A new DEA model was applied to a merged bank to adjust for cultural differences. *Journal of Productivity Analysis, 33*(2), 109–123. doi:10.100711123-009-0158-2

Park, H. J., & Zhang, Y. (2022). Technology readiness and technology paradox of unmanned convenience store users. *Journal of Retailing and Consumer Services, 65*, 102523. doi:10.1016/j.jretconser.2021.102523

Pasiouras, F., Sifodaskalakis, E., & Zopounidis, C. (2007). *Estimating and analyzing the cost efficiency of Greek cooperative banks: an application of two-stage data envelopment analysis.* Working Paper Series 2007.12, University of Bath, School of Management, Bath, UK.

Pasquale, F. A. (2010). *Trusting (and Verifying) Online Intermediaries' Policing (SSRN Scholarly Paper ID 1762236).* Social Science Research Network. https://papers.ssrn.com/abstract=1762236

Pastor, J. T., Asmild, M., & Lovell, C. K. (2011). The biennial Malmquist productivity change index. *Socio-Economic Planning Sciences, 45*(1), 10–15. doi:10.1016/j.seps.2010.09.001

Pastor, J. T., & Lovell, C. K. (2005). A global Malmquist productivity index. *Economics Letters, 88*(2), 266–271. doi:10.1016/j.econlet.2005.02.013

Patel, R., & Shah, D. (2016). Mergers and Acquisitions – The game of profit and Loss: A study on Indian banking sector. Journal of Arts. *Science and Commerce, 8*(3), 92–110.

Patkal, P. S., & Anasane, S. S. (2022). Implementation of Standard Work in Healthcare Industry. *Proceedings of the International Conference on Industrial Engineering and Operations Management*, 1110–1115. 10.46254/IN02.20220339

Paulden, M., McCabe, C., & Karnon, J. (2014). Achieving allocative efficiency in healthcare: Nice in theory, not so NICE in practice? In PharmacoEconomics (Vol. 32, Issue 4). doi:10.100740273-014-0146-x

Paul, S., Riffat, M., Yasir, A., Mahim, M. N., Sharnali, B. Y., Naheen, I. T., Rahman, A., & Kulkarni, A. (2021). Industry 4.0 applications for medical/healthcare services. *Journal of Sensor and Actuator Networks, 10*(3), 43. doi:10.3390/jsan10030043

Pavic, S., Koh, S. C. L., Simpson, M., & Padmore, J. (2007). Could e-business create a competitive advantage in UK SMEs? *Benchmarking, 14*(3), 320–351. doi:10.1108/14635770710753112

Peixoto, M. G. M., Musetti, M. A., & de Mendonça, M. C. A. (2020). Performance management in hospital organizations from the perspective of Principal Component Analysis and Data Envelopment Analysis: The case of Federal University Hospitals in Brazil. *Computers & Industrial Engineering, 150*, 106873. doi:10.1016/j.cie.2020.106873

Perry, P. (1992). Do banks gain or lose from inflation. *Journal of Retail Banking, 14*(2), 25–30.

Pham, M. T., Rajić, A., Greig, J. D., Sargeant, J. M., Papadopoulos, A., & McEwen, S. A. (2014). A scoping review of scoping reviews: Advancing the approach and enhancing the consistency. *Research Synthesis Methods, 5*(4), 371–385. doi:10.1002/jrsm.1123 PMID:26052958

Pinho, B. A. (2017). *The global airline industry: an assessment of the impact of low-cost carriers on the technical efficiency of full-service airlines.* ISCTE-Instituto Universitario de Lisboa.

Pitra, G. M., & Musti, K. S. S. (2021). Duck Curve with Renewable Energies and Storage Technologies. *13th International Conference on Computational Intelligence and Communication Networks (CICN)*, 66-71. 10.1109/CICN51697.2021.9574671

Popoola, J. J. (2009). Investigation on Quality of Service Provided by Third Tier Internet Service Providers in Nigeria: Akure Cybercafés as case study. *International Journal on Computer Science and Engineering, 1*(3), 186–191.

Potluri, R. M., & Thomas, S. J. (2023). Trends in E-Commerce During COVID-19: A Case of UAE. In Advancing SMEs Toward E-Commerce Policies for Sustainability (pp. 235-247). IGI Global.

Pourhejazy, P., Kwon, O., Chang, Y.-T., & Park, H. (2017). Evaluating Resiliency of Supply Chain Network: A Data Envelopment Analysis Approach. *Sustainability (Basel), 9*(2), 255. doi:10.3390u9020255

Pourmahmoud, J., & Bagheri, N. (2023). Uncertain Malmquist productivity index: An application to evaluate healthcare systems during COVID-19 pandemic. *Socio-Economic Planning Sciences, 87*, 101522. Advance online publication. doi:10.1016/j.seps.2023.101522 PMID:36777893

Prada, S. I., Garcia-Garcia, M. P., & Guzman, J. (2022). COVID-19 response in Colombia: Hits and misses. *Health Policy and Technology, 11*(2), 100621. Advance online publication. doi:10.1016/j.hlpt.2022.100621 PMID:35340774

Pradhan, R. P., Arvin, M. B., & Norman, N. R. (2015). The dynamics of information and communications technologies infrastructure, economic growth, and financial development: Evidence from Asian countries. *Technology in Society, 42*, 135–149. doi:10.1016/j.techsoc.2015.04.002

Pradhan, S., Patel, G., & Olfati, M. (2019). Integrationa and Application of Analytic Hierarchy Process with Data Envelopment Analysis - a Literature Review. *International Journal of Analytic Hierarchy Process, 11*(2), 228–268. doi:10.13033/ijahp.v11i2.632

Prasad Agrawal, K. (2023). Towards adoption of Generative AI in organizational settings. *Journal of Computer Information Systems*, 1–16. doi:10.1080/08874417.2023.2240744

Puliafito, A., Bruneo, D., Distefano, S., & Longo, F. (Eds.). (2017). Lecture Notes in Computer Science *Ad-hoc, Mobile, and Wireless Networks*. doi:10.1007/978-3-319-67910-5

Puyenbroeck, T. (2018). On the output orientation of the benefit-of-the-doubt-model. *Social Indicators Research, 139*(2), 415–431. doi:10.100711205-017-1734-x

Rahman, A., Lambkin, M., & Hussain, D. (2016). Value Creation and appropriation following M&A: A data envelopment analysis. *Journal of Business Research*, *69*(12), 5628–5635. doi:10.1016/j.jbusres.2016.03.070

Rajamani, M., & Ramakrishnan, P. R. (2015). A Study on Impact of Merger of Centurian Bank of Punjab on the Financial Performance of HDFC Bank. *IOSR Journal Of Humanities And Social Science*, *20*(5), 28–31.

Rajendran, S., Pan, W., Sabuncu, M. R., Chen, Y., Zhou, J., & Wang, F. (2023). *Patchwork Learning: A Paradigm Towards Integrative Analysis across Diverse Biomedical Data Sources*. Academic Press.

Rajeswari, A. R. (2020). *A Mobile Ad Hoc Network Routing Protocols: A Comparative Study, Recent Trends in Communication Networks, Pinaki Mitra*. IntechOpen. doi:10.5772/intechopen.92550

Ramezankhani, M. J., Torabi, S. A., & Vahidi, F. (2018). Supply chain performance measurement and evaluation: A mixed sustainability and resilience approach. *Computers & Industrial Engineering*, *126*, 531–548. doi:10.1016/j.cie.2018.09.054

Ranchal, R., Bastide, P., Wang, X., Gkoulalas-Divanis, A., Mehra, M., Bakthavachalam, S., Lei, H., & Mohindra, A. (2020). Disrupting healthcare silos: Addressing data volume, velocity and variety with a cloud-native healthcare data ingestion service. *IEEE Journal of Biomedical and Health Informatics*, *24*(11), 3182–3188. Advance online publication. doi:10.1109/JBHI.2020.3001518 PMID:32750932

Randolph, M. (2019). That will never work: The birth of Netflix and the amazing life of an idea. Hachette UK.

Rani, L. N., Sukmaningrum, P. S., & Salleh, M. C. M. (2020). A Comparative Analysis of the Productivity of Islamic Banking in Indonesia, Malaysia and Brunei Darussalam during the period 2012-2017. *International Journal of Innovation, Creativity and Change*, *11*(11), 470–491.

Rani, L. N., Widiastuti, T., & Rusydiana, A. S. (2017). Comparative Analysis of Islamic Bank's Productivity and Conventional Bank's in Indonesia Period 2008-2016. *1st International Conference on Islamic Economics, Business, and Philanthropy (ICIEBP 2017)*, 118–123. 10.5220/0007077901180123

Rashid, A., & Rehman, U. Z. (2016). Measurement and decomposition of productivity change in banking: Islamic and conventional banks in Pakistan. *Journal of Islamic Business and Management*, *6*(2), 55–75.

Rashid, B., & Rehmani, M. H. (2016). Applications of wireless sensor networks for urban areas: A survey. *Journal of Network and Computer Applications*, *60*, 192–219. doi:10.1016/j.jnca.2015.09.008

Ray, S. C. (2004). *Data Envelopment Analysis: Theory and Techniques for Economics and Operations Research*. Cambridge University Press. doi:10.1017/CBO9780511606731

Ray, S. C., & Das, A. (2010). Distribution of cost and profit efficiency: Evidence from Indian banking. *European Journal of Operational Research*, *201*(1), 297–307. doi:10.1016/j.ejor.2009.02.030

Rees, R. (1974). A reconsideration of the expense preference theory of the firm. *Econometrica*, *41*, 295–307.

Register, S., Brown, M., & White, M. L. (2019). Using healthcare simulation in space planning to improve efficiency and effectiveness within the healthcare system. *Health Systems (Basingstoke, England)*, *8*(3), 184–189. doi:10.1080/20476965.2019.1569482 PMID:31839930

Rezaei, A. H., & Adressi, A. (n.d.). *Supply Chain Performance Evaluation Using Data Envelopment Analysis*. Academic Press.

Riahi Dorcheh, F., Razavi Hajiagha, S. H., Rahbari, M., Jafari-Sadeghi, V., & Amoozad Mahdiraji, H. (2021). Identification, analysis and improvement of red meat supply chain strategies considering the impact of COVID-19 pandemic: A hybrid SWOT-QSPM approach in an emerging economy. *British Food Journal*, *123*(12), 4194–4223. doi:10.1108/BFJ-09-2020-0865

Rodoni, A., Salim, M. A., Amalia, E., & Rakhmadi, R. S. (2017). Comparing Efficiency and Productivity in Islamic Banking: Case Study Indonesia, Malaysia and Pakistan. *Al-Iqtishad: Journal of Islamic Economics*, *9*(2), 227–242. doi:10.15408/aiq.v9i2.5153

Romdhane, M., & Alhakimi, S. S. (2018). Productivity and technical efficiency in Islamic banks: Cross-country analysis. *Asian Journal of Economic Modelling*, *6*(1), 1–7. doi:10.18488/journal.8.2018.61.1.7

Rosenbäck, R. G., & Svensson, A. (2023). Resilience in keeping the balance between demand and capacity in the COVID-19 pandemic, a case study at a Swedish middle-sized hospital. *BMC Health Services Research*, *23*(1), 202. Advance online publication. doi:10.118612913-023-09182-4 PMID:36855122

Rosenthal, A., Mork, P., Li, M. H., Stanford, J., Koester, D., & Reynolds, P. (2010). Cloud computing: A new business paradigm for biomedical information sharing. *Journal of Biomedical Informatics*, *43*(2), 342–353. doi:10.1016/j.jbi.2009.08.014 PMID:19715773

Rostami, F., Kis, Z., Koppelaar, R., Jiménez, L., & Pozo, C. (2022). Comparative sustainability study of energy storage technologies using data envelopment analysis. *Energy Storage Materials*, *48*, 412–438. doi:10.1016/j.ensm.2022.03.026

Rowan, N. J., Murray, N., Qiao, Y., O'Neill, E., Clifford, E., Barceló, D., & Power, D. M. (2022). Digital transformation of peatland eco-innovations ('Paludiculture'): Enabling a paradigm shift towards the real-time sustainable production of 'green-friendly'products and services. *The Science of the Total Environment*, *838*, 156328. doi:10.1016/j.scitotenv.2022.156328 PMID:35649452

Rubin, D. B. (1993). Statistical Disclosure Limitation. *Journal of Official Statistics*, *9*(2), 461–468.

Ruiz, P., & Bouvry, P. (2015). Survey on broadcast algorithms for mobile ad hoc networks. *ACM Computing Surveys*, *48*(1), 1–35. doi:10.1145/2786005

Rusydiana, A. S., & Assalafiyah, A. (2021). Advancement and Setback in Islamic Banking Productivity in Asean: Do Technological Changes Matter? *Journal of Islamic Monetary Economics and Finance*, *7*(3), 583–604. doi:10.21098/jimf.v7i3.1322

Saadat, F., & Soltanifar, M. (2014). *The Role of Internet Service Providers (ISPS) in Encouraging Customers to Use Their Internet Services in Iran*. Academic Press.

Safdar, K. A., Emrouznejad, A., & Dey, P. K. (2020). An optimized queue management system to improve patient flow in the absence of appointment system. *International Journal of Health Care Quality Assurance*, *33*(7/8), 477–494. doi:10.1108/IJHCQA-03-2020-0052 PMID:33179461

Sah, B., Gupta, R., & Bani-Hani, D. (2021). Analysis of barriers to implement drone logistics. *International Journal of Logistics*, *24*(6), 531–550. doi:10.1080/13675567.2020.1782862

Salami, O. L., & Adeyemi, A. A. (2015). Malaysian Islamic banks' efficiency: An intra-bank comparative analysis of Islamic windows and full-fledged subsidiaries. *International Journal of Business and Society*, *16*(1), 19–38. doi:10.33736/ijbs.551.2015

Saleh, A. S., Moradi-Motlagh, A., & Zeitun, R. (2020). What are the drivers of inefficiency in the Gulf Cooperation Council banking industry? A comparison between conventional and Islamic banks. *Pacific Basin Finance Journal, 60*, 101266. https://doi.org/ doi:10.1016/j.pacfin.2020.101266

Salleh, M. C. M., & Rani, L. N. (2020). Productivity Comparation of Islamic and Conventional Banks in Indonesia. *Al-Uqud: Journal of Islamic Economics, 4*(28), 69–82. doi:10.26740/al-uqud.v4n1.p69-82

Samanta, A. K., Varaprasad, G., & Padhy, R. (2021). A systematic review of empirical studies pertaining to Lean, Six Sigma and Lean Six Sigma quality improvement methodologies in paediatrics. *International Journal of Business Excellence, 23*(1), 18–32. doi:10.1504/IJBEX.2021.111936

Sampat, B., Mogaji, E., & Nguyen, N. P. (2023). The dark side of FinTech in financial services: A qualitative enquiry into FinTech developers' perspective. *International Journal of Bank Marketing*. Advance online publication. doi:10.1108/IJBM-07-2022-0328

San Cristóbal, J. R. (2011). A multi criteria data envelopment analysis model to evaluate the efficiency of the Renewable Energy technologies. *Renewable Energy, 36*(10), 2742–2746. doi:10.1016/j.renene.2011.03.008

Sandfort, V., Yan, K., Pickhardt, P. J., & Summers, R. M. (2019). Data augmentation using generative adversarial networks (CycleGAN) to improve generalizability in CT segmentation tasks. *Scientific Reports, 9*(1), 16884. doi:10.103841598-019-52737-x PMID:31729403

Sankaranarayanan, S., Balaji, Y., Jain, A., Lim, S. N., & Chellappa, R. (2018). Learning from synthetic data: Addressing domain shift for semantic segmentation. In *Proceedings of the IEEE conference on computer vision and pattern recognition* (pp. 3752-3761). 10.1109/CVPR.2018.00395

Santiago, R., Koengkan, M., Fuinhas, J. A., & Marques, A. C. (2020). The relationship between public capital stock, private capital stock and economic growth in the Latin American and Caribbean countries. *International Review of Economics, 67*(3), 293–317. doi:10.100712232-019-00340-x

Santos, A. B., Calado, R. D., Zeferino, A. C. S., & Bourguignon, S. C. (2022). Queuing Theory: Contributions and Applications in the Field of Health Service Management - A Bibliometric Approach. *IFAC-PapersOnLine, 55*(10), 210–214. Advance online publication. doi:10.1016/j.ifacol.2022.09.392

Sapanji, R. A. E. V. T., Athoillah, A., Solehudin, E., & Mohamad, S. (2021). Analysis of the Technical Efficiency, Malmquist Productivity Index, and Tobit Regression of the eleven Islamic Commercial Banks in Indonesia between 2010 and 2019. *Turkish Journal of Computer and Mathematics Education, 12*(8), 505–522.

Saputri, V., Sutopo, W., Hisjam, M., & Ma'aram, A. (2019). Sustainable Agri-Food Supply Chain Performance Measurement Model for GMO and Non-GMO Using Data Envelopment Analysis Method. *Applied Sciences (Basel, Switzerland), 9*(6), 1199. doi:10.3390/app9061199

Sargam, S., Gupta, R., Sharma, R., & Jain, K. (2023). Adoption of 5G in developing economies: A supply side perspective from India. *Telematics and Informatics, 84*, 102034. doi:10.1016/j.tele.2023.102034

Sarrut, D., Etxebeste, A., Muñoz, E., Krah, N., & Létang, J. M. (2021). Artificial Intelligence for Monte Carlo Simulation in Medical Physics. *Frontiers in Physics (Lausanne), 9*, 738112. Advance online publication. doi:10.3389/fphy.2021.738112

Sastry Musti, K. S. (2023). Multicriteria Decision Analysis for Sustainable Green Financing in Energy Sector. In *Green Finance Instruments, FinTech, and Investment Strategies. Sustainable Finance.* Springer. doi:10.1007/978-3-031-29031-2_1

Sastry, M. K. S. (2007). Integrated Outage Management System: An effective solution for power utilities to address customer grievances. *International Journal of Electronic Customer Relationship Management*, *1*(1), 30–40. doi:10.1504/IJECRM.2007.014424

Sastry, M. K. S., & Van der Merwe, M. (2022). *A Novel MS Excel Tool for Multi-Criteria Decision Analysis in Energy Systems*. IGI-Global. doi:10.4018/978-1-6684-4012-4.ch003

Sato, R. C., & Zouain, D. M. (2010). Markov Models in health care. *Einstein (Sao Paulo, Brazil)*, *8*(3), 376–379. Advance online publication. doi:10.15901679-45082010rb1567 PMID:26760158

Sav, G. T. (2013). Effects of Financial Source Dependency on Public University Operating Efficiencies: Data Envelopment Single-Stage and Tobit Two-Stage Evaluations. *Revue d'Economie Financiere*, *3*, 63–73. https://api.semanticscholar.org/CorpusID:14860400

Schaffer, A. L., Dobbins, T. A., & Pearson, S. A. (2021). Interrupted time series analysis using autoregressive integrated moving average (ARIMA) models: A guide for evaluating large-scale health interventions. *BMC Medical Research Methodology*, *21*(1), 58. Advance online publication. doi:10.118612874-021-01235-8 PMID:33752604

Schecter, A. R. (2016). *For-Profit Walden U., Once Tied to Bill Clinton, Put Under Review*. NBC News https://www.nbcnews.com/news/us-news/student-sues-walden-university-i-wasted-six-years-my-life-n690706

Schonberger, R. J. (2018). Reconstituting lean in healthcare: From waste elimination toward 'queue-less' patient-focused care. *Business Horizons*, *61*(1), 13–22. Advance online publication. doi:10.1016/j.bushor.2017.09.001

Sealey, C. W. Jr, & Lindley, J. T. (1977). Inputs, Outputs, and a Theory of Production and Cost at Depository Financial Institutions. *The Journal of Finance*, *32*(4), 1251–1266. doi:10.1111/j.1540-6261.1977.tb03324.x

Seiford, L. M., & Thrall, R. M. (1990). Recent developments in DEA: The mathematical programming approach to frontier analysis. *Journal of Econometrics*, *46*(1–2), 7–38. doi:10.1016/0304-4076(90)90045-U

Seiford, L. M., & Zhu, J. (2002). Modeling Undesirable Factors in Efficiency Evaluation. *European Journal of Operational Research*, *142*(1), 16–20. doi:10.1016/S0377-2217(01)00293-4

Selby, L. M., & Bawa, A. (2018). Optimizing an Efficient Use of Internet Bandwidth for Higher Learning Institutions in Ghana. *International Journal of Scientific Research in Computer Sciencei, Engineering and Information Technology*, *3*(8), 50–65. doi:10.32628/CSEIT183819

Selzer, D. J. (2019). *Overview of Simulation in Surgery*. doi:10.1007/978-3-319-98276-2_2

Semih Yildirim, H., & Philippatos, G. C. (2007). Efficiency of banks: Recent evidence from the transition economies of Europe, 1993–2000. *European Journal of Finance*, *13*(2), 123–143. doi:10.1080/13518470600763687

Sensarma, R. (2005). Cost and profit efficiency of Indian banks during 1986–2003: A stochastic frontier analysis. *Economic and Political Weekly*, *40*(12), 1198–1208.

Senthil Kumar, T., Suresh, A., & Karumathil, A. (2014). Improvised classification model for cloud based authentication using keystroke dynamics. In *Frontier and Innovation in Future Computing and Communications* (pp. 885–893). Springer Netherlands. doi:10.1007/978-94-017-8798-7_97

Seol, H., Lee, H., Kim, S., & Park, Y. (2008). The impact of information technology on organizational efficiency in public services: A DEA-based DT approach. *The Journal of the Operational Research Society*, *59*(2), 231–238. doi:10.1057/palgrave.jors.2602453

Sethi, R., Yanamadala, V., Burton, D. C., & Bess, R. S. (2017). Using Lean Process Improvement to Enhance Safety and Value in Orthopaedic Surgery: The Case of Spine Surgery. *The Journal of the American Academy of Orthopaedic Surgeons*, *25*(11), e244–e250. doi:10.5435/JAAOS-D-17-00030 PMID:29059115

Setton, E., Yoo, T., Zhu, X., Goldsmith, A., & Girod, B. (2005). Cross-layer design of ad hoc networks for real-time video streaming. *IEEE Wireless Communications*, *12*(4), 59–65. doi:10.1109/MWC.2005.1497859

Sewpersadh, N. S. (2023). Disruptive business value models in the digital era. *Journal of Innovation and Entrepreneurship*, *12*(1), 1–27. doi:10.118613731-022-00252-1 PMID:36686335

Shah, A. A., Wu, D., & Korotkov, V. (2019). Are Sustainable Banks Efficient and Productive? A data Envelopment Analysis and Malmquist Productivity Index Analysis. *Sustainability (Basel)*, *11*(8), 2398. doi:10.3390u11082398

Shahhoseini, R., Tofighi, S., Jaafaripooyan, E., & Safiaryan, R. (2011). Efficiency measurement in developing countries: Application of data envelopment analysis for Iranian hospitals. *Health Services Management Research*, *24*(2), 75–80. doi:10.1258/hsmr.2010.010017 PMID:21471577

Shao, L., & Ehrgott, M. (2016). Discrete representation of non-dominated sets in multi-objective linear programming. *European Journal of Operational Research*, *255*(3), 687–698. Advance online publication. doi:10.1016/j.ejor.2016.05.001

Sharma, A. K., & Barua, M. K. (2013). Efficiency and productivity of banking sector. *Qualitative Research in Financial Markets*, *5*(2), 195–224. doi:10.1108/QRFM-10-2011-0025

Sherman, H. D., & Zhu, J. (2006). Benchmarking with quality-adjusted DEA (Q-DEA) to seek lower-cost high-quality service: Evidence from a US bank application. *Annals of Operations Research*, *145*(1), 301–319. doi:10.100710479-006-0037-4

Sherwood, R. M., Shepherd, G., & De Souza, C. M. (1994). Judicial systems and economic performance. *The Quarterly Review of Economics and Finance*, *34*, 101–116. doi:10.1016/1062-9769(94)90038-8

Shestalova, V. (2003). Sequential Malmquist indices of productivity growth: An application to OECD industrial activities. *Journal of Productivity Analysis*, *19*(2-3), 211–226. doi:10.1023/A:1022857501478

Shields, S. (2020). The EBRD, fail forward neoliberalism and the construction of the European periphery. *Economic and Labour Relations Review*, *31*(2), 230–248. doi:10.1177/1035304620916652

Shokri, A. (2017). Quantitative analysis of Six Sigma, Lean and Lean Six Sigma research publications in last two decades. *International Journal of Quality & Reliability Management*, *34*(5), 598–625. doi:10.1108/IJQRM-07-2015-0096

Shuwiekh, H. A. M., Kira, I. A., Sous, M. S. F., Ashby, J. S., Alhuwailah, A., Baali, S. B. A., Azdaou, C., Oliemat, E. M., & Jamil, H. J. (2022). The differential mental health impact of COVID-19 in Arab countries. *Current Psychology (New Brunswick, N.J.)*, *41*(8), 5678–5692. Advance online publication. doi:10.100712144-020-01148-7 PMID:33162726

Sıcakyuz, C. (2023). Bibliometric Analysis of Data Envelopment Analysis in Supply Chain Management. *Journal of Operational and Strategic Analytics*, *1*(1), 14–24. doi:10.56578/josa010103

Siddique, M. A., & Rahim, M. (2013). Efficiency analysis of full-fledged Islamic banks and standalone Islamic branches of conventional banks in Pakistan: A comparative study for the period of 2007-2012. *Journal of Islamic Business and Management*, *3*(2), 129–149. doi:10.12816/0005000

Siems, T. F., & Clark, J. A. (1997). Rethinking Bank Efficiency and Regulation: How Off-balance Sheet Activities Make a Difference. *Financial Industry Studies*, *3*(2), 1–11.

Sihotang, H. T., Marsoit, P. T., & Ortizan, K. G. (2022). *Data envelopment analysis for stochastic production and supply chain planning.* Academic Press.

Simeon, A., & Chowdhury, S. (2020). *Protection Challenges in a Stand-alone Microgrid: Case Study of Tsumkwe Microgrid.* . doi:10.1109/PowerAfrica49420.2020.9219972

Simplilearn. (2023). *What is R: Overview, its Applications and what is R used for?* Available online, https://www.simplilearn.com/what-is-r-article

Singh, S., & Das, S. (2018). Impact of post-merger and acquisition activities on the financial performance of banks: A study of Indian private sector and public sector banks. *Revista Espacios Magazine, 39,* 25.

Singh, S., Raghavendra, C. S., & Stepanek, J. (1999). Power-aware broadcasting in mobile ad hoc networks. *Proceedings of IEEE PIMRC, 99,* 22–31.

Singla, M. L. (2015). Merger and Acquisition in Indian Banking Industry. *International Journal of Research in Management, 662*(4), 77–94.

Sissoko, Y., Sloboda Brian, W., & Kone, S. (2018). Is it Factor Accumulation or Total Factor Productivity Explaining the Economic Growth in ECOWAS? An Empirical Assessment. *African Journal of Economic Review, 5*(2), 30–45.

Sloan, T., Fitzgerald, A., Hayes, K. J., Radnor, Z., Robinson, S., & Sohal, A. (2014). Lean in healthcare-- history and recent developments. In Journal of health organization and management (Vol. 28, Issue 2). doi:10.1108/JHOM-04-2014-0064

Sloboda, B. W., & Yao, V. W. (2008). Interstate spillovers of private capital and public spending. *The Annals of Regional Science, 42*(4), 505–518. doi:10.100700168-007-0181-z

Smith, A., Rupp, W., & Motley, D. (2013). Corporate reputation as strategic competitive advantage of manufacturing and service-based firms: Multi-industry case study. *International Journal of Services and Operations Management, 14*(2), 131–156. doi:10.1504/IJSOM.2013.051826

Snoke, J., Raab, G. M., Nowok, B., Dibben, C., & Slavkovic, A. (2018). General and specific utility measures for synthetic data. *Journal of the Royal Statistical Society. Series A, (Statistics in Society), 181*(3), 663–688. doi:10.1111/rssa.12358

Soheilirad, S., Govindan, K., Mardani, A., Zavadskas, E. K., Nilashi, M., & Zakuan, N. (2018). Application of data envelopment analysis models in supply chain management: A systematic review and meta-analysis. *Annals of Operations Research, 271*(2), 915–969. doi:10.100710479-017-2605-1

Sokolov, A., Veselitskaya, N., Carabias, V., & Yildirim, O. (2019). Scenario-based identification of key factors for smart cities development policies. *Technological Forecasting and Social Change, 148,* 119729. doi:10.1016/j.techfore.2019.119729

Solow, R. M. (1957). Technical change and the aggregate production function. *The Review of Economics and Statistics, 39*(3), 312–320. doi:10.2307/1926047

Song, C., Li, M., Zhang, F., He, Y., & Tao, W. (2015). A data envelopment analysis for energy efficiency of coal-fired power units in China. *Energy Conversion and Management, 102,* 121–130. doi:10.1016/j.enconman.2014.12.062

Song, M., An, Q., Zhang, W., Wang, Z., & Wu, J. (2012). Environmental efficiency evaluation based on data envelopment analysis: A review. *Renewable & Sustainable Energy Reviews, 16*(7), 4465–4469. doi:10.1016/j.rser.2012.04.052

Soni, R. (2012). Managerial efficiency-Key driver towards the profitability of Indian commercial banks in turbulent time. *International Journal of Applied Research and Studies, 1.*

Soyiri, I. N., & Reidpath, D. D. (2013). An overview of health forecasting. In Environmental Health and Preventive Medicine (Vol. 18, Issue 1). doi:10.100712199-012-0294-6

Srinivasan, N., & Eden, L. (2021). Going digital multinationals: Navigating economic and social imperatives in a post-pandemic world. *Journal of International Business Policy*, 4(2), 228–243. doi:10.105742214-021-00108-7

Srivastava, A., & Jain, V. (2006). Efficiency of banks in India: A DEA approach. *Review of Professional Management*, 4(2), 31–38.

Statice. (2022). *Types of synthetic data and 4 real-life examples*. Retrieved from https://www.statice.ai

Statista. (2023). *Health Care - Colombia | Statista Market Forecast*. https://es.statista.com/outlook/dmo/ecommerce/beauty-health-personal-household-care/health-care/colombia#revenue

Stefko, R., Gavurova, B., & Kocisova, K. (2018). Healthcare efficiency assessment using DEA analysis in the Slovak Republic. *Health Economics Review*, 8(1), 6. Advance online publication. doi:10.118613561-018-0191-9 PMID:29523981

Steinbuss, G., & Böhm, K. (2021). Benchmarking unsupervised outlier detection with realistic synthetic data. *ACM Transactions on Knowledge Discovery from Data (TKDD)*, 15(4), 1-20. 10.1145/3441453

Steins, K., & Persson, F. (2015). Identifying Factors for Successful Implementation of Simulation Modeling in Healthcare. *International Journal of Privacy and Health Information Management*, 3(1), 1–19. Advance online publication. doi:10.4018/IJPHIM.2015010101

Stimmel, C. L. (2015). Why Design Thinking? In Building Smart Cities (pp. 74–89). Auerbach Publications. doi:10.1201/b18827-11

Strang, K. D. (2012). Applied financial non-linear programming models for decision making. *International Journal of Applied Decision Sciences*, 5(4), 370–395. doi:10.1504/IJADS.2012.050023

Strang, K. D. (2019). Novel hydroelectricity data envelopment analysis model. *International Journal of Energy Technology and Policy*, 15(4), 436–456. doi:10.1504/IJETP.2019.102661

Straub, S., Vellutini, C., & Warlters, M. (2008). *Infrastructure and Economic Growth in East Asia* (Policy Research Working Paper 4589). World Bank.

Sturm, J. E., & De Haan, J. (1995). Is public expenditure really productive?: New evidence for the USA and The Netherlands. *Economic Modelling*, 12(1), 60–72. doi:10.1016/0264-9993(94)P4156-A

Sudarsanam, S. (2003). *Creating value from mergers and acquisitions: The Challenges: An integrated and international perspective*. Pearson Education.

Sufian, F. (2006). The Efficiency of Non-Bank Financial Institutions: Empirical Evidence from Malaysia. *International Research Journal of Finance and Economics*, 1(6), 49–65.

Sufian, F. (2007). Malmquist indices of productivity change in Malaysian Islamic banking industry: Foreign versus domestic banks. *Journal of Economic Cooperation*, 28(1), 115–150.

Sufian, F. (2009a). Sources of TFP growth in the Malaysian Islamic banking sector. *Service Industries Journal*, 29(9), 1273–1291. doi:10.1080/02642060801911128

Sufian, F. (2009b). Total factor productivity change of the Malaysian Islamic banking sector: An empirical study. *Journal of Islamic Economics. Banking and Finance*, 5(1), 73–88.

Sufian, F. (2010). Productivity, technology and efficiency of De Novo Islamic banks: Empirical evidence from Malaysia. *Journal of Financial Services Marketing*, 15(July), 241–258. doi:10.1057/fsm.2010.20

Sufian, F., & Haron, R. (2008). The sources and determinants of productivity growth in the Malaysian Islamic banking sector: A nonstochastic frontier approach. *International Journal of Accounting and Finance, 1*(2), 193–215. doi:10.1504/IJAF.2008.020303

Sufian, F., & Majid, M. A. (2007a). Singapore Banking Efficiency and its Relation to Stock Returns: A DEA Window Analysis Approach. *International Journal of Business Studies, 15*(1), 83–106.

Sufian, F., & Majid, M. A. (2007b). Deregulation, consolidation and banks efficiency in Singapore: Evidence from event study window approach and Tobit analysis. *International Review of Economics, 54*(2), 261–283. doi:10.100712232-007-0017-2

Suliman, K. R., Rahim, S. A., Ramayah, T., & Degeras, D. K. (2019). Measuring technical efficiency of dry bulk terminal performance using the frontier application of data envelopment analysis: A proposed framework. *Journal of Physics: Conference Series, 1366*(1), 012100. Advance online publication. doi:10.1088/1742-6596/1366/1/012100

Sultan, W. I., & Crispim, J. (2018). Measuring the efficiency of Palestinian public hospitals during 2010–2015: An application of a two-stage DEA method. *BMC Health Services Research, 18*(1), 1–17. doi:10.118612913-018-3228-1 PMID:29843732

Sun, H., Rabbani, M. R., Ahmad, N., Sial, M. S., Cheng, G., Zia-Ud-Din, M., & Fu, Q. (2020). CSR, co-creation and green consumer loyalty: Are green banking initiatives important? A moderated mediation approach from an emerging economy. *Sustainability (Basel), 12*(24), 10688. doi:10.3390u122410688

Sun, S. (2002). Measuring the relative efficiency of police precincts using data envelopment analysis. *Socio-Economic Planning Sciences, 36*(1), 51–71. doi:10.1016/S0038-0121(01)00010-6

Tabatabai, S. M., & Tabatabai, F. A.-S. (2024). Integrating Inverse Data Envelopment Analysis and Machine Learning for Enhanced Road Transport Safety in Iran. *Journal of Soft Computing in Civil Engineering, 8*(1), 141–160.

Tajbakhsh, A., & Hassini, E. (2015). A data envelopment analysis approach to evaluate sustainability in supply chain networks. *Journal of Cleaner Production, 105*, 74–85. doi:10.1016/j.jclepro.2014.07.054

Tanaka, F. H. K. D. S., & Aranha, C. (2019). *Data augmentation using GANs.* arXiv preprint arXiv:1904.09135.

Tanwar, J., Seth, H., Vaish, A. K., & Rao, N. V. M. (2020). Revisiting the efficiency of Indian banking sector: An analysis of comparative models through data envelopment analysis. *Indian Journal of Finance and Banking, 4*(1), 92–108. doi:10.46281/ijfb.v4i1.585

Teichert, R. (2019). Digital transformation maturity: A systematic review of literature. *Acta Universitatis Agriculturae et Silviculturae Mendelianae Brunensis, 67*(6), 1673–1687. doi:10.11118/actaun201967061673

Thaker, K., Charles, V., Pant, A., & Gherman, T. (2022). A DEA and random forest regression approach to studying bank efficiency and corporate governance. *The Journal of the Operational Research Society, 73*(6), 1258–1277. doi:10.1080/01605682.2021.1907239

Thanassoulis, E., Witte, K. D., Johnes, J., Karagiannis, J. G., & Portela, C. S. (2016). Applications of data envelopment analysis in education, In Data Envelopment Analysis: A Handbook of Empirical Studies and Application. Springer Science and Business Media.

Thasni, T., Kalaiarasan, C., & Venkatesh, K. A. (2020). Cloud Service Selection using DEA based on SMI Attributes. *International Journal of Engineering and Advanced Technology, 9*(4), 849–855.

Thumma, C. (2020). Impact of Operating efficiency of public sector banks on its profitability in India. *Indian Journal of Commerce and Management Studies, 8*, 54–62.

Tiku, S. (2023). *AI-Induced Labor Market Shifts and Aging Workforce Dynamics: A Cross-National Study of Corporate Strategic Responses in Japan, USA, and India*. Academic Press.

Tofallis, C. (2001). Combining two approaches to efficiency assessment. *The Journal of the Operational Research Society, 52*(11), 1225–1231. doi:10.1057/palgrave.jors.2601231

Tompkins, D. A., Hobelmann, J. G., & Compton, P. (2017). Providing chronic pain management in the "Fifth Vital Sign" Era: Historical and treatment perspectives on a modern-day medical dilemma. *Drug and Alcohol Dependence, 173*, S11–S21. doi:10.1016/j.drugalcdep.2016.12.002 PMID:28363315

Torfi, A., Fox, E. A., & Reddy, C. K. (2022). Differentially private synthetic medical data generation using convolutional GANs. *Information Sciences, 586*, 485–500. doi:10.1016/j.ins.2021.12.018

Toshiyuki, S., & Goto, M. (2019). Comparison among Three Groups of Solar Thermal Power Stations by Data Envelopment Analysis. *Energies, 12*(13), 2454. Advance online publication. doi:10.3390/en12132454

Tyxhari, G., & Martiri, E. (2022). A systematic review of synthetic data generation methods. *Circular Economy, 457*.

Ullah, Z., Al-Turjman, F., Mostarda, L., & Gagliardi, R. (2020). Applications of Artificial Intelligence and Machine learning in smart cities. *Computer Communications, 154*, 313–323. doi:10.1016/j.comcom.2020.02.069

Umezuruike, C., & Oludele, A. (2015). Broadband Internet Penetration in Nigeria: A Review. *International Journal of Research Studies in Computer Science and Engineering, 2*(1), 1–7.

University of Delaware. (2023). *The Cost Study: The National Study of Instructional Costs and Productivity*. Institutional Research and Effectiveness, Higher Education Consortia at the University of Delaware. https://ire.udel.edu/cost/reports/cost-study-reports/

USDE. (2023). *College Scorecard* [national data as of April 25, 2023]. U.S. Department of Education (USDE), https://collegescorecard.ed.gov/compare/?toggle%3Dinstitutions%26s%3D125231%26s%3D213543%26s%3D186399%26s%3D445188

USDOJ. (2020, July 31). *Lehigh University Agrees to Pay $200,000 Settlement to Resolve False Claims Act Allegations Arising from Convicted Professor's Grant Fraud* [Court Case]. U.S. Department of Justice, Attorney General's Office (USDOJ). https://www.justice.gov/usao-edpa/pr/lehigh-university-agrees-pay-200000-settlement-resolve-false-claims-act-allegations

Usman, H. (2018). *The Nature and Extent of Internet Service Providers' (ISPs) Liability in the European Union: Lessons for Nigerian Regulators* (SSRN Scholarly Paper ID 3204377). Social Science Research Network. https://papers.ssrn.com/abstract=3204377

Usman, N., Andriyani, L., & Pambuko, Z. B. (2019). Productivity of Islamic banks in Indonesia: Social funds versus financial funds. *Journal of Asian Finance. Economics and Business, 6*(3), 115–122. doi:10.13106/jafeb.2019.vol6.no3.115

Valavanidis, A. (2020). *Artificial Intelligence (AI)*. Applications.

Vanderbei, R. J. (2014). *Linear Programming* (Vol. 196). Springer US. doi:10.1007/978-1-4614-7630-6

Van-Voorhis, P. (2018, March 2). UC Merced charges College Republicans $17,000 for Ben Shapiro event. *Washington Examiner*. https://www.washingtonexaminer.com/uc-merced-charges-college-republicans-17-000-for-ben-shapiro-event

Vázquez-Serrano, J. I., Peimbert-García, R. E., & Cárdenas-Barrón, L. E. (2021). Discrete-Event Simulation Modeling in Healthcare: A Comprehensive Review. *International Journal of Environmental Research and Public Health, 18*(22), 12262. Advance online publication. doi:10.3390/ijerph182212262 PMID:34832016

Venkatesh, V., Morris, M. G., Davis, G. B., & Davis, F. D. (2003). User Acceptance of Information Technology: Toward a Unified View. *MIS Quarterly, 27*(3), 425–478. doi:10.2307/30036540

Verma, R., & Rathore, J. S. (2018). Mergers and Acquisitions (M&As) in the banking sector: A comparative study of the Indian and International literature. Journal of banking. *Information Technology Management, 15*(1), 22–36.

Villa, D. (2010). Automation, lean, six sigma: Synergies for improving laboratory efficiency. *Journal of Medical Biochemistry, 29*(4), 339–348. doi:10.2478/v10011-010-0038-3

Vitezic, N., Segota, A., & Setnikar Cankar, S. (2016). Measuring the efficiency of public health services by DEA. *Int'l Pub. Admin. Rev., 14*, 27.

Von Lohmann, F. (2017). Fair use as innovation policy. In *Copyright Law* (pp. 169–205). Routledge. doi:10.4324/9781315095400-6

Vyas, V., Narayanan, K., & Ramanathan, A. (2012). Determinants of mergers and acquisitions in Indian pharmaceuticals industry. *Eurasian Journal of Business and Economics, 5*(9), 79–102.

Waehama, W., McGrath, M., Korthaus, A., & Fong, M. (2014). ICT Adoption and the UTAUT Model. *International Journal of Information Technology : an Official Journal of Bharati Vidyapeeth's Institute of Computer Applications and Management*, 8.

Wahid, M. A., Bukhari, S. H. R., Daud, A., Awan, S. E., & Raja, M. A. Z. (2023). COVICT: An IoT based architecture for COVID-19 detection and contact tracing. *Journal of Ambient Intelligence and Humanized Computing, 14*(6), 7381–7398. doi:10.100712652-022-04446-z PMID:36281429

Wahid, M. A., & Harun, M. S. (2019). Productivity of Islamic and Conventional Banks in Malaysia –During the Pre and Post Global Financial Crisis. *The Journal of Muamalat and Islamic Finance Research, 16*(2), 86–95. doi:10.33102/jmifr.v16i2.225

Walia, K., Mendelson, M., Kang, G., Venkatasubramanian, R., Sinha, R., Vijay, S., Veeraraghavan, B., Basnyat, B., Rodrigues, C., Bansal, N., Ray, P., Mathur, P., Gopalakrishnan, R., & Ohri, V. C. (2023). How can lessons from the COVID-19 pandemic enhance antimicrobial resistance surveillance and stewardship? *The Lancet. Infectious Diseases, 23*(8), e301–e309. doi:10.1016/S1473-3099(23)00124-X PMID:37290476

Wang, Q., & Zhang, Y. (2018). Synthetic data in data envelopment analysis for supply chain efficiency evaluation. *International Journal of Production Economics, 135*(2), 265–276.

Wank, P. F., Barros, C., & Emrouznejad, A. (2015). Assessing Productive Efficiency of Banks Using integrated Fuzzy-DEA and bootstrapping: A Case of Mozambican Banks. *European Journal of Operational Research, 249*(1), 378–389. doi:10.1016/j.ejor.2015.10.018

Warner, A. M. (2014). *Public investment as an engine of growth*. Working Paper No. WP/14/148, International Monetary Fund. doi:10.1093/cjres/rsaa040

WhittakerG. (2014). Creation of Synthetic Microdata for Data Envelopment Analysis Using Nondominated Sorting. SSRN 2499012. doi:10.2139/ssrn.2499012

Widiarto, I., & Emrouznejad, A. (2015). Social and financial efficiency of Islamic microfinance institutions: A Data Envelopment Analysis application. *Socio-Economic Planning Sciences, 50*(1), 1–17. doi:10.1016/j.seps.2014.12.001

Wieselthier, J. E., Nguyen, G. D., & Ephremides, A. (2002). Energy-efficient broadcast and multicast trees in wireless networks. *Mobile Networks and Applications*, 7(6), 481–492. doi:10.1023/A:1020716919751

Williams, M. D., Rana, N. P., & Dwivedi, Y. K. (2015). The unified theory of acceptance and use of technology (UTAUT): A literature review. *Journal of Enterprise Information Management*, 28(3), 443–488. Advance online publication. doi:10.1108/JEIM-09-2014-0088

Williamson, O. (1963). Managerial discretion and business behavior. *The American Economic Review*, 53, 1032–1057.

Wolman, J. (2020, January 25). Class action lawsuit against Lehigh University, BASD asks for $54 million in damages. *The Brown and White*. https://thebrownandwhite.com/2020/01/25/breaking-class-actio n-lawsuit-against-lehigh-university-basd-asks-for-54-million -in-damages/

Wood, E., Baltrušaitis, T., Hewitt, C., Dziadzio, S., Cashman, T. J., & Shotton, J. (2021). Fake it till you make it: face analysis in the wild using synthetic data alone. In *Proceedings of the IEEE/CVF international conference on computer vision* (pp. 3681-3691). 10.1109/ICCV48922.2021.00366

Wu, S., Tang, H., Jing, X. Y., Qian, J., Sebe, N., Yan, Y., & Zhang, Q. (2022). Cross-view panorama image synthesis with progressive attention GANs. *Pattern Recognition*, 131, 108884. doi:10.1016/j.patcog.2022.108884

Xia, Y., & Chen, M. (2023). The Janus face of stateness: China's development-oriented equity investments in Africa. *World Development*, 162, 106133. doi:10.1016/j.worlddev.2022.106133

Xu, L. (2020). *Synthesizing tabular data using conditional GAN* [Doctoral dissertation]. Massachusetts Institute of Technology.

Xu, T., You, J., Li, H., & Shao, L. (2020). Energy Efficiency Evaluation Based on Data Envelopment Analysis: A Literature Review. *Energies*, 13(14), 3548. doi:10.3390/en13143548

Xu, L., Sanders, L., Li, K., & Chow, J. C. (2021). Chatbot for health care and oncology applications using artificial intelligence and machine learning: Systematic review. *JMIR Cancer*, 7(4), e27850. doi:10.2196/27850 PMID:34847056

Xu, L., Skoularidou, M., Cuesta-Infante, A., & Veeramachaneni, K. (2019). Modeling tabular data using conditional gan. *Advances in Neural Information Processing Systems*, 32.

Yang, B., Yang, S., Lv, Z., Wang, F., & Olofsson, T. (2022). Application of digital twins and metaverse in the field of fluid machinery pumps and fans: A review. *Sensors (Basel)*, 22(23), 9294. doi:10.339022239294 PMID:36501994

Yaumidin, U. K. (2007). Efficiency in Islamic Banking: A Non-Parametric Approach. *Buletin Ekonomi Moneter Dan Perbankan*, 9(4), 23–54. doi:10.21098/bemp.v9i4.213

Yaya, S., Xi, C., Xiaoyang, Z., & Meixia, Z. (2020). Evaluating the efficiency of China's healthcare service: A weighted DEA-game theory in a competitive environment. *Journal of Cleaner Production*, 270, 122431. doi:10.1016/j.jclepro.2020.122431

Yazdanparast, R., Tavakkoli-Moghaddam, R., Heidari, R., & Aliabadi, L. (2021). A hybrid Z-number data envelopment analysis and neural network for assessment of supply chain resilience: A case study. *Central European Journal of Operations Research*, 29(2), 611–631. doi:10.100710100-018-0596-x

Yıldırım, M., Yıldız, M. S., & Durak, İ. (2020). Industry 4.0 performances of OECD countries: a data envelope analysis. *İşletme Araştırmaları Dergisi*, 12(3), 2788-2798.

Yildirim, I. (2015). Financial efficiency analysis in Islamic banks: Turkey and Malaysia models. *Pressacademia*, *2*(3), 289–289. doi:10.17261/Pressacademia.2015312956

Yıldırım, İ. (2017). Financial Efficiency Analysis of Islamic Banks in the Qismut Countries. *Journal of Islamic Economics and Finance*, *3*(2), 187–216.

Yilmaz, M. K., Kusakci, A. O., Aksoy, M., & Hacioglu, U. (2022). The evaluation of operational efficiencies of Turkish airports: An integrated spherical fuzzy AHP/DEA approach. *Applied Soft Computing*, *119*, 108620. doi:10.1016/j.asoc.2022.108620

Yousefi Nayer, M., Fazaeli, A. A., & Hamidi, Y. (2022). Hospital efficiency measurement in the west of Iran: Data envelopment analysis and econometric approach. *Cost Effectiveness and Resource Allocation*, *20*(1), 5. Advance online publication. doi:10.118612962-022-00341-8 PMID:35139884

Yu, H., Zhang, Y., Zhang, A., Wang, K., & Cui, Q. (2019). A comparative study of airline efficiency in China and India: A dynamic network DEA approach. *Research in Transportation Economics*, *76*, 100746. doi:10.1016/j.retrec.2019.100746

Zarrin, M., Schoenfelder, J., & Brunner, J. O. (2022). Homogeneity and best practice analyses in hospital performance management: An analytical framework. *Health Care Management Science*, *25*(3), 406–425. doi:10.100710729-022-09590-8 PMID:35192085

Zavras, A. I., Tsakos, G., Economou, C., & Kyriopoulos, J. (2002). Using DEA to evaluate efficiency and formulate policy within a Greek national primary health care network. *Journal of Medical Systems*, *26*(4), 285–292. doi:10.1023/A:1015860318972 PMID:12118812

Zeng, Y., Guo, W., Wang, H., & Zhang, F. (2020). A two-stage evaluation and optimization method for renewable energy development based on data envelopment analysis. *Applied Energy*, *262*, 114363. doi:10.1016/j.apenergy.2019.114363

Zhai, G., Narazaki, Y., Wang, S., Shajihan, S. A. V., & Spencer, B. F. Jr. (2022). Synthetic data augmentation for pixel-wise steel fatigue crack identification using fully convolutional networks. *Smart Structures and Systems*, *29*(1), 237–250.

Zhang, H., Grimmer, M., Ramachandra, R., Raja, K., & Busch, C. (2021, May). On the applicability of synthetic data for face recognition. In *2021 IEEE International Workshop on Biometrics and Forensics (IWBF)* (pp. 1-6). IEEE. 10.1109/IWBF50991.2021.9465085

Zhu, J. (2003). Quantitative models for performance evaluation and benchmarking. Kluwer Academic Publishers Group.

Zhu, Y., & Reddi, V. J. (2013, February). High-performance and energy-efficient mobile web browsing on big/little systems. In *2013 IEEE 19th International Symposium on High Performance Computer Architecture (HPCA)* (pp. 13-24). IEEE.

Zhu, J. (2003). *Quantitative Models for Performance Evaluation and Benchmarking: Data Envelopment Analysis with Spreadsheets and DEA Excel Solver*. Kluwer Academic Publishers. doi:10.1007/978-1-4757-4246-6

Zhu, J. (2014). *Quantitative Models for Performance Evaluation and Benchmarking: Data Envelopment Analysis with Spreadsheets*. Springer.

Zhu, J. Y., Park, T., Isola, P., & Efros, A. A. (2017). Unpaired image-to-image translation using cycle-consistent adversarial networks. In *Proceedings of the IEEE international conference on computer vision (ICCV)* (pp. 2223-2232). 10.1109/ICCV.2017.244

Zhu, Z., Chu, Z., Wang, Z., & Lee, I. (2016). Outage constrained robust beamforming for secure broadcasting systems with energy harvesting. *IEEE Transactions on Wireless Communications*, *15*(11), 7610–7620. doi:10.1109/TWC.2016.2605102

Ziaee, O., & Falahati, B. (2017). *A data envelopment analysis (DEA)-based model for power interruption cost estimation for industrial companies. In IEEE Power & Energy Society Innovative Smart Grid Technologies Conference.* ISGT. doi:10.1109/ISGT.2017.8086058

Zitzler, E., & Thiele, L. (1999). Multiobjective evolutionary algorithms: A comparative case study and the strength Pareto approach. *IEEE Transactions on Evolutionary Computation, 3*(4), 257–271. Advance online publication. doi:10.1109/4235.797969

About the Contributors

Adeyemi Abel Ajibesin is a distinguished academic scholar with over two decades of extensive experience in research, teaching, and leadership, particularly in the field of Electrical and Computer Engineering. Currently serving as the Chair/HoD of Software Engineering at the School of IT & Computing (SITC) at the American University of Nigeria, he was the founding Interim Dean of the School of Engineering, the Interim Dean of SITC, and the Director of the African Centre for ICT Innovation and Training. Already, he has served in various capacities at Simon Fraser University, Canada; University of Cape Town, South Africa; and Pan African University Institute for Basic Sciences, Technology & Innovation, Kenya, among other places. His research interests are diverse, spanning data science, broadband networks, frontier analysis, AI applications for gender equity, community development, leadership, innovation, and transformation. Beyond academia, Dr. Ajibesin holds patents for engineering products and copyrights for computing software, showcasing his commitment to innovation and intellectual contributions in his field.

Narasimha Rao Vajjhala is working as the Dean of the Faculty of Engineering and Architecture at the University of New York Tirana, Albania. He had previously worked as the Chair of Computer Science and Software Engineering programs at the American University of Nigeria. He is a senior member of ACM and IEEE. He is the Editor-in-Chief (EiC) of the International Journal of Risk and Contingency Management (IJRCM). He is also a member of the Risk Management Society (RIMS), and the Project Management Institute (PMI). He has over 23 years of experience teaching programming and database-related courses at both graduate and undergraduate levels in Europe and Africa. He has also worked as a consultant in technology firms in Europe and has experience participating in EU-funded projects. He has completed a Doctorate in Information Systems and Technology (United States); holds a Master of Science in Computer Science and Applications (India), and a Master of Business Administration with a specialization in Information Systems (Switzerland).

* * *

Muhammed Abiodun Adebimpe earned his M.Sc. degree in Computer Science while serving at the University after five years of administrative university experience at the American University of Nigeria. He bagged his first degree at the Federal University of Technology, Minna, Niger State, Nigeria. He has other computing-related skills in data analysis, multimedia design, and Windows system administration.

Sachin Chaudhary completed his graduation from MJPRU and post-graduation from AKTU, Moradabad, U.P. Currently, he is pursuing his Ph.D. in Computer Science and Engineering from a government-recognized university. Presently, he is working as an Assistant Professor in the Department of Computer Science and Applications at IIMT University, Meerut, U.P, India. He has been awarded the Excellence in Teaching Award 2019. He is a reviewer member of some reputed journals. He has published several book chapters and national and international reputed journal research papers.

Philip Eappen is an Assistant Professor of Healthcare Management at Cape Breton University and a Director of Clinical Services and Transition to Community at the Breton Ability Center (LOA). He has over a decade of experience in hospital and healthcare management operations, along with his academic experience. Prior to teaching at Cape Breton University, Dr. Eappen taught healthcare management at the University of Toronto, Southern Alberta Institute of Technology, and Fanshawe College. Before moving to Canada, Dr. Eappen also worked as Director of Health Services and as a Chief Administrator of Healthcare Operations at the American University of Nigeria. He also worked as a faculty member at the American University and other universities and colleges. Dr. Eappen has a Doctorate in Healthcare Administration from Central Michigan University, United States, a Master of Business Administration in Health Care Management, and a Bachelor of Nursing. Dr. Eappen also has a post-graduate certificate in international health.

Natasha Cecilia Edeh works for EZ Career Consultant Pvt Ltd as an education consultant. Edeh's research focuses on human-centered topics such as open innovation, cybersecurity, and human-robot collaboration. She is now working on a chapter for the book Cybersecurity for Decision Makers on the topic "Cybersecurity frameworks and assessment models". Edeh graduated from the American University of Nigeria with a master's degree in Information Systems in 2018.

Khalid El Badraoui is a full professor of finance at Ibn Zohr University Business School (ENCG) in Agadir (Morocco). He received his Ph.D. in Finance from Rennes 1 University (France). Prof. El Badraoui is also an associate member of the Center for Research in Economics and Management (CREM) at Rennes 1 University and a member of the African Chair of Innovation and Sustainable Management (CAIMD) at Mohammed VI Polytechnic University (Morocco). Prof. El Badraoui has made several scholarly contributions, including peer-reviewed research papers published in journals such as Bankers, Markets & Investors, International Journal of Business, and Journal of Applied Business Research.

Laura Yeraldin Escobar Rodriguez is working as a Professor at Universidad Autonoma de Bucaramanga UNAB and Universidad Industrial de Santander. She has a M.Sc. in Industrial Engineering from Universidad Industrial de Santander. Her research interests include facility layout problems, simulation, and operational research applied to healthcare system design.

Vipul Gupta is an Assistant Professor in the School of Liberal Arts and Management- Humanities. Dr. Vipul Gupta received his Ph.D. in Economics from Panjab University Chandigarh and has an MA in Economics and a B.Com Hons. in Financial Management from Panjab University Chandigarh. Dr. Vipul Gupta's research interests canter upon macroeconomics, particularly money and banking, social responsibility, and Punjab Economy. He has written several research papers in the various areas of economics in Scopus, Web of Science, and UGC Care Journals. Before joining DIT, Dr. Vipul Gupta was an Assistant Professor at the Liberal Arts Department of Chandigarh University Gharuan.

Karim Iddouch is Assistant Professor of accounting and finance department at the International University of Casablanca's Business School. His teaching portfolio encompasses subjects like financial and management accounting, financial management, and business taxation. Currently, he is in the process of completing his PhD at Ibn Zohr University's Business School, under the primary guidance of Professor Khalid El Badraoui and co-supervision by Professor Jamal Ouenniche from the University of Edinburgh Business School.

Trilochan Jena is an Assistant Professor at the Rourkela Institute of Management Studies (RIMS), Rourkela. His current area of interest is Accounting and Finance, with more than 15 years Post Graduate Management Teaching experience in an MBA program. He teaches Corporate Finance, Financial Management, and Financial Derivatives. He has attended many National and International seminars and workshops conducted by Universities and Educational Institutions of repute. He also acts as a financial advisor and tax consultant to companies and individuals. His research interest is in the area of corporate finance and corporate restructuring.

Bhupendra Kumar completed his graduation and post-graduation from Chaudhary Charan Singh University, Meerut, U.P. and his PhD in Computer Science and Engineering from Mewar University, Hapur. Presently, he is working as a Professor in the Department of Computer Science and Applications, IIMT University, Meerut, U.P. He has a vast teaching experience of 19 years. He is a reviewer member of some reputed journals. He has published several book chapters and national and international reputable journal research papers.

Sree Kumar is a Professor at Rourkela Institute of Management Studies, Rourkela, India. He holds a Ph.D. in management from Sambalpur University. He works in the area of management decision-making. His areas of research interest include the application of DEA for efficiency analysis, multi-criteria decision-making, and fuzzy decision-making. He has around thirty years of teaching experience in management decision-making. He has published over fifty research papers in various international and national journals and conferences. He has also authored two books.

Senthil Kumar Thangavel completed his B.E(Computer Science and Engineering) from Sethu Institute of Technology, Madurai. He then completed his M.Tech(Distributed Computing Systems) from Pondicherry Engineering College, Pondicherry. He completed his Ph.D in Information and Communication Engineering from Anna University, Chennai. His areas of interest include video surveillance, Deep learning, cloud computing, software Engineering, Video processing, Wireless Sensor Networks, Big Data computing, Embedded Automation, and explainable AI. He works as an Associate Professor in the computer science and Engineering Department at Amrita School of Computing, Amrita Vishwa Vidyapeetham, Coimbatore. He is a reviewer for Elsevier Computers & Electrical Engineering Journal, IEEE Access, Inderscience, International Journal of Intelligent Information Systems IGI Global, Springer –Data Analysis, International Institute of Engineers Journal, Journal of Electronic Imaging, CMES: Computer Modeling in Engineering & Sciences. He has been working with Amrita Vishwa

Vidyapeetham, Coimbatore, since 2001. He is a part of funded projects with IBM, DST, Ministry of Tribal Affairs, Telesto Energy Pvt Ltd, and Multicoreware.

Uetutiza Cecilie Chantell Kuzatjike is currently with the Department of Electrical and Computer Engineering, Namibia University of Science and Technology. Her research interests include Energy Systems, Green Energy, and Computational alternatives.

Edlira Martiri graduated from the University of Tirana's Faculty of Natural Sciences with a bachelor's and a master's degree in "Computer Science." Since her early years in academia, her research interests have focused on information security. She is an associate professor and holds a double doctorate degree from UT (2016) and NTNU Norway (2022). Since January 2014, she has served as a national contact point at the European Association of Biometrics () for Albania. Being always enthusiastic about secure technologies, her research interest is focused on secure-by-design systems. She has participated in various projects in different international setups, such as H2020, FP7, COST actions, etc. Finally, she is an active member of the IT community, a team builder, consultant, and mentor, always trying to bridge the gap between academia and the IT industry.

K. S. Sastry Musti is with Namibia University of Science and Technology, Windhoek, Namibia. He has more than 30 years of professional experience. He obtained his BTech in Electrical Engineering from JNTU, Kakinada (A.P.) in 1990, his MTech, and his Ph.D. from NIT, Warangal, India, in 1996 and 2002, respectively. His earlier employments include the University of the West Indies, St Augustine, Trinidad, ESIGELEC, Rouen, France, and Sophia University, Tokyo, Japan. His research interests include Power and Energy Systems, Information Systems, and Engineering Education.

Jamal Ouenniche is Professor and Chair in Business Analytics at the University of Edinburgh Business School and a member of the African Chair of Innovation and Sustainable Management (CAIMD) at Mohammed VI Polytechnic University (Morocco). He was named 'a Leading Academic Data Leader in 2021 and 2023 by Chief Data Officer (CDO) Magazine. He holds BSc. in Mathematics and MSc. in Operational Research from the University of Montreal (Canada), and PhD in Operations Management from Laval University (Quebec, Canada). His research portfolio encompasses a broad range of applications and a variety of research methodologies in predictive and prescriptive analytics, and tackles important managerial issues in manufacturing, transport, public sector policy, banking, finance, and energy. Some of his research is concerned with methodological contributions to the fields of optimization, artificial intelligence, data envelopment analysis, multicriteria decision making, performance evaluation and benchmarking, risk modelling and analysis, and forecasting. He acts as a Referee for over 30 academic journals, several international conferences, and several national and foreign research councils.

Rajneesh Panwar graduated and post-graduated in Mathematics and Computer Applications from Chaudhary Charan Singh University, Meerut (U.P.), and received his M. Tech. in Computer Science from Shobhit University, Meerut. Presently, he is working as an Assistant Professor in the School of Computer Science and Application IIMT University, Meerut, U.P. He qualified for GATE 2021 and UGC-NET in June 2020 and December 2020. He has published several book chapters and research papers of national and international reputation.

Rajasekhara Mouly Potluri is a Professor of Management/Marketing at the School of Business of the Kazakh-British Technical University (KBTU), Almaty, Kazakhstan. Prof. Potluri, in his three decades of teaching and research experience, published around one hundred and twenty research papers, conference publications, books, and book chapters in many world-renowned peer-reviewed Scopus and ABDC-indexed journals. He presented more than thirty International Conference Presentations and won 12 Best Research Paper Awards and 10 Academic Excellence Awards at different conferences held in South Korea, UAE, Egypt, Georgia, and Vietnam. In his around two decades of International teaching and research career in multicultural and multi-ethnic environments in India, Ethiopia, Kazakhstan, South Korea, and Nigeria, he has been teaching courses in Management, Marketing, Strategy, HRM & OB, Entrepreneurship, and International Business. Finally, a confident, innovative faculty devoted to education and research with a quintessential career.

Ridwan Salahudeen was born in Nigeria in 1987. He received a B.Sc and M.Sc. degrees in computer science from Ahmadu Bello University, Zaria – Nigeria, in 2011 and 2016, respectively. He served as a teaching staff at the university until 2018, when he commenced his Ph.D. journey. He started the Ph.D. journey by enrolling in the American University of Nigeria. He later moved to Hong Kong in 2021, where he was engaged as a Research Associate in an Artificial Intelligence Laboratory under the Caritas Institute of Higher Education, Hong Kong. His research interest includes deep learning, blockchain technology, knowledge representation, and uncertainty resolution.

Pradipta Kumar Sanyal holds a Ph.D. in Business Management specializing in the area of Finance (Quantitative Finance and Financial Econometrics) with more than 23 years of Post Graduate Management Teaching experience at MBA in Business Schools ICFAI Group Institute Pune, Alliance University Bangalore, EIILM Calcutta and other reputed business schools. He teaches Corporate Finance, Business Valuation, Security Analysis, Portfolio Management, Financial Modelling, Financial Econometrics, Mathematical & Computational Finance, and Financial Derivatives. He also specializes in teaching all of his finance courses using Excel. His Research Interest is in the area of Financial Econometrics and Time Series Analysis. He has published various research papers in journals of national and international repute. He regularly conducts Faculty Development Programs (FDP), and Management Development Programs (MDP). He successfully completed Faculty Development Programs in Applied Financial Econometrics and Research Methodology. He conducts MDPs in the area of Financial Statements Analysis, Finance for Nonfinance Executives, Project Evaluation, Credit Management, and Financial Strategy and successfully completed the Management Development Program for NALCO, IFFCO, JSA Law Firm, and the National Council of Science Museum Kolkata. He has also been actively involved in Academic Administration.

Kewal Krishan Sharma is a professor of computer science at IIMT University, Meerut, U.P, India. He did his Ph.D. in computer networks and has an MCA, MBA, and Law degree. He did various certification courses also. He has an overall experience of around 33 years in academics, business, and industry. He wrote several research papers and books.

Vikas Sharma completed his graduation and post-graduation from Chaudhary Charan Singh University, Meerut, U.P. He is pursuing his Ph.D. in Computer Science and Engineering from a government-recognized university. Presently, he is working as an Assistant Professor in the Department of Computer Science and Applications at IIMT University, Meerut, U.P.

Yaya Sissoko has been a member of the Department of Finance and Economics since 2005. Sissoko received the People Award (2008) from the African American Cultural Center and served as a member of the board of directors of AACC for 10 years. He is the faculty advisor for both the Pan-African Student Association and the IUP Soccer Club. He is a member of both the Pan-African Studies and the Asian Studies programs. His fields of interest are economic development, monetary economics, international economics, managerial economics, environmental economics, and time series econometrics. Sissoko is a member of the editorial board of the African Journal of Accounting, Economics, Finance and Banking Research, the editorial board of the Pennsylvania Economic Review, the chair of the Pennsylvania Economic Association Best Undergraduate Paper Contest, and an ex-officio member of the PEA Board of Directors. Sissoko has published three-chapter books in the "Book Series of the International Finance Review and the Edwin Mellen Press" and more than a dozen articles in refereed journals such as Energy of Economics, International Advances in Economic Research, Review of Regional Studies, African Finance Journal, International Journal of Economic Sciences and Applied Research, Economic Systems, and the Pennsylvania Economic Review.

Brian Sloboda specializes in labor economics and microeconomic theory and has research interests in labor economics, performance measurement, and applied time series. He just finished the Post Doctoral Bridge (PDB) Program at the Warrington College of Business Administration Hough Graduate School at the University of Florida with a specialization in financial management and corporate finance. Brian has published articles in the African Journal Economic Review, Journal of Economics, Journal of Financial Issues, Advances in Econometrics, Crisis Management in Tourism (wrote a chapter on the effects of terrorism on Europe)) Tourism Economics, Journal of Transportation and Statistics, Pennsylvania Economic Review, International Journal of Transport Economics (2), Journal of Educators Online, the Journal of Transportation Research Forum, Public Administration(2), Journal of Business and Economic Studies, and the Virginia Economic Journal. He edited a volume for J Ross Publishers on Transportation Statistics. He is also a committee member for the Federal Forecasters Consortium (FFC) and a board member for the Pennsylvania Economics Association and the editorial board for the Pennsylvania Economic Review. He is the former president for the Society of Government Economists (SGE) and is now the executive director. He is currently an assistant editor for the Journal of Economics and a senior social science editor for the European Scientific Journal. He is also the book review editor for the Review of Regional Studies, the official journal of the Southern Regional Science Association.

Kenneth Strang has 300+ scholarly publications. He is a retired professor and active researcher across five disciplines: business administration, management information systems, marketing/consumer behavior, supply chain management and economics/statistics. Ken has a professional doctorate in project management (operations research), an MBA (strategic management), a BSBA (marketing), an AS (CS/IT) all with summa cum laude/honors plus he is an internationally licensed Project Management Professional (PMI, USA), a Certified Research Professional (IIPMR, USA), a Certified Network Administrator (Novell, USA), a Certified Supply Chain Specialist/Procurement Professional (IIPMR, USA) and a Fellow Life Management Institute with distinction (LOMA, USA). Dr. Strang has lifetime grant projects valued over $7 million+, and he has won several honors including a Behavior Energy Climate

Change Fellowship from the American Council for an Energy-Efficient Economy, two Emerald Literati awards and Duke of Edinborough community service medal, along with several presidential citations. He is Editor-in-Chief Emeritus of IGI's International Journal of Risk and Contingency Management (10 year tenure).

Leonardo H. Talero-Sarmiento is a Ph.D. candidate in Engineering at Universidad Autonoma de Bucaramanga. He specializes in mathematical modeling, data analytics, operational research and manufacturing, process improvement, and technology adoption. His work emphasizes decision-making and production planning. He has contributed to multiple scholarly articles in various fields. He has published articles in Digital Policy, Regulation and Governance, Heliyon, Revista Colombiana de Computacion, Suma de Negocios, IngeCUC, Apuntes del Cenes, Estudios Gerenciales, and Contaduría y Administración.

Franklin Tchakounte is an Associate Professor and researcher in computer science with more than 10 years of experience in cybersecurity and data intelligence. He received his M.Sc. in Computer engineering from the University of Ngaoundere (Cameroon, 2010) and his Ph.D. in Mobile Security from the University of Bremen (Germany, 2015). Franklin owns several IT certifications. He authored books, book chapters, and several research papers in cyber security. He is the founder of the Cybersecurity with Computational and Artificial Intelligence (CyComAI,) company. He has been involved in international projects. He is a fellow of DAAD Staff Exchange in Sub-Saharan Africa, Research Mobility grants in Cameroon, and the WebWeWant F.A.S.T project. He is a member of numerous societies: EAI, ISOC SIG Cybersecurity, ISOC SIG Cybersecurity Training and Education, Research Data Alliance (RDA), AuthorAID, and Africa Association of Entrepreneurs (AAE). He is currently the Cameroonian representative of Responsibility in AI in Africa (RAIN) and his interests include cyber security and artificial/digital intelligence.

Tarun Kumar Vashishth is an active academician and researcher in computer science with 21 years of experience. He earned a Ph.D. Mathematics degree specialized in Operations Research; served several academic positions such as HoD, Dy. Director, Academic Coordinator, Member Secretary of the Department Research Committee, Assistant Center Superintendent, and Head Examiner in university examinations. He is involved in academic development and scholarly activities. He is a member of the International Association of Engineers, The Society of Digital Information and Wireless Communications, the Global Professors Welfare Association, the International Association of Academic plus Corporate (IAAC), the Computer Science Teachers Association, and the Internet Society. His research interest includes Cloud Computing, Artificial Intelligence, Machine Learning, and Operations Research; he has published over 20 research articles with one book and ten book chapters in edited books. He is contributing as a member of editorial and reviewer boards in conferences and various computer journals published by CRC Press, Taylor and Francis, Springer, IGI Global, and other universities.

Index

A

Ad Hoc Wireless Networks 139, 141-143, 146, 148-151, 153-156, 160
Allocatively Efficient 16
Artificial Intelligence (AI) 145, 169, 174, 181-182, 244

B

Banking Efficiency 62, 70, 289, 303, 329
Banking Reforms 283, 301
Benchmarking 19, 24, 30, 38-39, 106-107, 110, 123, 125, 130, 136, 155-156, 158, 161, 168, 175, 177, 182-183, 203, 232-233, 238-239, 245-247, 249-250, 252, 254-258, 260, 268, 280-282, 303, 329
Big Data Analytics 161, 163, 182

C

Co-Creation 82-83, 89, 91, 96, 106-107, 116, 303
Coded Packet Algorithms 139, 160
Computational Complexity 87, 99, 107, 116
Constant Returns to Scale 5-6, 11, 16-18, 21, 26, 186, 228, 246, 268, 287, 315
Conventional Microeconomic Theory 289, 304
Convexity 6, 16, 213
Cost Efficiency 21, 51, 54, 63, 66, 283, 285-286, 291-294, 298, 300, 302, 304, 306, 310

D

Data Envelopment Analysis (DEA) 10, 17, 19, 39-40, 70, 83, 89, 91, 111-112, 116, 118, 125, 139, 141, 143-145, 159-160, 182, 184, 203, 206-215, 219-220, 222-224, 226-228, 231, 236, 242-245, 256, 259-261, 276, 282, 285, 305, 307, 312-313, 330
Data Generation Techniques 119, 123-126, 129-131
Data Privacy 118-120, 126, 129-130, 169

D (continued)

Decision Making 14, 37-38, 109, 137, 143-144, 157, 206, 214, 229, 255, 269, 276, 300, 314
Decision-Making Units (DMUs) 22, 39, 99, 144, 160, 162, 182, 206, 213, 226, 244-245, 260, 268, 270, 285, 311, 314
Design-Thinking 116
Digital Divide 261, 282
Disruptive Technologies 161-177, 183
Distance Function 6, 16
Drone Technology 163, 166, 170, 176

E

Economically Efficient 16, 199
Efficiency 1-7, 10, 12-17, 20-24, 26-28, 30-31, 33-34, 37-39, 41, 45-48, 51, 54-55, 57-71, 77, 82-89, 91, 97, 99-100, 102-117, 125-126, 133, 136, 139-146, 148-163, 166, 168, 170-177, 179-180, 182-183, 185-186, 188-189, 191, 193-196, 198, 200-215, 218-219, 222-236, 238-240, 242-271, 273-278, 280-296, 298-304, 306-308, 310-315, 318-330
Efficiency Assessment 115, 223-225, 228, 232, 234, 238-239, 243, 256, 259, 303
Efficiency Benchmarking 161, 183, 268
Efficiency Change 1, 7, 10, 12, 15-16, 45-48, 59, 281, 327
Efficiency Measurement 70, 115, 208, 245, 251-252, 258, 265, 267, 273, 305, 311, 313-314, 328
Efficiency Rating 151, 186, 194, 196, 201, 206, 273-275
Efficient Frontier 18, 21-22, 26-28, 30-32, 35, 39, 87, 97, 101, 103, 117, 144, 151, 153, 155-156, 208, 285, 292-293, 313
Electronic Health Records (EHR) 248, 260
Employer-Employee Relationships 161, 163, 175
Energy Efficiency 139-146, 148-149, 154-160, 173-174, 187, 203, 205-206, 222, 226, 229, 243
Energy Management 158, 173, 177, 185-186, 189
Energy Mix 201, 206

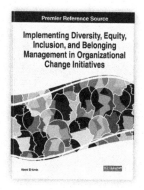

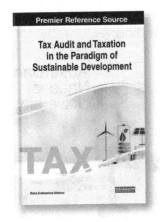

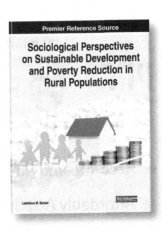

Printed in the United States
by Baker & Taylor Publisher Services